Discovering Psychology

A Guide to Active Study

Richard O. Straub

University of Michigan, Dearborn

to accompany

David G. Myers

Psychology Third Edition

WORTH PUBLISHERS

DISCOVERING PSYCHOLOGY: A Guide to Active Study
by Richard O. Straub
to accompany
Myers: **Psychology**, Third Edition

Printed in the United States of America
ISBN: 0-87901-507-1
  3 4 5 — 94 93

Cover: Pierre-Auguste Renoir, *The Luncheon of the Boating Party* (detail), 1881
Oil on canvas, 51" x 68", © The Phillips Collection, Washington, DC.
(Fine art consultant: Steven Diamond)

Worth Publishers
33 Irving Place
New York, New York 10003

Contents

Preface

This Study Guide is designed for use with *Psychology*, Third Edition, by David G. Myers. It is intended to help you evaluate your understanding of the text material, and then to review any problem areas. "How to Manage Your Time Efficiently, Study More Effectively, and Think Critically" provides detailed instructions on how to use the textbook and this Study Guide for maximum benefit. It also offers additional study suggestions based on principles of time management, effective notetaking, evaluation of exam performance, and an effective program for improving your comprehension while studying from textbooks. A new feature in this essay is a critical-thinking exercise that can help you to improve your ability to evaluate the arguments presented by others, as well as to more effectively formulate your own.

The third edition of this Study Guide offers other new features. Each chapter now includes three review tests: In addition to the two Progress Tests that focus on facts and definitions, there is a Challenge Test that evaluates your understanding of the text chapter's broader conceptual material and its application to real-world situations. The Challenge Test contains 20 multiple-choice questions and an essay question. For all three review tests, the correct answers are given, followed by textbook page references (so you can easily go back and reread the material), and complete explanations not only of why the answer is correct but also of why the other choices are incorrect. Detailed guidelines for the objectives in the Study Guide are provided. These guidelines are useful for a section-by-section review of each textbook chapter and as a source of additional essay questions.

I would like to thank all the students and instructors who used this Study Guide in its first two editions and provided such insightful and useful suggestions. Special thanks are also due to Christine Brune, Patricia Nankervis, and Betty Shapiro Probert for their extraordinary editorial contributions.

Richard O. Straub

September 1991

How to Manage Your Time Efficiently, Study More Effectively, and Think Critically

How effectively do you study? Good study habits make the job of being a college student much easier. Many students, who *could* succeed in college, fail or drop out because they have never learned to manage their time efficiently. Even the best students can usually benefit from an in-depth evaluation of their current study habits.

There are many ways to achieve academic success, of course, but your approach may not be the most effective or efficient. Are you sacrificing your social life or your physical or mental health in order to get A's on your exams? Good study habits result in better grades *and* more time for other activities.

Evaluate Your Current Study Habits

To improve your study habits, you must first have an accurate picture of how you currently spend your time. Begin by putting together a profile of your present living and studying habits. Answer the following questions by writing *yes* or *no* on each line.

_____ 1. Do you usually set up a schedule to budget your time for studying, recreation, and other activities?

_____ 2. Do you often put off studying until time pressures force you to cram?

_____ 3. Do other students seem to study less than you do, but get better grades?

_____ 4. Do you usually spend hours at a time studying one subject, rather than dividing that time between several subjects?

_____ 5. Do you often have trouble remembering what you have just read in a textbook?

_____ 6. Before reading a chapter in a textbook, do you skim through it and read the section headings?

_____ 7. Do you try to predict exam questions from your lecture notes and reading?

_____ 8. Do you usually attempt to paraphrase or summarize what you have just finished reading?

_____ 9. Do you find it difficult to concentrate very long when you study?

_____ 10. Do you often feel that you studied the wrong material for an exam?

Thousands of college students have participated in similar surveys. Students who are fully realizing their academic potential usually respond as follows: (1) yes, (2) no, (3) no, (4) no, (5) no, (6) yes, (7) yes, (8) yes, (9) no, (10) no.

Compare your responses to those of successful students. The greater the discrepancy, the more you could benefit from a program to improve your study habits. The questions are designed to identify areas of weakness. Once you have identified your weaknesses, you will be able to set specific goals for improvement and implement a program for reaching them.

Managing Your Time

Do you often feel frustrated because there isn't enough time to do all the things you must and want to do? Take heart. Even the most productive and successful people feel this way at times. But they establish priorities for their activities and they learn to budget time for each of them. There's much in the saying "If you want something done, ask a busy person to do it." A busy person knows how to get things done.

If you don't now have a system for budgeting your time, develop one. Not only will your academic accomplishments increase, but you will actually find more time in your schedule for other activities. And you won't have to feel guilty about "taking time off," because all your obligations will be covered.

Establish a Baseline

As a first step in preparing to budget your time, keep a diary for a few days to establish a summary, or baseline, of the time you spend in studying, socializing, working, and so on. If you are like many students, much of your "study" time is nonproductive; you may sit at your desk and leaf through a book, but the time is actually wasted. Or you may procrastinate. You are always getting ready to study, but you rarely do.

Besides revealing where you waste time, your diary will give you a realistic picture of how much time you need to allot for meals, commuting, and other fixed activities. In addition, careful records should indicate the times of the day when you are consistently most productive. A sample time-management diary is shown in Table 1.

Plan the Term

Having established and evaluated your baseline, you are ready to devise a more efficient schedule. Buy a calendar that covers the entire school term and has ample space for each day. Using the course outlines provided by your instructors, enter the dates of all exams, term paper deadlines, and other important academic obligations. If you have any long-range personal plans (concerts, weekend trips, etc.), enter the dates on the calendar as well. Keep your calendar up to date and refer to it often. I recommend carrying it with you at all times.

Table 1   Sample Time-Management Diary

	Monday	
Behavior	Time Completed	Duration Hours: Minutes
Sleep	7:00	7:30
Dressing	7:25	:25
Breakfast	7:45	:20
Commute	8:20	:35
Coffee	9:00	:40
French	10:00	1:00
Socialize	10:15	:15
Videogame	10:35	:20
Coffee	11:00	:25
Psychology	12:00	1:00
Lunch	12:25	:25
Study Lab	1:00	:35
Psych. Lab	4:00	3:00
Work	5:30	1:30
Commute	6:10	:40
Dinner	6:45	:35
TV	7:30	:45
Study Psych.	10:00	2:30
Socialize	11:30	1:30
Sleep		

Prepare a similar chart for each day of the week. When you finish an activity, note it on the chart and write down the time it was completed. Then determine its duration by subtracting the time the previous activity was finished from the newly entered time.

Develop a Weekly Calendar

Now that you have a general picture of the school term, develop a weekly schedule that includes all of your activities. Aim for a schedule that you can live with for the entire school term. A sample weekly schedule, incorporating the following guidelines, is shown in Table 2.

1. Enter your class times, work hours, and any other fixed obligations first. *Be thorough.* Using information from your time-management diary, allow plenty of time for such things as commuting, meals, laundry, and the like.

2. Set up a study schedule for each of your courses. The study habits survey and your time-management diary will direct you. The following guidelines should also be useful.

(a) Establish regular study times for each course. The 4 hours needed to study one subject, for example, are most profitable when divided into shorter periods spaced over several days. If you cram your studying into one 4-hour block, what you attempt to learn in the third or fourth hour will interfere with what you studied in the first 2 hours. Newly acquired knowledge is like wet cement. It needs some time to "harden" to become memory.

(b) Alternate subjects. The type of interference just mentioned is greatest between similar topics. Set up a schedule in which you spend time on several *different* courses during each study session. Besides reducing the potential for interference, alternating subjects will help to prevent mental fatigue with one topic.

(c) Set weekly goals to determine the amount of study time you need to do well in each course. This will depend on, among other things, the difficulty of your courses and the effectiveness of your methods. Many professors recommend studying at least 1 to 2 hours for each hour in class. If your time-management diary indicates that you presently study less time than that, do not plan to jump immediately to a much higher level. Increase study time from your baseline by setting weekly goals [see (4)] that will gradually bring you up to the desired level. As an initial schedule, for example, you might set aside an amount of study time for each course that matches class time.

(d) Schedule for maximum effectiveness. Tailor your schedule to meet the demands of each course. For the course that emphasizes lecture notes, schedule time for a daily review soon after the class. This will give you a chance to revise your notes and clean up any hard-to-decipher shorthand while the material is still fresh in your mind. If you are evaluated for class participation (for example, in a language course), allow time for a review just *before* the class meets. Schedule study time

Table 2   Sample Weekly Schedule

Time	Mon.	Tues.	Wed.	Thurs.	Fri.	Sat.
7–8	Dress Eat	Dress Eat	Dress Eat	Dress Eat	Dress Eat	
8–9	Psych.	Study Psych.	Psych.	Study Psych.	Psych.	Dress Eat
9–10	Eng.	Study Eng.	Eng.	Study Eng.	Eng.	Study Eng.
10–11	Study French	Free	Study French	Open Study	Study French	Study Stats.
11–12	French	Study Psych. Lab	French	Open Study	French	Study Stats.
12–1	Lunch	Lunch	Lunch	Lunch	Lunch	Lunch
1–2	Stats.	Psych. Lab	Stats.	Study or Free	Stats.	Free
2–3	Bio.	Psych. Lab	Bio.	Free	Bio.	Free
3–4	Free	Psych.	Free	Free	Free	Free
4–5	Job	Job	Job	Job	Job	Free
5–6	Job	Job	Job	Job	Job	Free
6–7	Dinner	Dinner	Dinner	Dinner	Dinner	Dinner
7–8	Study Bio.	Study Bio.	Study Bio.	Study Bio.	Free	Free
8–9	Study Eng.	Study Stats.	Study Psych.	Open Study	Open Study	Free
9–10	Open Study	Open Study	Open Study	Open Study	Free	Free

This is a sample schedule for a student with a 16-credit load and a 10-hour-per-week part-time job. Using this chart as an illustration, make up a weekly schedule, following the guidelines outlined here.

for your most difficult (or least motivating) courses during hours when you are the most alert and distractions are fewest.

(e) Schedule open study time. Emergencies, additional obligations, and the like could throw off your schedule. And you may simply need some extra time periodically for a project or for review in one of your courses. Schedule several hours each week for such purposes.

3. After you have budgeted time for studying, fill in slots for recreation, hobbies, relaxation, household errands, and the like.

4. Set specific goals. Before each study session, make a list of specific goals. The simple note "7-8 PM: study psychology" is too broad to ensure the most effective use of the time. Formulate your daily goals according to what you know you must accomplish during the term. If you have course outlines with advance assignments, set systematic daily goals that will allow you, for example, to cover fifteen chapters before the exam. And be realistic: Can you actually expect to cover a 78-page chapter in one session? Divide large tasks into smaller units; stop at the most logical resting points. When you complete a specific goal, take a 5- or 10-minute break before tackling the next goal.

5. Evaluate how successful or unsuccessful your studying has been on a daily or weekly basis. Did you reach most of your goals? If so, reward yourself immediately. You might even make a list of five to ten rewards to choose from. If you have trouble studying regularly, you may be able to motivate yourself by making such rewards contingent on completing specific goals.

6. Finally, until you have lived with your schedule for several weeks, don't hesitate to revise it. You may need to allow more time for chemistry, for example, and less for some other course. If you are trying to study regularly for the first time and are feeling burned out, you probably have set your initial goals too high. Don't let failure cause you to despair and abandon the program. Accept your limitations and revise your schedule so

that you are studying only 15 to 20 minutes more each evening than you are used to. The point is to *identify a regular schedule with which you can achieve some success.* Time management, like any skill, must be practiced to become effective.

Techniques for Effective Study

Knowing how to put study time to best use is, of course, as important as finding a place for it in your schedule. Here are some suggestions that should enable you to increase your reading comprehension and improve your notetaking. A few study tips are included as well.

Using SQ3R to Increase Reading Comprehension

How do you study from a textbook? If you are like many students, you simply read and reread in a *passive* manner. Studies have shown, however, that most students who simply read a textbook cannot remember more than half the material ten minutes after they have finished. Often, what is retained is the unessential material rather than the important points upon which exam questions will be based.

This Study Guide employs a program known as SQ3R (*Survey*, *Question*, *Read*, *Recite*, and *Review*) to facilitate, and allow you to assess, your comprehension of the important facts and concepts in *Psychology*, Third Edition, by David Myers.

Research has shown that students using SQ3R achieve significantly greater comprehension of textbooks than students reading in the more traditional passive manner. Once you have learned this program, you can improve your comprehension of any textbook.

Survey   Before reading a chapter, determine whether the text or the study guide has an outline or list of objectives. Read this material and the summary at the end of the chapter. Next, read the textbook chapter fairly quickly, paying special attention to the major headings and subheadings. This survey will give you an idea of the chapter's contents and organization. You will then be able to divide the chapter into logical sections in order to formulate specific goals for a more careful reading of the chapter.

In this Study Guide, the *Chapter Overview* summarizes the major topics of the textbook chapter. This section also provides a few suggestions for approaching topics you may find difficult.

Question   You will retain material longer when you have a use for it. If you look up a word's definition in order to solve a crossword puzzle, for example, you will remember it longer than if you merely fill in the letters as a result of putting other words in. Surveying

the chapter will allow you to generate important questions that the chapter will proceed to answer. These questions correspond to "mental files" into which knowledge will be sorted for easy access.

As you survey, jot down several questions for each chapter section. One simple technique is to generate questions by rephrasing a section heading. For example, the "Imprinting" head could be turned into "What is imprinting?" Good questions will allow you to focus on the important points in the text. Examples of good questions are those that begin as follows: "List two examples of. . . ." "What is the function of. . . ?" "What is the significance of. . . ?" Such questions give a purpose to your reading. Similarly, you can formulate questions based on the chapter outline.

The *Guided Study* section of this Study Guide provides the types of questions you might formulate while surveying each chapter. This section is a detailed set of objectives covering the points made in the text. Guidelines for answers to these objectives are provided at the end of each chapter.

Read   When you have established "files" for each section of the chapter, review your first question, begin reading, and continue until you have discovered its answer. If you come to material that seems to answer an important question you don't have a file for, stop and write down the question.

Using this Study Guide, read the chapter one section at a time. First, preview the section by skimming it, noting headings and boldface items. Next, study the appropriate section objectives in the *Guided Study*. Then, as you read the chapter section, search for the answer to each objective.

Be sure to read everything. Don't skip photo or art captions, graphs, or marginal notes. In some cases, what may seem vague in reading will be made clear by a simple graph. Keep in mind that test questions are sometimes drawn from illustrations and charts.

Recite   When you have found the answer to a question, close your eyes and mentally recite the question and its answer. Then *write* the answer next to the question. It is important that you recite an answer in your own words rather than the author's. Don't rely on your short-term memory to repeat the author's words verbatim.

In responding to the objectives, pay close attention to what is called for. If you are asked to identify or list, do just that. If asked to compare, contrast, or do both, you should focus on the similarities (compare) and differences (contrast) between the concepts or theories. Answering the objectives carefully will not only help you to focus your attention on the important concepts of the text, but it will also provide excellent practice for essay exams.

Recitation is an extremely effective study technique, recommended by many learning experts. In addition to increasing reading comprehension, it is useful for review. Trying to explain something in your own words clarifies your knowledge, often by revealing aspects of your answer that are vague or incomplete. If you repeatedly rely upon "I know" in recitation, you really *may not know*.

Recitation has the additional advantage of simulating an exam, especially an essay exam; the same skills are required in both cases. Too often students study without ever putting the book and notes aside, which makes it easy for them to develop false confidence in their knowledge. When the material is in front of you, you may be able to *recognize* an answer, but will you be able to *recall* it later, when you take an exam that does not provide these retrieval cues?

After you have recited and written your answer, continue with your next question. Read, recite, and so on.

Review When you have answered the last question on the material you have designated as a study goal, go back and review. Read over each question and your written answer to it. Your review might also include a brief written summary that integrates all of your questions and answers. This review need not take longer than a few minutes, but it is important. It will help you retain the material longer and will greatly facilitate a final review of each chapter before the exam.

In this Study Guide, the *Chapter Review* section contains fill-in questions for you to complete after you have finished reading the text and written answers to the objectives. The correct answers are given at the end of the chapter. Generally, your answer should match exactly (as in the case of important terms, theories, or people). In some cases, the answer is not a term or name, so a word close in meaning will suffice. You should go through the *Chapter Review* several times before taking an exam, so it is a good idea to mentally fill in the answers until you are ready for a final pretest review. Textbook page references are provided with each section title, in case you need to reread any of the material.

Also provided to facilitate your review are two *Progress Tests* that include multiple-choice questions and, where appropriate, matching or true-false questions. These tests are *not* to be taken until you have read the chapter, written answers to the objectives, and completed the *Chapter Review*. Correct answers, along with explanations of why each alternative is correct or incorrect, are provided at the end of the chapter. The relevant text page numbers for each question are also

given. If you miss a question, read these explanations and, if necessary, review the text pages to further understand why. The *Progress Tests* do not test every aspect of a concept, so you should treat an incorrect answer as an indication that you need to review the concept.

Following the two *Progress Tests* is a *Challenge Test*, which should be taken just prior to an exam. It includes questions that test your ability to analyze, integrate, and apply the concepts in the chapter. Each *Challenge Test* also includes an essay question dealing with a major concept covered in the chapter. As with the *Progress Tests*, answers for the *Challenge Test* are provided at the end of each chapter, along with relevant page numbers.

The chapter concludes with a list of *Key Terms*, with space provided for you to write a brief definition, or explanation, of each term, theory, or concept. As with the *Guided Study* objectives, it is important that these answers be written from memory, and in your own words. The *Answers* section at the end of the chapter gives a definition of each term, sometimes along with an example of its usage and/or a tip to help you remember its meaning.

In this Study Guide, an additional section called *Focus on Psychology* is provided to enrich your understanding of the textbook material. This section expands upon the text coverage by providing provocative issues for you to think about or by summarizing relevant research articles. In addition to serving as refreshing study breaks from the other sections of the Study Guide, the Focus items will enhance your understanding of the chapter's content by helping you to apply it to new information. Integrating what you've learned from the textbook with this new information is an excellent way to learn by actively participating, rather than by merely repeating information from the text.

One final suggestion: Incorporate SQ3R into your time-management calendar. Set specific goals for completing SQ3R with each assigned chapter. Keep a record of chapters completed, and reward yourself for being conscientious. Initially, it takes more time and effort to "read" using SQ3R, but with practice, the steps will become automatic. More important, you will comprehend significantly more material and retain knowledge longer than passive readers do.

Taking Lecture Notes

Are your class notes as useful as they might be? One way to determine their worth is to compare them with those taken by other good students. Are yours as thorough? Do they provide you with a comprehensible outline of each lecture? If not, then the following suggestions might increase the effectiveness of your notetaking.

1. Keep a separate notebook for each course. Use 8½ × 11-inch pages. Consider using a ring binder, which would allow you to revise and insert notes while still preserving lecture order.

2. Take notes in the format of a lecture outline. Use roman numerals for major points, letters for supporting arguments, and so on. Some instructors will make this easy by delivering organized lectures and, in some cases, by outlining their lectures on the board. If a lecture is disorganized, you will probably want to reorganize your notes soon after the class.

3. As you take notes in class, leave a wide margin on one side of each page. After the lecture, expand or clarify any shorthand notes while the material is fresh in your mind. Use this time to write important questions in the margin next to notes that answer them. This will facilitate later review and will allow you to anticipate similar exam questions.

Evaluating Your Exam Performance

How often have you received a grade on an exam that did not do justice to the effort you spent preparing for the exam? This is a common experience that can leave one feeling bewildered and abused. "What do I have to do to get an A?" "The test was unfair!" "I studied the wrong material!"

The chances of this happening are greatly reduced if you have an effective time-management schedule and use the study techniques described here. But it can happen to the best-prepared student and is most likely to occur on your first exam with a new professor.

Remember that there are two main reasons for studying. One is to learn for your own general academic development. Many people believe that such knowledge is all that really matters. Of course, it is possible, though unlikely, to be an expert on a topic without achieving commensurate grades, just as one can, occasionally, earn an excellent grade without truly mastering the course material. During a job interview or in the workplace, however, your A in Fortran won't mean much if you can't actually program a computer. In order to keep career options open after you graduate, you must know the material and maintain competitive grades. In the short run, this means performing well on exams, which is the second main objective in studying.

Probably the single best piece of advice to keep in mind when studying for exams is to *try to predict exam questions*. This means ignoring the trivia and focusing on the important questions and their answers (with your instructor's emphasis in mind).

A second point is obvious. How well you do on exams is determined by your mastery of *both* lecture and textbook material. Many students (partly because of poor time management) concentrate too much on one at the expense of the other.

To evaluate how well you are learning lecture and textbook material, analyze the questions you missed on the first exam. If your instructor does not review exams during class, you can easily do it yourself. Divide the questions into two categories: those drawn primarily from lectures and those drawn primarily from the textbook. Determine the percentage of questions you missed in each category. If your errors are evenly distributed and you are satisfied with your grade, you have no problem. If you are weaker in one area, you will need to set future goals for increasing and/or improving your study of that area.

Similarly, note the percentage of test questions drawn from each category. Although exams in most courses cover *both* lecture notes and the textbook, the relative emphasis of each may vary from instructor to instructor. While your instructors may not be entirely consistent in making up future exams, you may be able to tailor your studying for each course by placing *additional* emphasis on the appropriate area.

Exam evaluation will also point out the types of questions your instructor prefers. Does the exam consist primarily of multiple-choice, true-false, or essay questions? You may also discover that an instructor is fond of wording questions in certain ways. For example, an instructor may rely heavily on questions that require you to draw an analogy between a theory or concept and a real-world example. Evaluate both your instructor's style and how well you do with each format. Use this information to guide your future exam preparation.

Important aids, not only in studying for exams but also in determining how well prepared you are, are the *Progress* and *Challenge Tests* provided in this Study Guide. If these tests don't include all of the types of questions your instructor typically writes, make up your own practice exam questions. Spend extra time testing yourself with question formats that are most difficult for you. There is no better way to evaluate your preparation for an upcoming exam than by testing yourself under the conditions most likely to be in effect during the actual test.

A Few Practical Tips

Even the best intentions for studying sometimes fail. Some of these failures occur because students attempt to work under conditions that are simply not conducive to concentrated study. To help ensure the success of your time-management program, here are a few suggestions that should assist you in reducing the possibility of procrastination or distraction.

1. If you have set up a schedule for studying, make your roommate, family, and friends aware of this commitment, and ask them to honor your quiet study time. Close your door and post a "Do Not Disturb" sign.

2. Set up a place to study that minimizes potential distractions. Use a desk or table, not your bed or an extremely comfortable chair. Keep your desk and the walls around it free from clutter. If you need a place other than your room, find one that meets as many of the above requirements as possible—for example, in the library stacks.

3. Do nothing but study in this place. It should become associated with studying so that it "triggers" this activity, just as a mouth-watering aroma elicits an appetite.

4. Never study with the television on or with other distracting noises present. If you must have music in the background in order to mask outside noise, for example, play soft instrumental music. Don't pick vocal selections; your mind will be drawn to the lyrics.

5. Study by yourself. Other students can be distracting or can break the pace at which *your* learning is most efficient. In addition, there is always the possibility that group studying will become a social gathering. Reserve that for its own place in your schedule.

If you continue to have difficulty concentrating for very long, try the following suggestions.

6. Study your most difficult or most challenging subjects first, when you are most alert.

7. Start with relatively short periods of concentrated study, with breaks in between. If your attention starts to wander, get up immediately and take a break. It is better to study effectively for 15 minutes and then take a break than to fritter away 45 minutes out of an hour. Gradually increase the length of study periods, using your attention span as an indicator of successful pacing.

Critical Thinking

Having discussed a number of specific techniques for managing your time efficiently and studying effectively, let us now turn to a much broader topic: What exactly should you expect to learn as a student of psychology?

Most psychology courses have two major goals: (1) to help you acquire a basic understanding of psychology's knowledge base, and (2) to help you learn to think like a psychologist. Many students devote all of their efforts to the first of these goals, concentrating on memorizing as much of the course material as possible.

The second goal—learning to think like a psychologist—has to do with critical thinking. Critical thinking has many meanings. On one level, it refers to an attitude of healthy skepticism that should guide your study of psychology, or of any topic. As a critical thinker, you learn not to accept any explanation or conclusion about behavior as true until you have evaluated the evidence. On another level, critical thinking refers to a systematic process for examining the conclusions and arguments presented by others. In this regard, many of the features of the SQ3R technique for improving reading comprehension can be incorporated into an effective critical thinking system.

To learn to think critically, you must first recognize that psychological information is transmitted through the construction of persuasive *arguments*. An argument consists of three parts: an assertion, evidence, and an explanation (Mayer and Goodchild, 1990).

An assertion is a statement of relationship between some aspect of behavior, such as intelligence, and another factor, such as age. Learn to identify and evaluate the assertions about behavior and mental processes that you encounter as you read your textbook, listen to lectures, and engage in discussions with classmates. A good test of your understanding of an assertion is to try to restate it in your own words. As you do so, pay close attention to how terms and concepts are defined. When an article asserts that "intelligence declines with age," for example, what does it mean by "intelligence"? Assertions such as this one may be true when a critical term ("intelligence") is defined one way (for example, "speed of thinking"), but not when defined in another way (for example, "general knowledge"). One of the strengths of psychology is the use of *operational* definitions—definitions of terms and concepts that specify how they are to be measured, thus eliminating any ambiguity about their meaning. "Intelligence," for example, is often operationally defined as a person's score on a test that measures specific abilities. Whenever you encounter an assertion that is ambiguous, be skeptical of its accuracy.

When you have a clear understanding of an argument's assertion, evaluate its supporting evidence, the second component of an argument. Is it *empirical*; that is, is it based on actual experience—an observation or an experiment, for example? Does it, in fact, support the assertion? As you will learn in Chapter 1 of the textbook, psychologists accept only *empirical (observable) evidence* that is based on direct measurement of behavior. Hearsay, intuition, and personal experiences are not acceptable evidence. Chapter 1 contains a thorough discussion of the various research methods used by psychologists to gather empirical evidence. Some examples include surveys and tests, observations of behavior in natural settings, and experiments.

As you study psychology, you will become aware of another important issue in evaluating evidence — determining whether or not the research on which it is based is faulty. Research can be faulty for many reasons, including the use of an unrepresentative sample of subjects, experimenter bias, and inadequate control of unanticipated factors that might influence results. Evidence based on faulty research should be discounted. The textbook's Appendix, "Statistical Reasoning in Everyday Life," discusses these and other examples of faulty research.

The third component of an argument is the explanation provided for an assertion, which is based on the evidence that has been presented. While the argument's assertion merely *describes* how two things (such as intelligence and age) are related, the explanation tells *why*, often by proposing some theoretical mechanism that causes the relationship. Empirical evidence that thinking speed slows with age (the assertion), for example, may be explained as being caused by age-related changes in the activity of brain cells (a physiological explanation).

Be cautious in accepting explanations. In order to think critically about an argument's explanation, ask yourself three questions: (1) Can I restate the explanation in my own words?; (2) Does the explanation make sense based on the stated evidence?; and (3) Are there alternative explanations that adequately explain the assertion? Consider this last point in relation to our sample assertion: It is possible that the slower thinking speed of older adults is due to their having less recent experience than younger people with tasks that require quick thinking (a disuse explanation).

Because psychology is a relatively young science, its theoretical explanations are still emerging, and often change. For this reason, not all psychological arguments will offer explanations. Many arguments will only raise additional questions for further research to address.

Some Suggestions for Becoming a Critical Thinker

1. Adopt an attitude of healthy skepticism in evaluating psychological arguments.

2. Insist on unambiguous operational definitions of an argument's important concepts and terms.

3. Be cautious in accepting supporting evidence for an argument's assertion.

4. Refuse to accept evidence for an argument if it is based on faulty research.

5. Ask yourself if the theoretical explanation provided for an argument "makes sense" based on the empirical evidence.

6. Determine whether there are alternative explanations that adequately explain an assertion.

7. Use critical thinking to construct your own effective arguments when writing term papers, answering essay questions, and speaking.

8. Polish your critical thinking skills by applying them to each of your college courses, and to other areas of life as well. Learn to think critically about advertising, political speeches, and the material presented in popular periodicals.

A Critical Thinking Exercise

You should now be ready to test your understanding of critical thinking by evaluating an actual psychological argument from your textbook (pages 114–116). Carefully read the passage on Aging and Intelligence presented below. Next, answer the questions about the argument. Finally, compare your answers with those given on page xv. (Note: The full citations for references found in this section appear in the "References" section at the end of the text.)

What happens to our broader intellectual powers as we age? Do they gradually decline, like our ability to recall nonsense material? Or do they remain constant, like our ability to recognize meaningful material?

In cross-sectional studies, researchers test people of various ages at the same time. When giving intelligence tests to representative samples of people, researchers consistently find that older adults give fewer correct answers than younger adults (Figure 1).

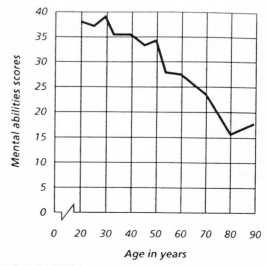

(From Geiwitz, 1980.)

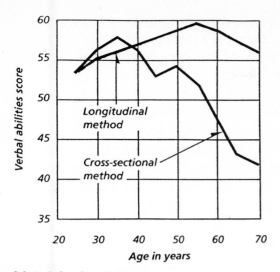

(From Schaie & Strother, 1968.)

David Wechsler (1972), creator of the widely used adult intelligence test, therefore concluded that "the decline of mental ability with age is part of the general (aging) process of the organism as a whole."

Colleges began giving intelligence tests to entering students about 1920, making it possible to retest older people who had taken an intelligence test years earlier. Several psychologists saw their chance to study intelligence longitudinally, by retesting the same people over a period of years. What they expected to find was the usual decrease in intelligence after about age 30 (Schaie & Geiwitz, 1982). What they actually found was a surprise: Until very late in life, intelligence remained stable, and on some tests it even increased.

How then are we to account for the findings from the cross-sectional studies? In retrospect, researchers saw the problem. When a cross-sectional study compares 70- and 30-year-olds, it compares not only people of two different ages, but of two different eras. It compares generally less educated people (born, say, in the early 1900s) with more educated people (born after 1950), people raised in large families with people raised in smaller families, people growing up in less affluent families with people raised in more affluent families.

Evaluate the Argument

1. State Wechsler's assertion in your own words, and give operational definitions of all important concepts and terms.

2. State the evidence for Wechsler's assertion, noting whether or not it is empirical, and whether or not it is based on faulty research.

3. Evaluate Wechsler's theoretical explanation for his assertion by:
a. restating it in your own words:

b. determining whether the explanation makes sense based on Wechsler's evidence:

c. stating an adequate alternative explanation for Wechsler's assertion:

Sample Answers to the Critical Thinking Exercise

1. State Wechsler's assertion in your own words, and give operational definitions of all important concepts and terms.

Wechsler asserts that mental ability, operationally defined as the number of correct answers on an intelligence test, declines with age.

2. State the evidence for Wechsler's assertion, noting whether or not it is empirical, and whether or not it is based on faulty research.

Wechsler's evidence is based on empirical cross-sectional research comparing intelligence test scores of people of various ages. It was later discovered that cross-sectional research is a faulty way to study age-related changes in intelligence. This is so because the comparison groups in cross-sectional studies typically differ not only in their ages, but also in their levels of education and affluence.

3. Evaluate Wechsler's theoretical explanation for his assertion by:
a. restating it in your own words:

Wechsler stated that age-related declines in mental

ability are a result of the normal physical aging of the body.

b. determining whether the explanation makes sense based on Wechsler's evidence:

Based on Wechsler's cross-sectional evidence alone, the physical explanation for his assertion that mental ability declines with age does seem to make sense. However, the cross-sectional evidence does not rule out alternative explanations.

c. stating an adequate alternative explanation for Wechsler's assertion:

Because cross-sectional research compares groups that differ not only in age, but also in education and affluence, it is possible that age alone does not cause a decline in mental ability. In the 1970s, older adults were more likely than younger adults to be less educated, and to have been raised in larger, less affluent families. These factors cannot be ruled out as explanations for the typical pattern found in cross-sectional studies of mental ability. Therefore, there is no reason to accept Wechsler's conclusion that the decline in intelligence is based on the physical effects of aging. Furthermore, longitudinal studies investigate age-related changes in mental ability while holding constant such factors as education and affluence. These studies demonstrate that mental ability remains stable until very late in life.

If you would like more information on critical thinking, consult one of the following sources.

Mayer, R., & Goodchild, F. (1990). *The critical thinker: Thinking and learning strategies for psychology students.* Dubuque, IA: Wm. C. Brown Publishers.

Paul, R. (1990). *Critical thinking: What every person needs to survive in a rapidly changing world.* Foundation for Critical Thinking.

Some Closing Thoughts

I hope that these suggestions not only help make you more successful academically, but also enhance the quality of your college life in general. Having the necessary skills makes any job a lot easier and more pleasant. Let me repeat my warning not to attempt to make too drastic a change in your life-style immediately. Good habits require time and self-discipline to develop. Once established they can last a lifetime.

1 / Introducing Psychology

Chapter Overview

Psychology's historical development and current activities lead us to define the field as the science of behavior and mental processes. Chapter 1 discusses the development of psychology and the range of behaviors and mental processes being investigated by psychologists in each of the various specialty areas. In addition, it explains how psychologists employ the research designs of description, correlation, and experimentation in order to objectively observe, predict, and understand behavior. Chapter 1 concludes with a discussion of several questions people often ask about psychology, including why animal research is relevant, whether laboratory experiments are ethical, whether psychological theories aren't simply based on common sense, and whether psychology's principles don't have the potential for misuse.

Chapter 1 should not be too difficult for you; there are not very many difficult terms or theories to remember. However, the chapter does introduce a number of concepts and issues that will play an important role in later chapters. Pay particular attention to the section "Psychology's Methods." Make sure you understand the method of experimentation, especially the importance of control conditions and the difference between independent and dependent variables.

NOTE: Answer guidelines for all Chapter 1 questions begin on page 14.

Guided Study

The text chapter should be studied one section at a time. Before you read, preview each section by skimming it, noting headings and boldface items. Then read the appropriate section objectives from the following outline. Keep these objectives in mind and, as you read the chapter section, search for the information that will enable you to meet each objective. Once you have finished a section, write out answers for its objectives.

What Is Psychology? (pp. 4–9)

1. Define psychology and trace its historical development.

   Psychology - Science of behavior & mental processes.

2. Explain the nature-nurture issue in psychology and identify its historical roots.

3. Describe the different perspectives from which psychologists examine behavior and mental processes.

   correlation
   description
   observation

4. Identify the major subfields of psychology.

   basic research
   applied "
   psychologist
   psychiatrist

1

The Scientific Approach (pp. 9–10)

5. Discuss the attitudes that characterize scientific inquiry and explain the scientific method.

Theory

hypothesis.

Psychology's Methods (pp. 10–17)

6. Identify the methods of psychology and discuss the descriptive research designs.

7. Explain why correlation enables prediction but not explanation.

8. Describe the nature and advantages of experimentation.

Commonly Asked Questions About Psychology (pp. 17–22)

9. Discuss questions regarding the artificiality of experimentation and whether psychological principles are culture-free.

10. Explain why psychologists study animals and discuss the ethics of experimentation.

11. Describe how psychologists' values influence their work and discuss whether psychological theories are merely common sense.

12. Discuss whether psychology is potentially dangerous.

How to Study This Book (pp. 22–23)

13. Explain the SQ3R study method.

Chapter Review

When you have finished reading the chapter, work through the material that follows to review it. Complete the sentences and answer the questions. As you proceed, evaluate your performance for each section by consulting the answers on page 16. Do not continue with the next section until you understand each answer. If you need to, review or reread the appropriate section in the textbook before continuing.

What Is Psychology? (pp. 4–9)

1. The historical roots of psychology include the fields of _physiology_ and _philosophy_.

2. The first psychological laboratory was founded in 1879 by Wilhelm _Wundt_.

3. Some early psychologists included Ivan Pavlov, who pioneered the study of _animal learning_. the personality theorist _Sigmund Freud._; Jean Piaget, who studied _child behavior_; and _William James_ the author of one of the first psychology textbooks.

4. In its earliest years, psychology was defined as the science of _mental_ life. From about 1920 until 1960, under the influence of _John Watson_, psychology in America was redefined as the science of _observable_ behavior. The author of your textbook defines psychology as the science of _mental_ and _behavioral_ processes.

5. The controversy over the relative contributions of genes, or _internal_ (internal/external) influences, and experience, or _external_ (internal/external) influences, on behavior is called the _nature_ – _nurture_ issue.

6. The Greek philosopher who assumed that character and intelligence are inherited is _Plato_. The Greek philosopher who argued that all knowledge comes from sensory experience is _Aristotle._ In the 1600s these views were revived by _John Locke._, who believed that most knowledge comes in through the senses, and _René Descartes_, who believed that knowledge does not depend on sense experience.

Give examples of how the phenomenon of intelligence might be explained by those who emphasize internal influences on behavior and by those who emphasize external influences.

7. Psychologists who study evolutionary and hereditary influences on behavior, for example, are working within the _biological_ perspective.

8. The _psychoanalytic_ perspective assumes that behavior is the product of unconscious drives and conflicts.

9. Psychologists who study the mechanisms by which observable responses are acquired and changed are working within the _behavioral_ perspective.

10. The emphasis on our capacity to choose our own life patterns and to grow to higher levels of maturity is characteristic of the _humanistic_ perspective.

11. The _cognitive_ perspective explores how our minds process, store, and retrieve information.

12. Psychologists who study how thinking and behavior vary in different situations are working within the _social-cultural_ perspective.

13. The different perspectives on behavior and mental processes _complement._ (contradict/complement) one another.

14. Psychologists who study, assess, and treat troubled people are called _clinical_ psychologists.

15. Psychologists may be involved in conducting _basic research_, which builds psychology's knowledge base, or _applied research_, which seeks solutions to practical problems.

Give examples of basic and applied research.

Basic	Applied
dev. psy.	ind. psy.
bio. psy.	

The Scientific Approach (pp. 9–10)

16. The scientific approach is characterized by the attitudes of open-minded _skepticism_ and _scrutiny_.

17. An integrated set of principles that explains something, organizes isolated facts, and predicts observable events is a _theory_ . Testable predictions that allow a scientist to evaluate a theory are called _hypothesis_ .

18. In order to prevent theoretical biases from influencing scientific observations, research must be reported precisely so that others can _test/replicate_ the findings.

19. Psychologists conduct research in the field, in the laboratory, and in other research _fields_ using people's self-report, direct observation, and other _assessment_ _technique_ .

Psychology's Methods (pp. 10–17)

20. The three basic research designs in psychology are _descriptive_ , _observation_ , and _correlation_ .

21. The research design in which one or more individuals is studied in depth in order to reveal general principles of behavior is the _case_ _study_ method.

22. The method in which a group of people is questioned about their attitudes or behavior is the _Survey_ method.

23. An important factor in the validity of survey research is the _wording_ of questions.

24. Surveys try to obtain a _random_ sample, one that will be representative of the _population_ being studied. In such a sample, every person _does_ (does/does not) have a chance of being included.

25. The research design in which people or animals are directly observed in their natural environments is called _naturalistic observations_ .

26. Case studies, surveys, and naturalistic observation do not explain behavior; they simply _describe_ it.

27. When changes in one factor are accompanied by changes in another, the two factors are said to be _correlation_ , and one is thus able to _predict_ the other. If the factors increase or decrease together, they are _positive_ _correlation_ . If, however, one decreases as the other increases, they are _negative_ _correlation_ .

28. A common error is to assume that a correlation between two factors means that one _causes_ the other. To study cause-and-effect relationships, psychologists conduct _experiments_ .

If your level of test anxiety goes down as your time spent studying for the exam goes up, would you say these events are positively or negatively correlated? Explain your reasoning.

29. An experiment must involve at least two conditions: the _control_ condition, in which the experimental treatment is absent, and the _experimental_ condition, in which it is present.

30. The factor that is being manipulated in an experiment is called the _independent_ variable. The factor that may change as a result of these manipulations is called the _dependent_ variable.

31. Experimenters rely on _random_ _assignment_ of individuals to experimental and control groups so that any difference between the two groups must be due to the experiment's _independent_ variable.

Explain at least one advantage of the experiment as a research design.

32. In the experiment investigating the impact of subliminal messages on self-esteem and memory, subjects in one condition received tapes without the expected message. This type of pseudo-treatment, or control, is called a ___placebo___.

33. In the ___double___-___bind___ procedures, neither the subjects nor the experimenter know which condition a subject is in.

Commonly Asked Questions About Psychology (pp. 17–22)

34. Laboratory experiments in psychology are sometimes criticized as being ___artificial___. However, psychologists' concern is not with the specific behaviors that occur in the experiments, but with the underlying theoretical ___principles___.

35. Although specific attitudes and behaviors vary across cultures, the underlying ___principles___ are the same.

36. Psychologists' values ___do___ (do/do not) influence their theories, observations, and professional advice.

37. The tendency to perceive an outcome that has occurred as being obvious and predictable is called ___hindsight bias___.

FOCUS ON PSYCHOLOGY:
A Career in Psychology

Preparing for a career in psychology usually requires a graduate degree. To earn a doctorate in psychology (Ph.D. or Psy.D.), students complete a four-to six-year program, at the end of which they must design and conduct an original research project. Although a doctorate is required for many jobs in psychology—indeed, more than 60 percent of all psychologists hold this degree—the degree of Master of Arts (M.A.) is sufficient for others, such as teaching at some community colleges or being a school psychologist. The M.A. degree program typically requires one or two years of training beyond the undergraduate curriculum. A bachelor's degree does not prepare students to work as psychologists any more than it prepares them to work as physicians or attorneys.

The figures on this page indicate the percentages of psychologists working in various settings and fields of specialization. Traditionally, most psychologists accepted teaching or research positions at universities and four-year colleges. Because of declining college enrollments and general economic trends, however, college faculty positions and jobs in areas dependent upon government funding (such as many research positions) are expected to decline. Many of the employment opportunities for doctorates in psychology will derive from society's increased emphasis on health maintenance and meeting the needs of particular groups, such as the elderly. Business, industry, and private clinical practice are also expected to be good sources of employment.

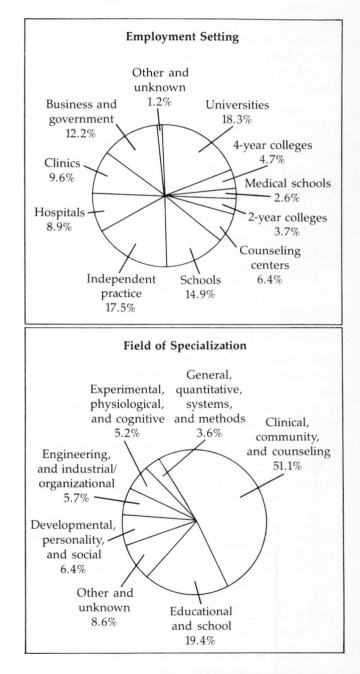

Employment Setting

Other and unknown 1.2%
Universities 18.3%
Business and government 12.2%
4-year colleges 4.7%
Clinics 9.6%
Medical schools 2.6%
Hospitals 8.9%
2-year colleges 3.7%
Counseling centers 6.4%
Independent practice 17.5%
Schools 14.9%

Field of Specialization

Experimental, physiological, and cognitive 5.2%
General, quantitative, systems, and methods 3.6%
Clinical, community, and counseling 51.1%
Engineering, and industrial/organizational 5.7%
Developmental, personality, and social 6.4%
Other and unknown 8.6%
Educational and school 19.4%

During the late 1980s approximately 97,000 psychologists were in the work force with a median annual salary of $40,000 for all those with doctoral degrees. Since the 1970s, however, the rate at which new doctorates have been conferred has increased faster in psychology than in any other field, creating a tremendous need for alternative sources of employment for psychologists, particularly those with only a master's degree.

Training in psychology can, of course, provide benefits other than employment. Many of the findings of psychologists have obvious practical applications helping you to understand the ways that groups influence a person's behavior, or helping you to eliminate undesirable habits. As a student of psychology, you may also develop the objective and skeptical eye of the behavioral scientist. This will help you evaluate information reported by the media. Developing this perspective will make you a more objective and better-informed citizen and consumer.

Sources: U.S. Census Bureau. (1990). *Statistical abstract of the United States*. Washington, DC.: Author.

Hopke, W. E. (1987). *The encyclopedia of careers and vocational guidance* (7th ed.). Chicago: J. G. Ferguson Publishing Company.

Stapp, J., Tucker, A. M., and VandenBos, G. R. (1985). Census of psychological personnel: 1983. *American Psychologist, 40* (12), 1317-1351.

American Psychological Association. (1986). *Careers in psychology*. Washington, DC: Author.
If you want information about how to prepare for a career in psychology and opportunities for employment, write to the American Psychological Association, 1200 Seventeenth St. N.W., Washington, D.C. 20036, and request this free pamphlet.

Progress Test 1

Multiple-Choice Questions

Circle your answers to the following questions and check them with the answers on page 16. If your answer is incorrect, read the explanation for why it is incorrect and then consult the appropriate pages of the text (in parentheses following the correct answer).

1. In its earliest days, psychology was defined as the:
   (a) study of mental phenomena.
   b. study of conscious and unconscious activity.
   c. science of observable behavior.
   d. science of behavior and mental processes.

2. Who would be most likely to agree with the statement, "Psychology should investigate only behaviors that can be observed?"
   a. Wilhelm Wundt
   b. Sigmund Freud
   (c) John Watson
   d. William James

3. Today, psychology is defined as the:
   a. study of mental phenomena.
   b. study of conscious and unconscious activity.
   c. science of behavior.
   (d) science of behavior and mental processes.

4. After detailed study of a gunshot wound victim, a psychologist concludes that the brain region destroyed is likely to be important for memory functions. Which research did the psychologist use to deduce this?
   (a) case study   c. correlational
   b. survey   d. experimental

5. In an experiment to determine the effects of exercise on motivation, exercise is the:
   (a) control condition.
   b. intervening variable.
   (c) independent variable.
   d. dependent variable.

6. In order to determine the effects of a new drug on memory, one group of subjects is given a pill that contains the drug. A second group is given a sugar pill that does not contain the drug. This second group constitutes the:
   a. random sample.   (c) control group.
   b. experimental group.   d. test group.

7. Theories are defined as:
   a. testable propositions.
   b. factors that may change in response to manipulation.
   c. statistical indexes.
   (d) principles that help to organize, predict, and explain facts.

8. A psychologist studies the play behavior of third-grade children by watching groups during recess at school. Which research design is being used?
   a. correlation
   b. case study
   c. experiment
   (d) naturalistic observation

9. Which of the following exemplifies the issue of the relative importance of internal and external influences on our behavior?
   (a) the issue of the relative influence of genes and experience on behavior
   b. the issue of the relative influence of rewards and punishments on behavior
   c. the debate as to the relative importance of heredity and instinct in determining behavior
   d. the debate as to whether mental processes are a legitimate area of scientific study

10. The seventeenth-century philosopher who believed that the mind is blank at birth and that most knowledge comes through sensory experience is:
    a. Plato.   c. Descartes.
    b. Aristotle.   (d) Locke.

11. Which psychological perspective emphasizes the interaction of the brain and body in behavior?
    a. biological perspective
    b. cognitive perspective
    c. behavioral perspective
    d. psychoanalytic perspective

12. Psychologists use experimental research in order to reveal or to understand:
    a. correlational relationships.
    b. hypotheses.
    c. theories.
    d. cause-and-effect relationships.

13. The scientific attitude of skepticism is based on the belief that:
    a. people are rarely candid in revealing their thoughts.
    b. mental processes cannot be studied objectively.
    c. the scientist's intuition about behavior is usually correct.
    d. ideas need to be tested against observable evidence.

14. Which of the following is *not* a basic research design used by psychologists?
    a. description   c. experimentation
    b. replication   d. correlation

15. A psychologist who explores how Asian and North American definitions of attractiveness differ is working within the _____ perspective.
    a. behavioral   c. cognitive
    b. psychoanalytic   d. social-cultural

16. Psychologists' personal values:
    a. have little influence on how their experiments are conducted.
    b. do not influence the interpretation of experi-

mental results because of the use of statistical techniques that guard against subjective bias.
    c. can bias both scientific observation and interpretation of data.
    d. have little influence on the methods of investigation but a significant effect on interpretation.

17. If shoe size and IQ are negatively correlated, which of the following is true?
    a. People with large feet tend to have high IQs.
    b. People with small feet tend to have high IQs.
    c. People with small feet tend to have low IQs.
    d. IQ is unpredictable based on a person's shoe size.

18. Which of the following research designs would be best to use to determine whether alcohol impairs memory?
    a. case study
    b. naturalistic observation
    c. survey
    d. experiment

19. Hypotheses are:
    a. integrated sets of principles that help organize observations.
    b. testable predictions, often derived from theories.
    c. hunches about mental processes.
    d. measures of relationships between two factors.

20. Well-done surveys measure attitudes in a representative subset, or _____, of an entire group, or _____.
    a. population; random sample
    b. control group; experimental group
    c. experimental group; control group
    d. random sample; population

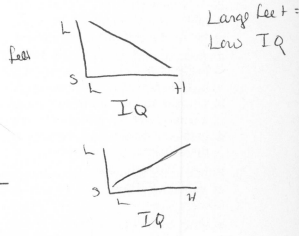

Matching Items

Match each subfield and psychological perspective with its definition or description.

Terms

___f___ 1. biological perspective
___b___ 2. social-cultural perspective
___j___ 3. psychiatry
___i___ 4. clinical psychology
___d___ 5. psychoanalytic perspective
___e___ 6. behavioral perspective
___a___ 7. humanistic perspective
___g___ 8. cognitive perspective
___h___ 9. basic research
___c___ 10. applied research

Definitions or Descriptions

a. emphasizes a person's capacity to grow to higher levels of fulfillment

b. concerned with how people differ as products of different environments

c. concerned with the study of practical problems

d. concerned with the role of unconscious drives and conflicts in determining human behavior

e. concerned with the mechanisms by which observable responses are acquired and changed

f. concerned with exploration of the links between biology and behavior

g. concerned with how the mind processes, stores, and retrieves information

h. concerned with adding to psychology's knowledge base

i. concerned with the study, assessment, and treatment of troubled people

j. concerned with the medical treatment of psychological disorders

Progress Test 2

Progress Test 2 should be completed during a final chapter review. Answer the following questions after you thoroughly understand the correct answers for the Chapter Review and Progress Test 1.

Multiple-Choice Questions

1. The first psychology laboratory was established by _____ in the year _____.
   a. Wundt; 1879   c. Freud; 1899
   b. James; 1890   d. Watson; 1913

2. In the experiment on subliminal perception, students listened for five weeks to tapes that they thought would enhance their memory or self-esteem. At the end of the experiment:
   a. students who thought they had a memory tape believed their memories had improved; but, in fact, there was no improvement.
   b. self-esteem, but not memory, improved.
   c. memory, but not self-esteem, improved.
   d. both self-esteem and memory improved over the course of the experiment.

3. Which of the following statements about the ethics of experimentation with people and animals is false?
   a. Only a small percentage of animal experiments use shock.
   b. Allegations that psychologists routinely subject animals to pain, starvation, and other inhumane conditions have not been found to be true.
   c. The American Psychological Association has set strict guidelines for the care and treatment of human and animal subjects.
   d. Animals are used as subjects in almost 25 percent of all psychology experiments.

4. In an experiment to determine the effects of attention on memory, memory is the:
   a. control condition.
   b. intervening variable.
   c. independent variable.
   d. dependent variable.

5. The group that receives the treatment of interest in an experiment is the:
   a. test group.
   b. random sample.
   c. experimental group.
   d. control group.

6. Which of the following best describes the hindsight bias?
   a. Events seem more predictable before they have occurred.
   b. Events seem more predictable after they have occurred.
   c. A person's intuition is usually correct.
   d. A person's intuition is usually not correct.

7. The procedure designed to ensure that the experimental and control groups do not differ in any way that might affect the experiment's results is called:
   a. variable controlling.
   b. random assignment.
   c. representative sampling.
   d. stratification.

8. Two historical roots of psychology are the disciplines of:
   a. philosophy and chemistry.
   b. physiology and chemistry.
   c. philosophy and physiology.
   d. philosophy and physics.

9. Which of the following individuals is also a physician?
   a. clinical psychologist
   b. experimental psychologist
   c. psychiatrist
   d. biological psychologist

10. The Greek philosopher who believed that intelligence was inherited was:
    a. Aristotle.   c. Descartes.
    b. Plato.   d. Simonides.

11. The way the mind processes, stores, and retrieves information is the primary concern of the _____ perspective.
    a. biological   c. behavioral
    b. psychoanalytic   d. cognitive

12. According to the textbook:
    a. because laboratory experiments are artificial, any principles discovered cannot be applied to everyday behaviors.
    b. no psychological theory can be considered true until tested.
    c. psychology's theories simply reflect common sense.
    d. psychology has few ties to other disciplines.

13. Dr. Jones's research centers on the relationship between changes in our thinking over the life span and changes in moral reasoning. Dr. Jones is most likely a:
    a. clinical psychologist.
    b. personality psychologist.
    c. social psychologist.
    d. developmental psychologist.

14. Which subfield is most directly concerned with studying human behavior in the workplace?
    a. clinical psychology
    b. personality psychology
    c. industrial/organizational psychology
    d. psychiatry

15. Dr. Ernst explains behavior in terms of unconscious drives. Dr. Ernst is working within the:
    a. behavioral perspective.
    b. humanistic perspective.
    c. psychoanalytic perspective.
    d. cognitive perspective.

16. Which perspective emphasizes the importance of environmental influences upon behavior?
    a. behavioral
    b. humanistic
    c. psychoanalytic
    d. cognitive

17. Which type of research design would allow you to determine whether students' college grades accurately predict later income?
    a. case study
    b. naturalistic observation
    c. experiment
    d. correlation

18. In a test of the effects of air pollution, groups of students performed a reaction-time task in either a polluted or unpolluted room. To what condition were students in the unpolluted room exposed?
    a. experimental   c. randomly assigned
    b. control   d. dependent

19. In order to study the effects of lighting on mood, Dr. Cooper had students fill out questionnaires in brightly lit or dimly lit rooms. In this study, the independent variable consisted of:
    a. the number of subjects assigned to each group.
    b. the students' responses to the questionnaire.
    c. the room lighting.
    d. the subject matter of the questions asked.

20. A psychologist who studies how worker productivity might be increased by changing office layout is engaged in _____ research.
    a. applied   c. clinical
    b. basic   d. developmental

Matching Items

Match each term with its definition or description.

Terms

_e_   **1.** hypothesis
_h_   **2.** theory
_b_   **3.** independent variable
_c_   **4.** dependent variable
_j_   **5.** experimental condition
_d_   **6.** control condition
_a_   **7.** case study
_k_   **8.** survey
_f_   **9.** replication
_g_   **10.** random assignment
_i_   **11.** experiment
_l_   **12.** double-blind

Definitions or Descriptions

a. an in-depth observational study of one person
b. the variable being manipulated in an experiment
c. the variable being measured in an experiment
d. the "treatment-absent" condition in an experiment
e. testable proposition
f. repeating an experiment to see whether the same results are obtained
g. the process in which subjects are selected by chance for different groups in an experiment
h. an integrated set of principles that organizes observations
i. the research design in which the effects of one or more variables on behavior are tested
j. the "treatment-present" condition in an experiment
k. the research design in which a representative sample of individuals is questioned
l. experimental procedure in which neither the subject nor the experimenter know which condition the subject is in

Challenge Test

Answer these questions the day before an exam as a final check on your understanding of the chapter's terms and concepts.

Multiple-Choice Questions

1. Psychology is defined as the "science of behavior and mental processes." Wilhelm Wundt would have omitted which of the following words from this definition?
   a. science
   b. behavior and
   c. and mental processes
   d. Wundt would have agreed with the definition as stated.

2. You decide to test your belief that men drink more soft drinks than women by finding out whether more soft drinks are consumed per day in the men's dorm than in the women's dorm. Your belief is a(n) _____, and your research prediction is a(n) _____ .
   a. hypothesis; theory
   b. theory; hypothesis
   c. independent variable; dependent variable
   d. dependent variable; independent variable

3. Your roommate is conducting a survey to learn how many hours the typical college student studies each day. She plans to pass out her questionnaire to the members of her sorority. You point out that her findings will be flawed because:

   a. she has not specified an independent variable.
   b. she has not specified a dependent variable.
   c. the sample will probably not be representative of the population of interest.
   d. of all the above reasons.

4. The concept of control is important in psychological research because:
   a. without control over independent and dependent variables, researchers cannot describe, predict, or explain behavior.
   b. experimental control allows researchers to study the influence of one or two independent variables on a dependent variable while holding other potential influences constant.
   c. without experimental control, results cannot be generalized from a sample to a population.
   d. of all the above reasons.

5. Martina believes that high doses of caffeine slow a person's reaction time. In order to test this belief, she has five friends each drink three 8-ounce cups of coffee and then measures their reaction time on a learning task. What is wrong with Martina's research design?
   a. No independent variable is specified.
   b. No dependent variable is specified.
   c. There is no control condition.
   d. There is no provision for replication of the findings.

6. A researcher was interested in determining whether her students' test performance could be predicted from their proximity to the front of the classroom. So she matched her students' scores on a math test with their seating position. This study is an example of:

   a. experimentation.
   b. correlational research.
   c. a survey.
   d. naturalistic observation.

7. Your best friend criticizes psychological research for being artificial and having no relevance to behavior in real life. In defense of psychology's use of laboratory experiments you point out that:

   a. psychologists make every attempt to avoid artificiality by setting up experiments that closely simulate real-world environments.
   b. psychologists who conduct basic research are not concerned with the applicability of their findings to the real world.
   c. most psychological research is not conducted in a laboratory environment.
   d. psychologists intentionally study behavior in simplified environments in order to gain greater control over variables and to test general principles that help explain many behaviors.

8. A professor constructs a questionnaire to determine how students at the university feel about nuclear disarmament. Which of the following techniques should be used in order to survey a random sample of the student body?

   a. Every student should be sent the questionnaire.
   b. Only students majoring in psychology should be asked to complete the questionnaire.
   c. Only students living on campus should be asked to complete the questionnaire.
   d. From an alphabetical listing of all students, every tenth (or fifteenth, or twentieth) student should be asked to complete the questionnaire.

9. Experimentation, which seeks to explain events, involves _____ factors, while correlation, which serves only to predict events, involves _____ factors.

   a. determining relationships between; direct manipulation of
   b. direct manipulation of; determining relationships between
   c. direct observation of; random selection of
   d. random selection of; direct observation of

10. If eating saturated fat and the likelihood of contracting cancer are positively correlated, which of the following is true?

   a. Saturated fat causes cancer.
   b. People who are prone to develop cancer prefer foods containing saturated fat.
   c. A separate factor links the consumption of saturated fat to cancer.
   d. None of the above is necessarily true.

11. Why are animals frequently used in psychology experiments?

   a. The processes that underlie behavior in animals and humans are often similar.
   b. Animal behavior is generally simpler to understand.
   c. Animals are worthy of study for their own sake.
   d. All of the above reasons are involved.

12. To say that "psychology is a science" means that:

   a. psychologists study only observable behaviors.
   b. psychologists approach the study of thoughts and actions with an attitude of skepticism, and derive their conclusions from direct observations.
   c. psychological research should be free of value judgments.
   d. all of the above are true.

13. Plato's philosophical position concerning the nature-nurture issue is to Locke's position as the position of _____ is to that of _____.

   a. Aristotle; Descartes   c. Watson; Aristotle
   b. Descartes; Aristotle   d. Aristotle; Watson

14. Which of the following psychological perspectives places the least emphasis on the objective measurement of behavior?

   a. biological perspective
   b. behavioral perspective
   c. cognitive perspective
   d. humanistic perspective

15. Rashad, who is participating in a psychology experiment on the effects of alcohol on perception, is truthfully told by the experimenter that he has been assigned to the "high-dose condition." What is wrong with this experiment?

   a. There is no control condition.
   b. Rashad's expectations concerning the effects of "high doses" of alcohol on perception may influence his performance.
   c. Knowing that Rashad is in the "high-dose" condition may influence the experimenter's interpretations of Rashad's results.
   d. Both b. and c. are correct.

16. A friend majoring in anthropology is critical of psychological research because it often ignores the influence of culture on thoughts and actions. You point out that:

   a. there is very little evidence that cultural diversity has a significant effect on specific behaviors and attitudes.

b. most researchers assign subjects to experimental and control conditions in such a way as to fairly represent the cultural diversity of the population under study.

c. it is impossible for psychologists to control for every possible variable that might influence the thoughts and actions of research participants.

d. even when specific thoughts and actions vary across cultures, as they often do, the underlying processes are much the same.

17. The scientific attitude of humility is based on the idea that:

a. researchers must evaluate new ideas and theories objectively, rather than accept them blindly.

b. scientific theories must be testable.

c. simple explanations of behavior make better theories than do complex explanations.

d. researchers must be prepared to reject their own ideas in the face of conflicting evidence.

18. Which of the following procedures is an example of the use of a placebo?

a. In a test of the effects of a drug on memory, a subject is led to believe that a harmless pill actually contains an active drug.

b. A subject in an experiment is led to believe that a pill, which actually contains an active drug, is harmless.

c. Subjects in an experiment are not told which treatment condition is in effect.

d. Neither the subjects nor the experimenter know which treatment condition is in effect.

19. During a dinner conversation a friend says that the psychoanalytic and humanistic perspectives are quite similar. You disagree and point out that the psychoanalytic perspective emphasizes _____, while the humanistic perspective emphasizes _____.

a. conscious processes; unconscious processes

b. unconscious processes; conscious processes

c. overt behaviors; covert behaviors

d. introspection; experimentation

20. Concerning the six psychological perspectives on behavior, the author of the textbook suggests that:

a. researchers should work within the framework of only one of the perspectives.

b. only those perspectives that emphasize objective measurement of behavior are useful.

c. the different perspectives often complement one another; together, they provide a fuller understanding of behavior than provided by any single perspective.

d. psychologists should avoid all of these traditional perspectives.

Essay Question

Esteban has a theory that regular exercise can improve thinking. Help him design an experiment evaluating this theory by answering questions a. through d.

a. How would you restate Esteban's theory as a testable hypothesis?

b. What are the independent and dependent variables and how could they be manipulated, or measured?

c. Do you need a control group? If so, why, and what should they do?

d. How should subjects be selected and assigned to the various conditions of the experiment?

Key Terms

Using your own words, write a brief definition or explanation of each of the following.

1. psychology

2. nature-nurture issue

3. biological perspective

4. psychoanalytic perspective

5. behavioral perspective

6. humanistic perspective

7. cognitive perspective

8. social-cultural perspective

9. clinical psychology

10. psychiatry

11. basic research

12. applied research

13. theory

14. hypothesis

15. replication

16. case study

17. survey

18. population

19. random sample

20. naturalistic observation

21. correlation

22. experiment

23. control condition

24. experimental condition

25. independent variable

26. dependent variable

27. random assignment

28. placebo

29. double-blind procedure

30. hindsight bias

31. SQ3R

ANSWERS

GUIDED STUDY

The following guidelines provide the main points that your answers should have touched upon.

1. Psychology, the science of behavior and mental processes, is a young science with roots in many disciplines. The earliest psychologists, including Wilhelm Wundt who founded the first psychology laboratory in 1879, were philosophers and physiologists. In its early years psychological research focused on inner sensations, feelings, and thoughts. From the 1920s to the 1960s, psychology in the United States was most influenced by John Watson and others who redefined it as the "science of observable behavior." In the 1960s, psychology began to recapture its interest in mental processes, so that today psychology encompasses the scientific study of both overt behavior and covert thoughts and feelings.

2. The nature-nurture issue in psychology is concerned with the relative contributions of internal influences, such as genes (nature), and external influences, such as experience (nurture). The nature-nurture debate has its roots in ancient Greek philosophy. Plato believed that much of human character and intelligence was inherited, whereas Aristotle believed that experience accounts for the contents of the mind. In the 1600s, John Locke and René Descartes revived the controversy, with Locke arguing that knowledge depends on experience and Descartes maintaining that knowledge is inborn.

3. Psychologists who work from a biological perspective study the influences of heredity and physiology on behavior. The psychoanalytic perspective

focuses on the influences of unconscious drives and conflicts on behavior. The behavioral perspective emphasizes how observable behaviors are acquired and changed in response to environmental influences. The humanistic perspective emphasizes how people attempt to understand and actively shape their lives, rather than respond passively to unconscious or environmental forces. The cognitive perspective explores how people process, store, and retrieve information. The social-cultural perspective calls attention to the importance of each person's social and cultural environment in shaping his or her thoughts, emotions, and behaviors.

4. Clinical psychologists study, assess, and treat troubled people. Psychiatrists are physicians who treat the physical causes of psychological disorders. Psychologists who work outside the mental health professions conduct basic research to increase our understanding of behavior or applied research to solve practical problems.

5. As scientists, psychologists attempt to study thoughts and actions with an attitude of open-minded skepticism. Scientists must also possess an attitude of humility. Scientists rely on theories to explain, organize, and predict behaviors under study. Good theories give direction to research by generating testable predictions, called hypotheses. Research findings are reported in the precise language of science, in order to allow other scientists to replicate (repeat) them.

6. Psychologists use varying combinations of certain assessment techniques (observation or self-report), research settings (laboratory or field), and research designs (description, correlation, experimentation). The simplest research design is description; examples include case studies, surveys, and naturalistic observation. In the case study one or more individuals is studied in great depth in the hope of revealing general principles underlying the behavior of all people. Surveys measure the self-reported attitudes of a representative sample of an entire group, or population. Naturalistic observation seeks to systematically observe and record the behavior of organisms (including humans) in their natural environments.

7. A correlation is a statistical measure of relationship, revealing how accurately one event predicts another. A correlation between two events or behaviors means only that one event can be predicted from the other. Because two events may both be caused by some other event, a correlation between the two events does not mean that one caused the other. Correlation thus does not enable explanation.

8. Conducting experiments allows psychologists to explain behaviors in terms of cause-and-effect relationships. This is because experiments allow researchers to manipulate just one experimental factor (the independent variable) while holding all other potential independent variables constant. If a subject's behavior (the dependent variable) changes, the change can be attributed to the influence of the independent variable under study. In the typical experiment, subjects are randomly assigned to either a control condition, in which the experimental treatment is absent, or an experimental condition, in which the treatment of interest is present. Two control techniques involve use of a placebo and the double-blind procedure. These help ensure that any changes in the dependent variable that occur are due to the independent variable, rather than to researchers' or subjects' expectations.

9. Psychologists intentionally conduct experiments on simplified behaviors in an artificial laboratory environment in order to gain control over the numerous independent and dependent variables present in more complex behaviors and the "real world." By studying simplified behaviors under controlled circumstances psychologists are able to test general principles of behavior that also operate in the real world.

For similar reasons, psychologists often apply their findings from psychological studies of people from one culture to people in general. Although attitudes and behaviors vary greatly from culture to culture, the underlying principles are much the same.

10. Some psychologists study animals simply because they want to understand animal behavior. For the same reasons that psychologists investigate human behavior in simplified laboratory environments before attempting to understand more complex everyday behaviors, other psychologists attempt to learn more about human behavior by studying simpler, yet similar, behaviors in animals.

Although animals in psychological research rarely experience pain, opposition to animal experimentation raises two important issues: (1) whether it is morally right to place the well-being of humans above that of animals, and (2) what safeguards should protect the well-being of animals.

Ethical standards developed by the American Psychological Association provide strict guidelines concerning the treatment of people and animals in psychology experiments.

11. No science, including psychology, is value-free. Psychologists' values influence their choice of re-

search topics, their observations, and their interpretations of research findings. Although psychological findings are sometimes criticized for merely
confirming what a person with common sense
knew all along, experiments reveal a hindsight
bias: After an experiment is completed, its findings
seem much more obvious than they were
beforehand.

12. Psychological knowledge is a power that, like all
powers, can be used for good or bad purposes.
Many psychologists conduct research aimed at
solving some of the world's most serious problems,
including war, prejudice, overpopulation, and
crime.

13. The SQ3R study method incorporates the idea that
mastery of a subject requires active processing of
it. SQ3R stands for the five steps of the method:
survey, question, read, rehearse, review. The text
and this study guide are organized to facilitate
your use of the SQ3R method.

CHAPTER REVIEW

1. physiology; philosophy
2. Wundt
3. learning; Sigmund Freud; children; William James
4. mental; John Watson; observable; behavior; mental
5. internal; external; nature-nurture
6. Plato; Aristotle; John Locke; René Descartes

An "internal" view of intelligence might emphasize
the importance of genetic predispositions, inborn
knowledge, and drives, while minimizing the influence
of sensory experiences and learning. An "external"
view would take the opposite position, maintaining
that knowledge develops in response to sensory experiences, environmental incentives, and other situational influences.

7. biological
8. psychoanalytic
9. behavioral
10. humanistic
11. cognitive
12. social-cultural
13. complement
14. clinical
15. basic research; applied research

An example of basic research would be the study of
how human memory is structured. In contrast, a psychologist engaged in applied research would focus on
how a person might improve his or her memory
through the use of better study techniques.

16. skepticism; humility
17. theory; hypotheses
18. replicate
19. settings; assessment techniques
20. description; correlation; experimentation
21. case study
22. survey
23. wording
24. random; population; does
25. naturalistic observation
26. describe
27. correlated; predict; positively correlated; negatively correlated
28. causes; experiments

This is an example of a negative correlation. As one
factor (time spent studying) increases, the other factor
(anxiety level) decreases.

29. control; experimental
30. independent; dependent
31. random assignment; independent

Experimentation has the advantage of increasing the
investigator's control of both relevant and irrelevant
variables that might influence behavior. Experiments
also permit the investigator to go beyond observation
and description to uncover cause-and-effect relationships in behavior.

32. placebo
33. double-blind
34. artificial; principles
35. principles
36. do
37. hindsight bias

PROGRESS TEST 1

Multiple-Choice Questions

1. **a.** is the answer. (p. 6)
   b. Psychology has never been defined in terms of
   conscious and unconscious activity.
   c. From about 1920 to 1960, under the influence
   of John Watson, psychology was defined as the
   science of observable behavior.
   d. Psychology today is defined as the science of
   behavior and mental processes. In its earliest days,
   however, psychology focused exclusively on mental phenomena.

2. **c.** is the answer. (p. 6)
   a. Wilhelm Wundt, the founder of the first psychology laboratory, used the method of introspection to study mental phenomena.

b. Sigmund Freud developed an influential theory of personality that focused on unconscious processes.

d. William James, author of the first psychology textbook, was a philosopher and therefore more interested in mental phenomena than observable behavior.

3. **d.** is the answer. (p. 6)

a. In its earliest days psychology was defined as the science of mental phenomena.

b. Psychology has never been defined in terms of conscious and unconscious activity.

c. From about 1920 to 1960, under the influence of John Watson, psychology was defined as the science of behavior.

4. **a.** is the answer. In a case study one subject is studied in depth. (p. 11)

b. In survey research a group of people are interviewed.

c. In correlational research an experimenter attempts to determine whether two factors are related.

d. In experimental research an investigator manipulates one variable to observe its effect on another.

5. **c.** is the answer. Exercise is the variable being manipulated by the experiment. (p. 15)

a. A control condition for this experiment would be a group of people not permitted to exercise.

b. An intervening variable is a variable other than those being manipulated that may influence behavior.

d. The dependent variable is the behavior measured by the experimenter, in this case, the effects of exercise.

6. **c.** is the answer. The control group is that for which the experimental treatment (the new drug) is absent. (p. 15)

a. A random sample is a subset of a population in which every person has an equal chance of being selected.

b. The experimental condition is the group for which the experimental treatment (the new drug) is present.

d. "Test group" is an ambiguous term; both the experimental and control group are tested.

7. **d.** is the answer. (p. 10)

a. Hypotheses are testable propositions.

b. Dependent variables are factors that may change in response to manipulated independent variables.

c. Statistical indexes, including averages, correlation coefficients, and measures of variability, may be used to test specific hypotheses (and therefore as indirect tests of theories), but they are merely mathematical tools, not general principles, as are theories.

8. **d.** is the answer. In this case the children are being observed in their normal environment, rather than in a laboratory. (pp. 12–13)

a. Correlation measures relationships between two factors. The psychologist may later want to use naturalistic observation to determine whether there are correlations between the variables that are studied.

b. In a case study one subject is studied in depth.

c. This is not an experiment because the psychologist is not directly controlling the variables being studied.

9. **a.** is the answer. Genes and experience are internal and external influences, respectively. (p. 6)

b. Rewards and punishments are both external influences on behavior.

c. Heredity and instinct are both internal influences on behavior.

d. The legitimacy of the study of mental processes does not relate to the internal/external issue.

10. **d.** is the answer. For Locke, the mind at birth was a blank slate. (p. 6)

a. Plato assumed that much of intelligence is inherited and therefore present at birth. Moreover, he was a philosopher of ancient Greece.

b. Aristotle held essentially the same viewpoint as Locke, but he lived in the fourth century B.C.

c. Descartes believed that knowledge does not depend on experience.

11. **a.** is the answer. (p. 7)

b. The cognitive perspective is concerned with how we process, store, and retrieve information.

c. The behavioral perspective studies the mechanisms by which observable responses are acquired and changed.

d. The psychoanalytic perspective emphasizes the influence of unconscious drives and conflicts on personality and behavior.

12. **d.** is the answer. (p. 14)

a. Correlational relationships can be revealed by statistical analyses of data; experimentation is not involved.

b. & c. Hypotheses and theories give direction to experimental research.

13. **d.** is the answer. (p. 9)

14. **b.** is the answer. Replication is the repetition of an experiment in order to determine whether its findings are reliable. It is not a research design. (p. 10)

15. d. is the answer. (p. 7)

a. Behavioral psychologists investigate how learned behaviors are acquired. They generally do not focus on subjective opinions, such as attractiveness.

b. The psychoanalytic perspective is concerned with unconscious phenomena, rather than conscious attitudes, such as attractiveness.

c. Cognitive psychologists study the mechanisms of thinking and memory, and generally do not investigate attitudes. Also, since the question specifies that the psychologist is interested in comparing two cultures, d. is clearly the best answer.

16. c. is the answer. (p. 21)

a. & b. Psychologists' personal values can influence both how experiments are conducted and how experimental findings are interpreted.

d. The issue of values is no less important in psychology than in other scientific fields.

17. b. is the answer. (p. 13)

a. & c. These answers would have been correct had the question stated that there is a *positive* correlation between shoe size and IQ. Actually, there is probably no correlation at all!

18. d. is the answer. In an experiment it would be possible to manipulate alcohol consumption and observe the effects, if any, on memory. (p. 14)

a., b., & c. These answers are incorrect because only by directly controlling the variables of interest can a researcher uncover cause-and-effect relationships.

19. b. is the answer. (p. 10)

a. This answer describes theories, not hypotheses.

c. Hypotheses are formal, testable propositions; they are not simply hunches.

d. This answer describes correlations between two events.

20. d. is the answer. (pp. 11–12)

a. A sample is a subset of a population.

b. & c. Control and experimental groups are used in experimentation, not in survey research.

Matching Items

1. f (p. 7)   **5.** d (p. 7)   **9.** h (p. 8)
2. b (p. 7)   **6.** e (p. 7)   **10.** c (p. 8)
3. j (p. 8)   **7.** a (p. 7)
4. i (p. 8)   **8.** g (p. 7)

PROGRESS TEST 2

Multiple-Choice Questions

1. a. is the answer. (p. 4)

2. a. is the answer. (pp. 16–17)

b., c., & d. There was no actual improvement in memory or self-esteem in this experiment.

3. d. is the answer. Only about 7 percent of all psychological experiments involve animals. (p. 19)

4. d. is the answer. (p. 15)

a. The control condition is the comparison group, in which the experimental treatment is absent.

b. Memory is a directly observed and measured dependent variable in this experiment.

c. Attention is the independent variable, which is being manipulated.

5. c. is the answer. (p. 15)

a. Both the experimental and control groups are test groups.

b. A random sample is a representative sample from the group under study. If one were to use a random sample in an experiment, one would use it for both the control and the experimental groups.

d. The control condition is the condition in which the treatment is absent.

6. b. is the answer. (pp. 21–22)

a. The phenomenon is related to hindsight rather than foresight.

c. & d. The phenomenon doesn't involve the correctness or incorrectness of intuitions but rather people's attitude that they had the correct intuition.

7. b. is the answer. If enough subjects are used in an experiment and they are randomly assigned to the two groups, any differences that emerge between the groups should stem from the experiment itself. (pp. 15–16)

a., c., & d. None of these terms describes precautions taken in setting up groups for experiments.

8. c. is the answer. Psychology emerged from these disciplines in particular. (p. 4)

a., b., & d. Chemistry and physics were not roots of psychology.

9. c. is the answer. After earning their M.D. degrees, psychiatrists specialize in the diagnosis and treatment of mental health disorders. (p. 8)

a., b., & d. These psychologists generally earn a Ph.D. rather than an M.D.

10. b. is the answer. (p. 6)

a. Aristotle believed that all knowledge originates with sensory experience.

c. Descartes was a philosopher of the seventeenth century.

d. Simonides was a well-known Greek orator.

11. d. is the answer. (p. 7)

a. The biological perspective studies the biological bases for a range of psychological phenomena.

b. The psychoanalytic perspective is concerned with how unconscious drives and conflicts may shape behavior.

c. The behavioral perspective studies the mechanisms by which observable responses are acquired and modified in particular environments.

12. **b.** is the answer. (p. 9)

a. In fact, the artificiality of experiments is part of an intentional attempt to create a controlled environment in which to test theoretical principles that are applicable to all behaviors.

c. Some psychological theories go against what we consider common sense; furthermore, on many issues that psychology addresses, it's far from clear what the "common sense" position is.

d. Psychology has always had ties to other disciplines, and in recent times, these ties have been increasing.

13. **d.** is the answer. The emphasis on change during the life span indicates that Dr. Jones is most likely a developmental psychologist. (p. 8)

a. Clinical psychologists study, assess, and treat people who are psychologically troubled.

b. Personality psychologists study our inner traits.

c. Social psychologists are concerned with the ways in which a person's behavior is influenced by others.

14. **c.** is the answer. (p. 8)

a. Clinical psychologists study, assess, and treat people with psychological disorders.

b. & d. Personality psychologists and psychiatrists do not usually study people in work situations.

15. **c.** is the answer. (p. 7)

a. Psychologists who follow the behavioral perspective emphasize observable, external influences on behavior.

b. The humanistic perspective reacts *against* the explanation of behavior in terms of unconscious drives.

d. The cognitive perspective places emphasis on conscious, rather than unconscious, processes.

16. **a.** is the answer. (p. 7)

b. The humanistic perspective emphasizes people's capacities to make choices and rejects the idea that specific environmental factors determine behavior.

c. & d. The psychoanalytic and cognitive perspectives each emphasize internal, rather than external, factors: unconscious drives in one case and cognitive processes in the other.

17. **d.** is the answer. Correlations show how well one factor can be predicted from another. (p. 13)

a. Since a case study focuses in great detail on the

behavior of an individual, it's unlikely to be useful in showing whether predictions are possible.

b. Naturalistic observation is a method of describing, rather than predicting, behavior.

c. In experimental research the effects of manipulated independent variables on dependent variables are measured. It is not clear how an experiment could help determine whether IQ tests predict academic success.

18. **b.** is the answer. The control condition is the one in which the treatment—in this case, pollution—is absent. (p. 15)

a. Students in the polluted room would be in the experimental condition.

c. Presumably, all students in both the experimental and control conditions were randomly assigned to their groups. Random assignment is a method for establishing groups, rather than a condition.

d. The word *dependent* refers to a kind of variable in experiments; conditions are either experimental or control.

19. **c.** is the answer. The lighting is the factor being manipulated. (p. 15)

a. & d. These answers are incorrect because they involve aspects of the experiment other than the variables.

b. This answer is the dependent, not the independent, variable.

20. **a.** is the answer. The research is addressing a practical issue. (p. 8)

b. Basic research is aimed at contributing to the base of knowledge in a given field, not at resolving particular practical problems.

c. & d. Clinical and developmental research would focus on issues relating to psychological disorders and life-span changes, respectively.

Matching Items

1. e (p. 10)	**5.** j (p. 15)	**9.** f (p. 10)
2. h (p. 10)	**6.** d (p. 15)	**10.** g (pp. 15–16)
3. b (p. 15)	**7.** a (p. 11)	**11.** i (p. 14)
4. c (p. 15)	**8.** k (pp. 11–12)	**12.** l (p. 17)

CHALLENGE TEST

Multiple-Choice Questions

1. **b.** is the answer. (p. 6)

a. As the founder of the first psychology laboratory, Wundt certainly based his research on the scientific method.

c. The earliest psychologists, including Wilhelm Wundt, were concerned with the self-examination of covert thoughts, feelings, and other mental processes.

2. **b.** is the answer. A general belief such as this one is a theory; it helps organize, explain, and generate testable predictions (hypotheses) such as "men drink more soft drinks than women." (p. 10)

c. & d. Independent and dependent variables are experimental treatments and behaviors, respectively. Beliefs and predictions may involve such variables, but are not themselves those variables.

3. **c.** is the answer. The members of one sorority are likely to share more interests, traits, and attitudes than will the members of a random sample of college students. (pp. 11–12)

a. & b. Unlike experiments, surveys do not specify or directly manipulate independent and dependent variables. In a sense, the questions of a survey are independent variables, and the answers, dependent variables.

4. **b.** is the answer. (p. 15)

a. Although case studies, surveys, naturalistic observation, and correlational research do not involve control of variables, they nevertheless enable researchers to describe and predict behavior.

c. Whether or not a sample is representative of a population, rather than control over variables, determines whether results can be generalized from a sample to a population.

5. **c.** is the answer. In order to determine the effects of caffeine on reaction time, Martina needs to measure reaction time in a control, or comparison, group that does not receive caffeine. (p. 15)

a. Caffeine is the independent variable.

b. Reaction time is the dependent variable.

d. Whether or not Martina's experiment can be replicated is determined by the precision with which she reports her procedures, which is not an aspect of research design.

6. **b.** is the answer. (p. 13)

a. This is not an experiment because the researcher is not manipulating the independent variable (seating position); she is merely measuring whether variation in this factor predicts test performance.

c. If the study were based entirely on students' self-reported responses, this would be a survey.

d. This study goes beyond naturalistic observation, which merely describes behavior as it occurs, to determine if test scores can be predicted from students' seating position.

7. **d.** is the answer. (p. 18)

8. **d.** is the answer. Selecting every tenth person would probably result in a representative sample of the entire population of students at the university. (pp. 11–12)

a. It would be difficult, if not impossible, to survey every student on campus.

b. Psychology students are not representative of the entire student population.

c. This answer is incorrect for the same reason as b. This would constitute a biased sample.

9. **b.** is the answer. (pp. 13–14)

a. Correlational research does not involve direct manipulation of factors.

c. & d. Both experimentation and correlational research involve hypotheses, which are testable predictions of relationships between specific, rather than random, factors.

10. **d.** is the answer. (p. 13)

a. Correlation does not imply causality.

b. Again, a positive correlation simply means that two factors tend to increase or decrease together; further relationships are not implied.

c. A separate factor may or may not be involved. That the two factors are correlated does not imply a separate factor, however. There may, for example, be a direct causal relationship between the two factors themselves.

11. **d.** is the answer. (p. 19)

12. **b.** is the answer. Psychology is a science because psychologists use the scientific method and approach the study of behavior and mental processes with attitudes of open-minded skepticism and humility. (p. 9)

a. Psychologists study both overt (observable) behaviors and covert thoughts and feelings.

c. Psychologists' values definitely *do* influence their research.

13. **b.** is the answer. Both Plato and Descartes believed that knowledge was inborn. Locke and Aristotle, on the other hand, believed that knowledge was based on experience. (p. 6)

c. & d. Watson, who championed psychology as the study of observable behavior, would surely have agreed with Aristotle that knowledge arises from experience. Because Plato and Locke held *opposing* viewpoints on this issue, these answers are incorrect.

14. **d.** is the answer. The humanistic perspective emphasizes each person's subjective understanding of his or her life experiences. (p. 7)

a., b., & c. Each of these perspectives is more objective than the humanistic perspective.

15. **d.** is the answer. (p. 17)

a. The low-dose comparison group is the control group.

16. **d.** is the answer. (pp. 18–19)

a. In fact, just the opposite is true.

b. Actually, psychological experiments tend to use the most readily available subjects, often White North American college students.

c. Although this may be true, psychological experiments remain important because they help explain underlying processes of human behavior everywhere. Therefore, d. is a much better response than c.

17. **d.** is the answer. (p. 9)

a. This follows from the attitude of open-minded skepticism, rather than humility.

b. & c. Although both of these are true of the scientific method, neither has anything to do with humility.

18. **a.** is the answer. (p. 17)

b. Use of a placebo tests whether the behavior of an experimental subject, who mistakenly believes that a treatment (such as a drug) is in effect, is the same as it would be if the treatment were actually present.

c. & d. These are examples of "blind" and "double-blind" control procedures.

19. **b.** is the answer. (p. 7)

c. Neither perspective places any special emphasis on overt or covert behaviors.

d. Introspection, or the self-examination of sensations, was a research method used by the earliest psychologists, not those working from the psychoanalytic perspective.

20. **c.** is the answer. (pp. 7–8)

a. The textbook suggests just the opposite: By studying behavior from several perspectives, psychologists gain a fuller understanding.

b. & d. Each perspective is useful in that it calls researchers' attention to different aspects of behavior. This is equally true of those perspectives that do not emphasize objective measurement.

Essay Question

a. Sample hypothesis: Daily aerobic exercise for one month will improve memory.

b. Exercise is the independent variable. The dependent variable is memory. Exercise could be manipulated by having people in an experimental group jog for 30 minutes each day. Memory could be measured by comparing the number of words subjects recall from a test list studied before the exercise experiment begins, and again afterward.

c. A control group that does not exercise *is* needed so that any improvement in the experimental group's memory can be attributed to exercise, and not to

some other factor, such as the passage of one month's time or familiarity with the memory test. The control group should engage in some nonexercise activity for the same amount of time each day that the experimental group exercises.

d. The subjects should be randomly selected from the population at large, and then randomly assigned to the experimental and control groups.

KEY TERMS

1. **Psychology** is the science of behavior and mental processes. (p. 6)

2. The **nature-nurture issue** is the controversy over the relative contributions of genes (nature) and experience (nurture) to the development of psychological traits and behaviors. (p. 6)

3. Psychologists who adopt the **biological perspective** emphasize the influences of heredity and physiology upon behavior, emotions, memories, and sensory experiences. (p. 7)

4. The **psychoanalytic perspective** maintains that behavior is determined by unconscious drives and conflicts. (p. 7)

5. The **behavioral perspective** emphasizes environmental influences on observable behavior. (p. 7)

6. The **humanistic perspective** emphasizes the individual's capacity for growth and studies people's subjective experiences. (p. 7)

7. The **cognitive perspective** emphasizes how people process, store, and retrieve information and use it to reason and solve problems. (p. 7)

   Example: A **cognitive psychologist** might be interested in, among other things, studying how experience affects the mental strategies people use to solve problems.

8. The **social-cultural perspective** focuses on our similarities and differences in thinking and behavior as the products of different social and cultural environments. (p. 7)

9. **Clinical psychology** is the branch of psychology concerned with the study, assessment, and treatment of people with psychological disorders. (p. 8)

10. **Psychiatry** is the branch of medicine concerned with the physical diagnosis and treatment of psychological disorders. (p. 8)

11. **Basic research** aims to increase psychology's knowledge base. (p. 8)

12. **Applied research** aims to solve specific practical problems. (p. 8)

13. A **theory** is an integrated set of principles that organizes a set of observations and makes testable predictions. (p. 10)

14. A **hypothesis** is a testable prediction derived from a theory; testing the hypothesis helps scientists to test the theory. (p. 10)

    Example: In order to test his theory of why people conform, Solomon Asch formulated the testable **hypothesis** that an individual would be more likely to go along with the majority opinion of a large group than with that of a smaller group.

15. **Replication** is the process of repeating an experiment, often with different subjects and in different situations, in order to test the reliability of experimental findings. (p. 10)

16. The **case study** is a descriptive research design in which one person is studied in great depth, often with the intention of discovering general principles. (p. 11)

    Example: When a psychologist studies the effects of a stroke on an individual's mental capacities, he or she is doing a **case study**.

17. The **survey** is a descriptive research design in which a sample of people are questioned about their attitudes or behavior. (pp. 11–12)

18. A **population** consists of all the members of a group being studied. (p. 11)

19. A **random sample** is one that is representative because every member of the population has an equal chance of being included. (p. 11)

20. **Naturalistic observation** involves observing and recording behavior in naturally occurring situations, without trying to influence the situation. (pp. 12–13)

21. The **correlation** is a statistical measure that indicates the extent to which two factors vary together and thus how well one factor can be predicted from the other; correlations can be positive or negative. (p. 13)

    Example: If there is a **positive correlation** between air temperature and ice cream sales, the warmer (higher) it is, the more ice cream is sold. If there is a **negative correlation** between air temperature and sales of cocoa, the cooler (lower) it is, the more cocoa is sold.

22. The **experiment** is the research design in which an investigator directly manipulates one or more factors (independent variables) in order to observe their effect on another factor (the dependent variable); experiments therefore make it possible to establish cause-and-effect relationships. (p. 14)

23. The **control condition** of an experiment is one in which the treatment of interest, or independent variable, is withheld so that comparison to the experimental group can be made. (p. 15)

    Example: The **control condition** for an experiment testing the effects of a new drug on reaction time would be a group of subjects given a placebo (inactive drug or sugar pill) instead of the drug being tested.

24. The **experimental condition** of an experiment is one in which subjects are exposed to the independent variable being studied. (p. 15)

    Example: In the study of the effects of a new drug on reaction time, subjects in the **experimental condition** would actually receive the drug being tested.

25. The **independent variable** of an experiment is the factor being manipulated and tested by the investigator. (p. 15)

    Example: In the study of the effects of a new drug on reaction time, the drug is the **independent variable**.

26. The **dependent variable** of an experiment is the factor being measured by the investigator. (p. 15)

    Example: In the study of the effects of a new drug on reaction time, the subjects' reaction time is the **dependent variable**.

27. **Random assignment** is the procedure of assigning subjects to the experimental and control groups by chance in order to minimize preexisting differences between the groups. (p. 15)

28. A **placebo** is an inert substance that is administered as a test of whether the behavior of an experimental subject, who mistakenly thinks a treatment is in effect, is the same as it would be if the treatment were actually present. (p. 17)

29. A **double-blind** is a control procedure in which neither the experimenter nor the research subjects are aware of which treatment condition is in effect. It is used to prevent experimenters' and subjects' expectations from influencing the results of an experiment. (p. 17)

30. **Hindsight bias** refers to the human tendency to exaggerate the obviousness of an outcome—including a psychological research finding—after one has heard about it. (pp. 21–22)

31. **SQ3R** is a study technique that stands for *s*urvey, *q*uestion, *r*ead, *r*ehearse, *r*eview. (p. 23)

2 / Biological Roots of Behavior

Chapter Overview

Chapter 2 is concerned with the functions of the nervous system, particularly the brain, which is the basis for all human behavior. Under the direction of the brain, the nervous and endocrine systems coordinate a variety of voluntary and involuntary behaviors and serve as the body's mechanisms for communication with the external environment.

The brain consists of three regions: the brainstem, the limbic system, and the cerebral cortex. Knowledge of the workings of the brain has increased with recent advances in neuropsychological methods. Studies of split-brain patients have also given researchers a great deal of information about the specialized functions of the brain's right and left hemispheres.

Many students find the technical material in this chapter difficult to master. Not only are there many terms for you to remember, but you must also know the organization and function of the various divisions of the nervous system. Learning this material will require a great deal of rehearsal. Working through the chapter review several times, drawing and labeling brain diagrams, and mentally reciting terms are all useful techniques for rehearsing this type of material.

NOTE: Answer guidelines for all Chapter 2 questions begin on page 38.

Guided Study

The text chapter should be studied one section at a time. Before you read, preview each section by skimming it, noting headings and boldface items. Then read the appropriate section objectives from the following outline. Keep these objectives in mind and, as you read the chapter section, search for the information that will enable you to meet each objective. Once you have finished a section, write out answers for its objectives.

The Nervous System (pp. 27–34)

1. Explain why psychologists are concerned with human biology.

2. Describe the structure of a neuron and the process by which an action potential is triggered.

3. Identify three types of neurons and describe their interaction in a simple reflex.

4. Describe how nerve cells communicate and discuss the importance of neurotransmitters for human behavior.

5. Discuss the significance of endorphins and explain how drugs influence neurotransmitters.

6. Identify the major divisions of the nervous system and their primary functions.

The Brain (pp. 34–53)

7. Identify and explain the methods used in studying the brain.

8. Discuss the organization of the brain from an evolutionary point of view, and describe the functions served by various structures within the brainstem.

9. Describe the functions served by various structures within the limbic system.

10. Discuss how the hypothalamus exerts its influence through the endocrine system.

11. Describe the structure and functions of the cerebral cortex.

12. Discuss how damage to several different cortical areas can impair language functioning and outline the process by which the brain directs reading aloud.

13. Discuss brain plasticity and what it reveals about brain reorganization.

14. Describe research on the split brain and discuss what it reveals regarding normal brain functioning.

15. (Close-Up) Describe the brain organization of left-handed people.

Chapter Review

When you have finished reading the chapter, work through the material that follows to review it. Complete the sentences and answer the questions. As you proceed, evaluate your performance for each section by consulting the answers on page 40. Do not continue with the next section until you understand each answer. If you need to, review or reread the appropriate section in the textbook before continuing.

1. The theory that linked our mental abilities to bumps on the skull was phrenology.

2. In the most basic sense, every idea, mood, memory, and behavior that an individual has ever experienced is a biological phenomenon.

3. Researchers who study the links between biology and psychology are called biological psychologists.

The Nervous System (pp. 27–34)

4. The circuitry of the body consists of billions of nerve cells, or neurons, that together comprise the nervous system.

5. The extensions of a neuron that receive impulses from other neurons are the dendrites.

6. The extensions of a neuron that transmit information to other neurons are the axons; some of these extensions are insulated by a layer of fatty cells called the myeline Sheath, which helps speed the nerve's impulses.

7. Identify the major parts of the neuron diagrammed below:
a. dendrites   c. axon
b. cell body   d. myelin Sheath.

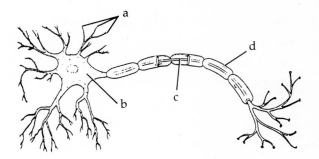

8. In order to trigger a neural impulse, or action potential, a stimulus must be greater in intensity than the neuron's threshold. Increasing a stimulus above this level will not (will/will not) increase the neural impulse's intensity. This phenomenon is called an all – or – nothing response.

Outline the sequence of reactions that occur when a neural impulse is generated and transmitted from one neuron to another.

9. The strength of a stimulus doesn't (does/does not) affect the speed of a neural impulse.

10. Information arriving in the central nervous system from the body travels in afferent, or Sensory, neurons.

11. The neurons involved in processing this information in the central nervous system are the interneurons.

12. The central nervous system sends instructions to the body's muscles by means of efferent, or motor, neurons.

13. Automatic responses to stimuli are called _reflexes_.

14. The junction between two neurons is called a _synapse_, and the gap is called the _synaptic cleft_.

15. The chemical messengers that convey information across the gaps between neurons are called _neurotransmitters_ These chemicals unlock "gates" on receptor sites, allowing electrically charged atoms, or _ions_, to enter the neuron.

16. Neurotransmitters influence neurons either by _exciting_ or _inhibiting_ their readiness to fire.

17. A neurotransmitter that is important in motor control and muscle contraction is _acetylcholine_. The poison _curare_ produces paralysis by blocking the activity of this neurotransmitter.

18. Naturally occurring morphinelike neurotransmitters that are present in the brain are called _endorphines_. When the brain is flooded with drugs such as _heroine_ or _morphine_, it may stop producing these neurotransmitters.

19. Cocaine produces its effects by flooding the brain with substitute _excitatory_ (excitatory/inhibitory) neurotransmitters.

20. The tremors of _Parkinson's_ disease are due to the degeneration of neurons that produce the neurotransmitter _dopamine_. The chemical _L-Dopa_ helps people with this condition regain control over their muscles.

21. The brain and spinal cord comprise the _central_ nervous system.

22. The neurons that link the brain and spinal cord to the rest of the body form the _peripheral_ nervous system.

23. The division of the PNS that transmits sensory input to the CNS and directs the movements of the skeletal muscles is the _somatic_ nervous system. These movements are usually under _voluntary_ control.

24. Involuntary, self-regulating responses—those of the glands and muscles of internal organs—are controlled by the _autonomic_ nervous system.

25. The body is made ready for action by the _sympathetic_ division of the autonomic nervous system.

26. The _parasympathetic_ division of the autonomic nervous system produces relaxation.

Describe and explain the sequence of physical reactions that occur in the body as an emergency is confronted and then passes.

The Brain (pp. 34–53)

27. Brain tissue is gray in color, due to the fact that its neurons are _unmyelinated_.

28. The oldest technique for studying the brain involves _clinical observation_ of patients with brain injuries or diseases.

29. Researchers have also studied brain function by producing _lesions_, or selectively destroyed areas of brain tissue.

30. The _EEG_ is a recording of the electrical activity of the whole brain.

31. A computer-generated image of a slice of the brain based on a series of x-rays taken from different positions is called a _CAT scan_.

32. The technique depicting the level of activity of brain areas by measuring the brain's consumption of glucose is called the _PET Scan_.

Write a sentence briefly explaining the purpose of the PET scan.

33. A technique that produces clearer images of the brain by using magnetic fields and radio signals is known as __MRI__.

34. The brain can be divided into regions corresponding to three stages of brain evolution; in order of increasing complexity of function, these regions are the __brain stem__, the __limbic system__, and the __cerebral cortex__.

35. In general, the more complex an organism's nervous system, the __less__ (more/less) its behavior is fixed genetically, and the __more__ (more/less) adaptable it is.

36. At the base of the brainstem, where the spinal cord enters the skull, lies the __medulla__, which controls __breathing__ and __heartbeat__.

37. At the top of the brainstem sits the __thalmus__, which serves as the brain's sensory switchboard.

38. The __reticular formation__ is contained inside the brainstem and helps control __arousal__ and __attention__.

39. At the rear of the brainstem lies the __cerebellum__. It influences __learning__ and memory, but its major function is coordination of voluntary movement and __balance__ control.

40. Between the brainstem and cerebral hemispheres is the __limbic__ system. Two components of this system that enable memory are the __amygdala__ and the __hippocampus__.

41. Rage or fear will result from stimulation of different regions of the __amygdala__.

42. Below the thalamus is the __hypothalmus__, which regulates bodily maintenance behaviors such as __thirst__ and __hunger__. Olds and Milner discovered that this region also contains __pleasure__ centers, which animals will work hard to have stimulated.

43. The hypothalamus also regulates behavior chemically by secreting __hormones__.

44. The body's chemical communication network is called the __endocrine system__. This system transmits messages at a much __slower__ (faster/slower) rate than the nervous system.

45. In a moment of danger, the __adrenal__ glands release __epinephrine__ and __norepinephrine__.

46. The most influential gland is the __pituitary__, which helps regulate __growth__ and the release of hormones by other endocrine glands.

Write a paragraph describing the feedback system that links the nervous and endocrine systems.

47. The most complex functions of human behavior are linked to the most developed part of the brain, the __cerebral cortex__, which is divided into two __hemispheres__, each of which consists of four lobes.

48. List the four lobes of the brain.
    a. __frontal__   c. __occipital__
    b. __parietal__   d. __temporal__

49. Electrical stimulation of one side of the __motor__ cortex, an arch-shaped region at the back of the __frontal__ lobe, will produce movement on the opposite side of the body.

50. At the front of the parietal lobe lies the __sensory__ cortex, which, when stimulated, elicits a sensation of __touch__.

Beginning with the sensory receptors in the skin, trace the course of the spinal reflex as a person reflexively jerks his or her hand away from an unexpectedly hot burner on a stove. Then, outline the brain pathways and endocrine response to the above situation.

51. Visual information is received in the _Occipital_ lobes, whereas auditory information is received in the _temporal_ lobes.

52. Areas of the brain that don't receive sensory information or direct movement but, rather, integrate and interpret information received by other regions are known as _Association areas_. Such areas in the _frontal_ lobe are involved in recognizing faces, making judgments, carrying out plans, and in some aspects of personality.

53. Brain injuries may produce an impairment in language use called _aphasia_. Studies of people with such impairments have shown that _Broca's area_ is involved in producing speech, _Wernicke's area_ is involved in understanding speech, and the _angular gyrus_ is involved in recoding printed words into auditory form.

54. Neurons in the CNS _will not_ (will/will not) regenerate.

55. The quality of the brain that makes it possible for undamaged brain areas to take over the functions of damaged regions is known as _plasticity_. After age _5_, left hemisphere damage permanently disrupts language.

56. Researchers are currently experimenting with _transplants_ of brain tissue as a possible cure for _Alzheimers_ disease, which involves a degeneration of acetylcholine-producing brain tissue.

57. Because damage to it will impair language and reasoning, the _left_ hemisphere came to be known as the _dominate_ hemisphere.

58. In treating several patients with severe epilepsy, Vogel and Bogan separated the two hemispheres of the brain by cutting the _corpus callosum_. When this structure is severed, the result is referred to as a _split_-_brain_.

59. In a split-brain patient, only the _right_ hemisphere will be aware of an unseen object held in the left hand. In this case, the person would not be able to _name_ the object. When different words are shown in the left and right visual fields, if the patient fixates on a point on the center line between the fields, the patient will be able to say only the word shown on the _right_.

Explain why a split-brain patient would be able to read aloud the word *pencil* flashed to his or her right visual field, but would be unable to identify a pencil by touch using only the left hand.

60. Identify which hemisphere is the more specialized for each of the following abilities:
    a. writing, _left_;

b. speaking, _____left_____ ;
c. emotion, _____right_____ ;
d. intuition, _____right_____ ;
e. perceptual tasks, _____right_____ .

FOCUS ON PSYCHOLOGY:
Magnetic Resonance Imaging Reveals Possible Cause of Autism

Autism, a devastating psychological disorder that occurs in 2 to 4 children out of every 10,000 under age 15, was first described in 1943 by Leo Kanner, a child psychiatrist. Since then, psychologists have been looking without success for its cause(s). Symptoms of autistic behavior include social withdrawal, language disturbance, and emotional detachment. One of the most striking characteristics of the disorder is the autistic child's noticeable lack of interest in other people. For this reason, one theory held that autism is a psychosocial disorder caused in part by an abnormal parent-child relationship. Recent findings, however, suggest that autism may be a disorder of the brain rather than a response to the environment.

A key piece to the puzzle of autism was found as a result of technological advances in brain study. Using MRI (magnetic resonance imaging), a computer-generated brain image based on magnetic fields and radio signals, neuroscientists at Children's Hospital in San Diego studied the brains of 18 autistic children. The MRI scans consistently showed that a particular region of the cerebellum—the "little brain" that is important in muscular control, learning, and memory—was unusually small. Although researchers have long suspected that some form of brain pathology was likely in those with autism—many autistic children develop epileptic seizures as they get older—this was the first specific abnormality ever found.

Several interpretations of these findings are possible. One is that because of the cerebellum's role in high-level mental functioning, damage during its critical period of prenatal development may directly cause autistic behavior. Another is that autism is controlled by some other region of the brain that is damaged along with the cerebellum.

Whatever the final conclusion regarding the link between the brain and autism, these findings illustrate the importance of biology to psychology and underscore an important theme in the history of the neurosciences: Our understanding of the brain and behavior is often paced by advances in the technologies on which scientists base their observations.

Sources: Rosenhan, D. L., & Seligman, M. E. P. (1989). *Abnormal Psychology* (2nd ed.). New York: W. W. Norton.

Wray, Herbert. (1989, June). New evidence: Autism is a brain disorder. *Psychology Today*.

Progress Test 1
Multiple-Choice Questions

Circle your answers to the following questions and check them with the answers on page 41. If your answer is incorrect, read the explanation for why it is incorrect and then consult the appropriate pages of the text (in parentheses following the correct answer).

1. Afferent is to efferent as _____ is to _____.
   a. central; peripheral   c. motor; sensory
   b. sensory; motor   d. peripheral; central

2. Heartbeat, digestion, glandular activity, and other self-regulating bodily functions are governed by the:
   a. voluntary nervous system.
   b. autonomic nervous system.
   c. sympathetic division of the autonomic nervous system.
   d. somatic nervous system.

3. A strong stimulus can increase:
   a. the speed of the impulse the neuron fires.
   b. the intensity of the impulse the neuron fires.
   c. the number of times the neuron fires.
   d. the threshold that must be reached before the neuron fires.

4. The pain of heroin withdrawal may be attributable to the fact that:
   a. under the influence of heroin, the brain ceases production of endorphins.
   b. under the influence of heroin, the brain ceases production of all neurotransmitters.
   c. during withdrawal, the brain's production of all neurotransmitters is greatly increased.
   d. heroin destroys endorphin receptors in the brain.

5. The brain research technique that involves monitoring the brain's usage of glucose is called the:
   a. PET scan.
   b. CAT scan.
   c. EEG.
   d. MRI.

6. The part of the neuron that generally carries messages away from the cell body is the:
   a. dendrite.   c. synapse.
   b. myelin sheath.   d. axon.

7. Though there is no single "control center" for emotions, their regulation is primarily attributed to the brain region known as the:
   a. limbic system.
   b. reticular formation.
   c. brainstem.
   d. cerebral cortex.

8. Which is the correct sequence in the transmission of a simple reflex?
   a. efferent neuron → interneuron → afferent neuron
   b. interneuron → efferent neuron → afferent neuron
   c. afferent neuron → interneuron → efferent neuron
   d. interneuron → afferent neuron → efferent neuron

9. Generally speaking, the brains of _____ exhibit greater plasticity than the brains of _____.
   a. adults; children   c. males; females
   b. children; adults   d. females; males

10. Damage to _____ will usually cause a person to lose the ability to comprehend language.
    a. the angular gyrus
    b. Broca's area
    c. Wernicke's area
    d. frontal lobe association areas

11. Which of the following is typically controlled by the right hemisphere?
    a. language
    b. learned voluntary movements
    c. arithmetic reasoning
    d. perceptual tasks

12. Dr. Hernandez is studying neurotransmitter abnormalities in depressed patients. She would most likely describe herself as a:
    a. psychiatrist.
    b. clinical psychologist.
    c. psychoanalyst.
    d. biological psychologist.

13. As the brain evolved, the increasing complexity of animals' behavior was accompanied by a(n):
    a. increase in the size of the brainstem.
    b. decrease in the ratio of brain to body weight.
    c. increase in the size of the frontal lobes.
    d. increase in the amount of association area.

14. Voluntary movements, such as writing with a pencil, are directed by:
    a. the sympathetic nervous system.
    b. the somatic nervous system.
    c. the parasympathetic nervous system.
    d. the autonomic nervous system.

15. A neuron will generate action potentials more often when:
    a. it remains below its threshold.
    b. it receives an excitatory input.
    c. it receives more excitatory than inhibitory inputs.
    d. it is stimulated by a neurotransmitter.

16. Which is the correct sequence in the transmission of a neural impulse?
    a. axon → dendrite → cell body → synapse
    b. dendrite → axon → cell body → synapse
    c. dendrite → cell body → axon → synapse
    d. axon → synapse → cell body → dendrite

17. Chemical messengers produced by endocrine glands are called:
    a. chromosomes.   c. hormones.
    b. neurotransmitters.   d. enzymes.

18. Following a head injury, a person has ongoing difficulties staying awake and focusing attention. Most likely, the damage occurred to the:
    a. thalamus.   c. reticular formation.
    b. corpus callosum.   d. cerebellum.

19. Based on the current research, which of the following seems true about the specialized functions of the right and left hemispheres?
    a. The specialization of the hemispheres is greater in men than in women.
    b. The specialization of the hemispheres is greater in women than in men.
    c. Most complex tasks emerge from the activity of one or the other hemispheres.
    d. Most complex activities emerge from the integrated activity of both hemispheres.

20. Cortical areas that are not primarily concerned with sensory, motor, or language functions are:
    a. called projection areas.
    b. called association areas.
    c. located mostly in the parietal lobe.
    d. located mostly in the temporal lobe.

Matching Items

Match each structure with its corresponding function or description.

Structures

d	**1.** hypothalamus
f	**2.** frontal lobe
e	**3.** parietal lobe
a	**4.** temporal lobe
g	**5.** reticular formation
b	**6.** occipital lobe
c	**7.** thalamus
h	**8.** corpus callosum
k	**9.** cerebellum
i	**10.** amygdala
j	**11.** medulla

Functions or Descriptions

a. includes auditory areas
b. includes visual areas
c. serves as sensory switchboard
d. contains pleasure centers
e. includes sensory cortex
f. includes motor cortex
g. controls arousal
h. links cerebral hemispheres
i. elicits rage and fear
j. regulates breathing and heartbeat
k. enables coordinated movement

Progress Test 2

Progress Test 2 should be completed during a final chapter review. Answer the following questions after you thoroughly understand the correct answers for the Chapter Review and Progress Test 1.

Multiple-Choice Questions

1. Following an injury, undamaged brain areas may take over the functions of damaged areas. This phenomenon results from the _____ of brain tissue.
   a. recombination
   b. regeneration
   c. enrichment
   d. plasticity

2. The visual cortex is located in the:
   a. occipital lobe.
   b. temporal lobe.
   c. frontal lobe.
   d. parietal lobe.

3. Which of the following is typically controlled by the left hemisphere?
   a. spatial reasoning
   b. arithmetic reasoning
   c. the left side of the body
   d. perceptual skills

4. When Sandy scalded her toe in a hot tub of water, the pain message was carried to her spinal cord by the _____ nervous system.
   a. somatic
   b. sympathetic
   c. parasympathetic
   d. central

5. Which of the following are governed by the simplest neural pathways?
   a. emotions
   b. physiological drives, such as hunger
   c. reflexes
   d. movements, such as walking

6. Melissa is so elated after running a marathon that she feels little fatigue or discomfort. Her lack of pain is probably the result of the release of:
   a. ACh.
   b. endorphins.
   c. serotonin.
   d. norepinephrine.

7. Parkinson's disease and Alzheimer's disease involve:
   a. a degeneration of brain tissue that produces vital neurotransmitters.
   b. impaired function in the right hemisphere only.
   c. impaired function in the left hemisphere only.
   d. excess production of the neurotransmitters dopamine and acetylcholine.

8. The technique that uses magnetic fields and radio signals to produce computer images of structures within the brain is called:
   a. the EEG.
   b. a CAT scan.
   c. a PET scan.
   d. MRI.

9. The myelin sheath that is present on some neurons:
   a. increases the speed of neural transmission.
   b. slows neural transmission.
   c. regulates the release of neurotransmitters.
   d. does a. and c.
   e. does b. and c.

10. The junction at which neural impulses communicate is called a:
    a. synapse.
    b. dendrite.
    c. myelin sheath.
    d. neurotransmitter.

11. The neurotransmitter acetylcholine (ACh) is most likely to be found:
    a. at the junction between sensory neurons and muscle fibers.
    b. at the junction between motor neurons and muscle fibers.
    c. at junctions between interneurons.
    d. in all of the above locations.

12. The gland that regulates body growth is the:
    a. adrenal.   c. hypothalamus.
    b. thyroid.   d. pituitary.

13. Epinephrine and norepinephrine are _____ that are released by the _____ gland.
    a. neurotransmitters; pituitary
    b. hormones; pituitary
    c. neurotransmitters; adrenal
    d. hormones; adrenal

14. Jessica experienced difficulty keeping her balance after receiving a blow to the back of her head. It is likely that she injured her:
    a. medulla.   c. hypothalamus.
    b. thalamus.   d. cerebellum.

15. Moruzzi and Magoun caused a cat to lapse into a coma by severing neural connections between the cortex and the:
    a. reticular formation.   c. thalamus.
    b. hypothalamus.   d. cerebellum.

16. In order of increasing complexity, the three stages of brain evolution are:
    a. cerebral cortex; brainstem; limbic system.
    b. brainstem; limbic system; cerebral cortex.

c. limbic system; brainstem; cerebral cortex.
d. limbic system; cerebral cortex; brainstem.

17. Which of the following is *not* one of the ways that drugs influence neural transmission?
    a. Drugs may cause the brain to stop producing certain neurotransmitters.
    b. Drugs may mimic a particular neurotransmitter.
    c. Drugs may block a particular neurotransmitter.
    d. Drugs may disrupt a neuron's all-or-none firing pattern.

18. The nerve fibers that have been severed in split-brain patients form a structure that is called the _____ _____.
    a. reticular formation   c. corpus callosum
    b. association areas   d. parietal lobes

19. Beginning at the front of the brain and working backward then down and around, which of the following is the correct order of cortical regions?
    a. occipital lobe; temporal lobe; parietal lobe; frontal lobe
    b. temporal lobe; frontal lobe; parietal lobe; occipital lobe
    c. frontal lobe; occipital lobe; temporal lobe; parietal lobe
    d. frontal lobe; parietal lobe; occipital lobe; temporal lobe

20. Following a gunshot wound to his head, Jack became more uninhibited, irritable, and profane. It is likely that his personality change was the result of injury to his:
    a. parietal lobe.   c. occipital lobe.
    b. temporal lobe.   d. frontal lobe.

Matching Items

Match each structure or term with its corresponding function or description.

Structures or Terms
___d___ 1. right hemisphere
___g___ 2. brainstem
___e___ 3. CAT scan
___f___ 4. aphasia
___i___ 5. EEG
___a___ 6. Broca's area
___j___ 7. Wernicke's area
___h___ 8. limbic system
___k___ 9. association areas
___b___ 10. left hemisphere
___c___ 11. angular gyrus

Functions or Descriptions
a. controls speech production
b. specializes in arithmetic reasoning
c. translates writing into speech
d. specializes in spatial relations
e. a series of x-rays of the brain taken from different positions
f. language disorder
g. oldest part of the brain
h. regulates emotion
i. recording of brain waves
j. responsible for language comprehension
k. brain areas involved in higher mental functions

In the diagrams to the right, the numbers refer to brain locations that have been damaged. Match each location with its probable effect on behavior.

Location		Behavioral Effect
a	1.	a. vision disorder
h	2.	b. insensitivity to touch
c/b	3.	c. motor paralysis
d	4.	d. hearing problem
e	5.	e. lack of coordination
b	6.	f. abnormal hunger
f	7.	g. split brain
g	8.	h. sleep/arousal disorder
k	9.	i. loss of smell
		j. loss of taste
		k. altered personality

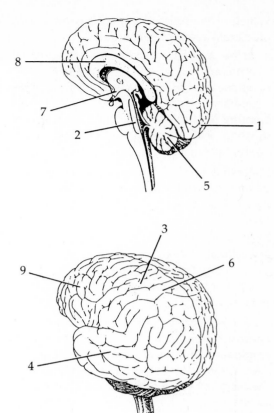

Challenge Test

Answer these questions the day before an exam as a final check on your understanding of the chapter's terms and concepts.

Multiple-Choice Questions

1. A biological psychologist would be *more* likely to study:
   a. how you learn to express emotions.
   b. how to help people overcome emotional disorders.
   c. life-span changes in the expression of emotion.
   d. the chemical changes that accompany emotions.

2. The part of the human brain that is most like that of a fish is the:
   a. cortex.
   b. limbic system.
   c. brainstem.
   d. right hemisphere.

3. You are able to pull your hand quickly away from hot water before a sensation of pain is felt because:
   a. movement of the hand is a reflex that involves intervention of the spinal cord only.
   b. movement of the hand does not require intervention by the central nervous system.
   c. the brain reacts quickly to prevent severe injury.
   d. the autonomic nervous system intervenes to speed contraction of the muscles of the hand.

4. In order to pinpoint the location of a tumor, a neurosurgeon electrically stimulated parts of the patient's sensory cortex. If the patient was conscious during the procedure, which of the following was probably experienced?
   a. "hearing" faint sounds
   b. "seeing" random visual patterns
   c. movement of the arms or legs
   d. a sense of having the skin touched

5. If Dr. Rogers wishes to conduct an experiment on the effects of stimulating the "pleasure center" of a rat's brain, he should insert an electrode into the:
   a. thalamus.
   b. sensory cortex.
   c. hypothalamus.
   d. corpus callosum.

6. A split-brain patient has a picture of a knife flashed to her left hemisphere and that of a fork to her right hemisphere. She will be able to:
   a. identify the fork using her left hand.
   b. identify a knife using her left hand.
   c. identify a knife using either hand.
   d. identify a fork using either hand.

7. Which of the following is *not* a correct description of a brain research technique?
   a. using a PET scan to examine the brain's structure
   b. using the EEG to record the brain's electrical activity
   c. using MRI to examine the brain's structure
   d. using a CAT scan to examine the brain's structure

8. Following Jayshree's near-fatal car accident, her physician noticed that the pupillary reflex of her eyes was abnormal. This *may* indicate that Jayshree's _____ was damaged in the accident.
   a. occipital cortex
   b. autonomic nervous system
   c. left temporal lobe
   d. cerebellum

9. Anton is applying for a technician's job with a neurosurgeon. In trying to impress his potential employer with his knowledge of the brain, he says, "After my father's stroke I knew immediately that the blood clot had affected his left cerebral hemisphere because he no longer recognized faces of friends and co-workers." Should Anton be hired?
   a. Yes. Anton obviously understands brain structure and function.
   b. No. The *right* hemisphere, not the left, specializes in facial recognition.
   c. Yes. Although blood clots never form in the left hemisphere, Anton should be rewarded for recognizing the left hemisphere's role in facial recognition.
   d. No. Blood clots never form in the left hemisphere, and the right hemisphere is more involved than the left in recognizing faces.

10. A stroke leaves a patient paralyzed on the left side of the body. Which region of the brain has been damaged?
    a. the reticular formation
    b. the limbic system
    c. the left hemisphere
    d. the right hemisphere

11. Dr. Johnson briefly flashed a picture of a key in the right visual field of a split-brain patient. The patient could probably:
    a. verbally report that a key was seen.
    b. write the word *key* using the left hand.
    c. draw a picture of a key using the left hand.
    d. do none of the above.

12. Following a gunshot wound to his left temporal lobe, 16-year-old Tyrone experienced aphasia. A young intern told his family not to give up hope for a full recovery because the damaged cortical neurons might regenerate. Is there anything wrong with the intern's advice?
    a. No.
    b. Yes. Aphasia results from *right* temporal lobe damage.
    c. Yes. Cortical neurons do not regenerate.
    d. Yes. People suffering from aphasia nearly always die within a few years of their injury.

13. As the brain evolved, genetic controls became _____ and the organism's adaptability _____.
    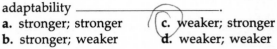
    a. stronger; stronger
    b. stronger; weaker
    c. weaker; stronger
    d. weaker; weaker

14. A scientist from another planet wishes to study the simplest brain mechanisms underlying emotion and memory. You recommend the scientist study the:
    a. brainstem of a frog.
    b. limbic system of a dog.
    c. cortex of a monkey.
    d. cortex of a human.

15. A major problem with phrenology was that:
    a. it was "ahead of its time" and no one believed it could be true.
    b. the brain is not neatly organized into structures that correspond to our categories of behavior.
    c. the brains of humans and animals are much less similar than the theory implied.
    d. All of the above were problems with phrenology.

16. I am a relatively slow-acting (but long-lasting) chemical messenger carried throughout the body by the bloodstream. What am I?
    a. a hormone   c. acetylcholine
    b. a neurotransmitter d. dopamine

17. Your brother has been taking prescription medication and experiencing a number of unpleasant side effects, including unusually rapid heartbeat and excessive perspiration. It is likely that the medication is exaggerating activity in the:
    a. reticular formation.
    b. sympathetic nervous system.
    c. parasympathetic nervous system.
    d. amygdala.

18. Dr. Frankenstein made a mistake during neurosurgery on his monster. After the operation, the monster "saw" with his ears and "heard" with his eyes. It is likely that Dr. Frankenstein "rewired" neural connections in the monster's:
    a. hypothalamus.   c. amygdala.
    b. cerebellum.   d. thalamus.

19. A bodybuilder friend of yours suddenly seems to have grown several inches in height. You suspect

that your friend has been using drugs that affect the:
a. pituitary gland.   **c.** adrenal glands.
b. thalamus.   **d.** medulla.

20. Raccoons have much more precise control of their paws than dogs. You would expect that raccoons have more cortical space dedicated to "paw control" in the _____ of their brains.
a. frontal lobes   **c.** temporal lobes
b. parietal lobes   **d.** occipital lobes

Essay Question

Discuss how the brainstem, limbic system, and cerebral cortex are each involved when a person plays a musical instrument. (Use the space below to list the points you want to make and organize them. Then write the essay on a separate sheet of paper.)

Key Terms

Using your own words, write a brief definition or explanation of each of the following terms.

1. biological psychology

2. nervous system

3. neuron

4. sensory neurons

5. interneurons

6. motor neurons

7. reflex

8. dendrites

9. axon

10. myelin sheath

11. threshold

12. synapse

13. neurotransmitters

14. acetylcholine (ACh)

15. endorphins

16. central nervous system (CNS)

17. peripheral nervous system (PNS)

18. somatic nervous system

19. autonomic nervous system

20. sympathetic nervous system

21. parasympathetic nervous system

22. lesion

23. electroencephalogram (EEG)

24. CAT (computerized axial tomograph) scan

25. PET (positron emission tomograph) scan

26. MRI (magnetic resonance imaging)

27. brainstem

28. medulla

29. cerebellum

30. thalamus

31. reticular formation

32. limbic system

33. amygdala

34. hypothalamus

35. hormones

36. endocrine system

37. adrenal glands

38. pituitary gland

39. cerebral cortex

40. frontal lobes

41. parietal lobes

42. occipital lobes

43. temporal lobes

44. motor cortex

45. sensory cortex

46. association areas

47. aphasia

48. Broca's area

49. Wernicke's area

50. plasticity

51. corpus callosum

52. split-brain

ANSWERS

GUIDED STUDY

The following guidelines provide the main points that your answers should have touched upon.

1. Biological processes underlie every aspect of our behavior and mental processes. By studying the links between biology and psychology, biological psychologists achieve a greater understanding of such basic behaviors as sleep, hunger, and stress, and gain new insights into how best to treat stress, disease, depression, and other human conditions.

2. Each neuron consists of a cell body, branching fibers called dendrites that receive information from sensory receptors or other neurons, and an extension fiber called an axon through which the neuron passes information to other neurons. Some neural fibers are insulated with a myelin sheath, which helps speed neural impulses.

   A neural impulse, or action potential, occurs when the neuron receives a message from excitatory neurons on its dendrites or cell body. When the stimulation exceeds the neuron's threshold, an electrical charge travels down the axon into junctions with other neurons and with the muscles and glands of the body.

3. Sensory, or afferent, neurons relay information from the body's tissues and sense organs to the brain and spinal cord. Interneurons of the brain and spinal cord (the central nervous system) are involved in processing sensory information. The central nervous system then sends instructions to the muscles of the body by means of the motor, or efferent, neurons.

   Reflexes, which are automatic responses to stimuli, are governed by the simplest neural connections. In response to a painful stimulus to the fingertips, for example, a sensory neuron conveys the message to an interneuron in the spinal cord. The interneuron triggers an action potential in motor neurons that cause muscles of your arm to jerk your hand away.

4. When an action potential reaches the end of the axon, chemical messengers called neurotransmitters are released into the synaptic gap between the sending and receiving neuron. This junction is called a synapse. Neurotransmitter molecules bind to receptor sites on the receiving neuron and have either an excitatory or inhibitory influence on that neuron's tendency to generate its own action potential. If the receiving neuron receives more excitatory than inhibitory inputs, more neural impulses are generated.

   A particular neural pathway may use only one or two neurotransmitters, each of which may have a specific effect on behavior. Acetylcholine (ACh), for example, is the neurotransmitter at every synapse between a motor neuron and a muscle.

5. Endorphins are morphinelike neurotransmitters found in the brain that are released in response to pain and vigorous exercise. The existence of endorphins may help explain good feelings such as the "runner's high," the analgesic effects of acupuncture, and the indifference to pain in some injured people.

   Drugs have a number of different effects on neurotransmitters. Some mimic or block a particular neurotransmitter. Others interfere with the breakdown or reabsorption of the neurotransmitter. Cocaine, for example, produces a psychological "rush" by flooding the brain with substitute neurotransmitters. Opiate drugs such as heroine may cause the brain to stop producing endorphins. When these drugs wear off, depression or painful withdrawal symptoms result due to the disruption of the activity of the brain's neurotransmitters.

6. The central nervous system (CNS) includes all the neurons in the brain and spinal cord. The peripheral nervous system (PNS), which links the CNS with the body's sense receptors, muscles, and glands, has two divisions: somatic and autonomic. The somatic nervous system transmits sensory input to the CNS and motor output controlling the voluntary movements of the skeletal muscles.

   The autonomic nervous system, which influences the glands and muscles of our internal organs, also is a dual system. The sympathetic nervous system arouses the body during emergencies by accelerating heart rate, slowing digestion, raising blood pressure, dilating arteries, and creating perspiration. When the emergency has passed, the parasympathetic nervous system relaxes the body by producing the opposite effects.

7. The oldest method of studying the brain is by observing the effects of brain disease and injuries. More recently, electrical stimulation and surgical lesions of brain tissue in animals have been used to study the brain. Another technique, the electroencephalogram (EEG), is a recording of the brain's electrical activity from electrodes placed on its surface. Scientists also examine the brain with CAT (computerized axial tomograph) scans, PET (positron emission tomograph) scans, and the newest method, magnetic resonance imaging (MRI). Although the text discusses the use of scanning and imaging on the brain only, these techniques are also used to diagnose problems elsewhere in the body.

8. The three principal layers of the brain—the brainstem, the limbic system, and the cerebral cortex—

correspond to three stages of brain evolution — primitive vertebrate animals, lower animals, and advanced mammals.

The brainstem is the oldest and innermost region of the brain. It begins where the spinal cord enters the skull and contains the medulla, thalamus, reticular formation, and the cerebellum. The medulla controls breathing and heartbeat and is the point where nerves to and from each side of the brain cross over to connect with the opposite side of the body. The thalamus serves as the brain's sensory switchboard, routing information from sensory neurons to higher brain regions dealing with vision, hearing, taste, and touch. The reticular formation helps control arousal and attention. The cerebellum influences learning and memory; its most obvious function is muscular control.

9. Two limbic system components, the amygdala and the hippocampus, have important roles in memory. The amygdala is also involved in regulating aggression and fear. When this region is surgically lesioned, aggressive behavior in animals is diminished. When one region of the amygdala is electrically stimulated, a normally docile animal will behave aggressively; when another area is stimulated, the animal will display signs of fear.

The hypothalamus contains neurons that regulate hunger, thirst, body temperature, and sexual behavior; it also contains the so-called "pleasure centers." The hypothalamus also secretes hormones that influence our interest in sex, food, aggression, and nurturance.

10. The hypothalamus secretes hormones, some of which have a direct influence on the pituitary, the "master" endocrine gland, through an elaborate feedback system (brain → pituitary → other glands → hormones) that coordinates behavior. The endocrine system is a relatively slow-acting chemical communication system of glands that secrete hormones influencing growth, reproduction, metabolism, mood, and reactions to stress. For example, the adrenal glands release epinephrine (adrenaline) and norepinephrine (noradrenaline) during emergencies. These hormones increase heart rate, blood pressure, and blood sugar, providing a source of energy.

11. The cerebral cortex is a thin sheet of nerve cells covering the left and right cerebral hemispheres. The cortex is divided into four regions called lobes: frontal, parietal, temporal, and occipital. The frontal lobes control movement through the motor cortex and contain association areas that are involved in making plans and judgments. When specific parts of the motor cortex in the left and right hemispheres are electrically stimulated, movement is triggered in specific body parts on the opposite side of the body.

The parietal lobes house the sensory cortex which, when electrically stimulated, triggers a sense of a particular body part having been touched. The more sensitive a body region, the greater the area of sensory cortex devoted to it.

The temporal lobes receive auditory information primarily from the opposite ear, and the occipital lobes similarly receive input from the eyes.

Approximately three-fourths of the cortex consists of uncommitted association areas that communicate with one another and with neurons of the sensory and motor areas. Association areas influence personality, recognition of faces, and many other "higher" mental abilities.

12. Damage to any one of several areas of the cortex can cause aphasia, an impaired use of language. Damage to Broca's area in the left frontal lobe disrupts speaking. Damage to Wernicke's area in the left temporal lobe disrupts language comprehension and leaves people able to speak words but in a meaningless way. Damage to the angular gyrus will disrupt the ability to read aloud.

When you read aloud, words are registered in the visual area of the cortex and then relayed to the angular gyrus, which transforms the words into an auditory code. This code is comprehended by Wernicke's area and then sent to Broca's area, which directs the motor cortex to produce speech.

13. When a particular area of the brain is damaged, such as occurs following a stroke, other areas may in time reorganize and assume its functions (plasticity). Neurons near damaged ones compensate for the damage by making new neural connections that replace the damaged ones. The brains of young children, in which regional functions are not yet fixed, exhibit the greatest plasticity. New neural connections are formed throughout life, however, and are the brain's way of compensating for the gradual loss of neurons with age.

14. In order to control severe epileptic seizures, surgeons sometimes sever the wide band of fibers (the corpus callosum) that connects the two hemispheres of the brain.

Sperry, Myers, and Gazzaniga studied such split-brain patients, revealing that the left and right hemispheres each have special functions. In a person with an intact brain, information in the left or right visual field of both eyes projects directly to the opposite hemisphere of the brain and is quickly passed to the other hemisphere through the corpus callosum. In the split-brain patient, however, a briefly flashed image on the subject's right, for example, will be perceived only in the left hemisphere. By flashing images in this way, researchers are able to send information to either the left or right hemisphere and thereby determine its capabilities.

These experiments demonstrate that the right hemisphere is superior to the left at copying drawings, recognizing faces, and reading emotions. The left hemisphere is more logical, verbal, and able to deal with things in sequence. Despite these specialized functions, the two hemispheres work together in an integrated manner during most activities.

15. Approximately 95 percent of right-handed people process speech primarily in the left hemisphere. In contrast, left-handers are more diverse in their processing of language. About half process speech in the left hemisphere, one-quarter in the right hemisphere, and one quarter in both hemispheres. This has led to the suggestion that left-handers may require better communication between the two hemispheres, which might explain why the corpus callosum is larger in left-handed people.

CHAPTER REVIEW

1. phrenology
2. biological
3. biological psychologists
4. neurons; nervous system
5. dendrites
6. axons; myelin sheath
7. **a.** dendrites
   b. cell body
   c. axon
   d. myelin sheath
8. action potential; threshold; will not; all-or-none

A neural impulse is generated by appropriate stimuli that exceed the neuron's threshold. The stimuli are received through the dendrites, combined in the cell body, and electrically transmitted in an all-or-none fashion down the length of the axon. When the combined signal reaches the end of the axon, chemical messengers called neurotransmitters are released into the synaptic cleft or gap between two neurons. Neurotransmitter molecules bind to receptor sites on the dendrites of neighboring neurons and have either an excitatory or inhibitory influence on that neuron's tendency to generate its own neural impulse.

9. does not
10. sensory
11. interneurons
12. motor
13. reflexes

14. synapse; synaptic cleft
15. neurotransmitters; ions (atoms)
16. exciting; inhibiting
17. acetylcholine (ACh); curare
18. endorphins; heroin; morphine
19. excitatory
20. Parkinson's; dopamine; L-Dopa
21. central
22. peripheral
23. somatic; voluntary
24. autonomic
25. sympathetic
26. parasympathetic

In response to an emergency, the sympathetic division of the autonomic nervous system becomes aroused. The physiological changes that occur include accelerated heart rate, elevated blood sugar, dilation of arteries, slowing of digestion, and increased perspiration to cool the body. When the emergency is over, the parasympathetic nervous system produces the opposite physical reactions.

27. unmyelinated
28. clinical observation
29. lesions
30. electroencephalogram (EEG)
31. CAT scan
32. PET scan

By depicting the brain's consumption of radioactively labeled glucose, the PET scan allows researchers to see which brain areas are most active as a person performs various tasks. This provides additional information on the specialized functions of various regions of the brain.

33. MRI (magnetic resonance imaging)
34. brainstem; limbic system; cerebral cortex
35. less; more
36. medulla; breathing; heartbeat
37. thalamus
38. reticular formation; arousal; attention
39. cerebellum; learning; balance
40. limbic; amygdala; hippocampus
41. amygdala
42. hypothalamus; hunger, thirst, body temperature, or sex; pleasure
43. hormones
44. endocrine system; slower
45. adrenal; epinephrine; norepinephrine
46. pituitary; growth

The hypothalamus, which takes its orders from the cortex, influences secretions by the pituitary. The pituitary regulates other endocrine glands, which release hormones that influence behavior. The hypothalamus monitors these changes in blood chemistry and thereby adjusts its inputs to the pituitary.

47. cerebral cortex; hemispheres

48. a. frontal lobe
   b. parietal lobe
   c. occipital lobe
   d. temporal lobe

49. motor; frontal

50. sensory; touch

From sensory receptors in the skin the message travels via sensory neurons to an interneuron in the spinal cord, which in turn activates a motor neuron. This motor neuron causes the muscles in the hand to contract, and the person jerks his or her hand away from the heat.

At the same time that the spinal reflex is initiated, other interneurons carry the message up the spinal cord to the brain, where the pain message will be processed. It reaches the thalamus, which routes it to the sensory cortex. Along the way to the thalamus, the sensory input would also reach the reticular formation, which would arouse the cerebral cortex, the hypothalamus, and the sympathetic division of the autonomic nervous system. Activation of these systems would cause the release of adrenal hormones that accelerate the heartbeat, dilate arteries, and produce other responses that mobilize the body's resources to meet this threat.

51. occipital; temporal

52. association areas; frontal

53. aphasia; Broca's area; Wernicke's area; angular gyrus

54. will not

55. plasticity; 5

56. transplants; Alzheimer's

57. left; dominant (major)

58. corpus callosum; split-brain

59. right; name; right

The word *pencil* when flashed to a split-brain patient's right visual field would project only to the opposite, or left, hemisphere of the patient's brain. Because the left hemisphere contains the language control centers of the brain, the patient would be able to read the word aloud. The left hand is controlled by the right hemisphere of the brain. Because the right hemisphere would not be aware of the word, it would not be able to guide the left hand in identifying a pencil by touch.

60. left; left; right; right; right

PROGRESS TEST 1

Multiple-Choice Questions

1. b. is the answer. Afferent means inward, and sensory neurons transmit information inward from the body's tissues to the CNS; efferent means outward, and efferent neurons transmit information outward from the CNS to the body's tissues. (p. 28)

a. & d. Afferent and efferent neurons are found in both the central and peripheral divisions of the nervous system.

c. If the question had read "Efferent is to afferent," this answer would have been correct.

2. b. is the answer. The autonomic nervous system controls internal functioning, including heartbeat, digestion, and glandular activity. (p. 33)

a. The functions mentioned are all automatic, rather than voluntary, so this answer cannot be correct.

c. This answer is incorrect since most organs are affected by both divisions of the autonomic nervous system.

d. The somatic nervous system transmits sensory input to the CNS and directs the movements of skeletal muscles.

3. c. is the answer. Stimulus strength can affect only the number of times a neuron fires or the number of neurons that fire. (p. 29)

a., b., & d. These answers are incorrect because firing is an all-or-none response, so intensity remains the same regardless of stimulus strength. Nor can stimulus strength change the neuronal threshold or the impulse speed.

4. a. is the answer. Endorphins are neurotransmitters that function as natural painkillers. When the body has a supply of artificial painkillers like heroin, endorphin production stops. (p. 32)

b. The production of neurotransmitters other than endorphins does not cease.

c. Neurotransmitter production does not increase during withdrawal.

d. Heroin makes use of the same receptor sites as endorphins.

5. a. is the answer. The PET scan measures glucose consumption in different areas of the brain to determine their levels of activity. (p. 36)

b. The CAT scan is a series of x-rays taken from different positions and then analyzed by a computer to create an image representing a slice through the brain.

c. The EEG is a measure of electrical activity in the brain.

d. MRI uses magnetic fields and radio signals to

produce computer-generated images of soft tissues of the body.

6. **d.** is the answer. (p. 29)

    a. The dendrite is the part of the neuron that *receives* information from other neurons.

    b. The myelin sheath insulates some axons and helps speed neural impulses, but it is the axon itself that carries neural messages.

    c. A synapse is a junction between two neurons, not part of either neuron's structure.

7. **a.** is the answer. (p. 39)

    b. The reticular formation is linked to arousal and attention.

    c. The brainstem governs the mechanisms of basic survival—heartbeat and breathing—and has many other roles.

    d. The cerebral cortex governs the "higher" functions of the brain.

8. **c.** is the answer. In a simple reflex, an afferent neuron carries the message that a sensory receptor has been stimulated to an interneuron in the spinal cord. The interneuron responds by activating motor neurons that will enable the appropriate response. (p. 28)

9. **b.** is the answer. The plasticity of the brain decreases with age. (p. 47)

    c. & d. There is no difference in the plasticity of male and female brains.

10. **c.** is the answer. Wernicke's area is involved in comprehension, and aphasics with damage to Wernicke's are unable to understand what is said to them. (p. 46)

    a. The angular gyrus translates printed words into speech sounds; damage would result in the inability to read.

    b. Broca's area is involved in the physical production of speech; damage would result in the inability to speak fluently.

    d. The association areas of the cortex are involved, among other things, in processing language; damage to these areas wouldn't specifically affect comprehension.

11. **d.** is the answer. (p. 51)

    a. In most persons, language is primarily a left hemisphere function.

    b. Learned movements are unrelated to hemispheric specialization.

    c. Arithmetic reasoning is generally a left hemisphere function.

12. **d.** is the answer. Biological psychologists study the links between biology (in this case, neurotransmitters) and psychology (depression, in this example). (p. 27)

a., b., & c. These mental health professionals are more involved in the *treatment* of troubled behavior than in research.

13. **d.** is the answer. As animals increase in complexity, there is an increase in the amount of association areas. (p. 44)

    a. The brainstem controls basic survival functions and is not related to the complexity of an animal's behavior.

    b. The ratio of body and brain weight is a poor predictor of behavior complexity.

    c. The frontal lobe is concerned with personality, planning, and other mental functions, but its size is unrelated to intelligence or the complexity of behavior.

14. **b.** is the answer. (p. 33)

    a., c., & d. The autonomic nervous system, which is divided into the sympathetic and parasympathetic divisions, is concerned with regulating basic bodily maintenance functions.

15. **c.** is the answer. (p. 29)

    a. An action potential will occur only when the neuron's threshold is *exceeded*.

    b. An excitatory input that does not reach the neuron's threshold will not trigger an action potential.

    d. This answer is incorrect because some neurotransmitters inhibit a neuron's readiness to fire.

16. **c.** is the answer. A neuron receives incoming stimuli on its dendrites and cell body. These electrochemical signals are combined in the cell body, generating an impulse that travels down the axon, causing the release of neurotransmitter substances into the synaptic cleft or gap. (pp. 29–30)

17. **c.** is the answer. (p. 41)

    a. Chromosomes are structures within the cell's nucleus, containing genetic material.

    b. Neurotransmitters are the chemicals involved in synaptic transmission in the nervous system.

    d. Enzymes are chemicals that facilitate various chemical reactions throughout the body but are not involved in communication within the endocrine system.

18. **c.** is the answer. The reticular formation plays an important role in the functions of arousal and attention. (pp. 38–39)

    a. The thalamus relays sensory input.

    b. The corpus callosum links the two cerebral hemispheres.

    d. The cerebellum is involved in coordination of voluntary movement.

19. **d.** is the answer. (p. 51)

20. **b.** is the answer. Association areas interpret, integrate, and act on information from other areas of the cortex. (pp. 44–45)

Matching Items

1. d (p. 40)
2. f (pp. 42–44)
3. e (p. 44)
4. a (p. 44)
5. g (pp. 38–39)
6. b (p. 44)
7. c (p. 38)
8. h (p. 48)
9. k (p. 38)
10. i (p. 39)
11. j (p. 37)

PROGRESS TEST 2

Multiple-Choice Questions

1. **d.** is the answer. Plasticity refers to the ability of other regions of the brain to assume the function of damaged areas. (pp. 46–47)

   a. Recombination is an unrelated process involved in the mechanisms of heredity.

   b. Regeneration is the ability of damaged tissue to repair itself or to regrow. Regeneration of neural tissue does not occur.

   c. Enrichment is a general description of growth-promoting experiences in the environment.

2. **a.** is the answer. The visual cortex is located at the very back of the brain. (pp. 43 and 44)

3. **b.** is the answer. (p. 51)

   a., c., & d. Spatial reasoning, perceptual skills, and the left side of the body are primarily influenced by the right hemisphere.

4. **a.** is the answer. Sensory neurons in the somatic nervous system relay such messages. (p. 33)

   b. & c. These divisions of the autonomic nervous system are concerned with the regulation of bodily maintenance functions such as heartbeat, digestion, and glandular activity.

   d. The spinal cord itself is part of the central nervous system, but the message is carried to the spinal cord by the somatic division of the peripheral nervous system.

5. **c.** is the answer. As automatic responses to stimuli, reflexes are the simplest complete units of behavior and require only simple neural pathways. (p. 28)

   a., b., & d. Emotions, drives, and voluntary movements are all behaviors that are much more complex than reflexes and therefore involve much more complicated neural pathways.

6. **b.** is the answer. Endorphins are neurotransmitters that function as natural painkillers and are evidently involved in the "runner's high" and other situations in which discomfort or fatigue are expected but not experienced. (p. 31)

   a. ACh is a neurotransmitter involved in muscular control.

   c. Serotonin is a neurotransmitter involved in, among other things, states of consciousness.

   d. Norepinephrine is an adrenal hormone released to help us respond in moments of danger.

7. **a.** is the answer. Parkinson's disease and Alzheimer's disease cause degeneration of brain tissue that produces dopamine and acetylcholine, respectively. (p. 47)

   b. & c. These diseases affect both hemispheres of the cortex.

   d. These diseases cause insufficient production of the neurotransmitters.

8. **d.** is the answer. (p. 36)

   a. The EEG is an amplified recording of the brain's electrical activity.

   b. The CAT scan involves a series of x-rays of the brain.

   c. The PET scan is a visual display of brain activity that detects the movement of a radioactive form of glucose as the brain performs a task.

9. **a.** is the answer. (p. 29)

   b. Myelin sheath speeds rather than slows neural transmission.

   c., d., & e. Myelin sheaths are not involved in regulating the release of neurotransmitters.

10. **a.** is the answer. (p. 30)

    b. Dendrites are the neuron extensions that receive incoming signals from other neurons.

    c. The myelin sheath is a layer of fatty cells covering many axons that speeds neural impulses.

    d. Neurotransmitters are chemical messengers that cross the synaptic gap between neurons.

11. **b.** is the answer. ACh is a neurotransmitter that causes the contraction of muscle fibers when stimulated by motor neurons. This function explains its location. (p. 31)

    a. & c. Sensory neurons and interneurons do not directly stimulate muscle fibers.

12. **d.** is the answer. The pituitary regulates body growth, and some of its secretions regulate the release of hormones from other glands. (p. 41)

    a. The adrenal glands are stimulated by the autonomic nervous system to release epinephine and norepinephrine.

    b. The thyroid gland produces a hormone that controls the rates of various chemical reactions in the body.

    c. The hypothalamus regulates the pituitary but does not itself directly regulate growth.

13. d. is the answer. Also known as adrenaline and noradrenaline, epinephrine and norepinephrine are hormones released by the adrenal glands. (p. 41)

14. d. is the answer. The cerebellum is involved in the coordination of voluntary muscular movements. (p. 38)

a. The medulla regulates breathing and heartbeat.

b. The thalamus relays sensory inputs to the appropriate higher centers of the brain.

c. The hypothalamus is concerned with the regulation of basic drives and emotions.

15. a. is the answer. The reticular formation controls arousal via its connections to the cortex. Thus, separating the two produces a coma. (pp. 38–39)

b., c., & d. None of these structures controls arousal. The hypothalamus regulates hunger, thirst, sexual behavior, and other basic drives, the thalamus is a sensory relay station, and the cerebellum is involved in coordination of voluntary movement.

16. b. is the answer. The oldest region, the brainstem, is present even in lower vertebrates; the limbic system is found in all mammals; and the most recently evolved structure, the cortex, is found only in higher mammals. (p. 37)

17. d. is the answer, by elimination of the other answer choices. (p. 32)

a., b., & c. Various drugs have each of these influences on neural transmission. For example, heroin causes the brain to stop producing endorphins.

18. c. is the answer. The corpus callosum is a thick band of neural fibers linking the right and left cerebral hemispheres. To sever the corpus callosum is in effect to split the brain. (p. 48)

19. d. is the answer. The frontal lobe is in the front of the brain. Just behind is the parietal lobe. The occipital lobe is located at the very back of the head and just below the parietal lobe. Next to the occipital lobe and toward the front of the head is the temporal lobe. (p. 42)

20. d. is the answer. As demonstrated in the case of Phineas Gage, injury to the frontal lobe may produce such changes in personality. (p. 45)

a. Damage to the parietal lobe might disrupt functions involving the sensory cortex.

b. Damage to the temporal lobe might impair hearing.

c. Occipital damage might impair vision.

Matching Items

1. d (p. 51)	**5.** i (p. 35)	**9.** k (pp. 44–45)
2. g (p. 37)	**6.** a (p. 46)	**10.** b (p. 51)
3. e (p. 36)	**7.** j (p. 46)	**11.** c (p. 46)
4. f (p. 45)	**8.** h (pp. 39–42)	

Brain Damage Diagram (pp. 37–47)

1. a	**4.** d	**7.** f
2. h	**5.** e	**8.** g
3. c	**6.** b	**9.** k

CHALLENGE TEST

Multiple-Choice Questions

1. d. is the answer. Biological psychologists study the links between biology (chemical changes in this example) and behavior (emotions in this example). (p. 27)

a., b., & c. Developmental, experimental, and clinical psychologists would be more concerned with life-span changes in emotions, learning of emotional expressions, and the treatment of emotional disorders, respectively.

2. c. is the answer. The brainstem is the oldest and most primitive region of the brain. It is found in lower vertebrates, such as fish, as well as in humans and other mammals. The structures mentioned in the other choices are associated with stages of brain evolution beyond that seen in the fish. (p. 37)

3. a. is the answer. Since this reflex is an automatic response and involves only the spinal cord, the hand is jerked away before the brain has even received the information that causes the sensation of pain. (p. 28)

b. The spinal cord, which organizes simple reflexes such as this one, *is* part of the central nervous system.

c. The brain is not involved in directing spinal reflexes.

d. The autonomic nervous system controls the glands and the muscles of the internal organs; it does not influence the skeletal muscles controlling the hand.

4. d. is the answer. Stimulation of the sensory cortex elicits a sense of touch, as the experiments of Penfield demonstrated. (p. 44)

a., b., & c. Hearing, seeing, or movement might be expected if the temporal, occipital, and motor regions of the cortex, respectively, were stimulated.

5. c. is the answer. As Olds and Milner discovered, electrical stimulation of the hypothalamus is a highly reinforcing event, because it is the location of the animal's pleasure centers. The other brain regions mentioned are not associated with pleasure centers. (p. 40)

6. **a.** is the answer. The left hand, controlled by the right hemisphere, would be able to identify the fork, the picture of which is flashed to the right hemisphere. (p. 50)

7. **a.** is the answer. The PET scan, which traces the brain's use of a radioactive form of glucose, measures brain *activity* in various regions. It does not reveal anything about the brain's structure. (p. 36)

 b., c., & d. Each of these techniques is utilized to study the structure of activity of the brain.

8. **b.** is the answer. Simple reflexes, such as this one, are governed by activity in the autonomic nervous system. (p. 33)

 a. The occipital lobes process sensory messages from the eyes; they play no role in the reflexive response of the pupils to light.

 c. The left temporal lobe specializes in processing language.

 d. The cerebellum specializes in coordinating movement.

9. **b.** is the answer. (p. 51)

 a., c., & d. The left hemisphere does not specialize in facial recognition. And blood clots can form anywhere in the brain.

10. **d.** is the answer. The motor cortex in each hemisphere controls movement on the opposite side of the body. If the left side is paralyzed, the damage occurred in the right hemisphere. (p. 40)

 a. The reticular formation is involved in arousal, not the control of movement.

 b. The limbic system regulates emotional states; it does not control movement.

 c. A stroke in the left hemisphere would result in paralysis on the right side of the body.

11. **a.** is the answer. The right visual field projects directly to the verbal left hemisphere. (p. 49)

 b. & c. The left hand is controlled by the right hemisphere, which, in this situation, would be unaware of the word since the picture has been flashed to the left hemisphere.

12. **c.** is the answer. (p. 46)

 b. & d. Neither is true of aphasia.

13. **c.** is the answer. With the evolution of each succeeding layer of the brain, tight genetic controls relaxed and the increased capacity for learning and thinking enabled greater behavioral adaptability. (p. 37)

14. **b.** is the answer. Two limbic system components, the amygdala and the hippocampus, play important roles in memory. The limbic system also regulates fear and anger. (p. 39)

 a. The brainstem controls vital functions such as breathing and heartbeat; it is not directly involved in either emotion or memory.

 c. & d. These answers are incorrect because the limbic system is an older brain structure than the cortex. Its involvement in emotions and memory is therefore more basic than that of the cortex.

15. **b.** is the answer. (p. 27)

 a. "Ahead of its time" implies the theory had merit, which later research clearly showed it did not. Moreover, phrenology *was* accepted as an accurate theory of brain organization by many scientists.

 c. Phrenology said nothing about the similarities of human and animal brains.

16. **a.** is the answer. (p. 41)

 b., c., & d. Acetylcholine and dopamine are fast-acting neurotransmitters released at synapses, not in the bloodstream.

17. **b.** is the answer. Arousal of the sympathetic nervous system produces a number of effects, including accelerated heartbeat and excessive perspiration. (pp. 33–34)

 a. Stimulation of the reticular formation increases alertness, but would not necessarily accelerate heartbeat or cause excessive perspiration.

 c. Arousal of the parasympathetic nervous system would have effects opposite those stated.

 d. If the medication were affecting his amygdala, your brother might experience emotions such as anger or fear at illogical times.

18. **d.** is the answer. The thalamus relays sensory messages from the eyes, ears, and other receptors to the appropriate projection areas of the cortex. "Rewiring" the thalamus, theoretically, could have the effects stated in this question. (p. 38)

 a., b., & c. These brain structures are not directly involved in brain processes related to sensation or perception.

19. **a.** is the answer. Hormones of the pituitary gland regulate body growth. (p. 41)

 b. & d. Because they are not endocrine glands, the thalamus and medulla are not influenced by hormones.

 c. The adrenal glands produce hormones that provide energy during emergencies; they are not involved in regulating body growth.

20. a. is the answer. The motor cortex, which determines the precision with which various parts of the body can be moved, is located in the frontal lobes. (p. 43)

b. The parietal lobes contain the sensory cortex, which controls sensitivity to touch.

c. The temporal lobes contain the primary projection areas for hearing and, on the left side, are also involved in language use.

d. The occipital lobes contain the primary projection areas for vision.

Essay Question

The brainstem contains the medulla, which controls heartbeat, breathing, and other vital life functions that keep the musician alive. It is also the crossover point, where nerves to and from each side of the brain mostly connect with the opposite side of the musician's body.

Atop the brainstem sits the thalamus, which routes sensory information from the musician's eyes, ears, and fingertips to the higher brain regions concerned with seeing, hearing, and touching. Through the thalamus the musician's brain receives the necessary sensory information to enable decision making regarding all aspects of playing the instrument. The thalamus also routes some of the higher brain responses to the cerebellum, which helps coordinate movements involved in playing the instrument.

Within the brainstem the reticular formation receives inputs from the thalamus and the cerebral cortex that help maintain the musician's arousal and attention, both of which are important elements of playing a musical instrument.

The limbic system's involvement in emotion, motivation, and memory will influence many aspects of a musical performance. The amygdala and hippocampus will have been involved in the formation of memories of how to play the musical instrument, as well as memories of the notes and lyrics for each song. The pleasure centers of the hypothalamus comprise the brain's reward system and will help maintain the musician's motivation for learning and playing the instrument.

The cerebral cortex will oversee all aspects of the musician's behavior. Sensory projection areas in the occipital, temporal, and parietal lobes will process messages from the musician's eyes, ears, and fingertips. The motor cortex of the frontal lobes will organize the body movements necessary for playing the instrument. Finally, association areas in the frontal lobes and other parts of the brain will be involved in the planning and decision making inherent in playing the musical instrument.

KEY TERMS

1. **Biological psychology** is the study of the links between biology and behavior. (p. 27)

2. The **nervous system** is the electrochemical system that underlies all thought, feeling, and behavior. (p. 27)

3. The **neuron**, or nerve cell, is the basic building block of the nervous system. (p. 27)

4. **Sensory neurons** transmit information about internal and external stimuli to the central nervous system for processing. (p. 28)

5. **Interneurons** are the neurons of the central nervous system that link the sensory and motor neurons in the transmission of sensory input and motor output. (p. 28)

6. **Motor neurons** carry information and instructions for action from the central nervous system to muscles and glands. (p. 28)

7. A **reflex** is an automatic response to a stimulus; it is governed by a very simple neural pathway. (p. 28)

8. The **dendrites** of a neuron are the extensions that receive incoming signals from other nerve cells and transmit them to the cell body. (p. 29)

9. The **axons** of a neuron are the extensions that transmit impulses away from the cell body and to other nerve cells. (p. 29)

10. The **myelin sheath** is a layer of fatty cells that covers many axons and helps speed neural impulses. (p. 29)

11. A neuron's **threshold** is the level of stimulation that must be exceeded in order for the neuron to fire, or generate an electrical impulse. (p. 29)

12. A **synapse** is the junction between the axon tip of the sending neuron and the dendrite or cell body of the receiving neuron. The tiny gap at this junction is called the synaptic cleft or gap. (p. 30)

13. **Neurotransmitters** are chemicals that, when released into synaptic gaps, *transmit neural messages* from neuron to neuron. (p. 30)

14. **Acetylcholine (ACh)** is a neurotransmitter that triggers muscle contractions. (p. 31)

15. **Endorphins** are naturally occurring neurotransmitters linked to pain control and pleasure. (p. 31) *Memory aid:* Endorphins *end* pain.

16. The **central nervous system (CNS)** consists of the brain and spinal cord; it is located at the *center*, or internal core, of the body. (p. 32)

17. The **peripheral nervous system (PNS)** connects the central nervous system to the rest of the body; it is at the *periphery* of the body relative to the brain and spinal cord. (p. 32)

18. The **somatic nervous system** is the division of the PNS that transmits sensory information to the CNS and directs voluntary movements of the skeletal muscles. (p. 33)

19. The **autonomic nervous system** is the division of the PNS that controls the glands and the muscles of internal organs and thereby controls internal functioning; it regulates the *automatic* behaviors necessary for survival. (p. 33)

20. The **sympathetic nervous system** is the division of the autonomic nervous system that arouses the body and mobilizes its resources in stressful situations. (p. 33)

21. The **parasympathetic nervous system** is the division of the autonomic nervous system that often calms the body. (p. 34)

22. A **lesion** is destruction of tissue; studying the consequences of lesions — both surgically produced in animals and naturally occurring — in different regions of the brain helps researchers to determine the normal functions of these regions. (p. 35)

23. An **electroencephalogram (EEG)** is an amplified recording of the waves of electrical activity of the brain. *Encephalo* comes from a Greek word meaning "related to the brain." (p. 35)

24. The **CAT (computerized axial tomograph) scan** is a series of x-rays of the brain taken from different positions and analyzed by computer, creating an image that represents a slice through the brain. (p. 35)

25. The **PET (positron emission tomograph) scan** measures the levels of activity of different areas of the brain by tracing their consumption of glucose, the brain's fuel. (p. 36)

26. **MRI (magnetic resonance imaging)** uses magnetic fields and radio signals to produce computer-generated images that show brain structures more clearly. (p. 36)

27. The **brainstem**, the oldest major subdivision of the brain, is an extension of the spinal cord and is the central core of the brain; its structures direct automatic survival functions. (p. 37)

    Memory aid: As a flower sits on top of its stem, the brain rests on its **brainstem**.

28. Located in the brainstem, the **medulla** is involved in the regulation of breathing and heart rate. (p. 37)

29. The **cerebellum**, also part of the brainstem, assists in balance and the coordination of movement. (p. 38)

30. Located on top of the brainstem, the **thalamus** routes incoming messages to the appropriate cortical centers and transmits replies to the medulla and cerebellum. (p. 38)

31. Also part of the brainstem, the **reticular formation** plays an important role in arousing the higher brain centers and in controlling attention. (p. 38)

32. The second oldest subdivision of the brain, the **limbic system** plays an important role in the regulation of emotions and basic physiological drives. (p. 39)

    Memory aid: Its name comes from the Latin word *limbus*, meaning "border"; the **limbic system** is at the border of the brainstem and cerebral hemispheres.

33. The **amygdala** is part of the limbic system and is involved in regulation of the emotions of fear and rage. (p. 39)

34. Also part of the limbic system, the **hypothalamus** regulates hunger, thirst, and body temperature and contains the so-called pleasure centers of the brain. It also helps govern the endocrine system through the pituitary gland. (p. 40)

35. **Hormones** are the chemical messengers of the endocrine system; they are secreted by endocrine glands and circulate via the bloodstream to their target tissues, on which they have specific effects. (p. 41)

36. The **endocrine system**, the body's "slower" communication system, consists of glands that secrete hormones into the bloodstream. (p. 41)

37. The **adrenal glands** produce epinephrine and norepinephrine, hormones that prepare the body to deal with emergencies or stress. (p. 41)

38. Sometimes called the "master gland," the **pituitary gland** regulates growth and directs the secretion of hormones by many other endocrine glands. (p. 41)

39. The **cerebral cortex** is the outer covering of the cerebral hemispheres. The cortex is the seat of information processing; it is responsible for those complex functions that make us distinctively human. (p. 42)

    Memory aid: *Cortex* in Latin means "bark." As bark covers a tree, the **cerebral cortex** is the "bark of the brain."

40. Located at the front of the brain, just behind the forehead, the **frontal lobes** contain the motor cortex and are involved in making plans and judgments. (p. 42)

41. Situated between the frontal and occipital lobes, the **parietal lobes** contain the sensory cortex. (p. 42)

42. Located at the back and base of the brain, the **occipital lobes** contain the visual cortex, which receives information from the eyes. (p. 42)

    Example: The "stars" that one sees when hit in the back of the head result from the activation of the cells in the visual cortex in the **occipital lobe**.

43. Located on the sides of the brain, the **temporal lobes** contain the auditory areas, which receive information from the ears. (p. 42)

    Memory aid: The **temporal lobes** are located near the *temples*.

44. Located at the back of the frontal lobe, the **motor cortex** controls voluntary movement. (p. 43)

    Example: When you have decided to hit a backhand in tennis, the **motor cortex** is alerted to initiate the sequence of motor neuron activity that results in the execution of the shot.

45. The **sensory cortex** is located at the front of the parietal lobes, just behind the motor cortex. It receives information from the skin senses. (p. 44)

46. Located throughout the cortex, **association areas** of the brain are involved in higher mental functions, such as learning, memory, and abstract thinking. (p. 44)

Memory aid: Among their other functions, **association areas** of the cortex are involved in integrating, or *associating*, information from different areas of the brain.

47. **Aphasia** is an impairment of language as a result of damage to any of several cortical areas, including Broca's area and Wernicke's area. (p. 45)

48. **Broca's area** is located on the left frontal lobe and is involved in controlling the motor ability to produce speech. (p. 46)

49. **Wernicke's area** is located on the left temporal lobe and is involved in language comprehension. (p. 46)

50. **Plasticity** refers to the ability of the brain to reorganize itself to compensate for destruction of brain tissue. The plasticity of the brain diminishes with age. (p. 46)

51. The **corpus callosum** is a thick band of nerve fibers that links the right and left cerebral hemispheres. Without this band of nerve fibers, the two hemispheres could not interact. (p. 48)

52. The **split-brain** patient has had the major connections between the two cerebral hemispheres (the corpus callosum) severed, literally resulting in a split brain. (p. 49)

3 / The Developing Child

Chapter Overview

Developmental psychologists study the life cycle, from conception to death, examining how we develop physically, cognitively, and socially. Chapter 3 covers prenatal, infant, and childhood development and examines three major issues in developmental psychology: (1) the relative impact of genes and experience on behavior, (2) whether development is best described as gradual and continuous or as a discontinuous sequence of stages, and (3) whether the individual's personality remains stable or changes over the life span.

Research and theoretical issues introduced in this first chapter on development provide a base for further study in Chapter 4. Pay particular attention to the research of Harlow and others on attachment and social deprivation, to Piaget's theory of cognitive development, to the studies of twins and adopted children, and to the controversy surrounding the developmental issues.

NOTE: Answer guidelines for all Chapter 3 questions begin on page 61.

Guided Study

The text chapter should be studied one section at a time. Before you read, preview each section by skimming it, noting headings and boldface items. Then read the appropriate section objectives from the following outline. Keep these objectives in mind and, as you read the chapter section, search for the information that will enable you to meet each objective. Once you have finished a section, write out answers for its objectives.

Developmental Issues (pp. 61–63)

1. Identify three major issues that pervade developmental psychology.

nature/nurture

stages or continuity.

stability or change.

Prenatal Development and the Newborn (pp. 63–66)

2. Identify the mechanisms of heredity and explain how sex is determined.

Sex is determined by the X & Y chrom. XX = girl XY = boy.

3. Outline the course of prenatal development.

zygote - conc. - 2 wks.
embryo - 2 wks - 8 wks.
fetus - 8 wks - birth

4. Discuss the possible effects of teratogens on the developing embryo and fetus.

5. Describe the capacities of the newborn.

Infancy and Childhood (pp. 67–86)

6. Describe brain and motor development from infancy through childhood and discuss the role of experience in each.

7. Discuss Piaget's view of how the mind develops and describe his cognitive stages.

8. Discuss current views of Piaget's theory of cognitive development.

9. Discuss the origins and effects of early attachment and temperament patterns on later life.

10. Discuss how parents and child care workers influence attachment and trust.

11. Explain how children's behavior provides evidence of an emerging self-concept and discuss possible effects of different parenting styles and culture on children.

Reflections on the Nature-Nurture Issue (pp. 86–91)

12. Explain the rationale for twin and adoption studies and discuss criticisms of them.

13. Summarize the results and implications of research on the nature-nurture issue.

Chapter Review

When you have finished reading the chapter, work through the material that follows to review it. Complete the sentences and answer the questions. As you proceed, evaluate your performance for each section by consulting the answers on page 64. Do not continue with the next section until you understand each answer. If you need to, review or reread the appropriate section in the textbook before continuing.

Developmental Issues (pp. 61–63)

1. Scientists who study physical, mental, and social changes throughout the life cycle are called _____ dev. _____ psy. _____.

2. One of the oldest debates in developmental psychology concerns the relative importance of genes and experience in determining behavior; this debate is called the _____ nature- _____ nurture _____ issue.

3. A second developmental issue, _continuity_ or _stages_, concerns whether developmental changes are gradual or abrupt.

4. A third controversial issue concerns the consistency of personality and whether development is characterized more by _stability_ over time or by change.

5. The biochemical units of heredity that make each of us a distinctive human being are called _genes_.

6. Biological growth processes that enable orderly changes in behavior are called _maturation_.

7. Today most developmentalists believe that behaviors are determined by the interaction of our _genes_ and our past and present _experiences_.

8. Psychologists who emphasize _maturation_ tend to see development not as a continuous process, but as a sequence of genetically predetermined stages.

9. Psychologists who emphasize _experience_ and _learning_ see development as a continuous process.

10. Most developmentalists believe that there _is_ (is/is not) an underlying continuity in certain traits.

Prenatal Development and the Newborn (pp. 63–66)

11. The reproductive cycle begins when an egg, or _ovum_, is released by the female's ovary.

12. The body's genetic plans are stored within the _chromosomes_. In number, each person inherits _46_ of these structures, _23_ from each parent. Each is composed of long threads of _DNA_.

13. The twenty-third pair of chromosomes are the sex chromosomes. The mother invariably contributes a(n) _X_ chromosome. When the father contributes a(n) _X or Y_ chromosome, the testes

begin producing the hormone _testosterone_, and the individual will be male.

Write several sentences describing the moment of conception and the beginning of prenatal development.

14. Fertilized human eggs are called _zygote_. From about 2 until 8 weeks of age the developing human is called a(n) _embryo_. During the final stage of prenatal development, the developing human is called a(n) _fetus_.

15. Along with nutrients, a range of harmful substances known as _teratogens_ can pass through the placenta.

16. If a mother drinks heavily, her baby is at risk for the birth defects and mental retardation that accompany _fetal alcohol syndrome_.

17. When an infant's cheek is touched, it will vigorously search for a nipple, a response known as the _rooting reflex_.

Give some evidence supporting the claim that a newborn's sensory equipment is biologically prewired to facilitate social responsiveness.

Infancy and Childhood (pp. 67–86)

18. At birth the human nervous system _is not_ (is/is not) fully mature. This helps explain why our earliest memories do not occur before age _2 or 3_.

19. Infants _can_ (can/cannot) learn before their nervous systems are mature.

20. Animals, whose brains are mature at birth, form their first memories _____ (earlier than/later than/at about the same age as) humans.

21. Rosenzweig and Krech discovered that rats raised from a young age in solitary confinement had _____ (thicker/thinner) cortexes than animals raised in groups.

Write several sentences describing the effects of sensory stimulation on neural development.

22. Infants pass the milestones of motor development at different rates, but the basic _Sequence_ of stages is fixed. As an example, maturation creates a readiness to learn walking in children at about age _1_. Until the necessary muscular and neural maturation is complete, experience has a _small_ (large/small) effect on behavior.

23. Physical growth and brain development tend to slow down in children after the age of _2_. The last areas of the brain to develop are the _association_ areas of the cortex, which are involved in thinking, memory, and language.

24. The term for all the mental activities associated with thinking, remembering and knowing, is _cognition_. The first researcher to show that the cognitive processes of adults and children are very different was _Piaget_.

25. To organize his or her experiences, the developing child constructs cognitive concepts called _Schemas_

26. The interpretation of new experiences in terms of existing ideas is called _assimilation_. The adaptation of existing ideas to fit new experiences is called _accomodation_

Explain why science, like cognitive development, is a process of assimilation and accommodation.

27. In Piaget's first stage of development, the _sensorymotor_ stage, children experience the world through their motor activities and sensory impressions. This stage occurs between infancy and age _2_.

28. The development of an awareness that things continue to exist even when they are removed from view is called _object permanence_. This awareness begins to develop at about _8_ months of age. At about this same time, a new fear, called _Stranger anxiety_, emerges.

29. Preschoolers are often unable to perceive things from another person's point of view. This inability is called _egocentrism_. According to Piaget, during the preschool years and up to age _6_, children are in the _pre-operational_ stage.

30. The principle that the quantity of a substance remains the same even when the appearance of its container changes is called _conservation_. Piaget believed that preschoolers _haven't_ (have/have not) developed this concept.

31. Piaget believed that children acquire the mental abilities needed to comprehend transformations and conservation by about _7_ years of age. At this time they enter the _concrete operational_ stage.

32. In Piaget's final stage, the _formal operations_ stage, reasoning expands from the purely concrete to encompass _critical_ thinking. Piaget believed most children begin to enter this stage by age _12_.

Explain how contemporary researchers have modified some of Piaget's ideas, and identify those ideas that continue to receive support.

Contrast the responses of securely and insecurely attached infants to strange situations.

33. The development of a strong social bond between infant and parent is called _Attachment_.

34. Harlow's studies of monkeys have shown that mother-infant attachment does not depend on the mother providing nourishment so much as it does on her providing the comfort of _body_ _contact_.

35. In some animals attachment will occur only during a restricted time called a _critical_ _period_. Lorenz discovered that young birds would follow almost any object if it were the first moving thing they observed. This phenomenon is called _imprinting_.

36. Human infants _do not_ (do/do not) have a precise critical period for becoming attached.

37. In terms of psychological benefits to the infant, breast-feeding _doesn't_ (does/does not) appear to convey an advantage over bottle-feeding.

38. The term that refers to the inborn rudiments of an infant's personality and emotional excitability is _temperment_.

39. Faced with a new or strange situation, high-strung infants become _more_ (more/less) physiologically aroused than less excitable infants.

40. Placed in a strange play situation, children show one of two patterns of attachment: _secure_ attachment or _insecure_ attachment.

41. Separation anxiety peaks in infants around _13_ months, then _grad. decl._ (gradually declines/ remains constant for about a year). This is true of children _____ (in North America/throughout the world). The development of separation anxiety in children placed in day care is _same as_ (the same as/different from) children who remain at home.

42. Infants who were securely attached at 12 to 18 months typically show greater social _competance_ as toddlers than infants who were insecurely attached.

43. According to Erikson, securely attached infants approach life with a sense of _basic_ _trust_.

44. Harlow found that monkeys reared in social isolation reacted with either fear or _aggression_ when placed with other monkeys.

45. Most abused children _do_ (do/do not) later become abusive parents.

46. Most adopted children _are_ (are/are not) able to form new attachments without permanent emotional scars.

47. Today, approximately _half_ of North American mothers of preschoolers are employed. Maternal employment _doesn't_ (does/does not) seem to have a major impact on children's development.

48. Some developmental psychologists, such as Belsky and Zigler, believe that day care may promote _insecure_ attachment in infants, and disobedience and _aggression_ when children are older.

Others disagree, claiming that greater disobedience signifies greater _Independence_ and _Self-conf._ in day care infants.

49. The primary social achievement of childhood is the development of a _Self-concept_, which occurs in most children by age _12_.

50. A child's self-image generally becomes stable between the ages of _8_ and _10_, when children begin to describe themselves in terms of gender, group memberships, and psychological _traits_.

Write a sentence describing several characteristics of children who have formed a positive self-image.

51. Parents who impose rules and expect blind obedience are exhibiting a(n) _authoritarian_ style of parenting.

52. Setting and enforcing standards after discussion with their children is the approach taken by _authoritative_ parents.

53. Parents who make few demands of their children and tend to submit to their children's desires are identified as _permissive_ parents.

54. "Disengaged" parents who expect little and invest little are identified as _neglecting-rejecting_ parents.

55. Studies have shown that there tends to be a correlation between high self-esteem on the part of the child and the _authoritative_ style of parenting. This may be because this parenting style gives children the greatest sense of _control_ over their lives.

56. While most Western parents place more emphasis on _independence_ (emotional closeness/independence) in their children, many Asian and African parents focus on cultivating _em. closeness_ (emotional closeness/independence).

Reflections on the Nature-Nurture Issue (pp. 86–91)

57. Animal breeders have found that temperamental differences _can_ (can/cannot) be selectively bred.

58. Research on the influence of heredity includes studies of twins who developed from a single egg and are therefore genetically _identical_. Twins who developed from different fertilized eggs are no more genetically alike than siblings and are called _fraternal_ twins.

Explain why identical twins are of particular interest to psychologists.

59. In terms of the personality traits of extraversion and neuroticism, identical twins are _more_ (more/no more) alike than are fraternal twins.

60. Through research on identical twins raised apart, psychologists are able to study the influence of the _environment_.

61. Studies tend to show that the personalities of adopted children _do not_ (do/do not) closely resemble those of their adoptive parents.

Write several sentences discussing the relative influences of genes and experience on development.

FOCUS ON PSYCHOLOGY:
You and Your Parents

Parental influence on the social, cognitive, and emotional development of children has been a favorite research topic of developmental psychologists. Here are several issues to start you thinking about your own upbringing and how it has affected your behavior.

Birth Order. First-born and only children tend to have higher IQs and to be more conservative, more concerned about social approval, and more achievement oriented than later-born children. Although birth order interacts with other factors, such as family size and how close the children are in age, many researchers believe that later-born children are raised and socialized very differently than first-born or only children. For example, parents are usually stricter and more encouraging of achievement with their first child than they are with later children. What other differences would you expect in the upbringing of only, first-born, and later-born children? What is your birth-order position? Compare your upbringing with that of your brothers and sisters. Note any behavioral differences. Take a survey of your friends. Are there any consistent effects of birth order?

Parental Style. The text identifies four types of parenting styles and discusses their effects on the social development of children. Authoritarian parents dictate rules and expect blind obedience. Authoritative parents set and enforce rules after discussion with their children. Permissive parents make few demands and tend to submit to the wishes of their children. Rejecting-neglecting parents are uninvolved in their children's lives, expecting little of them and investing little in their development. How would you characterize your parents and upbringing? What behavioral effects of this upbringing can you identify in yourself? How might you be different, had you been raised by other parents? How do you and your parents differ from close friends and their parents?

Parental Malpractice. In recent years, several children have attempted to sue their parents for "parental malpractice." For example, a son sued his parents for $350,000, claiming that their neglect of him as a child was responsible for his psychological problems. Should parents be held legally accountable for the way their children turn out? If so, for what reasons and to what extent? Under what circumstances would you decide such a case in favor of the child?

Progress Test 1

Circle your answers to the following questions and check them with the answers on page 65. If your answer is incorrect, read the explanation for why it is incorrect and then consult the appropriate pages of the text (in parentheses following the correct answer).

1. Piaget's theory is primarily concerned with:
   a. motor development.
   b. social development.
   c. biological development.
   d. cognitive development.

2. In Piaget's stage of concrete operational intelligence, the child acquires an understanding of the principle of:
   a. conservation.   **c.** attachment.
   b. deduction.   **d.** object permanence.

3. Piaget held that egocentrism is characteristic of the:
   a. sensorimotor stage.
   b. preoperational stage.
   c. concrete operational stage.
   d. formal operational stage.

4. Which parenting style usually produces children with the greatest confidence and self-esteem?
   a. permissive   **c.** authoritative
   b. authoritarian   **d.** rejecting-neglecting

5. Dr. Joan Goodman is studying how memory changes as people get older. She is most likely a(n) _____ psychologist.
   a. social   **c.** developmental
   b. cognitive   **d.** experimental

6. During which stage of cognitive development do children acquire object permanence?
   a. sensorimotor   **c.** concrete operations
   b. preoperational   **d.** formal operations

7. The rooting reflex occurs when a:
   a. newborn's foot is tickled.
   b. newborn's cheek is touched.
   c. newborn hears a loud noise.
   d. newborn makes eye contact with his or her caregiver.

8. Harlow's studies of attachment in monkeys showed that:
   a. provision of nourishment was the single most important factor motivating attachment.
   b. a cloth mother produced the greatest attachment response.
   c. whether a cloth or wire mother was present mattered less than the presence or absence of other infants.
   d. attachment in monkeys is based on imprinting.

9. *Cognition* is defined as:
   a. the study of memory.
   b. the study of how thinking emerges in children.
   c. mental operations such as mathematical transformations.
   d. all the mental activities associated with thinking, knowing, and remembering.

10. When psychologists discuss maturation, they are referring to stages of growth that are *not* influenced by:
    a. conservation.   **c.** nurture.
    b. nature.   **d.** continuity.

11. The phenomenon in which young birds follow the first moving object they observe is:
    a. imprinting.
    b. bonding.
    c. assimilation.
    d. accommodation.

12. The developmental theorist who suggests that securely attached children develop an attitude of basic trust is:
    a. Piaget.
    b. Erikson.
    c. Harlow.
    d. Freud.

13. Which of the following best describes the view of development taken by theorists who emphasize the role of learning and experience?
    a. Development is a sequence of stages that do not necessarily occur in any particular order.
    b. Development is a sequence of stages that occur in a specific order.
    c. Development is a slow, continuous shaping process.
    d. Development is a slow, discontinuous shaping process.

14. The fertilized egg will develop into a boy if, at conception:
    a. an X chromosome is contributed by the father's sperm.
    b. a Y chromosome is contributed by the father's sperm.
    c. an X chromosome is contributed by the mother's egg.
    d. a Y chromosome is contributed by the mother's egg.

15. Research findings on the development of walking in Hopi Indian children who spent much of their first year bound to cradleboards are consistent with the idea that:
    a. cognitive development lags significantly behind motor skills development.
    b. maturation of physical skills is unaffected by experience.
    c. in the absence of relevant earlier learning experiences, the emergence of motor skills will be slowed.
    d. in humans the process of maturation may be significantly altered by cultural factors.

16. The nature-nurture controversy considers the degree to which traits and behaviors are determined by:
    a. genes or heredity.
    b. genes or experience.
    c. continuity or stages.
    d. life-span stability or change.

17. The maturational view of development emphasizes:
    a. the continuity of development.
    b. the discontinuity of development.
    c. individual differences in development.
    d. the stability of traits over the life span.

18. The hormone testosterone:
    a. is found only in females.
    b. determines the sex of the zygote.
    c. stimulates growth of the female sex organs in the fetus.
    d. stimulates growth of the male sex organs in the fetus.

19. Fraternal twins result when:
    a. a single egg is fertilized by a sperm and then splits.
    b. a single egg is fertilized by two sperm.
    c. two eggs are fertilized by different sperm.
    d. either a single egg is fertilized by one sperm or two eggs are fertilized by different sperm.

20. Several studies of long-separated identical twins have found that these twins:
    a. have little in common, due to the different environments in which they were raised.
    b. have many similarities, in everything from medical histories to personality.
    c. have similar personalities, but very different likes, dislikes, and life-styles.
    d. are no more similar than are fraternal twins reared apart.

Progress Test 2

Progress Test 2 should be completed during a final chapter review. Answer the following questions after you thoroughly understand the correct answers for the Chapter Review and Progress Test 1.

1. Assimilation refers to:
    a. the application of existing schemas to new experiences.
    b. the modification of schemas to fit new experiences.
    c. the progression of a child through the various stages of cognitive development.
    d. the bonding of mother and infant.

2. Which of the following statements about child abuse is correct?
    a. Abused children generally come from high-income families.
    b. Most children are abused between 10 and 15 years of age.
    c. Abused children are more likely than others to become abusive parents.
    d. Most abused children have authoritative parents.

3. Each cell of the human body has a total of:
   a. twenty-three chromosomes.
   b. twenty-three genes.
   c. forty-six chromosomes.
   d. forty-six genes.

4. Stranger anxiety develops at the same time as:
   a. the concept of conservation.
   b. egocentrism.
   c. the ability to pretend.
   d. the concept of object permanence.

5. The primary social achievement of infancy is the development of:
   a. self-concept.   c. attachment.
   b. gender identity.   d. initiative.

6. Developmental theorists who emphasize the importance of maturation see development as a:
   a. sequence of predictable stages.
   b. slow, continuous shaping process.
   c. completely unpredictable process.
   d. sequence of stages, not necessarily in a particular order.

7. An authoritarian child-rearing style involves:
   a. discipline through give-and-take discussion.
   b. love without discipline.
   c. neither love nor discipline.
   d. discipline that demands unquestioning obedience.

8. Which is the correct sequence of stages in Piaget's theory of cognitive development?
   a. sensorimotor, preoperational, concrete operational, formal operational.
   b. sensorimotor, preoperational, formal operational, concrete operational.
   c. preoperational, sensorimotor, concrete operational, formal operational.
   d. preoperational, sensorimotor, formal operational, concrete operational.

9. A child can be born a drug addict because:
   a. drugs used by the mother will pass into the child's bloodstream.
   b. addiction is an inherited personality trait.
   c. drugs used by the mother create genetic defects in her chromosomes.
   d. the fetus's blood has not yet developed a resistance to drugs.

10. A child whose mother drank heavily when she was pregnant is at heightened risk of:
    a. being emotionally excitable during childhood.
    b. becoming insecurely attached.
    c. being born with the physical and cognitive abnormalities accompanying fetal alcohol syndrome.
    d. addiction to a range of drugs throughout life.

11. Which is the correct order of stages of prenatal development?
    a. zygote, fetus, embryo
    b. zygote, embryo, fetus
    c. embryo, zygote, fetus
    d. embryo, fetus, zygote

12. The term *critical period* refers to:
    a. prenatal development.
    b. the initial 2 hours after a child's birth.
    c. the preoperational stage.
    d. a restricted time for learning.

13. Which of the following was *not* found by Harlow in socially deprived monkeys?
    a. They had difficulty mating.
    b. They showed extreme fear or aggression when first seeing other monkeys.
    c. They showed abnormal physical development.
    d. The females were abusive mothers.

14. Children who in infancy formed secure attachments to their parents are more likely than other children to:
    a. prefer the company of adults to that of other children.
    b. become permissive parents.
    c. show a great deal of competence in social situations.
    d. be less achievement oriented.

15. Between the ages of 7 and 12 children are in the:
    a. sensorimotor stage.
    b. preoperational stage.
    c. concrete operational stage.
    d. formal operational stage.

16. Most people's earliest memories do not predate
    _____ of age.
    a. 6 months.   c. 2 years.
    b. 1 year.   d. 3 or 4 years.

17. Insecurely attached infants who are left by their mothers in an unfamiliar setting often will:
    a. hold fast to their mothers on their return.
    b. explore the new surroundings confidently.
    c. be indifferent or even hostile toward their mothers on their return.
    d. display little emotion under any circumstances.

18. Compared to those raised in Western societies, children raised in communal societies, such as Japan or China:
    a. grow up with a stronger integration of the sense of family into their self-concepts.
    b. exhibit greater shyness toward strangers.
    c. exhibit greater concern for loyalty and social harmony.
    d. have all of the above characteristics.
    e. have none of the above characteristics.

19. Research regarding the effects of day care on development in preschoolers suggests that children placed in day care:
    a. receive far less quality time from adults.
    b. are slower to develop clear self-concepts than children raised at home.
    c. are no less attached to their parents than children raised at home.
    d. show less social competence than children raised at home.

20. The term that refers to the rudiments of an individual's personality, especially emotional excitability, is:
    a. ego.   c. temperament.
    b. self-concept.   d. autonomy.

Challenge Test

Answer these questions the day before an exam as a final check on your understanding of the chapter's terms and concepts.

Multiple-Choice Questions

1. I am a segment of DNA found in every cell of the body. I direct the manufacture of proteins that control biological development. What am I?
    a. a chromosome   c. a teratogen
    b. a gene   d. a zygote

2. Calvin, who is trying to impress his psychology professor with his knowledge of infant motor development, asks why some infants learn to roll over before they lift their heads from a prone position, while others develop these skills in the opposite order. What should Calvin's professor conclude from this question?
    a. Calvin clearly understands that the sequence of motor development is not the same for all infants.
    b. Calvin doesn't know what he's talking about. Although some infants reach these developmental milestones ahead of others, the order is the same for all infants.
    c. Calvin needs to be reminded that rolling over is an inherited reflex, not a learned skill.
    d. Calvin understands an important principle: motor development is unpredictable.

3. "Infantile amnesia" is most likely caused by:
    a. prenatal exposure to teratogens.
    b. premature birth.
    c. the immature nervous system.
    d. prenatal malnutrition.

4. Children who become deaf at age 2, after being exposed to speech, are later more easily trained in sign language than those deaf from birth. This suggests:
    a. nothing, since wide variation in learning rates is common.
    b. that the first 2 years are a critical period for learning language.
    c. that children deaf from birth are likely to be learning disabled.
    d. that b. and c. are both correct.

5. I am a rat whose cortex is lighter and thinner and has smaller nerve cells and fewer glial cells than my litter mates. What happened to me?
    a. You were born prematurely.
    b. You suffer from fetal alcohol syndrome.
    c. You were raised in an enriched environment.
    d. You were raised in a deprived environment.

6. Before Piaget, people were more likely to believe that:
    a. the child's mind is a miniature model of the adult's.
    b. children think about the world in radically different ways than adults.
    c. the child's mind develops through a series of stages.
    d. children interpret their experiences in terms of their current understandings.

7. If a toddler's father points out the lion at the zoo and calls it "kittie," he is trying to help his son to _____, that is, to modify his schema for cat in order to incorporate the new experience.
    a. accommodate   c. use cognition
    b. assimilate   d. conserve

8. Two-year-old Naveed, who has a simple schema for "mom" and calls each new woman with a child he encounters "mom," is demonstrating Piaget's process of:
    a. accommodation.   c. cognition.
    b. assimilation.   d. conservation.

9. As a child observes, liquid is transferred from a tall, thin tube into a short, wide jar. The child is asked if there is now less liquid in order to determine if she has mastered:
    a. the processes of accommodation and assimilation.
    b. the concept of object permanence.
    c. the concept of conservation.
    d. the ability to reason abstractly.

10. I am 14 months old and quite fearful of strangers. I am in Piaget's _____ stage of cognitive development.
    a. sensorimotor   c. concrete operational
    b. preoperational   d. formal operational

11. I am 3 years old, love to pretend, and have trouble taking another person's perspective. I am in Piaget's _____ stage of cognitive development.
    a. sensorimotor
    b. preoperational
    c. concrete operational
    d. formal operational

12. In Piaget's theory, conservation is to egocentrism as the _____ stage is to the _____ stage.
    a. sensorimotor; formal operational
    b. formal operational; sensorimotor
    c. preoperational; sensorimotor
    d. concrete operational; preoperational

13. Despite growing up in the same home environment, Karen and her brother John have personalities as different from one another as two people selected randomly from the population. Why is this so?
    a. Personality is inherited. Since Karen and John are not identical twins, it is not surprising they have very different personalities.
    b. Gender is the most important factor in personality formation. If Karen had a sister, the two of them would probably be much more alike.
    c. The interaction of their individual genes and nonshared experiences accounts for the common finding that children in the same family are usually very different.
    d. Their case is unusual; children in the same family usually have similar personalities.

14. Four-year-old Jamail has a younger sister. When asked if he has a sister, he is likely to answer _____; when asked if his sister has a brother, Jamail is likely to answer _____.
    a. yes; yes
    b. no; no
    c. yes; no
    d. no; yes

15. The idea that parent-infant bonding in humans occurs shortly after birth arose from:
    a. observations of health care professionals in delivery rooms.
    b. animal studies.
    c. research on disturbed infants.
    d. adoption studies.

16. Your sister and brother-in-law, who are about to adopt a 1-year-old, are worried that the child will never "bond" to them. What advice should you offer?
    a. Tell them that, unfortunately, this is true; they would be better off waiting for a younger child who has not yet "bonded."
    b. Tell them that most year-old infants form new attachments without permanent emotional scars.

    c. Tell them that children younger than 5 usually have no difficulties relating to new parents.
    d. None; there is no way to predict how children will handle separation and new attachments.

17. "You will clean your room because I said so," would be a statement most typical of a(n) _____ parent.
    a. authoritarian
    b. authoritative
    c. permissive
    d. rejecting-neglecting

18. The relationship between a child's high self-esteem and authoritative parenting has been attributed to:
    a. the child's sense of basic trust.
    b. the child's secure attachment.
    c. the child's sense of control.
    d. a. and b. only.

19. Chad, who grew up in the United States, is more likely to encourage _____ in his future children than Asian-born Hidiyaki, who is more likely to encourage _____ in his future children.
    a. obedience; independence
    b. independence; emotional closeness
    c. emotional closeness; obedience
    d. loyalty; emotional closeness

20. One of the best ways to distinguish how much genetic and environmental factors affect behavior is to compare children who have:
    a. the same genes and environments.
    b. different genes and environments.
    c. similar genes and environments.
    d. similar genes and similar families.
    e. the same genes but different environments.

Essay Question

You have decided to open a school and day care center for children from 18 months to 12 years of age. You plan to base the curriculum for each age group on Piaget's theory of cognitive development. What kinds of activities should you plan for the 18-month-olds? the 5-year-olds? the 8-year-olds? the 12-year-olds? (Use the space below to list the points you want to make and organize them. Then write the essay on a separate sheet of paper.)

Key Terms

Using your own words, write a brief definition or explanation of each of the following terms.

1. developmental psychology

2. genes

3. maturation

4. ovum

5. chromosomes

6. DNA (deoxyribonucleic acid)

7. X chromosome

8. Y chromosome

9. testosterone

10. zygote

11. embryo

12. fetus

13. teratogens

14. fetal alcohol syndrome

15. rooting reflex

16. cognition

17. schema

18. assimilation

19. accommodation

20. sensorimotor stage

21. object permanence

22. stranger anxiety

23. egocentrism

24. preoperational stage

25. conservation

26. concrete operational stage

27. formal operational stage

28. attachment

29. critical period

30. imprinting

31. temperament

32. basic trust

33. identical twins

34. fraternal twins

ANSWERS

GUIDED STUDY

The following guidelines provide the main points that your answers should have touched upon.

1. The nature-nurture issue is concerned with how much our development is influenced by heredity and how much by our experience. The continuity or stage issue concerns whether development is a gradual, continuous process or a sequence of separate stages. The stability or change issue asks whether individual traits persist over the life span or people become different persons as they age.

2. When a mature ovum is fertilized by a sperm, the twenty-three chromosomes carried in the egg pair

up with the twenty-three chromosomes of the sperm. Each chromosome is composed of long threads of DNA; DNA is made of thousands of genes that determine development by directing the manufacture of proteins.

Sex is determined by the twenty-third pair of chromosomes, the sex chromosomes, one of which comes from each parent. The mother always contributes an X chromosome. The father's sperm contributes an X or a Y chromosome; with an X chromosome, the developing person becomes a girl; with a Y chromosome, a boy develops. The presence of a Y chromosome triggers development of the testes and the production of the principal male hormone, testosterone.

3. Prenatal development is divided into three stages: zygote (from conception to 2 weeks); embryo (2 weeks through 8 weeks); and fetus (9 weeks to birth).

During the period of the zygote, cell division is the primary task. Within two weeks of conception the increasingly numerous cells begin to differentiate and specialize in structure and function. At this time the zygote attaches to the mother's uterine wall. During the period of the embryo, body organs begin to form and function. By the end of the sixth month the fetus's internal organs have become sufficiently functional to allow a premature fetus a chance of survival.

4. Teratogens are damaging agents such as drugs and diseases that pass from the mother's bloodstream through the placenta into that of the embryo or fetus. Teratogens may result in a variety of physical and cognitive abnormalities in the developing child. For example, mothers who are heavy smokers often give birth to underweight infants. Mothers addicted to drugs such as heroin give birth to addicted newborns. If a mother is a heavy alcohol drinker her infant may suffer from fetal alcohol syndrome, which involves small misproportioned heads, brain abnormalities, and mental retardation.

5. Newborns are born with a variety of reflexes that help ensure their survival. When touched on its cheek, for example, a baby will open its mouth and search for food (rooting reflex).

The newborn's sensory capabilities facilitate social responsiveness. Newborns prefer human voices and drawings of human faces to artificial sounds and nonhuman visual patterns. Within days of birth, babies can distinguish their mother's facial expression, odor, and voice. By the second week infants can even imitate facial expressions.

6. All the brain cells a person will ever have are present at birth. However, the neural connections that enable walking, talking, and memory are only beginning to form. This neural immaturity may explain why we have no memories of events before 3 or 4 years of age. While lasting memories may not be formed before then, infants are capable of learning simple responses.

Sights, sounds, smells, touches, and other experiences foster the development of neural connections within the brain. Premature infants and laboratory animals who receive extra handling and a variety of experiences develop faster neurologically than those who are raised in deprived environments.

Although the age at which infants sit, stand, walk, and control bowel and bladder varies from child to child, the sequence in which babies develop these abilities is universal. Experiences before the necessary muscular and neural maturation has occurred have only a small effect on the acquisition of these abilities.

After the rapid pace of the first 2 years, physical growth and neural development proceeds at a slower pace during childhood. The association areas of the cortex are the last brain areas to develop.

7. Piaget believed that children actively construct their understanding of the world in radically different ways than adults. He further believed that children's minds develop through a series of stages in which they form increasingly complex schemas that organize their past experiences and provide a framework for understanding future experiences. New experiences that conform to existing schemas are assimilated. When new experiences do not fit existing schemas, children accommodate their schemas to incorporate the new experiences.

In the sensorimotor stage, from birth to about 2 years, children experience their world through their senses and actions. During this stage object permanence and stranger anxiety develop.

In the preoperational stage, from about 2 to 6 years, children are able to symbolically represent things with words and images but lack logical reasoning. During this stage pretend play and egocentrism develop.

In the concrete operational stage, from about 7 to 12 years, children are able to think logically about concrete events, grasp concrete analogies, and perform mathematical operations. Conservation also develops during this stage.

The formal operational stage, from age 12 through adulthood, is characterized by abstract and scientific reasoning, as well as by the potential for mature moral reasoning.

8. Today's researchers see development as more continuous than did Piaget. For example, object per-

manence, conservation, and the abilities to take another's perspective and perform mental operations unfold gradually and are not utterly absent in one stage and then suddenly present.

Researchers also believe that Piaget underestimated young children's competence. They have found rudiments of various cognitive abilities at an earlier age than Piaget supposed.

In many ways, however, Piaget's theory continues to receive support. Despite variations in the rate at which children develop, cross-cultural research reveals that human cognition everywhere unfolds in the basic sequence he proposed.

9. Harlow's research with monkeys reveals that attachment usually grows from body contact with parents, rather than by association with feeding. In many animals, attachment is also based on familiarity and forms during a critical period shortly after hatching or birth (a process called imprinting). Although human infants prefer faces and objects with which they are familiar, they do not have a critical period for becoming attached.

Attachment also depends on an infant's temperament, which includes inborn rudiments of personality and emotional excitability. The most emotionally reactive newborns tend also to be the most reactive, inhibited, and fearful 2-year-olds, shy 7-year-olds, and intense young adults. With age, these characteristics relax somewhat.

The mother's behavior is also a factor. Sensitive, responsive mothers tend to have infants who become securely attached. Insensitive, unresponsive mothers often have insecurely attached infants. Securely attached infants are less anxious and more socially competent, and these differences persist through early childhood.

10. Erik Erikson believed that infants with sensitive, loving caregivers form a lifelong attitude of basic trust—a sense that the world is predictable and reliable. Children who suffer parental neglect or abuse may form lasting scars—nightmares, depression, a troubled adolescence, and a greater tendency to later abuse their own children.

The impact of day care on children remains controversial. Some developmental psychologists believe that day care children are at heightened risk of insecure attachment and of being disobedient and aggressive at older ages. Others believe that quality day care does not hinder secure attachment and may actually promote greater independence and self-confidence.

11. Self-awareness emerges gradually over the first year, with the first sign being a child's self-recognition when staring into a mirror. By 15 to 18 months, children will wipe at a dab of makeup seen on their faces in a mirror's reflection. By school age, children begin to describe themselves in terms of gender, group memberships, and psychological traits.

Four parenting styles have been identified. Authoritarian parents impose rules and expect their children to be obedient. Authoritative parents are demanding, yet more responsive to their children. They set and enforce rules, but also are willing to explain and discuss the reasoning behind rules. Permissive parents make few demands of their children and submit to their wishes. Rejecting-neglecting parents expect little and invest little in their children's development. Children with the highest self-esteem, self-reliance, and social competence usually have authoritative parents, perhaps because their parents provide them with the greatest sense of self-control.

Social values vary from one culture to another. Most parents in Western societies value greater independence in their children than do parents in Asian and African cultures, who focus more on cultivating emotional closeness. Cross-cultural studies also reveal that people in Japanese and Chinese cultures exhibit greater shyness toward strangers and concern for social harmony and loyalty than do Westerners.

12. Since identical twins are genetically identical, the findings that they are more similar in a trait than fraternal twins or other siblings suggest that there is a substantial genetic influence on that trait. In this way, twin studies can give psychologists a greater understanding of the role of genes in development.

Adoption studies enable psychologists to determine the relative influence of nature and nurture on development by asking whether adopted children are more like their biological parents, who contribute their genes, or their adoptive parents, who contribute a home environment.

Critics of twin studies contend that twin similarities may merely be coincidental rather than a reflection of heredity. Moreover, because adoption agencies tend to place separated twins in similar homes, critics argue, similarities in traits may reflect the impact of similar experiences rather than heredity alone.

13. Twin and adoption studies reveal that genetic influences account for nearly 50 percent of the variation in traits such as outgoingness and emotional instability. The remaining variation has been attributed to each person's unique experiences in interacting with parents, peer, and cultural influences.

Because genes and experience interact in influencing development, it is incorrect to say that a certain trait is x percent due to genes and y percent due to experience. That genes direct experience can be seen in how people select environments that suit their natures, and how genetically influenced traits evoke certain responses in others.

CHAPTER REVIEW

1. developmental psychologists
2. nature-nurture
3. continuity; stages
4. stability
5. genes
6. maturation
7. genes; experiences
8. maturation
9. experience; learning
10. is
11. ovum
12. chromosomes; forty-six; twenty-three; DNA
13. X; Y; testosterone

An egg has been released by the ovary; during intercourse, millions of sperm are deposited and travel toward the egg. At the moment of conception, those few sperm that reach the egg release digestive enzymes that eat away the egg's protective coating, allowing one sperm to penetrate. An electrical charge then blocks the other sperm from entering. The fertilizing sperm is drawn into the egg, where the egg nucleus and sperm nucleus fuse and the chromosomes are paired. The process of cell division and differentiation begins.

14. zygotes; embryo; fetus
15. teratogens
16. fetal alcohol syndrome
17. rooting reflex

Newborns reflexively turn their heads in the direction of human voices, but not toward artificial sounds. They gaze longer at a drawing of a human face than at a geometric pattern. They focus best on objects about 8 to 12 inches away, which is about the distance between a nursing infant's eyes and the mother's.

18. is not; 3 or 4
19. can
20. earlier than
21. thinner

Research has shown that human and animal infants given extra sensory stimulation develop faster neurologically. Throughout life, sensory stimulation activates and strengthens particular neural connections,

while other connections weaken with disuse. In this way our experiences shape the very structure of the neural pathways that process those experiences.

22. sequence; 1; small
23. 2; association
24. cognition; Piaget
25. schemas
26. assimilation; accommodation

Scientists use existing theories to explain (assimilate) new findings. When new findings conflict with existing theories, the theories must be changed.

27. sensorimotor; 2
28. object permanence; 8; stranger anxiety
29. egocentrism; 7; preoperational
30. conservation; have not
31. 7; concrete operational
32. formal operational; abstract; 12

Contemporary researchers contend that Piaget underestimated the competence of young children. When tests of egocentrism and conservation are simplified, for example, 5- and 6-year-olds will exhibit some understanding of conservation and an emerging ability to take another's perspective. Researchers today also see development as more continuous than did Piaget. Despite these revisions to Piaget's theory, studies support the basic idea that cognitive development unfolds as a sequence of distinct stages.

33. attachment
34. body contact
35. critical period; imprinting
36. do not
37. does not
38. temperament
39. more
40. secure; insecure

Placed in a strange situation, securely attached infants play comfortably, happily exploring their new environment. In contrast, insecurely attached infants are less likely to explore their surroundings and may even cling to their mothers. When separated from their mothers, insecurely attached infants are much more distressed than securely attached infants. When reunited with their mothers, insecurely attached infants may be indifferent or even hostile.

41. 13; gradually declines; throughout the world; the same as
42. competence
43. basic trust
44. aggression

45. do not

46. are

47. half; does not

48. insecure; aggression; independence; self-confidence

49. self-concept; 12

50. 8; 10; traits

Children who have formed a positive self-concept tend to be more confident, independent, optimistic, assertive, and sociable.

51. authoritarian

52. authoritative

53. permissive

54. rejecting-neglecting

55. authoritative; control

56. independence; emotional closeness

57. can

58. identical; fraternal

Since identical twins are genetic replicas of each other, the findings that identical twins are highly similar in a trait—significantly more so than fraternal twins or other siblings—suggests that there is a substantial genetic influence on that trait. In this way, identical twins can give psychologists a greater understanding of the role of heredity.

59. more

60. environment

61. do not

Studies of twins and adopted children support the idea that genetic influences account for nearly 50 percent of individual variation in traits such as outgoingness and emotional instability. The remaining variation can be attributed to each individual's unique experiences. Therefore, genes *and* environment direct development, and their effects are intimately intertwined.

PROGRESS TEST 1

1. d. is the answer. Piaget's theory is concerned with the qualitatively different stages of thinking, or cognition, that occur in children. (p. 69)

2. a. is the answer. Understanding that an entity remains constant despite changes in appearance is the hallmark of the transition to concrete operational thought. (p. 74)

b. Deduction, or deductive reasoning, is a formal operational ability.

c. Piaget's theory is not concerned with attachment.

d. Attaining object permanence is the hallmark of preoperational thought.

3. b. is the answer. The preoperational child sees the world from his or her own vantage point. (p. 73)

a. As immature as egocentrism is, it represents a significant cognitive advance over the sensorimotor child, who knows the world only through senses and actions. Even simple self-awareness takes a while to develop.

c. & d. As children attain the operational stages, they become more able to see the world through the eyes of others.

4. c. is the answer. Children of authoritative parents tend to develop self-reliance and a positive self-image. (pp. 84–85)

a., b., & d. Children seem to fare best when they have been raised by parents who are not permissive, authoritarian, or rejecting-neglecting, but authoritative—exerting control without depriving their children of a sense of control over their own lives.

5. c. is the answer. Developmental psychologists study physical, cognitive (memory, in this example), and social change throughout the life span. (p. 61)

a. Social psychologists study how people influence and are influenced by others.

b. Cognitive psychologists *do* study memory; because Dr. Goodman is interested in life-span *changes* in memory, she is more likely a developmental psychologist.

d. Experimental psychologists study physiology, sensation, perception, learning, and other aspects of behavior. Only developmental psychologists focus on developmental changes in behavior and mental processes.

6. a. is the answer. Before object permanence is attained, "out of sight" is truly "out of mind." (p. 72)

b., c., & d. Developments associated with the preoperational, concrete operational, and formal operational stages include the ability to pretend, conservation, and abstract reasoning, respectively.

7. b. is the answer. The infant turns its head and begins sucking when its cheek is stroked. (p. 65)

a., c., & d. These stimuli produce other reflexes in the newborn.

8. b. is the answer. (p. 76)

a. When given the choice between a wire mother with a bottle and a cloth mother without, the monkeys preferred the cloth mother.

c. The presence of other infants made no difference.

d. Imprinting plays no role in the attachment of higher primates.

9. **d.** is the answer. (p. 69)

   a., b., & c. Memory, thinking, and mathematical reasoning are all aspects of cognition; each answer, however, is incomplete as a definition.

10. **c.** is the answer. Through maturation—an orderly sequence of biological growth processes that are relatively unaffected by experience—all humans develop. (p. 62)

    a. Conservation is the cognitive awareness that objects do not change with changes in appearance.

    b. The forces of nature *are* those that direct maturation.

    d. The continuity-discontinuity debate concerns whether development is a gradual and continuous process or a discontinuous, stagelike process. In fact, those who emphasize maturation see development as occurring in stages rather than continuously.

11. **a.** is the answer. (p. 77)

    b. Bonding refers to the more general process, seen in a number of species, of immediate mutual attachment between infant and parent, formed on the basis of physical contact.

    c. & d. Assimilation and accommodation refer to Piagetian processes by which cognitive schemas develop.

12. **b.** is the answer. Erikson proposed that development occurs in a series of stages, in the first of which the child develops an attitude of either basic trust or mistrust. (p. 80)

    a. Piaget's theory is concerned with cognitive development.

    c. Harlow conducted research on attachment and deprivation.

    d. Freud's theory is concerned with personality development.

13. **c.** is the answer. Theorists who emphasize the role of learning and experience see these as shaping experience in a gradual but continuous way. (p. 62)

    a. & d. These answers do not correspond to any of the commonly held views of development.

    b. The view of development as a series of fixed stages is generally associated with theorists who emphasize maturation.

14. **b.** is the answer. (p. 64)

    a. If the father's sperm contributes an X chromosome, a female will be produced.

    c. The mother's egg always contributes an X chromosome.

    d. This statement is factually incorrect. The mother's egg always contributes an X chromosome; a Y chromosome can be contributed only by the sperm.

15. **b.** is the answer. Although the Hopi children spent most of their first year restrained, they began to walk at a little over a year, just as other children do. Maturation of this physical skill was not affected by experience—or lack of it. (p. 68)

    a. The issue of cognitive versus motor development is not addressed by the research.

    c. & d. Despite a cultural practice that prevented extensive motor skills experience relevant to walking, the Hopi children began to walk at about the same time as children from other cultures. The maturation process is not affected by earlier learning or cultural differences.

16. **b.** is the answer. Nature = genes; nurture = experience. (p. 62)

    a. Genes and heredity both refer to the nature side of the nature-nurture controversy.

    c. & d. Whether development is continuous or occurs in stages and whether it is characterized by stability or change over the life span are two other developmental issues.

17. **b.** is the answer. Those who emphasize maturation tend to see development as occurring in stages, which by definition are steplike and discontinuous. (p. 62)

    a. The learning viewpoint emphasizes the continuity of development.

    c. The maturation view emphasizes similarities among individuals, since all go through the same maturational stages.

    d. The issue of stability over the life span is separate from the continuity versus stages issue addressed by the maturational view. However, since the maturational view emphasizes successive stages, it is more likely to focus on change over the life span than on stability.

18. **d.** is the answer. (p. 64)

    a. Testosterone is the principal *male* hormone.

    b. The zygote's sex is determined by the twenty-third pair of chromosomes, the sex chromosomes.

19. **c.** is the answer. (p. 87)

    a. This situation would produce identical twins.

    b. Only one sperm can fertilize an egg.

    d. This answer is incorrect because a single fertilized egg would not produce fraternal twins.

20. **b.** is the answer. (pp. 88–89)

    a., c., & d. Despite being raised in different environments, long-separated identical twins often have much in common, including likes, dislikes, and life-styles. This indicates the significant heritability of many traits.

PROGRESS TEST 2

1. **a.** is the answer. When new experiences are interpreted in terms of existing schemas, assimilation occurs. (p. 70)

b. This answer describes accommodation.

c. & d. These answers have no relationship to the cognitive process of assimilation.

2. **c.** is the answer. About 30 percent of abused children become abusive parents; this rate of child abuse is about four times the national figure. (p. 80)

a. Abusive parents are found in every socioeconomic group.

b. Abuse occurs to children of all ages.

d. There is no established relationship between authoritative parenting and abuse.

3. **c.** is the answer. (pp. 63–64)

b. & d. Each cell of the human body contains hundreds of genes.

4. **d.** is the answer. With object permanence, a child develops schemas for familiar objects, including faces, and may become upset when with a stranger who does not fit any of these schemas. (p. 72)

a. The concept of conservation develops during the concrete operational stage, whereas stranger anxiety develops during the earlier sensorimotor stage.

b. & c. Egocentrism and the ability to pretend both develop during the preoperational stage. This follows the sensorimotor stage, during which stranger anxiety develops.

5. **c.** is the answer. Attachment develops in infancy and has profound repercussions for the individual's subsequent psychosocial growth. (pp. 76–83)

a. & b. Self-concept and gender identity, which is part of self-concept, emerge during the preschool years.

d. In Erikson's theory, the emergence of initiative is associated with the preschool years.

6. **a.** is the answer. (p. 62)

b. This answer reflects the viewpoint of those who emphasize learning in development.

c. All researchers see behavior and development as somewhat predictable.

d. This answer is incorrect because the stages occur in an *ordered* sequence.

7. **d.** is the answer. Authoritarian parents impose rules that children are expected to follow in an unquestioning manner. (p. 84)

a. This is a description of authoritative parents.

b. Discipline is very much a part of the authoritarian style of child-rearing.

c. By definition, authoritarian parents discipline their children, but love or its absence is not correlated with any particular parenting style.

8. **a.** is the answer. (p. 71)

9. **a.** is the answer. Any drug taken by the mother passes through the placenta and enters the child's bloodstream. (p. 65)

b. Addiction cannot be inherited; it requires exposure to an addictive drug.

c. Drugs may disrupt the mechanisms of heredity, but there is no evidence that such changes promote addiction.

d. This answer is incorrect because at no age does the blood "resist" drugs.

10. **c.** is the answer. (p. 65)

a., b., & d. A child's emotional temperament, attachment, and addiction have not been linked to the mother's drinking while pregnant.

11. **b.** is the answer. (p. 64)

12. **d.** is the answer. A critical period is a restricted time during which an organism must be exposed to certain influences or experiences for a particular kind of learning to occur. (p. 77)

a. Critical periods refer to developmental periods after birth.

b. Critical periods vary from behavior to behavior, but they are not confined to the hours following birth.

c. Critical periods are not specifically associated with the preoperational period.

13. **c.** is the answer. Deprived monkeys were impaired in their social behaviors but not in their physical development. (p. 76)

a., b., & d. Each of these was found in socially deprived monkeys.

14. **c.** is the answer. Thus, for example, Sroufe found that children who were securely attached at 12 months of age were, as 2- to 3-year-olds, more outgoing than other children and more enthusiastic when working on challenging tasks. (p. 80)

a., b., & d. There is no indication that securely attached children prefer to be with adults, become permissive parents, or are less achievement oriented.

15. **c.** is the answer. (pp. 74–75)

a. The sensorimotor stage lasts from birth until age 2.

b. The preoperational stage lasts from age 2 to 6.

d. The formal operational stage begins during adolescence.

16. d. is the answer. (p. 67)

17. c. is the answer. (p. 78)

    a. Insecurely attached infants often cling to their mothers when placed in a new situation, yet, when the mother returns after an absence, the infant's reaction tends to be one of indifference or hostility.

    b. These behaviors are characteristic of securely attached infants.

    d. Insecurely attached infants in unfamiliar surroundings will often exhibit a range of emotional behaviors.

18. d. is the answer. (p. 86)

19. c. is the answer. Children's attachments to their parents do not seem to be disrupted by day care, which, like parenting, can be of high or low quality. (pp. 82–83)

    a. Studies indicate that preschoolers, whether or not their parents work, tend to receive relatively little quality time from their parents; hence, it's unlikely that children in day care receive far less quality time from adults.

    b. Studies have not shown that day care disrupts development of the self-concept.

    d. There is no evidence that day care lessens social competence.

20. c. is the answer. (p. 77)

    a. Ego is a Freudian term that has come to refer to an individual's sense of self.

    b. Self-concept refers to how individuals perceive themselves, rather than to their personality.

    d. Autonomy is only one factor of personality— specifically, that relating to an individual's independence, or self-determination.

CHALLENGE TEST

Multiple-Choice Questions

1. b. is the answer. (p. 64)

    a. Chromosomes are threadlike structures made of the DNA that contains the genes.

    c. Teratogens are potentially harmful agents, such as chemicals and diseases, that can reach the developing embryo or fetus.

    d. A zygote is a fertilized egg that will soon develop into an embryo and then a fetus.

2. b. is the answer. (pp. 68–69)

    a. & d. Although the rate of motor development varies from child to child, the basic sequence is universal and, therefore, predictable.

    c. Rolling over and head lifting are both learned movements.

3. c. is the answer. (p. 67)

    a., b., & d. "Infantile amnesia" is a normal developmental phenomenon unrelated to teratogens, premature birth, or prenatal malnutrition.

4. b. is the answer. (p. 67)

    a. Although variations in the rate of learning are common, the fact that the same experience (deafness) has a greater impact at one age than another implies that this is more than normal variation in development.

    c. There is no evidence that children deaf from birth are more likely to have learning disabilities.

5. d. is the answer (pp. 67–68)

    a. & b. Premature birth and fetal alcohol syndrome usually do not have these effects on the developing brain.

    c. If the question had stated "I have a thicker cortex with larger cell bodies and more glial cells," this answer would be correct.

6. a. is the answer. (p. 70)

    b., c., & d. Each of these is an understanding developed by Piaget.

7. a. is the answer. (p. 70)

    b. Assimilation is the process by which new experiences are incorporated into existing schemas.

    c. Cognition is a general term, referring to all mental activities associated with thinking, knowing, and remembering.

    d. Conservation is the ability to recognize that objects do not change whenever their appearances change.

8. b. is the answer. Naveed is assimilating each encounter with a new mother in his existing schema. (p. 70)

    a. Naveed is not accommodating because he does not have to adjust his schema to fit his new experiences.

    c. Cognition refers to all mental activities associated with thinking, knowing, and remembering.

    d. Conservation is the ability to recognize that objects do not change whenever their appearances change.

9. c. is the answer. This test is designed to determine if the child understands that the quantity of liquid is conserved, despite the shift to a container that is different in shape. (p. 74)

    a. These are general processes related to concept building.

    b. Object permanence is the concept that an object continues to exist even when not perceived; in this case, the water is perceived throughout the experiment.

d. This experiment does not require abstract reasoning, only the ability to reason logically about the concrete.

10. **a.** is the answer. This child's age and stranger anxiety clearly place him within Piaget's sensorimotor stage. (pp. 72–73)

11. **b.** is the answer. This child's age, ability to pretend, and egocentrism clearly place him within Piaget's preoperational stage. (pp. 73–74)

12. **d.** is the answer. Conservation is a hallmark of the concrete operational stage; egocentrism is a hallmark of the preoperational stage. (pp. 73–75)

13. **c.** is the answer. (pp. 89–90)

    a. Although heredity does influence certain traits, such as outgoingness and emotional instability, it is the interaction of heredity and experience that ultimately molds personality.

    b. There is no single "most important factor" in personality. Moreover, for the same reason two sisters or brothers often have dissimilar personalities, a sister and brother may be very much alike.

    d. Karen and John's case is not at all unusual.

14. **c.** is the answer. Being 4 years old, Jamail would be in Piaget's preoperational stage. Preoperational thinking is egocentric, which means Jamail would find it difficult to "put himself in his sister's shoes" and perceive that she has a brother. (p. 73)

15. **b.** is the answer. Studies of imprinting in animals led to the idea that there is a critical period for human bonding shortly after birth. (p. 77)

16. **b.** is the answer. (pp. 81–82)

    a. Unlike animals, human infants do not "bond" to a caregiver during a critical period shortly after birth.

    c. When children over 6 months of age are placed with new parents, they often have difficulties eating, sleeping, and relating to their new parents.

    d. The explanations for answers a. and c. demonstrate that there *is* a degree of predictability as to how children handle separation and new attachments.

17. **a.** is the answer. (p. 84)

    b. An authoritative parent would likely be firm in requiring room-cleaning, but would be more willing to explain why and discuss the issue with the child.

    c. Permissive parents would probably let the child do whatever she or he wanted.

    d. Rejecting-neglecting parents probably wouldn't care whether the child cleaned his or her room.

18. **c.** is the answer. Because authoritative parents openly discuss family rules, their children perceive that they, rather than their parents, control what happens to them. Studies reveal that people who perceive control over their lives become motivated and self-confident, thus the relationship between authoritative parenting and self-esteem. (p. 85)

    a. & b. Although a sense of basic trust and secure attachment are important to a child's well-being, neither explains the relationship between a particular style of parenting and children's high self-esteem.

19. **b.** is the answer. Although parental values differ from one time and place to another, studies reveal that Western parents today want their children to think for themselves, while Asian and African parents place greater value on emotional closeness. (p. 86)

    d. Both of these values are more typical of Asian than Western cultures.

20. **e.** is the answer. To separate the influences of heredity and experience on behavior, one of the two must be held constant. (pp. 88–89)

    a., b., c., & d. These situations would not allow one to separate the contributions of heredity and environment.

Essay Question

Eighteen-month-old children, who are in Piaget's sensorimotor stage, experience the world through their senses and actions. An appropriate "curriculum" for this age group would be the provision of an interesting sensorimotor environment filled with toys and other objects that foster touching, mouthing, crawling, and smelling.

Five-year-old children, who are in Piaget's preoperational stage, would enjoy a curriculum with lots of opportunities for pretend play. Dress-up and make-believe games of "go-to-work" and "school" would be appropriate activities.

Eight-year-old children, who are in Piaget's concrete operational stage, are able to think logically about concrete events. Arithmetic games, and other activities based on logical thinking about concrete events, would be appropriate activities for this age group.

Twelve-year-old children, who are on the threshold of formal operational thinking, are able to reason abstractly. Problem-solving activities based on hypothetical propositions and deductive reasoning would be stimulating activities for this age group.

KEY TERMS

1. **Developmental psychology** is the branch of psychology concerned with physical, cognitive, and social change throughout the life span. (p. 61)

2. **Genes** are the biochemical units of heredity; they are segments of the DNA molecules of which the chromosomes are composed. (p. 62)

3. **Maturation** is a biological growth process that is relatively uninfluenced by experience or other environmental factors. (p. 62)

   Example: The ability to walk depends on a certain level of neural and muscular **maturation**. For this reason, until the toddler's body is physically ready to walk, practice "walking" has little effect.

4. **Ovum** (the Latin word for "egg") refers to the female reproductive cell, which, if united with a sperm, develops into a new individual. (p. 63)

5. **Chromosomes** are made up of DNA molecules, which contain the genes. In conception, the twenty-three chromosomes in the egg are paired with the twenty-three chromosomes in the sperm. (p. 63)

6. **DNA (deoxyribonucleic acid)** is the chemical substance of which chromosomes are composed. (p. 64)

7. An **X chromosome** is found in both males and females. At conception, the egg always contributes an X sex chromosome; if the sperm also contributes an X chromosome, the child will be a girl. (p. 64)

8. A **Y chromosome** is found only in males. If, in addition to the X chromosome contributed by the egg, the sperm contributes a Y sex chromosome, the child will be a boy. (p. 64)

9. **Testosterone**, the most important male hormone, stimulates growth of the male sex organs and development of the male sex characteristics during puberty. (p. 64)

   Memory aid: *Test*osterone is produced by the male's *testes*.

10. The **zygote** (a term derived from the Greek word for "joint") is the fertilized egg, that is, the cluster of cells formed during conception by the union of sperm and egg. (p. 64)

11. The **embryo** is the developing prenatal organism from about 2 weeks until 2 months after conception. (p. 64)

12. The **fetus** is the developing prenatal human from 9 weeks after conception to birth. (p. 64)

13. **Teratogens** (literally, poisons) are any medications, drugs, viruses, or other substances that cross the mother's placenta and can harm the developing embryo or fetus. (p. 65)

14. The **fetal alcohol syndrome** refers to the physical and cognitive abnormalities that heavy drinking by a pregnant woman may cause in the developing child. (p. 65)

15. The **rooting reflex** is the newborn's tendency, when his or her cheek is stroked, to orient toward the stimulus and begin sucking. (p. 65)

16. **Cognition** refers to the mental processes associated with thinking, knowing, and remembering. (p. 69)

17. In Piaget's theory of cognitive development, **schemas** are mental concepts that help organize existing and new information. (p. 70)

18. **Assimilation** refers to the interpretation of new information in light of existing cognitive schemas. (p. 70)

   Example: When a young child points to buses, tractors, and other four-wheeled vehicles in a picture book and calls them "car," the child is **assimilating** new information to an existing schema.

19. **Accommodation** refers to the modification of existing schemas in order to incorporate new information. (p. 70)

   Example: **Accommodation** of the schema "car" will occur as the child gains information about vehicles: This schema will be narrowed, and new schemas ("buses," "tractors," etc.) will develop.

20. In Piaget's theory of cognitive stages, the **sensorimotor stage** lasts from birth to about age 2. During this stage, infants gain knowledge of the world through their senses and their motor activities. (p. 72)

21. **Object permanence**, which develops during the sensorimotor stage, is the awareness that things do not cease to exist when they are out of sight. (p. 72)

22. **Stranger anxiety** is the fear of strangers that infants begin to display at about 8 months of age. (pp. 72–73)

23. **Egocentrism** refers to the difficulty that preoperational children have in considering another's viewpoint. "Ego" means "self," and "centrism" indicates "in the center"; the preoperational child is "self-centered." (p. 74)

24. In Piaget's theory, the **preoperational stage** lasts from about 2 to 6 or 7 years of age. During this stage language development is rapid, but the child is unable to think logically or symbolically. (p. 74)

25. **Conservation** is the principle that properties such as number, volume, and mass remain constant despite changes in the appearance of objects; it is acquired during the concrete operational stage. (p. 74)

26. During the **concrete operational stage**, lasting from about ages 7 to 12, children can think logically about events and objects but are not able to reason abstractly. (pp. 74–75)

27. In Piaget's theory, the **formal operational stage** normally begins about age 12. During this stage people begin to think logically about abstract concepts. (p. 75)

    Memory aid: To help differentiate Piaget's stages remember that "operations" are mental transformations. *Pre*operational children, who lack the ability to perform transformations, are "before" this developmental milestone. Concrete operational children can operate on real, or concrete, objects. Formal operational children can perform logical transformations on abstract concepts.

28. **Attachment** refers to the process by which young children develop closeness to a caregiver. (p. 76)

29. A **critical period** is a limited time during which an organism must be exposed to certain experiences or influences if it is to develop properly. (p. 77)

30. **Imprinting** is the process by which certain animals form attachments early in life, usually during a limited critical period. (p. 77)

31. **Temperament** refers to the rudiments of personality and a child's characteristic emotional excitability. Temperament is a trait that is strongly linked to heredity. (p. 77)

32. According to Erikson, **basic trust** is a sense that the world is predictable and trustworthy—a concept that infants form if their needs are met by responsive caregiving. (p. 80)

33. **Identical twins** develop from a single fertilized egg that splits in two and therefore are genetically identical. (p. 87)

34. **Fraternal twins** develop from two separate eggs fertilized by different sperm and therefore are no more genetically similar than ordinary siblings. (p. 87)

    Memory aid: A *fraternity* is a group of nonidentical individuals.

4 / Adolescence and Adulthood

Chapter Overview

A key assumption of modern developmental psychology is that development is lifelong. Chapter 4 explores physical, cognitive, and social development during adolescence and adulthood. On the basis of this discussion, the final section reconsiders two major developmental issues: whether development is a continuous process or occurs in stages, and whether it is characterized more by stability over time or by change.

Although there are not too many terms to learn in this chapter, there are a number of important research findings to remember. Pay particular attention to the discussion of intellectual stability or decline during adulthood and social changes during adulthood. A major challenge in this chapter is to become familiar with two stage theories: Kohlberg's theory of moral development and Erikson's theory of psychosocial development. Writing carefully prepared answers to the guided study items should be especially helpful in mastering the material in this chapter.

NOTE: Answer guidelines for all Chapter 4 questions begin on page 83.

Guided Study

The text chapter should be studied one section at a time. Before you read, preview each section by skimming it, noting headings and boldface items. Then read the appropriate section objectives from the following outline. Keep these objectives in mind and, as you read the chapter section, search for the information that will enable you to meet each objective. Once you have finished a section, write out answers for its objectives.

Adolescence (pp. 95–107)

1. Identify the major physical changes that occur in adolescence.

2. Describe cognitive development during adolescence and identify two criticisms of Piaget's theory.

3. Describe Kohlberg's theory of moral development and its criticisms, and discuss the relationship of moral thinking to action.

4. Discuss Erikson's views on adolescence and the nature of social relationships, particularly with parents, during adolescence.

5. Discuss several factors that have contributed to the recent increase in adolescent pregnancy.

Adulthood (pp. 107–123)

6. Identify the major physical changes that occur in middle adulthood and later life.

7. Describe the major cognitive changes that occur in adulthood and old age.

8. Explain why stage theories of adult social development, such as that proposed by Levinson, are controversial.

9. Discuss the importance of family and career commitments in adult development.

10. Discuss the psychological reactions of the dying and of those who have lost a loved one.

Reflections on Life-Span Development (pp. 123–125)

11. State current views of psychologists on the issues of continuity versus discontinuity and stability versus change in lifelong development.

Chapter Review

When you have finished reading the chapter, work through the material that follows to review it. Complete the sentences and answer the questions. As you proceed, evaluate your performance for each section by consulting the answers on page 84. Do not continue with the next section until you understand each answer. If you need to, review or reread the appropriate section in the textbook before continuing.

1. The once popular belief that no important changes in personality occur after childhood has given way to an understanding that development is _lifelong_.

2. Today, sexual maturity is beginning _earlier_ (earlier/later), and adult independence _later_ (earlier/later) than in the past.

3. The "storm and stress" view of adolescence is credited to _Hall_, the first American psychologist to describe adolescence.

Adolescence (pp. 95–107)

4. Adolescence begins with the time of developing sexual maturity known as _puberty_. A two-year growth spurt begins in girls at about the age of _11_ and in boys at about the age of _13_.
This growth spurt is marked by the development of the reproductive organs, or _primary_ _sex_ characteristics, as well as by the development of traits such as pubic hair and enlarged breasts in females and facial hair in males. These nonreproductive traits are known as _secondary_ _sex_ characteristics.

5. The first menstrual period, called _menarche_, occurs by about age _13_. In boys the first ejaculation occurs by about age _14_.

6. The _sequence_ (timing/sequence) of pubertal changes is more predictable than their _timing_ (timing/sequence).

7. Boys who mature _early_ (early/late) tend to be more popular, self-assured, and independent. For girls, _early_ (early/late) maturation can be stressful.

8. During the early teen years, thinking continues to be _egocentric_, as adolescents often feel their experiences are unique.

9. Piaget's final stage of cognitive development is the stage of _formal operations_. The adolescent in this stage is capable of thinking logically about _abstract_ as well as concrete propositions. Some critics of Piaget suggest that this type of thinking may begin _earlier_ (earlier/later) than Piaget believed. Other critics believe Piaget _overestimated_ (overestimated/underestimated) the number of people who attain this stage.

10. The theorist who proposed that moral thought progresses through stages is _Kohlberg_. These stages are divided into three basic levels: _preconventional_, _conventional_, and _postconventional_

11. In the preconventional stages of morality, characteristic of children, the emphasis is on obeying rules in order to avoid _punishment_ or gain _rewards_.

12. Conventional morality usually emerges by early _adolescence_. The emphasis is on gaining social _approval_ or upholding the social _order_.

13. Individuals who base moral judgments on their own perceptions of universal ethical principles are said by Kohlberg to employ _postconv_ morality. Research has revealed that this level appears mostly in _educated_ (uneducated/educated) people who are in the _middle_ (lower/middle) class of countries that value _individualism_

Summarize the criticisms of Kohlberg's theory of moral development.

14. Studies _haven't_ (have/have not) found much difference between men and women's moral reasoning.

15. According to Gilligan, women are more likely than men to display an _ethic of care_.

16. The relationship between moral action and thinking _is not_ (is/is not) very strong.

17. Moral ideas grow _stronger_ (stronger/weaker) when acted on.

Complete the missing information in the following table of Erikson's stages of psychosocial development.

Approximate Age	Psychosocial Stage
Infancy	Trust vs. Mist
Toddler	Autonomy vs. shame and doubt
Preschooler	_Init. vs. guilt_
Elem. School	Competence vs. inferiority
Adolescence	_Ident. vs role conf_
Young Adulthood	Intimacy vs. isolation
Middle Adulthood	_Generativity vs. Stagn_
Late 11	Integrity vs. despair

18. According to Erikson, the task of adolescence is to develop a clear sense of self, or _identity_. Erikson sees this

development as a prerequisite for the development of ___intimacy___ in young adulthood.

19. Between 13 and 23 the individual's self-concept usually becomes ___more___ (more/less) positive.

20. Gilligan believes females are ___less___ (more/less) concerned than males with establishing individualistic identities.

21. Adolescence is typically a time of increasing influence from one's ___peers___ and decreasing influence from ___parents___. Studies have shown that the generation gap between adolescents and parents is quite ___small___ (small/large).

22. Sexual activity is ___higher___ (higher/lower) among adolescents who earn low grades, whose parents are not college graduates, who seldom attend religious services, and who use alcohol or marijuana.

Adulthood (pp. 107–123)

23. Early adulthood extends from the decade of the _____ into the _____, when _____ adulthood begins.

24. During adulthood, age _____ (is/is not) a very good predictor of a person's traits.

25. The cessation of the menstrual cycle, known as _____, occurs at about age _____. This biological change results from lowered levels of the hormone _____. A woman's experience during this time depends largely on her _____.

26. Although men experience no equivalent to the menopause, they do experience a gradual decline in _____ count and in the hormone _____ during later life.

27. With age, the eye's pupil _____ (shrinks/enlarges) and its lens becomes _____ (more/less) transparent. As a result, the amount of light that reaches the retina is _____ (increased/reduced).

28. Although older adults are _____ (more/less) susceptible to life-threatening ailments, they suffer from short-term ailments such as flu _____ (more/less) often than younger adults.

29. At birth the average American has a life expectancy of _____ years. People who reach age 65 can expect to live at least to age _____.

30. Aging _____ (slows/speeds/ has no effect on) neural processes.

31. The disease that causes progressive senility is _____ disease. This disease has been linked to a deterioration of neurons that produce the neurotransmitter _____.

32. Studies of developmental changes in learning and memory show that during adulthood there is a decline in the ability to _____ (recall/recognize) new information but not in the ability to _____ (recall/recognize) such information. One factor that influences the ease of memory in the elderly is the _____ of material.

33. The type of memory involved in remembering to do something shows _____ (great/little) decline with age.

34. Variation in the abilities of older people to learn and remember is _____ (greater/less) than that of younger people.

35. A research study in which people of various ages are tested at the same time is called a _____–_____ study. A research study in which the same people are retested several times over a period of years is called a _____ study. This first kind of study found evidence of intellectual _____ during adulthood; the second found evidence of intellectual _____.

Write several sentences explaining why studies of intellectual decline and aging yielded conflicting results.

36. The accumulation of stored information that comes with education and experience is called _____ intelligence, which tends to _____ with age.

37. The ability to reason abstractly is referred to as _____ intelligence, which tends to _____ with age.

38. Levinson has proposed a stage theory of adulthood in which adults progress through periods of _____, each interrupted by _____.

39. Contrary to popular opinion, job and marital dissatisfaction do not surge during the forties, thus suggesting that a midlife _____ need not occur.

40. The term used to refer to the culturally preferred timing for leaving home, getting a job, marrying, and so on is the _____. Today the timing of such life events is becoming _____ (more/less) predictable. More important than age are life events.

41. According to Freud, the healthy adult is one who can _____ and _____.

42. The "traditional family" of father, mother, and children represents a _____ (minority/majority) of American households.

43. The rise in the rate of divorces _____ (has/has not) been accompanied by an increase in happiness within marriages.

44. For most couples, the children's leaving home produces a feeling of greater freedom and marital satisfaction. Some, however, become distressed and feel a loss of purpose. This is called the _____ _____ syndrome.

45. Women who work _____ (do/do not) report being significantly happier than women who do not work.

46. According to studies, older people _____ (do/do not) report as much happiness and satisfaction with life as younger people do. Research has also found that the emotions of older adults tend to be _____ (more/less) extreme than those of younger people.

47. The theorist who proposed that dying patients experience an adjustment sequence of five stages is _____.

Write a sentence naming and describing each of these five stages.

48. A growing number of dying people are helped by _____ organizations that provide support and comfort for the terminally ill.

49. According to Erikson, the final task of adulthood is to achieve a sense of _____.

Reflections on Life-Span Development (pp. 123–125)

50. Stage theories that have been considered include the theory of cognitive development proposed by _____, the theory of moral development proposed by _____, and the theories of psychosocial development proposed by _____ and _____.

Summarize the major accomplishment or task of adolescence according to each of the relevant theories.

51. The first 2 years of life _____
(do/do not) provide a good basis for predicting a person's eventual traits.

52. Research on the consistency of personality shows that some traits, such as those related to _____, are more stable than others, such as social attitudes.

FOCUS ON PSYCHOLOGY:
The Changing Meanings of Age and Aging

In most societies, including our own, age is an important dimension of social organization, a determinant of how people relate to one another, and a major index by which individuals evaluate their lives. In an illuminating article, Bernice and Dail Neugarten discuss the historical development of life periods in Western societies and the blurring of these periods in contemporary society. With the emergence of the "young-old" and "hurried child" concepts and with changes in the pattern and timing of marriage, education, and career, age has become a poor predictor of life events. In the authors' words, today "we have conflicting images rather than stereotypes of age: the 70-year-old in a wheelchair, but also the 70-year-old on the tennis court; the 18-year-old who is married and supporting a family, but also the 18-year-old college student who brings his laundry home to his mother each week."

Research on aging has not helped clarify the situation very much, tending to emphasize age-related losses in function while neglecting the substantial variation in functional ability among older adults. Reviewing the literature on the relationship of aging to physical and mental health, researchers John Rowe and Robert Kahn argue that the effects of aging have been exaggerated, and that many age-related declines can be explained in terms of lifestyle, nutrition, exercise, and such psychosocial factors as individual autonomy and the presence or absence of social support. They suggest that researchers should refocus their efforts. By first distinguishing *usual aging*, or that which is statistically average, from *successful aging*, in which older people experience minimal physiological loss, researchers might help elucidate how the proportion of the elderly engaged in successful aging can be increased.

One thing is clear: The proportion of aged people is increasing and will continue to do so. As a result of declining birth rates and improved health habits and medical care, the fastest growing age group today is over 65; between 1950 and 1988, this group increased from about 7 to 12 percent of the population of the United States. During the same time period, the percentage of the population under age 14 decreased from 30 to 20 percent.

In the past, the shape of the population distribution was a pyramid, with the youngest (and largest) age groups at the bottom and the smallest (and oldest) at the top. If present trends continue, by the year 2030 the pyramid will become a rectangle and the population of the United States will be divided roughly into thirds—one-third aged 30 and younger, one-third aged 30 to 59, and one-third aged 60 and older.

Some experts warn that this "squaring" of the demographic pyramid will create many new social problems, including runaway health care costs for the elderly and a lessening concern for the education of children. In order to successfully face the challenges created by an aging population, policymakers, voters, and all members of society must be able to separate the true meanings of age and aging from ageist stereotypes. For this reason, research in developmental psychology is of increasing importance to everyone's well-being.

Sources: Berger, K. S. (1988). *The Developing Person Through the Life Span* (2nd ed.). New York: Worth, p. 528.

Neugarten, B.L., & Neugarten, D.A. (1987, May). The changing meanings of age. *Psychology Today*, 29–33.

Rowe, J.W., & Kahn, R.L. (1987, July 10). Human aging: Usual and successful. *Science*, 237, 143–149.

Progress Test 1

Circle your answers to the following questions and check them with the answers on page 85. If your answer is incorrect, read the explanation for why it is incorrect and then consult the appropriate pages of the text (in parentheses following the correct answer).

1. According to Erikson, the central psychological challenges pertaining to adolescence, young adulthood, and middle age, respectively, are:
a. identity formation; intimacy; generativity.
b. intimacy; identity formation; generativity.
c. generativity; intimacy; identity formation.
d. intimacy; generativity; identity formation.

2. Which of the following stage theorists is associated with the idea that adult development proceeds through cycles of stability and change?
a. Erikson   **c.** Kohlberg
b. Levinson   **d.** Kübler-Ross

3. In Kübler-Ross's theory, which of the following is the correct sequence of stages?
a. denial; anger; bargaining; depression; acceptance
b. anger; denial; bargaining; depression; acceptance
c. depression; anger; denial; bargaining; acceptance
d. bargaining; anger; depression; denial; acceptance

4. In preconventional morality:
   a. one obeys out of a sense of social duty.
   b. one conforms to gain social approval.
   c. one obeys to avoid punishment or to gain concrete rewards.
   d. one follows the dictates of one's conscience.

5. Which of the following is correct?
   a. Early maturation places both boys and girls at distinct social advantage.
   b. Early-maturing girls are more popular and self-assured than girls who mature late.
   c. Early maturation places both boys and girls at a distinct social disadvantage.
   d. Early-maturing boys are more popular and self-assured than boys who mature late.

6. A person's general ability to think abstractly is called _____ intelligence. This ability generally _____ with age.
   a. fluid; increases
   b. fluid; decreases
   c. crystallized; decreases
   d. crystallized; increases

7. An elderly person who can look back on life with satisfaction and reminisce with a sense of completion has attained Erikson's stage of:
   a. generativity.   c. integrity.
   b. intimacy.   d. acceptance.

8. According to Piaget, the ability to think logically about abstract propositions is indicative of the stage of:
   a. preoperational thought.
   b. concrete operations.
   c. formal operations.
   d. fluid intelligence.

9. Adolescence is marked by the onset of:
   a. an identity crisis.
   b. parent-child conflict.
   c. the concrete operational stage.
   d. puberty.

10. Which of the following cognitive abilities has been shown to decline during adulthood?
    a. ability to recall new information
    b. ability to recognize new information
    c. ability to learn meaningful new material
    d. ability to use judgment in dealing with daily life problems

11. Which of the following statements concerning the effects of aging is true?
    a. Aging almost inevitably leads to senility if the individual lives long enough.
    b. Aging increases susceptibility to short-term ailments such as the flu.

c. Significant increases in life satisfaction are associated with aging.
d. The aging process can be significantly affected by the individual's activity patterns.

12. Of the following, which is a possible cause of senility?
    a. stroke   c. alcoholism
    b. brain tumor   d. all of the above

13. Longitudinal tests:
    a. study people of different ages at the same time.
    b. study the same people at different times.
    c. usually involve a larger sample than do cross-sectional tests.
    d. usually involve a smaller sample than do cross-sectional tests.

14. In Levinson's theory, the early forties is a time of great struggle or even of feeling struck down by life. This has been referred to as the:
    a. midlife crisis.   c. menopause.
    b. identity crisis.   d. generativity crisis.

15. The ending of menstruation is called:
    a. menarche.   c. the midlife crisis.
    b. menopause.   d. generativity.

16. According to the textbook, some adolescents feel immune to the consequences of drug use or sexual promiscuity:
    a. because they are unaware of the dangers involved in these behaviors.
    b. because they are pressured by their peers to deny the dangers of these behaviors.
    c. because thinking during the early teen years is immature and egocentric.
    d. for all of the above reasons.

17. Among the landmark events of growing up are a boy's first ejaculation and a girl's first menstrual period, which also is called:
    a. puberty.   c. menarche.
    b. menopause.   d. generativity.

18. The average age at which puberty begins is _____ in boys; in girls, it is _____.
    a. 14; 13   c. 11; 10
    b. 13; 11   d. 10; 9

19. After puberty, the self-concept usually becomes:
    a. more positive in boys.
    b. more positive in girls.
    c. more positive in both boys and girls.
    d. more negative in both boys and girls.

20. "Hospice" refers to:
    a. a group of terminally ill patients involved in educating the general public as to the needs of the dying.

b. a group of physicians who believe that terminally ill patients should be allowed to die whenever they wish to.

c. a research institution studying the causes of Alzheimer's disease.

d. an organization that supports dying people and their families.

Progress Test 2

Progress Test 2 should be completed during a final chapter review. Answer the following questions after you thoroughly understand the correct answers for the Chapter Review and Progress Test 1.

1. In Kübler-Ross's theory, the first stage in dealing with one's dying is:
   a. anger.   **c.** depression.
   b. denial.   **d.** acceptance.

2. The cross-sectional method:
   a. studies people of different ages at the same time.
   b. studies the same group of people at different times.
   c. tends to paint too favorable a picture of the effects of aging on intelligence.
   d. is a more appropriate method for studying intellectual change over the life span than the longitudinal method.

3. The "social clock" refers to:
   a. an individual or society's distribution of work and leisure time.
   b. adulthood responsibilities.
   c. typical ages for starting a career, marrying, etc.
   d. age-related changes in one's circle of friends.

4. Who formulated a stage theory of moral development based on reasoning in ethical dilemmas?
   a. Erikson   **c.** Levinson
   b. Piaget   **d.** Kohlberg

5. In Erikson's theory, the achievement of integrity is the primary task of:
   a. adolescence.   **c.** middle adulthood.
   b. young adulthood.   **d.** late adulthood.

6. Which of the following is a true statement regarding the stage of formal operations?
   a. It must be attained before moral reasoning of any sort is possible.
   b. It is attained by everyone sooner or later.
   c. It is followed by the stage of concrete operations.
   d. It involves an ability to think abstractly.

7. To which of Kohlberg's levels would moral reasoning based on the existence of fundamental human rights pertain?

   a. preconventional morality
   b. conventional morality
   c. postconventional morality
   d. generative morality

8. In Erikson's theory, individuals generally focus on developing _____ during adolescence and then _____ during young adulthood.
   a. identity; intimacy   **c.** basic trust; identity
   b. intimacy; identity   **d.** identity; basic trust

9. Which of the following changes does not involve a secondary sex characteristic?
   a. breast development
   b. growth of pubic hair
   c. voice change in males
   d. onset of menstruation

10. After menopause, most women:
    a. experience anxiety and a sense of worthlessness.
    b. lose interest in sex.
    c. secrete unusually high levels of estrogen.
    d. feel a new sense of freedom.

11. Notable achievements in fields such as _____ are often made by younger adults in their late twenties or early thirties, when _____ intelligence is at its peak.
    a. mathematics; fluid   **c.** science; crystallized
    b. philosophy; fluid   **d.** literature; crystallized

12. The mid-twenties are usually the peak years for all but which of the following?
    a. physical strength
    b. reaction time
    c. recall memory
    d. professional achievements

13. Moral development is associated most closely with _____ development.
    a. perceptual   **c.** emotional
    b. physical   **d.** cognitive

14. After their grown children have left home, most couples experience:
    a. the distress of the "empty nest syndrome."
    b. increased strain in their marital relationship.
    c. both a. and b.
    d. greater happiness and enjoyment in their relationship.

15. Underlying Alzheimer's disease is a deterioration in neurons that produce:
    a. epinephrine.   **c.** serotonin.
    b. norepinephrine.   **d.** acetylcholine.

16. Sex education programs:
    a. are very effective in reducing teenage pregnancies.

b. have had a reverse effect and actually increased teenage pregnancies.

c. do not seem to be the critical factor in preventing teenage pregnancies.

d. are more effective for females than males.

17. A person's accumulation of stored information, called _____ intelligence, generally _____ with age.

    a. fluid; decreases

    b. fluid; increases

    c. crystallized; decreases

    d. crystallized; increases

18. In terms of incidence, susceptibility to short-term illnesses _____ with age and susceptibility to long-term ailments _____ with age.

    a. decreases; increases   **c.** increases; increases

    b. increases; decreases   **d.** decreases; decreases

19. One criticism of stage theories is that they fail to consider that development may be significantly affected by:

    a. variations in the social clock.

    b. each individual's experiences.

    c. each individual's historical and cultural setting.

    d. all of the above.

20. Research on the American family indicates that:

    a. fewer than 25 percent of unmarried adults, but nearly 40 percent of married adults, report being "very happy" with life.

    b. the divorce rate is now one-half the marriage rate.

    c. traditional families consisting of mother, father, and children under 18 comprise less than one-third of American households.

    d. all of the above are true.

Challenge Test

Answer these questions the day before an exam as a final check on your understanding of the chapter's terms and concepts.

Multiple-Choice Questions

1. Thirteen-year-old Irene has no trouble defeating her 11-year-old brother at a detective game that requires following clues in order to deduce the perpetrator of a crime. How might Piaget explain Irene's superiority at the game?

    a. Being older, Irene has had more years of schooling.

    b. Girls develop intellectually at a faster rate than boys.

    c. Being an adolescent, Irene is beginning to develop abstract reasoning skills.

    d. Girls typically have more experience than boys at playing games.

2. Which of the following *was not* mentioned in the textbook as a criticism of Kohlberg's theory of moral development?

    a. The development of moral reasoning is culture-specific.

    b. Postconventional morality appears mostly in educated, middle-class persons.

    c. The theory is biased against the moral reasoning of people in communal societies such as China.

    d. The theory is biased in favor of moral reasoning in men.

3. Fourteen-year-old Cassandra feels freer and more open with her friends than with her family. Knowing this is the case, Cassandra's parents should:

    a. be concerned, because deteriorating parent-adolescent relationships, such as this one, are often followed by a range of problem behaviors.

    b. encourage Cassandra to find new friends.

    c. seek family counseling.

    d. not worry, since adolescence is typically a time of growing peer influence and diminishing parental influence.

4. In one experiment, young and old rats were taught to swim to a platform just under the surface of a pool of cloudy water. When the rats' brain tissue was later examined, researchers found that some of the rats had fewer receptors in the part of the brain responsible for forming memories. Which of the following was the best predictor of which rats had neural degeneration?

    a. their ages

    b. the amount of practice on the task

    c. how quickly the rats learned to find the platform

    d. none of the above

5. Sixty-five-year-old Calvin can't reason as well as he could when he was younger. Evidently, Calvin's _____ intelligence has declined.

    a. analytic   **c.** fluid

    b. crystallized   **d.** both b. and c.

6. Cross-sectional studies of intelligence are potentially misleading because:

    a. they are typically based on a very small and unrepresentative sample of people.

    b. retesting the same people over a period of years allows test performance to be influenced by practice.

    c. they compare people who are not only different

in age, but of different eras, education levels, and affluence.

    d. of all the above reasons.

7. Based on the text's discussion of maturation and popularity, who among the following is probably the most popular sixth grader?

    a. Jessica, the most physically mature girl in the class

    b. Roger, the most intellectually mature boy in the class

    c. Rob, the tallest, most physically mature boy in the class

    d. Cindy, who is average in physical development and is on the school debating team

8. Which statement illustrates cognitive development during the course of adult life?

    a. Adults in their 40s have better recognition memory than adults in their 70s.

    b. Adults in their 40s have better recall memory than adults in their 70s.

    c. Recognition memory decreases sharply at midlife.

    d. Recall memory remains strong until very late in life.

9. Given the text discussion of life satisfaction patterns, which of the following people is likely to report the greatest life satisfaction?

    a. Billy, a 7-year-old second-grader

    b. Kathy, a 17-year-old high-school senior

    c. Mildred, a 70-year-old retired teacher

    d. too little information to tell

10. Which of the following statements is consistent with the current thinking of developmental psychologists?

    a. Development occurs in a series of sharply defined stages.

    b. The first two years are the most crucial in determining the individual's personality.

    c. The consistency of personality in most people tends to increase over the life span.

    d. Social and emotional style are among the characteristics that show the least stability over the life span.

11. Sam, a junior in high school, regularly attends church because his family and friends think he should. Which stage of moral reasoning is Sam in?

    a. preconventional

    b. conventional

    c. postconventional

    d. too little information to tell

12. Deborah is a mathematician and Willie is a philosopher. Considering the professions:

    a. Deborah will make her most significant career accomplishments at an earlier age than Willie will.

    b. Deborah will make her most significant career accomplishments at a later age than Willie will.

    c. Deborah will make her most significant career accomplishments at about the same time as Willie.

    d. there is still not enough information for predicting such accomplishments.

13. Research on social relationships between parents and their adolescent children shows that:

    a. parental influence on children increases during adolescence.

    b. parent-adolescent conflict is most common between mothers and daughters.

    c. parent-adolescent conflict is most common between fathers and sons.

    d. approximately 25 percent of U.S. teens report not getting along with their parents at all.

14. Most contemporary developmental psychologists believe that:

    a. personality is essentially formed by the end of infancy.

    b. personality continues to be formed until adolescence.

    c. the shaping of personality continues during adolescence and well beyond.

    d. adolescent development has very little impact on adult personality.

15. Research on personality development over the life span reveals that, all else being equal, an aggressive 8-year-old will probably become a(n) _____ 30-year-old.

    a. shy

    b. aggressive

    c. happy and well-adjusted

    d. aggressive or shy (There is no basis for such a prediction.)

16. After a series of unfulfilling relationships, 30-year-old Carlos tells a friend that he doesn't want to marry because he is afraid of losing his freedom and independence. Erikson would say that Carlos is having difficulty with the psychosocial task of:

    a. trust versus mistrust

    b. autonomy versus doubt

    c. intimacy versus isolation

    d. identity versus role confusion

17. Which of the following is false?

    a. Beginning in young adulthood there is a small, gradual loss of brain cells.

    b. Adults who remain mentally active retain more of their cognitive capacity in later years.

    c. The symptoms of Alzheimer's disease are merely an accelerated version of normal aging.

d. As people age, the speed of their neural processes slows.

18. The textbook defines "adolescence" as:
    a. the transition years between biological maturity and social independence.
    b. the age when reproductive maturity is attained.
    c. the years during which the secondary sex characteristics develop.
    d. the age at which the growth spurt begins.

19. Research on the relationship between self-reported happiness and employment in American women has revealed that:
    a. women who work tend to be happier.
    b. women who do not work tend to be happier.
    c. women today are happier than in the past, whether they are working or not.
    d. the quality of a woman's experience in her roles as paid worker, wife, and/or mother is more predictive of her happiness than the presence or absence of a given role.

20. Bill, a 75-year-old retired executive, feels that his life has been wasted. According to Erikson, Bill has not achieved a sense of:
    a. integrity.   **c.** competence.
    b. identity.   **d.** generativity.

Essay Question

Sheryl is 12 years old and in the sixth grade. Describe the developmental changes she is likely to be experiencing according to Piaget, Kohlberg, and Erikson. (Use the space below to list the points you want to make and organize them. Then write the essay on a separate sheet of paper.)

Key Terms

Using your own words, write a brief definition or explanation of each of the following terms:

1. adolescence

2. puberty

3. primary sex characteristics

4. secondary sex characteristics

5. menarche

6. identity

7. intimacy

8. menopause

9. Alzheimer's disease

10. cross-sectional study

11. longitudinal study

12. crystallized intelligence

13. fluid intelligence

14. social clock

15. hospice

ANSWERS

GUIDED STUDY

The following guidelines provide the main points that your answers should have touched upon.

1. Adolescence begins with puberty, a two-year period of rapid development that begins in girls at about age 11 and in boys at about age 13. Boys grow as much as 5 inches a year, compared with about 3 inches for girls. During the growth spurt sexual maturation also occurs, as the primary sex characteristics (reproductive organs) and secondary sex characteristics (nonreproductive traits) develop dramatically.

    The landmarks of puberty are the first ejaculation in boys at about age 14 and the first menstrual period, called menarche, in girls at about age 13. As in earlier life stages, the sequence of physical changes is more predictable than their timing.

2. During the early teen years reasoning continues to be immature and egocentric. Eventually, however, most adolescents attain Piaget's stage of formal operations and become capable of abstract, logical thinking.

    Developmental psychologists today believe that the rudiments of formal operational thinking begin earlier than Piaget proposed and that he overestimated the number of people who attain this stage.

3. Kohlberg believed that moral reasoning builds on cognitive development and proceeds through as many as six stages. Before age 9, most children obey rules either to avoid punishment or to gain rewards (preconventional morality). By early adolescence, they develop the conventional morality of abiding by laws simply because "those are the rules." Postconventional morality, achieved by those who develop the abstract reasoning of formal operations, affirms people's agreed-upon rights or follows a personal code of ethics.

    Critics note that morality also lies in actions, which are influenced by factors besides moral reasoning. For example, because of social influences, people's willingness to cheat, to discriminate racially, and to use drugs are not solely determined by their attitudes toward these behaviors. Critics also contend that the postconventional level appears mostly in the educated middle-class of countries that value individualism. Carol Gilligan further contends that Kohlberg's stages reflect a male bias, and that for women, moral maturity is less a matter of abstract justice than it is an ethic of caring relationships.

4. According to Erikson, the primary task of adolescence is the formation of identity. Many adolescents try out different "selves" by playing different roles in various situations until their sense of identity becomes clearer.

    Once adolescents have formed a sense of who they are, said Erikson, they focus on developing close relationships. Carol Gilligan believes that females are less concerned than males with developing a sense of identity as separate individuals *before* they strive to form close relationships.

    Adolescence is a time of growing peer influence and diminishing parental influence. Despite popular belief, only a very small percentage of teenagers report not getting on with their parents at all.

5. Most sexually active teenagers use contraception inconsistently, or not at all. Most teenagers are not knowledgeable about the safe and risky times of the menstrual cycle. Adolescents' guilt about sex makes it difficult for them to discuss contraception with their parents and to plan birth control with their partners. Sexually active teenagers often use alcohol, which depresses brain centers that control judgment and tends to break down normal sexual restraints. Television and the other media may contribute to increased adolescent pregnancy by redefining sexual norms, which today are "Go for it now. Don't worry about anything."

6. Muscular strength, reaction time, visual acuity, distance perception, hearing, and cardiac output all peak by the mid-twenties and begin to decline

thereafter. Lifestyle factors such as nutrition, smoking, drinking, and activity level are important factors in the rate of physical decline.

Decline in the functioning of the body's disease-fighting immune system makes the elderly more susceptible to life-threatening ailments such as cancer and pneumonia. Older people suffer short-term ailments, such as colds and the flu, less often, however.

For women, menopause is the foremost biological change related to aging. Despite popular belief, menopause usually does not create psychological problems for women. Men experience a gradual decline in sperm count and testosterone level as they get older.

Aging also slows neural processes and results in a small, gradual loss of brain cells. A small percentage of older adults suffer Alzheimer's disease, in which acetylcholine-producing neurons degenerate.

7. Individual variation in learning ability and memory throughout adulthood makes it difficult to generalize about age-related changes in cognition. Typically, however, the ability to recall (but not to recognize) new information, particularly material that is not meaningful to the individual, declines.

Longitudinal studies of intelligence have laid to rest the myth that intelligence sharply declines with age. Whether intelligent performance on a task increases or decreases with age depends largely on the task. Tests of accumulated knowledge reveal that crystallized intelligence increases up to old age. Tests measuring one's ability to reason abstractly reveal that fluid intelligence decreases with age. These differences help explain why people in different professions produce their most notable work at different ages.

8. Levinson suggested that adults progress through stages of stability alternating with times of upheaval and change. For example, the early 40s were supposedly a time of emotional instability, when a "midlife transition," or crisis, was likely. Research has not found, however, that emotional distress of this kind peaks at any particular age.

Researchers are skeptical of stage theories of adult social development for several reasons. For one, the settings of the social clock prescribing "proper" ages for various life events vary from culture to culture and from era to era. Even more important than one's age in defining new life stages are life events such as marriage, parenthood, job changes, divorce, and retirement. Increasingly, events such as these are occurring at unpredictable ages.

9. According to Erikson, the tasks of forming close relationships (intimacy) and feeling productive (generativity) dominate adulthood. Freud expressed the same viewpoint in saying that the healthy adult is one who can love and work.

Because of rising divorce rates, "traditional" nuclear families comprise a minority of U.S. households. Although those in today's surviving marriages are less likely to describe their marriages as "very happy," married adults *are* more likely than unmarried adults to report being "very happy" with life.

Despite the popular belief that the departure of adult children usually causes parents to feel great distress and a loss of purpose, research reveals that those whose nest has emptied generally report greater happiness and enjoyment of their marriage.

Studies of the relationship between happiness and having a career have compared employed and unemployed women. The results of these studies reveal that what matters is not which role(s) a woman occupies—as worker, wife, and/or mother—but the quality of her experience in each.

10. The normal range of reactions to loss of a loved one is much wider than most people suppose. Grief is especially severe when death comes before its expected time.

From her interviews with dying patients, Kübler-Ross proposed that the terminally ill pass through five stages: denial of death; anger; bargaining for more time; depression; and, finally, peaceful acceptance. Critics have questioned the generality of such stages, however, stressing that each person's experience is unique.

11. Although research casts doubt on the idea that life proceeds through neatly defined, age-linked stages of cognitive, moral, and social development, the concept of stage remains useful. Stage theories help focus awareness on how people of one age think and act differently when they arrive at a later age.

Recent research has revealed that there is a consistency to personality due to an underlying stability in basic social and emotional styles. Although the first two years of life provide a poor basis for predicting eventual traits, after age 30 dispositions become quite stable and attitudes much more predictable.

CHAPTER REVIEW

1. lifelong
2. earlier; later
3. G. Stanley Hall
4. puberty; 11; 13; primary sex; secondary sex
5. menarche; 13; 14
6. sequence; timing

7. early; early

8. egocentric

9. formal operations; abstract; earlier; overestimated

10. Kohlberg; preconventional; conventional; post-conventional

11. punishment; rewards

12. adolescence; approval; order

13. postconventional; educated; middle; individualism

Critics of Kohlberg's theory point out that morality also lies in a person's actions, which are influenced by factors besides moral reasoning. They also argue that the perception of postconventional moral reasoning as the highest level of moral development reflects a Western male cultural bias. Carol Gilligan has argued that for women, morality is less a matter of abstract, impersonal justice, and more an ethic of caring relationships.

14. have not

15. ethic of care

16. is not

17. stronger

Erikson's stages of psychosocial development

Approximate Age	Psychosocial Stage
Infancy	**Trust vs. mistrust**
Toddler	Autonomy vs. shame and doubt
Preschooler	**Initiative vs. guilt**
Elementary School	Competence vs. inferiority
Adolescence	**Identity vs. role confusion**
Young Adulthood	Intimacy vs. isolation
Middle Adulthood	**Generativity vs. stagnation**
Late Adulthood	Integrity vs. despair

18. identity; intimacy

19. more

20. less

21. peers; parents; small

22. higher

23. 20s; 40s; middle

24. is not

25. menopause; 50; estrogen; attitude

26. sperm; testosterone

27. shrinks; less; reduced

28. more; less

29. 75; 83

30. slows

31. Alzheimer's; acetylcholine

32. recall; recognize; meaningfulness

33. little

34. greater

35. cross-sectional; longitudinal; decline; stability

Because cross-sectional studies compare people not only of different ages but also of different eras, education levels, and affluence, it is not surprising that such studies reveal cognitive decline with age. In contrast, longitudinal studies test one group over a span of years. Research is also complicated by the fact that certain tests measure only one type of intelligence. Tests that measure fluid intelligence reveal decline with age; tests that measure crystallized intelligence reveal just the opposite.

36. crystallized; increase

37. fluid; decrease

38. stability; change or upheaval

39. crisis

40. social clock; less

41. love; work

42. minority

43. has not

44. empty nest

45. do not

46. do; less

47. Kübler-Ross

In her interviews with dying patients, Kübler-Ross identified five stages the dying move through: *denial* of the terminal condition, *anger* at the seeming unfairness of their situation, *bargaining* for more time, *depression* stemming from the impending loss, and finally, *acceptance* of their fate.

48. hospice

49. integrity

50. Piaget; Kohlberg; Erikson; Levinson

Piaget theorized that adolescents enter the stage of formal operations, which enables them to reason abstractly. Kohlberg contends that in adolescence moral reasoning evolves at least to the conventional level, and perhaps to the postconventional level. According to Erikson, the chief psychosocial task of adolescence is to form a sense of self, or identity.

51. do not

52. temperament

PROGRESS TEST 1

1. **a.** is the answer. (pp. 102, 103, 118)

2. **b.** is the answer. (p. 116)

a. Erikson is best known for his theory of psychosocial development over the life span.

c. Kohlberg is known for his work on the development of moral reasoning.

d. Kübler-Ross is known for her work on the emotional stages through which the terminally ill pass.

3. **a.** is the answer. (p. 122)

4. **c.** is the answer. At the preconventional level, moral reasoning centers on one's self-interest, whether this means obtaining rewards or avoiding punishment. (p. 100)

a. & b. Moral reasoning based on a sense of social duty or a desire to gain social approval is associated with the conventional level of moral development.

d. Reasoning based on one's own ethical principles is characteristic of the postconventional level of moral development.

5. **d.** is the answer. Boys who show early physical maturation are generally stronger and more athletic than boys who mature late; these qualities may lead to greater popularity and self-assurance. (p. 97)

a. & c. Early maturation tends to be socially advantageous for boys but not for girls.

b. Early-maturing girls often suffer embarrassment and are objects of teasing.

6. **b.** is the answer. (p. 115)

a. Fluid intelligence tends to decrease with age.

c. & d. Crystallized intelligence refers to the accumulation of facts and general knowledge that takes place during a person's life. Crystallized intelligence generally *increases* with age.

7. **c.** is the answer. (p. 123)

a. Generativity is associated with middle adulthood.

b. Intimacy is associated with young adulthood.

d. The term acceptance is not associated with Erikson's theory; rather, it is the final stage in Kübler-Ross's theory of emotions experienced by the terminally ill.

8. **c.** is the answer. Once formal operational thought has been attained, thinking is no longer limited to concrete propositions. (p. 98)

a. & b. Preoperational thought and concrete operational thought emerge before, and do not include, the ability to think logically about abstract propositions.

d. Fluid intelligence refers to abstract reasoning abilities; however, it is unrelated to Piaget's theory and stages.

9. **d.** is the answer. The physical changes of puberty mark the onset of adolescence. (p. 96)

a. & b. An identity crisis or parent-child conflict may or may not occur during adolescence; neither of these formally marks its onset.

c. Formal operational thought, rather than concrete reasoning, typically develops in adolescence.

10. **a.** is the answer. (pp. 112–113, 115)

b., c., & d. These cognitive abilities remain essentially unchanged as the person ages.

11. **d.** is the answer. "Use it or lose it" seems to be the rule: Often, changes in activity patterns contribute significantly to problems regarded as being part of usual aging. (p. 111)

a. Most elderly people do not become senile; even among the very old, senility is relatively uncommon.

b. Although the elderly are more subject to long-term ailments than younger adults, they actually suffer fewer short-term ailments.

c. There is no tendency for people of any particular age to report greater happiness or satisfaction with life.

12. **d.** is the answer. (p. 112)

13. **b.** is the answer. (p. 114)

a. This answer describes cross-sectional research.

c. & d. Sample size does not distinguish cross-sectional from longitudinal research.

14. **a.** is the answer. (p. 116)

b. Identity crises have generally been associated with adolescence, not middle adulthood.

c. Menopause usually comes about a decade later and refers specifically to cessation of the menstrual cycle in women.

d. Generativity, which is associated with Erikson's theory, refers to the impulse toward productivity.

15. **b.** is the answer. (p. 109)

a. Menarche refers to the onset of menstruation.

c. When it does occur, the midlife crisis is a psychological, rather than biological, phenomenon.

d. Generativity is Erikson's term for productivity during middle adulthood.

16. **c.** is the answer. Because their thinking is egocentric, young teens may feel invulnerable to the consequences of risky behavior. (p. 98)

a. Although adolescents typically are aware of the dangers of drug use and sexual promiscuity, their immature thinking may lead them to believe that dangerous consequences could never happen to them.

b. Peer pressure is an important factor in determining whether an adolescent begins using a drug. The textbook does not suggest, however, that peer pressure causes teens to deny the dangers of risky behaviors.

17. **c.** is the answer. (p. 96)

    a. Puberty refers to the early adolescent period during which accelerated growth and sexual maturation occur, not to the first menstrual period.

    b. Menopause is the cessation of menstruation, which typically occurs in the early fifties.

    d. In Erikson's theory, generativity, or the sense of contributing and being productive, is the task of middle adulthood.

18. **b.** is the answer. (p. 96)

19. **c.** is the answer. Because the late teen years provide many new opportunities for trying out possible roles, adolescents' identities typically incorporate an increasingly positive self-concept. (p. 103)

20. **d.** is the answer. Hospice staff and volunteers work in special facilities and in people's homes to support the terminally ill. (p. 123)

PROGRESS TEST 2

1. **b.** is the answer. (p. 122)

2. **a.** is the answer. (p. 114)

    b. This answer describes the longitudinal research method.

    c. & d. Cross-sectional studies have tended to exaggerate the effects of aging on intellectual functioning; for this reason they may not be the most appropriate method for studying life-span development.

3. **c.** is the answer. Different societies and eras have somewhat different ideas about the age at which major life events should ideally occur. (p. 117)

4. **d.** is the answer. (pp. 99–100)

    a. Erikson is known for his theory of psychosocial development.

    b. Piaget is known for his theory of cognitive development.

    c. Levinson is known for his stage theory of adult social development.

5. **d.** is the answer. (pp. 102, 123)

    a. The task of adolescence is achieving identity.

    b. The task of young adulthood is achieving intimacy.

    c. The task of middle adulthood is achieving generativity.

6. **d.** is the answer. (p. 98)

    a. Formal operational thought is required only for postconventional stages of morality; the other stages of moral reasoning may develop before formal operational thought.

    b. Not everyone reaches the stage of formal operations.

    c. Concrete operational thought precedes formal operational thought.

7. **c.** is the answer. (p. 100)

    a. Preconventional morality is based on avoiding punishment and obtaining rewards.

    b. Conventional morality is based on gaining the approval of others and/or on following the law and social convention.

    d. There is no such thing as generative morality.

8. **a.** is the answer. (pp. 102–103)

    b. According to Erikson, identity develops before intimacy.

    c & d. The formation of basic trust is the task of infancy.

9. **d.** is the answer. Menstruation directly involves the reproductive organs, which are primary sex characteristics. That is, the onset of menstruation reflects the development of body structures that enable reproduction. (p. 96)

    a., b., & c. These answers are incorrect because each is a secondary sex characteristic.

10. **d.** is the answer. (p. 109)

    a. Most women do not experience anxiety and distress following menopause; moreover, the woman's experience will depend largely on her attitude.

    b. Sexual interest does not decline in postmenopausal women.

    c. Menopause is caused by a *reduction* in estrogen.

11. **a.** is the answer. A mathematician's skills are likely to reflect abstract reasoning, or fluid intelligence, which declines with age. (pp. 115–116)

    b. & d. Philosophy and literature are fields in which individuals often do their most notable work later in life, after more experiential knowledge (crystallized intelligence) has accumulated.

    c. Scientific achievements generally reflect fluid, rather than crystallized, intelligence.

12. **d.** is the answer. In most fields, especially those in which crystallized intelligence is important, the greatest professional achievements occur later in life. (pp. 108, 112, 116)

    a., b., & c. Physical strength, reaction time, and recall memory all decline with age.

13. **d.** is the answer. Following Piaget's lead, Kohlberg proposed that moral reasoning develops in stages, paced by cognitive development. (p. 99)

a., b., & c. Kohlberg's theory does not claim that perceptual, physical, or emotional development play a role in the development of moral reasoning.

14. **d.** is the answer. (p. 119)

    a., b., & c. Most couples do not feel a loss of purpose or marital strain following the departure of grown children.

15. **d.** is the answer. Significantly, drugs that block the activity of the neurotransmitter acetylcholine produce Alzheimer-like symptoms. (p. 112)

    a. & b. Epinephrine and norepinephrine are hormones produced by glands of the endocrine system.

    c. Serotonin is a neurotransmitter, and hence produced by neurons, but it has not been implicated in Alzheimer's disease.

16. **c.** is the answer. (p. 106)

17. **d.** is the answer. (p. 115)

    a. & b. Fluid intelligence, which decreases with age, refers to the ability to reason abstractly.

    c. Crystallized intelligence increases with age.

18. **a.** is the answer. (p. 111)

19. **d.** is the answer. (p. 117)

20. **d.** is the answer. (p. 118)

    a., b., & c. Each of these is a correct statistic concerning the American family.

CHALLENGE TEST

Multiple-Choice Questions

1. **c.** is the answer. (p. 98)

    a., b., & d. Piaget did not link cognitive ability to amount of schooling, gender, or differences in how boys and girls are socialized.

2. **a.** is the answer. Children in various cultures do seem to progress through Kohlberg's preconventional and conventional levels, which indicates that some aspects of the development of moral reasoning are universal. (pp. 100–101)

    b., c., & d. Each of these *was* mentioned as a criticism of Kohlberg's theory.

3. **d.** is the answer. (p. 104)

    a. This description of Cassandra's feelings does not suggest that her relationship with her parents is deteriorating. Like most adolescents, Cassandra's social development is coming under increasing peer influence and diminishing parental influence.

    b. & c. Because Cassandra's feelings are quite normal, there is no reason for her to change her circle of friends or for her parents to seek family counseling.

4. **c.** is the answer. Compared with quick-to-learn rats (both young and old), slow-to-learn rats were found to have neural degeneration. (p. 113)

    a. & d. Neither age nor experience with the task predicted whether the rat's brain showed neural degeneration.

5. **c.** is the answer. Reasoning is based on fluid intelligence. (p. 115)

    a. There is no such thing as "analytic" intelligence.

    b. Crystallized intelligence increases up to old age.

6. **c.** is the answer. Because several variables (education, affluence, etc.) generally distinguish the various groups in a cross-sectional study, it is impossible to rule out that one or more of these, rather than aging, is the cause of the measured intellectual decrease. (pp. 114–115)

    a. Small sample size and unrepresentativeness generally are not limitations of cross-sectional research.

    b. This is a description of longitudinal research.

7. **c.** is the answer. Early-maturing boys tend to be more popular. (p. 97)

    a. Early-maturing girls may temporarily suffer embarrassment and be the objects of teasing.

    b. & d. The social benefits of early or late maturation are based on physical development, not on cognitive skills.

8. **b.** is the answer. (pp. 112–113)

    a. & c. In tests of recognition memory, the performance of older persons shows little decline.

    d. The ability to recall material, especially meaningless material such as nonsense syllables, declines with age.

9. **d.** is the answer. Research has not uncovered a tendency for people of any particular age group to report greater feelings of satisfaction or well-being. (p. 121)

10. **c.** is the answer. Although some researchers emphasize consistency and others emphasize potential for change, they all agree that consistency increases over the life span. (pp. 123–125)

    a. One criticism of stage theories is that development does not occur in sharply defined stages.

    b. Research has shown that individuals' adult personalities cannot be predicted from their first two years.

    d. Social and emotional style are two of the most stable traits.

11. **b.** is the answer. Conventional morality is based in part on a desire to gain others' approval. (p. 100)

    a. Preconventional reasoning is based on external

incentives such as gaining a reward or avoiding punishment.

c. Postconventional morality reflects an affirmation of agreed-upon rights or universal ethical principles.

d. Fear of others' disapproval is one of the bases of conventional moral reasoning.

12. **a.** is the answer. Mathematical and philosophical reasoning involve fluid and crystallized intelligence, respectively. Because fluid intelligence generally declines with age while crystallized intelligence increases, it is likely that significant mathematical accomplishments will occur at an earlier age than philosophical accomplishments. (pp. 115–116)

13. **b.** is the answer. (p. 104)

a. In fact, just the opposite is true: Parental influence on children *decreases* during adolescence.

d. Only about 4 percent of U.S. teens report not getting along with their parents at all.

14. **c.** is the answer. (pp. 124–125)

15. **b.** is the answer. Because basic social and emotional styles show an underlying stability, the most aggressive children typically become the most aggressive adults. (p. 124)

16. **c.** is the answer. Carlos's age and struggle to form a close relationship place him squarely in this stage. (pp. 102–103)

a. Trust versus mistrust is the psychosocial task of infancy.

b. Autonomy versus doubt is the psychosocial task of toddlerhood.

d. Identity versus role confusion is the psychosocial task of adolescence.

17. **c.** is the answer. The neural deterioration that accompanies Alzheimer's disease is an abnormality. (pp. 111–112)

18. **a.** is the answer. (pp. 95–96)

b., c., & d. Each of these is an aspect of the physical changes that accompany puberty. Adolescence incorporates changes in both physical and social development.

19. **d.** is the answer. (p. 120)

20. **a.** is the answer. Reflecting on life, the elderly person may experience integrity or, alternatively, a sense of failure (despair). (pp. 102, 123)

b. Identity is a sense of self; its development is associated with adolescence.

c. Competence is a sense of effectiveness; its development is associated with the elementary school years.

d. Generativity is a sense of making a contribution to the world through one's activities; its development is associated with middle adulthood.

Essay Question

Sheryl's age would place her at the threshold of Piaget's stage of formal operations. Although her thinking is probably still somewhat egocentric, Sheryl is becoming capable of abstract, logical thought. This will increasingly allow her to reason hypothetically and deductively. Because her logical thinking also enables her to detect inconsistencies in others' reasoning and between their ideals and actions, Sheryl and her parents may be having some heated debates about now.

According to Kohlberg, Sheryl is probably at the threshold of postconventional morality. When she was younger, Sheryl probably abided by rules in order to gain social approval, or simply because "rules are rules" (conventional morality). Now that she is older, Sheryl's moral reasoning will increasingly be based on her own personal code of ethics and an affirmation of people's agreed-upon rights.

According to Erikson, psychosocial development occurs in eight stages, each of which focuses on a particular task. As an adolescent, Sheryl's psychosocial task is to develop a sense of self by testing roles, then integrating them to form a single identity. Erikson called this stage "identity versus role confusion."

KEY TERMS

1. **Adolescence** refers to the life stage from puberty to independent adulthood, denoted physically by a growth spurt and maturation of primary and secondary sex characteristics, cognitively by the onset of formal operational thought, and socially by the formation of identity. (p. 95)

2. **Puberty** is the early adolescent period marked by accelerated growth and sexual maturation. (p. 96)

3. The **primary sex characteristics** are the body structures (ovaries and testes) that enable reproduction. (p. 96)

4. The **secondary sex characteristics** are the nonreproductive sexual characteristics, for example, female breasts, male voice change, and body hair. (p. 96)

5. **Menarche** is the first menstrual period. (p. 96)

6. In Erikson's theory, establishing an **identity**, or one's sense of self, is the primary task of adolescence. (p. 102)

7. In Erikson's theory, **intimacy**, or the ability to establish close relationships, is the primary task of late adolescence and early adulthood. (p. 103)

8. **Menopause** is the cessation of menstruation and typically occurs in the early fifties. It also refers to the biological and psychological changes experienced during a woman's years of declining ability to reproduce. (p. 109)

9. **Alzheimer's disease** is an irreversible brain disorder caused by deterioration in neurons that produce acetylcholine. It is characterized by a progressive loss of memory and general cognitive function. (p. 112)

10. In a **cross-sectional study**, people of different ages are tested at the same time. (p. 114)

11. In a **longitudinal study** the same people are tested and retested over a period of years. (p. 114)

    Memory aid: A *long*itudinal study takes a *long* time to complete because the same people are followed for many years.

12. **Crystallized intelligence** refers to those aspects of intellectual ability, such as vocabulary and general knowledge, that reflect accumulated learning. Crystallized intelligence tends to increase with age. (p. 115)

13. **Fluid intelligence** refers to a person's ability to reason abstractly. Fluid intelligence tends to decline with age. (p. 115)

14. The **social clock** refers to the culturally preferred timing of life events, such as leaving home, marrying, having children, and retiring. (p. 117)

15. A **hospice** is an organization that provides support for the terminally ill and for their families. (p. 123)

5 / Sensation

Chapter Overview

Sensation refers to the process by which our sense receptors and nervous system represent our external environment. This chapter describes the senses of vision, hearing, taste, touch, smell, kinesthesis, and equilibrium. It also presents research findings from studies of sensory restriction and subliminal stimulation.

In this chapter there are many terms to learn and several theories you must understand. Many of the terms are related to the structure of the eye, ear, and other sensory receptors. Doing the chapter review several times, labeling the diagrams, and rehearsing the material frequently will help you to memorize these structures and their functions. The theories discussed include the signal detection, Young-Helmholtz three-color, and opponent-process theories of color vision and the frequency and place theories of pitch. As you study these theories, concentrate on understanding the strengths and weaknesses (if any) of each.

NOTE: Answer guidelines for all Chapter 5 questions begin on page 104.

Guided Study

The text chapter should be studied one section at a time. Before you read, preview each section by skimming it, noting headings and boldface items. Then read the appropriate section objectives from the following outline. Keep these objectives in mind and, as you read the chapter section, search for the information that will enable you to meet each objective. Once you have finished a section, write out answers for its objectives.

1. Contrast the processes of sensation and perception.

Sensing the World: Some Basic Principles (pp. 132–137)

2. Distinguish between absolute and difference thresholds and discuss research findings on signal detection.

3. Discuss whether subliminal stimuli are sensed, and whether they are persuasive.

4. Describe the phenomenon of sensory adaptation and show how it focuses our attention on changing stimulation.

Vision (pp. 137–145)

5. Explain the visual process, including the stimulus input, the structure of the eye, and the transduction of light energy.

6. Discuss how visual information is processed in parallel and at increasingly abstract levels.

7. Discuss how both the Young-Helmholtz and the opponent-process theories contribute to our understanding of color vision.

8. Explain color constancy and discuss its significance to our understanding of vision.

Hearing (pp. 145–150)

9. Explain the auditory process, including the stimulus input and the structure and function of the ear.

10. Discuss how both the place and frequency theories contribute to our understanding of pitch perception.

11. Explain how sounds are located and discuss the nature and causes of hearing loss.

The Other Senses (pp. 151–157)

12. Describe the senses of touch and pain and explain the gate-control theory of pain.

13. Describe the senses of taste, smell, kinesthesis, and equilibrium. Comment on the nature of sensory interaction.

Sensory Restriction (pp. 157–158)

14. Discuss the effects of sensory restriction.

Chapter Review

When you have finished reading the chapter, work through the material that follows to review it. Complete the sentences and answer the questions. As you proceed, evaluate your performance for each section by consulting the answers on page 105. Do not continue with the next section until you understand each answer. If you need to, go back and review or reread the appropriate section in the textbook before continuing.

1. Three computer concepts that are useful in highlighting our response to environmental stimuli are __input__, __processing__, and __output__.

2. The process by which our sense receptors and nervous system represent our external environment is __Sensation__. The mental process by which sensations are organized and interpreted is __Perception__.

Sensing the World: Some Basic Principles (pp. 132–137)

3. The __absolute threshold__ refers to the minimum amount of stimulation necessary for a stimulus to be detected __50__ percent of the time.

4. The concept that absolute thresholds depend not only on the strength of the signal but also on a person's psychological state is called __Signal detection__.

5. Some weak stimuli may trigger in our sense receptors a response that is processed by the brain, even though the response doesn't cross the threshold into __conscious__ awareness.

6. Some entrepreneurs claim that exposure to these "below threshold," or __Subliminal__, stimuli can be persuasive, but their claims are probably unwarranted.

7. The minimum difference required to distinguish two stimuli 50 percent of the time is called the __difference threshold__. Another term for this value is the __just noticable difference__.

8. The principle that the difference threshold is not a constant amount, but a constant percentage, is known as __Webers law__. The proportion depends on the __Stimulus__.

9. After constant exposure to an unchanging stimulus, the receptor cells of our senses begin to fire less vigorously; this phenomenon is called __Sensory adaptation__.

Explain why sensory adaptation is beneficial.

Vision (pp. 137–145)

10. In the process of sensory __transduction__ stimulus energy is converted into __neural__ activity.

11. The visible spectrum of light is a small portion of the larger spectrum of __electromagnetic__ radiation.

12. The distance from one light wave peak to the next is called __wavelength__. This value determines the wave's color, or __hue__.

13. The amount of energy in light waves, or __intensity__, determines the __brightness__ of a light.

14. Light enters the eye through a small opening called the __pupil__; the size of this opening is controlled by the colored __iris__.

15. By changing its curvature, the __lens__ can focus the image of an object onto the __retina__, which lines the back of the eyeball.

16. The process by which the lens changes shape to focus light is called __accomodation__.

17. The retina's receptor cells are the __rods__ and __cones__.

18. From the rods and cones the neural signals pass to the neighboring __bipolar__ cells, then to a network of __ganglion__ cells. The ganglion cells converge to form the __optic nerve__, which carries the visual information to the __brain__.

19. Where this nerve leaves the eye, there are no receptors; thus the area is called the __blind spot__.

20. Most cones are clustered around the retina's point of central focus, called the

_fovea_____, whereas the rods are concentrated in more __peripheral____ regions of the retina. Many cones have their own __bipolar_____ cells to communicate with the visual cortex. It is the ___cones._____ (rods/cones) of the eye that permit the perception of color.

21. Unlike cones, in dim light the rods are __sensitive____ (sensitive/insensitive). Adapting to a darkened room will take the retina approximately __20____ minutes.

22. Hubel and Wiesel discovered that certain neurons in the _visual____ _cortex___ of the brain respond only to specific features of what is viewed. They called these neurons _feature____ _detectors.___.

23. The brain achieves its remarkable speed in visual perception by processing several subdivisions of a stimulus _sim.____ (simultaneously/sequentially). This procedure, called _parallel____ _processing_, may explain why people who have suffered a stroke may lose just one aspect of vision. Nevertheless, such people may demonstrate _blindsight____ by responding to a stimulus that is not consciously perceived.

24. That color deficiency is genetically sex-linked is indicated by the fact that it occurs most often in ___males____ (males/females).

25. According to the Young-Helmholtz trichromatic theory, the eyes have three color receptors: one reacts most strongly to __red____, one to __blue____, and one to __green____.

26. After staring at a green square for a while, you will see the color __red____, its _opponent processing_ color.

27. Hering's theory of color vision is called the _opponent____-_process___ theory. According to this theory, after visual information leaves the receptors it is analyzed in terms of pairs of opposing colors: _red___ versus _green___, _yellow___

versus __blue____, and __white__ versus __black____.

Summarize the two stages of color processing.

28. An object, such as an apple, appears red because it __reflect____ certain wavelengths. This indicates that color, like all aspects of vision, is a __mental____ construction.

29. The experience of color depends on the __context____ in which an object is seen.

30. In an unvarying context, a familiar object will be perceived as having consistent color, even as the light changes. This phenomenon is called __color____ _consistency._.

Hearing (pp. 145–150)

31. The stimulus for hearing is sound waves, created by the compression and expansion of __air____ _mol.____.

32. The amplitude of a sound wave determines the sound's __loudness____.

33. The pitch of a sound is derived from the __frequency____ of its wave.

34. The ear is divided into three main parts: the __outer____ ear, the __middle____ ear, and the __inner.____ ear.

35. The outer ear channels sound waves toward the __eardrum____, a membrane that then vibrates.

36. The middle ear amplifies the sound via the vibrations of three small bones: the __hammer____, __anvil____, and __stirrup.____.

37. In the inner ear a coiled tube called the __cochlea____ contains the receptor cells for hearing.

38. One theory of pitch perception proposes that different pitches activate different places on the cochlea's membrane; this is the _place_ theory. This theory has difficulty accounting for how we hear _low_-pitched sounds, which do not have such localized effects.

39. A second theory proposes that neural impulses, sent to the brain at the same frequency as the sound wave, allow the perception of different pitches. This is the _frequency_ theory. This theory fails to account for the perception of _high_-pitched sounds, because individual neurons cannot fire faster than _1000_ times per second.

40. For the higher pitches, cells may alternate their firing to match the sound's frequency, according to the _volley_ principle.

41. A sound that comes from directly ahead will be _harder_ (easier/harder) to locate than a sound that comes from off to one side.

42. Problems in the mechanical conduction of sound waves through the outer ear or the middle ear may cause _conduction deafness_.

43. Problems in the cochlea or the auditory nerve can cause _nerve_ deafness. This type of hearing loss is greatest in the _high_ frequency ranges.

The Other Senses (pp. 151–157)

44. The sense of touch is a mixture of at least four senses: _____, _____, _____, and _____. Other skin sensations, such as tickle, itch, hot, and wetness, are _____ of the basic ones.

45. A sensation of pain in an amputated leg is referred to as a _____ _____ sensation.

46. The pain system _____ (is/is not) triggered by one specific type of physical energy. The body _____

(does/does not) have specialized receptor cells for pain.

47. Melzack and Wall have proposed a theory of pain called the _____–_____ theory. This theory proposes that there is a neurological _____ in the _____ _____ that blocks pain signals or lets them through. It may be opened by activation of _____ (small/large) nerve fibers and closed by activation of _____ (small/large) fibers.

List some pain control techniques used in the Lamaze method of prepared childbirth.

48. The four basic taste sensations are _____, _____, _____, and _____.

49. The _____ of the tongue tends to be especially sensitive to sweet sensations, the _____ of the tongue to bitter sensations.

50. When the sense of smell is blocked, as when we have a cold, foods do not taste the same; this illustrates the principle of _____ _____.

51. Like taste, smell is a _____ sense. Unlike light, an odor _____ (can/cannot) be separated into more elemental odors.

52. The system for sensing the position and movement of body parts is called _____. The receptors for this sense are located in the _____, _____, and _____ of the body.

53. The sense that monitors the movement of the whole body is _____. The

receptors for this sense are located in the semicircular canals and vestibular sacs of the

_____   _____ .

Sensory Restriction (pp. 157–158)

54. Sensory restriction may involve either

_____ of a sense or simply

sensory _____ .

Summarize the psychological effects of sensory restriction and suggest some potential applications.

FOCUS ON PSYCHOLOGY:
The Sweet Taste of Stress

You've had a tough day at work or school and you're feeling stressed, tense, and irritable. What do you do? On the way home you stop at a local bakery or ice cream parlor for your favorite treat, right? Wrong! Recent experimental findings indicate that people do not crave sweets when under stress.

Neil Grunberg and Richard Straub asked groups of nonsmoking women and men seated in a comfortable living room to watch either a highly stressful film about wood shop accidents or a pleasant travelogue. Within the subjects' reach were bowls of peanuts (salty), rice cakes (bland), and M & M's (sweet). The bowls of food were weighed before and after each session to determine how much of each snack food the subjects consumed.

After watching one of the two films, the subjects filled out a battery of questionnaires that measured how stressful they found the film, their normal eating habits, and their concern about dieting.

Surprisingly, Grunberg and Straub found that the subjects who watched the stressful film consumed *fewer* sweet snacks than did the subjects who watched the nonstressful film. This was true for the entire group of men, and for women who reported few concerns about dieting and body weight. The only subjects who consumed more sweet snacks in the stressful condition than did those in the nonstressful condition were women who reported being especially conscious of their weight and who had a history of frequent dieting. Stress did not significantly influence the subjects' preferences for salty or bland snack foods.

Why should people have less of an appetite for sweets when they are stressed? One explanation of-

fered by the researchers is that stress may indirectly increase a person's blood sugar level by lowering the level of insulin, a hormone that regulates sugar in the body. The elevated blood sugar may eliminate or reduce the desire for additional sweets.

Although the researchers believe that their findings are preliminary, they are hopeful that their continuing research will one day prove helpful to people suffering from eating disorders. Says Grunberg, "If we can figure out what role stress is playing in eating disorders, it may highlight an important aspect of therapy for everything from bulimia to anorexia nervosa."

Sources: Fishman, B. (1989, March). Unsweetened stress. *Psychology Today*, p. 72.

Grunberg, N. E. & Straub, R. O. (1991). The role of gender and taste class in the effects of stress on eating. *Health Psychology* (in press).

Progress Test 1
Multiple-Choice Questions

Circle your answers to the following questions and check them with the answers on page 106. If your answer is incorrect, read the explanation for why it is incorrect and then consult the appropriate pages of the text (in parentheses following the correct answer).

1. Which of the following is true?
   a. The absolute threshold for any stimulus is a constant.
   b. The absolute threshold for any stimulus varies somewhat.
   c. The absolute threshold is defined as the minimum amount of stimulation necessary for a stimulus to be detected 75 percent of the time.
   d. The absolute threshold is defined as the minimum amount of stimulation necessary for a stimulus to be detected 60 percent of the time.

2. Stimuli that are too weak to cross the threshold for conscious awareness:
   a. cannot be processed at all.
   b. will not be processed by the brain.
   c. may trigger a small response in the sense receptors.
   d. may disrupt our concentration on stimuli of which we *are* aware.

3. If you can just notice the difference between 10- and 11-pound weights, which of the following weights could you differentiate from a 100-pound weight?
   a. 101-pound weight
   b. 105-pound weight
   c. 110-pound weight
   d. There is no basis for prediction.

4. A decrease in sensory responsiveness accompanying an unchanging stimulus is called:
   a. sensory fatigue.
   c. sensory restriction.
   b. accommodation.
   d. sensory adaptation.

5. The size of the pupil is controlled by the:
   a. lens.
   c. cornea.
   b. retina.
   d. iris.

6. The process by which the lens changes its curvature is:
   a. accommodation.
   c. focusing.
   b. sensory adaptation.
   d. transduction.

7. The receptor of the eye that functions best in dim light is the:
   a. fovea.
   c. cone.
   b. rod.
   d. bipolar cell.

8. The Young-Helmholtz theory proposes that:
   a. there are three different types of color-sensitive cones.
   b. retinal cells are excited by one color and inhibited by its complementary color.
   c. there are four different types of cones.
   d. rod, not cone, vision accounts for our ability to detect fine visual detail.

9. Frequency is to pitch as _____ is to _____.
   a. wavelength; loudness
   b. amplitude; loudness
   c. wavelength; intensity
   d. amplitude; intensity

10. The receptors for hearing are located:
    a. in the outer ear.
    c. in the inner ear.
    b. in the middle ear.
    d. throughout the ear.

11. The place theory of pitch perception cannot account for how we hear:
    a. low-pitched sounds.
    b. middle-pitched sounds.
    c. high-pitched sounds.
    d. chords (two pitches simultaneously).

12. The hearing losses that occur with age are especially pronounced for:
    a. low-pitched sounds.
    b. middle-pitched sounds.
    c. high-pitched sounds.
    d. chords.

13. According to the gate-control theory, a way to alleviate chronic pain would be to stimulate the

_____ nerve fibers that _____ the spinal gate.
   a. small; open
   c. large; open
   b. small; close
   d. large; close

14. The transduction of light energy into nerve impulses takes place in the:
    a. iris.
    c. lens.
    b. retina.
    d. optic nerve.

15. The brain breaks vision into separate dimensions such as color, depth, movement, and form, and works on each aspect simultaneously. This is called:
    a. feature detection.
    b. parallel processing.
    c. accommodation.
    d. opponent processing.

16. Kinesthesis involves:
    a. the bones of the middle ear.
    b. information from the muscles, tendons, and joints.
    c. membranes within the cochlea.
    d. the body's sense of balance.

17. If one light appears reddish and another greenish, the reason is that they differ in:
    a. wavelength.
    c. frequency.
    b. amplitude.
    d. opponent processes.

18. Which of the following explains why a rose appears equally red when viewed in bright and dim light?
    a. the Young-Helmholtz theory
    b. the opponent-process theory
    c. feature detection
    d. color constancy

19. Which of the following is an example of sensory adaptation?
    a. finding the cold water of a swimming pool warmer after you have been in it for a while
    b. developing an increased sensitivity to salt the more you use it in foods
    c. becoming very irritated at the continuing sound of a dripping faucet
    d. all of the above

20. A person who is color deficient will probably:
    a. be male.
    b. be unable to tell any colors apart.
    c. also suffer from poor vision.
    d. have above-average vision to compensate for the deficit.

Matching Items

Match each of the structures with its function or description.

Structures

_e_	**1.** lens
_d_	**2.** iris
_h_	**3.** pupil
_j_	**4.** rods
_i_	**5.** cones
_a_	**6.** middle ear
_k_	**7.** inner ear
_b_	**8.** tip of tongue
_g_	**9.** back of tongue
_c_	**10.** semicircular canals
_f_	**11.** sensors in joints

Functions or Descriptions

a. amplifies sounds
b. sweet receptors
c. sense of equilibrium
d. controls pupil
e. accommodation
f. kinesthetic sense
g. bitter receptors
h. admits light
i. color vision
j. vision in dim light
k. transduction of sound

Progress Test 2

Progress Test 2 should be completed during a final chapter review. Answer the following questions after you thoroughly understand the correct answers for the Chapter Review and Progress Test 1.

Multiple-Choice Questions

1. In his studies of the effects of sensory restriction, Peter Suedfeld found that:

   a. most people react negatively to reduced sensory stimulation.

   b. sensory restriction was experienced most negatively by people who were prone to addiction.

   c. sensory restriction helped smokers and overweight people modify their behavior.

   d. for most people, sensory restriction resulted in elevated absolute thresholds for vision and hearing.

2. Of the four distinct skin senses, the only one that has definable receptors is:

   a. warmth.   c. pressure.

   b. cold.   d. pain.

3. The process by which sensory information is converted into neural energy is:

   a. sensory adaptation.   c. signal detection.

   b. feature detection.   d. transduction.

4. The receptors for taste are located in the:

   a. taste buds.   c. fovea.

   b. cochlea.   d. cortex.

5. The inner ear contains receptors for:

   a. audition and kinesthesis.

   b. kinesthesis and equilibrium.

   c. audition and equilibrium.

   d. audition, kinesthesis, and equilibrium.

6. According to the opponent-process theory:

   a. there are three types of color-sensitive cones.

   b. the process of color vision begins in the cortex.

   c. neurons involved in color vision are stimulated by one color's wavelength and inhibited by another's.

   d. all of the above are true.

7. Nerve deafness is caused by:

   a. wax buildup in the outer ear.

   b. damage to the eardrum.

   c. blockage in the middle ear because of infection.

   d. damage to the cochlea.

8. What enables you to feel yourself wiggling your toes even with your eyes closed?

   a. sense of equilibrium   c. the skin senses

   b. sense of kinesthesis   d. sensory interaction

9. The frequency theory of hearing is more successful than place theory at explaining our sensation of:

   a. the lowest pitches.

   b. pitches of intermediate range.

   c. the highest pitches.

   d. all of the above.

10. Hubel and Wiesel discovered feature detectors in the _____ of a monkey's visual system.

    a. fovea   c. iris

    b. optic nerve   d. cortex

11. Weber's law states that:

    a. the absolute threshold for any stimulus is a constant.

    b. the jnd for any stimulus is a constant.

    c. the absolute threshold for any stimulus is a constant percentage.

    d. the jnd for any stimulus is a constant percentage.

12. The principle that one sense may influence another is:

    a. transduction.   c. Weber's law.

    b. sensory adaptation. d. sensory interaction.

13. Which of the following is the correct order of structures through which light passes after entering the eye?
    a. lens, pupil, cornea, retina
    b. pupil, cornea, lens, retina
    c. cornea, pupil, lens, retina
    d. cornea, retina, pupil, lens

14. In the opponent-process theory, the three pairs of processes are:
    a. red-green, blue-yellow, black-white
    b. red-blue, green-yellow, black-white
    c. red-yellow, blue-green, black-white
    d. dependent on the individual's past experience

15. Wavelength is to _____ as _____ is to brightness.
    a. hue; intensity
    b. intensity; hue
    c. frequency; amplitude
    d. brightness; hue

16. Concerning the evidence for subliminal stimulation, which of the following is the best answer?
    a. The brain processes some information without our awareness.
    b. Stimuli too weak to cross our thresholds for awareness may trigger a response in our sense receptors.
    c. Because the "absolute" threshold is a statistical average, we are able to detect weaker stimuli some of the time.
    d. All of the above are true.

17. Which of the following is the most accurate description of how we process color?
    a. Throughout the visual system, color processing is divided into separate red, green, and blue systems.
    b. Throughout the visual system, red-green, blue-yellow, and black-white opponent processes operate.
    c. Color processing occurs in two stages: (1) a three-color system in the retina and (2) opponent-process cells en route to the visual cortex.
    d. Color processing occurs in two stages: (1) an opponent-process system in the retina and (2) a three-color system en route to the visual cortex.

18. Which of the following is the most accurate explanation of how we discriminate pitch?
    a. For all audible frequencies, pitch is coded according to the place of maximum vibration on the cochlea's basilar membrane.
    b. For all audible frequencies, the rate of neural activity in the auditory nerve matches the frequency of the sound wave.
    c. For very high frequencies, pitch is coded according to place of vibration on the basilar membrane; for lower pitches, the rate of neural activity in the auditory nerve matches the sound's frequency.
    d. For very high frequencies, the rate of neural activity in the auditory nerve matches the frequency of the sound wave; for lower frequencies, pitch is coded according to the place of vibration on the basilar membrane.

19. One reason that your ability to detect fine visual details is greatest when scenes are focused on the fovea of your retina is that:
    a. there are more feature detectors in the fovea than in the peripheral regions of the retina.
    b. cones in the fovea are nearer to the optic nerve than those in peripheral regions of the retina.
    c. many rods, which are clustered in the fovea, have individual bipolar cells to relay their information to the cortex.
    d. many cones, which are clustered in the fovea, have individual bipolar cells to relay their information to the cortex.

20. Given normal sensory ability, a person can hear a watch ticking in a silent room from 20 feet away. This is a description of hearing's:
    a. difference threshold.   c. absolute threshold.
    b. jnd.   d. signal detection.

Labeling

Label the parts of the eye numbered in the diagram at right.

1. _____
2. _____
3. _____
4. _____
5. _____
6. _____
7. _____

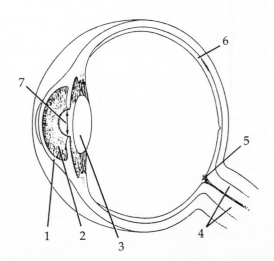

Label the parts of the ear numbered in the diagram at right.

1. _____

2. _____

3. _____

4. _____

5. _____

6. _____

7. _____

8. _____

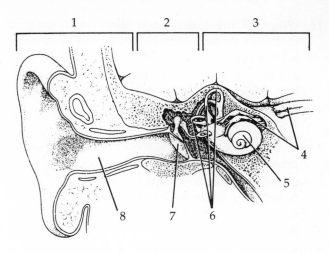

Challenge Test

Answer these questions the day before an exam as a final check on your understanding of the chapter's terms and concepts.

Multiple-Choice Questions

1. In shopping for a new stereo, you discover that you cannot differentiate between the sounds of models A and C. The difference between A and C is below your:
   a. absolute threshold.
   b. signal detection.
   c. receptor threshold.
   d. difference threshold.

2. In order to maximize your sensitivity to fine visual detail you should:
   a. stare off to one side of the object you are attempting to see.
   b. close one eye.
   c. decrease the intensity of the light falling upon the object.
   d. stare directly at the object.

3. The phantom limb sensation indicates that:
   a. pain is a purely sensory phenomenon.
   b. the central nervous system plays only a minor role in the experience of pain.
   c. pain involves the brain's interpretation of neural activity.
   d. all of the above are true.

4. While competing in the Olympic trials, marathoner Kirsten O'Brien suffered a stress fracture in her left leg. That she did not experience significant pain until the race was over is probably attributable to the fact that during the race:
   a. the pain gate in her spinal cord was closed by information coming from her brain.
   b. her body's production of endorphins decreased.
   c. an increase in the activity of small-diameter pain fibers closed the pain gate.
   d. a decrease in the activity of large-diameter pain fibers closed the pain gate.

5. Which of the following is an example of sensory interaction?
   a. finding that despite its delicious aroma, a weird-looking meal tastes awful
   b. finding that food tastes bland when you have a bad cold
   c. finding it difficult to maintain your balance when you have an ear infection
   d. all of the above

6. In comparing the human eye to a camera, the film would be analogous to the eye's:
   a. pupil.   c. cornea.
   b. lens.   d. retina.

7. Sensation is to _____ as perception is to _____.
   a. recognizing a stimulus; interpreting a stimulus
   b. detecting a stimulus; recognizing a stimulus
   c. interpreting a stimulus; detecting a stimulus
   d. seeing; hearing

8. I am a cell in the thalamus that is excited by red and inhibited by green. What am I?
   a. a feature detector
   b. a cone
   c. a bipolar cell
   d. an opponent-process cell

9. Which of the following correctly lists the order of structures through which sound travels after entering the ear?
   a. auditory canal, eardrum, middle ear, cochlea
   b. eardrum, auditory canal, middle ear, cochlea
   c. eardrum, middle ear, cochlea, auditory canal
   d. cochlea, eardrum, middle ear, auditory canal

10. Dr. Frankenstein has forgotten to give his monster an important part; as a result, the monster cannot transduce sound. Dr. Frankenstein omitted the:

   a. eardrum.
   b. middle ear.
   c. semicircular canals.
   d. basilar membrane.

11. Seventy-five-year-old Claude has difficulty hearing high-pitched sounds. Most likely his hearing problem involves:

   a. his eardrum.
   b. his auditory canal.
   c. the bones of his middle ear.
   d. the hair cells of his inner ear.

12. Which of the following is *not* true of cones?

   a. Cones enable color vision.
   b. Cones are highly concentrated in the foveal region of the retina.
   c. Cones have a higher absolute threshold for brightness than rods.
   d. Each cone has its own bipolar cell.

13. Assuming that the visual systems of humans and other mammals function similarly, you would expect that the retina of a nocturnal mammal (one active only at night) would contain:

   a. mostly cones.
   b. mostly rods.
   c. an equal number of rods and cones.
   d. more bipolar cells than an animal active only during the day.

14. As the football game continued into the night, LeVar noticed that he was having difficulty distinguishing the colors of the players' uniforms. This is because the _____, which enable color vision, have a _____ absolute threshold for brightness than the available light intensity.

   a. rods; higher
   b. cones; higher
   c. rods; lower
   d. cones; lower

15. After staring at a very intense red stimulus for a few minutes, Carrie shifted her gaze to a beige wall and "saw" the color _____. Carrie's experience provides support for the _____ theory.

   a. green; trichromatic
   b. blue; opponent-process
   c. green; opponent-process
   d. blue; trichromatic

16. Elderly Mrs. Martinez finds that she must spice her food heavily or she cannot taste it. Unfortunately, her son often finds her cooking inedible because it is so spicy. What is the likely explanation for the taste differences in the Martinez family?

   a. Women have higher taste thresholds than men.
   b. Men have higher taste thresholds than women.

   c. Being elderly, Mrs. Martinez probably has fewer taste buds than her son.
   d. All of the above are likely explanations.

17. When admiring the texture of a piece of fabric, Calvin usually runs his fingertips over the cloth's surface. He does this because:

   a. if the cloth were held motionless, sensory adaptation to the feel of the cloth would quickly occur.
   b. the sense of touch does not adapt.
   c. a relatively small amount of brain tissue is devoted to processing touch from the fingertips.
   d. of all the above reasons.

18. REST stands for:

   a. restricted environmental stimulation therapy
   b. remote extrasensory touch
   c. reversed enhancement (smell and touch)
   d. random environmental stimulus test

19. How does pain differ from other senses?

   a. It has no identifiable receptors.
   b. It has no single stimulus.
   c. It is influenced by both physical and psychological phenomena.
   d. All the above are true.

20. Tamiko hates the bitter taste of her cough syrup. Which of the following would she find most helpful in minimizing the syrup's bad taste?

   a. tasting something very sweet before taking the cough syrup
   b. keeping the syrup in her mouth for several seconds before swallowing it
   c. holding her nose while taking the cough syrup
   d. gulping the cough syrup so that it misses the tip of her tongue and stimulates only the taste buds in the back of her mouth

Essay Question

A dancer in a chorus line uses many sensory cues when performing. Discuss three senses that dancers rely on and explain why each is important. Use the space below to list the points you want to make and organize them. Then write the essay on a separate sheet of paper.

Key Terms

Using your own words, write a brief definition or explanation of each of the following terms.

1. sensation

2. perception

3. absolute threshold

4. signal detection

5. subliminal

6. difference threshold (jnd)

7. Weber's law

8. sensory adaptation

9. transduction

10. wavelength (hue)

11. intensity

12. pupil

13. iris

14. lens

15. accommodation

16. retina

17. rods and cones

18. optic nerve

19. blind spot

20. fovea

21. feature detectors

22. parallel processing

23. Young-Helmholtz trichromatic (three-color) theory

24. opponent-process theory

25. color constancy

26. audition

27. pitch (frequency)

28. middle ear

29. inner ear

30. cochlea

31. place theory

32. frequency theory

33. conduction deafness

34. nerve deafness

35. gate-control theory

36. sensory interaction

37. kinesthesis

38. equilibrium

ANSWERS
GUIDED STUDY

The following guidelines provide the main points that your answers should have touched upon.

1. Sensation refers to how our sense receptors and nervous system represent our external environment as neural information which is passed on to the brain. Perception refers to how we mentally organize and interpret sensory information.

2. An absolute threshold is the minimum stimulation necessary to detect a particular environmental stimulus 50 percent of the time. A difference threshold, or just noticeable difference (jnd), is the minimum difference a person can detect between any two stimuli 50 percent of the time. Weber's law states that the difference threshold is a constant proportion of the stimulus.

   Studies of signal detection indicate that thresholds depend not only on the strength of stimuli, but also on a person's experience, expectations, motivation, and fatigue. For this reason, thresholds are not constant.

3. Stimuli at or above the "absolute" threshold are detected half the time; subliminal stimuli, which are below the absolute threshold, are therefore detected *less* than half the time. Experiments show that under certain conditions, a weak stimulus may reach a part of the brain where it evokes a feeling but not conscious awareness. Claims that subliminal stimulation may lead to thought persuasion have not been supported, however.

4. Sensory adaptation refers to our diminishing sensitivity to an unchanging stimulus. By allowing us to focus our attention on informative changes in the environment, it keeps us from being distracted by the uninformative, constant stimulation of unchanging stimuli.

5. Visible light is a small portion of the larger spectrum of electromagnetic radiation. Light can be described by two physical characteristics, wavelength and intensity.

   Vision begins when light enters the eye through the opening in the iris called the pupil. Light passes through the lens, which changes its curvature (accommodation) in order to focus light on the retina. Within the retina are the rods and cones, which are responsible for the transduction of light energy into neural impulses. The optic nerve carries neural impulses from the retina to visual processing centers in the brain.

6. Visual information processing begins when light reaches the retina. As we view a scene, the rods and cones of the retina transduce the reflected light into neural impulses that are relayed to bipolar and ganglion cells and then sent to the brain by means of the optic nerve. The brain processes these visual stimuli relatively quickly by breaking them down into various subdimensions and working on each simultaneously (parallel processing). Thus, feature detectors break the image into bars, edges, gradients of light, and other elementary features. Higher-level brain cells reassemble the features and compare the resulting image with previously stored images until a match, and therefore recognition, occurs.

7. The Young-Helmholtz trichromatic theory states that the retina has three types of cones, each especially sensitive to one of three colors: red, green, or blue. To "see" other hues, such as yellow, there must be a unique combination of activity in two or three of these color receptors (red and green, in this case). This theory explains color processing at the level of the retina.

   According to the opponent-process theory, at a higher level in the brain visual information is analyzed in terms of the opponent colors red and green, blue and yellow, and black and white. This theory explains why we see afterimages following intense stimulation with a particular color.

8. Color constancy refers to the fact that, in an unvarying context, the color of an object remains roughly constant despite changes in lighting. If the context in which an object is viewed changes, the perceived color of the object changes. This demonstrates that the experience of color results not only from the light waves reflected from an object, but also from the light waves reflected by an object relative to surrounding objects.

9. The stimulus energy for hearing is the sound waves of compressed and expanded air that are created by vibrating objects. The length, or frequency, of sound waves determines their pitch; their strength, or amplitude, determines loudness.

   Hearing begins when the outer ear channels sound waves through the auditory canal to the eardrum. The middle ear transmits the eardrum's vibrations over three tiny bones (hammer, anvil, and stirrup) to the membrane entrance (oval window) of the fluid-filled cochlea of the inner ear. These vibrations cause ripples in the basilar membrane, which is lined with the hair cell receptors for audition. Movements of the basilar membrane cause the hair cells to bend, triggering nerve impulses in the adjacent nerve fibers.

10. According to the place theory, different sound wave frequencies trigger activity at different places along the cochlea's basilar membrane. The brain recognizes a sound's pitch by the place on the membrane from which it receives signals.

    Frequency theory suggests that the auditory nerve generates nerve impulses at the same rate as a sound's frequency. The brain recognizes pitch from the frequency of these impulses.

    Place theory best explains how we sense high pitches and frequency theory explains low pitches. A combination of the two processes accounts for the sensing of intermediate pitches.

11. Because of the distance between the two ears, a sound coming from one side of the body will arrive sooner at one ear and be slightly louder. That differences in loudness and arrival time are used in locating sounds is demonstrated by the difficulty we have in locating a sound that comes from directly ahead, behind, overhead, or beneath us. Such sounds strike the two ears simultaneously and with equal intensity.

    Damage to the eardrum or the bones of the middle ear causes conduction deafness, a problem in the mechanical system that conducts sound waves to the inner ear. A hearing aid that amplifies sound may partially correct this problem. Damage to the hair cells of the cochlea due to disease, aging, or prolonged exposure to loud sounds can cause nerve deafness, especially for high frequencies.

12. The sense of touch is a mixture of at least four skin senses—pressure, warmth, cold, and pain. Of these, only pressure has identifiable neural receptors. Other skin sensations, such as tickle, itch, wetness, and hot, are variations of the four basic ones.

    Pain is a property of the senses and the brain. Unlike other senses, pain does not have a single stimulus nor specialized receptors. According to the gate-control theory, the spinal cord contains a neural "gate" that either opens to permit pain signals to reach the brain or closes to prevent them from reaching the brain. This may explain why electrical stimulation, massage, and acupuncture relieve chronic pain—by triggering "gate-closing" activity in the spinal cord.

The gate-control theory also suggests that the pain gate can be closed by information from the brain. This may explain why thought distraction, hypnosis, and other psychological influences on pain are powerful.

13. Taste is a chemical sense comprised of four basic sensations—sweet, sour, salty, and bitter. Mixtures of these basic sensations give rise to other tastes. The receptors for taste (taste buds) are unevenly distributed so that different regions of the tongue are especially sensitive to one or more of the four basic tastes. Although the taste buds reproduce themselves every seven days, their number decreases with aging, smoking, and the use of alcohol.

    Smell (olfaction) occurs when air-carried molecules of a substance reach receptor cells in the nose. Unlike other senses, olfaction is not based on a small set of basic odors from which all other odors derive. Exactly how the olfactory receptors work remains a mystery.

    Sensors in the muscles, tendons, and joints of the body provide the brain with information about the position and movement of body parts (kinesthesis).

    Receptors in the semicircular canals and the vestibular sacs of the inner ear monitor the position and movement of the whole body and enable us to maintain balance (equilibrium).

    Sensory interaction is the principle that one sense may influence another. An example of sensory interaction is the enhancement of a food's taste that occurs when it smells delicious.

14. Surprisingly, researchers have found that sensory restriction—controlled exposure to monotonous sensory environments—does not disturb most people. More often, it reduces stress and helps people become more open to positive influences that promote behavior modification. Sensory restriction has helped people increase their self-control, quit smoking, and reduce alcohol consumption.

CHAPTER REVIEW

1. input; processing; output
2. sensation; perception
3. absolute threshold; 50
4. signal detection
5. conscious
6. subliminal
7. difference threshold; just noticeable difference
8. Weber's law; stimulus
9. sensory adaptation

Although sensory adaptation reduces our sensitivity, it enables us to focus our attention on informative changes in the environment without being distracted by the uninformative, constant stimulation that bombards our senses.

10. transduction; neural
11. electromagnetic
12. wavelength; hue
13. intensity; brightness
14. pupil; iris
15. lens; retina
16. accommodation
17. rods; cones
18. bipolar; ganglion; optic nerve; brain
19. blind spot
20. fovea; peripheral; bipolar; cones
21. sensitive; 20
22. visual cortex; feature detectors
23. simultaneously; parallel processing; blindsight
24. males
25. red; green; blue
26. red; opponent
27. opponent-process; red; green; yellow; blue; black; white

In the first stage of color processing, the retina's red, green, and blue cones respond in varying degrees to different color stimuli, as suggested by the three-color theory. The resulting signals are then processed by red-green, blue-yellow, and black-white opponent-process cells, which are stimulated by one wavelength and inhibited by its complement.

28. reflects; mental
29. context
30. color constancy
31. air molecules
32. loudness
33. frequency
34. outer; middle; inner
35. eardrum
36. hammer; anvil; stirrup
37. cochlea
38. place; low
39. frequency; high; 1000
40. volley
41. harder
42. conduction deafness
43. nerve; higher

44. pressure; warmth; cold; pain; variations
45. phantom limb
46. is not; does not
47. gate-control; gate; spinal cord; small; large

The Lamaze method of prepared childbirth combines several pain control techniques, including distraction, deep breathing and muscle relaxation, and counter-stimulation through gentle massage.

48. sweet; sour; salty; bitter
49. tip; back
50. sensory interaction
51. chemical; cannot
52. kinesthesis; muscles; tendons; joints
53. equilibrium; inner ear
54. loss; monotony

Although early experiments reported disorientation and hallucinations, subsequent research has found that most people are *not* negatively affected by sensory restriction. In many instances sensory restriction even seems to reduce stress and help people become more open to influences. For these reasons, sensory restriction may prove useful to people who want to modify their behavior, as indicated by experiments with smokers and overweight people.

PROGRESS TEST 1

Multiple-Choice Questions

1. **b.** is the answer. Psychological factors can affect the absolute threshold for a stimulus. (p. 133)

   a. The absolute threshold for detecting a stimulus depends not only on the strength of the stimulus, but also on psychological factors such as experience, expectations, motivation, and fatigue. Therefore, the threshold cannot be a constant.

   c. & d. The absolute threshold is defined as the minimum stimulus that is detected *50 percent* of the time.

2. **c.** is the answer. It appears that stimuli too weak to cross the threshold for conscious awareness may trigger a small response in sense receptors and even, in this way, be processed by the brain. But as shown by researchers' skepticism of subliminal persuasion, there is no evidence that such stimuli overpower stimuli of which we *are* consciously aware. (pp. 133–134)

3. **c.** is the answer. According to Weber's law, the difference threshold is a constant proportion of the stimulus. There is a 10 percent difference between 10 and 11 pounds; since the difference threshold is a constant proportion, the weight closest to 100 pounds that can nonetheless be differentiated

from it is 110 pounds (or 100 pounds plus 10 percent). (p. 135)

4. **d.** is the answer. (pp. 135–136)

a. "Sensory fatigue" is not a term in psychology.

b. Accommodation refers to an adaptive change in shape by the lens of the eye.

c. Sensory restriction refers to restricted sensory input because of sensory monotony or loss of a sense.

5. **d.** is the answer. (p. 138)

a. The lens lies behind the pupil and focuses light on the retina.

b. The retina lies at the back of the eyeball and contains the rods and cones.

c. The cornea lies in front of the pupil and is the first structure that light passes through as it enters the eye.

6. **a.** is the answer. (p. 138)

b. Sensory adaptation is our diminishing sensitivity to an unchanging stimulus.

c. Focusing is the process through which light converges onto the retina as a sharp image. The image is focused *because* the lens accommodates its shape.

d. Transduction refers to the conversion of an environmental stimulus, such as light, into a nerve impulse by a receptor—a rod or a cone.

7. **b.** is the answer. (p. 140)

a. The fovea is not a receptor; it is a region of the retina that contains only cones.

c. Cones have a higher threshold for brightness than rods and therefore do not function as well in dim light.

d. Bipolar cells are not receptors; they are neurons in the retina that link rods and cones with ganglion cells, which make up the optic nerve.

8. **a.** is the answer. The Young-Helmholtz theory proposes that there are red-, green-, and blue-sensitive cones. (p. 143)

b. This answer describes Hering's opponent-process theory.

c. The Young-Helmholtz theory proposes that there are *three* types of cones, not four.

d. The Young-Helmholtz theory concerns only color vision, not the detection of visual detail.

9. **b.** is the answer. Just as wave frequency determines pitch, so wave amplitude determines loudness. (p. 146)

a. Amplitude is the physical basis of loudness; wavelength determines frequency and thereby pitch.

c. & d. Wavelength, amplitude, and intensity, are *physical* aspects of light and sound. Because the question is based on a relationship between a physical property (frequency) of a stimulus and its psychological attribute (pitch), these answers are incorrect.

10. **c.** is the answer. The receptors for hearing—those cells that transduce sound energy into neural impulses—are the hair cells lining the basilar membrane of the cochlea. (pp. 146–147)

11. **a.** is the answer. (p. 147)

b. & c. Although the localization of low-pitched sounds along the basilar membrane is poor, that for sounds of middle and, especially, high pitch is good. Therefore, place theory accounts well for high-pitched sounds and, together with frequency theory, can account for middle-pitched sounds.

d. As long as the notes of a chord are within the range of responsiveness of the basilar membrane, chord perception can be accounted for by place theory.

12. **c.** is the answer. (p. 149)

d. Chord perception, except for chords comprised exclusively of high-frequency notes, shows no age-dependent decline.

13. **d.** is the answer. The small fibers conduct most pain signals; the large fibers conduct most other sensory signals from the skin. The gate either allows pain signals to pass on to the brain or blocks them from passing. When the large fibers are stimulated, the pain gate is closed and other sensations are felt in place of pain. (p. 152)

14. **b.** is the answer. (p. 139)

a. The iris controls the diameter of the pupil.

c. The lens accommodates its shape to focus images on the retina.

d. The optic nerve carries nerve impulses from the retina to the visual cortex.

15. **b.** is the answer. (p. 142)

a. Feature detection is the process by which nerve cells in the brain respond to specific visual features of a stimulus, such as movement, angle, or shape.

c. Accommodation is the process by which the lens changes its curvature to focus images on the retina.

d. The opponent-process theory suggests that color vision depends on the response of brain cells to red-green, yellow-blue, and black-white opposing colors.

16. **b.** is the answer. Kinesthesis, or the sense of the position and movement of body parts, is based on

information from the muscles, tendons, and joints. (p. 156)

a. & c. The ear and its parts play no role in kinesthesis.

d. Equilibrium, or the sense of balance, is not involved in kinesthesis but is, rather, a companion sense.

17. a. is the answer. Wavelength determines hue, or color. (p. 137)

b. The amplitude of light determines its brightness.

c. Frequency helps characterize the stimulus for hearing, not for vision.

d. Opponent processes are neural systems involved in color vision, not properties of light.

18. d. is the answer. Color constancy is the perception that familiar objects have consistent color, even if changing illumination alters the wavelengths reflected by that object. (p. 145)

a. & b. These theories explain how the visual system detects color; they do not address the issue of why colors do not seem to change when lighting does.

c. Feature detection explains how the brain recognizes visual images by analyzing their distinctive features of shape, movement, and angle.

19. a. is the answer. Sensory adaptation means a diminishing sensitivity to an unchanging stimulus. Only the adjustment to cold water involves a decrease in sensitivity; the other examples involve an *increase*. (p. 135)

20. a. is the answer. Color deficiency is genetically sex-linked. (p. 143)

b. Those who are color deficient are usually not "color blind" in a literal sense. Instead, they lack functioning red or green cones and have difficulty discriminating these two colors.

c. Failure to distinguish red and green is separate from, and does not usually affect, general visual ability.

d. Color deficiency does not enhance vision. A deficit in one sense often is compensated for by overdevelopment of another sense—for example, hearing in blind people.

Matching Items

1. e (p. 138)	**5.** i (p. 140)	**9.** g (p. 154)
2. d (p. 138)	**6.** a (p. 146)	**10.** c (p. 156)
3. h (p. 138)	**7.** k (pp. 146–147)	**11.** f (p. 156)
4. j (p. 140)	**8.** b (p. 154)	

PROGRESS TEST 2

Multiple-Choice Questions

1. c. is the answer. (p. 158)

a. In fact, researchers have found that most people are not affected negatively by sensory restriction.

b & d. There is no evidence that sensory restriction has a more negative impact on people prone to addiction or that it elevates absolute thresholds.

2. c. is the answer. Researchers have identified receptors for pressure but have been unable to do so for the other skin senses. (p. 151)

3. d. is the answer. (p. 137)

a. Sensory adaptation refers to the diminished sensitivity that occurs with unchanging stimulation.

b. Feature detection refers to the process by which nerve cells in the brain respond to specific aspects of visual stimuli, such as movement or shape.

c. Signal detection is a task in which the observer must judge whether a faint signal is present.

4. a. is the answer. (p. 154)

b. The cochlea contains receptors for hearing.

c. The fovea contains receptors for vision.

d. The cortex is the outer layer of the brain, where information detected by the receptors is processed.

5. c. is the answer. The inner ear contains the receptors for audition (hearing) and equilibrium; those for kinesthesis are located in the muscles, tendons, and joints. (pp. 146, 156)

6. c. is the answer. After leaving the receptor cells, visual information is analyzed in terms of pairs of opponent colors; neurons stimulated by one member of a pair are inhibited by the other. (p. 144)

a. The idea that there are three types of color-sensitive cones is the basis of the Young-Helmholtz three-color theory.

b. According to the opponent-process theory, and all other theories of color vision, the process of color vision begins in the retina.

7. d. is the answer. Nerve deafness is caused by destruction of neural tissue as a result of problems with the cochlea's receptors or the auditory nerve. (p. 149)

a. & c. Wax buildup and blockage because of infection are temporary states; nerve deafness is permanent. Moreover, nerve deafness involves the inner ear, rather than the outer or middle ear.

b. Damage to the eardrum impairs the mechanical system that conducts sound waves; it could therefore cause conduction deafness, but not nerve deafness.

8. **b.** is the answer. Kinesthesis, the sense of movement of body parts, would enable you to feel your toes wiggling. (p. 156)

a. Equilibrium is concerned with movement and position, or balance, of the whole body, not of its parts.

c. The skin, or tactile, senses are pressure, pain, warmth, and cold; they have nothing to do with movement of body parts.

d. Sensory interaction, the principle that the senses influence each other, does not play a role in this example, which involves only the sense of kinesthesis.

9. **a.** is the answer. Frequency theory best explains the lowest pitches. Place theory best explains the highest pitches, and some combination of the two theories probably accounts for our sensation of intermediate-range pitches. (p. 147)

10. **d.** is the answer. Feature detectors are cortical neurons and hence are located in the visual cortex. (p. 142)

a. The fovea contains cones.

b. The optic nerve contains neurons that relay nerve impulses from the retina to higher centers in the visual system.

c. The iris is simply a ring of muscle tissue, which controls the diameter of the pupil.

11. **d.** is the answer. Weber's law concerns difference thresholds (jnd's), not absolute thresholds, and states that these are constant proportions of the stimuli, not that they remain constant. (p. 135)

12. **d.** is the answer. (p. 154)

a. Transduction is the process by which stimulus energy is converted into neural impulses.

b. Sensory adaptation is diminished sensitivity to unchanging stimulation.

c. Weber's law states that the jnd is a constant proportion of a stimulus.

13. **c.** is the answer. (p. 138)

14. **a.** is the answer. (p. 144)

15. **a.** is the answer. Wavelength determines hue, and intensity determines brightness. (pp. 137–138)

16. **d.** is the answer. (pp. 133–134)

17. **c.** is the answer. (p. 144)

a. This answer is incorrect because separate red, green, and blue systems operate only in the retina.

b. This answer is incorrect because opponent-process systems operate en route to the brain, after visual processing in the receptors is completed.

d. This answer is incorrect because it reverses the correct order of the two stages of processing.

18. **c.** is the answer. (p. 147)

a. This answer describes how pitch is sensed in the case of high-pitched, but not low-pitched, sounds.

b. This answer describes how pitch is sensed in the case of low-pitched, but not high-pitched, sounds.

d. This answer is incorrect because it reverses the range of frequencies.

19. **d.** is the answer. (p. 140)

a. Feature detectors are nerve cells located in the visual cortex, not in the fovea of the retina.

b. The proximity of rods and cones to the optic nerve does not influence their ability to resolve fine details.

c. Rods are concentrated in the peripheral regions of the retina, not in the fovea; moreover, *several* rods share a single bipolar cell.

20. **c.** is the answer. The absolute threshold is the minimum stimulation needed to detect a stimulus. (p. 133)

a. & b. The difference threshold, which is also known as the jnd, is the minimum difference between *two* stimuli that a person can detect. In this example, there is only one stimulus — the sound of the watch.

d. Signal detection is a research task, not a sensory phenomenon.

Labeling

Eye Diagram (p. 138)

1. cornea
2. iris
3. lens
4. optic nerve
5. blind spot
6. retina
7. pupil

Ear Diagram (p. 146)

1. outer ear
2. middle ear
3. inner ear
4. auditory nerve
5. cochlea
6. semicircular canals
7. eardrum
8. auditory canal

CHALLENGE TEST

Multiple-Choice Questions

1. **d.** is the answer. (p. 135)

    a. The absolute threshold refers to whether a single stimulus can be detected, not to whether two stimuli can be differentiated.

    b. Signal detection is a task in which one must determine whether a faint stimulus is present or not.

    c. A receptor threshold is a minimum amount of energy that will elicit a neural impulse in a receptor cell.

2. **d.** is the answer. Greater sensitivity to fine visual detail is associated with the cones, which have their own bipolar cells to relay information to the cortex. The cones are concentrated in the fovea, the retina's point of central focus. For this reason, staring directly at an object maximizes sensitivity to fine detail. (p. 140)

    a. If you stare off to one side, the image falls onto peripheral regions of the retina, where rods are concentrated and sensitivity to fine visual detail is poor.

    b. Sensitivity to detail is not directly influenced by whether one or both eyes are stimulated.

    c. Decreasing the intensity of light would only impair the functioning of the cones, which are sensitive to visual detail but have a high threshold for light intensity.

3. **c.** is the answer. Since pain is felt in the limb that does not exist, the pain is simply the brain's (mis)interpretation of neural activity. (p. 152)

    a. If pain were a purely sensory phenomenon, phantom limb pain would not occur, since the receptors are no longer present.

    b. That pain is experienced when a limb is missing indicates that the central nervous system, especially the brain, *is* where pain is sensed.

4. **a.** is the answer. (p. 152)

    b. Since endorphins relieve pain, a decrease in their production would have made Kirsten more likely to experience pain. Moreover, because endorphins are released in response to pain, their production probably would have *increased*.

    c. Neural activity in small-diameter fibers tends to *open* the pain gate.

    d. An *increase* in large-fiber activity would tend to close the pain gate.

5. **d.** is the answer. Each of these is an example of the interaction of two senses—vision and taste in the case of a., taste and smell in the case of b., and hearing and equilibrium in the case of c. (p. 154)

6. **d.** is the answer. Just as light strikes the film of a camera, visual images entering the eye are projected onto the retina. (p. 138)

    a. The pupil would be analogous to the aperture of a camera, since both control the amount of light permitted to enter.

    b. The lens of the eye performs a focusing function similar to the lens of the camera.

    c. The cornea would be analogous to a camera's lens cap in that both protect delicate inner structures.

7. **b.** is the answer. (p. 132)

    a. Both recognition and interpretation are examples of perception.

    c. This answer would have been correct if the question had read, "Perception is to sensation as _____ is to _____."

    d. Sensation and perception are important processes in both hearing and seeing.

8. **d.** is the answer. (p. 144)

    a. Feature detectors are located in the visual cortex and respond to features such as movement, shape, and angle.

    b. & c. Cones and bipolar cells are located in the retina. Moreover, neither are excited by some colors and inhibited by others.

9. **a.** is the answer. (p. 146)

10. **d.** is the answer. The hair cells, which transduce sound energy, are located on the basilar membrane. (pp. 146–147)

    a. & b. The eardrum and bones of the middle ear merely conduct sound waves to the inner ear, where they are transduced.

    c. The semicircular canals are involved in the sense of equilibrium, not hearing.

11. **d.** is the answer. Hearing losses that result from aging are greatest in the higher frequencies and involve damage to the hair cells on the basilar membrane of the cochlea. (p. 149)

    a., b., & c. Damage to the eardrum, auditory canal, or bones of the middle ear would probably cause conduction deafness and reduced sensitivity to sounds of *all* frequencies.

12. **d.** is the answer. Many, but not all, cones are linked to their own bipolar cell. (p. 140)

13. **b.** is the answer. Rods and cones enable vision in dim and bright light, respectively. If an animal is active only at night, it is likely to have more rods than cones in its retinas. (p. 140)

    d. Bipolar cells link both cones and rods to ganglion cells. There is no reason to expect that a nocturnal mammal would have more bipolar cells than a mammal active both during the day and at night. If anything, because several rods share a single bipolar cell, whereas each cone has its own, a nocturnal animal (with a visual system consisting mostly of rods) might be expected to have *fewer* bipolar cells than an animal active during the day (with a visual system consisting mostly of cones).

14. **b.** is the answer. (pp. 133, 140)

    a. & c. It is the cones, rather than the rods, that enable color vision.

    d. If the cones' threshold were lower than the available light intensity, they *would* be able to function and therefore detect the colors of the players' uniforms.

15. **c.** is the answer. (p. 144)

    a. The trichromatic theory cannot account for the experience of afterimages.

    b. & d. Afterimages are experienced as the complementary color of a stimulus. Green, rather than blue, is red's complement.

16. **c.** is the answer. As people age they lose taste buds and their taste thresholds increase. For this reason, Mrs. Martinez needs more concentrated tastes than her son to find food palatable. (p. 154)

    a. & b. There is no evidence that women and men differ in their absolute thresholds for taste.

17. **a.** is the answer. (p. 151)

    b. The sense of touch (pressure) adapts very quickly.

    c. On the contrary, the extreme sensitivity of the fingertips is due to the relatively large amount of cortical tissue that processes neural impulses from the fingertips.

18. **a.** is the answer. (p. 158)

19. **d.** is the answer. (p. 152)

20. **c.** is the answer. Because of the powerful sensory interaction between taste and smell, eliminating the odor of the cough syrup should make its taste more pleasant. (p. 154)

    a. If anything, the contrasting tastes might make the bitter syrup even less palatable.

    b. If Tamiko keeps the syrup in her mouth for several seconds, it will ensure that her taste pores fully "catch" the stimulus, thus intensifying the bitter taste.

    d. Because the taste buds that respond mostly to bitter are at the back of the tongue, Tamiko would do well to *avoid* stimulating this area with the cough syrup.

Essay Question

The senses that are most important to dancers are vision, hearing, kinesthesis, and equilibrium. Your answer should refer to any three of these senses and include, at minimum, the following information.

Dancers rely on vision to gauge their body position relative to other dancers as they perform specific choreographed movements. Vision also helps dancers assess the audience's reaction to their performance. Whenever dance is set to music, hearing is necessary so that the dancers can detect musical cues for certain parts of their routines. Hearing also helps the dancers keep their movements in time with the music. Kinesthetic receptors in dancers' muscles, tendons, and joints provide their brains with information about the position and movement of body parts to determine if their hands, arms, legs, and heads are in the proper positions. Equilibrium receptors in the dancers' inner ears send messages to their brains that help them maintain their balance and determine the correctness of the position and movement of their bodies.

KEY TERMS

1. **Sensation** is the process by which our sense receptors and nervous system receive and represent stimulus energies from our environment. (p. 132)

2. **Perception** is the process by which the brain organizes and interprets sensory information. (p. 132)

3. The **absolute threshold** is the minimum stimulation needed to detect a stimulus 50 percent of the time. (p. 133)

4. **Signal detection** is the task of detecting a weak stimulus. Performance will vary, depending, for example, on a person's psychological state. (p. 133)

5. A stimulus that is **subliminal** is one that is below the threshold of awareness. (p. 134)

   Memory aid: Limen is the Latin word for "threshold." A stimulus that is **subliminal** is one that is *sub-* ("below") the *limen*, or threshold.

6. The **difference threshold**, or **just noticeable difference (jnd)**, is the minimum difference in two stimuli that a subject can detect 50 percent of the time. (p. 135)

   Example: Because trained musicians can hear very small differences in tones, they have lower **difference thresholds** for tones than do nonmusicians.

7. **Weber's law** states that the just noticeable difference between two stimuli is a constant minimum percentage. (p. 135)

   Example: If a difference of 10 percent in weight is noticeable, **Weber's law** predicts that a person could discriminate 10- and 11-pound weights or 50- and 55-pound weights.

8. **Sensory adaptation** refers to the decreased sensitivity that occurs with continued exposure to an unchanging stimulus. (p. 135)

   Example: When she left the steamy parking lot and first entered the air-conditioned shopping mall, Janice felt unbearably cold. After a few minutes she felt comfortable—**sensory adaptation** had taken place.

9. In the study of sensation, **transduction** refers to the process by which receptor cells in the eye, ear, skin, and nose convert environmental stimuli into neural impulses. (p. 137)

10. **Wavelength**, which refers to the distance from the peak of one light (or sound) wave to the next, gives rise to the perceptual experiences of **hue**, or color, in vision (and **pitch** in sound). (pp. 137, 146)

    Example: The visible spectrum consists of electromagnetic energy ranging between **wavelengths** of about 350 and 750 nanometers.

11. The **intensity** of light and sound is determined by the amplitude of the waves and is experienced as brightness and loudness, respectively. (pp. 137–138, 146)

    Example: Sounds that exceed 85 decibels in amplitude, or **intensity**, will damage the auditory system.

12. The **pupil** is the adjustable opening in the eye through which light enters. (p. 138)

13. The **iris** is the colored part of the eye that controls the diameter of the pupil. (p. 138)

    Example: Persons with light-colored eyes have **irises** that are less effective than those of darker-colored eyes in preventing light from entering the eye. As a result, they often find bright light more painful.

14. The **lens** is the structure of the eye behind the pupil that changes shape to focus images on the retina. (p. 138)

15. **Accommodation** is the process by which the lens of the eye changes shape to focus near or distant objects on the retina. (p. 138)

    Memory aid: To **accommodate** is to change in order to adapt to a new experience. The lens of the eye accommodates its shape in order to focus objects at varying distances.

16. The **retina** is the multilayered inner surface of the eye that contains the rods and cones, as well as neurons that form the beginning of the optic nerve. (p. 138)

17. The **rods** and **cones** are visual receptors that transduce light into neural impulses. The rods are concentrated in the periphery of the retina, the cones in the fovea. The rods have poor sensitivity, detect black and white, and function well in dim light. The cones have excellent sensitivity, enable color vision, and function best in daylight or bright light. (p. 139)

    Example: Further evidence of the function of **rods** and **cones** comes from the study of nocturnal animals, which possess only rods, and diurnal animals, which possess only cones.

18. Comprised of the axons of retinal ganglion cells, the **optic nerve** carries neural impulses from the eye to the brain. (p. 139)

    Example: At the optic chiasma, half the **optic nerve** fibers from each eye cross over to the opposite side, so information from the left and right visual fields projects directly to the right and left sides of the brain, respectively.

19. The **blind spot** is the region of the retina where the optic nerve leaves the eye. Because there are no rods or cones in this area, this is a spot where the eye is visually insensitive. (p. 140)

    Example: The fact that we are unaware of our **blind spots** indicates that the brain must perceptually "fill in" the missing visual detail.

20. The **fovea** is the retina's point of central focus. It contains only cones; therefore, images focused on the fovea are the clearest. (p. 140)

21. **Feature detectors**, located in the visual cortex of the brain, are nerve cells that selectively respond to specific visual features, such as movement, shape, or angle. Feature detectors are evidently the basis of visual information processing. (p. 142)

22. **Parallel processing** is information processing in which several aspects of a stimulus, such as light or sound, are processed simultaneously. (p. 142)

23. The **Young-Helmholtz trichromatic (three-color) theory** maintains that the retina contains red-, green-, and blue-sensitive color receptors that in combination can produce the perception of any color. This theory explains the first stage of color processing. (p. 143)

24. The **opponent-process theory** maintains that color vision depends on pairs of opposing retinal processes (red-green, yellow-blue, and white-black). This theory explains the second stage of color processing. (p. 144)

25. **Color constancy** is the perception that familiar objects have consistent color despite changes in illumination that shift the wavelengths they reflect. (p. 145)

26. **Audition** refers to the sense of hearing. (p. 145)

    Memory aid: An **audition** is a trial hearing of an actress, musician, or some other performer.

27. The **pitch** of a sound is determined by its **frequency**, that is, the number of complete wavelengths that can pass a point in a given time. Frequency, in turn, is directly related to wavelength: Longer waves produce lower pitch; shorter waves produce higher pitch. (p. 146)

28. The **middle ear** is the air-filled chamber between the eardrum and cochlea containing the three bones (hammer, anvil, and stirrup) that direct the

eardrum's vibrations into the inner ear. (p. 146)

Example: The "pop" that you feel in your ears when ascending or descending in an airplane occurs when the air pressure in the **middle ear** becomes equalized to the external pressure on your eardrums.

29. The **inner ear** contains the cochlea, the semicircular canals, and the receptors that transduce sound energy into neural impulses. Because it also contains the vestibular sac, the inner ear plays an important role in balance, as well as in audition. (p. 146)

30. The **cochlea** is the coiled, fluid-filled tube of the inner ear where the transduction of sound waves into neural impulses occurs. (p. 146)

31. The **place theory** of hearing states that we hear different pitches because sound waves of various frequencies trigger activity at different places on the cochlea's basilar membrane. (p. 147)

    Memory aid: **Place theory** maintains that the *place* of maximum vibration along the cochlea's membrane is the basis of pitch discrimination.

32. The **frequency theory** of hearing presumes that the rate, or frequency, of nerve impulses in the auditory nerve matches the frequency of a tone. (p. 147)

33. **Conduction deafness** refers to the hearing loss that results from damage to the mechanics of the outer or middle ear, which impairs the conduction of sound waves to the cochlea. (p. 149)

    Example: Because the source of the problem is diminished conduction, a hearing aid, which ampli-

fies the vibrations of sounds, may at least partially correct **conduction deafness**.

34. **Nerve deafness** is hearing loss caused by damage to the auditory receptors of the cochlea or to the auditory nerve. (p. 149)

    Example: Because neural tissue has been damaged, **nerve deafness** cannot be corrected by the use of a hearing aid.

35. The **gate-control theory** maintains that a "gate" in the spinal cord determines whether pain signals are permitted to reach the brain. When the neural activity in large nerve fibers exceeds that in smaller fibers, or when the brain so dictates, the gate is closed. (p. 152)

    Example: The **gate-control theory** gained support with the discovery of endorphins. Production of these morphine-like chemicals may be the brain's mechanism for closing the spinal gate.

36. **Sensory interaction** is the principle that one sense may influence another. (p. 154)

    Example: There is considerable **sensory interaction** between taste and smell. Food tastes bland when you have a cold and cannot savor aromas.

37. **Kinesthesis** is the sense of the position and movement of the parts of the body. (p. 156)

    Example: In performing their intricate exercises, gymnasts rely extensively on **kinesthetic** feedback from sensory receptors in their muscles, tendons, and joints.

38. The sense of body movement, position, and balance is called **equilibrium**. (p. 156)

6 / Perception

Chapter Overview

Chapter 6 explores how we organize and interpret our sensations into meaningful perceptions. The chapter introduces a wide range of terminology, especially in the Perceptual Organization section. Each of the two sections that follow deals with an important issue. The first issue is the role of experience, as opposed to heredity, in perception. Make sure you understand the results of studies of recovery from blindness, early sensory restriction, adaptation to distorted environments, and perceptual set. The second is the possible existence of ESP, or perception without sensation. You should be able to discuss both the claims made for ESP and the criticisms of these claims.

NOTE: Answer guidelines for all Chapter 6 questions begin on page 124.

Guided Study

The text chapter should be studied one section at a time. Before you read, preview each section by skimming it, noting headings and boldface items. Then read the appropriate section objectives from the following outline. Keep these objectives in mind and, as you read the chapter section, search for the information that will enable you to meet each objective. Once you have finished a section, write out answers for its objectives.

Perceptual Illusions (pp. 163–165)

1. Describe the nature-nurture debate on the nature of perception and explain how illusions help us to understand perception.

Perceptual Organization (pp. 165–174)

2. Discuss Gestalt psychology's contribution to our understanding of perception, including the figure-ground relationship and principles of perceptual grouping in form perception.

3. Discuss research on depth perception involving the use of the visual cliff and describe the binocular and monocular cues in depth perception.

4. Describe the perceptual constancies and show how they operate in visual illusions.

Interpretation (pp. 174–181)

5. Discuss research findings on sensory restriction and restored vision.

6. Explain what the use of distorting goggles indicates regarding the adaptability of perception.

7. Discuss the effects of assumptions, expectations, schemas, and contexts on our perceptions.

Is There Perception Without Sensation? (pp. 181–185)

8. State the claims of ESP and explain why most research psychologists remain skeptical.

Chapter Review

When you have finished reading the chapter, work through the material that follows to review it. Complete the sentences and answer the questions. As you proceed, evaluate your performance for each section by consulting the answers on page 125. Do not continue with the next section until you understand each answer. If you need to, go back and review or reread the appropriate section in the textbook before continuing.

1. When we focus on how people sense sights, sounds, smells, and tastes, we are working from the Bottom – up perspective. When we focus on how our knowledge and expectations help transform sensations into meaningful perceptions, we are working from the top – ~~bottom~~ down perspective.

2. The idea that knowledge comes from innate ways of organizing sensory experiences was proposed by the philosopher Kant.

3. On the other side were philosophers who maintained that we learn to perceive the world by experiencing it. One philosopher of this school was Locke, who believed that at birth the mind is blank.

Perceptual Illusions (pp. 163–165)

Explain how the study of illusions helps psychologists understand perception.

4. The tendency of vision to dominate the other senses is referred to as Visual Capture.

Perceptual Organization (pp. 165–174)

5. According to the Gestalt school of psychology, we tend to organize a separate set of sensations into a Whole form. This tendency can be illustrated using a figure called a Necker cube.

6. When we view a scene, we see the central object, or figure, as distinct from surrounding stimuli, or the ground.

Identify the major contributions of Gestalt psychology to our understanding of perception.

7. Proximity, similarity, closure, and continuity are examples of Gestalt rules of _grouping organ._

8. The principle that we organize stimuli into smooth, continuous patterns is called _continuity_. The principle that we fill in gaps to create a complete, whole object is _Closure connectedness_. The grouping of items that are close to each other is the principle of _proximity_; the grouping of items that look alike is the principle of _similarity_. The tendency to perceive uniform or connected items as a single unit is the principle of _connectedness_.

9. The ability to see objects in three dimensions despite their two-dimensional representations on our retinas is called _depth perception_.

10. Gibson and Walk developed the _visual cliff_ to test depth perception in infants.

Summarize the results of Gibson and Walk's studies of depth perception.

For questions 11–22, identify the depth perception cue that is defined.

11. Any cue that requires both eyes: _binocular_.

12. Any cue that requires only one eye: _monocular_.

13. The greater the difference between the images received by the two eyes, the nearer the object: _retinal disparity_.

14. The more our eyes focus inward when we view an object, the nearer the object: _convergance_.

15. If two objects are presumed to be the same size, the one that casts a smaller retinal image is perceived as farther away: _relative size_.

16. An object partially covered by another is seen as farther away: _overlaping_.

17. Objects that appear hazy are seen as farther away: _aerial perspective_.

18. As an object becomes increasingly distant, it appears progressively less distinct: _texture gradient_.

19. Objects lower in the visual field are seen as nearer: _relative height_.

20. As we move, objects at different distances appear to move at different rates: _relative motion_.

21. Parallel lines appear to converge in the distance: _linear perspective_.

22. Dimmer, or shaded, objects seem farther away: _relative brightness_.

23. Our tendency to see objects as unchanging while the stimuli from them change in size, shape, and brightness is called _perceptual consistancy_.

24. Several illusions, including the moon and Müller-Lyer illusions, are explained by the interplay between perceived _size_ and perceived _distance_. When distance cues are removed, these illusions are _diminished_ (diminished/strengthened).

Explain how the size-distance relationship accounts for the moon illusion.

25. People who have lived their lives in uncarpentered rural environments are _less_ (more/less) susceptible to the Müller-Lyer illusion.

26. The brain computes an object's brightness _relative_ (relative to/independent of) surrounding objects.

Interpretation (pp. 174–181)

27. Studies of cases in which vision has been restored to a person who was blind from birth

show that, upon *seeing* tactilely familiar objects for the first time, the person _Cannot_ (can/cannot) recognize them.

28. Studies of sensory restriction demonstrate that visual experiences during _infancy_ are crucial for perceptual development. Such experiences suggest that there is a _Critical Period._ for normal perceptual development.

Summarize the results of Blakemore and Cooper's studies of visual deprivation in kittens.

29. Humans given glasses that shift or invert the visual field _will_ (will/will not) adapt to the distorted perception. This is called _perceptual adaptation._

30. A mental predisposition that influences perception is called a _perceptual set_.

31. Through learning children acquire perceptual _schemas_, as reflected in their drawings at different ages.

32. How a stimulus is perceived depends on our perceptual schemas and the _context_ in which it is experienced, which may be colored by _stereotype_ about gender and culture.

33. (Close-Up) Psychologists who study the importance of considering perceptual principles in the design of machines, appliances, and work settings are called _human factors psychologists_.

Is There Perception Without Sensation? (pp. 181–185)

34. Perception outside the range of normal sensation is called _____ _____.

35. Psychologists who study ESP are called _____.

36. The form of ESP in which people claim to be capable of reading others' minds is called _____. A person who "senses" that a friend is in danger might claim to have the ESP ability of _____. An ability to "see" into the future is called _____. A person who claims to be able to levitate and move objects is claiming the power of _____.

37. Critics point out that a major difficulty for parapsychology is that ESP phenomena are not consistently _____.

38. When the clairvoyance experiment conducted by Layton and Turnbull was repeated, the results of both experiments were nearly identical to what one would expect on the basis of _____.

Explain why scientists are skeptical about ESP.

FOCUS ON PSYCHOLOGY:
Psychological Factors in Perception

As the Gestalt psychologists were fond of saying, "The whole is greater than the sum of its parts." Applying this statement to perception we can say that there is much more to perception than the stimulus information to which our senses are exposed. Perception is highly individualistic and influenced by experience, attitudes, and many other psychological factors.

One such factor, according to psychologist Paul Chance, is motivation. Several studies have shown that people are more likely to perceive ambiguous drawings as food when they are hungry than when they have recently eaten. This comes as no surprise to dieters, who "see" calorie-laden foods around every corner and in nearly every object.

Chance offers a convincing demonstration of how learnnig also influences what we see. In reading the previous sentence you probably were a victim of the "proofreader's illusion" and did not notice the misspelled word. Your retinas cannot be blamed for your insensitivity to this typographical error; rather, your knowledge of grammar caused you to see the word spelled correctly.

Our beliefs and biases also affect our perception. In another famous experiment, researchers showed pictures to groups of police officers, police cadets, and college students. One-half of each picture depicted an act of violence, such as a person holding a smoldering gun standing over an apparent victim lying on the ground. The other half was a nonviolent scene, such as a landscape or a person from a college yearbook. After each picture was flashed on a screen for a very brief period, the subjects were asked to describe what they saw. Although college students were about equally likely to report seeing the violent and nonviolent scenes, the police cadets—and even more so, the veteran police officers—were much more likely to report seeing the violent scenes.

Chance also offers a chilling, real-life example of the apparent operation of psychological factors in perception. On July 3, 1988, a United States naval warship shot down a civilian aircraft, resulting in the deaths of 290 people. Although the radar screen, which later functioned perfectly, showed that the aircraft was climbing as if it were taking off, the sailors apparently "saw" the plane descending, as if it were attacking their ship. As Chance notes, "What we see . . . also depends upon what we know, or think we know, about people. . . . Seeing is believing."

Source: Chance, Paul. (1989, January–February). Seeing is believing. *Psychology Today*, p. 26.

Progress Test 1

Circle your answers to the following questions and check them with the answers on page 125. If your answer is incorrect, read the explanation for why it is incorrect and then consult the appropriate pages of the text (in parentheses following the correct answer).

1. Which philosopher maintained that knowledge comes from innate ways of organizing our sensory experiences?
   a. Locke   c. Gibson
   b. Kant   d. Walk

2. The historical movement associated with the statement "The whole is different from the sum of its parts" is:
   a. parapsychology.
   b. behavioral psychology.
   c. functional psychology.
   d. Gestalt psychology.

3. Figures tend to be perceived as whole, complete objects, even if spaces or gaps exist in the representation, thus demonstrating the principle of:
   a. closure.   c. continuity.
   b. similarity.   d. proximity.

4. The figure-ground relationship demonstrates that:
   a. perception is largely innate.
   b. perception is simply a point-for-point representation of sensation.
   c. the same stimulus can trigger more than one perception.
   d. different people see different things when viewing a scene.

5. When we stare at an object, each of our eyes receives a slightly different image, providing a depth cue known as:
   a. convergence.   c. relative motion.
   b. linear perspective. d. retinal disparity.

6. As we move, viewed objects cast changing shapes on our retinas, although we do not perceive the objects as changing. This is part of the phenomenon of:
   a. perceptual constancy. c. linear perspective.
   b. relative motion.   d. continuity.

7. Which of the following illustrates the principle of visual capture?
   a. We tend to form first impressions of other people on the basis of appearance.
   b. Because visual processing is automatic, we can pay attention to a visual image and any other sensation at the same time.
   c. We cannot simultaneously attend to a visual image and another sensation.
   d. When there is a conflict between visual information and that from another sense, vision tends to dominate.

8. A person claiming to be able to read another's mind is claiming to have the ESP ability of:
   a. psychokinesis.   c. clairvoyance.
   b. precognition.   d. telepathy.

9. Which of the following was *not* mentioned in the text as a criticism of parapsychology?
   a. ESP effects have not been consistently reproducible.
   b. Parapsychology has suffered from a number of frauds and hoaxes.
   c. The tendency of people to recall only events that confirm their expectations accounts for much of the belief in ESP.
   d. There have been no laboratory-controlled studies of ESP.

10. Which of the following depth cues creates the impression of a visual cliff?

a. overlap   c. linear perspective
b. relative height   d. texture gradient

11. Kittens reared seeing only horizontal lines:
   a. later had difficulty perceiving both horizontal and vertical lines.
   b. later had difficulty perceiving vertical lines, but eventually regained normal sensitivity.
   c. later had difficulty perceiving vertical lines, and never regained normal sensitivity.
   d. showed no impairment in perception, indicating that neural feature detectors develop even in the absence of normal sensory experiences.

12. Congenitally blind adults who have had their vision restored:
   a. are almost immediately able to recognize familiar objects.
   b. typically fail to recognize familiar objects.
   c. are unable to follow moving objects with their eyes.
   d. have excellent eye-hand coordination.

13. The _____ perspective emphasizes how the physical characteristics of stimuli influence their interpretation.
   a. top-down
   b. bottom-up
   c. parapsychological
   d. human factors

14. Which of the following is *not* a monocular depth cue?
   a. texture gradient   c. retinal disparity
   b. relative height   d. overlap

15. The moon illusion occurs in part because distance cues at the horizon make the moon seem:
   a. farther away and therefore larger.
   b. closer and therefore larger.
   c. farther away and therefore smaller.
   d. closer and therefore smaller.

16. Figure is to ground as _____ is to _____.
   a. night; day
   b. top; bottom
   c. cloud; sky
   d. sensation; perception

17. The study of perception is primarily concerned with how we:
   a. detect sights, sounds, and other stimuli.
   b. sense environmental stimuli.
   c. develop sensitivity to illusions.
   d. interpret sensory stimuli.

18. Which of the following influences a person's perception?
   a. biological maturation
   b. the context in which stimuli are perceived

c. expectations
d. all of the above

19. Jack claims that he often has dreams that predict future events. He claims to have the power of:
   a. telepathy.   c. precognition.
   b. clairvoyance.   d. psychokinesis.

20. In their experiment on _____, Layton and Turnbull asked students to guess the contents of a sealed envelope.
   a. telepathy   c. precognition
   b. clairvoyance   d. psychokinesis

Progress Test 2

Progress Test 2 should be completed during a final chapter review. Answer the following questions after you thoroughly understand the correct answers for the Chapter Review and Progress Test 1.

1. According to the philosopher _____, we learn to perceive the world.
   a. Locke   c. Gibson
   b. Kant   d. Walk

2. The tendency to organize stimuli into smooth, uninterrupted patterns is called:
   a. closure.   c. similarity.
   b. continuity.   d. proximity.

3. Which of the following is a monocular depth cue?
   a. relative size
   b. convergence
   c. retinal disparity
   d. All of the above are monocular depth cues.

4. Which of the following statements is consistent with the Gestalt theory of perception?
   a. Perception develops largely through learning.
   b. Perception is the product of heredity.
   c. The mind organizes sensations into meaningful perceptions.
   d. Perception results directly from sensation.

5. Experiments with distorted visual environments demonstrate that:
   a. adaptation rarely takes place.
   b. animals adapt readily, but humans do not.
   c. humans adapt readily, while lower animals typically do not.
   d. adaptation is possible during a critical period in infancy but not thereafter.

6. The phenomenon that refers to the ways in which an individual's expectations influence perception is called:
   a. perceptual set.   c. convergence.
   b. retinal disparity.   d. visual capture.

7. (Close-Up) Psychologists who study the importance of considering perceptual phenomena in the design of machines and work settings are called:
   a. parapsychologists.
   b. human factors psychologists.
   c. psychokineticists.
   d. Gestalt psychologists.

8. The tendency to perceive hazy objects as being at a distance is known as _____.
   This is a _____ depth cue.
   a. linear perspective; binocular
   b. linear perspective; monocular
   c. aerial perspective; binocular
   d. aerial perspective; monocular

9. The phenomenon of size constancy is based upon the close connection between an object's perceived _____ and its perceived _____.
   a. size; shape   c. size; brightness
   b. size; distance   d. shape; distance

10. Which of the following statements best describes the effects of sensory restriction?
    a. It produces functional blindness when experienced for any length of time at any age.
    b. It has greater effects on humans than on animals.
    c. It has more damaging effects when experienced during infancy.
    d. It has greater effects on adults than on children.

11. Psychologists who study ESP are called:
    a. clairvoyants.   c. parapsychologists.
    b. telepaths.   d. levitators.

12. The depth cue that occurs when we watch stable objects at different distances as we are moving is:
    a. convergence.   c. aerial perspective.
    b. overlap.   d. relative motion.

13. Which of the following statements concerning ESP is true?
    a. Most ESP researchers are quacks.
    b. There have been a large number of reliable demonstrations of ESP.
    c. Most research psychologists are skeptical of the claims of defenders of ESP.
    d. There have been reliable laboratory demonstrations of ESP, but the results are no different from those that would occur by chance.

14. Each time you see your car, it projects a different image on the retinas of your eyes, yet you do not perceive it as changing. This is because of:
    a. perceptual set.
    b. retinal disparity.
    c. perceptual constancy.
    d. convergence.

15. The term *gestalt* means:
    a. grouping.   c. perception.
    b. sensation.   d. whole.

16. People asked to judge the distances of white disks under either clear or foggy conditions:
    a. estimated the disks to be more distant when viewed under clear conditions.
    b. estimated the disks to be nearer when viewed under clear conditions.
    c. took atmospheric conditions into consideration and judged the disks to be equally distant under the two viewing conditions.
    d. were much less accurate under foggy conditions.

17. Studies of the visual cliff have provided evidence that much of depth perception is:
    a. innate.
    b. learned.
    c. innate in lower animals but learned in humans.
    d. innate in humans but learned in lower animals.

18. All of the following are laws of perceptual organization *except*:
    a. proximity.   c. continuity.
    b. closure.   d. simplicity.

19. You probably perceive the diagram above as three separate objects due to the principle of:
    a. proximity.   c. closure.
    b. continuity.   d. connectedness.

20. The _____ perspective emphasizes how our knowledge and expectations influence perception.
    a. top-down   c. parapsychological
    b. bottom-up   d. human factors

Challenge Test

Answer these questions the day before an exam as a final check on your understanding of the chapter's terms and concepts.

Multiple-Choice Questions

1. Although carpenter Smith perceived a briefly viewed object as a screwdriver, police officer Wesson perceived the same object as a knife. This illustrates that perception is guided by:
   a. linear perspective.
   b. shape constancy.
   c. retinal disparity.
   d. perceptual set.

2. Because the flowers in the foreground had a

coarse, grainy appearance, the photographer decided that the picture was taken too near the subject. This conclusion was based on which depth cue?

a. relative size
b. overlap
c. retinal disparity
d. texture gradient

3. The fact that a white object under dim illumination appears lighter than a gray object under bright illumination is called:

a. relative luminance.
b. perceptual adaptation.
c. color contrast.
d. brightness constancy.

4. When two familiar objects of equal size cast unequal retinal images, the object that casts the smaller retinal image will be perceived as being:

a. closer than the other object.
b. more distant than the other object.
c. larger than the other object.
d. smaller than the other object.

5. If you slowly bring your finger toward your face until it eventually touches your nose, eye-muscle cues called _____ convey depth information to your brain.

a. retinal disparity   c. continuity
b. overlap   **d. convergence**

6. Jamal has been blind in one eye since birth. Nevertheless, he is able to perceive depth under most conditions by relying on:

a. relative size.
b. overlap.
c. texture gradient.
d. all of the above.

7. As her friend Milo walks toward her, Noriko perceives his size as remaining constant because his perceived distance _____ at the same time that her retinal image of him _____.

a. increases; decreases
b. increases; increases
c. decreases; decreases
d. decreases; increases

8. In the *absence* of perceptual constancy:

a. objects would appear to change size as their distance from us changed.
b. depth perception would be based exclusively on monocular cues.
c. depth perception would be based exclusively on binocular cues.
d. depth perception would be impossible.

9. The illusion that the St. Louis Gateway arch appears taller than it is wide (even though its height and width are equal) is based on our sensitivity to which monocular depth cue?

a. relative size   **c. relative height**
b. overlap   d. retinal disparity

10. How do we perceive a pole that partially covers a bush?

a. as farther away
b. as nearer
c. as larger
d. There is not enough information to determine the object's size or distance.

11. An artist paints a tree orchard so that the parallel rows of trees converge at the top of the canvas. Which cue has the artist used to convey distance?

a. overlap   **c. linear perspective**
b. aerial perspective   d. texture gradient

12. Objects higher in our field of vision are perceived as _____ due to the principle of _____.

a. nearer; relative height
b. nearer; linear perspective
c. farther away; relative height
d. farther away; linear perspective

13. According to the principle of relative brightness, if one of two identical objects reflects more light to your eyes it will be perceived as:

a. larger.   c. farther away.
b. smaller.   **d. nearer.**

14. Your friend tosses you a frisbee. You know that it is getting closer instead of larger because of:

a. shape constancy.   **c. size constancy.**
b. relative motion.   d. all of the above.

15. Which explanation of the Müller-Lyer illusion is offered in the textbook?

a. The corners in our carpentered world teach us to interpret outward- or inward- pointing arrowheads at the end of a line as a cue to the line's distance from us and so to its length.
b. The drawing's violation of linear perspective makes one line seem longer.
c. Top-down processing of the illusion is prevented because of the ambiguity of the stimuli.
d. All of the above were offered as explanations.

16. When the traffic light changed from red to green, the drivers on both sides of Leon's vehicle pulled quickly forward, giving Leon the disorienting feeling that his car was rolling backwards. Which principle explains Leon's misperception?

a. relative motion   **c. visual capture**
b. continuity   d. proximity

17. Regina claims that she can bend spoons, levitate furniture, and perform many other "mind over matter" feats. Regina apparently believes she has the powers of:
    a. telepathy.   c. precognition.
    b. clairvoyance.   d. psychokinesis.

18. The predictions of leading psychics:
    a. often are ambiguous prophecies later interpreted to match actual events.
    b. are no more accurate than guesses made by others.
    c. are nearly always inaccurate.
    d. are all of the above.

19. Studying the road map before her trip, Colleen had no trouble following the route of the highway she planned to travel. Colleen's ability illustrates the principle of:
    a. closure.   c. continuity.
    b. similarity.   d. proximity.

20. The insensitivity of many rural Africans to the Müller-Lyer illusion demonstrates that perception:
    a. is largely a "bottom-up" phenomenon.
    b. is unpredictable.
    c. is influenced by cultural experience.
    d. is characterized by all of the above.

Essay Question

In many movies from the 1930s, dancers performed seemingly meaningless movements which, when viewed from above, were transformed into intricate patterns and designs. Similarly, the formations of marching bands often create pictures and spell words. Identify and describe at least four Gestalt principles of grouping that explain the audience's perception of the images created by these types of formations. (Use the space below to list the points you want to make, and organize them. Then write the essay on a separate piece of paper.)

Key Terms

Using your own words, write a brief definition or explanation of each of the following terms.

1. visual capture

2. gestalt

3. figure-ground relationship

4. grouping

5. proximity

6. similarity

7. continuity

8. closure

9. connectedness

10. depth perception

11. visual cliff

12. binocular cue

13. monocular cue

14. retinal disparity

15. convergence

16. relative size

17. overlap

18. aerial perspective

19. texture gradient

20. relative height

21. relative motion

22. linear perspective

23. relative brightness

24. perceptual constancy

25. perceptual adaptation

26. perceptual set

27. extrasensory perception (ESP)

28. parapsychology

ANSWERS

GUIDED STUDY

The following guidelines provide the main points that your answers should have touched upon.

1. In the nature-nurture debate, philosophers argued about the origin of perceptual processes. On one side, the German philosopher Immanuel Kant maintained that knowledge comes from our innate ways of organizing sensory experiences. On the other side, the British philosopher John Locke argued that we learn how to perceive the world through our experiences of it.

   Understanding illusions requires an understanding of how we transform sensations into meaningful perceptions. Thus, for example, psychologists have learned a great deal about the interplay of size and distance from the Müller-Lyer and moon illusions, about the principle of relative height from the horizontal-vertical illusion, and about principles of grouping and depth perception from the study of other illusions.

2. The Gestalt psychologists demonstrated that perception involves the organization of sensations into meaningful whole forms, or Gestalts, that may be different from the sum of their individual parts and regrouped into more than one perception. They also showed that to recognize an object, we must first perceive it as a figure distinct from its surrounding stimuli, or ground. The Gestalt psychologists identified several principles by which sensations are organized into meaningful perceptions, including proximity, similarity, continuity, closure, and connectedness.

3. The visual cliff is a miniature cliff with an apparent drop-off on one side of a table. Gibson and Walk found that infants as young as 6 months of age refused to crawl out on the glass, despite their mother's coaxing. Newborn animals with virtually no visual experience respond similarly, thus indicating that the ability to perceive depth is innate.

   The binocular (two-eye) cues to depth include retinal disparity and convergence and the monocular (one-eye) cues to depth include relative size, overlap, aerial perspective, texture gradient, relative height, relative motion, linear perspective, and relative brightness.

4. Thanks to perceptual constancy we perceive familiar objects as having a constant form (shape constancy), brightness (brightness constancy), and size (size constancy) even when our retinal images of them change.

   There is a close interplay between an object's perceived size and its distance. As the retinal image of a familiar object decreases, we perceive its distance as increasing rather than that its size has changed. This size-distance relationship partially explains the "moon illusion": cues to objects' distances at the horizon make the moon behind them seem farther away, and seemingly larger, than when high in the sky. Similarly, one explanation of the Müller-Lyer illusion is that our experience with corners in our rectangularly carpentered world leads us to interpret a line segment ending in outward-pointing arrowheads as closer to us and therefore shorter than a line segment that ends in inward-pointing arrowheads.

5. In both humans and animals, infancy is a critical period during which normal visual stimulation must be experienced. Adults blinded with cataracts from birth, who later have their vision restored, are able to perceive figure, ground, and colors but are severely limited in their ability to distinguish shapes. Kittens and monkeys who have had their eyes surgically closed since infancy have similar visual impairments when their eyes are later opened. Kittens raised in a restricted visual environment that allowed them to see only horizontal lines later had difficulty perceiving vertical lines. Research also shows that early visual experience is critical to the normal development of the feature detector cells of the brain.

6. Studies in which people and animals are given goggles that shift the world to the left, right, or even upside down demonstrate that vision is remarkably adaptable. After a relatively brief period of adjustment, most subjects are able to function normally in the distorted visual environment. When the goggles are first removed, subjects experience a brief perceptual aftereffect, as their perceptual systems continue to compensate for the shifted visual input.

7. Our personal experiences, assumptions, and expectations may give us a perceptual set, or mental predisposition, that influences what we perceive. Perceptual sets, which are based on the concepts, or schemas, that we form through our experiences, help us organize and interpret unfamiliar or ambiguous information.

   The immediate context of a stimulus also influences how it is perceived. For example, a person or object is more quickly recognized in an expected context than in a novel one. The effects of context and perceptual sets show how our experiences help us to construct meaningful perceptions from our sensory experiences.

8. Extrasensory perception refers to the controversial claim that perception can occur outside sensory input. Telepathy is the claimed ability of mind-to-mind communication between two people. Psy-

chokinesis refers to the claimed ability to perform acts of "mind over matter." Precognition refers to the claimed ability to perceive future events. Clairvoyance refers to the claimed ability to perceive remote events.

Despite the efforts of parapsychologists to document ESP, most research psychologists argue that many so-called psychic demonstrations are nothing more than deceptive illusions that any magician could perform, and that no one has ever discovered a reproducible ESP phenomenon.

CHAPTER REVIEW

1. bottom-up; top-down
2. Kant
3. Locke

Perceptual illusions can provide valuable clues to the ordinary mechanisms of perception. Illusions mislead us by playing on the ways we organize and interpret our sensations. Understanding illusions requires deeper understanding of sensory and perceptual processes.

4. visual capture
5. Gestalt; whole; Necker
6. figure; ground

The Gestalt psychologists described some key principles of perceptual organization and, in so doing, demonstrated that perception is far more than a simple, sensory process. The reversible figure-ground relationship, for example, demonstrates that a single stimulus can trigger more than one perception. As Gestalt psychologists showed, we continually filter sensory information and construct our perceptions in ways that make sense to us.

7. grouping or perceptual organization
8. continuity; closure; proximity; similarity; connectedness
9. depth perception
10. visual cliff

Research on the visual cliff suggests that in many species the ability to perceive depth is present at, or very shortly after, birth.

11. binocular
12. monocular
13. retinal disparity
14. convergence
15. relative size
16. overlap
17. aerial perspective
18. texture gradient
19. relative height

20. relative motion
21. linear perspective
22. relative brightness
23. perceptual constancy
24. size; distance; diminished

A partial reason for the illusion that the moon at the horizon appears up to 50 percent larger than the moon directly overhead is that cues to the distance of objects at the horizon make the moon, behind them, seem farther away and therefore larger. When we see the moon overhead in the sky, these misleading cues are lacking.

25. less
26. relative to
27. cannot
28. infancy; critical period

After raising kittens in darkness, except 5 hours each day during which the kittens were placed in a horizontally or vertically striped environment, Blakemore and Cooper found that perceptual impairment resulted. In particular, the kittens had difficulty perceiving the kind of line—horizontal or vertical—to which they had not been exposed. Moreover, in these kittens, feature-detecting cells were found to respond mostly to one or the other kind of line.

29. will; perceptual adaptation
30. perceptual set
31. schemas
32. context; stereotypes
33. human factors psychologists
34. extrasensory perception
35. parapsychologists
36. telepathy; clairvoyance; precognition; psychokinesis
37. reproducible
38. chance

Skeptics of ESP point out that gullible audiences are easily duped into believing that stage tricks and illusions are examples of psychic powers. Scientists are especially skeptical of the existence of ESP because of the lack of a reliable, reproducible ESP effect.

PROGRESS TEST 1

1. **b.** is the answer. (p. 163)

    a. Locke argued that knowledge is not innate but comes through learning.

    c. & d. Gibson and Walk studied depth perception using the visual cliff; they made no claims about the source of knowledge.

2. **d.** is the answer. Gestalt psychology, which developed in Germany at the turn of the century, was interested in how clusters of sensations are organized into "whole" perceptions. (p. 165)

   a. Parapsychology is the study of ESP and other paranormal phenomena.

   b. & c. Behavioral and functional psychology were schools that developed later in the United States.

3. **a.** is the answer. (p. 166)

   b. Similarity refers to the tendency to group similar items.

   c. Continuity refers to the tendency to group stimuli into smooth, continuous patterns.

   d. Proximity refers to the tendency to group items that are close to each other.

4. **c.** is the answer. Although we always differentiate a stimulus into figure and ground, those elements of the stimulus we perceive as figure and those as ground may change. In this way, the same stimulus can trigger more than one perception. (p. 166)

   a. The figure-ground relationship has no bearing on the issue of whether perception is innate.

   b. Perception cannot be simply a point-for-point representation of sensation, since in figure-ground relationships a single stimulus can trigger more than one perception.

   d. Figure-ground relationships demonstrate the existence of general, rather than individual, principles of perceptual organization. Significantly, even the same person can see different figure-ground relationships when viewing a scene.

5. **d.** is the answer. The greater the retinal disparity, or difference between the images, the less the distance. (p. 168)

   a. Convergence is the extent to which the eyes move inward when looking at an object.

   b. Linear perspective is the monocular distance cue in which parallel lines appear to converge in the distance.

   c. Relative motion is the monocular distance cue in which objects at different distances change their relative positions in our visual image, with those closest moving most.

6. **a.** is the answer. Perception of constant shape, like perception of constant size, is part of the phenomenon of perceptual constancy. (p. 171)

   b. Relative motion is a monocular distance cue in which objects at different distances appear to move at different rates.

   c. Linear perspective is a monocular distance cue in which lines we know to be parallel converge in the distance, thus indicating depth.

   d. Continuity is the perceptual tendency to group items into continuous patterns.

7. **d.** is the answer. (p. 165)

   a., b., & c. Visual capture has nothing to do with forming impressions of people or whether we can attend to more than one stimulus at a time.

8. **d.** is the answer. (p. 181)

   a. Psychokinesis refers to the claimed ability to perform acts of "mind over matter."

   b. Precognition refers to the claimed ability to perceive future events.

   c. Clairvoyance refers to the claimed ability to perceive remote events.

9. **d.** is the answer. As discussed in the text, parapsychologists have conducted numerous experiments with both "psychic" and "normal" subjects. (pp. 182–184)

   a., b., & c. These are all valid criticisms of parapsychology mentioned in the text.

10. **d.** is the answer. There is, of course, no actual drop-off. The texture gradient of the checkerboard pattern beneath the glass table imparts the impression of depth. The other cues mentioned would not be relevant to the situation in this experiment. (pp. 167, 169)

11. **c.** is the answer. (pp. 175–176)

    a. & b. The kittens had difficulty only with lines they had never experienced, and never regained normal sensitivity.

    d. Both perceptual and feature-detector impairment resulted from visual deprivation.

12. **b.** is the answer. Because they have not had early visual experiences, these adults typically have great difficulty learning to perceive objects. (pp. 174–175)

    a. Such patients typically could not visually recognize objects with which they were familiar by touch, and in some cases this inability persisted.

    c. Being able to perceive figure-ground relationships, patients *are* able to follow moving objects with their eyes.

    d. This answer is incorrect because eye-hand coordination is an acquired skill and requires much practice.

13. **b.** is the answer. (p. 163)

    a. The top-down perspective emphasizes how our knowledge and expectations influence perception.

    c. Parapsychology is the study of perception outside normal sensory input.

    d. Human factors psychology is concerned with how best to design machines and work settings to take into account human perception.

14. **c.** is the answer. Retinal disparity is a *binocular* cue; all the other cues mentioned are monocular. (pp. 168–169)

15. **a.** is the answer. The moon appears larger at the horizon than overhead in the sky because objects at the horizon provide distance cues that make the moon seem farther away and therefore larger. In the open sky, of course, there are no such cues. (pp. 171–172)

16. **c.** is the answer. We see a cloud as a figure against the background of sky. (p. 166)

    a., b., & d. The figure-ground relationship refers to the organization of the visual field into objects (figures) that stand out from their surroundings (ground).

17. **d.** is the answer. (p. 163)

    a. & b. The study of sensation is concerned with these processes.

    c. Although studying illusions has helped psychologists understand ordinary perceptual mechanisms, it is not the primary focus of the field of perception.

18. **d.** is the answer. (p. 163)

19. **c.** is the answer. (pp. 181–182)

    a. This answer would be correct had Jack claimed to be able to read someone else's mind.

    b. This answer would be correct had Jack claimed to be able to sense remote events, such as a friend in distress.

    d. This answer would be correct had Jack claimed to be able to levitate objects or bend spoons without applying any physical force.

20. **b.** is the answer. As the contents of the envelope were not presented to the senses, the experiment involved clairvoyance. (pp. 181–182, 184)

    a. The experiment involved written numerals, not thoughts.

    c. The experiment did not require students to "see the future."

    d. The experiment had nothing to do with the mental manipulation of matter.

PROGRESS TEST 2

1. **a.** is the answer. (p. 163)

    c. & d. Gibson and Walk make no claims about the origins of perception.

    b. Kant claimed that knowledge is innate.

2. **b.** is the answer. (p. 166)

    a. Closure refers to the tendency to perceptually fill in gaps in recognizable objects in the visual field.

    c. Similarity refers to the tendency to group items that are similar.

    d. Proximity refers to the tendency to group items that are near one another.

3. **a.** is the answer. (p. 168)

    b. & c. Convergence and retinal disparity are both binocular cues that depend on information from both eyes.

4. **c.** is the answer. (p. 165)

    a. & b. The Gestalt psychologists did not deal with the origins of perception; they were more concerned with its form.

    d. In fact, they argued just the opposite: Perception is more than mere sensory experience.

5. **c.** is the answer. Humans and certain animals, such as monkeys, are able to adjust to upside-down worlds and other visual distortions, figuring out the relationship between the perceived and the actual reality; lower animals, such as chickens and fish, are typically unable to adapt. (pp. 176–177)

    a. Humans and certain animals are able to adapt quite well to distorted visual environments (and then to readapt).

    b. This answer is incorrect because humans are the most adaptable of creatures.

    d. Humans are able to adapt at any age to distorted visual environments.

6. **a.** is the answer. (p. 177)

    b. Retinal disparity is a binocular depth cue based on the fact that each eye receives a slightly different view of the world.

    c. Convergence is a binocular depth cue based on the fact that the eyes swing inward to focus on near objects.

    d. Visual capture refers to the tendency of vision to dominate the other senses.

7. **b.** is the answer. (p. 180)

    a. Parapsychologists study claims of ESP.

    c. Psychokineticists are people who claim ESP power of "mind over matter."

    d. Gestalt psychologists emphasize the organization of sensations into meaningful perceptions.

8. **d.** is the answer. (p. 168)

    a. & b. Linear perspective, which is a monocular cue, refers to the tendency of parallel lines to converge in the distance.

    c. Aerial perspective requires only one eye and is therefore a monocular cue.

9. **b.** is the answer. (p. 171)

10. **c.** is the answer. There appears to be a critical period for perceptual development, in that sensory restriction has severe, even permanently, disrup-

tive effects when it occurs in infancy but not when it occurs later in life. (p. 175)

a. & d. Sensory restriction does not have the same effects at all ages, and it is more damaging to children than to adults. This is because there is a critical period for perceptual development; whether functional blindness will result depends in part on the nature of the sensory restriction.

b. Research studies have not indicated that sensory restriction is more damaging to humans than to animals.

11. **c.** is the answer. (p. 181)

a., b., & d. These are different kinds of psychics, who claim to exhibit the phenomena studied by parapsychologists.

12. **d.** is the answer. When we move, stable objects we see also appear to move, and the distance and speed of the apparent motion cue us to the objects' relative distances. (p. 169)

a., b., & c. These depth cues are unrelated to movement and thus work even when we are stationary.

13. **c.** is the answer. (pp. 183–184)

a. Many ESP researchers are sincere, reputable researchers.

b. & d. There have been no reliable demonstrations of ESP.

14. **c.** is the answer. Because of perceptual constancy, we see the car's shape and size as always the same. (p. 171)

a. Perceptual set is a mental predisposition to perceive one thing and not another.

b. Retinal disparity refers to the fact that our right and left eyes each receive slightly different images.

d. Convergence is a form of muscular feedback in which the eyes swing in, or out, as we view objects at different distances.

15. **d.** is the answer. Gestalt means a "form" or "organized whole." (p. 165)

16. **b.** is the answer. We perceive hazy objects as farther away than sharp, clear objects: This cue to depth is aerial perspective. (p. 164)

a. & c. The disks were estimated to be *nearer* when viewed under clear conditions.

d. As shown by the chart on p. 164, foggy conditions increase the perceived distance but by no means necessarily reduce accuracy.

17. **a.** is the answer. Most infants refused to crawl out over the "cliff" even when coaxed, suggesting that much of depth perception is innate. Studies with the young of "lower" animals show the same thing. (p. 167)

18. **d.** is the answer. (p. 166)

19. **d.** is the answer. (p. 166)

a. Proximity is the tendency to group objects near to one another. The diagram is perceived as three distinct units, even though the points are evenly spaced.

b. Continuity is the tendency to group stimuli into smooth, uninterrupted patterns. There is no such continuity in the diagram.

c. Closure is the perceptual tendency to fill in gaps in a form. In the diagram, three disconnected units are perceived rather than a single whole.

20. **a.** is the answer. (p. 163)

b. The bottom-up perspective focuses on the physical characteristics of stimuli rather than their perceptual interpretation.

c. Parapsychology is the study of perception outside normal sensory input.

d. Human factors psychology is concerned with how best to design machines and work settings to take into account human perception.

CHALLENGE TEST

Multiple-Choice Questions

1. **d.** is the answer. The two people interpreted a briefly perceived object in terms of their perceptual sets, or mental predispositions, in this case conditioned by their work experiences. (p. 177)

a. Since both Smith and Wesson had the same sensory experience of the object, linear perspective cues would not cause their differing perceptions.

b. Shape constancy refers to the perception that objects remain constant in shape even when our retinal images of them change.

c. Retinal disparity refers to the fact that each of a person's eyes views the world from a slightly different angle; it has nothing to do with individual differences in perception.

2. **d.** is the answer. When the texture of an object is coarse and grainy, we perceive the object as nearer than when its texture is finer and less distinct. (p. 169)

a. & b. Relative size and overlap are used to judge the relative distances of two or more objects; because only one photograph was involved, these cues are irrelevant.

c. Retinal disparity refers to the different images our eyes receive; whether the photograph's texture was coarse or fine, the retinal disparity would be the same.

3. **d.** is the answer. Although the amount of light reflected from a white object is less in dim light

than in bright light—and may be less than the amount of light reflected from a brightly lit gray object—the brightness of the white object is perceived as remaining constant. Because a white object reflects a higher percentage of the light falling on it than does a gray object, and the brightness of objects is perceived as constant despite variations in illumination, white is perceived as brighter than gray even under dim illumination. (p. 174)

a. Relative luminance refers to the relative intensity of light falling on surfaces that are in close proximity. Brightness constancy is perceived despite variations in illumination.

b. Perceptual adaptation refers to the ability to adjust to an artificially modified perceptual environment, such as an inverted visual field.

c. Color contrast has not been discussed in this text.

4. b. is the answer. The phenomenon described is the basis for the monocular cue of relative size. (p. 168)

a. The object casting the *larger* retinal image would be perceived as closer.

c. & d. Because of size constancy, familiar objects remain constant in perceived size, despite changes in their retinal image size.

5. d. is the answer. As an object comes closer in our field of vision, the eyes swing inward (converge) and provide muscular cues as to the object's distance. (p. 168)

a. Retinal disparity refers to the slightly different images of an object received by the two eyes due to their different angles of viewing.

b. Overlap is a monocular cue to distance in which an object that partially blocks another is seen as closer.

c. Continuity is a Gestalt grouping principle, rather than a distance cue.

6. d. is the answer. Relative size, overlap, and texture gradient are all *monocular* depth cues. (pp. 168–169)

7. d. is the answer. (p. 171)

8. a. is the answer. Because we perceive the size of a familiar object as constant even as its retinal image grows smaller, we perceive the object as being farther away. (p. 171)

b. & c. Perceptual constancy is a cognitive, rather than sensory, phenomenon. Therefore, the absence of perceptual constancy would not alter a person's sensitivity to monocular or binocular cues.

d. Although the absence of perceptual constancy would impair depth perception based on the size-distance relationship, other cues to depth, such as texture gradient and overlap, could still be used.

9. c. is the answer. We perceive objects higher in our field of vision as farther away. Thus, the brain perceives a vertical line the same length as a horizontal line to be more distant and mentally adjusts its apparent length to make it seem longer. (p. 169)

a. & b. These monocular cues are irrelevant in this particular illusion.

d. Retinal disparity is a *binocular* cue to depth.

10. b. is the answer. This is an example of the principle of overlap in depth perception. (p. 168)

a. The partially *obscured* object is perceived as farther away.

c. The perceived size of an object is not altered when that object overlaps another.

11. c. is the answer. (p. 170)

a. Overlap is a monocular depth cue in which an object that partially covers another is perceived as closer.

b. Had the artist painted the trees so that the images of some were sharp and others hazy, the artist would have been conveying distance through aerial perspective.

d. Had the artist painted the trees so that there was a gradual change from a coarse, distinct to a fine, indistinct texture a texture gradient would have been used to convey depth.

12. c. is the answer. (p. 169)

b. & d. Linear perspective is the apparent convergence of parallel lines as a cue to distance.

13. d. is the answer. Nearby objects reflect more light to eyes. Thus, given two identical objects, the brighter one seems nearer. (p. 170)

a. & b. Because of the principle of size constancy, an object's perceived size is unaffected by its distance, angle of viewing, or illumination.

14. c. is the answer. This is an illustration of the size-distance relationship in depth perception. (p. 171)

a. Although the frisbee's shape is perceived as constant (even as the shape of its retinal image changes), this is not a cue to its distance.

b. Relative motion is the perception that when we move, stationary objects at different distances change their relative positions in our visual image, with those closest moving most. In this example, only the frisbee is moving.

15. a. is the answer. (pp. 172–173)

b. & c. These were not offered as explanations of the Müller-Lyer illusion.

16. c. is the answer. Although Leon's other senses

would have told him his car was not moving, the visual images of the other cars moving forward "captured" his awareness and created the perception that he was rolling backwards. (p. 165)

b. & d. Continuity and proximity are Gestalt principles of grouping, rather than cues to distance.

a. Relative motion is a distance cue that occurs when stationary objects appear to move as we move. Just the opposite is happening to Leon.

17. d. is the answer. (p. 182)

a. Telepathy is the claimed ability to "read" minds.

b. Clairvoyance refers to the claimed ability to perceive remote events.

c. Precognition refers to the claimed ability to perceive future events.

18. d. is the answer. (p. 183)

19. c. is the answer. She perceives the line for the road as continuous, even though it is interrupted by lines indicating other roads. (p. 166)

a. Closure refers to the perceptual filling in of gaps in a stimulus to create a complete, whole object.

b. Similarity is the tendency to perceive similar objects as belonging together. On a road map, all of the lines representing roads appear similar. Thus, this cue could not be the basis for Colleen's ability to trace the route of a particular road.

d. Proximity is the tendency to group objects near to one another as a single unit.

20. c. is the answer. (p. 173)

a. If perception were entirely based on the physical characteristics of a stimulus ("bottom-up"), lack of experience with a carpentered environment would not reduce sensitivity to the illusion.

b. Principles of grouping, depth perception, and sensitivity to illusions all demonstrate that perception often *is* predictable.

Essay Question

1. *Proximity.* We tend to perceive items that are near each other as belonging together. Thus, a small section of dancers or members of a marching band may separate themselves from the larger group in order to form part of a particular image.

2. *Similarity.* Because we perceive similar figures as belonging together, choreographers and band directors often create distinct visual groupings within the larger band or dance troupe by having the members of each group wear a distinctive costume or uniform.

3. *Continuity.* Because we perceive smooth, continuous patterns rather than discontinuous ones,

dancers or marching musicians moving together (as in a column, for example) are perceived as a separate unit.

4. *Closure.* If a figure has gaps, we complete it, filling in the gaps to create a whole image. Thus, we perceptually fill in the relatively wide spacing between dancers or marching musicians in order to perceive the complete words or forms they are creating.

KEY TERMS

1. Visual capture is the tendency for vision to dominate other senses. (p. 165)

2. Gestalt means "organized whole." The Gestalt psychologists emphasized our tendency to integrate sensory impressions into meaningful perceptions. (p. 165)

3. The **figure-ground relationship** refers to the organization of the visual field into two parts: the figure, which stands out from its surroundings, and the surroundings, or background. (p. 166)
Example: Sometimes **figure-ground relationships** are ambiguous, so that what is first perceived as figure is then perceived as ground, and vice versa.

4. Grouping is the process by which we organize stimuli in order to arrive at meaningful forms. Gestalt psychologists identified various principles of grouping. (p. 166)

5. Proximity is the Gestalt principle that we tend to group together sensory stimuli that are near one another. (p. 166)
Example: The **proximity** of individual notes in a piece of music leads to the perception of measure and other musical groupings based on intervals of time.

6. Similarity is the Gestalt principle that we tend to group together sensory stimuli that are similar. The basis for the similarity may be appearance, size, color, or any of many other dimensions. (p. 166)

7. The Gestalt principle of **continuity** is the perceptual tendency to group stimuli into smooth, continuous patterns. (p. 166)

8. Closure is the perceptual tendency to fill in incomplete figures to create the perception of a whole object, as identified by the Gestalt psychologists. (p. 166)

9. Connectedness is the Gestalt principle that we perceive spots, lines, or areas as a single unit when uniform and linked. (p. 166)

10. Depth perception is the ability to create three-dimensional perceptions from the two-dimensional images that strike the retina. (p. 167)

11. The **visual cliff** is a laboratory device for testing depth perception, especially in infants and animals. In their experiments with the visual cliff, Gibson and Walk found strong evidence that depth perception is at least in part innate. (p. 167)

12. **Binocular cues** are depth cues that depend on information from both eyes. (p. 168)

    Memory aid: Bi- indicates "two"; *ocular* means something pertaining to the eye. **Binocular cues** are cues for the "two eyes."

13. **Monocular cues** are depth cues that depend on information from only one eye. (p. 168)

    Memory aid: *Mono-* means one; a monocle is an eyeglass for one eye. A **monocular cue** is one that is available to either the left or the right eye.

14. **Retinal disparity** refers to the differences between the images received by the left eye and the right as a result of viewing the world from slightly different angles. It is a binocular depth cue, since the greater the difference between the two images, the nearer the object. (p. 168)

    Example: A forerunner of the 3-D movie, the stereoscope is an optical instrument that presents slightly different images of the same scene to the two eyes. The **retinal disparity** that results imparts a three-dimensional effect.

15. **Convergence** is a binocular depth cue based on the extent to which the eyes converge, or turn inward, when looking at near or distant objects. The more the eyes converge, the nearer the objects. (p. 168)

16. **Relative size** is a monocular depth cue; when two objects are presumed to be the same, the one producing the smaller retinal image is judged to be more distant. (p. 168)

    Example: As you stare at a person walking away from you, the **relative size** of the image their body projects onto your retinas decreases.

17. **Overlap** is a monocular depth cue; nearby objects often partially obscure more distant objects. (p. 168)

18. A monocular depth cue, **aerial perspective** refers to the tendency of distant objects to appear less distinct than nearer objects. (p. 168)

    Example: Atmospheric properties, such as water vapor and pollution, distort the clarity of distant objects; this **aerial perspective** creates a tendency to perceive blurry objects as more distant.

19. **Texture gradients** are monocular depth cues; we perceive a gradual change from a coarse, distinct texture to a finer, less distinct one as indicating increasing distance. (p. 169)

    Example: When we gaze up the Empire State Building, the **texture gradient** created by the windows

and building facade helps give us a feeling for the phenomenal height of the building.

20. A monocular cue for depth, **relative height** refers to our tendency to perceive higher objects as more distant. (p. 169)

    Example: Before the development of perspective in art, artisans indicated distance by the **relative height** of an object in the visual plane.

21. A monocular cue for perceiving distance, **relative motion** refers to the fact that, when we move, closer objects appear to shift more rapidly than distant objects. (p. 169)

22. A monocular depth cue, **linear perspective** refers to our tendency to perceive the convergence of parallel lines as indicating increasing distance. (p. 170)

23. A monocular depth cue, **relative brightness** refers to our tendency to perceive brighter objects as closer and dimmer objects as more distant. (p. 170)

24. **Perceptual constancy** is the perception that objects have consistent brightness, color, shape, and size, even as illumination and retinal images change. (p. 171)

    Example: As the sun passed from behind a cloud, the hood of Brenda's car suddenly glowed brightly; if not for **brightness constancy**, she would have feared the engine was about to explode!

25. **Perceptual adaptation** refers to our ability to adapt to visual distortions. Given distorting lenses, we perceive things accordingly, but soon adjust by learning the relationship between our distorted perceptions and the reality. (p. 176)

26. **Perceptual set** is a mental predisposition to perceive the environment in a particular way. (p. 177)

    Example: When police officers and college students were shown ambiguous scenes, their different **perceptual sets** were indicated by the greater tendency of the officers to perceive violence in the images.

27. **Extrasensory perception (ESP)** refers to perception that occurs without sensory input. Supposed ESP powers include telepathy, clairvoyance, and precognition. (p. 181)

    Memory aid: Extra- means "beyond" or "in addition to"; **extrasensory perception** is perception outside or beyond the normal senses.

28. **Parapsychology** is the study of ESP, psychokinesis, and other paranormal forms of interaction between the individual and the environment. (p. 181)

    Memory aid: *Para-*, like *extra-*, indicates "beyond"; thus, paranormal is beyond the normal and **parapsychology** is the study of phenomena beyond the realm of psychology and known natural laws.

7 / States of Consciousness

Chapter Overview

Consciousness—selective attention to perceptions, thoughts, and feelings—can be experienced in various states. Chapter 7 examines not only waking consciousness, but also covers sleep and dreaming, daydreaming, fantasies, meditation, hypnotic states, drug-altered states, and near-death experiences.

Most of the terminology in this chapter is introduced in the sections on Sleep and Dreams and on Drugs and Consciousness. Among the issues discussed in the chapter are why we sleep and dream, whether hypnosis is a unique state of consciousness, and possible psychological and social roots of drug use.

NOTE: Answer guidelines for all Chapter 7 questions begin on page 146.

Guided Study

The text chapter should be studied one section at a time. Before you read, preview each section by skimming it, noting headings and boldface items. Then read the appropriate section objectives from the following outline. Keep these objectives in mind and, as you read the chapter section, search for the information that will enable you to meet each objective. Once you have finished a section, write out answers for its objectives.

Studying Consciousness (pp. 189–191)

1. Discuss the nature of consciousness and its significance in the history of psychology.

Sleep and Dreams (pp. 191–200)

2. Describe the cyclical nature of sleep.

3. Discuss possible functions of sleep and the effects of sleep deprivation.

4. Identify and describe the major sleep disorders.

5. Describe the normal content of dreams.

6. Discuss the possible functions of dreams as revealed in various theories.

Daydreams, Fantasies, and Meditation (pp. 200–202)

7. Discuss the nature and potential functions of daydreams, fantasies, and meditation.

Hypnosis (pp. 202–209)

8. Define hypnosis and discuss several popular misconceptions about hypnosis.

9. Discuss the controversy over whether hypnosis is an altered state of consciousness.

Drugs and Consciousness (pp. 210–218)

10. Describe the physiological and psychological effects of psychoactive drugs.

11. Discuss the biological, psychological, and social roots of drug use.

Near-Death Experiences (pp. 218–220)

12. Describe the near-death experience and the controversy over the separability of mind and body.

Chapter Review

When you have finished reading the chapter, work through the material that follows to review it. Complete the sentences and answer the questions. As you proceed, evaluate your performance for each section by consulting the answers on page 148. Do not continue with the next section until you understand each answer. If you need to, go back and review or reread the appropriate section in the textbook before continuing.

Studying Consciousness (pp. 189–191)

1. The study of _____ was central in the early years of psychology and in recent decades, but for quite some time it was displaced by the study of observable

   _____.

Define consciousness in a sentence.

2. At any moment our conscious attention is focused on only a very limited aspect of all the sensory stimuli present; this indicates that our attention is _____.

3. The ability to attend selectively to one voice among many is referred to as the

   _____ _____

   effect. We _____ (can/cannot) react to stimuli that have not been consciously perceived.

4. In comparison with unconscious processing, conscious processing has a(n)

   _____ (limited/unlimited) capacity, is relatively _____ (fast/slow), and processes information

   _____ (simultaneously/successively).

Sleep and Dreams (pp. 191–200)

5. The sleep-waking cycle follows a 24-hour clock called the _____ _____. We may experience _____ _____ if it is interrupted by travel across time zones.

6. When clocks and daylight cues are absent, the sleep-waking cycle shifts to a _____-hour day.

7. The sleep cycle consists of _____ distinct stages.

8. The rhythm of sleep cycles was discovered when Aserinsky noticed that, at periodic intervals during the night, the _____ of a sleeping child moved rapidly.

9. The relatively slow brain waves of the awake but relaxed state are known as _____ waves.

Describe Stage 1 sleep.

10. The bursts of brain-wave activity that occur during Stage 2 sleep are called _____ _____.

11. Large, slow brain waves are called _____ waves. These predominate during Stage _____ sleep. A person in this stage of sleep generally will be _____ (easy/difficult) to awaken. It is during this stage that people may engage in sleep _____ and sleep _____.

Describe the bodily changes that accompany REM sleep.

12. During REM sleep, the motor cortex is _____ (active/relaxed), while the muscles are _____ (active/relaxed). For this reason, REM is often referred to as _____ sleep.

13. The rapid eye movements generally signal the beginning of a _____.

14. The sleep cycle repeats itself about every _____ minutes. As the night progresses, Stage 4 sleep becomes _____ (longer/briefer) and REM periods become _____ (longer/briefer). Approximately _____ percent of a night's sleep is spent in REM sleep.

Describe the effects of sleep deprivation.

15. Studies have indicated that, after strenuous exercise, we tend to sleep for longer periods and to increase our Stage _____ sleep.

16. During sleep a growth hormone is released by the _____ gland. Adults spend _____ (more/less) time in deep sleep than children and so release _____ (more/less) growth hormone.

17. Newborns spend about _____ of their time asleep; adults, only about _____.

18. Webb and Campbell found that the sleep patterns of identical twins were similar, suggesting a possible _____ basis for individual differences in sleep habits.

19. A recurring difficulty in falling asleep is characteristic of _____. Sleeping pills and alcohol may make the problem worse since they tend to _____ (increase/reduce) REM sleep.

20. The sleep disorder in which a person experiences uncontrollable sleep attacks is _____.

21. Individuals suffering from

_____ _____

stop breathing while sleeping.

22. The sleep disorder characterized by extreme fright and rapid heartbeat and breathing is called _____ _____. Unlike nightmares, these episodes usually happen early in the night, during Stage _____ sleep.

23. The genital arousal that typically occurs during REM sleep usually _____ (does/does not) reflect a sexual dream.

24. Although females tend to dream equally often about males and females, males tend to dream more about _____. This gender difference _____ (is/is not) found in cultures worldwide.

25. Freud referred to the actual content of a dream as its _____ content. Freud believed that this is a censored, symbolic version of the true meaning, or _____ _____, of the dream. According to Freud, most of the dreams of adults reflect _____ wishes.

26. A second theory of dreams is that they serve an _____-processing function. Support for this theory is provided by the fact that after intense learning experiences, _____ (REM/Stage 4) sleep tends to increase.

27. Other theories propose that dreaming serves some _____ function, for example, that REM sleep provides the brain with needed _____. Such an explanation is supported by the fact that _____ (infants/adults) spend the most time in REM sleep.

28. Yet other theories propose that dreams are elicited by _____ activity originating in lower regions of the brain, such as the _____.

Summarize Seligman and Yellen's theory of dreaming.

29. After being deprived of REM sleep, a person spends more time in REM sleep; this is the _____ _____ effect.

30. REM sleep _____ (does/does not) occur in other mammals.

Daydreams, Fantasies, and Meditation (pp. 200–202)

31. Most people _____ (do/do not) daydream every day. Compared to older adults, young adults spend _____ (more/less) time daydreaming. About 4 percent of the population has such vivid fantasies and daydreams that they are referred to as _____-_____ personalities.

Explain why some psychologists consider daydreaming to be adaptive.

32. A more focused, yet fully conscious state of awareness is _____. Physically, experienced meditators exhibit changes in

_____ _____,

_____ _____,

_____ _____,

and _____ similar to those of deeply relaxed people. Meditation can be helpful in relieving _____,

_____, and _____-_____ illnesses.

Hypnosis (pp. 202–209)

33. The suggestion that a person forget things that occurred while he or she was under hypnosis may produce _____

_____.

34. The discovery of hypnosis is attributed to _____, who claimed to have discovered the principle of body _____.

35. Most people are _____ (somewhat/not at all) hypnotically suggestible.

Describe people who are the most susceptible to hypnosis.

36. If people are led to expect that they are hypnotizable, their responsiveness under hypnosis _____ (will/will not) increase.

37. The hypnotic demonstration in which a subject supposedly relives earlier experiences is referred to as _____ _____. Research studies show that the subjects in such demonstrations have memories that are _____ (more/no more) accurate than the memories of fully conscious persons.

38. The weight of research evidence suggests that hypnosis _____ (does/does not) allow a person to perform dangerous feats that are impossible in the normal waking state.

39. Hypnotherapists have helped some people control headaches and quit smoking through the use of _____ suggestions.

40. For voluntary disorders, such as smoking, a subject's hypnotic responsiveness _____ (does/does not) make a difference in the effectiveness of hypnosis. As therapy for involuntary disorders, hypnosis _____ (is/is not) more effective

in speeding recovery than techniques promoting relaxation and positive images.

41. One theory of hypnotic pain relief is that hypnosis separates, or _____, the sensory and emotional aspects of pain. Another is that hypnotic pain relief is due to selective _____, that is, to the person's focusing on stimuli other than pain.

Summarize the argument that hypnosis is not an altered state of consciousness.

42. Hilgard has advanced the idea that during hypnosis there is a _____, or split, between different levels of consciousness. The existence of a separate consciousness, which is aware of what takes place during hypnosis, is expressed in the concept of the

_____ _____.

Drugs and Consciousness (pp. 210–218)

43. Drugs that alter moods and perceptions are called _____ drugs.

44. Drug users who require increasing doses to experience a drug's effects have developed _____ for the drug.

45. If a person begins experiencing withdrawal symptoms after ceasing to use a drug, the person has developed a physical _____. Regular use of a drug to relieve stress is an example of a _____ dependence.

46. The three broad categories of drugs discussed in the textbook include _____,

which tend to slow body functions; _____, which speed body functions; and _____, which alter perception. These drugs all work by mimicking or affecting the activity of the brain's _____.

47. Low doses of alcohol, which is classified as a _____, slow the activity of the _____ nervous system.

48. Alcohol facilitates urges that might otherwise be resisted because it focuses attention on the _____ situation and away from _____ consequences. Alcohol also affects memory by interfering with the process of transferring experiences into _____–_____ memory. Thus, alcohol may make a person more _____, more _____, more _____–_____, or more _____ daring.

Describe how a person's expectations can influence the behavioral effects of alcohol.

49. Tranquilizers, which are also known as _____, have effects similar to those of alcohol.

50. Opium, morphine, and heroin all _____ (excite/depress) neural functioning. Together, these drugs are called the _____. When they are present, the brain eventually stops producing _____.

51. The most widely used stimulants are _____, _____, _____, and _____. Stimulants _____ (are/are not) habit forming.

52. Cocaine and crack deplete the brain's supply of the neurotransmitters _____

and _____, and result in depression as the drugs' effects wear off.

53. Cocaine's psychological effects depend not only on dosage and form but also on _____, _____, and the _____.

54. Hallucinogens are also referred to as _____. Two common synthetic hallucinogens are _____ and _____.

55. The active ingredient in marijuana is abbreviated _____. Marijuana has been used therapeutically with those who suffer from _____ and cancer.

Describe some of the physical and psychological effects of marijuana.

56. Tolerance and withdrawal may be explained in part by the principle that emotions trigger _____ _____.

57. That attitudes toward drug use are changing is shown by the fact that drug use _____ (declined/increased) during the 1980s.

58. Adopted individuals are more susceptible to alcoholism if they had an alcoholic _____ (adoptive/biological) parent.

Identify some of the psychological and social roots of drug use.

Near-Death Experiences (pp. 218–220)

59. The reports of people who have had near-death experiences are very similar to the

_____ reported by drug users. These experiences may be the result of a deficient supply of _____ or other traumas to the brain.

60. That the mind and body are distinct entities is the position of the theorists known as

_____. In contrast, the

_____ believe that the mind and body are one.

FOCUS ON PSYCHOLOGY:
Cycles of Craving in Drug Abuse

Drug experts are generally cautious in identifying historical trends in the use of specific drugs. Harvard psychiatrist Norman Zinberg, after studying drug-abuse patterns in the United States for the past quarter century, contends, however, that society's drug of choice has shifted four times: LSD and other hallucinogens dominated the early 1960s, marijuana took over through the late 1960s, heroin was the most popular drug during the early 1970s, and today cocaine leads the way. Zinberg believes that drugs become popular when they do because they fit the public mood. "Cocaine became the drug of the '80s because it's a stimulant. People were looking for action," says the psychiatrist.

Experts are less reluctant to specify patterns of drug use. For example, they all agree that drug use typically begins with more affluent individuals looking for a new thrill, filters down into the middle classes, and finally reaches the lower socioeconomic groups. Cocaine use in the 1980s provides a good example of this pattern. Researchers noted the social class of all callers to 1-800-COCAINE, a national hot line for the abusers of the powerful stimulant. In 1983, more than half the calls came from college-educated individuals with incomes of at least $25,000; by 1987, fewer than 20 percent of the calls were from this group.

Experts also agree that certain categories of drugs tend to be abused simultaneously. Cocaine abusers, for example, often use an opiate such as heroin to counteract the stimulating effects of cocaine. Officials at the United States Drug Enforcement Agency were not surprised to find that both cocaine- and heroin-related deaths increased dramatically between 1984 and 1988. This pattern of drug use may best be explained in terms of the opposing physiological effects of certain psychoactive drugs on the nervous system.

Davis Musto, a medical historian at Yale University, has observed another, more positive trend over the past decade: a growing public intolerance toward illegal drugs that has led to decreased drug use by the middle class. Musto attributes this trend largely to society's outrage at the epidemic abuse of "crack," a smokable, relatively inexpensive yet highly addictive form of cocaine, which "created a consensus in society against drugs and ended the ambivalence that had been prevalent for decades."

And what does the future hold? Although drug use has declined, the problem is still enormous, particularly in relation to crimes committed to get money for drugs. Historian Musto is concerned that drug abuse is being swept under the historical carpet in the American educational system. For example, the California school system recently revised its syllabus for teaching American history. In the revised syllabus the history of drug abuse is not mentioned. Musto fears that "a society that forgets its history of abuse is doomed to repeat it." If children are made to read the devastating effects of the widespread abuse of cocaine during the 1920s and the 1980s, they might avoid the mistakes of earlier generations.

One thing is clear: the problem of drug abuse has many biological, social, and psychological roots, each of which must be understood before the problem can be solved. As Zinberg and Musto make clear, social and historical trends in drug abuse offer important insights into these roots. Failing to understand and remember our history may bring us into yet another orbit within the vicious cycle of drug abuse.

Source: Hurley, D. (1989, August). Cycles of craving. *Psychology Today*, 54–60.

Progress Test 1
Multiple-Choice Questions

Circle your answers to the following questions and check them with the answers on page 149. If your answer is incorrect, read the explanation for why it is incorrect and then consult the appropriate pages of the text (in parentheses following the correct answer).

1. As defined by the text, consciousness includes which of the following?
   a. daydreaming   c. hypnosis
   b. sleeping   d. all of the above

2. Which of the following groups tends to daydream the most?
   a. elderly men   c. middle-aged adults
   b. elderly women   d. young adults

3. When our _____ is disrupted, we experience jet lag.
   a. daydreaming   c. circadian rhythm
   b. REM sleep   d. Stage 4 sleep

4. Sleep spindles predominate during which stage of sleep?
   a. Stage 2   c. Stage 4
   b. Stage 3   d. REM sleep

5. During which stage of sleep does the body experience increased heart rate, rapid breathing, and genital arousal?
   a. Stage 2   c. Stage 4
   b. Stage 3   d. REM sleep

6. The duration of the sleep cycle is approximately _____ minutes.
   a. 30   c. 75
   b. 50   d. 90

7. Sleep deprivation typically leads to:
   a. disruption of muscular coordination.
   b. hallucinations and other abnormal conditions.
   c. misperceptions on monotonous tasks.
   d. all of the above.

8. One effect of sleeping pills is to:
   a. depress REM sleep.
   b. increase REM sleep.
   c. depress Stage 2 sleep.
   d. increase Stage 2 sleep.

9. Cocaine and crack produce a euphoric rush by:
   a. stimulating an increase in the release of norepinephrine.
   b. depressing neural activity in the brain.
   c. blocking the reabsorption of excess dopamine, norepinephrine, and serotonin.
   d. stimulating the brain's production of endorphins.

10. Which of the following is classified as a depressant?
    a. amphetamines   c. marijuana
    b. LSD   d. alcohol

11. The modern discovery of hypnosis is generally attributed to:
    a. Freud.   c. Orne.
    b. Mesmer.   d. Hilgard.

12. Which of the following statements concerning hypnosis is true?
    a. People will do anything under hypnosis.
    b. Hypnosis is the same as sleeping.
    c. Hypnosis is not associated with a distinct physiological state.
    d. Hypnosis improves memory recall.

13. The cocktail party effect refers to:
    a. the effects of random noise on a person's perception of low pitches.
    b. the effects of random noise on a person's mood.
    c. the ability to attend selectively to one stimulus.
    d. the cumulative effect of multiple uses of a depressant drug.

14. According to Freud, dreams are:
    a. a symbolic fulfillment of erotic wishes.
    b. the result of random neural activity in the brainstem.
    c. the brain's mechanism for self-stimulation.
    d. transparent representations of the individual's conflicts.

15. Psychoactive drugs affect behavior and perception through:
    a. the power of suggestion.
    b. the placebo effect.
    c. alteration of neural activity in the brain.
    d. psychological, rather than physiological, influences.

16. When students closely attended to a prose passage presented to one ear:
    a. they failed to notice, and were unaffected by, simple tunes played to the other ear.
    b. they were able to divide their attention and comprehend both the prose passage and a simple message presented to the other ear.
    c. they were able to divide their attention and comprehend both the prose passage and a message presented to the other ear, but only if the two messages were spoken by different people.
    d. they later were unable to recognize simple tunes played to the other ear, but preferred them to tunes they had not heard before.

17. At its beginning, psychology focused on the study of:
    a. observable behavior.   c. abnormal behavior.
    b. consciousness.   d. all of the above.

18. Which of the following is not a theory of dreaming mentioned in the textbook?
    a. Dreams facilitate information processing.
    b. Dreaming stimulates the developing brain.
    c. Dreams result from random neural activity originating in the brainstem.
    d. Dreaming is an attempt to escape from social stimulation.

19. The sleep-waking cycles of people isolated without clocks or daylight typically are _____ hours in duration.
    a. 23   c. 25
    b. 24   d. 26

20. Meditation is best described as:
    a. daydreaming.
    b. an altered state of consciousness that is not accompanied by physiological change.
    c. a focused, conscious state of awareness accompanied by physiological changes characteristic of deep relaxation.
    d. all of the above.

Matching Items

Match each term with its appropriate definition or description.

Definitions or Descriptions

_____ **1.** surface meaning of dreams
_____ **2.** deeper meaning of dreams
_____ **3.** stage of sleep associated with delta waves
_____ **4.** stage of sleep associated with muscular relaxation
_____ **5.** sleep disorder in which breathing stops
_____ **6.** sleep disorder occurring in Stage 4 sleep
_____ **7.** depressant
_____ **8.** hallucinogen
_____ **9.** stimulant
_____ **10.** twilight stage of sleep associated with imagery resembling hallucinations
_____ **11.** disorder in which sleep attacks occur

Terms

a. marijuana
b. alcohol
c. Stage 1 sleep
d. night terrors
e. manifest content
f. cocaine
g. narcolepsy
h. sleep apnea
i. Stages 3 and 4 sleep
j. REM sleep
k. latent content

Progress Test 2

Progress Test 2 should be completed during a final chapter review. Answer the following questions after you thoroughly understand the correct answers for the Chapter Review and Progress Test 1.

Multiple-Choice Questions

1. Which of the following statements regarding REM sleep is true?
   a. Adults spend more time than infants in REM sleep.
   b. REM sleep deprivation results in a REM rebound.
   c. People deprived of REM sleep adapt easily.
   d. After a stressful experience, a person's REM sleep decreases.

2. Which theorists believe that the mind and the body are separate entities?
   a. the behaviorists   **c.** the dualists
   b. the monists   **d.** the Freudians

3. Alcohol has the most profound effect on:
   a. the transfer of experiences to long-term memory.
   b. immediate memory.
   c. previously established long-term memories.
   d. all of the above.

4. A person whose EEG shows a high proportion of alpha waves is most likely:
   a. dreaming.
   b. in Stage 2 sleep.
   c. in Stage 4 sleep.
   d. awake and relaxed.

5. Circadian rhythms are the:
   a. brain waves that occur during Stage 4 sleep.
   b. muscular tremors that occur during opiate withdrawal.
   c. regular body cycles that occur on a 24-hour schedule.
   d. brain waves that are indicative of Stage 2 sleep.

6. A person who requires increasing amounts of a drug in order to feel its effect has developed:
   a. tolerance.
   b. physical dependency.
   c. psychological dependency.
   d. resistance.

7. Meditation:
   a. can help relieve pain and stress-related illnesses.
   b. produces blood pressure, heart rate, and brain wave levels like those of deeply relaxed people.
   c. is a focused state in which a person remains fully conscious.
   d. is all of the above.

8. Which of the following is characteristic of REM sleep?
   a. genital arousal
   b. increased muscular tension
   c. night terrors
   d. slow, regular breathing

9. Which of the following is *not* a stimulant?
   a. amphetamines   **c.** nicotine
   b. caffeine   **d.** alcohol

10. Hypnotic responsiveness:
    a. is the same in all people.
    b. is generally greater in women than men.
    c. is generally greater in men than women.
    d. is greater when people are led to *expect* it.

11. According to Hilgard, hypnosis is:
    a. no different from a state of heightened motivation.
    b. a hoax perpetrated by frauds.
    c. the same as dreaming.
    d. a dissociation between different levels of consciousness.

12. Which of the following is a psychoactive drug?
    a. LSD
    b. sleeping pills
    c. caffeine
    d. All of the above are psychoactive drugs.

13. As a form of therapy for relieving problems such as headaches and allergies, hypnosis is:
    a. ineffective.
    b. no more effective than positive suggestions given without hypnosis.
    c. highly effective.
    d. more effective with adults than children.

14. Which of the following is usually the most powerful determinant of whether teenagers begin using drugs?
    a. family strength
    b. religiosity
    c. school adjustment
    d. peer influence

15. THC is the major active ingredient in:
    a. nicotine.   c. marijuana.
    b. LSD.   d. cocaine.

16. Those who believe that hypnosis is a social phenomenon argue that "hypnotized" individuals are:
    a. consciously faking their behavior.
    b. merely acting out a role.

    c. underachievers striving to please the hypnotist.
    d. all of the above.

17. "Consciousness" is defined in the textbook as:
    a. mental life.
    b. selective attention to ongoing perceptions, thoughts, and feelings.
    c. information processing.
    d. a vague concept no longer useful to contemporary psychologists.

18. Which of the following is true?
    a. REM sleep tends to increase following intense learning periods.
    b. Non-REM sleep tends to increase following intense learning periods.
    c. REM-deprived people remember less presleep material than people deprived of Stage 1–4 sleep.
    d. Sleep control centers are located in the higher, association areas of the cortex, where memories are stored.

19. According to Seligman and Yellen, dreaming represents:
    a. the brain's efforts to integrate unrelated bursts of activity in the visual cortex with emotional tone provided by activity in the limbic system.
    b. a mechanism for coping with the stresses of daily life.
    c. a symbolic depiction of a person's unfulfilled wishes.
    d. an information-processing mechanism for converting the day's experiences into long-term memory.

20. How a particular psychoactive drug affects a person depends on:
    a. the dosage and form in which the drug is taken.
    b. the user's expectations and personality.
    c. the situation in which the drug is taken.
    d. all of the above.

Matching Items

Match each term with its appropriate definition or description.

Definitions or Descriptions

_____ 1. early name for hypnosis

_____ 2. drugs that increase energy and stimulate neural activity

_____ 3. brain wave of awake, relaxed person

_____ 4. brain-wave activity during Stage 2 sleep

_____ 5. sleep stage associated with dreaming

_____ 6. drugs that reduce anxiety and depress central nervous system activity

_____ 7. natural painkiller produced by the brain

_____ 8. neurotransmitter that LSD resembles

_____ 9. ongoing perceptions, thoughts, and feelings

_____ 10. theory that dreaming reflects erotic drives

_____ 11. theory that hypnosis is a split in consciousness

Terms

a. Freud's theory
b. serotonin
c. mesmerism
d. alpha
e. dissociation
f. amphetamines
g. consciousness
h. sleep spindle
i. endorphin
j. REM
k. barbiturates

Challenge Test

Answer these questions the day before an exam as a final check on your understanding of the chapter's terms and concepts.

Multiple-Choice Questions

1. A person who falls asleep in the midst of a heated argument probably suffers from:
   a. sleep apnea.   **c.** night terrors.
   b. narcolepsy.   **d.** insomnia.

2. Which of the following was *not* suggested by the text as an important aspect of drug prevention and treatment programs?
   a. education about the long-term costs of a drug's temporary pleasures
   b. efforts to boost people's self-esteem and purpose in life
   c. attempts to modify peer associations
   d. "scare tactics" that frighten prepubescent children into avoiding drug experimentation

3. REM sleep is referred to as "paradoxical sleep" because:
   a. studies of people deprived of REM sleep indicate that REM sleep is unnecessary.
   b. the body's muscles remain relaxed while the brain and eyes are active.
   c. it is very easy to awaken a person from REM sleep.
   d. the body's muscles are very tense while the brain is in a nearly meditative state.

4. An attorney wants to know if the details and accuracy of an eyewitness's memory for a crime would be improved under hypnosis. Given the results of relevant research, what should you tell the attorney?
   a. Most hypnotically retrieved memories are either false or contaminated.
   b. Hypnotically retrieved memories are usually more accurate than conscious memories.
   c. Hypnotically retrieved memories are purely the product of the subject's imagination.
   d. Hypnosis only improves memory of anxiety-provoking childhood events.

5. Dan has recently begun using an addictive, euphoria-producing drug. Which of the following will probably occur if he repeatedly uses this drug?
   a. As tolerance to the drug develops, Dan will experience increasingly pleasurable "highs."
   b. The dosage needed to produce the desired effect will decrease.
   c. After each use, he will become more and more depressed.
   d. All of the above will probably occur.

6. Bruce has just completed his first day of military basic training. Physically exhausted from the strenuous exercise, he will probably spend an increased amount of time in which stage of sleep?
   a. REM   **c.** Stage 2
   b. Stage 1   **d.** Stage 4

7. Being engrossed in reading her new novel, Kathy isn't easily distracted by the usual dormitory noise. Her behavior is best explained in terms of:

a. fantasy-prone behavior.

b. selective attention.

c. dissociation.

d. divided consciousness.

8. Roberto is moderately intoxicated by alcohol. Which of the following changes in his behavior is likely to occur?

   a. If angered, he is more likely to become aggressive than when he is sober.

   b. He will be less self-conscious about his behavior.

   c. If sexually aroused, he will be less inhibited about engaging in sexual activity.

   d. All of the above are likely.

9. Jill dreams that her boyfriend pushes her into the path of an oncoming car. Her psychoanalyst suggests that the dream might symbolize her fear that her boyfriend is rushing her into sexual activity she is not yet ready for. The analyst is evidently attempting to interpret the _____ content of Jill's dream.

   a. manifest   **c.** dissociated

   b. latent   **d.** overt

10. Barry has just spent four nights as a subject in a sleep study in which he was awakened each time he entered REM sleep. Now that the experiment is over, which of the following can be expected to occur?

    a. Barry will be extremely irritable until his body has made up the lost REM sleep.

    b. Barry will sleep so deeply for several nights that dreaming will be minimal.

    c. There will be an increase in sleep Stages 1–4.

    d. There will be an increase in Barry's REM sleep.

11. Of the following individuals, who is likely to be the most hypnotically suggestible?

    a. Bill, a reality-oriented stockbroker

    b. Janice, a fantasy-prone actress

    c. Megan, a sixth-grader who has trouble focusing her attention on a task

    d. Darren, who has never been able to really "get involved" in movies or novels

12. Which of the following statements concerning alcoholism is *not* true?

    a. Adopted individuals are more susceptible to alcoholism if they had an alcoholic adoptive parent.

    b. Having an alcoholic identical twin puts one at increased risk of becoming alcoholic.

    c. Compared to children of nonalcoholics, children of alcoholics are more sensitive to alcohol's intoxicating pleasure.

    d. Researchers have bred animals that prefer alcohol to water.

13. Research studies of the effectiveness of hypnosis as a form of therapy have demonstrated that:

    a. for problems of self-control, such as smoking, hypnosis is equally effective with subjects who can be deeply hypnotized and those who cannot.

    b. posthypnotic suggestions have helped alleviate headaches, asthma, warts, and certain skin disorders.

    c. positive suggestions given without hypnosis are often as effective as hypnosis as a form of therapy.

    d. all of the above are true.

14. As a child, Jane enjoyed intense make-believe play with dolls, stuffed animals, and imaginary companions. As an adult, she spends an unusually large amount of time fantasizing. She is sometimes uncertain whether an event was real or imagined. A psychologist would most likely describe Jane as:

    a. highly suggestible.   **c.** a daydreamer.

    b. fantasy prone.   **d.** a dissociator.

15. Levar believes that once the body has died, the mind ceases to exist as well. Evidently, Levar is a(n):

    a. behaviorist.   **c.** dualist.

    b. monist.   **d.** atheist.

16. Which of the following statements concerning marijuana is *not* true?

    a. The by-products of marijuana are cleared from the body more quickly than the by-products of alcohol.

    b. Long-term marijuana use may depress male sex hormone and sperm levels.

    c. Marijuana is not as addictive as nicotine or cocaine.

    d. Large doses of marijuana hasten the loss of brain cells.

17. Which of the following statements concerning near-death experiences is true?

    a. Fewer than 1 percent of patients who come close to dying report having them.

    b. They typically consist of fantastic, mystical imagery.

    c. They are more commonly experienced by females than by males.

    d. They are more commonly experienced by males than by females.

18. Those who consider hypnosis a social phenomenon contend that:

    a. hypnotic phenomena are merely an extension of everyday social behavior.

    b. although hypnosis is an altered state of consciousness, hypnotic phenomena are not unique to hypnosis.

c. if a hypnotist eliminates the motivation for acting, hypnotized subjects become unresponsive.

d. all of the above are true.

19. Which of the following statements concerning the roots of drug use is *not* true?

a. Heavy users of alcohol, marijuana, and cocaine often are depressed.

b. If an adolescent's friends use drugs, odds are that he or she will too.

c. Teenagers who come from happy families and do well in school seldom use drugs.

d. It is nearly impossible to predict whether or not an adolescent will experiment with drugs.

20. Which of the following statements concerning daydreaming is true?

a. People prone to violence or drug use tend to have fewer vivid daydreams.

b. Most daydreaming involves the familiar details of our everyday lives.

c. Psychologists consider children's daydreams to be a form of imaginative play.

d. All of the above are true.

Essay Question

You have just been assigned the task of writing an article tentatively titled "Alcohol and Alcoholism: Roots, Effects, and Prevention." What information should you include in your article? (Use the space below to list the points you want to make, and organize them. Then write the essay on a separate piece of paper.)

Key Terms

Using your own words, write a brief definition or explanation of each of the following terms.

1. consciousness

2. selective attention

3. circadian rhythm

4. REM sleep

5. alpha waves

6. hallucinations

7. delta waves

8. insomnia

9. narcolepsy

10. sleep apnea

11. night terrors

12. manifest content

13. latent content

14. REM rebound

15. fantasy-prone personality

16. hypnosis

17. posthypnotic amnesia

18. age regression

19. posthypnotic suggestion

20. dissociation

21. hidden observer

22. psychoactive drugs

23. tolerance

24. withdrawal

25. physical dependence

26. psychological dependence

27. depressants

28. stimulants

29. hallucinogens

30. barbiturates

31. opiates

32. amphetamines

33. LSD (lysergic acid diethylamide)

34. THC

35. near-death experience

36. dualism

37. monism

ANSWERS
GUIDED STUDY

The following guidelines provide the main points that your answers should have touched upon.

1. At its beginning, psychology focused on the description and explanation of states of consciousness. The difficulty of scientifically studying consciousness and the emergence of the school of behaviorism, however, caused psychology to shift to the study of overt behavior. By 1960, advances in neuroscience made it possible to relate brain activity to various mental states and mental concepts began to reenter psychology.

   Contemporary psychologists define consciousness as "selective attention to ongoing perceptions, thoughts, and feelings," and conduct research on attention, sleeping, meditation, dreaming, and altered states of consciousness induced by hypnosis and drugs.

2. The sleep-waking cycle is a circadian (24-hour) rhythm. The cycle of sleep is a 90-minute rhythm that consists of five distinct stages. During Stage 1 sleep, which lasts about two minutes, breathing rate slows, brain waves become light and irregular, and people often experience hallucination-like sensations. The approximately 20 minutes of Stage 2 sleep is characterized by bursts of brain-wave activity (sleep spindles). Starting in Stage 3 and increasingly in Stage 4, the sleeper's brain emits large, slow delta waves. During Stage 4 sleep, which lasts about 30 minutes, it is difficult to awaken a sleeper. During REM sleep, brain waves, heart rate, and breathing become more rapid, genital arousal and rapid eye movements occur, and dreaming is common. Over the course of a night's sleep, REM sleep increases in duration, while Stages 3 and 4 become shorter.

3. Why people need sleep is not fully understood. Sleep helps restore body tissues, especially those of the brain. An example of the restorative effect of sleep is the increase in Stage 4 sleep that occurs following strenuous exercise. That sleep also plays a role in the growth process is indicated by evidence that during deep sleep, the pituitary gland releases a growth hormone.

   The major effect of sleep deprivation is sleepiness. Other effects include impaired creativity and concentration, diminished immunity to disease, irritability, slight hand tremors, and occasional inattention on monotonous tasks. On short, highly motivating tasks, however, sleep deprivation has little effect.

4. Approximately 10 to 15 percent of adults suffer recurring problems in falling or staying asleep (insomnia). People with narcolepsy suffer overwhelming bouts of sleepiness and collapse directly into a brief period of REM sleep. Those who suffer from sleep apnea intermittently stop breathing for a minute or so when they sleep. Unlike nightmares, which typically occur during early morning REM sleep, night terrors usually occur early in the

night and during Stage 4 sleep; they are characterized by high arousal and an appearance of being terrified.

5. REM dreams are more vivid, emotional, and bizarre than daydreams. Many dreams, however, are rather ordinary and deal with daily life events. People commonly dream of failure, of being attacked, pursued, or rejected, or of experiencing misfortune. Sexual imagery in dreams is less common than is popularly believed. Women dream of males and females equally often, but 65 percent of men's dream characters are males. Occasionally, people experience "lucid dreams," in which they are sufficiently aware during a dream to wonder whether they are, in fact, dreaming and are able to test their state of consciousness.

6. Freud argued that dreams are a psychic safety valve that discharges threatening feelings. According to this view, a dream's manifest content is a symbolic version of its true underlying meaning (latent content) which consists of unacceptable drives and erotic wishes.

   According to the information-processing theory, dreams help with the processing and storage of daily experiences. In support of this theory is evidence that following stressful or intense learning periods, REM sleep increases.

   Another theory holds that dreams provide the brain with needed stimulation that promotes development of neural pathways. In support of this theory is evidence that infants spend more time in REM sleep than adults.

   Seligman and Yellen believe that dreams are the brain's attempt to integrate unrelated bursts of activity in the visual cortex, imposing meaning on meaningless stimuli. The emotional "tone" of dreams is provided by activity in the limbic system.

7. Daydreams help people prepare for future events by serving as mental rehearsals. For children, daydreaming is a form of imaginative play that fosters social and cognitive development. Daydreams may also substitute for impulsive behavior.

   Approximately 4 percent of people can be characterized as fantasy-prone. These individuals spend more than half their time fantasizing and may have trouble separating fantasy from reality.

   Meditation is a more focused, yet fully conscious state of awareness that can help relieve pain, anxiety, and stress-related illnesses. Experienced meditators exhibit physical changes typical of deeply relaxed people.

8. Hypnosis is an apparently heightened suggestibility that may enable a hypnotist's directions to trigger specific behaviors, perceptions, and per-

haps even memories. Approximately 20 percent of people are highly susceptible to hypnosis, although studies show that anyone can experience hypnotic responsiveness if led to expect it.

   Studies of hypnotic memory refreshment and age regression demonstrate that hypnosis does not boost memory. Age-regressed people merely act as they believe appropriate for a certain age.

   The belief that hypnosis can force people to act against their will, or perform acts that fully conscious people cannot, is also unsubstantiated.

   Posthypnotic suggestions have been used to help people control headaches, asthma, and other physical disorders. But controlled studies demonstrate that giving patients positive suggestions without hypnosis is equally effective.

   Hypnosis can relieve pain, perhaps by allowing a person to dissociate the pain from conscious awareness, or by focusing attention elsewhere. Several studies have shown that hypnosis relieves pain no better than relaxing and distracting people without hypnosis.

9. Most studies have found that hypnosis does not produce any unique physiological changes that would indicate it is an altered state of consciousness. Nor is the behavior of hypnotized people fundamentally different from that of fully conscious people. Therefore, hypnosis may be mainly a social phenomenon, with hypnotized subjects acting out the role of a "good hypnotic subject."

   The controversial divided-consciousness theory is based on Hilgard's idea that during hypnosis consciousness splits into a cooperating, suggestible component and a hidden observer that is passively aware of what is happening.

10. Depressants such as alcohol, barbiturates, and opiates calm activity in the sympathetic nervous system and slow down body functions. Like all psychoactive drugs, depressants can produce both physical and psychological dependence. Behaviorally, alcohol promotes aggressive, sexual, or helpful urges that the user's normal restraints might otherwise inhibit. Alcohol also disrupts the processing of recent experiences into long-term memories, reduces self-awareness, and suppresses REM sleep. The barbiturate drugs have effects similar to those of alcohol. With repeated use of artificial opiates, the brain stops producing endorphins, which leads to the agony of withdrawal when the drug is withdrawn.

    The stimulants, which include caffeine, nicotine, amphetamines, and cocaine, speed up body functions. When stimulants wear off, there is a compensatory slowdown of behavior that includes symptoms of tiredness, headaches, irritability, and depression. Cocaine produces its effects by blocking the reabsorption of excess dopamine, norepinephrine, and serotonin. Amphetamines produce their effects by stimulating the release of excess norepinephrine.

Hallucinogens such as marijuana, PCP, and LSD distort perceptions and evoke unpredictable psychological effects. Many hallucinogens produce their effects by blocking the actions of the neurotransmitter serotonin. Like alcohol, marijuana relaxes, disinhibits, and impairs memory and perceptual and motor skills. Marijuana may also depress male sex hormones and hasten the loss of brain cells.

11. Drug use among teenagers and adults declined during the 1980s, indicating a changing national attitude toward drugs. Nevertheless, biological, social, and psychological factors may lead some individuals to experiment with drugs.

That some people may be biologically vulnerable to drug use is indicated by evidence that heredity influences alcoholic tendencies. Having an alcoholic biological parent or identical twin, for example, puts one at increased risk of becoming alcoholic.

Several psychological factors may promote addiction, including feeling that one's life is meaningless, experiencing significant stress or failure, low self-esteem, and depression.

Especially for teenagers, social influences on drug use are strong. Peers influence attitudes about drugs, provide drugs, and establish the social context for their use. If an adolescent's friends use drugs, the odds are that he or she will too.

12. Approximately 30 to 40 percent of people who have come close to death report some sort of near-death experience involving visions of tunnels, bright lights, out-of-body sensations, or replays of old memories. Dualists, who believe the mind can exist separate from the body, have glorified such experiences as evidence of life after death. Monists, who contend that the mind and body are inseparable, argue that near-death experiences are similar to the hallucinations people experience while using drugs, or when their brains are deprived of oxygen. Monists believe that near-death experiences mean nothing more than that the brain has been traumatized.

CHAPTER REVIEW

1. consciousness; behavior

Consciousness can be defined as selective attention to ongoing perceptions, thoughts, and feelings.

2. selective
3. cocktail party; can
4. limited; slow; successively
5. circadian rhythm; jet lag
6. 25
7. 5
8. eyes
9. alpha

During Stage 1 sleep, breathing rate slows and brain waves become light and irregular. Stage 1 is a twilight state in which people often have sensory experiences very similar to hallucinations. During this stage of sleep the person is easily awakened.

10. sleep spindles
11. delta; 4; difficult; walking; talking

During REM sleep, brain waves become as rapid as those of Stage 1 sleep, heart rate and breathing become more rapid and irregular, and genital arousal and rapid eye movements occur.

12. active; relaxed; paradoxical
13. dream
14. 90; briefer; longer; 20 to 25

The major effect of sleep deprivation is sleepiness. Other effects include impaired creativity and concentration, diminished immunity to disease, irritability, and occasional misperceptions on monotonous tasks.

15. 4
16. pituitary; less; less
17. two-thirds; one-fourth
18. genetic or hereditary
19. insomnia; reduce
20. narcolepsy
21. sleep apnea
22. night terrors; 4
23. does not
24. males; is
25. manifest; latent content; erotic
26. information; REM
27. physiological; stimulation; infants
28. neural; brainstem

Seligman and Yellen believe that dreams are the brain's attempt to integrate unrelated bursts of activity in the visual cortex, imposing meaning on meaningless stimuli. The emotional "tone" of the particular dream is provided by the activity of the limbic system.

29. REM rebound

30. does

31. do; more; fantasy-prone

Daydreams help us prepare for future events by serving as mental rehearsals. For children, daydreaming in the form of imaginative play is important to social and cognitive development. Daydreams may also substitute for impulsive behavior (delinquents and drug users tend to have fewer vivid fantasies).

32. meditation; blood pressure; heart rate; brain waves; metabolism; pain; anxiety; stress-related

33. posthypnotic amnesia

34. Mesmer; magnetism

35. somewhat

Those who are most susceptible share with the fantasy-prone personality the capability of becoming deeply absorbed in the imaginary. They also tend to be very creative individuals and to have rich fantasy lives.

36. will

37. age regression; no more

38. does not

39. posthypnotic

40. does not; is not

41. dissociates; attention

Although the issue is still unsettled, most studies have found that hypnosis does not produce any unique changes in physiological processes—and we would expect such changes if hypnosis is an altered state of consciousness. Nor is the behavior of hypnotized subjects fundamentally different from that of other people. Therefore, hypnosis may be mainly a social phenomenon, with hypnotized subjects acting out the role of a "good hypnotic subject."

42. dissociation; hidden observer

43. psychoactive

44. tolerance

45. dependence; psychological

46. depressants; stimulants; hallucinogens; neurotransmitters

47. depressant; sympathetic

48. immediate; future; long-term; aggressive; helpful; self-disclosing; sexually

Studies have found that if people believe that alcohol affects social behavior in certain ways, then, when they drink alcohol (or even mistakenly think that they have been drinking alcohol), they will behave according to their expectations. For example, if people believe alcohol promotes sexual feeling, on drinking they will be likely to behave in a sexually aroused way.

49. barbiturates

50. depress; opiates; endorphins

51. caffeine; nicotine; amphetamines; cocaine; are

52. dopamine; norepinephrine

53. expectations; personality; situation

54. psychedelics; LSD; PCP

55. THC; glaucoma

Like alcohol, marijuana relaxes, disinhibits, and may produce a euphoric feeling. Also like alcohol, marijuana impairs perceptual and motor skills. Marijuana is a mild hallucinogen; it can slow the perceived passage of time and amplify sensitivity to colors, sounds, tastes, and smells.

56. opposing emotions

57. declined

58. biological

A psychological factor in drug use is the feeling that one's life is meaningless and lacks direction. Regular users of psychoactive drugs often have experienced stress or failure and are somewhat depressed. Drug use often begins as a temporary way to relieve depression, anger, anxiety, or insomnia. A powerful social factor in drug use, especially among adolescents, is peer influence. Peers shape attitudes about drugs, provide drugs, and establish the social context for their use.

59. hallucinations; oxygen

60. dualists; monists

PROGRESS TEST 1

Multiple-Choice Questions

1. **d.** is the answer. (p. 189)

2. **d.** is the answer. (p. 201)

3. **c.** is the answer. Jet lag is experienced because, having traveled across time zones, we are awake at a time when our biological clock says, "Sleep!" This biological clock is the circadian rhythm. (p. 192)

4. **a.** is the answer. (p. 193)

   b. & c. Delta waves predominate during Stages 3 and 4. Stage 3 is the transition between Stages 2 and 4 and is associated with a pattern that has elements of both these stages.

   d. Faster, nearly waking brain waves occur during REM sleep.

5. **d.** is the answer. (p. 193)

   a., b., & c. During non-REM Stages 1–4 heart rate and breathing are slow and regular and the genitals are not aroused.

6. **d.** is the answer. (p. 194)

7. **c.** is the answer. Sleep deprivation can have serious consequences for monotonous tasks like long-distance driving, although short, highly motivated tasks are evidently unaffected. No significant physical, emotional, or cognitive effects have been found. (p. 195)

8. **a.** is the answer. Like alcohol, sleeping pills carry the undesirable consequence of reducing REM sleep and may make insomnia worse in the long run. (p. 196)

   b., c., & d. Sleeping pills do not produce these effects.

9. **c.** is the answer. (p. 213)

   a. This answer describes the effect of amphetamines.

   b. Depressants such as alcohol have this effect. Cocaine and crack are classified as stimulants.

   d. None of the psychoactive drugs has this effect. Opiates, however, *suppress* the brain's production of endorphins.

10. **d.** is the answer. Alcohol, which slows body functions and neural activity, is a depressant. (p. 210)

    a. Amphetamines are stimulants.

    b. & c. LSD and marijuana are hallucinogens.

11. **b.** is the answer. Hypnosis was originally referred to as "mesmerism." (p. 203)

    a. In the area of consciousness, Freud is best known for his theory of dreaming.

    c. Orne is best known for his contention that hypnosis is a social phenomenon involving role playing.

    d. Hilgard is known for his theory of dissociation and the hidden observer in hypnosis.

12. **c.** is the answer. (pp. 205, 208)

    a. Hypnotized subjects usually perform only acts they might perform normally.

    b. The brain waves of hypnotized subjects are like those seen in relaxed, awake states, not like those associated with sleeping.

    d. Hypnosis typically *disrupts*, or contaminates, memory.

13. **c.** is the answer. An example of selective attention, the cocktail party effect is the ability to attend to one voice among many. (p. 190)

14. **a.** is the answer. Freud saw dreams as psychic escape valves that discharge unacceptable feelings that are often related to erotic wishes. (p. 198)

    b. & c. These physiological theories of dreaming are not associated with Freud.

    d. According to Freud, dreams represent the individual's conflicts and wishes but in disguised, rather than transparent, form.

15. **c.** is the answer. Such drugs work primarily at synapses, altering neural transmission. (p. 210)

    a. What people believe will happen after taking a drug will be likely to have some effect on their individual reaction, but psychoactive drugs actually work by altering neural transmission.

    b. Since a placebo is a substance without active properties, this answer is incorrect.

    d. This answer is incorrect because the effects of psychoactive drugs on behavior, perception, and so forth have a physiological basis.

16. **d.** is the answer. The results of this study demonstrate that although attention is selective, even unattended-to stimuli can affect our behavior, in this case by increasing the subjects' fondness for previously played tunes. (pp. 190–191)

17. **b.** is the answer. (p. 189)

    a. The behaviorists' emphasis on observable behavior occurred much later in the history of psychology.

    c. Psychology has never been primarily concerned with abnormal behavior.

18. **d.** is the answer. (pp. 198–199)

    a., b., & c. Each of these describes a valid theory of dreaming that was mentioned in the textbook.

19. **c.** is the answer. In the absence of these cues, the normal circadian (24-hour) rhythm shifts to a 25-hour cycle. (p. 192).

20. **c.** is the answer. (p. 202)

    a. Meditation is a more focused state of awareness than daydreaming.

    b. Experienced meditators do exhibit physiological changes in blood pressure, heart rate, brain waves, and metabolism.

Matching Items

1. e (p. 198)   **5.** h (p. 197)   **9.** f (p. 212)
2. k (p. 198)   **6.** d (p. 197)   **10.** c (p. 193)
3. i (p. 193)   **7.** b (p. 210)   **11.** g (p. 196)
4. j (p. 194)   **8.** a (p. 214)

PROGRESS TEST 2

Multiple-Choice Questions

1. **b.** is the answer. Following REM deprivation, people temporarily increase their amount of REM sleep, in a phenomenon known as REM rebound. (p. 200)

a. Just the opposite is true: The amount of REM sleep is greatest in infancy.

c. Deprived of REM sleep by repeated awakenings, people return more and more quickly to the REM stages after falling back to sleep. They by no means adapt easily to the deprivations.

d. Just the opposite occurs: Following stressful experiences, REM sleep tends to increase.

2. **c.** is the answer. (p. 220)

a. Behaviorists focus on observable behaviors and avoid concepts like the mind.

b. The monists believe that the mind and body are one.

d. Freudians focus on unconscious and conscious aspects of the mind and have little to say regarding the mind-body relationship.

3. **a.** is the answer. Alcohol disrupts the processing of experiences into long-term memory but has little effect on either immediate or previously established memories. (p. 211)

4. **d.** is the answer. (p. 193)

a. The brain waves of REM sleep (dream sleep) are more like those of nearly awake, Stage 1 sleepers.

b. Stage 2 is characterized by sleep spindles.

c. Stage 4 is characterized by slow, rolling delta waves.

5. **c.** is the answer. Since circadian rhythms occur regularly over a 24-hour period, the other answers cannot be correct. (p. 192)

6. **a.** is the answer. (p. 210)

b. Physical dependence may occur in the absence of tolerance. The hallmark of physical dependence is the presence of withdrawal symptoms when off the drug.

c. Psychological dependence refers to a felt, or psychological, need to use a drug, for example, a drug that relieves stress.

d. There is no such thing as drug "resistance."

7. **d.** is the answer. (p. 202)

8. **a.** is the answer. (p. 194)

b. During REM sleep, muscular tension is low.

c. Night terrors are associated with Stage 4 sleep.

d. During REM sleep, respiration is rapid and irregular.

9. **d.** is the answer. Alcohol is a depressant. (p. 210)

10. **d.** is the answer. (p. 204)

a. Hypnotic responsiveness varies greatly from person to person.

b. & c. There is no evidence of a gender difference in hypnotic responsiveness.

11. **d.** is the answer. Hilgard believes that hypnosis reflects a dissociation, or split, in consciousness, as occurs normally, only to a much greater extent. (p. 209)

12. **d.** is the answer. All of these are psychoactive drugs. (pp. 210–216)

13. **b.** is the answer. (p. 207)

a. & c. Hypnosis *can* be helpful in treating these problems, but it is no more effective than other forms of therapy.

d. Adults are not more responsive than children to hypnosis.

14. **d.** is the answer. If adolescents' friends use drugs, the odds are that they will, too. (p. 218)

a., b., & c. These are also predictors of drug use but seem to operate mainly through their effects on peer association.

15. **c.** is the answer. (p. 215)

16. **b.** is the answer. (p. 208)

a. & c. There is no evidence that hypnotically responsive individuals fake their behaviors, or that they are underachievers.

17. **b.** is the answer. (p. 189)

18. **a.** is true. The fact that REM sleep tends to increase following intense learning periods has led to the theory that dreams may help sift, sort, and fix in memory the day's experiences. (p. 199)

b. Non-REM Stage 4 sleep tends to increase following strenuous physical exertion, but non-REM sleep usually does *not* increase following intense learning periods.

c. There is no evidence that REM-deprived people have poorer recall of presleep experiences than non-REM-deprived people.

d. Sleep control centers are actually located in the lower centers of the brainstem, not in the association areas of the cortex.

19. **a.** is the answer. Seligman and Yellen believe that the brain's attempt to make sense of random neural activity is consistent with people's well-established tendencies to impose meaning on even meaningless stimuli they experience. (p. 200)

b. & c. These essentially Freudian explanations of the purpose of dreaming are based on the idea that a dream is a psychic safety valve that harmlessly discharges otherwise inexpressible feelings.

d. This explanation of the function of dreaming is associated with the information-processing viewpoint, but not with Seligman and Yellen.

20. **d.** is the answer. (p. 213)

Matching Items

1. c (p. 203)   5. j (p. 194)   9. g (p. 189)
2. f (p. 212)   6. k (p. 212)   10. a (p. 198)
3. d (p. 193)   7. i (p. 212)   11. e (p. 207)
4. h (p. 193)   8. b (p. 215)

CHALLENGE TEST

Multiple-Choice Questions

1. **b.** is the answer. Narcolepsy is the sleep disorder characterized by uncontrollable sleep attacks. (p. 196)

   a. Sleep apnea is characterized by the temporary cessation of breathing while asleep.

   c. Night terrors are characterized by high arousal and terrified behavior, occurring during Stage 4 sleep.

   d. Insomnia refers to chronic difficulty in falling or staying asleep.

2. **d.** is the answer. (p. 218)

   a., b., & c. Each of these was suggested by the text as an important aspect of drug prevention and treatment programs.

3. **b.** is the answer. Although the body is aroused internally, the messages of the activated motor cortex do not reach the muscles. (p. 194)

   a. Studies of REM-deprived subjects indicate just the opposite.

   c. It is difficult to awaken a person from REM sleep.

   d. Just the opposite occurs in REM sleep: The muscles are relaxed, yet the brain is aroused.

4. **a.** is the answer. Although people recall more under hypnosis, they "recall" a lot of fiction along with fact and appear unable to distinguish between the two. (p. 205)

   b. Hypnotically refreshed memories are usually no more accurate than conscious memories.

   c. Although the hypnotized subject's imagination may influence the memories retrieved, some actual memory retrieval also occurs.

   d. Hypnotically retrieved memories don't normally focus on anxiety-provoking events.

5. **c.** is the answer. Continued use of a drug produces a tolerance, so, to experience the same "high," Dan will have to use larger and larger doses. As the doses become larger, the negative aftereffects, or withdrawal symptoms, become worse. (p. 210)

6. **d.** is the answer. The amount of time a person spends in Stage 4 sleep often increases following strenuous exercise, such as military basic training. This indicates that sleep helps to restore exhausted body tissues. (p. 195)

   a. REM sleep tends to increase following stressful experiences or intense learning periods.

   b. & c. The amount of time a person spends in Stage 1 or 2 sleep does not increase following strenuous exercise.

7. **b.** is the answer. Selective attention means focusing on a particular stimulus—the novel in Kathy's case. (p. 190)

   a. Becoming engrossed in a novel is characteristic of a fantasy-prone person but is not, in itself, enough to indicate this personality type.

   c. & d. Dissociation and divided consciousness refer to splits in consciousness, which allow different mental activities to occur simultaneously. In the example, Kathy is engaged in one activity.

8. **d.** is the answer. Alcohol reduces self-consciousness and it loosens inhibitions, making people more likely to act on their feelings of anger or sexual arousal. (p. 211)

9. **b.** is the answer. The analyst is evidently trying to go beyond the events in the dream and understand the dream's hidden meaning, or the dream's latent content. (p. 198)

   a. The manifest content of a dream is its actual story line.

   c. Dissociation refers to a split in levels of consciousness.

   d. There is no such term. In any case, "overt" would be the same as "manifest" content.

10. **d.** is the answer. Because of the phenomenon known as REM rebound, Barry, having been deprived of REM sleep, will now increase his REM sleep. (p. 200)

    a. Increased irritability is an effect of sleep deprivation in general, not of REM deprivation specifically.

    b. REM rebound will cause Barry to dream more than normal.

    c. The increase in REM sleep is necessarily accompanied by decreases in Stages 1–4 sleep.

11. **b.** is the answer. Fantasy-prone people have essentially the characteristics associated with hypnotic suggestibility: rich fantasy lives, the ability to become imaginatively absorbed, etc. The fact that Janice is an actress also suggests she possesses such traits. (pp. 203–204)

    a. Bill's reality orientation makes him an unlikely candidate for hypnosis.

    c. The hypnotically suggestible are generally able to focus on tasks or on imaginative activities.

    d. People who are hypnotically suggestible tend to become deeply engrossed in novels and movies.

12. **a.** is the answer. Adopted individuals are more susceptible to alcoholism if they had an alcoholic *biological* parent. (p. 217)

b., c., & d. Each of these is true, which indicates that susceptibility to alcoholism is at least partially determined by heredity.

13. **d.** is the answer. (pp. 205–207)

14. **b.** is the answer. Although all people daydream, people with fantasy-prone personalities daydream far more and far more vividly. (p. 201)

a. Jane may very well also be suggestible to hypnosis; fantasy-prone personalities tend to be. The stated characteristics, however, do not necessarily indicate that she is.

c. The description indicates that Jane's behavior involves much more than simple daydreaming.

d. There is no such personality as a "dissociator." Dissociation refers to a split in consciousness that allows some thoughts and behaviors to occur simultaneously with others.

15. **b.** is the answer. Monists such as Levar believe that the mind and body are inseparable. Thus, when the body dies, the mind ceases to exist. (p. 220)

a. Behaviorists avoid references to the mind.

c. Dualists believe that the mind can exist apart from the body.

d. The text does not discuss the relationship between religious belief and near-death experiences.

16. **a.** is the answer. THC, the active ingredient in marijuana, and its by-products linger in the body for a month or more. (p. 216)

17. **b.** is the answer. (p. 219)

a. Approximately 30 to 40 percent of people who have come close to death report some sort of near-death experience.

c. & d. There is no gender difference in the prevalence of near-death experiences.

18. **d.** is the answer. (p. 208)

19. **d.** is the answer. As answers a., b., & c. (which are true) indicate, it *is* possible to predict whether or not an adolescent will experiment with drugs. (p. 218)

20. **d.** is the answer. (pp. 201–202)

Essay Question

As a depressant, alcohol slows neural activity and body functions. Although low doses of alcohol may produce relaxation, with larger doses reactions slow, speech slurs, skilled performance deteriorates, and the processing of recent experiences into long-term memo-

ries is disrupted. Alcohol also reduces self-awareness and may facilitate sexual and aggressive urges the individual might otherwise resist.

Some people may be biologically vulnerable to alcoholism. This is indicated by the fact that individuals who have an alcoholic biological parent, or an alcoholic identical twin, are more susceptible to alcoholism.

Stress, depression, and the feeling that life is meaningless and without direction are common feelings among heavy users of alcohol and may create a psychological vulnerability to alcoholism.

Especially for teenagers, peer group influence is strong. If an adolescent's friends use alcohol, odds are that he or she will too.

Research suggests three important channels of influence for drug prevention and treatment programs: (1) education about the long-term consequences of alcohol use; (2) efforts to boost people's self-esteem and purpose in life; and (3) attempts to counteract peer pressure that leads to experimentation with drugs.

KEY TERMS

1. The textbook defines **consciousness** as selective attention to ongoing perceptions, thoughts, and feelings. (p. 189)

   Example: The study of **consciousness** includes not only alert wakefulness, but also altered states, such as sleep and dreaming, daydreams, and states induced by hypnosis and drugs.

2. **Selective attention** refers to the fact that at any given moment our conscious awareness is focused on only a small amount of what we could be experiencing. (p. 190)

3. A **circadian rhythm** is any regular biological rhythm, such as body temperature and sleep-wakefulness, that follows a 24-hour cycle. (p. 192)

   Memory aid: In Latin, *circa* means "about" and *dies* means "day." A **circadian rhythm** is one that is about a day, or 24 hours, in duration.

4. **REM sleep** is the sleep stage in which the brain and eyes are active, the muscles are relaxed, and dreaming occurs. (p. 193)

   Memory aid: **REM** is an acronym for rapid eye movement, the distinguishing feature of this sleep stage that led to its discovery.

5. **Alpha waves** are the relatively slow brain waves characteristic of an awake, relaxed state. (p. 193)

6. **Hallucinations** are illusions, or false sensory experiences; they occur without a sensory stimulus. (p. 193)

   Example: The fantastic imagery of the near-death experience and that of drug-induced **hallucinations** are often quite similar.

7. **Delta waves** are the larger, slow brain waves associated with deep, Stage 4 sleep. (p. 193)

8. **Insomnia** is a sleep disorder in which the person regularly has difficulty in falling or staying asleep. (p. 196)

   Example: Taking sleeping pills to cure **insomnia** is usually counterproductive because they suppress REM sleep.

9. **Narcolepsy** is a sleep disorder in which the victim suffers sudden, uncontrollable sleep attacks, characterized by entry directly into REM. (p. 196)

10. **Sleep apnea** is a sleep disorder in which the person ceases breathing while asleep, briefly arouses to gasp for air, falls back asleep, and repeats this cycle throughout the night. (p. 197)

    Example: One theory of the Sudden Infant Death Syndrome is that it is caused by **sleep apnea**.

11. A person suffering from **night terrors** experiences episodes of high arousal with apparent terror. Night terrors usually occur during Stage 4 sleep. (p. 197)

12. In Freud's theory of dreaming, the **manifest content** is the remembered story line. (p. 198)

13. In Freud's theory of dreaming, the **latent content** is the underlying meaning of a dream. (p. 198)

    Memory aids for 12 and 13: Manifest means "clearly apparent, obvious"; *latent* means "hidden, concealed." A dream's **manifest content** is that which is obvious; its **latent content** remains hidden until its symbolism is interpreted.

14. The **REM rebound** is the tendency for REM sleep to increase following deprivation resulting from, say, the use of sleeping pills. (p. 200)

15. The **fantasy-prone personality** is one who has a vivid imagination and spends an unusual amount of time fantasizing. (p. 201)

16. **Hypnosis** is the state of heightened suggestibility in some people that enables a hypnotist's directions to trigger specific behaviors, perceptions, and possibly memories. (p. 202)

17. **Posthypnotic amnesia** is the condition in which, in response to the hypnotist's suggestion, subjects are unable to recall what happened while they were under hypnosis. (p. 203)

18. In hypnosis, **age regression** is the supposed retrieval of earlier memories and experiences. (p. 204)

19. A **posthypnotic suggestion** is a suggestion made by a hypnotist that is to be carried out when the subject is no longer hypnotized. (p. 205)

    Example: To help clients curb their desire for nicotine, the hypnotist gave them the **posthypnotic suggestion** that when awake, the mere thought of smoking a cigarette would make them nauseated.

20. **Dissociation** is a split between different levels of consciousness, allowing a person to divide attention between two or more thoughts. (p. 207)

21. According to Hilgard, the **hidden observer** is a part of a hypnotized person's consciousness that remains aware of happenings even under hypnosis. Hilgard believes the hidden observer is an example of dissociation. (p. 209)

22. **Psychoactive drugs**—stimulants, depressants, hallucinogens—are chemical substances that alter mood and perception. They work by affecting or mimicking the activity of neurotransmitters. (p. 210)

23. **Tolerance** is the diminishing of a psychoactive drug's effect that occurs with repeated use and the need for progressively larger doses in order to produce the same effect. (p. 210)

24. **Withdrawal** refers to the unpleasant physical and psychological symptoms that accompany the discontinued use of some drugs. (p. 210)

    Example: The painful symptoms of opiate **withdrawal** may occur because, while the opiate was available, the drug user's body stopped its production of pain-reducing endorphins.

25. **Physical dependence** is a physiological need for a drug that is indicated by the presence of withdrawal symptoms when the drug is not taken. (p. 210)

26. The psychological need to use a drug is referred to as **psychological dependence**. (p. 210)

27. **Depressants** are psychoactive drugs, such as alcohol, opiates, and barbiturates, that reduce neural activity and slow down body functions. (p. 210)

28. **Stimulants** are psychoactive drugs, such as caffeine, nicotine, amphetamines, and cocaine, that speed up body functions. (p. 210)

29. **Hallucinogens** are psychoactive drugs, such as LSD and marijuana, that distort perception and evoke sensory imagery in the absence of sensory input. (p. 210)

30. **Barbiturates** are depressants, sometimes used to induce sleep or reduce anxiety. (p. 212)

31. **Opiates** are depressants derived from the opium poppy, such as opium, morphine, and heroin; they reduce neural activity and relieve pain. Opiates are among the most strongly addictive of all psychoactive drugs. (p. 212)

32. **Amphetamines** are a type of stimulant and, as such, speed up body functions and neural activity. (p. 212)

33. **LSD (lysergic acid diethylamide)** is a powerful hallucinogen capable of producing vivid false perceptions and disorganization of thought processes. LSD produces its unpredictable effects partially

because it blocks the action of the neurotransmitter serotonin. (p. 215)

34. The active ingredient in marijuana, **THC** is classified as a mild hallucinogen. (p. 215)

35. The **near-death experience** is an altered state of consciousness that has been reported by some people who have had a close brush with death. (p. 218)

36. **Dualism** is the philosophical belief that the mind and body are distinct entities — the mind nonphysical, the body physical. (p. 220)

Example: Those who believe that **near-death experiences** are proof of immortality are expressing the **dualist** position that mind and body are separate entities.

37. **Monism** is the philosophical belief that the mind and body are different aspects of the same thing. (p. 220)

Example: The belief that death is final and that no afterlife exists is a reflection of the **monist** position that mind and body are one.

8 / Learning

Chapter Overview

No topic is closer to the heart of psychology than learning, a relatively permanent change in an organism's behavior due to experience. Chapter 8 covers the basic principles of three forms of learning: classical conditioning, in which we learn associations between events; operant conditioning, in which we learn to engage in behaviors that are rewarded and to avoid behaviors that are punished; and observational learning, in which we learn by observing and imitating others.

The chapter also covers several important issues, including the generality of principles of learning, the role of cognitive processes in learning, and the ways in which learning is constrained by the biological predispositions of different species.

NOTE: Answer guidelines for all Chapter 8 questions begin on page 169.

Guided Study

The text chapter should be studied one section at a time. Before you read, preview each section by skimming it, noting headings and boldface items. Then read the appropriate section objectives from the following outline. Keep these objectives in mind and, as you read the chapter section, search for the information that will enable you to meet each objective. Once you have finished a section, write out answers for its objectives.

Classical Conditioning (pp. 228–235)

1. Describe the nature of classical conditioning and show how it demonstrates learning by association.

2. Explain the processes of acquisition, extinction, spontaneous recovery, generalization, and discrimination.

3. Discuss cognitive and biological constraints on classical conditioning.

4. Discuss the importance of Pavlov's work in classical conditioning and explain how Pavlov paved the way for the behaviorist position.

Operant Conditioning (pp. 236–247)

5. Describe the process of operant conditioning, including the procedure of shaping.

6. Identify the different types of reinforcers and describe the major schedules of partial reinforcement.

7. Discuss the effects of punishment on behavior.

8. Discuss evidence of the importance of cognitive and biological processes in operant conditioning.

9. Describe some major applications of operant conditioning.

Learning by Observation (pp. 247–248)

10. Describe the process of observational learning.

Chapter Review

When you have finished reading the chapter, work through the material that follows to review it. Complete the sentences and answer the questions. As you proceed, evaluate your performance for each section by consulting the answers on page 170. Do not continue with the next section until you understand each answer. If you need to, review or reread the appropriate section in the textbook before continuing.

1. A relatively permanent change in an organism's behavior due to experience is called
   learning.

2. During the seventeenth century, philosophers, such as John Locke, argued that an important factor in learning is our tendency to
   associate events that occur in a sequence. Even simple animals, such as the sea snail *Aplysia*, can learn simple
   associations between stimuli.

3. The type of learning in which the organism learns to anticipate and prepare for significant events is _Classical_ conditioning.

4. The tendency of organisms to repeat acts that produce favorable outcomes forms the basis of
   operant conditioning.

5. Learning by watching others is called
   observational learning.

6. Early in this century, psychologist
   John Watson urged psychologists to discard references to mental concepts in favor of studying observable behavior. This view, called
   behaviorism, influenced American psychology during the first half of the century.

Classical Conditioning (pp. 228–235)

7. Classical conditioning was first explored by the Russian physiologist _Ivan Pavlov_

8. In Pavlov's classic experiment, a bell, or
   conditioned stimulus,
   is sounded just before food, the
   unconditioned stimulus,
   is placed in the animal's mouth.

9. An animal will salivate when food is placed in its mouth. This salivation is called the
   unconditioned response.

10. Eventually, the dogs in Pavlov's experiment would salivate on hearing the tone. This salivation is called the _conditioned response_

Explain why learning theorists consider classically conditioned behaviors to be biologically adaptive.

11. For many conditioning situations, the optimal interval between a neutral stimulus and the UCS is _one-half   second_.

12. When the UCS is presented prior to a neutral stimulus, conditioning _does   not_ (does/does not) occur.

13. If a CS is repeatedly presented without the UCS, _extinction_ soon occurs; that is, the CR diminishes.

14. Following a rest, however, the CR reappears in response to the CS; this phenomenon is called _spontaneous   recovery_.

15. Subjects often respond to a similar stimulus as they would to the original CS. This phenomenon is called _generalization_. Subjects can, however, also be trained not to respond to these similar stimuli. This learned ability is called _discrimination_.

16. Experiments by Rescorla and Wagner found that when a CS and a UCS are randomly paired, conditioning _does not._ (does/does not) take place. This demonstrates that a CS must reliably _predict_ the UCS for an association to develop and, more generally, that _cognitive._ processes play a role in conditioning.

Describe two issues that have led to the recent reconsideration of behaviorism.

17. The importance of cognitive processes in human conditioning is demonstrated by the failure of classical conditioning as a treatment for _alcoholism_.

18. Garcia discovered that rats would associate _sickness_ with taste, but not with other stimuli. Garcia found that taste-aversion conditioning _would_ (would/would not) occur when the delay between the CS and the UCS was more than an hour. Results such as these demonstrate that the principles of learning are constrained by the _biological_ predispositions of each animal species and that they help each species _adapt_ to its environment.

Explain why the study of classical conditioning is important.

19. In their famous experiment, Watson and Rayner used _classical_ conditioning to train an infant to fear a rat.

Describe the Watson and Rayner experiment.

Operant Conditioning (pp. 236–247)

20. Classical conditioning involves _involuntary_ (voluntary/involuntary) responses. For _voluntary_ (voluntary/involuntary) responses, _operant._ conditioning is more relevant.

21. Skinner has referred to the automatic responses of classical conditioning as _respondent_

behavior. In contrast, he labels behavior that is more spontaneous and that is influenced by its consequences as _operant_ behavior.

22. Using Thorndike's _law of effect_ as a starting point, Skinner developed a behavioral technology. He designed an apparatus, called the _Skinner Box_, to investigate learning in animals.

23. The procedure in which a person teaches an animal to perform an intricate behavior by building up to it in small steps is called _Shaping_. This method involves reinforcing successive _approximations_ of the desired behavior.

24. An event that strengthens the behavior it follows is a _reinforcer_.

25. According to _Premaks principle_, any activity can be reinforced by a more preferred activity.

26. A stimulus that strengthens behavior that leads to its presentation is a _positive reinforcer_.

27. A stimulus that reinforces behavior that leads to its termination is a _negative reinforcer_.

28. Reinforcers, such as food and shock, that are related to basic needs and therefore do not rely on learning are called _primary reinforcers_. Reinforcers that must be conditioned and therefore derive their power through association are called _secondary reinforcers_.

29. Children who are able to delay gratification tend to become _more_ (more/less) socially competent and high achieving.

30. Immediate reinforcement _is_ (is/is not) more effective than its alternative, _delayed_ reinforcement.

31. The procedure involving reinforcement of each and every response is called _Continuous_

reinforcement. Under these conditions, learning is _rapid_ (rapid/slow). When this type of reinforcement is discontinued, extinction is _rapid_ (rapid/slow).

32. The procedure in which responses are only intermittently reinforced is called _partial_ reinforcement. Under these conditions, learning is generally _slower_ (faster/slower) than it is with continuous reinforcement. Behavior reinforced in this manner is _very_ (very/not very) resistant to extinction.

33. When behavior is reinforced after a set number of responses, a _fixed-ratio_ schedule is in effect.

34. Three-year-old Yusef knows that if he cries when he wants a treat, his mother will sometimes give in. When, as in this case, reinforcement occurs after an unpredictable number of responses, a _variable-ratio_ schedule is being used.

35. Reinforcement of the first response after a set interval of time defines the _fixed-interval_ schedule. An example of this schedule is _checking mail_.

36. When the first response after varying amounts of time is reinforced, a _variable-interval_ schedule is in effect.

Describe the typical patterns of response under fixed-interval, fixed-ratio, variable-interval, and variable-ratio schedules of reinforcement.

37. An aversive consequence that decreases the likelihood of the behavior that preceded it is called _Punishment_.

Describe some drawbacks to the use of punishment.

38. When a well-learned route in a maze is blocked, rats sometimes choose an alternative route, acting as if they were consulting a _cognitive_ _map_.

39. Animals may learn from experience even when reinforcement is not available. When learning is not apparent until reinforcement has been provided, _latent_ _learning_ is said to have occurred.

40. When people are rewarded for doing what they already enjoy, their intrinsic motivation may be undermined; this is the _overjustification_ _effect_.

41. Operant conditioning _is_ (is/is not) constrained by an animal's biological predispositions.

42. The use of teaching machines and programmed textbooks was an early application of the operant conditioning procedure of _shaping_ to education.

List some of the advantages of computer-assisted instruction.

43. In boosting productivity in the workplace, positive reinforcement is _more_ (more/less) effective when applied to specific behaviors than when given to reward general merit. For such behaviors, immediate reinforcement is _more_ (more/ no more) effective than delayed reinforcement.

Learning by Observation (pp. 247–248)

44. Learning by imitation is called modeling, or _observational learning_. The psychologist best known for research in this area is _Bandura_.

45. In one experiment, the child who viewed an adult punch an inflatable doll played _more_ (more/less) aggressively than the child who had not observed the adult.

46. Children will also model positive, or _prosocial_, behaviors.

FOCUS ON PSYCHOLOGY:
The Prenatal University

René Van de Carr is a California obstetrician who became interested in "prenatal psychology" after a patient reported that when she poked her baby through her abdomen it poked back. This observation, as well as extensive research, led him to establish a course for prospective parents who want to "teach" their unborn children.

Van de Carr claims that his course, which involves a complex program of words, sounds, and tactile stimulation, teaches the developing child to attend to specific stimuli, a skill that supposedly facilitates the later acquisition of a variety of intellectual abilities. The training begins during the fifth month of pregnancy when parents are urged to respond to the baby's natural kicking by gently pushing back and verbally reinforcing the movement by saying, "Good baby, kick again!" The first evidence of learning occurs within several weeks when kicking, like any voluntary response subjected to positive reinforcement, becomes more frequent.

In the seventh month of prenatal development parents begin to teach their babies to associate spoken words with touch. Twice a day, in five-minute sessions, parents say, "Rub, rub, rub, rub," as they rub the mother's abdomen, or "Shake, shake, shake, shake," as the mother (and baby) gently wiggle.

Some of Van de Carr's prenatal students continue on for "postgraduate education" as their parents attempt to teach more difficult words, such as "hot," "cold," and "wet," and give their children an early advantage in auditioning for the school orchestra by playing various instruments and saying the note names aloud.

Does Van de Carr's program work? In a recent longitudinal study, he compared the development of children who were graduates of his program with that of children who had some exposure to the training techniques and children who had not participated in the program. The findings indicated that graduates spoke their first words earlier, advanced to the two-word stage of language at a younger age, and demonstrated object constancy (the awareness that objects continue to exist even when out of sight) earlier than did the partially trained babies. Babies who had not participated in the prenatal program developed each of these abilities even later.

Although Van de Carr contends that more than 1500 babies have been helped by his program, other psychologists are skeptical of its effectiveness. For one thing, parents who stimulate their babies before birth are more likely to provide above-average intellectual stimulation after birth as well. It may be this later stimulation, rather than the prenatal program, that leads to the developmental advantage.

Clinical psychologist Amy Altenhaus also notes that, "It is often difficult to predict behavior from developmental milestones before the age of 3. A 6-month-old who achieves exceptional development may not necessarily be exceptional down the road." The meaning of early attainment of these abilities is therefore not clear.

The opposing views on the prenatal program reflect the controversy over the value of early learning. On one side are those who believe that children have a much greater capacity to learn at an early age than was previously thought. Parents who take this position are flocking to enroll in programs that help them teach their infants to swim, read, do math, learn a foreign language, play chess, and master musical instruments.

Taking the opposite viewpoint are those parents, psychologists, and educators who believe—as David Elkind, the author of *The Hurried Child*, does—that many parents are pushing their children too hard. These people maintain that while there is little evidence of early instruction having lasting benefits, evidence of its potential for lasting harm is considerable.

What then are prospective parents to believe? As with many other issues, the truth probably lies somewhere between the two extremes. Intellectually, "too much, too soon" may very well be unhealthy for the child. Yet, some aspects of the programs may be beneficial. As psychologist Altenhaus says, "Such things as music and massage, if they calm the mother down, can only be positive for the fetus."

Sources: Prentice, K. (1988, March 2). Toddling onto the fast track? *Detroit Free Press*, 1B, 3B.

Weintraub, P. (1989, August). Preschool? *Omni*, 34–38, 42–47.

Progress Test 1

Multiple-Choice Questions

Circle your answers to the following questions and check them with the answers on page 171. If your answer is incorrect, read the explanation for why it is incorrect and then consult the appropriate pages of the text (in parentheses following the correct answer).

1. Learning is best defined as:
   a. any behavior emitted by an organism without being elicited.
   b. a change in the behavior of an organism.
   c. a relatively permanent change in the behavior of an organism due to experience.
   d. behavior based on operant rather than respondent conditioning.

2. The type of learning associated with B. F. Skinner is:
   a. classical conditioning.
   b. operant conditioning.
   c. respondent conditioning.
   d. observational learning.

3. In Pavlov's original experiment with dogs, the meat served as a(n):
   a. conditioned stimulus.
   b. conditioned response.
   c. unconditioned stimulus.
   d. unconditioned response.

4. In Pavlov's original experiment with dogs, the tone was initially a(n) _____ stimulus; after it was paired with meat, it became a(n) _____ stimulus.
   a. conditioned; neutral
   b. neutral; conditioned
   c. conditioned; unconditioned
   d. unconditioned; conditioned

5. In order to obtain a reward a monkey learns to press a lever when a 1000-Hz tone is on but not when a 1200-Hz tone is on. What kind of training is this?
   a. extinction
   b. generalization
   c. discrimination
   d. classical conditioning

6. Which of the following statements concerning reinforcement is correct?
   a. Learning is most rapid with partial reinforcement, but continuous reinforcement produces the greatest resistance to extinction.
   b. Learning is most rapid with continuous reinforcement, but partial reinforcement produces the greatest resistance to extinction.
   c. Learning is fastest and resistance to extinction is greatest following continuous reinforcement.
   d. Learning is fastest and resistance to extinction is greatest following partial reinforcement.

7. Cognitive processes are:
   a. unimportant in classical and operant conditioning.
   b. important in both classical and operant conditioning.
   c. more important in classical than in operant conditioning.
   d. more important in operant than in classical conditioning.

8. Which of the following schedules of reinforcement produces the highest and most consistent rate of response?
   a. fixed-ratio
   b. variable-ratio
   c. fixed-interval
   d. variable-interval

9. A response that leads to the removal of an unpleasant stimulus is one being:
   a. positively reinforced.
   b. negatively reinforced.
   c. punished.
   d. extinguished.

10. When a conditioned stimulus is presented without an accompanying unconditioned stimulus, _____ will soon take place.
    a. generalization   c. extinction
    b. discrimination   d. aversion

11. One difference between classical and operant conditioning is that:
    a. in classical conditioning the responses are voluntary.
    b. in operant conditioning the responses are triggered by preceding stimuli.
    c. in classical conditioning the responses are involuntary.
    d. in operant conditioning the responses are involuntary.

12. In Garcia and Koelling's studies of taste-aversion learning, rats learned to associate:
    a. taste with electric shock.
    b. sights and sounds with sickness.
    c. taste with sickness.
    d. taste and sounds with electric shock.

13. In Pavlov's original experiment with dogs, salivation to meat was the:
    a. conditioned stimulus.
    b. conditioned response.
    c. unconditioned stimulus.
    d. unconditioned response.

14. Learning by imitating others' behaviors is called _____ learning. The researcher best known for studying this type of learning is:
    a. secondary; Skinner.
    b. observational; Bandura.
    c. secondary; Pavlov.
    d. observational; Watson.

15. When people are paid for performing tasks they enjoy, their self-motivation may actually decrease. This is called:
    a. latent learning.
    b. the overjustification effect.
    c. primary reinforcement.
    d. modeling.

16. Punishment is a controversial way of controlling behavior because:
    a. behavior is not forgotten and may return.
    b. punishing stimuli often create fear.
    c. punishment often increases aggressiveness.
    d. of all of the above reasons.

17. Classical conditioning experiments by Rescorla and Wagner demonstrate that an important factor in conditioning is:
    a. the subject's age.
    b. the strength of the stimuli.
    c. the predictability of an association.
    d. all of the above.

18. Which of the following is an example of reinforcement?
    a. presenting a positive stimulus after a response
    b. removing an unpleasant stimulus after a response
    c. permitting an individual to engage in a preferred activity after a response
    d. All of the above are examples.

19. Premack's principle states that:
    a. any stimulus can be associated with any response.
    b. not all stimuli and responses can easily be associated.
    c. any activity can be reinforced by a more preferred activity.
    d. the predictability of a CS and UCS occurring together determines the strength of conditioning.

20. For the most rapid conditioning, a CS should be presented:
    a. about 1 second after the UCS.
    b. about one-half second before the UCS.
    c. about 15 seconds before the UCS.
    d. at the same time as the UCS.

Matching Items

Match each definition or description with the appropriate term.

Definitions or Descriptions

_____ e **1.** presenting a desired stimulus
_____ h **2.** tendency for similar stimuli to evoke a CR
_____ f **3.** terminating an aversive stimulus
_____ g **4.** an innately reinforcing stimulus
_____ i **5.** an acquired reinforcer
_____ k **6.** responses are reinforced after an unpredictable amount of time
_____ j **7.** each and every response is reinforced
_____ a **8.** reinforcing closer and closer approximations of a behavior
_____ c **9.** the reappearance of an extinguished CR
_____ b **10.** presenting an aversive stimulus
_____ d **11.** learning that becomes apparent only after reinforcement is provided

Terms

a. shaping
b. punishment
c. spontaneous recovery
d. latent learning
e. positive reinforcement
f. negative reinforcement
g. primary reinforcer
h. generalization
i. secondary reinforcer
j. continuous reinforcement
k. variable-interval schedule

Progress Test 2

Progress Test 2 should be completed during a final chapter review. Answer the following questions after you thoroughly understand the correct answers for the Chapter Review and Progress Test 1.

Multiple-Choice Questions

1. During extinction, the _____ is omitted; as a result, the _____ seems to disappear.
  a. UCS; UCR   **c.** UCS; CR
  b. CS; CR   **d.** CS; UCR

2. In Watson and Rayner's experiment, the loud noise was the _____ and the white rat was the _____.
  a. CS; CR   **c.** CS; UCS
  b. UCS; CS   **d.** UCS; CR

3. Classical conditioning may play a role in:
  a. emotional disorders.
  b. the body's immune response.
  c. how animals adapt to the environment.
  d. all of the above.

4. Shaping is a(n) _____ technique for _____ a behavior.
  a. operant; establishing
  b. operant; suppressing
  c. respondent; establishing
  d. respondent; suppressing

5. In Pavlov's studies of classical conditioning of a dog's salivary responses, spontaneous recovery occurred:

a. during acquisition, when the CS was first paired with the UCS.
b. during extinction, when the CS was first presented by itself.
c. when the CS was reintroduced following extinction of the CR and a rest period.
d. during discrimination training, when several conditioned stimuli were introduced.

6. For classical conditioning to be effective, when should the reinforcers be presented in relation to the desired response?
  a. immediately before
  b. immediately after
  c. at the same time as
  d. in any of the above sequences

7. In distinguishing between negative reinforcers and punishment, we note that:

a. punishment, but not negative reinforcement, involves use of an aversive stimulus.
b. in contrast to punishment, with negative reinforcement the likelihood of a response is decreased by the presentation of an aversive stimulus.
c. in contrast to punishment, with negative reinforcement the likelihood of a response is increased by the presentation of an aversive stimulus.
d. in contrast to punishment, with negative reinforcement the likelihood of a response is increased by the termination of an aversive stimulus.

8. The "piecework," or commission, method of payment is an example of which reinforcement schedule?
   a. fixed-interval
   b. variable-interval
   c. fixed-ratio
   d. variable-ratio

9. Putting on your coat when it is cold outside is a behavior that is maintained by:
   a. discrimination learning.
   b. punishment.
   c. negative reinforcement.
   d. classical conditioning.

10. On a partial reinforcement schedule, reinforcement is given:
    a. in very small amounts.
    b. randomly.
    c. for successive approximations of a desired behavior.
    d. only some of the time.

11. You teach your dog to fetch the paper by giving him a cookie each time he does so. This is an example of:
    a. operant conditioning.
    b. classical conditioning.
    c. secondary reinforcement.
    d. partial reinforcement.

12. To be effective in promoting observational learning, models should be:
    a. perceived as similar to the observers.
    b. respected and admired.
    c. consistent in their actions and words.
    d. all of the above.

13. A cognitive map is a:
    a. mental representation of one's environment.
    b. sequence of thought processes leading from one idea to another.
    c. set of instructions detailing the most effective means of teaching a particular concept.
    d. biological predisposition to learn a particular skill.

14. After exploring a complicated maze for several days, a rat subsequently ran the maze with very few errors when food was placed in the goal box for the first time. This performance illustrates:
    a. classical conditioning.
    b. discrimination learning.
    c. observational learning.
    d. latent learning.

15. Leon's psychology instructor has scheduled an exam every third week of the term. Leon will probably study the most just before an exam and the least just after an exam. This is because the sched-

ule of exams is reinforcing studying according to which schedule?
   a. fixed-ratio
   b. variable-ratio
   c. fixed-interval
   d. variable-interval

16. Operant conditioning is to _____ as respondent conditioning is to _____.
    a. Pavlov; Watson
    b. Skinner; Bandura
    c. involuntary behavior; voluntary behavior
    d. voluntary behavior; involuntary behavior

17. Computer-assisted instruction (CAI) is an application of the operant conditioning principles of:
    a. shaping and immediate reinforcement.
    b. immediate reinforcement and punishment.
    c. shaping and primary reinforcement.
    d. continuous reinforcement and punishment.

18. Fishing is reinforced according to which schedule?
    a. fixed-interval
    b. fixed-ratio
    c. variable-interval
    d. variable-ratio

19. Which of the following is the best example of a secondary reinforcer?
    a. putting on a coat on a cold day
    b. relief from pain after the dentist stops drilling your teeth
    c. receiving a cool drink after washing your mother's car on a hot day
    d. receiving an approving nod from the boss for a job well done

20. Experiments on taste-aversion learning demonstrate that:
    a. for the conditioning of certain stimuli, the UCS need not immediately follow the CS.
    b. any perceivable stimulus can become a CS.
    c. all animals are biologically primed to associate illness with the taste of a tainted food.
    d. all of the above are true.

True-False Items

Indicate whether each statement is true or false by placing *T* or *F* in the blank next to the item.

_____ 1. Operant conditioning involves behavior that is primarily involuntary.

_____ 2. The optimal interval between CS and UCS is about 15 seconds.

_____ 3. Negative reinforcement decreases the likelihood that a response will recur.

_____ 4. The learning of a new behavior proceeds most rapidly with continuous reinforcement.

_____I_____ 5. As a rule, variable schedules of reinforcement produce more consistent rates of responding than fixed schedules.

_____F_____ 6. Cognitive processes are of relatively little importance in learning.

_____I_____ 7. Although punishment may be effective in suppressing behavior, it can have several undesirable side effects.

_____F_____ 8. All animals, including rats and birds, are biologically predisposed to associate taste cues with sickness.

_____F_____ 9. Whether the CS or UCS is presented first seems not to matter in terms of the ease of classical conditioning.

_____T_____ 10. Spontaneous recovery refers to the tendency of extinguished behaviors to reappear suddenly.

CHALLENGE TEST

Answer these questions the day before an exam as a final check on your understanding of the chapter's terms and concepts.

Multiple-Choice Questions

1. You always rattle the box of dog biscuits before giving your dog a treat. As you do so, your dog salivates. Rattling the box is a(n) _____; your dog's salivation is a(n) _____.
   a. conditioned stimulus; conditioned response
   b. conditioned stimulus; unconditioned response
   c. unconditioned stimulus; conditioned response
   d. unconditioned stimulus; unconditioned response

2. You are expecting an important letter in the mail. As the regular delivery time approaches you glance more and more frequently out the window, searching for the letter carrier. Your behavior in this situation typifies that associated with which schedule of reinforcement?
   a. fixed-ratio
   b. variable-ratio
   c. fixed-interval
   d. variable-interval

3. Jack finally takes out the garbage in order to get his father to stop pestering him. Jack's behavior is being influenced by:
   a. positive reinforcement.
   b. negative reinforcement.
   c. Premack's principle.
   d. punishment.

4. Mrs. Ramirez often tells her children that it is important to buckle their seat belts while riding in the car, but she rarely does so herself. Her children will probably learn to:
   a. use their seat belts and tell others it is important to do so.
   b. use their seat belts but not tell others it is important to do so.
   c. tell others it is important to use seat belts but rarely use them themselves.
   d. neither tell others that seat belts are important nor use them.

5. A pigeon can easily be taught to flap its wings in order to avoid shock but not for food reinforcement. According to the textbook, this is most likely so because:
   a. pigeons are biologically predisposed to flap their wings in order to escape aversive events and to use their beaks to obtain food.
   b. shock is a more motivating stimulus for birds than food is.
   c. hungry animals have difficulty delaying their eating long enough to learn _any_ new skill.
   d. of all of the above reasons.

6. From a casino owner's viewpoint, which of the following jackpot-payout schedules would be the most desirable for reinforcing customer use of a slot machine?
   a. variable-ratio   c. variable-interval
   b. fixed-ratio   d. fixed-interval

7. After discovering that her usual route home was closed due to road repairs, Sharetta used her knowledge of the city and sense of direction to find an alternate route. Her behavior is an example of:
   a. latent learning.
   b. observational learning.
   c. shaping.
   d. using a cognitive map.

For questions 8 to 11, use the following information.
   As a child you were playing in the yard one day when a neighbor's cat wandered over. Your mother (who has a terrible fear of animals) screamed and snatched you into her arms. Her behavior caused you to cry. You now have a fear of cats.

8. Identify the CS.
   a. your mother's behavior
   b. your crying
   c. the cat
   d. your fear today

9. Identify the UCS.
   a. your mother's behavior
   b. your crying
   c. the cat
   d. your fear today

10. Identify the CR.
    a. your mother's behavior
    b. your crying
    c. the cat
    d. your fear today

11. Identify the UCR.
    a. your mother's behavior
    b. your crying
    c. the cat
    d. your fear today

12. The manager of a manufacturing plant wishes to use positive reinforcement to increase the productivity of her workers. Which of the following procedures would probably be the most effective?
    a. Deserving employees are given a general merit bonus at the end of each fiscal year.
    b. A productivity goal that seems attainable, yet actually is unrealistic, is set for each employee.
    c. Employees are given immediate bonuses for specific behaviors related to productivity.
    d. Employees who fail to meet standards of productivity receive pay cuts.

13. Which of the following would be most likely to result in the overjustification effect?
    a. Each day that her son fails to clean his room, Mrs. Shih adds an additional chore he must complete.
    b. Kim's mother decides to reward her daughter's enjoyment of karate by paying her 75 cents for each hour that she practices.
    c. The manager of a shoe store decides to give a bonus to the employee who sells the most shoes each week.
    d. After her soccer team's poor performance, the coach scolds the players.

14. Bill once had a blue car that was in the shop more than it was out. Since then he will not even consider owning blue- or green-colored cars. Bill's aversion to green cars is an example of:
    a. discrimination.
    b. generalization.
    c. latent learning.
    d. the overjustification effect.

15. After watching coverage of the Olympics on television recently, Lynn and Susan have been staging their own "summer games." Which of the following best accounts for their behavior?
    a. classical conditioning
    b. observational learning
    c. latent learning
    d. shaping

16. Two groups of rats receive classical conditioning trials in which a tone and electric shock are pre-sented. For Group 1 the electric shock always follows the tone. For Group 2 the tone and shock occur randomly. Which of the following is likely to result?
    a. The tone will become a CS for Group 1 but not for Group 2.
    b. The tone will become a CS for Group 2 but not for Group 1.
    c. The tone will become a CS for both groups.
    d. The tone will not become a CS for either group.

17. Last evening May-ling ate her first cheeseburger and french fries at an American fast-food restaurant. A few hours later she became ill. It can be expected that:
    a. May-ling will develop an aversion to the sight of a cheeseburger and french fries.
    b. May-ling will develop an aversion to the taste of a cheeseburger and french fries.
    c. May-ling will not associate her illness with the food she ate.
    d. May-ling will associate her sickness with something she experienced immediately before she became ill.

18. Reggie's mother tells him that he can watch TV after he cleans his room. Evidently, Reggie's mother is attempting to use _____ to increase room cleaning.
    a. operant conditioning
    b. Premack's principle
    c. positive reinforcement
    d. all of the above

19. Which of the following is an example of shaping?
    a. A dog learns to salivate at the sight of a box of dog biscuits.
    b. A new driver learns to stop at an intersection when the light changes to red.
    c. A parrot is rewarded first for making any sound, then for making a sound similar to "Laura," and then for "speaking" its owner's name.
    d. A psychology student reinforces a laboratory rat only occasionally, to make its behavior more resistant to extinction.

20. Lars is paid for his job every two weeks, whereas Tom receives a commission for each pair of shoes he sells. Evidently, Lars is paid on a _____ schedule of reinforcement, and Tom on a _____ schedule of reinforcement.
    a. fixed-ratio; fixed-interval
    b. continuous; intermittent
    c. fixed-interval; fixed-ratio
    d. variable-interval; variable-ratio

34. observational learning

35. modeling

36. prosocial behavior

ANSWERS
GUIDED STUDY

The following guidelines provide the main points that your answers should have touched upon.

1. Through classical conditioning, organisms learn to anticipate and prepare for significant events, such as the delivery of food or a painful stimulus. Classical conditioning occurs when a neutral stimulus becomes associated with an unconditioned stimulus (UCS). By itself, the UCS will automatically trigger an involuntary, or reflexive, unconditioned response (UCR). If the association between the CS and UCS is predictable, conditioning will occur and the CS alone will eventually elicit a conditioned response (CR) similar to the UCR.

2. Acquisition refers to the initial stage of learning, during which the CR is established and gradually strengthened. Extinction refers to the gradual disappearance of a CR when the CS is repeatedly presented without a UCS. Spontaneous recovery refers to the reappearance, after a period of rest, of an extinguished CR. Generalization is the tendency for stimuli similar to the CS to evoke a CR. Discrimination is the ability to distinguish between an actual CS and similar stimuli that have not been paired with the UCS.

3. Pavlov, Watson, and the early behaviorists underestimated the importance of cognitive processes and biological constraints on learning.

   Research by Rescorla and Wagner demonstrated that classical conditioning occurs best when the association between a CS and UCS is predictable. This indicates that subjects develop a cognitive expectancy, or an awareness of how likely it is that the UCS will follow the CS.

Garcia and Koelling's studies of conditioned taste aversion demonstrated that animals are biologically primed to learn to associate certain CSs with certain UCSs. Rats, for example, develop aversions to the taste, but not the appearance, of tainted foods. In contrast, birds are biologically primed to develop aversions to the sight of tainted food. This violates the behaviorist tenet that any perceivable stimulus can become a CS.

4. Pavlov's work in classical conditioning showed how a significant internal process, such as learning, could be studied objectively. Pavlov's findings also provided a basis for the behaviorist idea that human behavior consists, in part, of stimulus-response connections.

   The original behaviorist philosophy, as stated by John Watson, was that psychology should be an objective science that studied only observable behaviors and avoided references to all mental processes. Watson argued that by studying how organisms respond to stimuli in their environments, psychologists would eventually become able to understand, predict, and control behavior.

5. In contrast to classical conditioning, which works on involuntary behaviors, *operant* conditioning works on voluntary behaviors. Operant behaviors *operate* on the environment to produce consequences that influence the future occurrence of those behaviors. Behaviors followed by favorable events (reinforcers) tend to be repeated. Behaviors followed by unpleasant stimuli (punishment) tend not to be repeated.

   Shaping is a systematic technique for establishing a new response in which successive approximations of a desired behavior are reinforced.

6. A positive reinforcer is a stimulus that strengthens a response that leads to its presentation. A negative reinforcer is an aversive stimulus that strengthens a response that leads to its removal. Primary reinforcers are innately reinforcing stimuli that satisfy biological needs. Secondary reinforcers acquire their effectiveness by being associated with primary reinforcers.

   Fixed-interval schedules deliver reinforcement for the first response that follows a specified amount of time. Variable-interval schedules deliver reinforcement for a response following unpredictable time intervals. Fixed-ratio schedules deliver reinforcement after a set number of responses. Variable-ratio schedules deliver reinforcement after an unpredictable number of responses.

7. A punisher is any consequence that decreases the frequency of a behavior that it follows. Although

punishment may be effective in the short run, it has its drawbacks. Because punished behavior is merely suppressed rather than forgotten, it may reappear in safe settings. Punishment may also promote aggressiveness as a way of coping with problems, fear of the person who administers it, or fear of the situation in which it occurs. Because punishment does not teach positive behaviors, it is usually more effective when used in combination with positive reinforcement.

8. Latent learning is learning that occurs without reinforcement. Rats allowed to explore a maze without reinforcement nevertheless learn a cognitive map of its layout. When they later are rewarded, they immediately perform as well as rats that have been reinforced with food all along.

Overjustification occurs when people, who are offered a reward for a task they already enjoy, lose their intrinsic motivation for the task.

Latent learning and overjustification demonstrate that there is more to learning than the association of a response with a reinforcer. Cognitive processes must be taken into consideration.

Evidence for biological processes in operant conditioning comes from studies demonstrating that animals have biologically predisposed response patterns that influence the effectiveness of operant procedures with certain behaviors.

9. Operant principles of shaping and immediate reinforcement have been applied in school settings through the use of computer-assisted instruction for some drill and practice tasks. Operant principles have also helped business managers reduce absenteeism and increase productivity among their employees. Operant principles also have helped people take charge of their own behavior by creating self-management programs to stop smoking, lose weight, study, or exercise.

10. Observational learning, in which people observe and imitate, or model, others' behaviors, explains how many social behaviors are acquired. Research studies have shown that children will imitate both antisocial and prosocial models. Models are most effective when their actions and words are consistent. We are most likely to imitate people we respect, those we perceive as similar to ourselves, and those we perceive as successful.

CHAPTER REVIEW

1. learning
2. associate; associations
3. classical
4. operant
5. observational learning

6. John Watson; behaviorism
7. Ivan Pavlov
8. conditioned stimulus; unconditioned stimulus
9. unconditioned response
10. conditioned response

Learning theorists consider classical conditioning to be adaptive because conditioned responses help organisms to prepare for good or bad events (unconditioned stimuli) that are about to occur.

11. one-half second
12. does not
13. extinction
14. spontaneous recovery
15. generalization; discrimination
16. does not; predict; cognitive

The early behaviorists believed that all learned behavior could be reduced to stimulus-response mechanisms. This discounting of mental (cognitive) processes has been strongly challenged by experiments suggesting that even in animals cognition is important for learning. Second, the behaviorists' belief that learning principles would generalize from one response to another and from one species to another has been questioned by research indicating that conditioning principles are constrained by each organism's biological predispositions.

17. alcoholism
18. sickness; would; biological; adapt

Classical conditioning led to the discovery of general principles of learning that are the same for all species tested, including people. Classical conditioning also provided an example to the young field of psychology of how complex behaviors could be studied objectively. In addition, classical conditioning has proven to have many helpful applications to human health and well-being.

19. classical

In Watson and Rayner's experiment, classical conditioning was used to condition a fear of a rat in Albert, an 11-month-old infant. When Albert touched the white rat (neutral stimulus), a loud noise (unconditioned stimulus) was sounded. After several pairings of the rat with the noise, Albert began crying at the mere sight of the rat. The rat had become a conditioned stimulus, eliciting a conditioned response of fear.

20. involuntary; voluntary; operant
21. respondent; operant
22. law of effect; Skinner box
23. shaping; approximations
24. reinforcer
25. Premack's principle

26. positive reinforcer
27. negative reinforcer
28. primary reinforcers; secondary reinforcers
29. more
30. is; delayed
31. continuous reinforcement; rapid; rapid
32. partial; slower; very
33. fixed-ratio
34. variable-ratio
35. fixed-interval; checking the mail as delivery time approaches
36. variable-interval

Following reinforcement on a fixed-interval schedule, there is a pause in responding and then an increasing rate of response as time for the next reinforcement draws near. On a fixed-ratio schedule there also is a post-reinforcement pause, followed, however, by a return to a consistent, high rate of response. Both kinds of variable schedules produce steadier rates of response, without the pauses associated with fixed schedules.

37. punishment

Because punished behavior is merely suppressed, it may reappear. Punishment can lead to fear and a sense of helplessness, as well as to the association of the aversive event with the person who administers it. Punishment also often increases aggressiveness, anger, and hostility. Finally, punishment alone does not guide the organism toward more desirable behavior.

38. cognitive map
39. latent learning
40. overjustification effect
41. is
42. shaping

For some types of educational tasks, such as teaching reading, math, and other skills based on "drill and practice" techniques, CAI is very effective. The computer engages students actively, paces material individually, provides immediate feedback, and keeps detailed records of achievement.

43. more; more
44. observational learning; Bandura
45. more
46. prosocial

PROGRESS TEST 1

Multiple-Choice Questions

1. **c.** is the answer. (p. 227)
   a. This answer is incorrect because it simply describes any behavior that is voluntary rather than being triggered, or elicited, by a specific stimulus.
   b. This answer is too general, since behaviors can change for reasons other than learning.
   d. Respondently conditioned behavior also satisfies the criteria of our definition of learning.

2. **b.** is the answer. (pp. 236–237)
   a. & c. Classical conditioning is associated with Pavlov; respondent conditioning is the same thing as classical conditioning.
   d. Observational learning is most closely associated with Bandura.

3. **c.** is the answer. Meat automatically triggers the response of salivation and is therefore an unconditioned stimulus. (p. 229)
   a. A conditioned stimulus acquires its response-eliciting powers through learning. A dog does not learn to salivate to meat.
   b. & d. Responses are behaviors elicited in the organism, in this case the dog's salivation. The meat is a stimulus.

4. **b.** is the answer. Prior to its pairing with meat (the UCS), the tone did not elicit salivation and was therefore a neutral stimulus. Afterwards, the tone elicited salivation (the CR) and was therefore a conditioned stimulus (CS). (p. 229)
   c. & d. Unconditioned stimuli, such as meat, innately elicit responding. Pavlov's dogs had to learn to associate the tone with the food.

5. **c.** is the answer. In learning to distinguish between the conditioned stimulus and another, similar stimulus, the monkey has received training in discrimination. (p. 232)
   a. In extinction training, a stimulus and/or response is allowed to go unreinforced.
   b. Generalization training involves responding to stimuli similar to the conditioned stimulus; here the monkey is being trained not to respond to a similar stimulus.
   d. This cannot be classical conditioning since the monkey is acting in order to obtain a reward. Thus, this is an example of operant conditioning.

6. **b.** is the answer. A continuous association will naturally be easier to learn than one that occurs on only some occasions, so learning is most rapid with continuous reinforcement. Yet once the continuous association is no longer there, as in extinction training, extinction will occur more rapidly than it would have, had the organism not always experienced reinforcement. (p. 239)

7. **b.** is the answer. (pp. 232, 242)
   c. & d. The textbook does not present evidence

regarding the relative importance of cognitive processes in classical and operant conditioning.

8. **b.** is the answer. (pp. 240–241)

a. Response rate is high with fixed-ratio schedules, but there is a pause following each reinforcement.

c. & d. Because reinforcement is not contingent on the rate of response, interval schedules, especially fixed-interval schedules, produce lower response rates than ratio schedules.

9. **b.** is the answer. (p. 238)

a. Positive reinforcement involves presenting a favorable stimulus following a response.

c. Punishment involves presenting an unpleasant stimulus following a response.

d. In extinction, a previously reinforced response is no longer followed by reinforcement. In this situation, a response causes a stimulus to be terminated or removed.

10. **c.** is the answer. In this situation, the CR will decline, a phenomenon known as extinction. (p. 231)

a. Generalization occurs when the subject makes a CR to stimuli similar to the original CS.

b. Discrimination is when the subject does not make a CR to stimuli other than the original CS.

d. An aversion is a CR to a CS that has been associated with an unpleasant UCS, such as shock or a nausea-producing drug.

11. **c.** is the answer. (p. 236)

a. In *operant* conditioning the responses are voluntary.

b. In *classical* conditioning responses are triggered, or elicited, by preceding stimuli.

d. In *classical* conditioning responses are involuntary.

12. **c.** is the answer. (p. 233)

a. & d. These studies also indicated that rats are biologically predisposed to associate visual and auditory stimuli, but not taste, with shock.

b. Rats are biologically predisposed to associate taste with sickness.

13. **d.** is the answer. A dog does not have to learn to salivate to food; therefore, this response is unconditioned. (p. 229)

a. & c. Salivation is a response, not a stimulus.

14. **b.** is the answer. (p. 247)

a. Skinner is best known for studies of *operant* learning. Moreover, there is no such thing as secondary learning.

c. Pavlov is best known for classical conditioning.

d. Watson is best known as an early proponent of behaviorism.

15. **b.** is the answer. (p. 243)

a. Latent learning is learning that occurs but is not apparent until there is an incentive to demonstrate it.

c. Primary reinforcement involves the presentation of a stimulus that satisfies some biological need. Money is an acquired, or secondary, reinforcer.

d. Modeling is the process of learning by watching and imitating the behavior of others.

16. **d.** is the answer. (p. 241)

17. **c.** is the answer. (p. 232)

a. & b. Rescorla and Wagner's research did not address the importance of these factors in classical conditioning.

18. **d.** is the answer. a. is an example of positive reinforcement, b. is an example of negative reinforcement, and c. is an example of the Premack principle. (p. 238)

19. **c.** is the answer. (p. 238)

20. **b.** is the answer. (p. 230)

a. Backward conditioning, in which the UCS precedes the CS, is ineffective.

c. This interval is longer than is optimum for the most rapid acquisition of a CS-UCS association.

d. Simultaneous presentation of CS and UCS is ineffective because it does not permit the subject to anticipate the UCS.

Matching Items

1. e (p. 238)
2. h (p. 231)
3. f (p. 238)
4. g (p. 239)
5. i (p. 239)
6. k (p. 241)
7. j (p. 239)
8. a (p. 237)
9. c (p. 231)
10. b (p. 241)
11. d (p. 243)

PROGRESS TEST 2

Multiple-Choice Questions

1. **c.** is the answer. (p. 231)

2. **b.** is the answer. The loud noise automatically elicited Albert's fear and therefore functioned as a UCS. After being associated with the UCS, the white rat acquired the power to elicit fear and thus became a CS. (p. 235)

3. **d.** is the answer. (p. 234)

4. **a.** is the answer. Shaping operates on voluntary, operant behaviors by reinforcing successive approximations to a desired goal. (p. 237)

5. **c.** is the answer. (p. 231)

a., b., & d. Spontaneous recovery occurs after a CR has been extinguished, and in the absence of the UCS. The situations described here all involve the continued presentation of the UCS and, therefore, the further strengthening of the CR.

6. **b.** is the answer. (p. 230)

a. & c. Reinforcement that is delayed, presented before a response, or at the same time as a response, does not increase the frequency of occurrence of the response.

7. **d.** is the answer. (pp. 238, 241)

a. Both involve an aversive stimulus.

b. All reinforcers, including negative reinforcers, increase the likelihood of a response.

c. In negative reinforcement an aversive stimulus is withdrawn following a desirable response.

8. **c.** is the answer. Payment is given after a fixed number of pieces have been completed. (p. 240)

a. & b. Interval schedules reinforce according to the passage of time, not the amount of work accomplished.

d. Fortunately for those working on commission, the work ratio is fixed and therefore predictable.

9. **c.** is the answer. By learning to put on your coat before going outside, you have learned to terminate the aversive stimulus of the cold. (p. 238)

a. Discrimination learning involves learning to make a response in the presence of the appropriate stimulus and not other stimuli.

b. Punishment is the suppression of an undesirable response by the presentation of an aversive stimulus.

d. Putting on a coat is a voluntary response. Therefore, this is an example of operant, not classical, conditioning.

10. **d.** is the answer. (p. 239)

a. Partial reinforcement refers to the ratio of responses to reinforcers, not the overall quantity of reinforcement delivered.

b. Unlike partial reinforcement, in which the delivery of reinforcement is contingent on responding, random reinforcement is delivered independently of the subject's behavior.

c. This defines the technique of shaping, not partial reinforcement.

11. **a.** is the answer. You are teaching your dog by rewarding him when he produces the desired behavior. (pp. 236–237)

b. This is not classical conditioning because the cookie is a primary reinforcer presented after the operant behavior of the dog fetching the paper.

c. Food is a primary reinforcer; it satisfies an innate need.

d. Because you reward your dog each time he fetches the paper, this is continuous reinforcement.

12. **d.** is the answer. (p. 248)

13. **a.** is the answer. (p. 242)

14. **d.** is the answer. The rat had learned the maze but did not display this learning until reinforcement became available. (pp. 242–243)

a. Negotiating a maze is clearly voluntary, emitted, operant behavior.

b. This example does not involve learning to distinguish between stimuli.

c. This is not observational learning because the rat has no one to observe!

15. **c.** is the answer. Because reinforcement (earning a good grade on the exam) is available according to the passage of time, studying is reinforced according to an interval schedule. Because the interval between exams is constant, this is an example of a fixed-interval schedule. (p. 241)

16. **d.** is the answer. Operant conditioning works on voluntary behaviors, and respondent (classical) conditioning works on involuntary behaviors. (p. 236)

a. Pavlov and Watson are both associated with respondent conditioning.

b. Skinner is associated with operant conditioning, and Bandura is associated with observational learning.

17. **a.** is the answer. CAI applies operant principles such as reinforcement, immediate feedback, and shaping to the teaching of new skills. (p. 245)

b. & d. CAI provides immediate, and continuous, reinforcement for correct responses, but does not make use of aversive control procedures such as punishment.

c. CAI is based on feedback for correct responses; this feedback constitutes secondary, rather than primary, reinforcement

18. **c.** is the answer. In fishing, an unpredictable amount of time passes between catches. (p. 241)

a. This answer is incorrect because the interval between catching successive fish is unpredictable.

b. & d. There is no contingency between "fishing rate" and when the next fish reinforcement will occur.

19. **d.** is the answer. An approving nod from the boss is a secondary reinforcer, in that it doesn't satisfy an innate need but has become linked with desirable consequences. Cessation of cold, cessation of pain, and a drink are all primary reinforcers, which meet innate needs. (p. 239)

20. **a.** is the answer. Taste-aversion experiments demonstrate conditioning even with CS-UCS intervals as long as several hours. (p. 233)

b. Despite being perceivable, a visual or auditory stimulus cannot become a CS for illness in some animals, such as rats.

c. Some animals, such as birds, are biologically primed to associate the *appearance* of food with illness.

True-False Items

1. F (p. 236)   **5.** T (p. 240)   **9.** F (p. 232)
2. F (p. 230)   **6.** F (pp. 232, 242)   **10.** T (p. 231)
3. F (p. 238)   **7.** T (p. 241)
4. T (p. 239)   **8.** F (p. 233)

CHALLENGE TEST

Multiple-Choice Questions

1. a. is the answer. Your dog had to learn to associate the rattling sound with the food. Rattling is therefore a conditioned, or learned, stimulus, and salivation in response to this rattling is a learned, or conditioned, response. (p. 229)

2. c. is the answer. Reinforcement (the letter) comes after a fixed interval, and as the likely end of the interval approaches, your behavior (glancing out the window) becomes more frequent. (p. 241)

a. & b. These answers are incorrect because with ratio schedules, reinforcement is contingent upon the number of responses rather than on the passage of time.

d. Assuming that the mail is delivered at about the same time each day, the interval is fixed rather than variable. Your behavior reflects this, since you glance out the window more often as the delivery time approaches.

3. b. is the answer. By taking out the garbage, Jack terminates an aversive stimulus — his father's nagging. (p. 238)

a. Positive reinforcement would involve a desirable stimulus that increases the likelihood of the response that preceded it.

c. This answer would have been correct if Jack's father had rewarded Jack for taking out the garbage by making it possible for Jack to engage in a preferred activity, such as attending a rock concert.

d. Punishment suppresses behavior; Jack is emitting a behavior in order to obtain reinforcement.

4. c. is the answer. Studies indicate that when a model says one thing but does another, subjects do the same and learn not to practice what they preach. (p. 248)

5. a. is the answer. As in this example, conditioning must be consistent with the particular organism's biological predispositions. (p. 244)

b. Some behaviors, but certainly not all, are acquired more rapidly than others when shock is used as negative reinforcement.

c. Pigeons are able to acquire many new behaviors when food is used as reinforcement.

6. a. is the answer. Ratio schedules maintain higher rates of responding — gambling in this example — than do interval schedules. Furthermore, variable schedules are not associated with the pause in responding following reinforcement that is typical of fixed schedules. The slot machine would therefore be used more often, and more consistently, if jackpots were scheduled according to a variable-ratio schedule. (p. 241)

7. d. is the answer. Sharetta is guided by her mental representation of the city, or cognitive map. (p. 242)

a. Latent learning, or learning in the absence of reinforcement that is demonstrated when reinforcement becomes available, has no direct relevance to the example.

b. Observational learning refers to learning from watching others.

c. Shaping is the technique of reinforcing successive approximations of a desired behavior.

8. c. is the answer. Because the cat was associated with your mother's scream, it elicited a fear response, and is thus the CS. (p. 229)

9. a. is the answer. Your mother's scream and evident fear, which naturally caused you to cry, was the UCS. (p. 229)

10. d. is the answer. Your fear of cats is the CR. An acquired fear, or phobia, is always a conditioned response. (p. 229)

11. b. is the answer. Your crying, automatically elicited by your mother's scream and fear, was the UCR. (p. 229)

12. c. is the answer. (pp. 245–246)

a. Positive reinforcement is most effective in boosting productivity in the workplace when specific behavior, rather than vaguely defined general merit, is rewarded. Also, immediate reinforcement is much more effective than the delayed reinforcement described in a.

b. Positive reinforcement is most effective in boosting productivity when performance goals are achievable, rather than unrealistic.

d. The text does not specifically discuss the use of punishment in the workplace. However, it makes the general point that although punishment may temporarily suppress unwanted behavior, it does not guide one toward more desirable behavior. Therefore, workers who receive pay cuts for poor performance may learn nothing about how to improve their productivity.

13. **b.** is the answer. Paying a person for doing what he or she already enjoys may undermine the person's intrinsic motivation for the task and lead to the overjustification effect. (p. 243)

   a. This example of negative reinforcement of room cleaning may motivate the son to get the job done, but since the job apparently is not intrinsically rewarding, it is doubtful that Mrs. Shih's additional incentives will lead to an overjustification effect.

   c. Presumably the salespeople work in order to make money; a bonus should therefore serve as additional positive reinforcement for selling shoes.

   d. The coach's scolding may make soccer less enjoyable for the players, but not as a result of overjustification provided by additional reinforcement.

14. **b.** is the answer. Not only is Bill extending a learned aversion to a specific blue car to all blue cars but also to cars that are green. (p. 231)

   a. Whereas discrimination involves responding only to a particular stimulus, Bill is extending his aversive response to other stimuli (green cars) as well.

   c. Latent learning is learning that becomes apparent only after reinforcement becomes available.

   d. The overjustification effect refers to the counterproductive effects of reinforcement on behavior that is self-reinforcing.

15. **b.** is the answer. The girls are imitating behavior they have observed and admired. (p. 247)

   a. Because these behaviors are clearly voluntary rather than elicited, classical conditioning plays no role.

   c. Latent learning plays no role in this example.

   d. Shaping is a procedure for teaching the acquisition of a new response by reinforcing successive approximations of the behavior.

16. **a.** is the answer. Classical conditioning proceeds most effectively when the CS and UCS are reliably paired and therefore appear predictably associated. Only for Group 1 is this likely to be true. (p. 232)

17. **b.** is the answer. (p. 234)

   a., c., & d. Taste-aversion research demonstrates that humans and some other animals, such as rats, are biologically primed to associate illness with the taste of tainted food, rather than with other cues, such as the food's appearance. Moreover, taste aversions can be acquired even when the interval between the CS and the illness is several hours.

18. **d.** is the answer. By making a more preferred activity (watching TV) contingent on a less preferred activity (room cleaning), Reggie's mother is employing Premack's principle, which is a variation of the operant conditioning technique of positive reinforcement. (pp. 236, 238)

19. **c.** is the answer. The parrot is reinforced for making successive approximations of a goal behavior. This defines shaping. (pp. 237–238)

   a. Shaping is an operant conditioning procedure; salivation at the sight of dog biscuits is a classically conditioned response.

   b. Shaping involves the systematic reinforcement of successive approximations of a more complex behavior. In this example there is no indication that the response of stopping at the intersection involved the gradual acquisition of simpler behaviors.

   d. This is an example of the partial reinforcement of an established response, rather than the shaping of a new response.

20. **c.** is the answer. Whereas Lars is paid (reinforced) after a fixed period of time (fixed-interval), Tom is reinforced for each sale (fixed-ratio) he makes. (pp. 240–241)

   b. Lars and Tom are both being reinforced intermittently.

   d. In this example Lars's pay interval and Tom's work ratio are both fixed, rather than variable.

Essay Question

The first step in shaping an operant response, such as rolling over, is to find an effective reinforcer. Some sort of biscuit or dog treat is favored by animal trainers. This primary reinforcement should be accompanied by effusive praise (secondary reinforcement) whenever the dog makes a successful response.

   Rolling over (the goal response) should be divided into a series of simple approximations, the first of which is a response, such as lying down on command, that is already in the dog's repertoire. This response should be reinforced several times. The next step is to issue a command, such as "Roll over," and withhold reinforcement until the dog (usually out of frustration) makes a closer approximation (such as rotating slightly in one direction). Following this example, the trainer should gradually require closer and closer approximations until the goal response is attained. When the new response has been established, the trainer should switch from continuous to partial reinforcement, in order to strengthen the skill.

KEY TERMS

1. **Learning** is defined as any relatively permanent change in an organism's behavior as the result of experience. (p. 227)

2. **Behaviorism** is the school of thought maintaining that psychology should be an objective science, study only observable behaviors, and avoid references to mental processes. (p. 228)

   Example: Because he was an early advocate of the study of overt behavior, John Watson is often called the father of **behaviorism**.

3. Also know as respondent conditioning, **classical conditioning** is a type of learning in which a neutral stimulus becomes capable of eliciting a conditioned response after having become associated with an unconditioned stimulus. (p. 228)

4. In classical conditioning, the **unconditioned response (UCR)** is the unlearned, involuntary response to the unconditioned stimulus. (p. 229)

   Memory aid: A behavior that is **unconditioned** is one that did not require training, or conditioning. Examples of such reflexive and involuntary responses are shivering, changes in pupil size, and blinking.

5. In classical conditioning, the **unconditioned stimulus (UCS)** is the stimulus that naturally and automatically elicits the reflexive unconditioned response. (p. 229)

   Example: Cold temperatures, changes in light intensity, and puffs of air to the eye are the **unconditioned stimuli** that elicit the unconditioned responses of shivering, changes in pupil size, and blinking.

6. In classical conditioning, the **conditioned response (CR)** is the learned response to a conditioned stimulus, which results from the acquired association between the CS and UCS. (p. 229)

7. In classical conditioning, the **conditioned stimulus (CS)** is an originally neutral stimulus that comes to elicit a CR after being paired with an unconditioned stimulus. (p. 229)

8. In a learning experiment, **acquisition** refers to the initial stage of conditioning in which the new response is gradually strengthened. (p. 230)

   Example: The operant procedure of shaping is a technique for facilitating the **acquisition** of a new response.

9. **Extinction** refers to the weakening of a CR when the CS is no longer followed by the UCS; in operant conditioning extinction occurs when a response is no longer reinforced. (p. 231)

   Example: In order to **extinguish** the child's tantrum behavior, the teacher ignored it until it ceased.

10. **Spontaneous recovery** is the reappearance of an extinguished CR after a rest period. (p. 231)

    Example: Although Craig hadn't smoked in years, he still often found himself tempted to have a cigarette with his after-dinner coffee. This **spontaneous recovery** of his former habit seemed impossible to extinguish.

11. **Generalization** refers to the tendency for stimuli similar to the original CS to evoke a CR. (p. 231)

    Example: After Little Albert had been conditioned to fear a rat, his fear **generalized** to rabbits, hamsters, and even fur pieces.

12. **Discrimination** in classical conditioning refers to the ability to distinguish the CS from other similar stimuli. (p. 232)

    Example: In an early experiment, Pavlov taught a dog to **discriminate** a circle from an ellipse.

13. **Operant conditioning**. is a type of learning in which voluntary behavior becomes more or less probable when followed by reinforcing or punishing stimuli. (p. 236)

    Example: Unlike classical conditioning, which works on involuntary behaviors, **operant conditioning** works on voluntary behaviors that are willfully emitted by an organism.

14. **Respondent behavior** is that which occurs as an automatic, involuntary response to some stimulus. (p. 236)

    Example: Conditioned and unconditioned responses, in classical conditioning, are examples of **respondent behavior** in that they are involuntary responses elicited by specific stimuli.

15. In Skinner's theory, **operant behavior** is voluntary behavior the organism emits that operates on the environment and produces consequences such as reinforcement and punishment. (p. 236)

16. A **Skinner box** is an experimental chamber for the operant conditioning of an animal such as a pigeon or rat. The controlled environment enables the investigator to present visual or auditory stimuli, deliver reinforcement or punishment, and precisely measure simple responses such as bar presses or key pecking. (p. 237)

17. **Shaping** is the operant conditioning procedure for establishing a new response by reinforcing successive approximations of the desired behavior. (p. 237)

18. A **reinforcer** is any event that increases the likelihood of the behavior it follows. (p. 238)

19. **Premack's principle** is that a more preferred activity, such as swimming, can reinforce a less preferred activity, such as studying. (p. 238)

20. **Positive reinforcement** refers to the presentation of a rewarding stimulus following a response. The effect of positive reinforcement is to strengthen the response. (p. 238)

21. **Negative reinforcement** refers to the withdrawal of an unpleasant stimulus, the effect of which is to reinforce, or strengthen, the preceding response. (p. 238)

    Memory aid: In operant conditioning, "positive" and "negative" do *not* mean good and bad, but to present or withdraw a stimulus, respectively.

22. The powers of **primary reinforcers** are automatic, inborn, and do not depend on learning. (p. 239)

    Example: To a hungry organism, food is a **primary reinforcer**.

23. **Secondary reinforcers** are stimuli that acquire their reinforcing power through their association with an established reinforcer. (p. 239)

    Example: Because money can be exchanged for a variety of primary reinforcers, such as food or shelter, it is a powerful **secondary reinforcer**.

24. **Continuous reinforcement** is the operant procedure of reinforcing each and every response. In promoting the acquisition of a new response it is best to use continuous reinforcement. (p. 239)

25. **Partial (or intermittent) reinforcement** is the operant procedure of reinforcing a response intermittently. A response that has been partially reinforced is much more resistant to extinction than one that has been continuously reinforced. (p. 239)

26. In operant conditioning, a **fixed-ratio schedule** is one in which reinforcement is presented after a set number of responses. (p. 240)

    Example: Continuous reinforcement is a special kind of **fixed-ratio schedule**: Reinforcement is presented after *each* response, so the ratio of reinforcements to responses is one to one.

27. In operant conditioning, a **variable-ratio schedule** is one in which reinforcement is presented after a varying number of responses. (p. 241)

    Example: Because reinforcement is contingent on the rate of responding even though the ratio of responses to reinforcements is unpredictable, **variable-ratio schedules** of reinforcement produce the highest and most stable rates of response.

28. In operant conditioning, a **fixed-interval schedule** is one in which a response is reinforced after a specified time has elapsed. (p. 241)

    Example: Weekly quizzes are an example of a **fixed-interval schedule**. Studying tends to be minimal just after the previous exam and to peak just before the next one.

29. In operant conditioning, a **variable-interval schedule** is one in which responses are reinforced after varying intervals of time. (p. 241)

    Example: Pop quizzes are an example of a **variable-interval schedule**. Because the exact time of reinforcement is unpredictable on such a schedule, studying will tend to take place much more consistently.

30. In operant conditioning, **punishment** is the presentation of an aversive stimulus, such as shock, which weakens the behavior it follows. (p. 241)

    Memory aid: Many people confuse negative reinforcement with **punishment**. The former strengthens behavior, while the latter weakens it.

31. A **cognitive map** is a mental picture of one's environment. (p. 242)

    Example: The discovery that rats in mazes often behave as though they were employing **cognitive maps** led to a renewed interest in animal cognition.

32. **Latent learning** is learning that occurs in the absence of reinforcement but only becomes apparent when there is an incentive to demonstrate it. (p. 243)

33. The undermining effect of being rewarded for something enjoyable is called the **overjustification effect**. (p. 243)

    Memory aid: **Overjustification** is like overkill; if something is so heavily rewarded, it must not be very enjoyable.

34. **Observational learning** is learning by watching and imitating others. (p. 247)

35. **Modeling** is the process of watching and then imitating a specific behavior and is thus an important means through which observational learning occurs. (p. 247)

36. The opposite of antisocial behavior, **prosocial behavior** is positive, helpful, and constructive, and is subject to the same principles of observational learning as is undesirable behavior, such as aggression. (p. 248)

    Example: In an effort to promote **prosocial behavior** among sports fans, professional clubs offer public service announcements describing courteous conduct in the stands. Their slogan: "Courtesy is contagious."

9 / Memory

Chapter Overview

Chapter 9 explores human memory as a system that processes information in three steps. Encoding refers to the process of putting information into the memory system. Storage is the purely passive mechanism by which information is maintained in memory. Retrieval is the process by which information is accessed from memory through recall or recognition.

Chapter 9 also discusses the importance of imagery and organization in encoding new memories, how memory is represented physically in the brain, and how forgetting may result from failure to encode or store information or to find appropriate retrieval cues. As you study this chapter, try applying some of the memory and studying tips discussed in the text.

NOTE: Answer guidelines for all Chapter 9 questions begin on page 190.

Guided Study

The text chapter should be studied one section at a time. Before you read, preview each section by skimming it, noting headings and boldface items. Then read the appropriate section objectives from the following outline. Keep these objectives in mind and, as you read the chapter section, search for the information that will enable you to meet each objective. Once you have finished a section, write out answers for its objectives.

The Phenomenon of Memory (pp. 253–257)

1. Explain memory in terms of information processing.

2. Distinguish between iconic and echoic memory.

How We Encode Information (pp. 257–265)

3. Explain the process of encoding and distinguish between automatic and effortful processing.

4. Discuss the importance of rehearsal, spacing, and serial position in encoding.

5. Explain the importance of meaning, imagery, and organization in the encoding process.

6. Discuss forgetting as a form of encoding failure.

11. Discuss the evidence for memory's being constructive.

Long-Term Memory (pp. 266–280)

7. Describe memory capacity and duration.

12. Discuss the role of interference in the process of forgetting.

13. Describe motivated forgetting and explain the concept of repression.

8. Discuss research findings on the physical basis of memory.

Improving Memory (pp. 280–281)

9. Discuss what research with amnesics reveals about memory.

14. Discuss strategies for improving memory.

10. Contrast recall, recognition, and relearning measures of memory and describe the importance of retrieval cues.

Chapter Review

When you have finished reading the chapter, work through the material that follows to review it. Complete the sentences and answer the questions. As you proceed, evaluate your performance for each section by consulting the answers on page 192. Do not continue with the next section until you understand each answer. If you need to, review or reread the appropriate section in the textbook before continuing.

1. Learning that persists over time indicates the existence of _____ for that learning.

The Phenomenon of Memory (pp. 253–257)

2. Memories for emotional moments that are especially clear are called _____ memories.

3. Both human memory and computer memory can be viewed as _____– _____ systems that perform three tasks: _____, _____, and _____.

4. Similar to a computer's permanent storage, we maintain vast amounts of information in _____–_____ memory. From this storehouse we can retrieve a(n) _____ (limited/unlimited) amount of information into _____– _____ memory.

5. Our short-term memory capacity is about _____ chunks of information.

6. Short-term memory for information we hear is somewhat _____ (better/ worse) than that for information we see. The memory span of an adult is _____ (greater than/equal to/less than) that of a child.

7. George Sperling found that when people were briefly shown three rows of letters, they could recall _____ (virtually all/ about half) of them. When Sperling sounded a tone immediately after a row of letters was flashed to indicate which letters were to be recalled, the subjects were much _____ (more/less) accurate. This suggests that people have a brief photographic, or _____, memory lasting about _____.

8. Sensory memory for sounds is called _____ memory. This memory fades _____ (more/less) rapidly than photographic memory, lasting for as long as _____.

How We Encode Information (pp. 257–265)

9. Encoding the meaning of words is referred to as _____ encoding; encoding by sound is called _____ encoding; encoding the image of words is _____ encoding.

10. A distinction is made between memory processing that does not require conscious attention and is therefore _____ and that which is _____.

Give examples of material encoded by automatic processing and by effortful processing.

11. Peterson and Peterson found that when _____ was prevented by asking subjects to count backwards, memory for letters was gone after 12 seconds.

12. A pioneering researcher in verbal memory was _____. In one experiment he found that the longer he studied a list of nonsense syllables, the _____ (fewer/greater) the number of repetitions he required to relearn it later.

13. After material has been learned, additional repetition, or overlearning, usually _____ (will/will not) increase retention.

14. Memory studies also reveal a _____ _____: Distributed study is more effective than cramming.

15. The tendency to remember the first and last items in a list best is called the _____ _____. Following a delay, first items are remembered _____ (better/less well) than last items.

16. Craik and Tulving's study comparing visual, acoustic, and semantic encoding showed that memory was best with _____ encoding.

17. Memory that consists of mental pictures is based on the use of _____.

18. Your earliest memories are most likely of events that occurred when you were about _____ years old.

19. Concrete, high-imagery words tend to be remembered _____ (better/less well) than abstract, low-imagery words.

20. Memory aids are known as _____ devices. One such device involves forming associations between a familiar series of locations and to-be-remembered words; this technique is called the _____ _____.

21. Using a jingle, such as the one that begins "one is a bun," is an example of the _____-_____ system.

22. Memory may be aided by grouping information into meaningful units called _____. An example of this technique involves forming words from the first letters of to-be-remembered words; the resulting word is called an _____.

23. In addition, material may be processed into _____, which are composed of a few broad concepts divided into lesser concepts, categories, and facts.

24. Of all the material that is sensed, much of it never actually enters the memory system. This type of "forgetting" is known as _____ _____.

Long-Term Memory (pp. 266–280)

25. If you are able to retrieve something from memory, you must have engaged in the passive process of _____.

26. In contrast to short-term memory—and contrary to popular belief—the capacity of permanent memory is essentially _____.

27. Studies by Ebbinghaus and by Bahrick indicate that most forgetting occurs _____ (soon/a long time) after the material is learned.

28. Penfield's electrically stimulated patients _____ (do/do not) provide reliable evidence that our stored memories are precise and durable.

29. It is likely that forgetting occurs because new experiences _____ with our retrieval of old information and that the physical memory trace _____ with the passage of time.

30. Lashley attempted to locate memory by cutting out pieces of rats' _____ after they had learned a maze. He found that no matter where he cut, the rats _____ (remembered/forgot) the maze.

31. Gerard found that a hamster's memory remained even after its body temperature was lowered to a point where the brain's _____ activity stopped.

32. A blow or electrical shock to the brain will disrupt _____ (recent/old) memories.

33. Researchers believe that memory involves a strengthening of certain neural connections, which occurs at the _____ between neurons.

34. Alkon, Lynch, and colleagues have found that conditioning makes the receiving _____ of animals' neurons _____ (more/less) sensitive.

35. Kandel and Schwartz have found that when learning occurs in the sea snail *Aplysia*, the neurotransmitter _____ is released in greater amounts, making synapses more efficient.

36. Certain disorders, such as _____ disease, disrupt memory through the loss of brain tissues that secrete important neurotransmitters.

37. Alcohol and other drugs classified as _____ impede memory formation.

38. Hormones released under stress often _____ (facilitate/impair) learning and memory.

39. Studies of amnesics suggest that there _____ (is/is not) a single unified system of memory.

40. Although amnesics typically _____ (have/have not) lost their capacity for learning, which is called _____ memory, they _____ (are/are not) able to declare their memory, suggesting a deficit in their _____ memory systems.

41. Amnesic patients typically have suffered damage to the _____ of their limbic system. This brain structure is important in the processing and storage of _____ memories. More primitive regions of the brain are important in the processing of _____ memories.

42. The dual explicit-implicit memory system helps explain _____ amnesia. We do not have explicit memories of our first two years because the _____ is one of the last brain structures to mature.

43. The ability to retrieve information that is not present in conscious awareness is called _____.

44. Bahrick found that, 25 years after graduation, people were not able to _____ (recall/recognize) the names of their classmates but were able to _____ (recall/recognize) both their names and their yearbook picture.

45. If you have learned something and then forgotten it, you will probably be able to _____ it _____ (more/less) quickly than you did originally.

46. The process by which associations can lead to retrieval is called _____.

47. Studies have shown that retention is best when learning and testing are done in _____ (the same/different) contexts.

Summarize the textbook's explanation of the déjà vu experience.

48. The type of memory in which emotions serve as retrieval cues is referred to as _____– _____ memory.

Describe the effects of mood on memory.

49. Research has shown that recall of an event is often influenced by general schemas, other past experiences, present assumptions, and so forth. The workings of these influences illustrate the process of memory _____.

50. When witnesses to an event receive misleading information about it, they may experience a _____ _____ and misremember the event.

Describe what Loftus's studies have shown about the effects of misleading postevent information on eyewitness reports.

51. Eyewitnesses' confidence in their memories _____ (is/is not) related to the accuracy of those memories.

Identify several memory phenomena that memory construction helps explain.

52. When information that is stored in memory temporarily cannot be found, _____ failure has occurred.

53. Research suggests that memories are also lost as a result of _____, which is especially possible if we simultaneously learn similar, new material.

54. The disruptive effect of previous learning on current learning is called _____ _____. The disruptive effect of learning new material on efforts to recall material previously learned is called

_____ _____.

55. Jenkins and Dallenbach found that if subjects went to sleep after learning, their memory for a list of nonsense syllables was

_____ (better/worse) than it was if they stayed awake.

56. Freud proposed that motivated forgetting, or _____, may protect a person from painful memories.

Improving Memory (pp. 280–281)

Identify strategies for improving memory.

FOCUS ON PSYCHOLOGY:
How the Brain Records a Memory

Memories consist of patterns of individual pieces of information linked in such a way that awareness of one piece often triggers awareness of the entire pattern. A single feature on the face of a passerby, for example, may remind us of the face of a friend.

Recent studies of neural functioning are beginning to reveal how associative memories are formed. Daniel Alkon and his colleagues at the National Institute of Neurological and Communicative Disorders and Stroke have found that when the brain records a memory, a sequence of molecular changes occurs in certain neurons that permanently changes their electrical excitability.

Alkon and his co-workers studied the acquisition of conditioned responses in rabbits and the marine snail *Hermissenda crassicornis*. In the rabbit conditioning procedure, an audible tone was paired with a blink-triggering puff of air to the animal's eye. Learning was demonstrated when the rabbit consistently blinked its eye in response to the conditioned stimulus (the tone), which preceded the unconditioned stimulus (the puff of air). The memory formed in order to learn the conditioned response involved an association between the separate neural pathways underlying the responses to the tone and the puff of air.

Alkon's experiments demonstrated that these separate pathways converged on and stimulated increased electrical activity in specialized neurons in the hippocampus of the rabbit brain. These hippocampal neurons are exceedingly complex and may each possess as many as 200,000 dendritic inputs from other nerve cells. A few days of conditioning trials, however, may alter the structure of these neurons in such a way as to limit the number of inputs. This "neural streamlining," similar to that observed during early brain development when neurons compete for limited synaptic opportunities, presumably allows each neuron to store thousands of separate memories.

Although our understanding of the physical basis of memory is far from complete, the pioneering research of Daniel Alkon and his colleagues has led to many important findings, not the least of which is that neurons involved in memory are dynamic and capable of dramatic changes in structure and function in order to represent the range of phenomena that constitute memory.

Source: Alkon, Daniel L. (1989, July). Memory storage and neural systems. *Scientific American*, 42–50.

Progress Test 1

Multiple-Choice Questions

Circle your answers to the following questions and check them with the answers on page 193. If your answer is incorrect, read the explanation for why it is incorrect and then consult the appropriate pages of the text (in parentheses following the correct answer).

1. The three steps in memory information processing are:
   a. input, processing, output.
   b. input, storage, output.
   c. input, storage, retrieval.
   d. encoding, storage, retrieval.

2. Visual sensory memory is referred to as:
   a. iconic memory.   c. photomemory.
   b. echoic memory.   d. semantic memory.

3. Iconic memories fade after approximately:
   a. 1 hour.   c. 1 second.
   b. 1 minute.   d. 3 to 4 seconds.

4. Which of the following is *not* a measure of retention?
   a. recall   c. relearning
   b. recognition   d. retrieval

5. Our immediate memory span is approximately _____ items.
   a. 2   c. 7
   b. 5   d. 15

6. Memory techniques such as the method of loci, acronyms, and the peg-word system are called:
   a. consolidation techniques.
   b. imagery techniques.
   c. encoding strategies.
   d. mnemonic devices.

7. One way to increase the amount of information in memory is to group it into larger, familiar units. This process is referred to as:
   a. consolidating.
   b. chunking.
   c. memory construction.
   d. encoding.

8. Kandel and Schwartz have found that when learning occurs, more of the neurotransmitter _____ is released into synapses.
   a. ACh   c. serotonin
   b. dopamine   d. noradrenaline

9. Research on memory construction reveals that:
   a. memories are stored as exact copies of experience.
   b. memories reflect a person's biases and assumptions.
   c. memories may be chemically transferred from one organism to another.
   d. long-term memories usually decay within about five years.

10. Context cues are important in memory. In one study, people learned words while on land or under water. In a later test of recall, those with the best retention had:
    a. learned the words on land, that is, in the more familiar context.
    b. learned the words under water, that is, in the more exotic context.
    c. learned the words and been tested on them in different contexts.
    d. learned the words and been tested on them in the same context.

11. Forgetting can be attributed to:
    a. retrieval failure.   c. interference.
    b. encoding failure.   d. all of the above.

12. The spacing effect means that:
    a. distributed study yields better retention than cramming.
    b. retention is improved when encoding and retrieval are separated by no more than 1 hour.
    c. learning causes a reduction in the size of the synaptic gap between certain neurons.
    d. delaying retrieval until memory has consolidated improves recall.

13. Alkon, Lynch, and colleagues found that learning causes structural changes in the _____ of animals' neurons.

    a. axons   c. dendrites
    b. cell bodies   d. axon terminals

14. In Sperling's memory experiment, subjects were shown three rows of three letters, followed immediately by a low-, medium-, or high-pitched tone. The subjects were able to report:
    a. all three rows with perfect accuracy.
    b. only the top row of letters.
    c. only the middle row of letters.
    d. any one of the three rows of letters.

15. Studies of victims of amnesia suggest that:
    a. memory is a single, unified system.
    b. there are two distinct types of memory.
    c. there are three distinct types of memory.
    d. memory losses following brain trauma are unpredictable.

16. Memory for skills is called:
    a. explicit memory.   c. episodic memory.
    b. declarative memory.   d. implicit memory.

17. The eerie feeling of having been somewhere before is an example of:
    a. state dependency.   c. priming.
    b. encoding failure.   d. déjà vu.

18. When Gordon Bower presented subjects with words grouped by category or in random order, recall was:
    a. the same for all words.
    b. better for the categorized words.
    c. better for the random words.
    d. improved when subjects developed their own mnemonic devices.

19. Which of the following has been proposed as a neurophysiological explanation of infantile amnesia?
    a. The slow maturation of the hippocampus leaves the infant's brain unable to store images and events.
    b. The deficient supply of serotonin until about age 3 makes encoding very limited.
    c. The limited availability of association areas of the cortex until about age 3 impairs encoding and storage.
    d. All of the above explanations have been proposed.

20. Hypnotically "refreshed" memories may prove inaccurate—especially if the hypnotist asks leading questions—because of:
    a. encoding failure.
    b. state-dependent memory.
    c. proactive interference.
    d. memory construction.

Matching Items

Match each definition or description with the appropriate term.

Definitions or Descriptions

_____ **1.** the type of sensory memory that decays more slowly than visual sensory memory

_____ **2.** the process by which information gets into the memory system

_____ **3.** mental pictures that aid memory

_____ **4.** the blocking of painful memories

_____ **5.** the phenomenon in which one's mood can influence retrieval

_____ **6.** memory for a list of words is affected by word order

_____ **7.** "one is a bun, two is a show" mnemonic device

_____ **8.** "The Magical Number Seven, plus or minus two"

_____ **9.** new learning interferes with previous knowledge

_____ **10.** a measure of memory

_____ **11.** old knowledge interferes with new learning

Terms

a. repression

b. relearning

c. serial position effect

d. peg-word system

e. memory span

f. proactive interference

g. retroactive interference

h. encoding

i. imagery

j. state-dependent memory

k. echoic memory

Progress Test 2

Progress Test 2 should be completed during a final chapter review. Answer the following questions after you thoroughly understand the correct answers for the Chapter Review and Progress Test 1.

Multiple-Choice Questions

1. Which of the following best describes the typical forgetting curve?

a. a steady, slow decline in retention over time

b. a steady, rapid decline in retention over time

c. a rapid initial decline in retention becoming stable thereafter

d. a slow initial decline in retention becoming rapid thereafter

2. Jenkins and Dallenbach found that memory was better in subjects who were _____ during the retention interval, presumably because _____ was reduced.

a. awake; decay

b. asleep; decay

c. awake; interference

d. asleep; interference

3. Which of the following measures of retention is the least sensitive in triggering retrieval?

a. recall

b. recognition

c. relearning

d. déjà vu

4. Victims of amnesia typically have experienced damage to the _____ of the brain.

a. frontal lobes

b. cerebellum

c. thalamus

d. hippocampus

5. According to the serial position effect, when recalling a list of words you should have the greatest difficulty with those:

a. at the beginning of the list.

b. in the middle of the list.

c. at the end of the list.

d. at the end and in the middle of the list.

6. Craik and Watkins gave subjects a list of words to be recalled. When subjects were tested after a delay, the items that were best recalled were:

a. at the beginning of the list.

b. in the middle of the list.

c. at the end of the list.

d. at the beginning and the end of the list.

7. Craik and Tulving had subjects process words visually, acoustically, or semantically. In a subsequent recall test, which type of processing resulted in the greatest retention?

a. visual

b. acoustic

c. semantic

d. Acoustic and semantic processing were equally beneficial.

8. Lashley's studies, in which rats learned a maze and then had various parts of their brains surgically removed, showed that:
   a. the memory was lost when surgery took place within 1 hour of learning.
   b. the memory was lost when surgery took place within 24 hours of learning.
   c. the memory was lost when any region of the brain was removed.
   d. the memory remained no matter which area of the brain was tampered with.

9. The disruption of memory caused by Alzheimer's disease or excessive consumption of alcohol provides evidence for the importance of:
   a. neurotransmitters in the formation of new memories.
   b. neurotransmitters in the retrieval of long-term memories.
   c. nutrition in normal neural functioning.
   d. all of the above.

10. Which category of substance tends to disrupt memory formation?
    a. stimulants   c. depressants
    b. stress hormones   d. opiates

11. Repression is an example of:
    a. encoding failure.
    b. memory decay.
    c. motivated forgetting.
    d. all of the above.

12. Studies by Loftus and Palmer, in which subjects were quizzed about a film of an accident, indicate that:
    a. when quizzed immediately, subjects can recall very little, due to the stress of witnessing an accident.
    b. when questioned as little as one day later, their memory was very inaccurate.
    c. most subjects had very accurate memories as much as 6 months later.
    d. subjects' recall may easily be affected by misleading information.

13. Which of the following was *not* recommended as a strategy for improving memory?
    a. active rehearsal
    b. distributed study
    c. speed reading
    d. encoding meaningful associations

14. The process of getting information out of memory storage is called:
    a. encoding.   c. rehearsal.
    b. retrieval.   d. storage.

15. Amnesic patients typically experience disruption of:
    a. implicit memories.   c. iconic memories.
    b. explicit memories.   d. echoic memories.

16. Information is maintained in short-term memory only briefly unless it is:
    a. encoded.   c. iconic or echoic.
    b. rehearsed.   d. retrieved.

17. Textbook chapters are often organized into _____ in order to facilitate information processing.
    a. mnemonic devices   c. hierarchies
    b. chunks   d. recognizable units

18. The passive maintenance of information over time is called:
    a. encoding.   c. rehearsal.
    b. storage.   d. retrieval.

19. It is easier to recall information that has just been presented when:
    a. the information consists of random letters rather than words.
    b. the information is seen rather than heard.
    c. the information is heard rather than seen.
    d. the information is experienced in an unusual context.

20. The misinformation effect provides evidence that memory:
    a. is constructed during encoding.
    b. is unchanging once established.
    c. may be reconstructed during recall according to how questions are framed.
    d. is highly resistant to misleading information.

True-False Items

Indicate whether each statement is true or false by placing *T* or *F* in the blank next to the item.

_____ 1. Studying that is distributed over time produces better retention than cramming.

_____ 2. Generally speaking, memory for pictures is better than memory for words.

_____ 3. Studies of age regression through hypnosis indicate that memory is permanent, due to the reliability of such reports.

_____ 4. Most people do not have memories of events that occurred before the age of 2.

_____ 5. Studies by Ebbinghaus show that most forgetting takes place soon after learning.

_____ 6. There is no evidence that people repress memories as Freud suggested.

_____ 7. Recall of newly acquired knowledge is no better after sleeping than after being awake for the same period of time.

_____ 8. Time spent in developing imagery, chunking, and associating material with what you already know is more effective than time spent repeating information again and again.

_____ **9.** The final step in the SQ3R technique is "recite."

_____ **10.** Overlearning material by continuing to restudy it beyond mastery often disrupts recall.

Challenge Test

Answer these questions the day before an exam as a final check on your understanding of the chapter's terms and concepts.

Multiple-Choice Questions

1. Complete this analogy: Fill-in-the-blank test questions are to multiple-choice questions as:
   a. encoding is to storage.
   b. storage is to encoding.
   c. recognition is to recall.
   d. recall is to recognition.

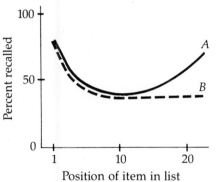

2. The above figure depicts the recall of a list of words under two conditions. Which of the following best describes the difference between the conditions?
   a. In *A*, the words were studied and retrieved in the same context; in *B*, the contexts were different.
   b. In *B*, the words were studied and retrieved in the same context; in *A*, the contexts were different.
   c. The delay between presentation of the last word and the test of recall was longer for *A* than for *B*.
   d. The delay between presentation of the last word and the test of recall was longer for *B* than for *A*.

3. Darren was asked to memorize a list of letters that included *v*, *q*, *y*, and *j*. He later recalled these letters as *e*, *u*, *i*, and *k*, suggesting that the original letters had been encoded:
   a. automatically.   c. semantically.
   b. visually.   d. acoustically.

4. After finding her old combination lock, Janice can't remember its combination because she keeps confusing it with the combination of her new lock. She is experiencing:
   a. proactive interference.
   b. retroactive interference.
   c. encoding failure.
   d. storage failure.

5. Which of the following sequences would be best to follow if you wanted to minimize interference-induced forgetting in order to improve your recall on the psychology midterm?
   a. study, eat, test
   b. study, sleep, test
   c. study, listen to music, test
   d. study, exercise, test

6. Being in a bad mood after a hard day of work, Susan could think of nothing positive in her life. This is best explained as an example of:
   a. priming.
   b. memory construction.
   c. state-dependent memory.
   d. retrieval failure.

7. In an effort to remember the name of the classmate who sat behind her in fifth grade, Martina mentally recited the names of other classmates who sat near her. Martina's effort to refresh her memory by activating related associations is an example of:
   a. priming.   c. encoding.
   b. déjà vu.   d. relearning.

8. Walking through the halls of his high school 10 years after graduation, Tom experienced a flood of old memories. Tom's experience showed the role of:
   a. state-dependent memory.
   b. context effects.
   c. retroactive interference.
   d. echoic memory.

9. The first thing Karen did when she discovered that she had misplaced her keys was to recreate in her mind the sequence of the day's events. That she had little difficulty in doing so illustrates:
   a. automatic processing.
   b. effortful processing.
   c. state-dependent memory.
   d. priming.

10. Which of the following is the best example of a flashbulb memory?
    a. suddenly remembering to buy bread while standing in the checkout line at the grocery store
    b. recalling the name of someone from high school while looking at his or her yearbook snapshot
    c. remembering to make an important phone call
    d. remembering what you were doing the day President Bush declared war on Iraq

11. When Carlos was promoted, he moved into a new office with a new phone extension. When asked for his phone number, Carlos first thinks of his old extension, illustrating the effects of:
    a. proactive interference.
    b. retroactive interference.
    c. encoding failure.
    d. storage failure.

12. Elderly Mr. Flanagan can easily recall his high school graduation, but he can't remember the name of the president of the United States. Evidently, Mr. Flanagan's _____ memory is better than his _____ memory.
    a. implicit; explicit
    b. explicit; implicit
    c. episodic; semantic
    d. semantic; episodic

13. Although you can't recall the answer to a question on your psychology midterm, you have a clear mental image of the textbook page on which it appears. Evidently, your _____ encoding of the answer was _____.
    a. semantic; automatic
    b. visual; automatic
    c. semantic; effortful
    d. visual; effortful

14. At your high school reunion you cannot remember the last name of your homeroom teacher. Your failure to remember is most likely the result of:
    a. encoding failure.
    b. storage failure.
    c. retrieval failure.
    d. state-dependent memory.

15. Brenda has trouble remembering her new five-digit ZIP plus four-digit address code. What is the most likely explanation for Brenda's difficulty?
    a. Nine digits are at or above the upper limit of most people's short-term memory capacity.
    b. Nine digits are at or above the upper limit of most people's iconic memory capacity.
    c. The extra four digits cannot be organized into easily remembered chunks.
    d. Brenda evidently has an impaired implicit memory.

16. Lewis cannot remember the details of the torture he experienced as a prisoner of war. Lewis's failure to remember these painful memories is an example of:
    a. repression.
    b. retrieval failure.
    c. state-dependent memory.
    d. flashbulb memory.

17. Which of the following illustrates the constructive nature of memory?
    a. Janice keeps calling her new boyfriend by her old boyfriend's name.
    b. After studying all afternoon and then getting drunk in the evening, Don can't remember the material he studied.
    c. After getting some good news, elated Kareem has a flood of good memories from his younger years.
    d. Although elderly Mrs. Harvey, who has Alzheimer's disease, has many gaps in her memory, she invents sensible accounts of her activities so that her family will not worry.

18. To help him remember the order of ingredients in difficult recipes, master chef Giulio often associates them with the route that he walks to work each day. Giulio is using which mnemonic technique?
    a. peg-word system
    b. acronyms
    c. the method of loci
    d. chunking

19. During basketball practice Jan's head was painfully elbowed. If the trauma to her brain disrupts her memory, we would expect that Jan would be most likely to forget:
    a. the name of her teammates.
    b. her telephone number.
    c. the name of the play during which she was elbowed.
    d. the details of events that happened shortly after the incident.

20. After suffering damage to the hippocampus, a person would probably:
    a. lose memory for skills such as bicycle riding.
    b. be incapable of being classically conditioned.
    c. lose the ability to store new facts.
    d. experience all of the above changes.

Essay Question

Describe the stages of information processing in memory. (Use the space below to list points you want to make and organize them. Then write the essay on a separate piece of paper.)

Key Terms

Using your own words, write a brief definition or explanation of each of the following terms.

1. memory

2. flashbulb memory

3. encoding (acoustic, visual, semantic)

4. storage

5. retrieval

6. long-term memory

7. short-term memory

8. sensory memory

9. iconic memory

10. echoic memory

11. automatic processing

12. effortful processing

13. rehearsal

14. spacing effect

15. serial position effect

16. imagery

17. mnemonic device

18. chunking

19. implicit memory

20. explicit memory

21. hippocampus

22. recall

23. recognition

24. relearning

25. priming

26. déjà vu

27. state-dependent memory

28. misinformation effect

29. proactive interference

30. retroactive interference

31. repression

ANSWERS

GUIDED STUDY

The following guidelines provide the main points that your answers should have touched upon.

1. To remember any event requires that we somehow get information into our brain (encoding), retain it (storage) as short- or long-term memory, and get it back out (retrieval). These three steps apply not only to human memory but also to other information-processing systems, such as computers.

2. Iconic memory is momentary photographic memory in which the eyes register an exact representation of a scene. George Sperling first demonstrated the existence of this type of sensory memory, which lasts for only about one second. Sensory memory for sound, called echoic memory, disappears after 3 or 4 seconds.

3. Encoding is the process by which sensory information is transferred into the memory system. We may encode images (visual encoding), sounds (acoustic encoding), and the meaning of material (semantic encoding).

   Information about space, time, and frequency is encoded with little or no effort (automatic processing). Encoding of most information, however, requires conscious rehearsal (effortful processing).

4. Ebbinghaus demonstrated that the amount of material remembered depends on the time spent rehearsing it. Even after material is learned, additional rehearsal (overlearning) increases retention.

   Experiments show that distributed study yields better long-term retention than cramming (spacing effect).

   The serial position effect refers to the finding that people often remember the first and last items in a list better than they do items in the middle.

5. Studies by Craik and Tulving demonstrate that the processing of meaning (semantic encoding) yields better memory of verbal information than visual or acoustic encoding.

   The imagery principle—that people have excellent memory for pictures and picture-evoking words—is at the heart of memory-enhancing mnemonic devices. In the method of loci and the "peg-word" system, we associate to-be-remembered items with visual codes.

   Organizing information into meaningful units, or chunks, also improves memory. The use of acronyms and hierarchies, for example, can facilitate both retention and retrieval.

6. We sense so much during a lifetime that it is fortunate that we forget some things. Much of the material we think of as having been forgotten was never "remembered." Although it was sensed, it never entered the memory system because it was not encoded; therefore, its "loss" can be attributed to encoding failure.

7. Our capacity for storing long-term memories is essentially limitless. Ebbinghaus' famous "forgetting curve" studies and Bahrick's study of long-term retention of Spanish vocabulary showed that most forgetting occurs relatively soon after learning. Two possible explanations for the forgetting curve are that new experiences interfere with retrieval and that the physical memory trace gradually decays.

8. Lashley's studies demonstrated that memories do not reside in single, specific parts of the cortex. Gerard demonstrated that lowering animals' body temperatures until their brains' electrical activity ceased did not disrupt long-term memories. Alkon, Lynch, and colleagues observed molecular changes in animals' dendrite receptors following conditioning that made the receiving neurons more sensitive. Kandel and Schwartz found that when learning occurs in sea snails, more of the neurotransmitter serotonin is released at certain synapses, and neural transmission is more efficient. Other studies have shown that when neurotransmitters are blocked by depressant drugs, information storage is disrupted.

9. Although amnesics often can't recall new facts or recent experiences, most are capable of learning new skills. This suggests that there are two distinct types of memory: implicit (or nondeclarative) memory of skills, preferences, and dispositions; and explicit (declarative) memory of facts and experiences that are consciously known.

   The fact that most amnesics have suffered damage to the hippocampus suggests that this limbic structure plays a crucial role in the processing of explicit memories. Because older memories remain intact in amnesics, the hippocampus cannot be the permanent storehouse for such memories. It is likely that the hippocampus functions as a relay station that feeds new information to other brain circuits for permanent storage.

10. Recall is the ability to retrieve information not in conscious awareness. Recognition is a measure of memory in which one need only identify previously learned information. Relearning measures the amount of time saved when previously learned information is learned for a second time. Tests of recognition and relearning typically reveal that people remember more than they can recall.

    Recognition tests of memory are "easier" because they provide retrieval cues that serve as reminders of information that could not otherwise be recalled. Priming and context effects, too, indicate the importance of retrieval cues in memory. Emotions also trigger memories. State-dependent memory is the phenomenon that things learned in one emotional state are more easily recalled when we are again in the same state. Another aspect of this phenomenon is that our current mood influences our retrieval of past experiences.

11. Memory retrieval does not consist merely of a literal reporting of stored information. Instead, memories are constructed as we encode them, then alter them in the face of new experiences. Loftus and Palmer have shown that after exposure to subtle misinformation, eyewitnesses to an incident incorrectly recalled the actual incident (the misinformation effect). Memory construction also explains why "hypnotically refreshed" memories often incorporate false information and why patients with memory loss so readily invent sensible-sounding accounts of their activities.

12. Proactive interference refers to the disruptive effect of previous learning on the recall of new information. Retroactive interference refers to the disruptive effect of new information on the recall of previous information. Jenkins and Dallenbach's classic study demonstrated that retroactive interference was reduced when subjects slept following a learning episode, presumably because the number of potentially interfering events was minimized.

13. Motivated forgetting refers to the irretrievability of memories that are embarrassing to remember. Similarly, with his concept of repression Freud proposed that memory is self-censoring. According to this viewpoint, repressed memories remain intact and may be retrieved at some later time. Evidence of repression comes from clinical cases of torture and war victims who cannot remember painful moments.

14. Suggestions for improving memory include rehearsing material over many separate and distrib-

uted study sessions with the objective of over-learning material. Studying should also involve active rehearsal, rather than mindless repetition of information. Organizing information, relating material to what is already known, developing numerous retrieval cues, and using mnemonic devices that incorporate vivid imagery are helpful too. Frequent activation of retrieval cues, such as the context and mood in which the original learning occurred, can also help strengthen memory, as can recalling events while they are fresh, before possible misinformation is encountered. Studying should also be arranged to minimize potential sources of interference. Finally, self-tests in the same format (recall or recognition) that will later be used on the actual test are useful.

CHAPTER REVIEW

1. memory
2. flashbulb
3. information-processing; encoding; storage; retrieval
4. long-term; unlimited; short-term
5. 7
6. better; greater than
7. about half; more; iconic; 1 second
8. echoic; less; 3 or 4 seconds
9. semantic; acoustic; visual
10. automatic; effortful

Automatic processing includes the encoding of information about space, time, and frequency—encoding that is evidently innate. Automatic processing also includes the encoding of word meaning, a type of encoding that appears to be learned. Effortful processing, or encoding that requires attention and effort, is used to encode material like telephone numbers, word lists, textbook chapters, etc.

11. rehearsal
12. Ebbinghaus; fewer
13. will
14. spacing effect
15. serial position effect; better
16. semantic
17. imagery
18. 3 or 4
19. better
20. mnemonic; method of loci
21. peg-word
22. chunks; acronym
23. hierarchies

24. encoding failure
25. storage
26. unlimited
27. soon
28. do not
29. interfere; decays
30. cortices; remembered
31. electrical
32. recent
33. synapses
34. dendrites; more
35. serotonin
36. Alzheimer's
37. depressants
38. facilitate
39. is not
40. have not; implicit; are not; explicit
41. hippocampus; explicit; implicit
42. infantile; hippocampus
43. recall
44. recall; recognize
45. relearn; more
46. priming
47. the same

The déjà vu experience is most likely the result of being in a context similar to one that we *have* actually been in before. If we have previously been in a similar situation, though we cannot recall what it was, the current situation may present cues that unconsciously help us to retrieve the earlier experience.

48. state-dependent

The effect of state-dependent memory is that things learned in one state are most easily recalled when we are again in the same state. Moods also affect both our encoding of present experiences and our retrieval of past experiences. When happy, for example, we perceive things in a positive light and recall happy events; these perceptions and memories, in turn, prolong our good mood.

49. construction
50. misinformation effect

When subjects viewed a film of a traffic accident and were quizzed a week later, misleading postevent information was found to influence recall of the event (although it did not affect people's ability to recognize what they had witnessed). Phrasing of questions affected answers; the word "smashed," for instance, made subjects mistakenly think they had seen broken glass.

51. is not

Memory construction explains, for example, why hypnotically refreshed memories are often inaccurate, and why patients with memory loss, such as those suffering from Alzheimer's disease, are able to invent accounts of their activities.

52. retrieval

53. interference

54. proactive interference; retroactive interference

55. better

56. repression

Strategies for improving memory include active and spaced rehearsal, organized encoding based on meaningful and vivid associations, use of mnemonic devices, minimizing interference, and frequent self-testing and rehearsal.

PROGRESS TEST 1

Multiple-Choice Questions

1. d. is the answer. Information must be encoded, or put into appropriate form; stored, or retained over time; and retrieved, or located and gotten out when needed. (p. 255)

2. a. is the answer. Iconic memory is our fleeting memory of visual stimuli. (p. 257)

b. Echoic memory is auditory sensory memory.

c. There is no such thing as photomemory.

d. Semantic memory is memory for meaning, not a form of sensory memory.

3. c. is the answer. Echoic memories last 3 to 4 seconds. (p. 257)

4. d. is the answer. Retrieval refers to the *process* of remembering. (p. 272)

5. c. is the answer. (p. 263)

6. d. is the answer. (p. 262)

a. There is no such term as "consolidation techniques."

b. & c. Imagery and encoding strategies are important in storing new memories, but mnemonic device is the general designation of techniques that facilitate memory, such as acronyms and the pegword system.

7. b. is the answer. (p. 263)

a. There is no such process of "consolidating."

c. Memory construction refers to the ways in which memories are altered by the individual's basic assumptions and experiences.

d. Encoding refers to the processing of information into the memory system.

8. c. is the answer. Kandel and Schwartz found that when learning occurred in the sea snail *Aplysia*, serotonin was released at certain synapses, which then became more efficient at signal transmission. (p. 269)

a., b., & d. These are all neurotransmitters, but none played a role in Kandel and Schwartz's studies.

9. b. is the answer. In essence, we construct our memories, bringing them into line with our biases and assumptions, as well as with our subsequent experiences. (pp. 275–276)

a. If this were true, it would mean that memory construction does not occur. Through memory construction, memories may deviate significantly from the original experiences.

c. There is no evidence that such chemical transfers occur.

d. Many long-term memories are apparently unlimited in duration.

10. d. is the answer. In general, being in a context similar to that in which you experienced something will tend to help you recall the experience. (p. 273)

a. & b. The learning environment per se—and its familiarity or exoticness—had no effect on retention.

11. d. is the answer. (pp. 265, 277–278)

12. a. is the answer. (p. 259)

b. & d. The textbook does not suggest that there is an optimal interval between encoding and retrieval.

c. Learning increases the efficiency of synaptic transmission in certain neurons, but not by altering the size of the synapse.

13. c. is the answer. (p. 269)

14. d. is the answer. When asked to recall all the letters, subjects could recall only about half; however, if immediately after the presentation they were signaled to recall a particular row, their recall was near perfect. This showed that they had a brief photographic memory—so brief that it faded in less time than it would have taken to say all nine letters. (pp. 256–257)

15. b. is the answer. Because amnesics lose their fact (explicit) memories but not their skill (implicit) memories or their capacity to learn, it appears that human memory can be divided into two distinct types. (p. 270)

d. As studies of victims of amnesia show, memory losses following damage to the hippocampus are quite predictable.

16. d. is the answer. (p. 270)

a. & b. Explicit memory (also called declarative memory) is memory of facts and experiences that one can consciously know and declare.

c. Episodic memory is explicit memory for personally experienced events.

17. **d.** is the answer. (p. 274)

a. State-dependent memory is the phenomenon in which information is best retrieved when the person is in the same emotional or physiological state he or she was in when the material was learned.

b. Encoding failure occurs when a person has not processed information sufficiently for it to enter the memory system.

c. Priming is the process by which a memory is activated through retrieval of an associated memory.

18. **b.** is the answer. When the words were organized into categories recall was two to three times better, indicating the benefits of hierarchical organization in memory. (p. 264)

d. This study did not examine the use of mnemonic devices by subjects.

19. **a.** is the answer. We remember skills acquired in infancy, as such memories are recorded in earlier developing brain regions, but declarative memories involve the hippocampus. (p. 271)

b., c., & d. There is no evidence that serotonin levels or association areas are deficient until age 3. Moreover, such proposals are unlikely, as they wouldn't explain why we remember skills learned in infancy while forgetting events experienced.

20. **d.** is the answer. It is in both encoding and retrieval that we construct our memories, and as Loftus's studies showed, leading questions affect people's memory construction. (pp. 275–276)

a. The memory encoding occurred at the time of the event in question, not during questioning by the hypnotist.

b. State-dependent memory refers to the influence of one's own emotional or physiological state on encoding and retrieval, and would not apply here.

c. Proactive interference is the interfering effect of prior learning on the recall of new information.

Matching Items

1. k (p. 257)
2. h (p. 255)
3. i (pp. 261–262)
4. a (p. 279)
5. j (p. 274)
6. c (p. 259)
7. d (p. 262)
8. e (p. 256)
9. g (p. 278)
10. b (p. 272)
11. f (p. 278)

PROGRESS TEST 2

Multiple-Choice Questions

1. **c.** is the answer. As Ebbinghaus and Bahrick both showed, most of the forgetting that is going to occur happens soon after learning. (pp. 266–267)

2. **d.** is the answer. (p. 278)

a. & b. This study did not find evidence that memories fade (decay) with time.

c. When one is awake, there are many *more* potential sources of memory interference than when one is asleep.

3. **a.** is the answer. A test of recall presents the fewest retrieval cues and usually produces the most limited retrieval. (p. 272)

4. **d.** is the answer. (p. 271)

5. **b.** is the answer. According to the serial position effect, items at the beginning and end of a list tend to be remembered best. (p. 259)

6. **a.** is the answer. (p. 259)

b. In the serial position effect, the items in the middle of the list always show the *poorest* retention.

c. & d. Delayed recall erases the memory facilitation for items at the end of the list.

7. **c.** is the answer. Processing a word in terms of its meaning (semantic encoding) produces much better retention than does visual or acoustic encoding. (pp. 260–261)

8. **d.** is the answer. Surprisingly, Lashley found that no matter where he cut, the rats had at least a partial memory of how to solve the maze. (p. 268)

a. & b. Lashley's studies did not investigate the significance of the interval between learning and cortical lesioning.

9. **a.** is the answer. Both alcohol and Alzheimer's disease disrupt memory by interfering with the neurotransmitter serotonin. (p. 269)

b. The disruptive effects of alcohol and Alzheimer's disease are on the formation, rather than the retrieval, of memories.

c. Although nutrition plays an important role in brain chemistry, the effects of Alzheimer's disease and alcohol are independent of nutrition.

10. **c.** is the answer. Alcohol is a prime example of the effect of depressants on memory formation. (p. 269)

a. & b. These often facilitate encoding and retention.

d. Opiates do not have a reliable influence, one way or the other, on memory.

11. **c.** is the answer. According to Freud, we repress painful memories to preserve our self-concepts. (pp. 279–280)

a. & b. The fact that repressed memories can sometimes be retrieved suggests that they were encoded and have not decayed with time.

12. **d.** is the answer. When misled by the phrasings of questions, subjects incorrectly recalled details of the film and even "remembered" objects that weren't there. (pp. 275–276)

a., b., & c. These were not findings of Loftus and Palmer.

13. **c.** is the answer. Speed reading, which entails little active rehearsal, yields poor retention. (p. 280)

14. **b.** is the answer. (p. 255)

a. Encoding is the processing of information *into* memory.

c. Rehearsal is the conscious repetition of information in order to maintain it in memory.

d. Storage is the maintenance of encoded material over time.

15. **b.** is the answer. Amnesics typically have suffered damage to the hippocampus, a brain structure involved in processing explicit memories for facts. (p. 271)

a. Amnesics do retain implicit memories for how to do things; these are processed in the more ancient parts of the brain.

c. & d. Amnesics generally do not experience impairment in their iconic and echoic sensory memories.

16. **b.** is the answer. (p. 258)

a. Information in short-term memory has *already* been encoded.

c. Iconic and echoic are types of *sensory* memory.

d. Retrieval is the process of getting material out of storage and into conscious, working memory. Thus, all material in short-term memory has either already been retrieved, or is about to be placed in storage.

17. **c.** is the answer. By breaking concepts down into subconcepts and yet smaller divisions and showing the relationships among these, hierarchies facilitate information processing. Use of main heads and subheads is an example of the organization of textbook chapters into hierarchies. (pp. 263–264)

a. Mnemonic devices are the method of loci, acronyms, and other memory *techniques* that facilitate retention.

b. Chunks are organizations of knowledge into familiar, manageable units.

d. Recognition is a measure of retention.

18. **b.** is the answer. (pp. 255–256)

a. Encoding is the processing of information into memory.

c. Rehearsal is conscious repetition of material in order to maintain it in memory.

d. Retrieval is the activation of information *from* memory storage.

19. **c.** is the answer. Short-term recall is slightly better for information we hear rather than see, because echoic memory momentarily outlasts iconic memory. (p. 257)

a. Meaningful stimuli, such as words, are usually remembered more easily than meaningless stimuli, such as random letters.

b. Iconic memory does not last as long as echoic memory in short-term recall.

d. Although context is a powerful retrieval cue, there is no general facilitation of memory in an unusual context.

20. **c.** is the answer. Loftus and Palmer found that eyewitness testimony could easily be altered when questions were phrased to imply misleading information. (pp. 275–276)

a. Although memories *are* constructed during encoding, the misinformation effect is a retrieval, rather than an encoding, phenomenon.

b. & d. In fact, just the opposite is true.

True-False Items

1. True (p. 259)
2. True (p. 257)
3. False (p. 267)
4. True (p. 271)
5. True (pp. 266–267)
6. False (pp. 279–280)
7. False (p. 278)
8. True (pp. 280–281)
9. False (p. 280)
10. False (p. 259)

CHALLENGE TEST

Multiple-Choice Questions

1. **d.** is the answer. (p. 272)

a. & b. In order to correctly answer either type of question, the knowledge must have been encoded and stored.

c. With fill-in-the blank questions, the answer must be recalled with no retrieval cues other than the question. With multiple-choice questions, the correct answer merely has to be recognized from among several alternatives.

2. **d.** is the answer. (p. 259)

a. & b. These answers are incorrect because a serial position effect would presumably occur whether the study and retrieval contexts were the same or different.

c. As Craik and Watkins found, when recall is delayed, only the first items in a list are recalled more accurately than the others. With immediate recall, both the first and last items are recalled more accurately.

3. **d.** is the answer. That all four mistakes are based on a sound confusion suggests that the letters were encoded acoustically. (p. 260)

a. Memorizing a list of letters would involve effortful, rather than automatic, processing.

b. The mistakes do not involve letters that are similar in appearance.

c. Semantic encoding would have been suggested by errors based on similarities in meaning.

4. **b.** is the answer. Retroactive interference is the disruption of something you once learned by new information. (p. 278)

a. Proactive interference occurs when old information makes it difficult to correctly remember new information.

c. & d. Interference produces forgetting even when the forgotten material was effectively encoded and stored. Janice's problem is at the level of retrieval.

5. **b.** is the answer. (p. 278)

a., c., & d. Involvement in other activities, even just eating or listening to music, is more disruptive than sleeping.

6. **c.** is the answer. Susan's memories are affected by her state, in this case her bad mood. (pp. 274–275)

a. Priming refers to the conscious or unconscious activation of particular associations in memory.

b. Memory construction refers to changes in memory as new experiences occur.

d. Although Susan's difficulty in recalling the good could be considered retrieval failure, it is caused by the state-dependent effect, which is therefore the best explanation.

7. **a.** is the answer. Priming is the conscious or unconscious activation of particular associations in memory. (p. 273)

b. Déjà vu is the false impression of having previously experienced a current situation.

c. That Martina is able to retrieve her former classmates' names implies that they already have been encoded.

d. Relearning is a measure of retention based on how long it takes to relearn something already mastered. Martina is recalling her former classmates' names, not relearning them.

8. **b.** is the answer. Being back in the context in which the original experiences occurred triggered memories of these experiences. (p. 273)

a. The memories were triggered by similarity of place, not mood.

c. Retroactive interference would involve difficulties in retrieving old memories.

d. Echoic memory refers to momentary memory of auditory stimuli.

9. **a.** is the answer. Time and space—and therefore sequences of events—are often automatically processed. (p. 257)

b. That she had *little difficulty* indicates that the processing was automatic, rather than effortful.

c. & d. State-dependent memory and priming have nothing to do with the automatic processing of space and time.

10. **d.** is the answer. Flashbulb memories are unusually clear memories of emotionally significant moments in life. (p. 254)

11. **a.** is the answer. Proactive interference occurs when old information makes it difficult to recall new information. (p. 278)

b. If Carlos were having trouble remembering the old extension, this answer would be correct.

c. & d. Carlos has successfully encoded and stored the extension; he's just having problems retrieving it.

12. **c.** is the answer. Episodic memory is memory for personal life experiences, such as a high school graduation; semantic memory is memory for facts, such as the name of the president. (p. 270)

a. & b. Implicit memories are memories for skills. Both of these examples involve explicit memory, which is memory for facts and experiences.

13. **b.** is the answer. (p. 257)

a. & c. Your failure to recall the answer indicates that it was never encoded semantically.

d. Spatial information, such as the location of an answer (but not the actual answer) on a textbook page, is often encoded automatically.

14. **c.** is the answer. (p. 272)

a. & b. The name of your homeroom teacher, which you probably heard at least once each day of school, was surely processed into memory (encoded) and maintained there for some time (stored).

d. State-dependent memory is the tendency to recall information best in the same emotional or physiological state as when the information was learned. It is unlikely that any single state was associated with learning your homeroom teacher's name.

15. **a.** is the answer. Short-term memory capacity is approximately seven digits. (p. 256)

b. Because iconic memory lasts no more than a second or so, regardless of how much material is experienced, this cannot be the explanation for Brenda's difficulty.

c. The final four digits should be no more difficult to organize into chunks than the first five digits of the address code.

d. Memory for digits is an example of explicit, rather than implicit, memory.

16. **a.** is the answer. (pp. 279–280)

b. Although Lewis's difficulty in recalling these memories could be considered retrieval failure, it is caused by repression, which is therefore the *best* explanation.

c. This answer is incorrect because it is clear that Lewis fails to remember these experiences because they are painful memories and not because he is in a different emotional or physiological state.

d. Flashbulb memories are especially *vivid* memories for emotionally significant events. Lewis has no memory at all.

17. **d.** is the answer. (p. 276)

a. This is an example of proactive interference.

b. This is an example of the disruptive effects of depressant drugs, such as alcohol, on the formation of new memories.

c. This is an example of state-dependent memory.

18. **c.** is the answer. (p. 262)

a. The peg-word system involves developing associations between rhyming words in a jingle and to-be-remembered items.

b. Acronyms are words created from the first letters of to-be-remembered words.

d. Chunking is the organization of information into meaningful units, such as acronyms.

19. **c.** is the answer. Blows to the head usually disrupt the most recent experiences, such as this one, rather than long-term memories like those in answers a. and b., or new learning such as that in answer d. (p. 268)

20. **c.** is the answer. The hippocampus is involved in processing new facts for storage. (p. 271)

a., b., & d. Studies of amnesics with hippocampal damage show that neither classical conditioning nor skill memory are impaired, indicating that these aspects of memory are controlled by more primitive regions of the brain.

Essay Question

Information is first held briefly as iconic (visual) or echoic (auditory) sensory memory. Information that is attended to is further processed (encoded) into short-term memory. Information that pertains to space, time, and frequency is encoded automatically; other information is effortfully encoded through conscious rehearsal of the material's sound (auditory encoding), appearance (visual encoding), or meaning (semantic encoding). Encoding is facilitated through the use of imagery, mnemonic devices, chunking, and the organization of material into hierarchies.

Short-term, or working, memory briefly stores about 7 chunks of information (give or take 2) until the information is either forgotten (due to decay or interference from other information) or placed into more permanent storage. Long-term memory holds an unlimited amount of information indefinitely. For this reason, much of forgetting is actually due to a failure in encoding or retrieval.

KEY TERMS

1. **Memory** is simply any indication in an organism's behavior that learning has persisted over time. (p. 253)

2. A **flashbulb memory** is an unusually vivid memory of an emotionally important moment in one's life. (p. 254)

    Example: As if a photographer had snapped a picture of him at the moment he heard John Lennon had been killed, the **flashbulb memory** of where he was and what he was doing is forever stored in his mind.

3. **Encoding** is the first step in memory; information is translated into some form that enables it to enter our memory system. Encoding may be **acoustic**, when sound is encoded; **visual**, when images are encoded; or **semantic**, when meaning is encoded. (pp. 255–257)

4. **Storage** refers to the passive process by which encoded information is maintained over time. (p. 255)

5. **Retrieval** is the process of bringing to consciousness information from memory storage. (p. 255)

    Example: We often think we have forgotten something when what actually has occurred is **retrieval** failure: At another time, in another place, the desired information may readily come to mind.

6. **Long-term memory** is the relatively permanent and unlimited capacity memory system into which information from short-term memory may pass. (p. 256)

7. **Short-term memory** is conscious, working memory, which can hold about seven items for a short time and often represents information acoustically. (p. 256)

8. **Sensory memory** is the immediate, initial recording of sensory information in the memory system. (p. 256)

9. **Iconic memory** is the visual sensory memory consisting of a perfect photographic memory, which lasts no more than a second or so. (p. 257)

   Memory aid: *Icon* means "image," or "representation." **Iconic memory** consists of brief visual images.

10. **Echoic memory** is the momentary sensory memory of auditory stimuli, lasting about 3 or 4 seconds. (p. 257)

    Memory aid: An echo is the repetition of a sound; **echoic memory** is the persistence of sounds in our sensory register.

11. **Automatic processing** refers to our effortless encoding of incidental information such as space, time, and frequency. (p. 257)

    Example: Because of our dependence on language, the encoding of word meaning is an example of **automatic processing**, which does not require conscious control.

12. **Effortful processing** is encoding that requires conscious attention and some degree of effort. (p. 258)

    Example: Study techniques such as recitation, rehearsal, chunking, and SQ3R can often facilitate **effortful processing**.

13. **Rehearsal** is the conscious, effortful repetition of information that you are trying to encode for storage. (p. 258)

14. The **spacing effect** is the tendency for distributed practice to yield better retention than massed practice, or cramming. (p. 259)

15. The **serial position effect** is the tendency for items at the beginning and end of a list to be more easily retained than those in the middle. (p. 259)

    Memory aid: An item's *position* within a *series* affects the ease with which it is retained.

16. **Imagery** refers to mental pictures and can be an important aid to memory. For example, concrete words, which can be associated with images, are better remembered than abstract words. (p. 261)

17. **Mnemonic devices** are memory aids (the method of loci, acronyms, peg-words, etc.), which often use visual imagery. (p. 262)

    Example: The mnemonist, or professional memorizer, depends on a large repertoire of **mnemonic** devices in order to quickly encode to-be-remembered information.

18. **Chunking** is the memory technique of organizing material into familiar, meaningful units. (p. 263)

Example: In a classic experiment, the capacity of short-term memory was determined to be 7 ± 2 chunks of information. By regrouping, or **chunking**, single digits into groups of 3 and 4, subjects were able to increase the amount of information they could retain without rehearsal.

19. **Implicit memories** are memories of skills, or procedures for how to do things. These memories are evidently processed, not by the hippocampus, but by more primitive parts of the brain. They are also called nondeclarative memories. (p. 270)

20. **Explicit memories** are memories of facts, including names, images, and events. They are also called declarative memories. (p. 270)

21. The **hippocampus** is a neural region within the limbic system that is important in the processing of names, images, events, and other facts in memory. (p. 271)

    Example: Many amnesic patients have suffered damage to the **hippocampus** and are unable to store new declarative memories.

22. **Recall** is a measure of retention in which the person must remember, with few retrieval cues, information learned earlier. (p. 272)

    Example: Because fill-in-the-blank questions provide virtually no retrieval cues, they are tests of **recall**.

23. **Recognition** is a measure of retention in which one need only identify, rather than recall, previously learned information. (p. 272)

    Example: Matching and multiple-choice test items require **recognition** of correct answers from among a set of alternatives.

24. **Relearning** is also a measure of retention in that the less time it takes to relearn information, the more that information has been retained. (p. 272)

25. **Priming** is the activation of a web of associations in memory in order to retrieve a specific memory. (p. 273)

    Example: In order to answer the trivia question about the 1968 Detroit Tigers, Denny **primed** his memory by mentally reciting the batting lineup.

26. **Déjà vu** is the false sense that you have already experienced a current situation. (p. 274)

27. **State-dependent memory** is the tendency to best recall information when in the same emotional or physiological state one was in at the time of learning. (p. 274)

28. The **misinformation effect** is the tendency of eyewitnesses to an event to incorporate misleading information about the event into their memories. (p. 276)

29. **Proactive interference** is the disruptive effect of something you already have learned on your efforts to learn or recall new information. (p. 278)

30. **Retroactive interference** is the disruptive effect of something recently learned on old knowledge. (p. 278)

Memory aid: Retro means "backward." ***Retro*active interference** is "backward-acting" interference.

31. **Repression** is an example of motivated forgetting in that painful memories are prevented from entering consciousness. (p. 279)

10 / Thinking and Language

Chapter Overview

Most of Chapter 10 deals with thinking, with emphasis on how people logically—or at times illogically—use tools such as algorithms and heuristics when making decisions and solving problems. Also discussed are several common obstacles to problem solving, including fixations that prevent us from taking a fresh perspective on a problem and our bias to seek information that confirms rather than challenges existing hypotheses.

The chapter also explores how the new generation of computer systems has been constructed to simulate the neural networks of the human brain. By mimicking the ways in which human neural networks interconnect, computers enable scientists to study how human systems process sensations and memories and how the thought process works.

The rest of the chapter is concerned with language, including its structure, development in children, and relationship to thinking. Two theories of language acquisition are evaluated: Skinner's theory that language acquisition is based entirely on learning, and Chomsky's theory that humans have a biological predisposition to acquire language.

NOTE: Answer guidelines for all Chapter 10 questions begin on page 211.

Guided Study

The text chapter should be studied one section at a time. Before you read, preview each section by skimming it, noting headings and boldface items. Then read the appropriate section objectives from the following outline. Keep these objectives in mind and, as you read the chapter section, search for the information that will enable you to meet each objective. Once you have finished a section, write out answers for its objectives.

Thinking (pp. 286–301)

1. Describe the nature, function, and formation of concepts.

2. Discuss the major problem-solving strategies and describe the nature of insight.

3. Identify obstacles to problem solving.

4. Describe the heuristics that guide decision making and explain how overconfidence and framing can affect judgment.

5. Describe how our beliefs influence our logical reasoning.

6. Contrast the human mind and the computer as information processors and describe recent advances in artificial intelligence.

Language (pp. 301–310)

7. Describe the structure of language.

8. Trace the course of language acquisition and discuss alternative theories of language development.

9. Describe the research on animal communication and discuss the controversy over whether animals have language.

Thinking and Language (pp. 310–313)

10. Discuss the relationship between thought and language.

Chapter Review

When you have finished reading the chapter, work through the material that follows to review it. Complete the sentences and answer the questions. As you proceed, evaluate your performance for each section by consulting the answers on page 212. Do not continue with the next section until you understand each answer. If you need to, review or reread the appropriate section in the textbook before continuing.

Thinking (pp. 286–301)

1. Cognition, or _____, can be defined as _____

   _____.

   Scientists who study these mental activities are called _____ _____.

2. People tend to organize specific items into mental groupings called _____, and many such groupings often are further organized into _____.

3. Concepts are typically formed through the development of a best example, or _____, of a category.

4. Although humans may not always think logically, we are especially capable of using our reasoning powers for coping with new situations, for _____ _____.

5. Finding a problem's solution by trying each possibility is called _____ _____.

6. Logical, methodical, step-by-step procedures for solving problems are called _____.

7. Rule-of-thumb strategies that provide us with problem-solving shortcuts are referred to as _____.

8. When you suddenly realize a problem's solution, _____ has occurred. Many psychologists believe that animals _____ (have/have not) been shown to possess this capability.

9. The tendency of people to look for information that verifies their preconceptions is called the _____ _____.

10. Not being able to take a new perspective when attempting to solve a problem is referred to as _____. One example of this obstacle to problem solving is the tendency to repeat solutions that have worked previously; this phenomenon is known as the development of a _____ _____.

11. When a person is unable to envision using an object in an atypical way, _____ _____ is operating.

12. People judge how well something matches a particular prototype; this is the _____ _____.

13. When we judge the likelihood of something occurring in terms of how readily it comes to mind, we are using the _____ _____.

Explain how these two heuristics may lead us to make judgmental errors.

14. The tendency of people to overestimate the accuracy of their knowledge results in _____.

15. Research has shown that, when subjects are given feedback on the accuracy of their judgments, such feedback generally _____ (does/does not) help them become more realistic about how much they know.

16. Decision making can be significantly **affected by** the phrasing, or _____, of an issue.

17. The tendency for our beliefs to distort logical reasoning is called _____ _____. This phenomenon makes it _____ (easier/more difficult) for us to see the illogic of conclusions that run counter to our beliefs.

18. Research has shown that once we form a belief or a concept, it may take more convincing evidence for us to change the concept than it **did** to create it; this is because of _____ _____.

19. The science involving the development of computers and programs that mimic human thinking is called _____ _____.

20. Unlike the computer, which processes information _____ (serially/simultaneously), humans can process many bits of information _____ (serially/simultaneously).

21. Computer systems that imitate the brain's **neural** organization are called _____ _____. Such systems increase the computer's capacity for _____ processing _____ (and so/but do not) enable the computer to "learn" simple concepts.

Language (pp. 301–310)

22. The basic sound units of language are its _____. English has approximately _____ of these units.

23. Phonemes are grouped into units of meaning called _____.

24. The system of rules that enables us to use our language to speak to and understand others is called _____.

25. The system by which meaning is derived from words is the _____ of a language.

26. The system of rules we use to combine words together into sentences is called

_____.

27. The first stage of language development, in which children spontaneously utter different sounds, is the _____ stage. This stage typically begins at about

_____ months of age. The sounds children make during this stage

_____ (do/do not) include only the phonemes of the language that they hear.

28. During the second stage, called the

_____–_____ stage, children convey complete thoughts using single words. This stage begins at about

_____ year(s) of age.

29. During the two-word stage children speak in sentences containing mostly nouns and verbs. This type of speech is called

_____ speech.

30. Skinner believes that language development follows the general principles of learning, including _____,

_____, and _____.

31. Other theorists believe that humans are biologically predisposed to learn language. One such theorist is _____.

Give several examples of linguistic behavior in children that support the argument that humans are biologically predisposed to acquire language.

32. Honeybees communicate by means of a

_____, which researchers

_____ (do/do not) consider to have its own syntax and semantics.

33. The Gardners attempted to communicate with the chimpanzee Washoe by teaching her

_____ _____.

Summarize some of the arguments of skeptics of the "talking apes" research.

Thinking and Language (pp. 310–313)

34. According to the _____

_____ hypothesis, language shapes our thinking. The linguist who proposed this hypothesis is _____.

35. In several studies researchers have found that using the pronoun "he" (instead of "he or she")

_____ (does/does not) influence people's thoughts concerning gender.

36. It appears that thinking _____ (can/cannot) occur without the use of language.

Summarize the probable relationship between thinking and language.

FOCUS ON PSYCHOLOGY:
Deaf Babies Babble Manually

Attempts to answer the question of how children acquire language have sparked a spirited debate, at the center of which is the nature-nurture issue.

According to behaviorist B.F. Skinner, language acquisition is the product of imitation, reinforcement, and other principles of operant conditioning. In contrast, linguists such as Noam Chomsky maintain that children have an innate "language acquisition device" that biologically predisposes the development of language. According to Chomsky, we use our inborn "universal grammar" to string together units into what eventually become words, phrases, and sentences.

Support for Chomsky's position has come from evidence of *linguistic universals* that cannot easily be accounted for by the behaviorists. For example, they cannot account for the predictability with which children acquire the rules of grammar. If, as they say, language is the product of learning, its acquisition should be fundamentally different for each child since no two children experience the same learning environment. Grammatical rules should be mastered by different children in different orders and a child's language should be a direct reflection of his or her linguistic environment. There is substantial evidence, however, that children acquire the rules of grammar in a predictable order. They begin adding -ing to words before they begin using the prepositions in and on, for example.

Further support for Chomsky's position comes from evidence that children are more active in mastering the rules of grammar than would be expected by the behaviorists. Instead of merely parroting what they hear, children seem to operate as "little scientists" as they form and test hypotheses about grammar. This explains why children make grammatical errors they have never heard from their caregivers, such as overgeneralizing the rule about adding -ed to a verb to form the past tense.

Another linguistic universal is that children the world over, including those who are deaf, enter a babbling stage at about 4 months. Some recent evidence shows that deaf babies who are raised with deaf parents who use sign language, babble with their hands in the same rhythmic fashion that hearing infants babble vocally. Just as hearing babies experiment by duplicating monosyllables such as "babababa" or "mamamama," so deaf infants repeat several key motions over and over, including one gesture that resembles the sign for "1" and another resembling the sign for "OK."

According to Dr. Laura Petitto of McGill University, "the motions seem to be the deaf babies' fledgling attempts to master language. The brain will progress from one stage to another regardless of whether language is conveyed through speaking, hand-signing, or presumably any other method of communication."

Petitto's findings are significant for two reasons. First, they contradict "a widespread assumption among linguists that the maturation of the vocal cords affects language development among infants." In showing that deaf babies babble with their hands in a manner that contains all the basic elements of vocal babbling, Petitto has separated language from speech. Second, Petitto's results provide further evidence that biology and experience work together in promoting the acquisition of language. "Babies babble regardless of whether the language spoken at home is English, Japanese, French, or, it seems, sign language."

Staff. (March 22, 1991). Deaf babies shown to babble manually. *Detroit Free Press*, p. 3A.

Progress Test 1

Multiple-Choice Questions

Circle your answers to the following questions and check them with the answers on page 213. If your answer is incorrect, read the explanation for why it is incorrect and then consult the appropriate pages of the text (in parentheses following the correct answer).

1. The textbook defines thinking as:
   a. silent speech.
   b. all mental activity.
   c. mental activity associated with understanding, processing, and communicating knowledge.
   d. logical reasoning.

2. A mental grouping of similar things, events, or people is called a(n):
   a. prototype.   c. algorithm.
   b. concept.   d. heuristic.

3. When forming a concept, people often develop a best example, or _____, of a category.
   a. denoter   c. prototype
   b. heuristic   d. algorithm

4. Confirmation bias refers to the tendency to:
   a. allow preexisting beliefs to distort logical reasoning.
   b. cling to one's initial conceptions after the basis on which they were formed has been discredited.
   c. search randomly through alternative solutions when problem solving.
   d. look for information that is consistent with one's beliefs.

5. The English language has approximately _____ phonemes.
   a. 25   c. 40
   b. 30   d. 50

6. Which of the following is *not* true of babbling?
   a. It is imitation of adult speech.
   b. It is the same in all cultures.
   c. It typically occurs from about age 4 months to 1 year.
   d. Babbling increasingly comes to resemble a particular language.

7. Mental set and functional fixedness are two types of:
   a. algorithms.   c. fixation.
   b. heuristics.   d. insight.

8. Which of the following has been argued by critics of ape language research?
   a. Ape language is merely imitation of the trainer's behavior.
   b. There is little evidence that apes can equal even a 3-year-old's ability to order words with proper syntax.
   c. By seeing what they wish to see, trainers attribute greater linguistic ability to apes than actually exists.
   d. All of the above have been argued.

9. Whorf's linguistic relativity hypothesis states that:
   a. language is primarily a learned ability.
   b. language is partially an innate ability.
   c. the size of a person's vocabulary reflects his or her intelligence.
   d. our language shapes our thinking.

10. Which of the following *best* describes Chomsky's view of language development?
    a. Language is an entirely learned ability.
    b. Language is an innate ability.
    c. Humans have a biological predisposition to acquire language.
    d. There are no cultural influences on the development of language.

11. Failing to solve a problem that requires using an object in an unusual way illustrates the phenomenon of:
    a. mental set.
    b. functional fixedness.
    c. framing.
    d. belief perseverance.

12. Which of the following is an example of the use of heuristics?
    a. trying every possible letter ordering when unscrambling a word
    b. considering each possible move when playing chess
    c. using the formula "area = length × width" to find the area of a rectangle
    d. playing chess using a defensive strategy that has often been successful for you

13. The chimpanzee Sultan used a short stick to pull a longer stick that was out of reach into his cage. He then used the longer stick to reach a piece of fruit. Researchers hypothesized that Sultan's discovery of the solution to his problem was the result of:
    a. insight.
    b. trial and error.
    c. functional fixedness.
    d. mental set.

14. You hear that one of the Smith children is an outstanding Little League player and immediately conclude it's their one son rather than any of their four daughters. You reached your quite possibly erroneous conclusion as the result of:
    a. the confirmation bias.
    b. the availability heuristic.
    c. the representativeness heuristic.
    d. belief perseverance.

15. Because of their lightning speed, computers can retrieve and manipulate stored data faster than people can, but the human brain beats the computer hands down when it comes to:

   a. using heuristics.
   b. following algorithms.
   c. serial processing.
   d. simultaneous processing.

16. Neural networks are:
    a. computer circuits that mimic the brain's neural circuitry.
    b. obstacles to effective problem solving.
    c. heuristics that make problem solving more efficient.
    d. biologically programmed synaptic connections that enable simple responses.

17. According to the textbook, language acquisition is best described as:
    a. the result of conditioning and reinforcement.
    b. a biological process of maturation.
    c. an interaction between biology and experience.
    d. a mystery of which researchers have no real understanding.

18. Biologist Karl von Frisch won the Nobel prize for his discovery that honeybees communicate with each other by:
    a. varying the acoustic pitch of their buzzing noises.
    b. secreting chemical odors called pheromones.
    c. performing an intricate dance.
    d. leading other worker bees on lengthy flights to find nectar.

19. The linguistic relativity hypothesis is challenged by the finding that:
    a. chimps can learn to communicate with one another spontaneously by using sign language.
    b. people with no word for a certain color can still perceive that color accurately.
    c. the Eskimo language contains a number of words for snow, whereas English has only one.
    d. infants' babbling contains many phonemes that do not occur in their own language and that they therefore cannot have heard.

20. Several studies have indicated that the generic pronoun "he":
    a. tends for children and adults alike to trigger images of both males and females.
    b. tends for adults to trigger images of both males and females, but for children to trigger images of males.
    c. tends for both children and adults to trigger images of males but not females.
    d. for both children and adults triggers images of females about one-fourth of the time it is used.

Matching Items

Match each definition or description with the appropriate term.

Definitions or Descriptions

_____ 1. the basic units of sound in a language
_____ 2. the way an issue or question is posed
_____ 3. rules for combining words into sentences
_____ 4. the system by which meaning is derived from sentences
_____ 5. presuming that something is likely if it comes readily to mind
_____ 6. the tendency to overestimate the accuracy of one's judgments
_____ 7. being unable to see a problem from a different angle
_____ 8. haphazard problem solving by trying one solution after another
_____ 9. the sudden realization of the solution to a problem
_____ 10. the tendency to repeat problem-solving techniques that worked in the past even though a fresh approach may be more appropriate
_____ 11. the basic units of meaning in a language

Terms

a. syntax
b. morphemes
c. mental set
d. trial and error
e. availability heuristic
f. phonemes
g. semantics
h. insight
i. framing
j. overconfidence
k. fixation

Progress Test 2

Progress Test 2 should be completed during a final chapter review. Answer the following questions after you thoroughly understand the correct answers for the Chapter Review and Progress Test 1.

Multiple-Choice Questions

1. A common problem in everyday reasoning is our tendency to:
   a. accept as logical those conclusions that agree with our own opinions.
   b. accept as logical those conclusions that disagree with our own opinions.
   c. underestimate the accuracy of our knowledge.
   d. accept as logical conclusions that involve unfamiliar concepts.

2. Phonemes are the basic units of _____ in language.
   a. sound   c. grammar
   b. meaning   d. syntax

3. Syntax refers to:
   a. the sounds in a word.
   b. the rules by which words are grouped into sentences.
   c. the rules by which meaning is derived from sentences.
   d. the overall rules of a language.

4. Skinner and other behaviorists have argued that language development is the result of:
   a. imitation.   c. association.
   b. reinforcement.   d. all of the above.

5. Many psychologists are skeptical of claims that chimpanzees can acquire language because the chimps have not shown the ability to:
   a. use symbols meaningfully.
   b. acquire speech.
   c. acquire even a limited vocabulary.
   d. use syntax in communicating.

6. Representativeness and availability are examples of:
   a. mental sets.   c. algorithms.
   b. heuristics.   d. fixation.

7. The basic units of cognition are:
   a. phonemes.   c. prototypes.
   b. concepts.   d. morphemes.

8. Which of the following describes artificial intelligence?
   a. the science of low-temperature phenomena
   b. the study of animal behavior in its natural habitat
   c. the study of control processes in electronic and biological systems
   d. the science that explores human thought by attempting to model it on the computer

9. Assume that Congress is considering revising its approach to welfare and to this end is hearing a range of testimony. A member of Congress who uses the availability heuristic would be most likely to:

   a. want to experiment with numerous possible approaches to see which of these seems to work best.
   b. want to cling to approaches to welfare that seem to have had some success in the past.
   c. refuse to be budged from his or her beliefs despite persuasive testimony to the contrary.
   d. base his or her ideas on the most vivid, memorable testimony, even though many statistics presented run counter to this testimony.

10. If you want to be absolutely certain that you will find the solution to a problem you know *is* solvable, you should use:

    a. a heuristic.   c. insight.
    b. an algorithm.   d. trial and error.

11. Complete the following: *-ed* is to *sh* as _____ is to _____.

    a. phoneme; morpheme
    b. morpheme; phoneme
    c. grammar; syntax
    d. syntax; grammar

12. Which of the following is *not* cited by Chomsky as evidence that language acquisition cannot be explained by learning alone?

    a. Children master the complicated rules of grammar with ease.
    b. Children create sentences they have never heard.
    c. Children make the kinds of mistakes that suggest they are attempting to apply rules of grammar.
    d. Children raised in isolation from language spontaneously begin speaking words.

13. Telegraphic speech is typical of the _____ stage.

    a. babbling   c. two-word
    b. one-word   d. three-word

14. Children first demonstrate a rudimentary understanding of syntax during the _____ stage.

    a. babbling   c. two-word
    b. one-word   d. three-word

15. The study in which people who immigrated to the United States at various ages were compared in terms of their ability to understand English grammar found that:

    a. age of arrival had no effect on mastery of grammar.
    b. those who immigrated as children understood grammar as well as native speakers.
    c. those who immigrated as adults understood grammar as well as native speakers.
    d. whether or not English was spoken in the home was the most important factor in mastering the rules of grammar.

16. Researchers taught the chimpanzee Washoe and the gorilla Koko to communicate by using:

    a. various sounds.
    b. plastic symbols of various shapes and color.
    c. sign language.
    d. all of the above.

17. Neural network computers:

    a. can be programmed to mimic excitatory and inhibitory neural messages.
    b. have a greater capacity than conventional computers to learn from experience.
    c. are not limited to serial processing.
    d. can do all of the above.
    e. can do none of the above.

18. The rules most directly involved in permitting a person to derive meaning from words and sentences are rules of:

    a. syntax.   c. phonemic structure.
    b. grammar.   d. semantics.

19. Which of the following is true regarding the relationship between thinking and language?

    a. "Real" thinking requires the use of language.
    b. People sometimes think in images rather than in words.
    c. A thought that cannot be expressed in a particular language cannot occur to speakers of that language.
    d. All of the above are true.

20. One reason an English-speaking adult may have difficulty pronouncing Russian words is that:

    a. the vocal tracts of English- and Russian-speaking people develop differently in response to the demands of the two languages.
    b. although English and Russian have very similar morphemes, their phonemic inventories are very different.
    c. although English and Russian have very similar phonemes, the morphemic inventories are very different.
    d. after the babbling stage, a child who hears only English stops producing other phonemes.

True-False Items

Indicate whether each statement is true or false by placing *T* or *F* in the blank next to the item.

_____ 1. The order in which children acquire an understanding of various morphemes is unpredictable.

_____ 2. According to the confirmation bias, people often interpret ambiguous evidence as support for their beliefs.

_____ 3. Most human problem solving involves the use of heuristics rather than reasoning that systematically considers every possible solution.

_____ 4. When asked, most people underestimate the accuracy of their judgments.

_____ 5. Studies have shown that, in certain instances, even animals may have insight reactions.

_____ 6. Mental set is the tendency to repeat problem-solving solutions that have worked in the past.

_____ 7. Although the morphemes differ from language to language, the phonemes for all languages are the same.

_____ 8. Children of all cultures babble using the same phonemes.

_____ 9. Thinking without using language is not possible.

_____ 10. Unlike computers, which are limited to processing information serially, humans can process many different bits of information simultaneously.

Challenge Test

Answer these questions the day before an exam as a final check on your understanding of the chapter's terms and concepts.

Multiple-Choice Questions

1. The word "predates" contains _____ phonemes and _____ morphemes.
   a. 7; 3   **c.** 7; 2
   b. 3; 7   **d.** 3; 2

2. Which of the following utterances is an example of overgeneralization?
   a. "We goed to the store."
   b. "Ball pretty."
   c. "The sky is crying."
   d. "We eat 'paghetti."

3. A listener hearing a recording of Japanese, Spanish, and North American children babbling would:
   a. not be able to tell them apart.
   b. be able to tell them apart if they were older than 6 months.

   c. be able to tell them apart if they were older than 8 to 10 months.
   d. be able to tell them apart at any age.

4. Which of the following illustrates belief perseverance?
   a. Your belief remains intact even in the face of evidence to the contrary.
   b. You refuse to listen to arguments counter to your beliefs.
   c. You tend to become flustered and angered when your beliefs are refuted.
   d. You tend to search for information that supports your beliefs.

5. Complete the following analogy: Rose is to flower as:
   a. concept is to prototype.
   b. prototype is to concept.
   c. concept is to hierarchy.
   d. hierarchy is to concept.

6. Your stand on an issue such as the use of nuclear power involves personal judgment. In such a case, one memorable occurrence can weigh more heavily than a bookful of data, thus illustrating:
   a. belief perseverance.
   b. confirmation bias.
   c. the representativeness heuristic.
   d. the availability heuristic.

7. A dessert recipe that gives you the ingredients, their amounts, and the steps to follow is an example of a(n):
   a. prototype.   **c.** heuristic.
   b. algorithm.   **d.** mental set.

8. Marilyn was asked to solve a series of five math problems. The first four problems could only be solved by a particular sequence of operations. The fifth problem could also be solved following this sequence; however, a much simpler solution was possible. Marilyn did not realize this simpler solution and solved the problem in the way she had solved the first four. Her problem-solving strategy was hampered by:
   a. functional fixedness.
   b. the overconfidence phenomenon.
   c. mental set.
   d. her lack of a prototype for the solution.

9. Dr. Mendoza is studying the mental strategies people use when solving problems. Dr. Mendoza is clearly a(n):
   a. cognitive psychologist.
   b. experimental psychologist.
   c. organizational psychologist.
   d. developmental psychologist.

10. Boris the chess master selects his next move by considering moves that would threaten his opponent's queen. His opponent, a chess-playing computer, selects its next move by considering *all* possible moves. Boris is using a(n) _____ and the computer is using a(n) _____.
    a. algorithm; heuristic
    b. prototype; mental set
    c. mental set; prototype
    d. heuristic; algorithm

11. During a televised political debate, the Republican and Democratic candidates each argued that the results of a recent public opinion poll supported their party's platform. Because both candidates saw the information as supporting their belief, it is clear that both were victims of:
    a. functional fixedness.
    b. mental set.
    c. belief bias.
    d. confirmation bias.

12. The child who says "Milk gone" is engaging in _____. This type of utterance demonstrates that children are actively experimenting with the rules of _____.
    a. babbling; syntax
    b. telegraphic speech; syntax
    c. babbling; semantics
    d. telegraphic speech; semantics

13. Experts in a field prefer heuristics to algorithms because heuristics:
    a. guarantee solutions to problems.
    b. prevent mental sets.
    c. often save time.
    d. do all of the above.

14. Rudy is 6 feet 6 inches tall, weighs 210 pounds, and is very muscular. If you think that Rudy is more likely to be a professional basketball player than a computer programmer, you are a victim of:
    a. belief bias.
    b. the availability heuristic.
    c. the representativeness heuristic.
    d. functional fixedness.

15. Failing to see that an article of clothing can be inflated as a life preserver is an example of:
    a. belief bias.
    b. the availability heuristic.
    c. the representativeness heuristic.
    d. functional fixedness.

16. Airline reservations typically decline after a highly publicized airline crash because people overestimate the incidence of such disasters. In such instances, people's decisions are being influenced by:
    a. belief bias.

    b. the availability heuristic.
    c. the representativeness heuristic.
    d. functional fixedness.

17. Most people tend to:
    a. accurately estimate the accuracy of their knowledge and judgments.
    b. underestimate the accuracy of their knowledge and judgments.
    c. overestimate the accuracy of their knowledge and judgments.
    d. lack confidence in their decision-making strategies.

18. In relation to ground beef, consumers respond more positively to an ad describing it as "75 percent lean" than to one referring to its "25 percent fat" content. This is an example of:
    a. the framing effect.
    b. confirmation bias.
    c. mental set.
    d. overconfidence.

19. The sentence "Blue jeans wear false smiles" has correct _____ but incorrect _____.
    a. morphemes; phonemes
    b. phonemes; morphemes
    c. semantics; syntax
    d. syntax; semantics

20. Regarding the relationship between thinking and language, which of the following most accurately reflects the position taken in the textbook?
    a. Language determines everything about our thinking.
    b. Language determines the *way* we think.
    c. Thinking without language is not possible.
    d. Thinking affects our language, which then affects our thought.

Essay Question

The lectures of your linguistics professor, who happens to be a staunch behaviorist, clearly imply that she believes language development can be explained according to principles of conditioning. What evidence should you present to convince her that she is wrong? (Use the space below to list the points you want to make and organize them. Then write the essay on a separate piece of paper.)

Key Terms

Using your own words, write a brief definition or explanation of each of the following terms.

1. thinking (or cognition)

2. cognitive psychology

3. concept

4. prototype

5. algorithm

6. heuristic

7. insight

8. confirmation bias

9. fixation

10. mental set

11. functional fixedness

12. representativeness heuristic

13. availability heuristic

14. overconfidence

15. framing

16. belief bias

17. belief perseverance

18. artificial intelligence (AI)

19. neural networks

20. language

21. phonemes

22. morphemes

23. grammar

24. semantics

25. syntax

26. babbling stage

27. one-word stage

28. two-word stage

29. telegraphic speech

30. linguistic relativity

ANSWERS

GUIDED STUDY

The following guidelines provide the main points that your answers should have touched upon.

1. Concepts are mental groupings of events, people, or things that share common features. Because they provide a great deal of information with a minimum of cognitive effort, concepts are the basic units of thinking. Most concepts are formed around a best example, or prototype, of a particular category. Concepts are often organized into hierarchies that further increase cognitive efficiency.

2. Trial and error is a haphazard strategy for solving problems, in which one solution after another is tried until success is achieved. Algorithms are methodical and logical rules for solving problems; they often are laborious and inefficient. Heuristics are based on rules-of-thumb and/or past experience. Although formally not a problem-solving strategy, a sudden flash of inspiration (insight) often helps us to solve problems. Insight has been observed in chimpanzees who are given challenging problems to solve.

3. The confirmation bias is an obstacle to problem solving in which people seek information that validates their beliefs. Another common obstacle to problem solving is fixation, an inability to approach a familiar problem in a new way. One example of fixation is the tendency to continue applying a particular problem-solving strategy even when it is no longer useful (mental set). Another example is functional fixedness, in which a person is unable to perceive unusual functions for familiar objects.

4. The representativeness heuristic is the tendency to judge the likelihood of things in terms of how well they represent particular prototypes. The availability heuristic occurs when we base our judgments on how readily certain information comes to mind.

The overconfidence phenomenon is the tendency of people to overestimate the accuracy of their knowledge and judgments. Although overconfidence may blind us to our vulnerability to error in reasoning, it has adaptive value in that it makes decision making somewhat easier.

Framing refers to the way an issue or question

is posed, which can greatly influence our perception of the issue or answer to the question.

5. Belief bias is the tendency for our beliefs to distort logical reasoning. An example of this common error is our tendency to accept as logical those conclusions that agree with our opinions. Belief perseverance is our tendency to cling to our beliefs even in the face of contrary evidence. Once beliefs are formed, it takes stronger evidence to change them than it did to create them.

6. Although both the mind and the computer process input from the environment, only humans truly think and feel. Computers excel at tasks that require the manipulation of large amounts of data. Unlike the human brain, which can process unrelated bits of information simultaneously, most computers process information sequentially. A new generation of computer neural networks has been designed to more closely simulate the brain's interconnected neural units and their functions. Compared with conventional artificial intelligence systems, neural network computers show greater capacity for parallel processing and "learning" from environmental experience.

7. Phonemes are the basic units of sound in a language. Morphemes are the smallest units of speech that convey meaning. Most morphemes are combinations of two or more phonemes. Each language has a system of rules, or grammar, that enables people to use and understand it. Semantics refers to the grammatical rules used to derive meaning from the elements of language. Syntax specifies the rules for combining words into sentences.

8. At about 4 months of age, babies enter a babbling stage in which they spontaneously utter phonemes of all languages. By 1 year children enter the one-word stage. In this stage, single-syllable words are used to name things and may even be inflected to convey the meaning of an entire sentence. By age 2 most children enter the two-word stage. At this time their speech consists of telegraphic utterances containing mostly nouns and verbs, yet placed in a sensible syntactic order. Children then quickly begin uttering longer and more complex phrases and sentences.

   According to B. F. Skinner, language development can be explained according to the learning principles of association, imitation, and reinforcement. In contrast, Noam Chomsky believes that children are biologically prepared to learn language as they interact with their caregivers.

9. Numerous studies demonstrate that animals communicate effectively amongst themselves. Karl von Frisch, for example, discovered that explorer bees convey to other bees the direction and distance of a food source by means of an intricate dance.

Several attempts have been made to teach sign language and other symbolic languages to chimpanzees. Although apes have a capacity to learn a relatively large vocabulary of sign words, critics contend that much of their signing is nothing more than imitation of their trainer's signs and shows little evidence of syntax.

10. According to Whorf's linguistic relativity hypothesis, language determines the way we think. Critics of this idea claim that our language *reflects* rather than creates the way we think. Studies of the ability of vocabulary enrichment to enhance thinking reveal that it is more accurate to say that language *influences*, rather than determines, thought. Some thoughts, such as the imagery involved in art, music, and athletics, do not depend on language.

CHAPTER REVIEW

1. thinking; the mental activity associated with understanding, processing, and communicating knowledge; cognitive psychologists
2. concepts; hierarchies
3. prototype
4. problem solving
5. trial and error
6. algorithms
7. heuristics
8. insight; have
9. confirmation bias
10. fixation; mental set
11. functional fixedness
12. representativeness heuristic
13. availability heuristic

Using these heuristics often prevents us from processing other relevant information, and because we overlook this information, we make judgmental errors. Thus, in the text example, the representativeness heuristic leads people to overlook the fact that there are many more truck drivers than Ivy League classics professors and, as a result, to wrongly conclude that the poetry reader is more likely to be an Ivy League classics professor. Also as noted in the text, the availability heuristic leads us to incorrectly think that words beginning with *k* are more common than words having *k* as their third letter.

14. overconfidence
15. does
16. framing
17. belief bias; easier
18. belief perseverance
19. artificial intelligence

20. serially; simultaneously

21. neural networks; parallel; and so

22. phonemes; 40

23. morphemes

24. grammar

25. semantics

26. syntax

27. babbling; 4; do not

28. one-word; 1

29. telegraphic

30. association; imitation; reinforcement

31. Chomsky

The rate at which children acquire vocabulary and grammar is too rapid to be explained solely by learning. Children create sentences that they have never heard and therefore could not be imitating. Children's linguistic errors are often logical overextensions of grammatical rules.

32. dance; do not

33. sign language

Chimps have acquired only limited vocabularies and—in contrast to children—have acquired these vocabularies only with great difficulty. Also in contrast to children, it's unclear that chimps can use syntax to express meaning. Even simpler animals, such as birds, are capable of learning behavioral sequences that some chimp researchers consider language. Much of the signing of chimps is nothing more than imitation of the trainer's actions. People tend to interpret such ambiguous behavior in terms of what they want to see.

34. linguistic relativity; Whorf

35. does

36. can

The relationship is probably a two-way one: The linguistic relativity hypothesis suggests that language helps shape thought; that words come into the language to express new ideas indicates that thought also shapes language.

PROGRESS TEST 1

Multiple-Choice Questions

1. **c.** is the answer. (p. 286)

2. **b.** is the answer. (p. 286)

    a. A prototype is the best example of a particular category, or concept.

    c. & d. Algorithms and heuristics are problem-solving strategies.

3. **c.** is the answer. (p. 287)

    a. There is no such thing as a "denoter."

b. & d. Heuristics and algorithms are problem-solving strategies.

4. **d.** is the answer. A major obstacle to problem-solving, the confirmation bias refers to the common tendency to search for evidence that confirms one's beliefs and not for evidence that would disconfirm them. (p. 288)

    a. & b. These refer to belief bias and belief perseverance, respectively.

    c. This is trial-and-error problem solving.

5. **c.** is the answer. (p. 302)

6. **a.** is the answer. Babbling is not the imitation of adult speech since babbling infants produce phonemes from languages they have not heard and could not be imitating. (p. 303)

7. **c.** is the answer. Both are examples of failing to see a problem from a new perspective. (pp. 290–291)

    a. & b. Algorithms and heuristics are problem-solving strategies.

    d. Insight is the sudden realization of a problem's solution.

8. **d.** is the answer. Each of these arguments has been made by skeptics of ape language research. (pp. 308–309)

9. **d.** is the answer. (pp. 310–311)

    a. This is Skinner's position regarding language development.

    b. This is Chomsky's position regarding language development.

    c. The linguistic relativity hypothesis is concerned with the content of thought, not intelligence.

10. **c.** is the answer. (pp. 305–306)

    a. This is the position of a behaviorist, such as Skinner.

    b. According to Chomsky, although the *ability* to acquire language is innate, the child can only acquire language in association with others.

    d. Cultural influences are an important example of the influence of learning on language development, an influence Chomsky fully accepts.

11. **b.** is the answer. Functional fixedness is the tendency to think of things only in terms of their usual functions. (p. 291)

    a. Mental set is the tendency to approach a problem in a particular way that worked previously.

    c. Framing refers to the way an issue is posed; this often influences our judgment.

    d. Belief perseverance is the tendency to cling to one's beliefs even after they have been refuted.

12. **d.** is the answer. Heuristics are rule-of-thumb strategies—such as playing chess defensively—

that are based on past successes in similar situations. (p. 287)

a., b., & c. These are all algorithms.

13. **a.** is the answer. Sultan suddenly arrived at a novel solution to his problem, thus displaying apparent insight. (pp. 287–288)

b. Sultan did not randomly try various strategies of reaching the fruit; he demonstrated the "light bulb" reaction that is the hallmark of insight.

c. & d. Functional fixedness and mental set are impediments to problem solving. Sultan obviously solved his problem.

14. **c.** is the answer. Your conclusion is based on sex stereotypes, that is, athletic ability and participation are for you more *representative* of boys. Your conclusion is by no means necessarily right, however, especially since the Smiths have four daughters and only one son. (p. 291)

a. The confirmation bias is the tendency to look for information that confirms one's preconception.

b. The availability heuristic involves judging the probability of an event in terms of how readily it comes to mind.

d. Belief perseverance is the tendency to cling to beliefs, even when the evidence has shown that they are wrong.

15. **d.** is the answer. People can process millions of different bits of information at the same time; computers must generally process information one step at a time. (p. 300)

a., b., & c. Both computers and people are capable of these.

16. **a.** is the answer. (pp. 300–301)

17. **c.** is the answer. Children are biologically prepared to learn language as they and their caregivers interact. (pp. 305–307)

a. This is Skinner's position.

b. No psychologist, including Chomsky, believes that language is entirely a product of biological maturation.

d. Although language acquisition is not completely understood, research has shed sufficient light on it to render it less than a complete mystery.

18. **c.** is the answer. The dance's direction and duration inform worker bees of the direction and distance of a food source. (p. 307)

19. **b.** is the answer. The evidence that absence of a term for a color does not affect ability to perceive the color challenges the idea that language always shapes thought. (pp. 310–312)

a. & d. These findings would not be relevant to the linguistic relativity hypothesis, which addresses the relationship between language and thought.

c. This finding is in keeping with the linguistic relativity hypothesis.

20. **c.** is the answer. The generic pronoun *he* evidently tends, for both adults and children, to conjure up images of males. (p. 311)

Matching Items

1. f (p. 302)	**5.** e (p. 292)	**9.** h (p. 287)
2. i (p. 296)	**6.** j (p. 294)	**10.** c (p. 290)
3. a (p. 302)	**7.** k (p. 290)	**11.** b (p. 302)
4. g (p. 302)	**8.** d (p. 287)	

PROGRESS TEST 2

Multiple-Choice Questions

1. **a.** is the answer. Reasoning in daily life is often distorted by our beliefs, which may lead us, for example, to accept conclusions that haven't been arrived at logically. (p. 297)

b. & d. These are just the opposite of what we tend to do.

c. In fact, people tend to overestimate the accuracy of their knowledge.

2. **a.** is the answer. (p. 302)

b. Morphemes are the basic units of meaning.

c. & d. The text does not refer to basic units of grammar or syntax.

3. **b.** is the answer. (p. 302)

a. Phonemes are the sounds in a word.

c. Such rules are known as semantics.

d. Such rules are the language's grammar, which would include its syntax as well as its semantics.

4. **d.** is the answer. These are all basic principles of learning and explain language development. (p. 305)

5. **d.** is the answer. Syntax is one of the fundamental aspects of language, and chimps seem unable, for example, to use word order to convey differences in meaning. (pp. 308–309)

a. & c. Chimps' use of sign language demonstrates both the use of symbols and the acquisition of fairly sizable vocabularies.

b. No psychologist would require the use of speech as evidence of language; significantly, all the research and arguments focus on what chimps are and are not able to do in acquiring other facets of language.

6. **b.** is the answer. Both are rule-of-thumb strategies that allow us to make quick judgments. (p. 287)

a. & d. Mental sets and fixation are obstacles to

problem solving, in which the person tends to repeat solutions that have worked in the past and is unable to conceive of other possible solutions.

c. Algorithms are methodical strategies that guarantee a solution to a particular problem.

7. **b.** is the answer. (p. 286)

a. & d. Phonemes and morphemes are units of sound and meaning in language, respectively.

c. Prototypes are the best examples of specific categories.

8. **d.** is the answer. Artificial intelligence researchers attempt to design and program computers to do things that appear "intelligent." (p. 299)

9. **d.** is the answer. If we use the availability heuristic, we base judgments on the availability of information in our memories, and more vivid information is often the most readily available. (p. 292)

a. This would exemplify use of the trial-and-error approach to problem solving.

b. This would exemplify a mental set.

c. This would exemplify belief perseverance.

10. **b.** is the answer. Because they involve the systematic examination of all possible solutions to a problem, algorithms guarantee that a solution will be found. (p. 287)

a., c., & d. None of these methods guarantees that a problem's solution will be found.

11. **b.** is the answer. The morpheme *-ed* changes the *meaning* of a regular verb to form its past tense; the phoneme *sh* is a unique *sound* in the English language. (p. 302)

c. & d. Syntax, which specifies rules for combining words into sentences, is one aspect of the grammar of a language.

12. **d.** is the answer. Chomsky believes that the inborn capacity for language acquisition must be activated by exposure to language. And in fact, children raised in isolation will *not* begin to speak spontaneously. (pp. 305–306)

13. **c.** is the answer. (p. 304)

14. **c.** is the answer. Although the child's utterances are only two words long, the words are placed in a sensible order. In English, for example, adjectives are placed before nouns. (p. 304)

a & b. These answers are incorrect because syntax specifies rules for *combining* two or more units in speech.

d. There is no three-word stage.

15. **b.** is the answer. (p. 306)

16. **c.** is the answer. (pp. 307–308)

17. **d.** is the answer. (pp. 300–301)

18. **d.** is the answer. Semantic rules are directly concerned with the derivation of meaning from morphemes, words, and sentences. (p. 302)

a. Syntax is the set of rules for a language that permits the combination of words into sentences.

b. Grammar is the overall system of rules for using a language and, as such, includes syntax as well as semantics.

c. Phonemic structure concerns the basic sounds, or phonemes, of a language.

19. **b.** is the answer. (p. 312)

a. Researchers do not make a distinction between "real" and other thinking, nor do they consider nonlinguistic thinking less valid than linguistic thinking.

c. As indicated by several studies cited in the textbook, this is not true.

20. **d.** is the answer. Following the babbling stage, the child's ability to produce all phonemes becomes in a sense shaped and limited to the ability to produce those phonemes he or she hears. (p. 303)

a. The vocal tract of Homo sapiens does not develop in specialized ways for different languages.

b. & c. English and Russian differ significantly in both their phonemes and their morphemes. Nor is there any reason why differences in morphemes would in and of themselves cause pronunciation difficulties.

True-False Items

1. False (p. 305)
2. True (p. 288)
3. True (p. 287)
4. False (p. 294)
5. True (pp. 287–288)

6. True (p. 290)
7. False (p. 302)
8. True (p. 303)
9. False (p. 312)
10. True (p. 300)

CHALLENGE TEST

Multiple-Choice Questions

1. **a.** is the answer. Each sound of the word is a phoneme (note that the second letter "e" does not itself represent a sound); the morphemes are "pre," which means before, "date," and "s," which indicates the plural. (p. 302)

2. **a.** is the answer. Adding *-ed* to the irregular verb go results in the ungrammatical *goed*—an overgeneralization of the rule by which the past tense of regular verbs is formed. (p. 305)

b. This is an example of telegraphic speech.

c. This is a grammatical statement.

d. "'paghetti" is simply an immature pronunciation of "spaghetti"; young children often have difficulty with consonant clusters like "sp."

3. a. is the answer. (p. 303)

4. a. is the answer. (pp. 297–298)

b. & c. These may very well occur, but they do not define belief perseverance.

d. This is the confirmation bias.

5. b. is the answer. A rose is a prototypical example of the concept *flower.* (p. 287)

c. & d. Hierarchies are organized clusters of concepts. In this example, there is only the single concept *flower.*

6. d. is the answer. The availability heuristic is the judgmental strategy that estimates the likelihood of events in terms of how readily they come to mind, and the most vivid information is often the most readily available. (p. 292)

7. b. is the answer. Follow the directions precisely and you can't miss! (p. 287)

a. A prototype is the best example of a concept.

c. Heuristics are rules of thumb that help solve problems but, in contrast to a recipe that is followed precisely, do not guarantee success.

d. A mental set is a tendency to approach a problem in a way that has been successful in the past.

8. c. is the answer. By simply following a strategy that has worked well in the past, Marilyn is hampered by the type of fixation called mental set. (p. 290)

a. Functional fixedness is being unable to conceive of an unusual function for an object.

b. Overconfidence is exhibited by the person who overestimates the accuracy of his or her judgments.

d. Prototypes are best examples of categories, not strategies for solving problems.

9. a. is the answer. Cognitive psychologists study how we process, understand, and communicate knowledge. Problem solving involves processing information and is therefore a topic explored by cognitive psychologists. (p. 286)

b. Cognitive psychologists often use experimentation to study phenomena but, because not all experimental psychologists study cognition, a. is the best answer.

c. Organizational psychologists study behavior in the workplace.

d. Developmental psychologists study the ways in which behavior changes over the life span.

10. d. is the answer. (p. 287)

b. & c. If Boris always attacks his opponent's queen when playing chess, he is a victim of mental set; prototypes, however, have nothing to do with chess playing.

11. d. is the answer. The confirmation bias is the tendency to search for information that confirms one's preconceptions. In this example, the politicians' preconceptions are biasing their interpretation of the survey results. (p. 288)

a. Functional fixedness is the inability to perceive an unusual use for a familiar object.

b. Mental set is the tendency to approach a problem in a particular way. There is no problem per se in this example.

c. Belief bias is the tendency for one's preexisting beliefs to distort logical reasoning. This answer is incorrect because it is not clear, in this example, whether either politician is reasoning illogically.

12. b. is the answer. Such utterances, characteristic of a child of about 2 years, are like telegrams, in that they consist mainly of nouns and verbs and show use of syntax. (p. 304)

a. & c. Babbling consists of phonemes, not words.

d. Semantics refers to the rules by which meaning is derived from sentences; this speech example indicates nothing in particular about the child's understanding of semantics.

13. c. is the answer. (pp. 287, 291)

a. & b. Heuristics do not guarantee solutions or prevent mental sets.

14. c. is the answer. Your conclusion is based on the stereotype that muscular build is more *representative* of athletes than computer programmers. (pp. 291–292)

a. Belief bias is the tendency for one's preexisting beliefs to distort logical reasoning.

b. The availability heuristic involves judging the probability of an event in terms of how readily it comes to mind.

d. Functional fixedness is the tendency to think of things only in terms of their usual functions.

15. d. is the answer. (p. 291)

16. b. is the answer. The publicity surrounding disasters makes such events vivid and seemingly more probable than they actually are. (p. 292)

a. The belief bias is the tendency for preexisting beliefs to distort logical thinking.

c. The representativeness heuristic operates when we judge the likelihood of things in terms of how well they represent particular prototypes. This example does not involve such a situation.

d. Functional fixedness operates in situations in which effective problem solving requires using an object in an unfamiliar manner.

17. c. is the answer. This is referred to as overconfidence. (p. 294)

18. **a.** is the answer. In this example, the way the issue is posed, or framed, has evidently influenced consumers' judgments. (p. 296)

    b. Confirmation bias is the tendency to search for information that confirms one's preconceptions.

    c. Mental set is the tendency to approach a problem in a particular way.

    d. Overconfidence is the tendency to be more confident than correct.

19. **d.** is the answer. This sentence, although semantically meaningless, nevertheless follows the grammatical rules of English syntax for combining words into sentences. (p. 302)

    a. & b. The phonemes (smallest units of sound) and morphemes (smallest units of meaning) of this sentence are equally correct.

20. **d.** is the answer. (p. 313)

Essay Question

You should point out that the rate at which children acquire words and grammar is too extraordinary to be explained solely according to principles of learning. Children also utter all sorts of word forms they have never heard and could not, therefore, be imitating. Furthermore, children begin using morphemes in a predictable order, which learning theorists would not expect since each child experiences a unique linguistic environment. Children also make predictable errors that result from overuse of grammatical rules, rather than from imitation. It therefore seems clear that children are biologically prepared to acquire language and that the behaviorist position is incorrect.

KEY TERMS

1. **Thinking**, or **cognition**, refers to mental activity associated with understanding, processing, and communicating knowledge. (p. 286)

2. **Cognitive psychology** is the branch of psychology that studies mental activities that underlie problem solving, judgments, decision making, and language. (p. 286)

3. A **concept** is a mental grouping, or category, of similar things, events, or people. (p. 286)

4. A **prototype** is the best example of a particular category. (p. 287)

   Example: A robin, but not a goose, is a **prototypical** bird; an apple, but not a tomato, is a **prototypical** fruit.

5. An **algorithm** is a methodical problem-solving strategy that, while sometimes slow, guarantees success. (p. 287)

6. A **heuristic** is any problem-solving strategy based on rules of thumb and/or past experience. Although heuristics are more efficient than algorithms, they do not guarantee success and sometimes even impede problem solving. (p. 287)

7. **Insight** is a sudden and often creative solution to a problem. Insight contrasts with trial and error and, indeed, may often follow an unsuccessful episode of trial and error. (p. 287)

8. The **confirmation bias** is an obstacle to problem solving in which people seek information that validates their beliefs. (p. 288)

   Example: **Confirmation bias** can often be observed in politicians as they automatically, yet unintentionally, interpret ambiguous statistics as supporting their ideas and proposals.

9. **Fixation** is an inability to approach a problem in a new way. (p. 290)

10. **Mental set** refers to the tendency to continue applying a particular problem-solving strategy even when it is no longer helpful. (p. 290)

    Example: Brainstorming is a technique designed to break **mental sets** and generate novel solutions to problems.

11. **Functional fixedness** is a type of fixation in which a person can think of things only in terms of their usual functions. (p. 291)

    Example: In a creativity test that requires using a pair of pliers as a support for a small board, subjects' **functional fixedness** might prevent them from thinking of pliers as anything other than a tool for grasping.

12. The **representativeness heuristic** is the tendency to judge the likelihood of things in terms of how well they conform to one's prototypes. (p. 291)

    Example: The diagnostic process of an experienced doctor provides a good example of the **representativeness heuristic**: The likelihood of a patient's having a particular disease is based on how closely his or her symptoms correspond to the prototypical symptoms for that disease.

13. The **availability heuristic** is based on estimating the probability of certain events in terms of how readily they come to mind. (p. 292)

    Example: In attempting to convince legislators to adopt their viewpoints, lobbyists take advantage of the **availability heuristic**: In-person arguments are more persuasive than written correspondence because, later, they tend to come more readily to mind.

14. Another obstacle to problem solving, **overconfidence** refers to the tendency to overestimate the accuracy of one's beliefs. (p. 294)

15. **Framing** refers to the way an issue or question is

posed. It can affect people's perception of the issue or answer to the question. (p. 296)

16. **Belief bias** is the tendency for a person's preexisting beliefs to distort his or her logical reasoning. (p. 297)

17. **Belief perseverance** is the tendency for people to cling to a particular belief even after the information that led to the formation of the belief is discredited. (p. 297)

18. **Artificial intelligence (AI)** is the science of programming computers to perform practical operations and to model human information processing. (p. 299)

19. **Neural networks** are computer circuits that simulate the brain's interconnected nerve cells and perform tasks such as learning to recognize visual patterns. (p. 300)

20. **Language** refers to words and how we combine them to communicate meaning. (p. 301)

21. **Phonemes** are the smallest units of sound in a language that are distinctive for speakers of the language. (p. 302)

22. **Morphemes** are the smallest units of speech that convey meaning. (p. 302)

    Example: The word "dogs," which contains four phonemes, contains only two **morphemes**— "dog" and "-s." Although most morphemes are combinations of two or more phonemes, the plural "-s" conveys a distinctive meaning of "more than one."

23. **Grammar** is the set of rules that enables people to use and understand a language. (p. 302)

24. **Semantics** is the aspect of grammar that specifies the rules used to derive meaning from morphemes, words, and sentences. (p. 302)

    Example: One **semantic** rule of English is that adding -ed to a verb gives the verb a past-tense meaning.

25. **Syntax** is the aspect of grammar specifying the rules for combining words into grammatical sentences. (p. 302)

    Example: One **syntactic** rule of English is that adjectives are positioned before nouns.

26. The **babbling stage** of speech development, which begins at about 4 months, is characterized by the spontaneous utterance of speech sounds. During the babbling stage, children the world over sound alike. (p. 303)

27. Between 1 and 2 years of age children speak mostly in single words; they are therefore in the **one-word stage** of linguistic development. (p. 303)

28. Beginning about age 2, children are in the **two-word stage** and speak mostly in two-word sentences. (p. 304)

29. **Telegraphic speech** is the economical, telegram-like speech of children in the two-word stage. Utterances consist mostly of nouns and verbs; however, words occur in the correct order, showing that the child has learned some of the language's syntactic rules. (p. 304)

30. **Linguistic relativity** is Benjamin Whorf's hypothesis that language influences the way we think. (p. 310)

11 / Intelligence

Chapter Overview

An enduring controversy in psychology involves attempts to define and measure intelligence. Chapter 11 describes the historical origins of intelligence tests and discusses several important issues concerning their use. These include the methods by which intelligence tests are constructed and whether such tests are valid, reliable, and free of cultural bias. The chapter also discusses research that attempts to assess the stability of intelligence, whether intelligence is a single general ability or several specific ones, and the extent of genetic and environmental influences on intelligence.

NOTE: Answer guidelines for all Chapter 11 questions begin on page 231.

Guided Study

The text chapter should be studied one section at a time. Before you read, preview each section by skimming it, noting headings and boldface items. Then read the appropriate section objectives from the following outline. Keep these objectives in mind and, as you read the chapter section, search for the information that will enable you to meet each objective. Once you have finished a section, write out answers for its objectives.

Assessing Intelligence (pp. 318–327)

1. Trace the origins of intelligence tests.

2. Distinguish between aptitude and achievement tests and describe modern tests of mental abilities.

3. Identify the major principles of good test construction and illustrate their application to intelligence tests.

What Is Intelligence? (pp. 327–332)

4. Describe the nature of intelligence and discuss whether it is culturally defined or culture-free.

5. Describe the factor-analysis approach to understanding intelligence and discuss evidence regarding intelligence as a general mental ability and/or as many specific abilities.

6. Discuss the information-processing approach to intelligence.

11. Discuss whether intelligence tests are biased and/or discriminatory.

The Dynamics of Intelligence (pp. 332–336)

7. Discuss the stability of intelligence test scores and the two extremes of intelligence.

Chapter Review

When you have finished reading the chapter, work through the material that follows to review it. Complete the sentences and answer the questions. As you proceed, evaluate your performance for each section by consulting the answers on page 233. Do not continue with the next section until you understand each answer. If you need to, review or reread the appropriate section in the textbook before continuing.

8. Identify the factors associated with creativity.

1. Tests that assess a person's mental capacities and compare them to others' are called

   _____ tests.

Assessing Intelligence (pp. 318–327)

2. The early Greek philosopher

   _____ concluded that individuals differed in their natural endowments.

Genetic and Environmental Determinants of Intelligence (pp. 336–345)

9. Discuss evidence for both genetic and environmental influences on intelligence.

3. The English scientist _____ developed the idea of improving humankind by selectively breeding persons with superior traits; this idea is called _____. It assumes that most important human traits are

   _____.

4. The French psychologist who devised a test to predict the success of children in school was

   _____. Predictions were made by comparing children's chronological ages with their _____ ages, which were determined by the test. This test

   _____ (was/was not) designed to measure inborn intelligence.

10. Describe group differences in intelligence test scores and show how they can be explained in terms of environmental factors.

5. Lewis Terman's revision of Binet's test is referred to as the _____–_____. This test enables one to derive an

   _____ _____

   for an individual.

Give the original formula for computing IQ and explain any items used in the formula.

Describe the normal curve and explain its significance in the standardization process.

6. Today's tests compute IQ by comparing the individual's performance to the average performance of people _____ (the same/of different) age(s). These tests are designed so that a score of _____ is considered average.

7. When given intelligence tests in the early 1900s, immigrants arriving in the United States often scored _____ (above/below) average. This is because the tests were based on a particular _____ background.

8. Tests designed to predict your ability to learn something new are called _____ tests. Tests designed to measure what you already have learned are called _____ tests.

9. The most widely used intelligence test is the

_____ _____

_____ _____.

Consisting of eleven subtests, it provides not only a general intelligence score but also _____ and _____ intelligence scores.

10. Two tests of general ability that are designed to predict a student's academic performance in college are the _____ and the _____.

11. Three requirements of a good test are

_____, _____, and

_____.

12. The administering of a test to a representative comparison group is called

_____.

13. When scores on a test are compiled, they generally result in a bell-shaped, or _____, distribution.

14. During the 1960s and 1970s, SAT scores in the United States showed a steady _____ (increase/decline).

15. Since the 1930s, performance on the WAIS has generally _____ (increased/declined).

Cite several proposed reasons for these trends in SAT and WAIS performance.

16. If a test yields consistent results, it is said to be

_____.

17. When a test is administered more than once to the same people, the psychologist is determining its _____ - _____ reliability.

18. When a person's scores for the odd- and even-numbered questions on a test are compared, _____ - _____ reliability is being assessed.

19. The Stanford-Binet, Wechsler, SAT, and ACT have reliabilities of about _____.

20. The degree to which a test measures or predicts what it is supposed to is referred to as the test's

_____.

21. The degree to which a test measures the behavior it was designed to measure is referred to as the test's _____ _____.

22. The degree to which a test predicts future performance, called the test's _____, is referred to as the test's _____ _____.

Choose a specific example and use it to illustrate and explain the concept of criterion and its relationship to predictive validity.

23. Generally speaking, the predictive validity of general aptitude tests _____ (is/is not) as high as their reliability. The predictive validity of these tests _____ (increases/diminishes) as individuals move up the educational ladder.

What Is Intelligence? (pp. 327–332)

24. Psychologists _____ (do/do not) agree on a definition of intelligence.

25. To regard an abstract concept as a concrete entity is to commit the error known as _____.

26. According to the textbook, intelligence can be defined as _____ _____.

Describe the controversy surrounding intelligence as a culturally defined or a culture-free ability.

27. A second controversy regarding the nature of intelligence centers on whether intelligence is one _____ ability or several _____ abilities.

28. The statistical procedure used to identify groups of items that appear to measure a common ability is called _____ _____. Charles Spearman, one of the developers of this technique, believed that a factor called *g*, or _____ _____, runs through the more specific aspects of intelligence.

29. Opposing Spearman, _____ identified eight clusters of _____ _____.

30. People with _____ _____ score at the low end of intelligence tests but possess extraordinary specific skills.

31. Howard Gardner proposes that there are _____ _____, each independent of the others.

32. Sternberg and Wagner distinguish three types of intelligence: _____ intelligence, _____ intelligence, and _____ intelligence. Similarly, Cantor and Kihlstrom distinguish between _____ intelligence and _____ intelligence. Support for this distinction comes from evidence that college grades _____ (do/do not) accurately predict later achievement in careers.

33. When solving a problem, highly intelligent persons spend more time _____ the problem than do those labeled less intelligent.

34. Studies looking at a range of tasks have found that people with high intelligence scores tend to process and retrieve information _____ (faster/more slowly) than people with low intelligence scores.

The Dynamics of Intelligence (pp. 332–336)

35. Two- to 6-month-old infants who quickly become bored when looking at a picture score _____ (higher/lower) on intelligence tests several years later.

36. Traditional intelligence tests before age _____ generally do not predict future scores.

37. During childhood, the stability of intelligence scores _____ (increases/decreases) with age. By adolescence, intelligence scores are _____ (extremely/not very) stable.

38. Individuals whose intelligence scores fall below 70 and who have difficulty adapting to life may be labeled _____ _____. This label applies to approximately _____ percent of the population.

39. Severe retardation generally has a physical basis, such as _____ _____, a genetic disorder caused by an extra chromosome.

Discuss criticisms of programs that sort children into gifted and nongifted tracks.

40. The ability to produce novel ideas is called _____. The relationship between intelligence and creativity holds only up to a certain point—an intelligence score of about _____.

Describe four components of creativity other than intelligence.

Genetic and Environmental Determinants of Intelligence (pp. 336–345)

41. The position that both heredity and environment exert some influence on intelligence is _____ (controversial/generally accepted) among psychologists.

42. Two kinds of studies that have been undertaken to shed light on the nature-nurture issue with regard to intelligence are _____ studies and _____ studies.

43. The intelligence scores of identical twins reared together are _____ (more/no more) similar than those of fraternal twins.

44. Children's intelligence scores are more like those of their _____ (biological/adoptive) parents than their _____ (biological/adoptive) parents. The strength of this relationship _____ (increases/remains stable/decreases) as the children get older.

45. The amount of variation in a trait within a group that is attributed to genetic factors is called its _____. For intelligence, this has been estimated at roughly _____ percent.

46. Studies indicate that neglected children _____ (do/do not) show signs of recovery in intelligence and behavior when placed in more nurturing environments.

47. If we know a trait has perfect heritability, this knowledge _____ (does/does not) enable us to rule out environmental factors in explaining differences between groups.

48. High-quality programs for disadvantaged children, such as the government-funded _____ _____ program, produce at least short-term gains on intelligence tests.

49. Most psychologists believe that racial gaps in intelligence are due primarily to _____ (genetic/environmental) factors.

Explain why heredity may contribute to individual differences in intelligence but not necessarily contribute to group differences.

50. In the sense that they detect differences caused by cultural experiences, intelligence tests probably _____ (are/are not) biased.

51. Most psychologists agree that, in terms of predictive validity, the major aptitude tests _____ (are/are not) racially biased.

FOCUS ON PSYCHOLOGY:
Becoming a Mental Calculator

Steven Smith (1983) refers to individuals who can perform complex calculations in their heads as *mental calculators*. For example, Shyam Marathe determined that the twenty-third root of 24,242,900,770,553, 981,941,874,678,268,486,966,725,193 was 57—and he performed the calculation mentally, in only 50 seconds.

Although people once believed that the ability to perform complex mental calculations was a sign of superior intelligence, we now know that almost anyone willing to learn a few systematic steps can do such calculations. As an illustration, consider the digits 0 through 9 and their cubes.

Digit (root)	Cube
0	0
1	1
2	8
3	27
4	64
5	125
6	216
7	343
8	512
9	729

Except in the cases of 2, 3, 7, and 8, the last digit of each cube is the same as its root. For these four numbers, the last digit of the cube is equal to the root subtracted from 10. For example, the last digit of the cube of 8 is 2 (10 − 8). Once you have committed the above ten cubes to memory, you can easily find the root of any perfect cube less than 1,000,000. In every case, the root will have only 1 or 2 digits. The last digit of the cube is either the root itself or the root subtracted from 10. Suppose you want to find the cube root of 274,625. The last digit is 5, which is also the second digit of its root. To find the first digit you need to remember the table and one additional rule. Determine which two cubes the digits to the left of the comma fall between. These digits, 274, fall between the cubes of 6 and 7 in the table. The first digit of the cube root you seek is simply the smaller of the two.

Therefore, the cube root of 274,625 is 65. Try using this technique to determine the cube roots of 10,648 and 132,651.

Smith, S. B. (1983). *The great mental calculators: The psychology, methods, and lives of calculating prodigies, past and present.* New York: Columbia University Press.

Progress Test 1

Multiple-Choice Questions

Circle your answers to the following questions and check them with the answers on page 234. If your answer is incorrect, read the explanation for why it is incorrect and then consult the appropriate pages of the text (in parentheses following the correct answer).

1. The English scientist who considered assessing intelligence by measuring head size was:
   a. Galton.   c. Terman.
   b. Binet.   d. Wechsler.

2. A 6-year-old child has a mental age of 9. The child's IQ is:
   a. 100.   c. 150.
   b. 125.   d. 166.

3. Which of the following tests consists of eleven subtests and yields separate intelligence scores for verbal and performance categories?
   a. WAIS   c. ACT
   b. SAT   d. Stanford-Binet

4. Most psychologists believe that racial gaps in test scores:
   a. have been exaggerated when they are, in fact, insignificant.
   b. indicate that intelligence is in large measure inherited.
   c. are in large measure caused by environmental factors.
   d. are decreasing.

5. Standardization refers to the process of:
   a. determining the accuracy with which a test measures what it is supposed to.
   b. defining meaningful scores relative to a representative pretested group.
   c. determining the consistency of test scores obtained by retesting people.
   d. measuring the success with which a test predicts the behavior it is designed to predict.

6. Down syndrome is normally caused by:
   a. an extra chromosome in the person's genetic makeup.
   b. a missing chromosome in the person's genetic makeup.
   c. malnutrition during the first months of life.
   d. prenatal exposure to an addictive drug.

7. Which of the following is *not* a requirement of a good test?
   a. reliability
   b. standardization
   c. reification
   d. validity

8. Scarr and Weinberg found that Black children adopted and raised by White middle-class families had intelligence scores:
   a. comparable to those of adopted White children.
   b. lower than those of adopted White children.
   c. higher than those of adopted White children.
   d. higher than those of Black children in general but lower than those of adopted White children.

9. Which of the following statements is true?
   a. The predictive validity of intelligence tests is not as high as their reliability.
   b. The reliability of intelligence tests is not as high as their predictive validity.
   c. Modern intelligence tests have extremely high predictive validity and reliability.
   d. The predictive validity and reliability of most intelligence tests is very low.

10. Before about age _____, intelligence tests generally do not predict future scores.
    a. 1
    b. 3
    c. 5
    d. 10

11. Sorting children into gifted and nongifted educational groups:
    a. presumes that giftedness is a single trait.
    b. does not result in higher academic achievement scores.
    c. promotes racial segregation and prejudice.
    d. has all of the above effects.

12. Which of the following best describes the relationship between creativity and intelligence?
    a. Creativity appears to depend on the ability to think imaginatively and has little if any relationship to intelligence.
    b. Creativity is best understood as a certain kind of intelligence.
    c. The more intelligent a person is, the greater his or her creativity.
    d. A certain level of intelligence is necessary but not sufficient for creativity.

13. Studies of 2- to 6-month-old babies show that babies who quickly become bored with a picture:
    a. often develop learning disabilities later on.
    b. score lower on infant intelligence tests.
    c. score higher on intelligence tests several years later.
    d. score very low on intelligence tests several years later.

14. The existence of _____ reinforces the generally accepted notion that intelligence is a multidimensional quality.
    a. adaptive skills
    b. mental retardation
    c. general intelligence
    d. savant syndrome

15. Which of the following provides the strongest evidence of the role of heredity in determining intelligence?
    a. The intelligence scores of identical twins raised separately are more similar than those of fraternal twins raised together.
    b. The intelligence scores of fraternal twins are more similar than those of ordinary siblings.
    c. The intelligence scores of identical twins raised together are more similar than those of identical twins raised apart.
    d. The intelligence scores of children who have been adopted show relatively weak correlations with scores of adoptive as well as biological parents.

16. Current estimates are that _____ percent of the total variation among intelligence scores can be attributed to genetic factors.
    a. less than 10
    b. approximately 25
    c. between 50 and 60
    d. over 75

17. Over the past 50 years, SAT scores have _____ and WAIS scores have _____.
    a. declined; remained stable
    b. remained stable; declined
    c. risen; declined
    d. declined; risen

18. Reported racial gaps in average intelligence scores are most likely attributable to:
    a. the use of biased tests of intelligence.
    b. the use of unreliable tests of intelligence.
    c. genetic factors.
    d. environmental factors.

19. The bell-shaped distribution of intelligence scores in the general population is called a:
    a. *g* distribution.
    b. standardization curve.
    c. bimodal distribution.
    d. normal distribution.

20. Research on the effectiveness of Head Start suggests that enrichment programs:
    a. produce permanent gains in intelligence scores.
    b. improve school readiness, but have no measurable impact on intelligence scores.
    c. improve intelligence scores but *not* school readiness.
    d. produce temporary gains in intelligence scores.

Matching Items

Match each term with its definition or description.

Terms

_____ 1. intelligence score
_____ 2. *g*
_____ 3. eugenics
_____ 4. savant syndrome
_____ 5. factor analysis
_____ 6. aptitude test
_____ 7. achievement test
_____ 8. Stanford-Binet
_____ 9. SAT
_____ 10. content validity
_____ 11. reliability

Definitions or Descriptions

a. a test designed to predict a person's ability to learn something new
b. a test designed to measure current knowledge
c. the consistency with which a test measures performance
d. the degree to which a test measures what it is designed to measure
e. Terman's revision of Binet's original intelligence test
f. an aptitude test designed to predict academic performance in college
g. an underlying, general intelligence factor
h. a person's score on an intelligence test based on performance relative to the average performance of people the same age
i. a very low intelligence score accompanied by one extraordinary skill
j. a program for the selective breeding of the most intelligent individuals
k. a statistical technique that identifies related items on a test

Progress Test 2

Progress Test 2 should be completed during a final chapter review. Answer the following questions after you thoroughly understand the correct answers for the Chapter Review and Progress Test 1.

Multiple-Choice Questions

1. The test created by Alfred Binet was designed specifically to:
   a. measure inborn intelligence in adults.
   b. measure inborn intelligence in children.
   c. predict school performance in children.
   d. identify mentally retarded children so that they could be institutionalized.

2. Which of the following provides the strongest evidence of the role of environmental factors in intelligence?
   a. Adopted children's intelligence scores are more like their adoptive parents' scores than their biological parents'.
   b. Children's intelligence scores are more strongly related to their mothers' scores than to their fathers'.
   c. Children moved from a deprived environment into an intellectually enriched one show gains in intellectual development.
   d. The intelligence scores of identical twins raised separately are no more alike than those of siblings.

3. If a test designed to indicate which applicants are likely to perform the best on the job fails to do so, the test has:
   a. low reliability.
   b. low content validity.
   c. low predictive validity.
   d. not been standardized.

4. By creating a label such as "gifted," we begin to act as if all children are naturally divided into two categories, gifted and nongifted. This logical error is referred to as:
   a. rationalization.
   b. nominalizing.
   c. factor analysis.
   d. reification.

5. The formula for the intelligence quotient was devised by:
   a. Galton.
   b. Stern.
   c. Binet.
   d. Terman.

6. Current intelligence tests compute an individual's intelligence score as:
   a. the ratio of mental age to chronological age multiplied by 100.
   b. the ratio of chronological age to mental age multiplied by 100.
   c. the amount by which the test-taker's performance deviates from the average performance of others the same age.
   d. the ratio of the test-taker's verbal intelligence score to his or her nonverbal intelligence score.

7. J. McVicker Hunt found that institutionalized children given "tutored human enrichment":
   a. showed no change in intelligence test performance compared with institutionalized children who did not receive such enrichment.
   b. responded so negatively as a result of their impoverished early experiences that he felt it necessary to disband the program.
   c. thrived intellectually and socially on the benefits of positive caregiving.
   d. actually developed greater intelligence than control subjects who had lived in foster homes since birth.

8. The concept of a *g* factor implies that intelligence:
   a. is a single overall ability.
   b. is several specific abilities.
   c. cannot be defined or measured.
   d. is both a. and c.

9. On tests of simple information processing, people with high intelligence scores:
   a. spend less time analyzing problems than low-scoring people.
   b. take more time to react than low-scoring people, and thus avoid foolish errors.
   c. react more quickly than low-scoring people.
   d. do both a. and b.

10. By what age does a child's performance on an intelligence test become stable?
   a. 2
   b. 4
   c. 6
   d. 7

11. If we compare the performance of a recent standardization sample of Americans who took the WAIS to that of the original 1930 sample, we find that performance has:
   a. remained stable.
   b. declined.
   c. improved.
   d. declined in men but improved in women.

12. In his study of children with high intelligence scores, Terman found that:
   a. the children were more emotional and less healthy than a control group.
   b. the children were ostracized by classmates.
   c. the children were healthy and well-adjusted, and did well academically.
   d. later, as adults, they nearly all achieved great vocational success.

13. Which of the following is *not* one of the types of intelligence proposed by Sternberg and Wagner?
   a. academic
   b. social
   c. practical
   d. creative

14. Most experts view intelligence as a person's:
   a. ability to perform well on intelligence tests.
   b. innate mental capacity.
   c. capacity for goal-directed adaptive behavior.
   d. diverse skills acquired throughout life.

15. Which of the following statements is true?
   a. About 1 percent of the population is mentally retarded.
   b. More males than females are mentally retarded.
   c. A majority of the mentally retarded can learn basic reading skills.
   d. All of the above are true.

16. Which of the following has *not* been offered as a reason SAT scores declined during the 1960s?
   a. A combination of grade inflation, nonacademic electives, and simplified textbooks lowered the quality of education.
   b. Television displaced reading.
   c. The number and academic diversity of students taking the test greatly increased.
   d. Because the SAT is restandardized every 5 years, it has become more difficult.

17. Of the following, who would probably be the most skeptical about the prospects for a "culture-free" test of intelligence?
   a. those who view intelligence as successful adaptation to the environment
   b. those who view intelligence as a single entity
   c. those who view intelligence as multifaceted
   d. those who view intelligence as largely innate

18. Originally, IQ was defined as:
   a. mental age divided by chronological age and multiplied by 100.
   b. chronological age divided by mental age and multiplied by 100.
   c. mental age subtracted from chronological age and multiplied by 100.
   d. chronological age subtracted from mental age and multiplied by 100.

19. Tests of _____ measure what an individual can do now, whereas tests of _____ predict what an individual will be able to do later.
   a. aptitude; achievement
   b. achievement; aptitude
   c. reliability; validity
   d. validity; reliability

20. Which of the following statements most accurately reflects the textbook's position regarding the relative contribution of genes and environment in determining intelligence?
   a. Except in cases of a neglectful early environment, each individual's basic intelligence is largely the product of heredity.
   b. With the exception of those with genetic disorders such as Down syndrome, intelligence is primarily the product of environmental experiences.
   c. Both genes and life experiences significantly influence performance on intelligence tests.
   d. Because intelligence tests have such low predictive validity, the question cannot be addressed until psychologists agree on a more valid test of intelligence.

True-False Items

Indicate whether each statement is true or false by placing *T* or *F* in the blank next to the item.

_____ 1. In the current version of the Stanford-Binet intelligence test, one's performance is compared only with the performance of others the same age.

_____ 2. Intelligence scores in the United States have been dropping over the past 50 years.

_____ 3. Most of the major aptitude tests have higher validity than reliability.

_____ 4. People with high intelligence scores tend to process sensory information more quickly.

_____ 5. The gap in intelligence scores between Black and White children is increasing.

_____ 6. The intelligence scores of adopted children are more similar to those of their adoptive parents than their biological parents.

_____ 7. The consensus among psychologists is that most intelligence tests are extremely biased.

_____ 8. Most psychologists agree that intelligence is primarily determined by heredity.

_____ 9. Unlike the SAT, the Stanford-Binet test and the Wechsler scales are periodically restandardized.

_____ 10. The variation in intelligence scores within a racial group is much larger than that between racial groups.

Challenge Test

Answer these questions the day before an exam as a final check on your understanding of the chapter's terms and concepts.

Multiple-Choice Questions

1. Vanessa is a very creative sculptress. We would expect that Vanessa also:
   a. has an exceptionally high intelligence score.
   b. is quite introverted.
   c. has a venturesome personality and is intrinsically motivated.
   d. lacks expertise in most other skills.

2. To say that the heritability of a trait is approximately 50 percent means:
   a. that genes are responsible for 50 percent of the trait in an individual, and the environment is responsible for the rest.
   b. that the trait's appearance in a person will reflect approximately equal genetic contributions from both parents.
   c. that of the variation in the trait within a group of people, 50 percent can be attributed to heredity.
   d. all of the above.

3. Twenty-two-year-old Dan has an intelligence score of 63 and the academic skills of a fourth-grader, and is unable to live independently. Dan *probably*:
   a. has Down syndrome.
   b. has savant syndrome.
   c. is mentally retarded.
   d. will eventually achieve self-supporting social and vocational skills.

4. At age 16, Angel's intelligence score was 110. What will her score probably be at age 32?
   a. 105
   b. 110
   c. 115
   d. There is no basis for predicting an individual's future IQ.

5. A school psychologist found that 85 percent of those who scored above 115 on an aptitude test were "A" students and 75 percent of those who scored below 85 on the test were "D" students. The psychologist concluded that the test had high _____ validity because scores on it correlated highly with the _____ behavior.
   a. content; criterion
   b. predictive; criterion
   c. content; target
   d. predictive; target

6. In terms of his viewpoint on the determinants of intelligence, Lewis Terman would probably have allied himself most closely with:
   a. Galton.
   b. Binet.
   c. Sternberg.
   d. Gardner.

7. Benito was born in 1937. In 1947, he scored 130 on an intelligence test. What was Benito's mental age when he took the test?
   a. 9
   b. 10
   c. 11
   d. 13

8. Randy is disappointed in his SAT score and so is taking a test-preparation course prior to retaking the test. On the basis of information in the textbook, what advice should you offer Randy?
   a. Randy should take the course; research predicts his score could improve at least 50 points on the 200- to 800-point scale.
   b. Test-preparation courses typically produce only modest score increases; thus Randy should simply brush up on his math and vocabulary by taking the sample test he will receive when he registers for the test.
   c. Randy should rethink his decision to attend college since his test score clearly indicates he lacks the necessary skills.
   d. It is impossible to make a recommendation since there has been no research on the effectiveness of crash test-preparation courses.

9. The contribution of environmental factors to racial gaps in intelligence scores is indicated by:
   a. evidence that as educational opportunities in the United States have become more equal, the Black/White SAT difference has shrunk.
   b. evidence that the intelligence scores of Black children raised in privileged, White middle-class homes are comparable to White middle-class scores.
   c. the fact that on tests of mathematical competence, fifth-grade Asian children scored roughly one standard deviation above American children.
   d. all of the above.

10. One reason that the similarity in the intelligence scores of identical twins raised apart is not conclusive proof of heredity's role in determining intelligence is that:
    a. the similarity in their intelligence scores before separation is not known.
    b. the intelligence scores of such twins are somewhat less similar than the intelligence scores of fraternal twins raised together.
    c. twins are often placed in adoptive homes that provide very similar environments.
    d. the correlation between the intelligence scores of such twins is only marginally significant.

11. Jack takes the same test of mechanical reasoning on several different days and gets virtually identical scores. This suggests that the test has:
    a. high content validity.
    b. high reliability.
    c. high predictive validity.
    d. all of the above qualities.

12. You would not use a test of hearing acuity as an intelligence test because it would lack:
    a. content reliability.
    b. predictive reliability.
    c. predictive validity.
    d. content validity.

13. Before becoming attorneys, law students must pass a special licensing exam, which is an _____ test. Before entering college, high school students must take either the ACT or the SAT, both of which are _____ tests.
    a. achievement; aptitude
    b. aptitude; achievement
    c. achievement; achievement
    d. aptitude; aptitude

14. If you compare the same trait in people of similar heredity who live in very different environments, heritability for that trait will be _____; heritability is most likely to be _____ among people of very different heredities who live in similar environments.
    a. low; high
    b. high; low
    c. environmental; genetic
    d. genetic; environmental

15. A high-school psychologist who is looking at a student's intelligence score finds a jump of 30 points between the earliest score at age 2 and the most recent at age 17. The psychologist's knowledge of testing would probably lead her to conclude that such a jump:
   a. indicates that different tests were used, creating an apparent change in intelligence although it actually remained stable.
   b. signals a significant improvement in the child's environment over this period.
   c. is unsurprising, since intelligence scores do not become stable until late adolescence.
   d. is mainly the result of the age at which the first test was taken.

16. If you wanted to develop a test of musical aptitude in North American children, which would be the appropriate standardization group?
   a. children all over the world
   b. North American children
   c. children of musical parents
   d. children with known musical ability

17. Although Don's intelligence scores were only average, he has been enormously successful as a corporate manager. Psychologists Sternberg and Wagner would probably suggest that Don's _____ intelligence exceeds his _____ intelligence.
   a. verbal; performance   c. academic; practical
   b. performance; verbal   d. practical; academic

18. According to the textbook, what can be concluded from early intelligence testing in the United States?
   a. Most European immigrants were "feeble-minded."
   b. Army recruits of other than West European heritage were intellectually deficient.
   c. The tests were unfairly biased against people who did not share the culture assumed by the test.
   d. Both a. and b. could be concluded.

19. If asked to guess the intelligence score of a stranger, your best guess would be:
   a. 75.
   b. 100.
   c. 125.
   d. "I don't know, intelligence scores vary too widely."

20. Which of the following is true of people who score high on aptitude tests?
   a. They achieve greater success in their occupations.
   b. They are likely to be happier.
   c. They always do well in college.
   d. None of the above is true.

Essay Question

For your psychology honors project you have been given the assignment of devising a "Psychology Achievement Test (PAT)" that will be administered to freshmen who declare psychology as their major. What steps will you take to ensure that the PAT is a good intelligence test? (Use the space below to list the points you want to make and organize them. Then write the essay on a separate piece of paper.)

Key Terms

Using your own words, write a brief definition or explanation of each of the following terms.

1. intelligence test

2. mental age

3. Stanford-Binet

4. intelligence quotient (IQ)

5. aptitude tests

6. achievement tests

7. Wechsler Adult Intelligence Scale (WAIS)

8. standardization

9. normal curve (normal distribution)

10. reliability

11. validity

12. content validity

13. criterion

14. predictive validity

15. intelligence

16. factor analysis

17. general intelligence (g)

18. savant syndrome

19. mental retardation

20. Down syndrome

21. creativity

22. heritability

ANSWERS

GUIDED STUDY

The following guidelines provide the main points that your answers should have touched upon.

1. Sir Francis Galton was the first to attempt to measure individual mental abilities. Galton, who

founded the eugenics movement, assumed that intelligence was inherited and attempted (without success) to equate intelligence with head size and later with reaction time, sensory acuity, muscular power, and body proportion. Modern intelligence testing began when Alfred Binet developed a test to predict children's future school performance. Binet's test was designed to compute a mental age for each child. Lewis Terman's revision of Binet's test, known as the Stanford-Binet, computed an IQ score as the ratio of mental age to chronological age. Modern intelligence tests no longer compute an intelligence quotient and are classified as either achievement or aptitude tests.

2. Aptitude tests, such as the SAT and ACT, are intended to predict a person's ability to learn new skills. Achievement tests, such as a final exam in a college course, are intended to measure what already has been learned.

   The most widely used intelligence tests, the WAIS for adults and the WISC for children, consist of a number of subtests and yield an overall intelligence score as well as separate verbal and performance scores. The SAT and ACT tests measure both aptitude and achievement and aim to predict high school students' potential for academic achievement in college.

3. Good intelligence tests have been standardized and are reliable and valid. Standardization is the process of defining meaningful scores on the test relative to a pretested group. A random group of test results should form a normal distribution.

   Reliability is the extent to which a test yields consistent results. To check a test's reliability, people are tested twice using the same or a different form of the test. If the scores correlate, the test is reliable. The Stanford-Binet, WAIS, WISC, SAT, and ACT all have high reliabilities of about +.9.

   Validity is the extent to which a test actually measures the behavior (content validity) it claims to, or predicts some criterion, such as future performance (predictive validity). The predictive validity of general aptitude tests is not as high as their reliability.

4. Most experts view intelligence as a person's capacity for "goal-directed adaptive behavior" that reflects an ability to learn from experience, solve problems, and reason clearly. Psychologists who view intelligence as successful adaptation to the environment contend that what is considered highly intelligent behavior in one culture may not be in another. Others view intelligence as basic problem-solving abilities that are important in any culture.

5. Factor analysis is a statistical technique used to identify clusters of test items that measure a common ability, such as spatial or reasoning ability.

   Although psychologists agree that people have specific abilities, such as verbal or mathematical intelligence, they do not agree about the existence of an underlying general intelligence factor. People with savant syndrome, who score very low on intelligence tests but possess extraordinary specific abilities, provide support for the viewpoint that there are multiple intelligences, each independent of the others. Sternberg and Wagner, for example, distinguish among three intelligences — academic, practical, and creative — and Cantor and Kihlstrom distinguish between academic and social intelligence.

6. The information-processing approach to intelligence is based on the idea that differences in intelligence are reflected in measurable differences in people's capacities for processing information. Robert Sternberg found that highly intelligent people spend more time analyzing problems than those who score lower on intelligence tests, but they then recognize correct answers faster. Other researchers have found that people with high intelligence scores react faster than low-scoring people on tests that measure speed of processing simple information.

7. The stability of intelligence test scores increases with age. Infants who become quickly bored with a picture score higher on intelligence tests several years later. By age 3, children's performances on intelligence tests begin to predict their adolescent and adult scores. By late adolescence, aptitude scores are quite stable.

   Approximately 1 percent of the population have very low intelligence scores, experience difficulty adapting to the normal demands of living independently, and are labeled as mentally retarded. Severe mental retardation usually results from physical causes, such as Down syndrome.

   Approximately 3 to 5 percent of children are labeled "gifted." Contrary to popular myth, gifted children are not frequently maladjusted. The segregation of children into gifted and nongifted educational tracks remains controversial. Critics of ability tracking contend that it does not result in higher achievement scores, that it lowers all students' self-concepts, and that it promotes racial segregation and prejudice. Ability tracking also is based on the possibly erroneous notion that giftedness is a single trait rather than any one of many specific abilities.

8. Creativity is the ability to produce novel and valuable ideas. Although people with high intelligence scores do well on tests of creativity, beyond an

intelligence score of about 120, the correlation between intelligence scores and creativity disappears.

Studies of creativity suggest four components to creativity other than intelligence: expertise, imaginative thinking skills, a venturesome personality, and intrinsic motivation.

9. Both genes and environment influence intelligence. Studies of twins and adopted children point to the influence of heredity. For example, the most genetically similar people have the most similar intelligence scores, and adopted children's intelligence scores are more like their biological parents' scores than their adoptive parents' scores. It is estimated that the *heritability* of intelligence is about 50 to 60 percent; that is, 50 to 60 percent of the variation in intelligence within a *group* of people can be attributed to heredity.

The impact of the environment is also revealed in twin studies: identical twins reared apart test somewhat less alike than those reared together. Other studies that compare children reared in neglectful environments with those reared in enriched environments, or in different cultures, also point to the impact of environmental experiences on intelligence scores. The jury is still out on the full value of Head Start programs, but some believe that high-quality programs can generate long-term positive effects.

10. On average, there *are* group differences in intelligence scores. For example, males outscore females on the math portion of the SAT, Japanese children score higher than American children on math achievement tests, and White Americans tend to score higher than African-Americans on the SAT verbal and math tests.

Although heredity contributes to individual differences in intelligence, it does not necessarily contribute to group differences. Most experts believe that the intelligence score gaps between groups are the result of differences between privileged and disadvantaged groups around the world, as well as cultural differences in educational enrichment.

11. In the sense that intelligence scores are sensitive to differences caused by cultural experience, aptitude tests are certainly biased. In terms of predictive validity, however, most experts agree that the major intelligence tests are not racially biased.

Because intelligence tests are designed to distinguish different levels of aptitude, their purpose in this sense *is* to discriminate among individuals. In another sense, however, intelligence tests reduce discrimination by reducing the use of subjective criteria in school and job placement.

CHAPTER REVIEW

1. intelligence
2. Plato
3. Galton; eugenics; inherited
4. Binet; mental; was not
5. Stanford-Binet; intelligence quotient

In the original formula for IQ, measured mental age is divided by chronological age and the result is multiplied by 100. "Mental age" refers to the chronological age that most typically corresponds to a given level of performance.

6. the same; 100
7. below; cultural
8. aptitude; achievement
9. Wechsler Adult Intelligence Scale (WAIS); verbal; performance
10. SAT; ACT
11. standardization; reliability; validity
12. standardization
13. normal

The normal curve describes the distribution of many physical phenomena and psychological attributes (including IQ scores), with most scores falling near the average and fewer and fewer near the extremes. When a test is standardized on a normal curve, individual scores are assigned according to how much they deviate above or below the distribution's average.

14. decline
15. increased

Part of the decline in SAT scores has been attributed to the greater academic diversity of students who began taking the test during the 1960s. Other explanations that have been offered include the displacement of reading by TV, grade inflation, simplified textbooks, and reduced homework. In contrast to the SAT, the WAIS has always been taken by a diverse group of people. Americans as a whole have become more literate and better educated. Thus, while SAT performance has declined, performance on the WAIS has improved. Further, the SAT measures higher-level academic skills, which, unlike the simpler problem-solving skills required by the IQ tests, have not improved.

16. reliable
17. test-retest
18. split-half
19. +.9
20. validity
21. content validity
22. criterion; predictive validity

The criterion is the particular behavior that a predictive test, such as an aptitude test, is intended to predict. For example, performance in a relevant job situation would be the criterion for a test measuring managerial aptitude. The criterion determines whether a test has predictive validity. In the example, the on-the-job success of those who did well on the test would indicate the test has predictive validity.

23. is not; diminishes

24. do not

25. reification

26. a person's capacity for "goal-directed adaptive behavior"

Some researchers argue that intelligent behavior is culturally defined and therefore varies with the situation. In different environments, different behaviors would be considered intelligent. Others view intelligence as those cognitive abilities that would in *any* environment help people solve problems and achieve their goals.

27. overall (general); specific

28. factor analysis; general intelligence

29. Thurstone; primary mental abilities

30. savant syndrome

31. multiple intelligences

32. academic; practical; creative; academic; social; do not

33. analyzing

34. faster

35. higher

36. 3

37. increases; extremely

38. mentally retarded; 1

39. Down syndrome

By labeling and segregating "gifted" and "nongifted" groups we presume that giftedness is a single objective trait rather than one of many potentials. Critics of ability tracking contend that it does not result in higher intelligence scores, that it lowers students' self-concepts, and that it promotes racial segregation and prejudice.

40. creativity; 120

Creative people tend to have *expertise*, or a solid base of knowledge, *imaginative thinking skills*, which allow them to see things in new ways, to recognize patterns, and to make connections, *intrinsic motivation*, or the tendency to focus on the pleasure and challenge of their work, and a *venturesome personality* that tolerates ambiguity and risk and seeks new experiences.

41. generally accepted

42. twin; adoption

43. more

44. biological; adoptive; increases

45. heritability; 50 to 60

46. do

47. does not

48. Head Start

49. environmental

Because of the impact of environmental factors such as education and nutrition on intelligence test performance, even if the heritability of intelligence is high within a particular group, differences in intelligence *among* groups may be environmentally caused. One group may, for example, thrive in an enriched environment while another of the same genetic predisposition may falter in an impoverished one.

50. are

51. are not

PROGRESS TEST 1

Multiple-Choice Questions

1. **a.** is the answer. Galton's early and unsuccessful efforts to quantify "superiority" included the idea of using head size as a yardstick. (p. 318)

   b. Binet was the first to develop questions to help predict a child's future progress in school.

   c. Terman developed the Stanford-Binet by revising Binet's test.

   d. Wechsler created the WAIS, the most widely used test of intelligence.

2. **c.** is the answer. If we divide 9, the measured mental age, by 6, the chronological age, and multiply the result by 100, we obtain 150. (p. 320)

3. **a.** is the answer. (p. 322)

   b. & c. The SAT and ACT yield separate math and verbal scores, but not an overall intelligence score.

   d. The Stanford-Binet yields an overall IQ score only.

4. **c.** is the answer. (p. 342)

   a. On the contrary, many *group* differences are highly significant, even though they tell us nothing about specific *individuals*.

   b. Although heredity contributes to individual differences in intelligence, it does not necessarily contribute to group differences.

   d. The textbook does not present evidence that group differences are decreasing.

5. **b.** is the answer. (p. 322)

   a. This answer refers to a test's validity.

   c. This answer refers to test-retest reliability.

   d. This answer refers to predictive validity.

6. **a.** is the answer. (p. 334)

   b. Down syndrome is normally caused by an extra, rather than a missing, chromosome.

   c. & d. Down syndrome is a genetic disorder that is manifest during the earliest stages of prenatal development, well before malnutrition and exposure to drugs would produce their harmful effects on the developing fetus.

7. **c.** is the answer. Reification is a reasoning error, in which an abstract concept like IQ is regarded as though it were real. (pp. 322, 324–327)

8. **a.** is the answer. Scarr and Weinberg's study indicates that a privileged, middle-class upbringing results in the same range of intelligence scores, regardless of one's race. (p. 343)

9. **a.** is the answer. (p. 326)

   c. & d. Most modern tests have high reliabilities of about +.9; their validity scores are much lower.

10. **b.** is the answer. (p. 333)

11. **d.** is the answer. (pp. 334–335)

12. **d.** is the answer. Up to an intelligence score of about 120, there is a positive correlation between intelligence and creativity. But beyond this point the correlation disappears, indicating that factors other than intelligence are also involved. (p. 335)

   a. The ability to think imaginatively and intelligence are *both* components of creativity.

   b. Creativity, the capacity to produce ideas that are novel and valuable, is related to and depends in part on intelligence but cannot be considered simply a kind of intelligence.

   c. Beyond an intelligence score of about 120 there is no correlation between intelligence scores and creativity.

13. **c.** is the answer. (p. 333)

14. **d.** is the answer. That people with savant syndrome excel in one area but are intellectually retarded in others suggests that there are multiple intelligences. (p. 330)

   a. The ability to adapt defines the capacity we call intelligence.

   b. Mental retardation is an indicator of the *range* of human intelligence.

   c. A general intelligence factor was hypothesized by Spearman to underlie each specific factor of intelligent behavior, but its existence is controversial and remains to be proved.

15. **a.** is the answer. Identical twins who live apart have the same genetic makeup but different environments; if their scores are more similar than those of fraternal twins (with their somewhat different genetic makeups) raised together, this is evidence for the role of heredity. (p. 337)

   b. Since fraternal twins are no more genetically alike than ordinary siblings, this could not provide evidence for the role of heredity.

   c. That twins raised together have more similar scores than twins raised apart provides evidence for the role of the environment.

   d. As both sets of correlations are weak, little evidence is provided either for or against the role of heredity.

16. **c.** is the answer. Recent estimates are generally in the range of 50 to 60 percent. (p. 338)

17. **d.** is the answer. The SAT is a complex test that is not periodically restandardized. The WAIS, a more basic test that is periodically restandardized so that the average is always 100, also reflects the performance of a more diverse group. (p. 325)

18. **d.** is the answer. Findings from a range of studies —including studies of SAT trends, cross-cultural studies, and adoption studies—have led experts to focus on environmental factors. (p. 342)

   a. Most experts believe that in terms of predictive validity, the major tests are not racially biased.

   b. The reliability of the major tests is actually very high.

   c. The bulk of the evidence on which experts base their findings points to environmental factors.

19. **d.** is the answer. (p. 324)

   a. *g* is Spearman's term for "general intelligence"; there is no such thing as a "*g* distribution."

   b. There is no such thing as a "standardization curve."

   c. A bimodal distribution is one having two (bi-) modes, or averages. The normal distribution has only one mode.

20. **d.** is the answer. The benefits of enrichment programs like Head Start dissipate over time. (p. 340)

   b. & c. Enrichment programs *do* improve school readiness and result in measurable, but temporary, gains in intelligence scores.

Matching Items

1. h (p. 320)	**5.** k (p. 329)	**9.** f (p. 322)
2. g (p. 329)	**6.** a (p. 321)	**10.** d (p. 326)
3. j (p. 318)	**7.** b (p. 321)	**11.** c (p. 325)
4. i (p. 330)	**8.** e (p. 320)	

PROGRESS TEST 2

Multiple-Choice Questions

1. **c.** is the answer. French compulsory education laws brought more children into the school system, and the government didn't want to rely on teachers' subjective judgments to determine which children would require special help. (p. 319)

   a. & b. Binet's test was intended for children, and Binet specifically rejected the idea that his test measured inborn intelligence, which is an abstract capacity that cannot be quantified.

   d. This was not a purpose of the test, which dealt with children in the school system.

2. **c.** is the answer. (pp. 339–340)

   a., b., & d. None of these are true.

3. **c.** is the answer. Predictive validity is the extent to which tests predict what they are intended to predict. (p. 326)

   a. Reliability is the consistency with which a test samples the particular behavior of interest.

   b. Content validity is the degree to which a test measures what it is designed to measure.

   d. Standardization is the process of defining meaningful test scores based on the performance of a representative group.

4. **d.** is the answer. Reification is the error of creating a concept and then assuming the created concept has a concrete reality. (p. 328)

   a. To rationalize is to develop self-satisfying explanations of one's behavior.

   b. The term "nominalizing" has no relevance to psychology.

   c. Factor analysis is a statistical procedure that identifies clusters of related items, or factors, on a test.

5. **b.** is the answer. (p. 320)

6. **c.** is the answer. (p. 320)

   a. This is William Stern's original formula for the intelligence quotient.

   b. & d. Neither of these formulas is used to compute the score on current intelligence tests.

7. **c.** is the answer. Enrichment led to dramatic results and thereby testified to the importance of environmental factors. (p. 339)

   a. & d. The study involved neither intelligence tests nor comparisons with control groups.

   b. The children showed a dramatic positive response.

8. **a.** is the answer. (p. 329)

9. **c.** is the answer. (p. 332)

   a. In fact, just the opposite is true.

10. **d.** is the answer. Intelligence test performances begin to become predictive at about age 3 and become stable by about age 7. (p. 333)

11. **c.** is the answer. A raw score that would earn an IQ score of 100 today would have earned a score of 114 in the 1930s. (p. 325)

12. **c.** is the answer. (p. 334)

    a. & b. There was no evidence of either of these in Terman's subjects.

    d. Vocational success in adulthood varied.

13. **b.** is the answer. (p. 330)

14. **c.** is the answer. (p. 328)

    a. Performance ability and intellectual ability are separate traits.

    b. This has been argued by some, but certainly not most, experts.

    d. Although many experts believe that there are multiple intelligences, this would not be the same thing as diverse acquired skills.

15. **d.** is the answer. (pp. 333–334)

16. **d.** is the answer. Unlike the Stanford-Binet test and the Wechsler scales, the SAT is *not* periodically restandardized. (p. 325)

    a., b., & c. All of these reasons have been offered as explanations for the decline in SAT scores.

17. **a.** is the answer. In this view, what is "intelligent" in one environment may not be in another, and tests are necessarily making judgments about what's adaptive (p. 328)

    b., c., & d. The issues of whether intelligence is innate and whether it is a single entity or multifaceted have relatively little bearing on the question of the potential for culture-free tests.

18. **a.** is the answer. (p. 320)

19. **b.** is the answer. (p. 321)

    c. & d. Reliability and validity are characteristics of good tests.

20. **c.** is the answer. (p. 339)

    a. & b. Studies of twins, family members, and adopted children point to a significant hereditary contribution to intelligence scores. These same studies, plus others comparing children reared in neglectful or enriched environments, indicate that life experiences also significantly influence test performance.

    d. Although the issue of how intelligence should be defined is controversial, intelligence tests generally have very high predictive validity.

True-False Items

1. True (p. 324)
2. False (p. 325)
3. False (p. 326)
4. True (p. 332)
5. False (p. 343)

6. False (p. 338)
7. False (p. 345)
8. False (pp. 341–342)
9. True (p. 325)
10. True (p. 341)

CHALLENGE TEST

Multiple-Choice Questions

1. **c.** is the answer. (p. 335)

   a. Beyond an intelligence score of about 120, creativity and intelligence scores are not correlated.

   b. & d. There is no evidence that creative people are more likely to be introverted.

2. **c.** is the answer. Heritability is a measure of the extent to which a trait's variation within a group of people can be attributed to heredity. (p. 338)

   a. & b. Heritability is *not* a measure of how much of an *individual's* behavior is inherited, nor of the relative contribution of genes from that person's mother and father. Further, the heritability of any trait depends on the context, or environment, in which that trait is being studied.

3. **c.** is the answer. To be labeled mentally retarded a person must have a test score below 70 and experience difficulty adapting to the normal demands of living independently. (p. 334)

   a. Down syndrome is a common cause of *severe* mental retardation; Dan's test score places him in the range of mild retardation.

   b. There is no indication that Dan possesses one extraordinary skill, as do people with savant syndrome.

   d. The textbook does not suggest that mentally retarded people eventually become self-supporting.

4. **b.** is the answer. Intelligence scores become quite stable during adolescence. (p. 333)

5. **b.** is the answer. (p. 326)

   a. & c. Content validity is the degree to which a test measures what it claims to measure. Furthermore, "target behavior" is not a term used by intelligence researchers.

6. **a.** is the answer. Terman and Galton both believed that important traits, such as intelligence, are inherited. (pp. 318, 320)

   b., c., & d. The textbook does not describe the viewpoints of Binet, Sternberg, or Gardner concerning the determinants of intelligence.

7. **d.** is the answer. At the time he took the test, Benito's chronological age (CA) was 10. Knowing that IQ = 130 and CA = 10, solving the equation for mental age yields a value of 13. (p. 320)

8. **b.** is the answer. (p. 327)

9. **d.** is the answer. These reasons, along with other historical and cross-cultural reasons, all argue for the role of environment in creating and perpetuating the gap. (pp. 342–344)

10. **c.** is the answer. Because studies show that such twins were often selectively placed in similar environments, the importance of environment can't be ruled out. (p. 338)

    a. Such comparisons are not usually made and this information would not be necessary.

    b. The intelligence scores of identical twins raised apart are more similar than those of fraternal twins raised together.

    d. In fact, the correlation is highly significant.

11. **b.** is the answer. (pp. 325–326)

12. **d.** is the answer. Because the hearing acuity test would in no way sample behaviors relevant to intelligence, it would not have content validity as a test of intelligence. (p. 326)

    a. & b. There is no such thing as content reliability or predictive reliability.

    c. There is nothing to indicate that, used to test hearing, this test would lack predictive validity.

13. **a.** is the answer. An exam for a professional license is intended to measure whether you have gained the overall knowledge and skill to practice the profession. The SAT and ACT are designed to predict ability, or aptitude, for learning a new skill. (p. 321)

14. **a.** is the answer. If everyone has nearly the same heredity, then heritability—the variation in a trait attributed to heredity—must be low. If individuals within a group come from very similar environments, environmental differences cannot account for variation in a trait; heritability, therefore, must be high. (p. 338)

15. **d.** is the answer. It is not until after age 3 that intelligence test performance begins to predict adult scores. (p. 333)

    a. Such a conclusion is unlikely, given the high validity of the commonly used intelligence tests.

    b. No such conclusion is possible, because intelligence test performance before age 3 does not predict later aptitude.

    c. Stability in intelligence scores is generally established by age 7—long before adulthood.

16. **b.** is the answer. A standardization group provides a representative comparison for the trait being measured by a test. Since this test will measure musical aptitude in North American children, the standardization group should be limited to North American children but should include children of all degrees of musical aptitude. (p. 322)

17. **d.** is the answer. Sternberg and Wagner distinguish among *academic* intelligence, as measured by intelligence tests, *practical* intelligence, which is involved in everyday life and tasks, such as managerial work, and *creative* intelligence. (p. 330)

    a. & b. Verbal and performance intelligence are both measured by standard intelligence tests like the WAIS and would be included in Sternberg and Wagner's academic intelligence.

    c. Academic intelligence refers to skills assessed by intelligence tests; practical intelligence applies to skills required for everyday tasks and, often, for occupational success.

18. **c.** is the answer. (p. 321)

    a. & b. Although at the time the tests were administered some individuals reached these conclusions, they were of course misled.

19. **b.** is the answer. Modern intelligence tests are periodically restandardized so that the average remains near 100. (p. 324)

20. **d.** is the answer. (p. 321)

Essay Question

The first step in constructing the test is to create a valid set of questions that measure psychological knowledge and therefore give the test content validity. If your objective is to predict students' future achievement in psychology courses, the test questions should be selected to measure a criterion, such as information faculty members expect all psychology majors to master before they graduate.

To enable meaningful comparisons, the test must be standardized. That is, the test should be administered to a representative sample of incoming freshmen at the time they declare psychology to be their major. From the scores of your pretested sample you will then be able to assign an average score and evaluate any individual score according to how much it deviates above or below the average.

To check your test's reliability you might retest a sample of people using the same test or another version of it. If the two scores are correlated, your test is reliable. Alternatively, you might split the test in half and determine whether scores on the two halves are correlated.

KEY TERMS

1. **Intelligence tests** measure people's mental aptitudes and compare them to others' through numerical scores. (p. 317)

2. A concept introduced by Binet, **mental age** is the chronological age that most typically corresponds to a given level of performance. (p. 319)

3. The **Stanford-Binet** is Lewis Terman's widely used revision of Binet's original intelligence test. (p. 320)

4. The **intelligence quotient**, or **IQ**, was defined originally as the ratio of mental age to chronological age multiplied by 100. Contemporary tests of intelligence assign a score of 100 to the average performance for a given age and define other scores as deviations from this average. (p. 320)

5. **Aptitude tests** are designed to predict future performance. They measure your capacity to learn new information, rather than measuring what you already know. (p. 321)

6. **Achievement tests** measure a person's current knowledge. (p. 321)

7. The **Wechsler Adult Intelligence Scale (WAIS)** is the most widely used intelligence test. It is individually administered, contains eleven subtests, and yields separate verbal and performance intelligence scores, as well as an overall intelligence score. (p. 322)

8. **Standardization** is the process of defining meaningful scores on a test by administering it to a large representative sample of people. (p. 322)

9. The **normal curve** (or **distribution**) is a bell-shaped curve that represents the distribution (frequency of occurrence) of many traits, such as intelligence scores. The curve is symmetrical, with most scores near the average and fewer near the extremes. (p. 324)

10. **Reliability** is the extent to which a test produces consistent results. (p. 325)

    Memory aid: If someone is **reliable**, he or she can be depended on. A reliable test is one that can be depended on to produce consistent measurements.

11. **Validity** is the degree to which a test measures what it is supposed to measure or predicts what it is supposed to predict. (p. 326)

12. The **content validity** of a test is the extent to which it measures the behavior that it is designed to measure. (p. 326)

    Example: A computer-generated real estate exam in which half the questions were concerned with preparing income tax returns would have low **content validity**: it would not do a good job of measuring test-takers' knowledge of real estate.

13. A test's **criterion** is the behavior the test is designed to predict. (p. 326)

    Example: Determining a test's predictive validity involves assessing the correlation between test scores and **criterion** behavior—for example, seeing whether those who did well on a clerical aptitude test are successful in clerical jobs.

14. **Predictive validity** is the extent to which a test predicts the behavior it is designed to predict. (p. 326)

    Example: Because their admissions committees have been unhappy with the **predictive validity** of standardized tests, some graduate schools no longer require the GRE. They feel other methods are more successful in predicting which applicants will do well in graduate programs.

15. Most experts define **intelligence** as the capacity for goal-directed adaptive behavior. (p. 328)

16. **Factor analysis** is a statistical procedure that identifies factors, or clusters of items, that seem to define a common ability. Using this procedure, psychologists have identified several clusters, including verbal intelligence, spatial ability, and reasoning ability factors. (p. 329)

17. **General intelligence**, or **g** factor, underlies each of the more specific intelligence clusters identified through factor analysis. (p. 329)

    Example: Although people often have special abilities, people who score high on one factor typically score higher than average on other related factors. This commonality, according to Spearman, is the **general intelligence** factor.

18. A person with **savant syndrome** has a very low intelligence score, yet possesses one exceptional ability, for example, in music, drawing, or mathematics. (p. 330)

19. The two criteria that designate **mental retardation** are an IQ below 70 and difficulty adapting to the normal demands of independent living. Approximately 1 percent of the population satisfies both these criteria. (p. 333)

20. A common cause of severe retardation, **Down syndrome** is usually the result of an extra chromosome in the person's genetic makeup. (p. 334)

21. Although many definitions of **creativity** have been proposed, most experts agree that it refers to an ability to generate novel and valuable ideas. People with high IQs may or may not be creative, which indicates that intelligence is only one component of creativity. (p. 335)

22. **Heritability** is the amount of variation in a trait that is attributable to genetic factors. Current estimates place the heritability of intelligence at about 50 to 60 percent. (p. 338)

12 / Motivation

Chapter Overview

Perhaps no topic is more fundamental to psychology than motivation—the study of forces that energize and direct our behavior. Chapter 12 discusses various concepts of motivation and looks closely at three motives: hunger, sex, and achievement. Research on hunger points to the interplay between physiological and psychological (internal and external) factors in motivation. Sexual motivation in men and women is triggered less by physiological factors and more by external incentives. Achievement motivation, in particular, demonstrates that a drive theory is of limited usefulness in explaining human behavior: Although this motivation serves no apparent physiological need, it may be extremely forceful nonetheless.

NOTE: Answer guidelines to all Chapter 12 questions begin on page 254.

Guided Study

The text chapter should be studied one section at a time. Before you read, preview each section by skimming it, noting headings and boldface items. Then read the appropriate section objectives from the following outline. Keep these objectives in mind and, as you read the chapter section, search for the information that will enable you to meet each objective. Once you have finished a section, write out answers for its objectives.

Concepts of Motivation (pp. 352–355)

1. Define motivation and discuss the role of biological states and external incentives in motivated behavior.

2. Discuss Maslow's hierarchy of needs.

Hunger (pp. 355–360)

3. Discuss the basis of hunger in terms of both physiology and external incentives.

4. Describe the symptoms and possible causes of anorexia nervosa and bulimia nervosa.

Sexual Motivation (pp. 360–370)

5. Discuss whether survey research has contributed to our understanding of sexual behavior and describe the human sexual response cycle.

6. Discuss the basis of sexual motivation in terms of both internal physiology and external incentives.

7. Identify some common sexual dysfunctions and their possible treatment.

8. Describe research findings on the nature and dynamics of sexual orientation.

9. Discuss the place of values in research and education on sexual behavior.

Achievement Motivation (pp. 370–378)

10. Describe the nature and origin of achievement motivation.

11. Distinguish between extrinsic and intrinsic achievement motivation and identify factors that encourage each type.

12. Discuss how managers can create a motivated, productive, and satisfied workforce.

Chapter Review

When you have finished reading the chapter, work through the material that follows to review it. Complete the sentences and answer the questions. As you proceed, evaluate your performance for each section by consulting the answers on page 256. Do not continue with the next section until you understand each answer. If you need to, review or reread the appropriate section in the textbook before continuing.

1. To motivate is to _____ behavior and _____ it toward goals.

Concepts of Motivation (pp. 352–355)

2. As a result of Darwin's influence, there was an increasing focus on the role of _____ forces in behavior.

3. A rigid, biologically determined behavior that is characteristic of a species is called an _____.

Discuss why instinct theory failed as an explanation of human behavior.

4. According to another view of motivation, organisms may experience a deprivation, or _____, which creates a state of arousal, or _____.

5. The aim of drive reduction is to maintain a constant internal state, called _____.

6. Behavior is often not so much pushed by our drives as it is pulled by _____ in the environment. This demonstrates that human motives _____ (do/do not) always satisfy some biological need.

7. Starting from the idea that some needs take precedence over others, Maslow constructed a _____ of needs.

8. According to Maslow, the _____ needs are the most pressing, whereas the highest-order needs relate to _____–_____. Critics of Maslow's theory point out that the sequence is _____ and not _____ experienced.

Hunger (pp. 355–360)

9. Ancel Keys observed that men became preoccupied with thoughts of food when they underwent _____.

10. Cannon and Washburn's experiment using a balloon indicated that there is an association between hunger and _____.

11. When an animal has had its stomach removed, hunger _____ (does/does not) continue.

12. Feelings of hunger are decreased when _____ is injected into the bloodstream. Blood sugar is lowered and hunger is increased when _____ is injected.

13. Taste preferences for sweet and salty are _____ (genetic/learned). Other influences on taste include _____, _____, and _____.

14. Carbohydrates boost levels of the neurotransmitter _____, which _____ (calms/arouses) the body.

15. The brain area that plays a role in hunger and other bodily maintenance functions is the _____. Animals will begin eating when the _____ is electrically stimulated. When this region is destroyed, hunger _____ (increases/decreases). Animals will stop eating when the _____ is stimulated. When this area is destroyed, animals _____ (overeat/ undereat).

16. The weight level that an individual's body is programmed to stay at is referred to as the body's _____ _____. A person whose weight goes beyond this level will tend to feel _____ (more/less) hungry than usual and expend _____ (more/less) energy.

17. The rate of energy expenditure in the body is the _____ rate. When food intake is reduced, the body compensates by _____ (raising/lowering) this rate.

18. Rodin refers to people whose eating is more affected by food stimuli than by internal cues as _____. Rodin found that such individuals showed a particularly marked increase in blood _____ level when confronted with the sight, smell, and sound of a steak being grilled.

19. Eating disorders are perhaps the best example of the influence of _____ factors on eating behavior.

20. The disorder in which a person becomes significantly underweight and yet feels fat is known as _____. In terms of sex and age, this disorder tends to develop in _____ who are in their _____.

21. A more common disorder is

_____ _____,

which is characterized by repeated

_____–_____ episodes
and by feelings of depression.

22. The families of bulimia patients have a high
incidence of _____,

_____, and _____. The
families of anorexia patients tend to be

_____ and _____.

23. Fallon and Rozin found a discrepancy between
_____ (men's/women's) ideal
body weight and the weight actually preferred
by members of the opposite sex.

24. Women with low _____–
_____ are especially vulnerable
to eating disorders.

Sexual Motivation (pp. 360–370)

25. In the 1940s and 1950s, a biologist named
_____ surveyed the sexual
practices of thousands of men and women. One
of his major findings was that there
_____ (was/was not) great
diversity in "normal" sexual behavior.

26. Many popular sexual surveys cannot be taken
seriously because they are based on
_____ samples of respondents.

27. The two researchers who identified a four-stage
sexual response cycle are _____ and
_____. In order, the stages of
the cycle are the _____ phase,
the _____ phase,
_____, and the _____
phase.

28. During resolution, males experience a

_____ _____,

during which they are not capable of another
orgasm.

29. In most mammals, females are sexually receptive
only during ovulation, when the hormone
_____ has peaked.

30. The importance of the hormone
_____ to male sexual arousal is

confirmed by the fact that sexual interest
declines in animals if their _____
are removed.

31. Normal hormonal fluctuations in humans have
_____ (little/significant) effect
on sexual motivation. In later life, frequency of
intercourse _____ (increases/
decreases) as sex hormone levels
_____ (increase/decline).

32. The region of the brain through which hormones
help trigger sexual arousal is the

_____.

33. The only unlearned stimulus for human arousal
is _____.

34. Studies by Heiman have shown that erotic
stimuli _____ (are/are not) as
arousing for women as for men.

Explain some of the possible harmful consequences of
sexually explicit material.

35. The importance of the brain in sexual motivation
is indicated by the fact that people who, because
of injury, have no genital sensation
_____ (do/do not) feel sexual
desire.

36. Problems that consistently impair sexual
functioning are called _____
_____. Examples of such
problems include _____
_____, _____, and

_____ _____.

Personality disorders _____
(have/have not) been linked with most of the
problems impairing sexual functioning, and so
the usual psychotherapeutic methods
_____ (are/are not) effective.

37. A person's sexual attraction to the same or
opposite sex is referred to as

_____.

38. Historically, _____ (virtually

all/a slight majority) of the world's cultures have been predominantly heterosexual.

39. Studies in Western Europe and the United States indicate that approximately _____ percent of men and _____ percent of women are exclusively homosexual. This finding suggests that popular estimates of the rate of homosexuality are _____ (high/low/accurate).

40. A person's sexual orientation _____ (does/does not) appear to be voluntarily chosen.

41. Childhood events and family relationships _____ (are/are not) important factors in determining a person's sexual orientation.

42. Sex hormone levels _____ (do/do not) predict sexual orientation.

43. Homosexuality _____ (does/ does not) involve a fear of the other sex that leads people to direct their sexual desires toward members of their own sex.

44. As children, most homosexuals _____ (were/were not) sexually victimized.

45. One theory proposes that sexual orientation emerges as the objects, smells, and sights associated with early sexual experiences become _____ cues for arousal. The fact that early homosexual behavior _____ (does/does not) make people homosexual _____ (supports/conflicts with) this theory.

46. In animals and some rare human cases, sexual orientation has been altered by abnormal _____ conditions during prenatal development. In humans, prenatal exposure to hormone levels typical of _____, particularly between _____ and _____ months after conception, may predispose an attraction to males.

Explain why many experts feel that the study of sex cannot and should not be free of values.

Achievement Motivation (pp. 370–378)

47. The drive theory of motivation is contradicted by the existence of many behaviors that appear to satisfy no apparent biological _____.

48. Psychologists Murray, McClelland, and Atkinson studied achievement motivation by having people create _____ about ambiguous pictures.

49. In experiments, individuals who chose extremely difficult tasks tended to have a _____ (low/high) need for achievement.

50. Increasing achievement motivation in people _____ (does/does not) tend to increase achievement.

51. Achievement motivation has both _____ roots and _____ roots.

52. In terms of performance in school and on intelligence tests, first-born children do slightly _____ (better/worse) than later-born children. Other studies have shown that first-born children tend to be _____ (more/less) socially relaxed and popular. Compared with later-borns, who tend to be _____ (more/less) creative and accepting of new ideas, first-borns are more _____.

53. Motivation to perform a behavior for its own sake is referred to as _____

_____. Motivation based on external rewards and punishments is called

_____ _____.

Of the two, _____

_____ appears to be more successful in fueling achievement.

54. Spence and Helmreich found that people who tend to achieve the most are those oriented toward _____ and hard _____. They also found that there is an _____ effect between these factors and competitiveness.

Explain the relationship between work-mastery orientation and competitiveness.

55. The field of _____ psychology studies how managers might best motivate employees.

56. Studies have shown that rewards lower intrinsic motivation when they are used to _____ but raise it when they are used to _____.

57. Managers who are directive, set clear standards, organize work, and focus attention on specific goals are said to employ _____ _____. More democratic managers who aim to build teamwork and mediate conflicts in the workforce employ _____ _____.

58. In experiments, women tended to excel at _____ leadership, while men tended to excel at _____ leadership.

59. McGregor refers to managers who assume that workers are basically lazy and motivated only by money as _____ managers. Managers who assume that people are

intrinsically motivated in their work are referred to as _____ managers.

Give several pieces of advice offered in the textbook to managers who wish to motivate employees.

FOCUS ON PSYCHOLOGY:
Motivation for Listening to Rock Music

Many motivation researchers now believe that motivated behavior involves three basic components: learning, cognition, and biology. The word "component" implies that each factor influences the behavior in question and is, in turn, influenced by the other factors.

Motivation researcher Robert Franken offers an example of the components approach in explaining why people enjoy listening to rock music. Franken begins with the assumption that cognitive processes obviously play a role in the appreciation of music. We enjoy new songs not only for their lyrics, but also because they involve novel melodies, rhythms, and combinations of voices and instruments. The motivating properties of curiosity and the reinforcing value of novel stimuli are both well-documented in humans.

Learning also plays a significant role in the enjoyment of music. Our taste in music can be attributed, at least in part, to past musical exposure and reinforcement. We are more likely to enjoy music that has been associated with feelings of well-being, for example, than music that has been associated with less desirable psychological states.

For many of us, music may serve as a conditioned stimulus. It can, for example, elicit emotional memories as classically conditioned responses. Upon hearing a song that was popular during our youth, for example, we may vividly re-experience feelings of well-being, self-confidence, or rebelliousness, if the song was at one time associated with these emotions. Perhaps the clearest example of music as a conditioned stimulus is the fact that people often play particular pieces of music to trigger specific moods.

The role of the biological component in listening to rock music is less obvious than that of learning or cognition, but no less significant. For many listeners, rock music is best appreciated when played very loud. Indeed, live rock music is often played at loudness levels in excess of 100 decibels. Sounds louder than approximately 80 decibels produce a number of physiological changes in the body, including arousal of the reticular formation, stimulation of the cortex of the brain, and the outpouring of stress hormones and neurotransmitters that accompany the "fight-or-flight" reaction of the autonomic nervous system.

Numerous studies have shown that moderate increases in arousal are pleasurable. Higher levels of arousal, although not always pleasurable, have been shown to intensify prevailing emotions. It may be, therefore, that listening to loud rock music is at least partially motivated by a desire to experience increased arousal. And, if the listener is already in a good mood —perhaps enjoying the company of friends at a concert or party—the increased arousal associated with loud music may enhance the good mood.

Franken's example strongly suggests that motivation involves the interaction of biological, learned, and cognitive factors. The pleasure derived from the moderate increases in arousal associated with listening to music is evidence for the biological component. Yet, as Franken notes, "The fact that people listen to rock music when they could more readily obtain the same arousal level by running around the block indicates that something more is involved. Obviously the structure of the music and the associations it elicits are important factors in the total reaction to it. Somehow all these factors interact to produce a particular sensation. The joining together—or, more precisely, the pooling—of motivation is a fascinating thing to note about human behavior."

Source: Franken, R. E. (1988). *Human motivation* (2nd ed.). Pacific Grove, CA: Brooks/Cole, 44–47.

Progress Test 1

Multiple-Choice Questions

Circle your answers to the following questions and check them with the answers on page 257. If your answer is incorrect, read the explanation for why it is incorrect and then consult the appropriate pages of the text (in parentheses following the correct answer).

1. Motivation is best understood as a state that:
   a. reduces a drive.
   b. aims at satisfying a biological need.
   c. energizes an organism to act.
   d. energizes and directs behavior.

2. Which of the following is a difference between a drive and a need?
   a. Needs are learned; drives are inherited.
   b. Needs are physiological states; drives are psychological states.
   c. Drives are generally stronger than needs.
   d. Needs are generally stronger than drives.

3. One problem with the idea of motivation as drive reduction is that:
   a. because some motivated behaviors do not seem to be based on physiological needs, they cannot be explained in terms of drive reduction.
   b. it fails to explain any human motivation.
   c. it cannot account for homeostasis.
   d. it does not explain the hunger drive.

4. Which of the following needs are at the top of Maslow's hierarchy?
   a. physiological needs
   b. safety needs
   c. belongingness needs
   d. self-actualization needs

5. Injections of insulin will:
   a. lower blood sugar and trigger hunger.
   b. raise blood sugar and trigger hunger.
   c. lower blood sugar and trigger satiety.
   d. raise blood sugar and trigger satiety.

6. Electrical stimulation of the lateral hypothalamus will cause an animal to:
   a. begin eating.
   b. stop eating.
   c. become obese.
   d. begin copulating.

7. Recent evidence suggests that the lateral hypothalamus:
   a. interferes with testosterone and estrogen levels.
   b. affects the body's water balance.
   c. decreases the available amount of serotonin in the brain.
   d. plays an important role in stabilizing body weight.

8. Rodin found that, in response to the sight and smell of a steak being grilled:
   a. overweight people had a greater insulin response than people of normal weight.
   b. people of normal weight had a greater insulin response than overweight people.
   c. externals had a greater insulin response than internals.
   d. internals had a greater insulin response than externals.

9. Instinct theory and drive theory both emphasize _____ factors in motivation.
   a. environmental   c. biological
   b. cognitive   d. social

10. The correct order of the stages of Masters and Johnson's sexual response cycle is:
    a. plateau; excitement; orgasm; resolution.
    b. excitement; plateau; orgasm; resolution.
    c. excitement; orgasm; resolution; refractory.
    d. plateau; excitement; orgasm; refractory.

11. Few human behaviors are sufficiently automatic to qualify as:
    a. needs.   c. instincts.
    b. drives.   d. incentives.

12. Theory _____ managers tend to adopt a style of _____ leadership.
    a. X; task   c. Y; autocratic
    b. X; social   d. Y; directive

13. In his study of men on a semistarvation diet, Keys found that:
    a. the metabolic rate of the subjects increased.
    b. the subjects eventually lost interest in food.
    c. the subjects became obsessed with food.
    d. the subjects' behavior directly contradicted predictions made by Maslow's hierarchy.

14. When people restrict their intake of food, as when dieting, their:
    a. metabolism increases.
    b. metabolism decreases.
    c. metabolism stays the same.
    d. insulin decreases.

15. Bulimia involves:
    a. binging.
    b. purging.
    c. dramatic weight loss.
    d. a. and b.
    e. a., b., and c.

16. Castration of male rats results in:
    a. reduced testosterone and sexual interest.
    b. reduced testosterone, but no change in sexual interest.
    c. reduced estrogen and sexual interest.
    d. reduced estrogen, but no change in sexual interest.

17. Most sexual dysfunctions are caused by:
    a. personality disorders.
    b. hormone imbalances.
    c. a very restricted upbringing.
    d. none of the above.

18. It has been said that the body's major sex organ is the brain. With regard to sex education:
    a. transmission of value-free information about the wide range of sexual behaviors should be the primary focus of the educator.
    b. transmission of technical knowledge about the biological act should be the classroom focus, free from the personal values and attitudes of researchers, teachers, and students.
    c. the home, not the school, should be the focus of all instruction about reproductive behavior.
    d. attitudes, values, and morals cannot be divorced from the biological aspects of sexuality.

19. Kinsey's studies of sexual behavior showed that:
    a. males enjoy sex more than females.
    b. females enjoy sex more than males.
    c. premarital sex is less common than is popularly believed.
    d. sexual behavior is enormously varied.

20. To increase employee motivation and productivity, industrial/organizational psychologists advise managers to:
    a. adopt an autocratic leadership style.
    b. adopt a participative leadership style.
    c. instill competitiveness in each employee.
    d. deal with employees according to their individual motives.

Matching Items

Match each term with its definition or description.

Terms

_____ **1.** intrinsic motivation
_____ **2.** set point
_____ **3.** drive
_____ **4.** orgasmic dysfunction
_____ **5.** extrinsic motivation
_____ **6.** estrogen
_____ **7.** homeostasis
_____ **8.** sexual orientation
_____ **9.** need
_____ **10.** incentive
_____ **11.** impotence

Definitions or Descriptions

a. a hormone secreted more by females than males
b. the body's tendency to maintain a balanced internal state
c. an environmental stimulus that motivates behavior
d. a person's attraction to members of a particular sex
e. the motivation to perform a behavior for its own sake
f. a desire to perform a behavior due to promised rewards
g. an inability to have or maintain an erection
h. an inability to experience orgasm
i. an aroused state arising from some state of deprivation
j. a state of deprivation
k. the body's weight-maintenance setting

Progress Test 2

Progress Test 2 should be completed during a final chapter review. Answer the following questions after you thoroughly understand the correct answers for the Chapter Review and Progress Test 1.

Multiple-Choice Questions

1. Sexual motivation in women is most influenced by:
   a. the level of progesterone.
   b. the level of estrogen.
   c. the phase of the menstrual cycle.
   d. social and psychological factors.

2. Homeostasis refers to:
   a. the tendency to maintain a steady internal state.
   b. the tendency to seek external incentives for behavior.
   c. the setting of the body's "weight thermostat."
   d. a theory of the development of sexual orientation.

3. Which of the following tends to foster a high need for achievement?
   a. the frequent use of extrinsic controls on behavior
   b. encouraging young children to remain dependent
   c. the use of punishment for failures
   d. rewards that provide feedback

4. Which of the following is true concerning the relationship between birth order and achievement?
   a. First-born children tend to do better on various measures of academic achievement.

   b. Later-born children tend to do better on various measures of academic achievement.
   c. Later-born children tend to be more intrinsically motivated to achieve; first-born children tend to be more extrinsically motivated.
   d. Compared to later-born children, first-born children are more competitive but have a lower work-mastery orientation.

5. Although the cause of eating disorders is still unknown, explanations that have been proposed focus on all of the following *except*:
   a. metabolic factors.
   b. personality factors.
   c. family background factors.
   d. cultural factors.

6. The brain area that when stimulated suppresses eating is the:
   a. lateral hypothalamus.
   b. ventromedial hypothalamus.
   c. lateral thalamus.
   d. ventromedial thalamus.

7. Exposure of a fetus to the hormones typical of females between _____ and _____ months after conception may predispose the developing human to become attracted to males.
   a. 1; 3   **c.** 4; 7
   b. 2; 5   **d.** 9; 11

8. Which of the following statements concerning homosexuality is true?
   a. Homosexuals have abnormal hormone levels.

b. As children, most homosexuals were molested by an adult homosexual.

c. Homosexuals had a domineering opposite-sex parent.

d. The basis for sexual orientation is largely unknown.

9. Investigations of men and women's view of body image found that:

a. men and women alike expressed significant self-dissatisfaction.

b. men and women alike accurately assessed the body weight for their own sex that the other sex preferred.

c. men tended to rate their current weight as corresponding both to their ideal weight and to women's ideal weight for men.

d. women tended to be satisfied with their current body weight but to think that men preferred a thinner body shape for women.

10. According to Maslow's theory:

a. the most basic motives are based on physiological needs.

b. needs are satisfied in a specified order.

c. the highest motives relate to self-actualization.

d. all of the above are true.

11. Which of the following is *inconsistent* with the drive theory of motivation?

a. When an individual's body temperature drops below 98.6° Fahrenheit, blood vessels constrict to conserve warmth.

b. A person is driven to seek a drink when his or her cellular water level drops below its optimum point.

c. Monkeys will work puzzles even if not given a food reward.

d. A person becomes hungry when body weight falls below its biological set point.

12. Which of the following is true of the relationship between competitiveness and a work-mastery orientation?

a. Work-mastery orientation and competitiveness are positively correlated, so individuals who are high in one are high in the other.

b. People tend to be motivated either by competitiveness or by work-mastery, so few individuals are high in both.

c. Among those who have a high work-mastery orientation, less competitive individuals achieve more.

d. Among those who have a low work-mastery orientation, less competitive individuals achieve more.

13. Sexual orientation refers to:

a. a person's tendency to display behaviors typical of males or females.

b. a person's sense of identity as a male or female.

c. a person's enduring sexual attraction toward members of a particular sex.

d. all of the above.

14. Which of the following is *not* an aspect of Murray's definition of achievement motivation?

a. the desire to master skills

b. the desire for control

c. the desire to gain approval

d. the desire to attain a high standard

15. The power of external stimuli in sexual motivation is illustrated in Julia Heiman's experiment, which recorded subjects' responses to various romantic, erotic, or neutral audio tapes. Which of the following was among the findings?

a. The women were more aroused by the romantic tape; the men were more aroused by the sexually explicit tape.

b. The sexually experienced subjects reported greater arousal when the tape depicted a sexual encounter in which a woman is overpowered by a man and enjoys being dominated.

c. Whereas the men's physical arousal was both obvious and consistent with their verbal reports, the women's verbal reports did not correspond very directly with their measured physical arousal.

d. Both men and women were aroused most by the sexually explicit tape.

16. According to Masters and Johnson, the sexual response of males is most likely to differ from that of females during:

a. the excitement phase.

b. the plateau phase.

c. orgasm.

d. the resolution phase.

17. In animals, destruction of the lateral hypothalamus results in _____, whereas destruction of the ventromedial hypothalamus results in _____.

a. overeating; loss of hunger

b. loss of hunger; overeating

c. an elevated set point; a lowered set point

d. increased thirst; loss of thirst

18. Why do people with a high need for achievement prefer tasks of moderate difficulty?

a. They are afraid of failing at more difficult tasks.

b. They want to avoid the embarrassment of failing at easy tasks.

c. Moderately difficult tasks present an attainable goal in which success is attributable to their own skill.

d. They have high extrinsic motivation.

19. Beginning with the most fundamental needs, which of the following represents the correct sequence of needs in the hierarchy described by Maslow?
    a. safety; physiological; esteem; love; self-fulfillment
    b. safety; physiological; love; esteem; self-fulfillment
    c. physiological; safety; esteem; love; self-fulfillment
    d. physiological; safety; love; esteem; self-fulfillment

20. Hunger is to food deprivation as _____ is to _____.
    a. drive; need
    b. need; drive
    c. incentive; need
    d. incentive; drive

True-False Items

Indicate whether each statement is true or false by placing *T* or *F* in the blank next to the item.

_____ 1. When body weight rises above set point, hunger increases.

_____ 2. According to Masters and Johnson, only males experience a plateau period in the cycle of sexual arousal.

_____ 3. Testosterone affects the sexual arousal of the male only.

_____ 4. Unlike men, women tend not to be aroused by sexually explicit material.

_____ 5. All taste preferences are conditioned.

_____ 6. Later-born children tend to be more social and more popular than first-born children.

_____ 7. An injection of insulin increases blood glucose levels and triggers hunger.

_____ 8. Most types of sexual dysfunction are associated with personality disorders.

_____ 9. Intrinsic motivation fuels achievement more than does extrinsic motivation.

_____ 10. One's sexual orientation is not voluntarily chosen.

Challenge Test

Answer these questions the day before an exam as a final check on your understanding of the chapter's terms and concepts.

Multiple-Choice Questions

1. Because Brent believes that his employees are intrinsically motivated to work for reasons beyond money, Brent would be described as a(n) _____ manager.
    a. directive
    b. autocratic
    c. theory X
    d. theory Y

2. Although Noriko is a very successful corporate manager in Japan, she probably would be less successful in _____, unless she altered her management style to be more sensitive to the greater value workers in that country place on _____.
    a. China; individualism
    b. China; communalism
    c. the United States; individualism
    d. the United States; communalism

3. Mary loves hang-gliding. It would be *most* difficult to explain Mary's behavior according to:
    a. incentives.
    b. achievement motivation.
    c. drive theory.
    d. Maslow's hierarchy of needs.

4. For two weeks Orlando has been on a hunger strike in order to protest his country's involvement in what he perceives as an immoral war. Orlando's willingness to starve himself in order to make a political statement conflicts with the theory of motivation advanced by:
    a. Kinsey.
    b. Murray.
    c. Keys.
    d. Maslow.

5. Kathy has been undergoing treatment for bulimia. There is an above-average probability that one or more members of Kathy's family are:
    a. high-achieving.
    b. overprotective.
    c. alcoholic.
    d. all of the above.

6. Compared with his younger brother, first-born Virgil is more likely to:
    a. do poorly in school.
    b. develop low expectations of himself.
    c. be socially relaxed and popular.
    d. identify with his parents' views.

7. One shortcoming of the instinct theory of motivation is that:
    a. it places too much emphasis on environmental factors.
    b. it focuses only on cognitive aspects of motivation.
    c. it applies only to animal behavior.
    d. it does not explain human behaviors; it simply names them.

8. Which of the following is *not* typical of both anorexia and bulimia?

a. far more frequent occurrence in women than in men

b. preoccupation with food and fear of being overweight

c. weight significantly and noticeably outside normal ranges

d. low self-esteem and feelings of depression

9. Which of the following is *not* an example of homeostasis?

a. perspiring in order to restore normal body temperature

b. feeling hungry and eating to restore the level of blood glucose to its normal level

c. feeling hungry at the sight of an appetizing food

d. All of the above are examples of homeostasis.

10. Two rats have escaped from their cages in the neurophysiology laboratory. The technician needs your help in returning them to their proper cages. One rat is grossly overweight; the other is severely underweight. You confidently state that the overweight rat goes in the "_____ -lesion" cage, while the underweight rat goes in the "_____ -lesion" cage.

a. hippocampus; amygdala

b. amygdala; hippocampus

c. lateral hypothalamus; ventromedial hypothalamus

d. ventromedial hypothalamus; lateral hypothalamus

11. Two students are shown the same picture of a diver standing at the edge of a diving board. They each write a story describing what they see. One says the diver is concentrating on making a successful dive that will qualify her for her country's Olympic team. The other student sees the diver as balking from the intense pressure and training required to be a competitive diver. The two students probably differ in their:

a. intrinsic motivation.

b. extrinsic motivation.

c. need for achievement.

d. work-mastery orientation.

12. A cologne manufacturer claims to have developed a scent that automatically triggers sexual interest in members of the opposite sex. Your parents ask you whether you think it is a good idea for them to invest their retirement savings on the promise that the new cologne will make them rich. What advice should you give them?

a. "Go for it!" Although no one has yet isolated the scent, psychologists are sure that there is an unlearned scent that triggers sexual arousal in humans.

b. "Invest cautiously." There already are several colognes and perfumes on the market that automatically trigger sexual interest.

c. "Don't waste your money!" The only unlearned stimulus for human sexual arousal appears to be touch.

d. "This is a scam!" Everyone knows that only males are automatically aroused by scent. Colognes that supposedly arouse females are nothing more than hoaxes.

13. Darren, a sales clerk at a tire store, enjoys being a salesman not so much for the money as for its challenge and the opportunity to interact with a variety of people. The store manager asks you to recommend a strategy for increasing Darren's motivation. Which of the following is most likely to be effective?

a. Create a competition among the salespeople so that whoever has the highest sales each week receives a bonus.

b. Put Darren on a week-by-week employment contract, promising him continued employment only if his sales increase each week.

c. Leave Darren alone unless his sales drop and then threaten to fire him if his performance doesn't improve.

d. Involve Darren as much as possible in company decision making and use rewards to inform him of his successful performance.

14. At the local factory, the boss began rewarding the most productive workers with special recognition pins. This practice illustrates the use of:

a. incentives.

b. drives.

c. intrinsic motivation.

d. work-mastery orientation.

15. Of the following individuals, who might be most prone to developing an eating disorder?

a. Jason, an adolescent boy who is somewhat overweight and is unpopular with his peers

b. Jennifer, a teenage girl who has a poor self-image and a fear of not being able to live up to her parents' high standards

c. Susan, a 35-year-old woman who is a "workaholic" and devotes most of her energies to her high-pressured career

d. Bill, a 40-year-old man who has had problems with alcoholism and is seriously depressed after losing his job of 20 years

16. Lucille has been sticking to a strict diet but can't seem to lose weight. What is the most likely explanation for her difficulty?
    a. Her body has a very low set point.
    b. Her prediet weight was near her body's set point.
    c. Her weight problem is actually caused by an underlying eating disorder.
    d. Lucille is an "external."

17. Randy, who has been under a lot of stress lately, has intense cravings for sugary junk foods, which tend to make him feel more relaxed. Which of the following is the most likely explanation for his craving?
    a. Randy feels that he deserves to pamper himself with sweets because of the stress he is under.
    b. The extra sugar gives Randy the energy he needs to cope with the demands of daily life.
    c. Carbohydrates boost levels of serotonin, which have a calming effect.
    d. The extra sugar tends to lower Randy's blood insulin level, which promotes relaxation.

18. A course that Janice wants very much to take is being offered by three instructors. Janice chooses the instructor with a reputation for being moderately difficult over one perceived as impossibly difficult and another viewed as very easy. It is most likely that Janice's choice reflects her:
    a. being a later-born child.
    b. having a low need for achievement.
    c. having a high need for achievement.
    d. having a high level of extrinsic motivation.

19. Nancy decided to take introductory psychology because she has always been interested in human behavior. Jack enrolled in the same course because he thought it would be easy. Nancy's behavior was motivated by _____, Jack's by _____.
    a. extrinsic motivation; intrinsic motivation
    b. intrinsic motivation; extrinsic motivation
    c. drives; incentives
    d. incentives; drives

20. For as long as she has been the plant manager, Juanita has welcomed input from employees and has delegated authority. Bill, in managing his department, takes a more authoritarian, iron-fisted approach. Juanita's style is one of _____ leadership, whereas Bill's is one of _____ leadership.
    a. task; social
    b. social; task
    c. autocratic; democratic
    d. democratic; participative

Essay Question

Explain the instinct and drive theories of motivation, discuss their origins, and explain why they cannot fully account for human behavior. (Use the space below to list the points you want to make and organize them. Then write the essay on a separate sheet of paper.)

Key Terms

Using your own words, write a brief definition or explanation of each of the following terms.

1. motivation

2. instinct

3. drive

4. homeostasis

5. incentive

6. hierarchy of needs

7. glucose

8. insulin

9. set point

10. metabolic rate

11. anorexia nervosa

12. bulimia nervosa

13. sexual response cycle

14. refractory period

15. estrogen

16. testosterone

17. sexual dysfunctions

18. sexual orientation

19. achievement motivation

20. intrinsic motivation

21. extrinsic motivation

22. interaction effect

23. task leadership

24. social leadership

25. theory X

26. theory Y

ANSWERS

GUIDED STUDY

The following guidelines provide the main points that your answers should have touched upon.

1. Motivation is a need or desire that energizes behavior and directs it toward a goal. Most physiological needs create psychological drives, which motivate behaviors that gratify those needs and preserve homeostasis. Many motives do not satisfy biological needs, however, indicating that behavior is also motivated by external incentives based on our personal and cultural experiences.

2. Maslow's hierarchy of needs expresses the idea that some needs are more fundamental than others. Maslow proposed that physiological needs, such as for food, water, and shelter, are the most basic and must be met before we are motivated to meet "higher" needs for safety, love, self-esteem, and self-actualization. Critics of Maslow's theory contend that the proposed sequence of needs is arbitrary and not universally fixed.

3. Although stomach pangs correlate with feelings of hunger, they are not the only source. Hunger also increases when blood levels of glucose and insulin are low and high, respectively. Blood chemistry is monitored by the lateral and ventromedial areas of the hypothalamus, which therefore control body weight. Animal research shows that when the LH is electrically stimulated, hunger increases; when the LH is destroyed, hunger decreases. Stimulation of the VMH depresses hunger, while its destruction will increase hunger and trigger rapid weight gain. The body also adjusts its metabolic rate to maintain its weight set point.

   Studies by Judith Rodin indicate that, especially in "external" people, the sights and smells of food can increase hunger, in part because these stimuli trigger increases in blood levels of insulin.

4. Anorexia nervosa is a disorder in which a person becomes significantly underweight yet feels fat. The disorder usually develops in adolescent females. Anorexia patients tend to come from high-achieving and protective families.

   Bulimia nervosa is a more common disorder characterized by repeated episodes of overeating followed by vomiting or using a laxative ("binge-purge" episodes). The families of bulimia patients have a higher than usual incidence of alcoholism, obesity, and depression.

   Several factors may contribute to these eating disorders—for example, the increasingly stringent cultural standards of thinness for women. In addition, studies have demonstrated that women's self-reported ideal weights tend to be lighter than their current weights and that women tend to think that men prefer them to weigh less than the weight men actually prefer. Another indication of the impact of psychological factors in eating disorders is evidence that women with low self-esteem are especially vulnerable to eating disorders.

5. Biologist Alfred Kinsey interviewed more than 10,000 men and women in an effort to describe human sexual behavior. Although Kinsey's sample was not random, his statistics showed that sexual behavior is enormously varied. Other sex reports have been prepared, but because they were based on biased samples of people, they cannot be taken seriously.

   Masters and Johnson outlined four stages in the sexual response cycle. During the initial excitement phase, the genital areas become engorged with blood, causing the penis and clitoris to swell and the vagina to expand and secrete lubricant. In the plateau phase, breathing, pulse, and blood pressure rates increase along with sexual excitement. During orgasm, rhythmic genital contractions create a pleasurable feeling of sexual release. During the resolution phase, the body gradually returns to its unaroused state and males enter a refractory period during which they are incapable of another orgasm.

6. Sex hormones direct the development of male and female sex characteristics, and (especially in nonhuman animals) they activate sexual behavior. In most mammals, sexual activity coincides with ovulation and peak level of estrogen in the female. Sexual behavior in male animals is directly related to the level of testosterone in their bodies.

   In humans, normal fluctuations in hormone levels have little effect on sex drive once the pubertal surge in sex hormones has occurred. In later life, however, the frequency of intercourse decreases as sex hormone levels decline.

   External stimuli, such as touch and erotic material, can trigger sexual arousal in both men and women, although sexually explicit materials may lead people to devalue their partners. Our imagination—in dreams and fantasies—can also lead to arousal.

7. Sexual dysfunctions are problems that consistently

impair sexual functioning, such as premature ejaculation, the inability to have or maintain an erection (impotence), or infrequent orgasms (orgasmic dysfunction).

Sexual dysfunctions do not appear to be linked to personality disorders; it is therefore not surprising that traditional psychotherapy is ineffective in treating them. Sexual dysfunctions are most effectively treated by methods that assume that people can learn and therefore modify their sexual responses.

8. Sexual orientation is an individual's enduring sexual attraction toward members of a particular sex. Although virtually all cultures in all times have been predominantly heterosexual, studies suggest that 4 percent of men and 1 percent of women are exclusively homosexual.

Most homosexuals report first being aware of same-gender sexual feelings around puberty, but they typically do not think of themselves as gay or lesbian until nearer their twenties. The ostracism homosexuals often face may cause them to struggle with their sexual motivation. Because sexual orientation is neither willfully chosen nor willfully changed, however, homosexual feelings generally persist.

There are many myths about the causes of homosexuality, including that it is linked with levels of sex hormones; as a child, being molested or seduced by an adult homosexual; having a domineering mother and an ineffectual father; or fearing or hating members of the opposite sex. Some researchers believe that sexual orientation is the result of the conditioning of erotic associations with homosexual or heterosexual cues. Others believe that people develop sexual attachments to those who are different from the sex they have mostly associated with while growing up. In animals and some exceptional human cases, sexual orientation has been altered by abnormal prenatal hormone conditions, leading some researchers to suggest that exposure to hormone levels typical of females during a critical period of brain development may predispose the individual to become attracted to males.

9. Most sex educators and researchers aim for objectivity and strive to keep their writings on sexuality value-free. Critics contend that the study of sex cannot, and should not, be free of values. For example, the words we use to describe sexual behavior often reflect our personal values. Second, when sexual information is separated from the context of human values, young people are sent a message that sexual behavior is merely recreational activity or a biological act. Therefore, sex-related values should be discussed openly, rather than avoided.

10. As defined by Henry Murray, achievement motivation is the desire for significant accomplishment, for mastering skills or ideas, for control, and for rapidly attaining a high standard. People with a low need for achievement prefer very easy or very difficult tasks, where failure is either unlikely or unembarrassing. People with a high need for achievement prefer moderately difficult tasks, where success is attainable and attributable to their own effort.

Children with a high need for achievement often have parents who encourage their independence from an early age and praise them for their successes. Achievement motivation has both emotional and cognitive roots, as children learn to associate achievement with positive emotions and to attribute their achievements to their own competence.

First-born and only children tend to be more conscientious, and perform slightly better in school and on intelligence tests, perhaps because of the greater parental attention they receive. Later-born children tend to be more socially relaxed, creative, and accepting of new ideas.

11. Intrinsic motivation is the desire to perform a behavior for its own sake. Extrinsic motivation is seeking external rewards and avoiding punishments. Intrinsic motivation promotes high achievement, while extrinsic motivation often does not. Among people who do not intrinsically enjoy mastery of tasks and hard work, competitiveness promotes achievement; among those driven to master tasks and work hard, competitiveness does not promote achievement.

Tasks that challenge and trigger curiosity stimulate intrinsic motivation, as does the use of extrinsic rewards that *inform* people of their successes. Extrinsic rewards that are delivered to *control* people's behaviors, however, undermine intrinsic motivation.

12. Effective managers assess workers' motives (accomplishment, recognition, affiliation, power, etc.) and adjust their managerial style accordingly. Regardless of the managerial style, setting clear objectives, establishing challenging goals, and providing feedback on progress motivate high productivity.

The appropriate leadership style depends on the situation, the strengths of the manager, and his or her assumptions about employees' motives. Those who excel at task leadership are directive, goal-oriented managers who are good at keeping a group centered on its mission. Those who excel at social leadership take a more democratic approach as they promote teamwork, mediate conflicts, and support their work force. Theory X managers, who assume that workers are basically lazy and extrinsically motivated, monitor employees closely and provide incentives to work harder. Theory Y managers, who assume that workers are intrinsically motivated, encourage employee participation in decision making. Effective managers combine goal-oriented task leadership with group-oriented social leadership, adjusting their managerial style in response to workers' motives.

CHAPTER REVIEW

1. energize; direct
2. biological
3. instinct

According to instinct theory, any human behavior could be regarded as an instinct. The only evidence for each such "instinct" was the behavior used to identify it. Thus, instinct theory offered only circular explanations; it labeled behaviors but did not explain them.

4. need; drive
5. homeostasis
6. incentives; do not
7. hierarchy
8. physiological; self-actualization; arbitrary; universally
9. semistarvation
10. stomach contractions
11. does
12. glucose; insulin
13. genetic; body chemistry; culture; conditioning
14. serotonin; calms
15. hypothalamus; lateral hypothalamus; decreases; ventromedial hypothalamus; overeat
16. set point; less; more
17. metabolic; lowering
18. externals; insulin
19. psychological
20. anorexia nervosa; females; teens
21. bulimia nervosa; binge-purge
22. alcoholism; obesity; depression; high-achieving; protective
23. women's
24. self-esteem
25. Kinsey; was
26. biased
27. Masters; Johnson; excitement; plateau; orgasm; resolution
28. refractory period
29. estrogen
30. testosterone; testes

31. little; decreases; decline
32. hypothalamus
33. touch
34. are

Erotic material may lead people to devalue their partners and relationships. It may create unrealistic expectations and as a result make people feel sexually inadequate. Material that is both sexually explicit and violent may promote violent behavior toward women.

35. do
36. sexual dysfunctions; premature ejaculation; impotence; orgasmic dysfunction; have not; are not
37. sexual orientation
38. virtually all
39. 4; 1; high
40. does not
41. are not
42. do not
43. does not
44. were not
45. conditioned; does not; conflicts with
46. hormone; females; 2; 5

Because the words we use to describe behavior often reflect our values, sex research can never be value-free. When sexual information is taught apart from a context of human values, students may get the message that intercourse is merely a biological act of recreation. Sex education that places equal emphasis on respect for oneself and for one's friends and lovers can resolve for adolescents and for adults questions about when to "just say no" to sexual intimacy.

47. need
48. stories
49. low
50. does
51. emotional; cognitive
52. better; less; more; conscientious
53. intrinsic motivation; extrinsic motivation; intrinsic motivation
54. mastery; work; interaction

The effect of competitiveness depends on the degree of work-mastery orientation. Among people who do not intrinsically enjoy mastery and hard work, it pays to be highly competitive; however, among those who *are* oriented toward mastery and hard work, it pays to be less competitive.

55. industrial/organizational
56. control; inform
57. task leadership; social leadership
58. social; task

59. theory X; theory Y

Effective managers use extrinsic rewards to *inform* employees of their successes and boost intrinsic motivation. They also adjust their managerial style to suit their employees, assessing workers' motives (accomplishment, recognition, affiliation, power) and challenging and rewarding them accordingly.

PROGRESS TEST 1

Multiple-Choice Questions

1. d. is the answer. (p. 351)

a. & b. Although motivation is often aimed at reducing drives and satisfying biological needs, this is by no means always the case, as achievement motivation illustrates.

c. Motivated behavior is not only energized but also directed at a goal.

2. b. is the answer. A drive is the psychological consequence of a physiological need. (p. 353)

a. Needs are unlearned states of deprivation.

c. & d. Since needs are physical and drives psychological, their strengths cannot be compared directly.

3. a. is the answer. The curiosity of a child or a scientist is an example of behavior apparently motivated by something other than a physiological need. (p. 354)

b. & d. Some behaviors, such as thirst and hunger, *are* partially explained by drive reduction.

c. Drive reduction is directly based on the principle of homeostasis.

4. d. is the answer. The other needs mentioned were for Maslow more fundamental then self-actualization. (p. 355)

5. a. is the answer. Insulin injections increase hunger directly and also indirectly by lowering blood sugar, or glucose. It is glucose injections, as in d., that would raise blood sugar and increase satiety. (p. 356)

6. a. is the answer. This area of the hypothalamus seems to elevate hunger. (p. 357)

b. Stimulating the ventromedial hypothalamus has this effect.

c. Lesioning the ventromedial hypothalamus has this effect.

d. The hypothalamus *is* involved in sexual motivation, but not in this way.

7. d. is the answer. The fact that even animals whose lateral hypothalamus has been destroyed will eat once their weight drops far enough below the set point suggests that the LH and the VMH aren't simple hunger on-off switches but work through

their influence on the body's "weight thermostat." (p. 357)

a., b., & c. None of these are effects of activity in the lateral hypothalamus.

8. c. is the answer. Externals—those whose eating is especially triggered by food stimuli—showed a greater insulin response than did internals. (p. 358)

a. & b. The greater insulin response occurred in people who were especially sensitive to external cues, regardless of whether they were overweight.

d. Blood insulin levels rose less in internal subjects.

9. c. is the answer. (p. 353)

10. b. is the answer. (p. 362)

11. c. is the answer. (p. 353)

a. & b. Needs and drives are biologically based states that stimulate behaviors but are not themselves behaviors.

d. Incentives are the external pulls that motivate behavior.

12. a. is the answer. Because they assume that workers are basically lazy and extrinsically motivated, theory X managers tend to be task-oriented. (p. 377)

c. & d. Theory Y managers tend to be democratic/participative leaders.

13. c. is the answer. The deprived subjects focused on food almost to the exclusion of anything else. (p. 355)

a. In order to conserve energy, the men's metabolic rate actually *decreased*.

b. & d. Far from losing interest in food, the subjects came to care only about food—a finding consistent with Maslow's hierarchy, in which physiological needs are at the base.

14. b. is the answer. (p. 358)

15. d. is the answer. (p. 359)

16. a. is the answer. (p. 362)

c. & d. Castration of the testes, which produce testosterone, does not alter estrogen levels.

17. d. is the answer. (p. 365)

18. d. is the answer. Sex is much more than just a biological act and its study therefore inherently involves values, attitudes, and morals, which should thus be discussed openly. (p. 369)

19. d. is the answer. (p. 360)

a., b., & c. Kinsey's data do not support any of these statements.

20. d. is the answer. As different people are motivated by different things, to increase motivation and thus productivity, managers are advised to learn what motivates individual employees and to challenge and reward them accordingly. (p. 376)

a. & b. The most effective management style will depend on the situation.

c. This might be an effective strategy with some, but not all, employees.

Matching Items

1. e (p. 373)   5. f (p. 373)   9. j (p. 353)
2. k (p. 357)   6. a (p. 362)   10. c (p. 354)
3. i (p. 353)   7. b (pp. 353–354) 11. g (p. 365)
4. h (p. 365)   8. d (p. 365)

PROGRESS TEST 2

Multiple-Choice Questions

1. **d.** is the answer. In contrast to the sexual behavior of other animals, which is largely controlled by hormones, human sexual motivation is primarily influenced by social and psychological factors. (pp. 363–364)

2. **a.** is the answer. (p. 353)

   b. This describes extrinsic motivation.

   c. This describes set point.

   d. Homeostasis has nothing to do with sexual orientation.

3. **d.** is the answer. If used to inform rather than to control, rewards can increase intrinsic motivation and the need for achievement. (p. 375)

   a., b., & c. Each of these has been shown to *discourage* the development of intrinsic motivation.

4. **a.** is the answer. The differences found between first-born and later-born children are in measures of achievement, with first-born children doing slightly better than their siblings in grades, intelligence tests, and school admissions. (p. 372)

   b. Later-born children tend to be more socially relaxed and popular.

   c. & d. First-born and later-born children do not differ in their competitiveness, work-mastery orientation, or intrinsic motivation.

5. **a.** is the answer. The text does not indicate whether their metabolism is higher or lower than most. (pp. 358–360)

   b., c., & d. Personality, family background, and cultural influence have all been proposed as factors in eating disorders.

6. **b.** is the answer. (p. 357)

   a. Stimulation of the lateral hypothalamus triggers eating.

   c. & d. The thalamus is a sensory relay station; stimulation of it has no effect on eating.

7. **b.** is the answer. The time between 2 and 5 months after conception may be a critical period for the brain's neuro-hormonal control system. Exposure to abnormal hormonal conditions at other times has no effect on sexual orientation. (p. 368)

8. **d.** is the answer. Researchers have not been able to find any clear differences, psychological or otherwise, between homosexuals and heterosexuals. Thus the basis for sexual orientation remains unknown. (pp. 367–368)

9. **c.** is the answer. (pp. 359–360)

   a. It has been found that women tend to express greater dissatisfaction with their body image than do men.

   b. Men tend to judge more accurately the body weight they think women prefer.

   d. Women tend to be dissatisfied with their body weight, and to think, erroneously, that men would prefer them thinner.

10. **d.** is the answer. (p. 355)

11. **c.** is the answer. Such behavior, presumably motivated by curiosity rather than any biological need, is inconsistent with a drive theory of motivation. (pp. 353–354)

    a., b., & d. Each of these examples is consistent with a drive theory of motivation.

12. **c.** is the answer. (p. 373)

    a. & b. People may or may not be both competitive and oriented toward work-mastery.

    d. Among those who have a low work-mastery orientation, less competitive people achieve less.

13. **c.** is the answer. (p. 365)

14. **c.** is the answer. (p. 370)

15. **d.** is the answer. (p. 364)

16. **d.** is the answer. During the resolution phase males experience a refractory period. (p. 362)

    a., b., & c. The male and female responses are very similar in each of these phases.

17. **b.** is the answer. (p. 357)

    a. These effects are the reverse of what takes place.

    c. If anything, set point is lowered by destruction of the lateral hypothalamus and elevated by destruction of the ventromedial hypothalamus.

    d. These effects do not occur.

18. **c.** is the answer. (p. 371)

19. **d.** is the answer. (p. 355)

20. **a.** is the answer. Hunger is the drive that arises in response to the need of food deprivation. (p. 353)

    b. Hunger is a drive, or psychological state of arousal; food deprivation is a physical need.

c. & d. Incentives are positive or negative environmental stimuli that motivate behavior.

True-False Items

1. False (p. 357)
2. False (p. 362)
3. False (p. 363)
4. False (p. 364)
5. False (p. 356)
6. True (p. 372)
7. False (p. 356)
8. False (p. 365)
9. True (p. 373)
10. True (p. 367)

CHALLENGE TEST

1. **d.** is the answer. (p. 377)

   a. & b. Directive managers, who often have an autocratic management style, are likely to favor theory X assumptions regarding worker motivation.

   c. Theory X managers assume that workers are basically lazy, error-prone, and extrinsically motivated by money.

2. **c.** is the answer. (p. 376)

   a. Values in Asian countries, such as China, lean toward communalism rather than individualism.

   b. Because of the country's similar cultural values, Noriko would likely be quite successful in China.

   d. Cultural values in Europe and the United States lean toward individualism rather than communalism.

3. **c.** is the answer. Drive theory maintains that behavior is motivated when a biological need creates an aroused state, driving the individual to satisfy the need. It is difficult to believe that Mary's hang-gliding is gratifying a biological need. (pp. 353–354)

   a., b., & d. Mary may enjoy hang-gliding because it is a challenge that "is there" (incentive), because it satisfies a need to accomplish something challenging (achievement), or because it increases her self-esteem and sense of fulfillment in life (Maslow's hierarchy of needs).

4. **d.** is the answer. According to Maslow's theory, physiological needs, such as the need to satisfy hunger, must be satisfied before a person pursues loftier needs, such as making political statements. (p. 355)

   a. Kinsey was concerned with sexual behavior.

   b. Murray was concerned with achievement motivation.

   c. Keys was concerned with hunger.

5. **c.** is the answer. (p. 359)

   a. & b. These are more typical of the families of anorexia patients.

6. **d.** is the answer. (p. 372)

   a. & b. First-borns tend to do better in school and develop higher personal expectations.

   c. Later-borns tend to be more socially relaxed and popular.

7. **d.** is the answer. (p. 353)

   a. & b. Instinct theory emphasizes biological factors, rather than environmental or cognitive factors.

   c. Instinct theory applies to both humans and other animals.

8. **c.** is the answer. Although anorexics are significantly underweight, bulimics often are not unusually thin or overweight. (p. 359)

   a., b., & d. Both anorexics and bulimics are more likely to be women than men, preoccupied with food, fearful of becoming overweight, and suffer from depression or low self-esteem.

9. **c.** is the answer. This is an example of salivating in response to an incentive, rather than to maintain a balanced internal state. (pp. 353–354)

   a. & b. Both of these are examples of behavior that maintains a balanced internal state (homeostasis).

10. **d.** is the answer. Lesions of the ventromedial hypothalamus produce overeating and rapid weight gains. Lesions of the lateral hypothalamus suppress hunger and produce weight loss. (p. 357)

    a. & b. The hippocampus and amygdala are not involved in regulating eating behavior.

11. **c.** is the answer. Achievement researchers regard people whose stories about ambiguous pictures express fantasies about the pursuit of goals, performing heroic acts, or feeling pride in success, as indicating achievement concerns. (pp. 370–371)

    a., b., & d. There is nothing in the stated information that would allow us to conclude that the students differ in their intrinsic, extrinsic, or work-mastery orientation.

12. **c.** is the answer. (p. 363)

13. **d.** is the answer. Because Darren evidently has a high intrinsic and work-mastery orientation, giving him feedback about his work and involving him in participative management are probably all he needs to be very satisfied with his situation. (pp. 373, 375–377)

    a., b., & c. Creating competitions and using controlling, rather than informing, rewards may have the opposite effect and actually undermine Darren's intrinsic motivation.

14. **a.** is the answer. The pins are an external stimulus that can motivate behavior. (pp. 353, 354, 373)

    b. Drives are states of arousal that arise from physiological needs.

c. Intrinsic motivation is the desire to perform a behavior for its own sake; external incentives are unnecessary.

d. A work-mastery orientation is characteristic of people who are intrinsically motivated.

15. **b.** is the answer. Adolescent females with low self-esteem and high-achieving families seem especially prone to eating disorders such as anorexia nervosa. (p. 359)

a. & d. Eating disorders occur much more frequently in women than in men.

c. Eating disorders usually develop during adolescence, rather than during adulthood, as in this example.

16. **b.** is the answer. The body acts to defend its set point, or the weight to which it is predisposed. If Lucille was already near her set point, weight loss would prove difficult. (p. 358)

a. If the weight level to which her body is predisposed is low, weight loss upon dieting should not be difficult.

c. The eating disorders relate to eating behaviors and psychological factors and would not explain a difficulty with weight loss.

d. Externals might have greater problems losing weight, since they tend to respond to food stimuli, but this can't be the explanation in Lucille's case, since she has been sticking to her diet.

17. **c.** is the answer. Serotonin is a neurotransmitter that is elevated by the consumption of carbohydrates and has a calming effect. (p. 357)

a. & b. These answers do not explain the feelings of relaxation that Randy associates with eating junk food.

d. The consumption of sugar tends to elevate insulin level rather than lower it.

18. **c.** is the answer. Individuals with a high need for achievement tend to choose moderately difficult tasks at which they can succeed if they work. (p. 371)

a. The choice described is characteristic of those with a high need for achievement, which in turn tends to be more characteristic of first-born than of later-born children.

b. People with a low need for achievement might be more likely to prefer either the easy or the very difficult course.

d. That she chooses the course because it interests her implies that she is *intrinsically* motivated.

19. **b.** is the answer. Wanting to do something for its own sake is intrinsic motivation; wanting to do something for a reward (in this case, presumably, a high grade) is extrinsic motivation. (p. 373)

a. The opposite is true. Nancy was motivated to take the course for its own sake, whereas Jack was evidently motivated by the likelihood of a reward in the form of a good grade.

c. & d. A good grade, such as the one Jack is expecting, is an incentive. Drives, however, are aroused states that result from physical deprivation; they are not involved in this example.

20. **b.** is the answer. (pp. 376–377)

a. Bill's style is one of task leadership, whereas Juanita's is one of social leadership.

c. Juanita's style is democratic/participative, whereas Bill's is autocratic/directive.

d. The terms democratic and participative refer to the same style of leadership.

Essay Question

Under the influence of Darwin's evolutionary theory, it became fashionable to classify all sorts of behaviors as instincts. Instinct theory fell into disfavor for several reasons. First, instincts do not explain behaviors, they merely name them. Second, to qualify as an instinct, a behavior must have a fixed and automatic pattern and occur in all people, regardless of differing cultures and experiences. Apart from a few simple reflexes, however, human behavior is not sufficiently automatic and universal to meet these criteria.

Instinct theory was replaced by drive theory and the idea that biological needs create aroused drive states that motivate the individual to satisfy these needs and preserve homeostasis. Drive theory failed as a complete account of human motivation because many human motives do not satisfy any obvious biological need. Instead, such behaviors are motivated by incentives in the environment.

KEY TERMS

1. **Motivation** is a force, internal or external, that energizes and directs behavior. (p. 351)

   Example: A classic debate in the study of **motivation** concerns whether behavior is more pushed from within by biological drives or pulled from without by incentives.

2. An **instinct** is a stereotyped behavior pattern that is rigid, characteristic of an entire species, and unlearned. (p. 353)

3. A **drive** is an energized state that arises from an underlying need. (p. 353)

4. **Homeostasis** refers to the body's tendency to maintain a constant, and optimum, internal state. (p. 353)

5. An **incentive** is an environmental stimulus that motivates behavior by "pulling" it from without. (p. 354)

   Example: Under the company's employee **incentive** plan, low absenteeism was rewarded with bonus pay.

6. Maslow's **hierarchy of needs** proposes that human motives may be ranked from the basic, physiological level through higher-level needs for safety, love, esteem, and self-fulfillment, and that until they are satisfied, the more basic needs are more compelling than the higher-level ones. (p. 355)

7. **Glucose**, or blood sugar, is the major source of energy for the body. Elevating the level of glucose in the body will reduce hunger. (p. 356)

8. **Insulin** is a hormone that helps the body convert glucose into fat. Elevating the level of insulin in the body will trigger hunger. (p. 356)

9. **Set point** is an individual's regulated weight level, which is maintained by adjusting food intake and energy output. (p. 357)

10. **Metabolic rate** is the body's rate of energy expenditure. (p. 358)

11. **Anorexia nervosa** is an eating disorder, most common in adolescent females, in which a person restricts food intake to become significantly underweight and yet still feels fat. (p. 359)

12. **Bulimia nervosa** is an eating disorder characterized by repeated "binge-purge" episodes of overeating followed by vomiting or laxative use. (p. 359)

13. The **sexual response cycle** described by Masters and Johnson consists of four stages of bodily reaction: excitement, plateau, orgasm, and resolution. (p. 362)

    Example: Perhaps the most important result of Masters and Johnson's study of the **sexual response cycle** is the finding that except for the resolution phase, males and females have very similar responses.

14. The **refractory period** is a resting period after orgasm, during which a male cannot be aroused to another orgasm. (p. 362)

15. **Estrogen** is a sex hormone secreted in greater amounts by females than by males. In mammals other than humans, estrogen levels peak during ovulation and trigger sexual drive. (p. 362)

16. **Testosterone** is the most important male sex hormone; it stimulates the growth of male sex characteristics. (p. 362)

17. **Sexual dysfunctions** are problems—such as impotence, premature ejaculation, and orgasmic dysfunction—that consistently impair sexual functioning. (p. 365)

18. **Sexual orientation** refers to a person's attraction to members of either the same or the opposite sex. (p. 365)

    Example: Although theories of the origins of **sexual orientation** abound, few conclusions exist, other than that one's orientation does not seem to be a voluntary choice.

19. **Achievement motivation** is the degree to which a person is motivated internally by a desire for significant accomplishment and attaining a high standard. (p. 370)

20. **Intrinsic motivation** is the desire to perform a behavior for its own sake, rather than for some external reason. (p. 373)

    Memory aid: Intrinsic means "*in*ternal": A person who is **intrinsically** motivated is motivated from within.

21. **Extrinsic motivation** is the desire to perform a behavior in order to obtain a reward or avoid a punishment. (p. 373)

    Memory aid: Extrinsic means "*ex*ternal": A person who is **extrinsically** motivated is motivated by some outside factor.

22. An **interaction effect** occurs when the effect of one factor depends on the level of another factor. (p. 373)

    Example: In achievement motivation there is an **interaction effect** between work-mastery and competitiveness. Whether competitiveness is advantageous or not depends on the level of the individual's work-mastery orientation.

23. **Task leadership** is goal-oriented leadership that sets standards, organizes work, and often is adopted by theory X managers. (p. 376)

24. **Social leadership** is group-oriented leadership that builds teamwork, mediates conflict, and often is adopted by theory Y managers. (pp. 376–377)

25. **Theory X** managers assume that employees are basically lazy and extrinsically motivated. (p. 377)

26. **Theory Y** managers assume that, under the proper conditions, employees are intrinsically motivated to work for reasons other than money. (p. 377)

13 / Emotion

Chapter Overview

Emotions are responses of the whole individual, involving physiological arousal, expressive reactions, and conscious feelings and thoughts. Chapter 13 examines each of these components in detail, particularly as they relate to three specific emotions: fear, anger, and happiness. In addition, the chapter discusses several theoretical controversies concerning the relationship and sequence of the components of emotion. Primary among these are whether body response to a stimulus causes the emotion that is felt and whether thinking is necessary to and must precede the experience of emotion.

NOTE: Answer guidelines for all Chapter 13 questions begin on page 273.

Guided Study

The text chapter should be studied one section at a time. Before you read, preview each section by skimming it, noting headings and boldface items. Then read the appropriate section objectives from the following outline. Keep these objectives in mind and, as you read the chapter section, search for the information that will enable you to meet each objective. Once you have finished a section, write out answers for its objectives.

The Physiology of Emotion (pp. 384–388)

1. Identify the three components of emotion and describe the physiological changes that occur during emotional arousal, including the relationship between arousal and performance.

2. Discuss the research findings on the relationship between body states and specific emotions.

3. Discuss the effectiveness of the polygraph in detecting lies.

Expressing Emotion (pp. 388–392)

4. Discuss the extent to which nonverbal expressions of emotion are universally understood and describe the effects of facial expressions on emotion.

Experiencing Emotion (pp. 392–402)

5. Identify three dimensions of emotional experience; discuss the significance of biological and environmental factors in the acquisition of fear.

6. Discuss the catharsis hypothesis and identify some of the advantages and disadvantages of openly expressing anger.

7. Identify some potential causes and consequences of happiness and discuss reasons for the relativity of happiness.

8. (Close-Up) Explain the opponent-process theory of emotion.

Theories of Emotion (pp. 402–406)

9. Contrast and critique the James-Lange and Cannon-Bard theories of emotion.

10. Describe Schachter's two-factor theory of emotion and discuss evidence suggesting that some emotional reactions involve no conscious thought.

Chapter Review

When you have finished reading the chapter, work through the material that follows to review it. Complete the sentences and answer the questions. As you proceed, evaluate your performance for each section by consulting the answers on page 275. Do not continue with the next section until you understand each answer. If you need to, review or reread the appropriate section in the textbook before continuing.

1. Of all the species, _____ are the most emotional.

2. Three aspects of any emotion are _____ _____ _____.

The Physiology of Emotion (pp. 384–388)

3. Describe the major physiological changes that each of the following undergoes during emotional arousal:
   a. heart: _____
   b. muscles: _____
   c. liver: _____
   d. breathing: _____
   e. digestion: _____
   f. pupils: _____
   g. blood: _____

4. The responses of arousal are activated by the _____ nervous system. In response to its signal, the _____ glands release the hormones _____ and _____, which increase heart rate and blood pressure.

5. When the need for arousal has passed, the body is calmed through activation of the _____ nervous system.

Explain the relationship between performance and arousal.

6. The various emotions are associated with _____ (similar/different) forms of physiological arousal.

7. Generally, psychologists _____ (believe/do not believe) that different patterns of brain activity underlie different emotions. For example, negative emotions are accompanied by increased activity in the _____ hemisphere, while positive emotions are accompanied by increased activity in the _____ hemisphere.

8. Individuals with more active _____ (right/left) _____ lobes tend to be more cheerful than those in whom this pattern of brain activity is reversed.

9. The emotions _____ and _____ are accompanied by differing _____ temperatures and _____ secretions.

10. The physical accompaniments of emotion _____ (are/are not) innate and universal.

11. The technical name for the "lie detector" is the _____.

Explain how lie detectors supposedly indicate whether a person is lying.

12. How well the lie detector works depends on whether a person exhibits _____ while lying.

13. Those who criticize lie detectors feel that the tests are particularly likely to err in the case of the _____ (innocent/guilty), because different _____ all register as _____.

14. By and large, experts _____ (agree/do not agree) that lie detector tests are highly accurate.

15. A test that assesses a suspect's knowledge of

details of a crime that only the guilty person should know is the _____

_____ _____.

Today many employees are required to take paper-and-pencil _____ tests that question their past behavior.

Expressing Emotion (pp. 388–392)

16. Emotions may be communicated in words and/or through body expressions, referred to as _____ communication.

17. Most people are especially good at interpreting nonverbal _____.

18. Women are generally _____ (better/worse) than men at detecting nonverbal signs of emotion.

19. Various emotions may be linked with specific

_____ _____.

20. Gestures have _____ (the same/different) meanings in different cultures.

21. Studies of adults indicate that in different cultures facial expressions have _____ (the same/different) meanings. Studies of children indicate that the meaning of their facial expressions _____ (varies/does not vary) across cultures.

22. According to _____, human emotional expressions evolved because they helped our ancestors communicate before language developed.

23. In cultures that encourage _____, emotional expressions are often intense and prolonged. In cultures that emphasize _____, emotions such as _____, _____, and _____ are more common than in the _____ (East/West).

24. Darwin believed that when an emotion is accompanied by an outward facial expression, the emotion is _____ (intensified/diminished).

25. In one study, students who were induced to smile _____ (found/did not find) cartoons more humorous.

26. Ekman and colleagues found that imitating emotional facial expressions resulted in _____ changes characteristic of emotional arousal.

27. Studies have found that imitating another person's facial expressions _____ (leads/does not lead) to greater empathy with that person's feelings.

Experiencing Emotion (pp. 392–402)

28. Cross-cultural research reveals three dimensions that distinguish various emotions:

_____, _____, and _____.

29. Izard believes that there are _____ basic emotions, most of which _____ (are/are not) present in infancy.

30. Fear can by and large be seen as a(n) _____ (adaptive/maladaptive) response.

31. Most human fears are acquired through _____. In addition, some fears are acquired by _____ parents and friends.

Explain why researchers believe that some fears are biologically predisposed.

32. People differ _____ (little/ significantly) in their level of fearfulness.

33. Averill has found that most people become angry several times per _____.

34. The belief that expressing pent-up emotion is adaptive is most commonly found in cultures that emphasize _____. This is the _____ hypothesis. In cultures that emphasize _____,

such as those of _____ or _____, expressions of anger are less common.

35. Psychologists have found that when anger has been provoked, retaliation may have a calming effect under certain circumstances. List these circumstances below.

a. _____

b. _____

c. _____

Identify some potential problems of expressing anger.

36. List two suggestions offered by experts for handling anger.

a. _____

b. _____

37. Psychologists have consistently found that people become more willing to help others when they themselves are _____.

38. After experiencing tragedy, people generally _____ (regain/do not regain) their previous degree of happiness.

39. When Europeans were surveyed, researchers found that levels of happiness _____ (do/do not) mirror differences in standards of living. Since the 1950s, spendable income in the United States has doubled; personal happiness has _____ (increased/decreased/ remained unchanged).

40. The idea that happiness is relative to one's recent experience is stated by the

_____-_____

principle.

Explain how this principle accounts for the fact that, for some people, material desires can never be satisfied.

41. The idea that "every emotion triggers its opposite" is the basis of the _____–_____ theory of emotion. According to this theory, the opposing emotion is most intense immediately _____ (before/after) an emotion-arousing event. With repeated experience of the event, the primary emotion becomes _____ (weaker/stronger) and the opposing emotion becomes _____ (weaker/stronger).

42. The principle that one's happiness is relative to others' is known as _____ _____.

43. List six factors that have been shown to be positively correlated with feelings of happiness.

_____ _____

_____ _____

_____ _____

44. List six factors that are evidently unrelated to happiness.

_____ _____

_____ _____

_____ _____

45. When people were interrupted during their daily activities and asked to report their feelings, they reported being happier when they were engaged in _____ _____ or _____ _____.

Theories of Emotion (pp. 402–406)

46. According to the James-Lange theory, emotional states _____ (precede/follow) body arousal.

Describe two problems that Walter Cannon identified with the James-Lange theory.

47. Cannon proposed that emotional stimuli in the environment are routed simultaneously to the _____, which results in awareness of the emotion, and to the _____ nervous system, which

causes the body's reaction. Because another scientist concurrently proposed similar ideas, this theory has come to be known as the _____–_____ theory.

48. For victims of spinal cord injuries who have lost all feeling below the neck, the intensity of emotions tends to _____. This result supports the _____–_____ theory of emotion.

49. The two-factor theory of emotion proposes that emotion has two components: _____ arousal and a _____ label. This theory was proposed by _____.

50. Schachter and Singer found that physically aroused subjects told that an injection would cause arousal _____ (did/did not) become emotional in response to an accomplice's aroused behavior. Physically aroused subjects not expecting arousal _____ (did/did not) become emotional in response to an accomplice's behavior.

51. Robert Zajonc believes that the feeling of emotion _____ (can/cannot) precede our cognitive labeling of that emotion.

Cite two pieces of evidence that support Zajonc's position.

52. The researcher who disagrees with Zajonc and argues that most emotions require cognitive processing is _____.

Express some general conclusions that can be drawn about cognition and emotion.

FOCUS ON PSYCHOLOGY:
Does Unhappiness Run in Families?

Researchers investigating human emotions have recently come to the surprising conclusion that happiness (a subjective sense of well-being) and unhappiness (or sadness) are separate feelings, rather than opposite endpoints on one emotional continuum. Edward Diener, psychology professor at the University of Illinois, believes that the two emotions can exist simultaneously in each of us, much as we can have mixed or conflicting feelings about a partner in a close relationship.

Evidence for the independence of happiness and unhappiness comes from research showing that while a predisposition toward sadness may be inherited, happiness is more situationally controlled. In one study, researchers at the University of Southern California measured levels of happiness and unhappiness in more than 100 pairs of twins, as well as in several generations of other families. They found that family members were much more similar in level of unhappiness than in level of happiness. Furthermore, identical twins were more similar than fraternal twins, but *only in levels of unhappiness*. These results suggest that unhappiness may run in families, while happiness is more a matter of personal control and environmental influence.

In another study, researchers at the University of Minnesota compared the personalities of identical twins who had been raised together with those who had not. Twins who had grown up together had much more similar levels of happiness than did twins who had been raised apart. In terms of unhappiness, however, twins raised together were no more similar than twins raised separately.

Science writer Diane Swanbrow believes that these findings offer useful clues to people wishing to live happier lives. Because happiness and unhappiness are independent emotions, "changing or avoiding things that make you miserable may well make you less miserable but probably won't make you any happier." Instead, Swanbrow suggests you should do those things that make you happy. In one experiment, people were asked to spend more time doing things they enjoyed for one month. At the end of the month, average happiness levels increased significantly as compared with happiness levels of control subjects, who did not change their monthly activities.

Although psychologists have only recently begun to investigate happiness, their initial findings are important to all of us. By planning to be happy, making the pursuit of a happy life a priority, and making time to do the things that make us happy, each of us can discover that whatever our emotional heritage, happiness is something attainable and under our control.

Source: Swanbrow, D. (1989, July-August). The paradox of happiness. *Psychology Today*, 37–39.

Progress Test 1
Multiple-Choice Questions

Circle your answers to the following questions and check them with the answers on page 276. If your answer is incorrect, read the explanation for why it is incorrect and then consult the appropriate pages of the text (in parentheses following the correct answer).

1. Which of the following is correct regarding the relationship between arousal and performance?
   a. Generally, performance is optimal when arousal is low.
   b. Generally, performance is optimal when arousal is high.
   c. On easy tasks, performance is optimal when arousal is low.
   d. On easy tasks, performance is optimal when arousal is high.

2. Which division of the nervous system is especially involved in bringing about emotional arousal?
   a. somatic nervous system
   b. peripheral nervous system
   c. sympathetic nervous system
   d. parasympathetic nervous system

3. Concerning emotions and their accompanying body responses, which of the following appears to be true?
   a. Each emotion has its own body response and underlying brain activity.
   b. All emotions involve the same body response as a result of the same underlying brain activity.
   c. Many emotions involve similar body responses but have different underlying brain activity.
   d. All emotions have the same underlying brain activity but different body responses.

4. The Cannon-Bard theory of emotion states that:
   a. emotions have two ingredients: physical arousal and a cognitive label.
   b. the conscious experience of an emotion occurs at the same time as the body's physical reaction.
   c. emotional experiences are based on an awareness of body responses to an emotion-arousing stimulus.
   d. emotional ups and downs tend to balance in the long run.

5. Electrical stimulation of which brain region can produce terror or rage in cats?
   a. limbic system   c. cortex
   b. hypothalamus   d. cerebellum

6. The body's response to danger is triggered by the release of _____ by the _____ glands.
   a. acetylcholine; adrenal
   b. epinephrine and norepinephrine; adrenal
   c. acetylcholine; pituitary
   d. epinephrine and norepinephrine; pituitary

7. Which of the following was *not* raised as a criticism of the James-Lange theory of emotion?
   a. Body responses are too similar to trigger the various emotions.
   b. Emotional reactions occur before body responses can take place.
   c. The cognitive activity of the cortex plays a role in the emotions we experience.
   d. People with spinal cord injuries at the neck typically experience less emotion.

8. Current estimates are that the polygraph is inaccurate approximately _____ of the time.
   a. three-fourths   c. one-third
   b. one-half   d. one-tenth

9. In the Schachter-Singer experiment, which subjects reported feeling an emotional change in the presence of the experimenter's highly emotional confederate?
   a. those receiving epinephrine and expecting to feel physical arousal
   b. those receiving a placebo and expecting to feel physical arousal
   c. those receiving epinephrine but not expecting to feel physical arousal
   d. those receiving a placebo and not expecting to feel physical arousal

10. Which of the following is true?
    a. People with more education tend to be happier.
    b. Highly intelligent people tend to be happier.
    c. Women tend to be happier than men.
    d. People who are socially outgoing or who exercise regularly tend to be happier.

11. Catharsis will be most effective in reducing anger toward another person if:
    a. you wait until you are no longer angry before confronting the person.
    b. the target of your anger is someone you feel has power over you.
    c. your anger is directed specifically toward the person who angered you.
    d. the other person is able to retaliate by also expressing anger.

12. Emotions are:
    a. physiological reactions.
    b. behavioral expressions.

c. conscious feelings.
d. all of the above.

13. Law enforcement officials sometimes use a lie detector to assess a suspect's responses to details of the crime believed to be known only to the perpetrator. This is known as the:
    a. inductive approach.
    b. deductive approach.
    c. guilty knowledge test.
    d. screening examination.

14. Research on nonverbal communication has revealed that:
    a. it is easy to hide your emotions by controlling your facial expressions.
    b. facial expressions tend to be the same the world over, while gestures vary from culture to culture.
    c. most authentic expressions last between 7 and 10 seconds.
    d. most gestures have universal meanings; facial expressions vary from culture to culture.

15. In laboratory experiments, facial expressions of fear and anger have been found to result in:
    a. an increase in skin temperature.
    b. increases in both skin temperature and heart rate.
    c. strong feelings of fear and anger.
    d. subtly different body reactions.

16. Which of the following is *not* one of the basic dimensions of emotion?
    a. duration   c. pleasantness
    b. intensity   d. specificity

17. Research indicates that a person is most likely to be helpful to others if he or she:
    a. is feeling guilty about something.
    b. is happy.
    c. recently received help from another person.
    d. recently offered help to another person.

18. Darwin believed that:
    a. the expression of emotions helped our ancestors to survive.
    b. all humans express basic emotions using similar facial expressions.
    c. human facial expressions of emotion retain elements of animals' emotional displays.
    d. all of the above are true.

19. Research supporting the opponent-process theory of emotion suggests that:
    a. the price of pleasure is pain.
    b. with repetition a task that arouses fear will become more tolerable.
    c. suffering can pay emotional dividends.
    d. all of the above are true.

20. Evidence that changes in facial expression can directly affect people's feelings and body states has convinced Robert Zajonc that:

    a. the heart is always subject to the mind.

    b. emotional reactions involve deliberate rational thinking.
    c. cognition is not necessary for emotion.
    d. the interpretation of facial expressions is a learned skill.

Matching Items

Match each definition or description with the appropriate term.

Definitions or Descriptions

_____ 1. the tendency to react to changes on the basis of recent experience

_____ 2. we are sad because we cry

_____ 3. emotional release

_____ 4. the tendency to evaluate our situation negatively against that of other people

_____ 5. the reason emotions may balance in the short run

_____ 6. emotions consist of both physical arousal and a cognitive label

_____ 7. an emotion-arousing stimulus triggers cognitive and body responses simultaneously

_____ 8. the division of the nervous system that calms the body following arousal

_____ 9. the division of the nervous system that activates arousal

_____ 10. a device that measures the physiological correlates of emotion

Terms

a. adaptation-level principle
b. opponent-process theory
c. two-factor theory
d. catharsis
e. sympathetic nervous system
f. James-Lange theory
g. polygraph
h. Cannon-Bard theory
i. parasympathetic nervous system
j. relative deprivation principle

Progress Test 2

Progress Test 2 should be completed during a final chapter review. Answer the following questions after you thoroughly understand the correct answers for the Chapter Review and Progress Test 1.

Multiple-Choice Questions

1. Which of the following most accurately describes emotional arousal?

    a. Emotions prepare the body to fight or flee.
    b. Emotions are voluntary reactions to emotion-arousing stimuli.
    c. Because all emotions have the same physiological basis, emotions are primarily psychological events.
    d. All are accurate descriptions.

2. Schachter's two-factor theory emphasizes that emotion involves both:

    a. the sympathetic and parasympathetic divisions of the nervous system.
    b. verbal and nonverbal expression.
    c. physical arousal and a cognitive label.
    d. universal and culture-specific aspects.

3. Dermer found that students who had seen others worse off than themselves felt greater satisfaction with their own lives; this is the principle of:

    a. relative deprivation.
    b. adaptation level.
    c. behavioral contrast.
    d. opponent processes.

4. Which theory of emotion emphasizes the simultaneous experience of body response and emotional feeling?

    a. James-Lange theory
    b. Cannon-Bard theory
    c. two-factor theory
    d. opponent-process theory

5. Izard believes that there are _____ basic emotions.

    a. 3   c. 7
    b. 5   d. 10

6. The polygraph measures:

    a. lying.
    b. brain rhythms.
    c. chemical changes in the body.
    d. physiological indexes of arousal.

7. According to the opponent-process theory, as an emotion is repeatedly experienced:
   a. the primary emotional experience becomes stronger.
   b. the opposing emotional experience becomes weaker.
   c. both a. and b. occur.
   d. the primary emotional experience becomes weaker; the opposing emotional experience becomes stronger.

8. Which of the following is true?
   a. Gestures are universal; facial expressions, culture-specific.
   b. Facial expressions are universal; gestures, culture-specific.
   c. Both gestures and facial expressions are universal.
   d. Both gestures and facial expressions are culture-specific.

9. Which theory of emotion implies that every emotion is associated with a unique physiological reaction?
   a. James-Lange theory
   b. Cannon-Bard theory
   c. two-factor theory
   d. opponent-process theory

10. For which of the following fears do humans appear biologically prepared?
    a. fear of electricity
    b. fear of cliffs
    c. fear of thunder
    d. fear of flying

11. Which of the following was *not* presented in the text as evidence that some emotional reactions involve no deliberate, rational thinking?
    a. Some of the neural pathways involved in emotion are separate from those involved in thinking and memory.
    b. Emotional reactions are sometimes quicker than our interpretations of a situation.
    c. People can develop an emotional preference for visual stimuli to which they have been unknowingly exposed.
    d. Arousal of the sympathetic nervous system will trigger an emotional reaction even when artificially induced by an injection of epinephrine.

12. Concerning the catharsis hypothesis, which of the following is true?
    a. Expressing anger can be temporarily calming if it does not leave one feeling guilty or anxious.
    b. The arousal that accompanies unexpressed anger never dissipates.
    c. Expressing one's anger always calms one down.
    d. Psychologists agree that under no circumstances is catharsis beneficial.

13. In an emergency situation, emotional arousal will result in:
    a. increased rate of respiration.
    b. increased blood sugar.
    c. a slowing of digestion.
    d. all of the above.

14. A relatively high level of arousal would be most likely to facilitate:
    a. remembering the lines of a play.
    b. shooting free throws in basketball.
    c. sprinting 100 meters.
    d. taking a final exam in introductory psychology.

15. Several studies have shown that physical arousal can intensify just about any emotion. For example, when people who have been physically aroused by exercise are insulted, they often misattribute their arousal to the insult. This finding illustrates the importance of:
    a. cognitive labels of arousal in the conscious experience of emotions.
    b. a minimum level of arousal in triggering emotional experiences.
    c. the simultaneous occurrence of physical arousal and cognitive labeling in emotional experience.
    d. all of the above.

16. Psychologist David Lykken is opposed to the use of lie detectors because:
    a. they represent an invasion of privacy and could easily be used for unethical purposes.
    b. there are often serious discrepancies among the various indicators such as perspiration and heart rate.
    c. the polygraph cannot distinguish the various possible causes of arousal.
    d. it is only accurate about 50 percent of the time.

17. Most human fears are:
    a. universal.
    b. biologically determined.
    c. present at birth.
    d. learned.

18. How often do most people become angry?
    a. once a day
    b. several times a week
    c. several times a month
    d. There is no common pattern to anger.

19. Which of these factors have researchers *not* found to correlate with happiness?
    a. a satisfying marriage or other love relationship
    b. high self-esteem
    c. religious faith
    d. intelligence

20. In cultures that emphasize social interdependence:
    a. emotional displays are typically intense.
    b. emotional displays are typically prolonged.
    c. negative emotions are more rarely displayed.
    d. all of the above are true.

True-False Items

Indicate whether each statement is true or false by placing *T* or *F* in the blank next to the item.

_____ 1. For easy tasks, the optimal level of arousal is higher than for difficult tasks.

_____ 2. Men are generally better than women at detecting nonverbal emotional expression.

_____ 3. The sympathetic nervous system triggers physiological arousal during an emotion.

_____ 4. The adrenal glands produce the hormones epinephrine and norepinephrine.

_____ 5. When one imitates an emotional facial expression, the body may experience physiological changes characteristic of that emotion.

_____ 6. Paraplegics who have lost sensation only in their lower bodies experience a considerable decrease in the intensity of their emotions.

_____ 7. Wealthy people tend to be much happier than middle-income people.

_____ 8. Physical arousal can intensify emotion.

_____ 9. All emotions involve conscious thinking.

_____ 10. According to the two-factor theory, emotions are labeled cognitively before physical arousal occurs.

Challenge Test

Answer these questions the day before an exam as a final check on your understanding of the chapter's terms and concepts.

Multiple-Choice Questions

1. You are on your way to school to take a big exam. Suddenly, on noticing that your pulse is racing and that you are sweating, you feel nervous. With which theory of emotion is this experience most consistent?
    a. Cannon-Bard theory
    b. James-Lange theory
    c. opponent-process theory
    d. adaptation-level theory

2. When Professor Simon acquired a spacious new office, he was overjoyed. Six months later, however, he was taking the office for granted. His behavior illustrates the:

    a. relative deprivation principle.
    b. adaptation-level principle.
    c. opponent-process theory.
    d. optimum arousal principle.

3. After Brenda scolded her brother for forgetting to pick her up from school, the physical arousal that had accompanied her anger diminished. Which division of her nervous system mediated her physical *relaxation*?
    a. sympathetic division
    b. parasympathetic division
    c. somatic division
    d. peripheral nervous system

4. Two years ago Maria was in an automobile accident in which her spinal cord was severed, leaving her paralyzed from her neck down. Today, Maria finds that she experiences emotions less intensely than she did before her accident. This tends to support which theory of emotion?
    a. James-Lange theory
    b. Cannon-Bard theory
    c. opponent-process theory
    d. adaptation-level theory

5. The candidate stepped before the hostile audience, panic written all over his face. It is likely that the candidate's facial expression caused him to experience:
    a. a lessening of his fear.
    b. an intensification of his fear.
    c. a surge of digestive enzymes in his body.
    d. increased body temperature.

6. Jane was so mad at her brother that she exploded at him when he entered her room. That she felt less angry afterward is best explained by the principle of:
    a. adaptation level.   c. relative deprivation.
    b. opponent processes.   d. catharsis.

7. After hitting a grand-slam home run, Mike noticed that his heart was pounding. Later that evening, after nearly having a collision while driving on the freeway, Mike again noticed that his heart was pounding. That he interpreted this reaction as fear, rather than as ecstasy, can best be explained by the:
    a. James-Lange theory.
    b. Cannon-Bard theory.
    c. opponent-process theory.
    d. two-factor theory.

8. As part of her job interview, Jan is asked to take a lie-detector test. Jan politely refuses and points out that:
    a. a guilty person can be found innocent by the polygraph.

    b. an innocent person can be found guilty.

    c. a liar can learn to fool a lie-detector test.

    d. all of the above are true.

9. A subject in an experiment concerned with physical responses that accompany emotions reports that her mouth is dry, her heart is racing, and she feels flushed. What emotion is the subject experiencing?

    a. anger

    b. fear

    c. ecstasy

    d. It cannot be determined from the information given.

10. Who will probably be angrier after learning that he or she has received a parking ticket?

    a. Bob, who has just awakened from a nap

    b. Veronica, who has just finished eating a big lunch

    c. Dan, who has just completed a tennis match

    d. It cannot be determined from the information given.

11. Children in New York, Nigeria, and New Zealand smile when they are happy and frown when they are sad. This suggests that:

    a. the Cannon-Bard theory is correct.

    b. some emotional expressions are learned at a very early age.

    c. the two-factor theory is correct.

    d. some facial expressions of emotion are universal and biologically determined.

12. Who is the *least* likely to display negative emotions openly?

    a. Paul, a game warden in Australia

    b. Niles, a stockbroker in Belgium

    c. Deborah, a physicist in Toronto

    d. Yoko, a dentist in Japan

13. Nine-month-old Nicole's left frontal lobe is more active than her right frontal lobe. We can expect that, all other things being equal, Nicole:

    a. may suffer from mild depression for most of her life.

    b. may have trouble "turning off" upsetting feelings later in her life.

    c. may be more cheerful than those with more active right frontal lobes.

    d. may have trouble expressing feelings later in her life.

14. Julio was extremely angry when he came in for a routine EEG of his brain activity. When he later told this to the doctor, she was no longer concerned about the:

    a. increased electrical activity in Julio's right hemisphere.

    b. increased electrical activity in Julio's left hemisphere.

    c. decreased electrical activity in Julio's amygdala.

    d. increased electrical activity in Julio's amygdala.

15. When the scientist electrically stimulated one area of a monkey's brain, the monkey became enraged. When another electrode was activated, the monkey cowered in fear. The electrodes were most likely implanted in the:

    a. pituitary gland.   c. limbic system.

    b. adrenal glands.   d. right hemisphere.

16. As elderly Mr. Hooper crosses the busy intersection, he stumbles and drops the packages he is carrying. Which passerby is most likely to help Mr. Hooper?

    a. Drew, who has been laid off from work for three months

    b. Leon, who is on his way to work

    c. Bonnie, who graduated from college the day before

    d. Nancy, whose father recently passed away

17. Expressing anger can be adaptive when you:

    a. retaliate immediately.

    b. have mentally rehearsed all the reasons for your anger.

    c. count to ten, then blow off steam.

    d. first wait until the anger subsides, then deal with the situation in a civil manner.

18. Cindy was happy with her promotion until she found out that Janice, who has the same amount of experience, receives a higher salary. Cindy's feelings are *best* explained according to the:

    a. adaptation-level phenomenon.

    b. opponent-process theory.

    c. catharsis hypothesis.

    d. principle of relative deprivation.

19. The first time Rosalina used cocaine she enjoyed it. After taking the drug several times a day for several months, she no longer enjoys its effects; she continues to take it, however, in order not to feel shaky and depressed. Which theory best accounts for her behavior?

    a. James-Lange theory

    b. Cannon-Bard theory

    c. opponent-process theory

    d. two-factor theory

20. Margaret has written a children's story that deals with fear, joy, and anger. One theme of the story is that different emotions have different durations. To symbolically represent the three emotions, she asks the illustrator to depict each as an animal, with the animal's size signifying the duration of the emotion it represents. In order, from largest

(longest-lasting) to smallest (briefest), the "emotion animals" should be:

a. fear, anger, joy
b. anger, fear, joy
c. joy, anger, fear
d. fear, joy, anger

Essay Question

Discuss biological and cultural influences on emotions. (Use the space below to list the points you want to make and organize them. Then write the essay on a separate sheet of paper.)

Key Terms

Using your own words, write a brief definition or explanation of each of the following terms.

1. emotion

2. polygraph

3. catharsis

4. adaptation-level phenomenon

5. relative deprivation

6. James-Lange theory

7. Cannon-Bard theory

8. two-factor theory

ANSWERS

GUIDED STUDY

The following guidelines provide the main points that your answers should have touched upon.

1. Emotions involve a mixture of physiological arousal, expressive behavior, and conscious experience. Physiological arousal occurs when the sympathetic nervous system directs the adrenal glands to release epinephrine and norepinephrine. These hormones trigger increased heart rate, blood pressure, and blood sugar levels.

   Our performance on a task is usually best when arousal is moderate. However, the difficulty of the task affects optimum arousal level. A relatively high level of arousal is best on easy or well-learned tasks; a relatively low level of arousal is best on difficult or unrehearsed tasks.

2. The heart rate, blood pressure, and breathing patterns that accompany the different emotions often are *not* different. Scientists increasingly agree, however, that different brain regions and distinct patterns of brain activity underlie different emotions. Limbic stimulation, for example, will trigger rage or terror in an animal. These emotions are also accompanied by different hormone secretions. Negative emotions and positive emotions tend to be accompanied by greater activity in the right and left hemispheres, respectively. Infants and adults with greater activity in their left frontal lobes tend to be more cheerful than those with more active right frontal lobes.

3. The polygraph, or lie detector, measures the physiological responses that accompany emotions. How well it works depends on whether liars become anxious and exhibit detectable physiological arousal. Critics of the use of lie detectors argue that

the tests are inaccurate about one-third of the time because they can't distinguish among anxiety, irritation, and guilt. Thus, they may label the innocent guilty when a question is upsetting. The polygraph may be somewhat more effective in criminal investigations that use the guilty knowledge test, which assesses a subject's response to details of the crime known only to the police and the guilty person.

4. People differ in their abilities to detect nonverbal expressions of emotion; women, for example, tend to be better at it than men. Although there are many cultural variations in the meaning of gestures, facial expressions have universal meaning. Cultures differ in how and how much they use nonverbal expressions, however. In cultures that encourage individuality, emotional displays often are more intense and prolonged than in communal cultures that value interdependence.

   Research demonstrates that facial expressions intensify emotions and also trigger physiological changes in the autonomic nervous system.

5. People from various cultures place emotions along three dimensions: pleasantness, intensity, and duration.

   Fear is an adaptive response that prepares the body to flee from danger, protects us from harm, and constrains us from harming other people. Although most fears are the product of learning, we are biologically prepared to acquire certain fears, such as those that probably helped our ancestors to survive. Biological factors also influence specific emotional tendencies, such as a person's level of fearfulness.

6. The catharsis hypothesis maintains that expressing emotion results in emotional release. Research shows that the cathartic expression of anger is most likely to *temporarily* reduce anger when it is specifically directed against the provoker, when it is justifiable, and when the provoker is not intimidating. Other studies show that openly expressing anger can have the opposite effect and amplify underlying hostility. Angry outbursts may also be habit-forming if they temporarily calm the individual.

   Anger experts recommend that the best way to handle anger is: first, bring down the level of physiological arousal by waiting; then, deal with the anger in a way that involves neither being chronically angry nor passively sulking.

7. People who are happy perceive the world as safer, make decisions more easily, rate job applicants more favorably, report greater satisfaction with their lives, and are more willing to help others. Factors that predict happiness include having high self-esteem, a satisfying love relationship, a mean-

ingful faith, being optimistic and outgoing, sleeping well, exercising, and engaging in challenging work and leisure activities.

   The effect of dramatically positive or negative events on happiness is typically temporary. Happiness is also relative to our recent experiences (adaptation-level phenomenon) and to how we compare ourselves with others (relative deprivation principle). These principles help explain why middle- and upper-income people in a given country tend to be slightly more satisfied with life than the relatively poor, even though happiness does not directly increase with affluence.

8. (Close-Up) According to the opponent-process theory, every emotion triggers an opposing emotion that causes our emotions to balance. Repetitions of the event that arouses the primary emotion strengthen the opposing emotion and weaken the experience of the primary emotion, explaining why with repetition the afterreaction, such as the pain of drug withdrawal, becomes stronger.

9. According to the James-Lange theory, the experience of emotion results from awareness of the physiological responses to emotion-arousing stimuli. According to the Cannon-Bard theory, an emotion-arousing stimulus is simultaneously routed to the cortex, which causes the subjective experience of emotion, and to the sympathetic nervous system, which causes the body's physiological arousal.

   In criticizing the James-Lange theory, Walter Cannon argued that the body's responses were not sufficiently distinct to trigger the different emotions. The James-Lange theory has recently received support from evidence showing that there *are* physiological distinctions among the emotions and that emotions are diminished when the brain's awareness of body reactions is reduced. However, many researchers continue to agree with Cannon and Bard that the experience of emotion also involves cognitive activity.

10. Schachter's two-factor theory of emotion proposes that emotions have two components: physical arousal and a cognitive label. Like the James-Lange theory, the two-factor theory presumes that our experience of emotion stems from our awareness of physical arousal. Like the Cannon-Bard theory, the two-factor theory presumes that emotions are physiologically similar and require a conscious interpretation of the arousal.

   Although the more important emotions, such as anger, guilt, happiness, and love, clearly arise from conscious thought, there is evidence that some simple emotional responses may not involve conscious thinking. When people repeatedly view stimuli they are not consciously aware of (subliminal stimuli), for example, they come to prefer those stimuli. Furthermore, some neural pathways involved in emotion, such as the one that links the eye to the amygdala, bypass cortical areas involved in thinking and enable an automatic emotional response.

CHAPTER REVIEW

1. humans
2. physiological arousal, expressive behavior, conscious experience
3. **a.** Heart rate increases.
   b. Muscles become tense.
   c. The liver releases sugar into the bloodstream.
   d. Breathing rate increases.
   e. Digestion slows.
   f. Pupils dilate.
   g. Blood tends to clot more rapidly.
4. sympathetic; adrenal; adrenaline (epinephrine); noradrenaline (norepinephrine)
5. parasympathetic

Performance on a task is usually best when arousal is moderate. However, the difficulty of the task affects optimum arousal level. A relatively high level of arousal is best on easy tasks; a relatively low level of arousal is best on difficult tasks.

6. similar
7. believe; right; left
8. left; frontal
9. fear; anger; finger; hormone
10. are
11. polygraph

The polygraph measures several of the physiological responses that accompany emotion, such as changes in breathing, pulse rate, blood pressure, and perspiration. The assumption is that lying is stressful, so a person who is lying will become physiologically aroused.

12. anxiety
13. innocent; emotions; arousal
14. do not agree
15. guilty knowledge test; integrity
16. nonverbal
17. threats
18. better
19. facial muscles
20. different
21. the same; does not vary
22. Darwin

23. individuality; interdependence; sympathy; respect; shame; West
24. intensified
25. found
26. physiological
27. leads
28. pleasantness; intensity; duration
29. 10; are
30. adaptive
31. learning (conditioning); observing

The fact that humans quickly learn and slowly unlearn to fear snakes, spiders, and cliffs — fears that were presumably very useful to our ancestors — suggests that these are biologically predisposed fears that develop with little or no learning.

32. significantly
33. week
34. individuality; catharsis; interdependence; Tahiti; Japan
35. **a.** Retaliation must be directed against the person who provoked the anger.
    b. Retaliation must be justifiable.
    c. The target of the relation must not be someone who is intimidating.

One problem with expressing anger is that it breeds more anger, in part because it may trigger retaliation. Expressing anger can also magnify anger and reinforce its occurrence.

36. **a.** Wait to calm down.
    b. Deal with anger in a civil way that promotes reconciliation rather than retaliation.
37. happy
38. regain
39. do not; remained unchanged
40. adaptation-level

If we acquire new possessions, we feel an initial surge of pleasure. But we then adapt to having these new possessions, come to see them as normal, and require other things to give us another surge of happiness.

41. opponent-process; after; weaker; stronger
42. relative deprivation
43. high self-esteem; satisfying marriage or other love relationship; meaningful religious faith; outgoing personality; good sleeping habits; regular exercise; employment
44. age; race; gender; education; intelligence; parenthood
45. challenging tasks; leisure activities
46. follow

Cannon argued that the body's responses were not sufficiently distinct to trigger the various different emotions and, furthermore, that physiological changes occur too slowly to trigger sudden emotion.

47. cortex; sympathetic; Cannon-Bard

48. diminish; James-Lange

49. physiological; cognitive; Schachter

50. did not; did

51. can

First, experiments on subliminal perception indicate that although shapes or sounds are not consciously perceived, subjects later prefer these shapes or sounds to others they have never been exposed to. Second, there is some separation of the neural pathways involved in emotion and cognition.

52. Lazarus

It seems that some emotional responses—especially simple likes, dislikes, and fears—involve no conscious thinking. Other emotions are greatly affected by our interpretations, memories, and expectations.

PROGRESS TEST 1

Multiple-Choice Questions

1. d. is the answer. Generally speaking, performance is optimal when arousal is moderate; for easy tasks, however, performance is optimal when arousal is high. For difficult tasks, performance is optimal when arousal is low. (pp. 384–385)

2. c. is the answer. (p. 384)

a. The somatic division of the peripheral nervous system carries sensory and motor signals to and from the CNS.

b. The peripheral nervous system is too general an answer, since it includes the sympathetic and parasympathetic divisions, as well as the somatic division.

d. The parasympathetic nervous system restores the body to its unaroused state.

3. c. is the answer. Although many emotions have the same general body arousal, resulting from activation of the sympathetic nervous system, they appear to be associated with different brain regions and different patterns of brain activity. (pp. 385–386)

4. b. is the answer. (p. 403)

a. This expresses the two-factor theory.

c. This expresses the James-Lange theory.

d. This expresses the opponent-process theory.

5. a. is the answer. (p. 385)

b. The hypothalamus is involved in eating, thirst, and sexual motivation.

c. The cortex is the center of higher cognitive functions, such as memory and thinking.

d. The cerebellum is involved in motor coordination.

6. b. is the answer. (p. 384)

a. & c. Acetylcholine, a neurotransmitter involved in motor responses, is not a hormone and therefore is not secreted by a gland.

7. d. is the answer. The finding that people whose brains can't sense body responses experience considerably less emotion in fact supports the James-Lange theory, which claims that experienced emotion follows from body responses. (p. 403)

a., b., & c. All these statements go counter to the theory's claim that experienced emotion is essentially just an awareness of a body response.

8. c. is the answer. (p. 387)

9. c. is the answer. Subjects who received epinephrine without an explanation felt arousal and, moreover, experienced this arousal as whatever emotion the experimental confederate in the room with them was displaying. (p. 404)

a. Epinephrine recipients who expected arousal attributed their arousal to the drug and reported no emotional change in reaction to the confederate's behavior.

b. & d. In addition to the two groups discussed in the text, the experiment involved placebo recipients; these subjects were not physically aroused and did not experience an emotional change.

10. d. is the answer. Education level, intelligence, and gender seem unrelated to happiness. (p. 402)

11. c. is the answer. (p. 395)

a. This would not be an example of catharsis, since catharsis involves releasing, rather than suppressing, aggressive energy.

b. Expressions of anger in such a situation tend to cause the person anxiety and thus tend not to be effective.

d. One of the dangers of expressing anger is that it will lead to retaliation and an escalation of anger.

12. d. is the answer. These are the three components of emotions identified in the textbook. (p. 383)

13. c. is the answer. If the suspect becomes physically aroused while answering questions about details only the perpetrator of the crime could know, it is presumed that he or she committed the crime. (p. 387)

14. b. is the answer. (pp. 389–390)

a. The opposite is true; relevant facial muscles are hard to control voluntarily.

c. Authentic facial expressions tend to fade within 5 seconds.

d. Facial expressions are generally universal; many gestures vary from culture to culture.

15. **d.** is the answer. Facial expressions of fear were associated with increased heart rate only, facial expressions of anger with increases in both heart rate and finger temperature. (p. 392)

a. & b. Skin temperature increases were associated only with expressions of anger.

c. Such feelings did not occur.

16. **d.** is the answer. (p. 392)

17. **b.** is the answer. (p. 396)

a., c., & d. Research studies have not found these factors to be related to altruistic behavior.

18. **d.** is the answer. (p. 391)

19. **d.** is the answer. According to the theory, with repeated stimulations the primary emotion becomes weaker and the opponent emotion becomes stronger. (p. 400)

20. **c.** is the answer. (p. 405)

a. & b. These answers imply that cognition *always* precedes emotion.

d. That changes in facial expression can directly affect people's feelings and body states does not imply a learned ability to interpret facial expressions. In fact, facial expressions apparently speak a universal language, which implies that the ability to interpret them is inborn.

Matching Items

1. a (p. 398)
2. f (p. 402)
3. d (p. 395)
4. j (p. 401)
5. b (p. 400)
6. c (p. 404)
7. h (p. 403)
8. i (p. 384)
9. e (p. 384)
10. g (p. 386)

PROGRESS 2

Multiple-Choice Questions

1. **a.** is the answer. Emotional arousal activates the sympathetic nervous system, causing the release of sugar into the blood for energy, pupil dilation, and the diverting of blood from the internal organs to the muscles, all of which help prepare the body to meet an emergency. (p. 384)

b. Being autonomic responses, most emotions are *involuntary* reactions.

c. All emotions do *not* have the same physiological basis.

2. **c.** is the answer. According to Schachter, the two factors in emotion are (1) body arousal and (2) conscious interpretation of the arousal. (p. 404)

3. **a.** is the answer. The principle of relative deprivation states that happiness is relative to others' attainments. This helps explain why those who are relatively well off tend to be slightly more satisfied than the relatively poor, with whom the better-off can compare themselves. (p. 401)

b. Adaptation level is the tendency for our judgments to be relative to our prior experience.

c. This phenomenon has nothing to do with the interpretation of emotion.

d. Opponent processes are opposing emotional states that tend to balance each other.

4. **b.** is the answer. (p. 403)

a. The James-Lange theory states that the experience of an emotion is an awareness of one's physical response to an emotion-arousing stimulus.

c. The two-factor theory states that to experience emotion one must be physically aroused and attribute the arousal to an emotional cause.

d. The opponent-process theory states that every emotion tends to trigger an opposing emotion.

5. **d.** is the answer. (pp. 392–393)

6. **d.** is the answer. No device can literally measure lying. The polygraph measures breathing, pulse rate, blood pressure, and perspiration for changes indicative of physiological arousal. (p. 386)

7. **d.** is the answer. (p. 400)

8. **b.** is the answer. Whereas the meanings of gestures vary from culture to culture, facial expressions seem to have the same meanings around the world. (p. 390)

9. **a.** is the answer. If, as the theory claims, emotions are triggered by physiological reactions, then each emotion must be associated with a unique physiological reaction. (pp. 402–403)

b. According to the Cannon-Bard theory, the same general body response accompanies many emotions.

c. The two-factor theory states that the cognitive interpretation of a general state of physical arousal determines different emotions.

d. The opponent-process theory states that every emotion triggers its opposite emotion.

10. **b.** is the answer. The fears for which humans seem biologically prepared are fears that probably were useful to our ancestors. (p. 394)

11. **d.** is the answer. As the Schachter-Singer study indicated, physical arousal is not always accompanied by an emotional reaction. Only when arousal was attributed to an emotion was it experienced as such. The results of this experiment, therefore, support the viewpoint that conscious interpretation of arousal must precede emotion. (p. 404)

a., b., & c. Each of these was presented as a supporting argument in the text.

12. **a.** is the answer. (pp. 395–396)

b. In fact, the opposite is true. Any emotional arousal will simmer down if you wait long enough.

c. Catharsis often magnifies anger, escalates arguments, and leads to retaliation.

d. When counterattack is justified and can be directed at the offender, catharsis may be helpful.

13. **d.** is the answer. (p. 394)

14. **c.** is the answer. Easy or well-rehearsed tasks, such as sprinting, are best performed when arousal is high; more difficult tasks are best performed when arousal is lower. (pp. 384–385)

15. **a.** is the answer. That physical arousal can be misattributed demonstrates that it is the cognitive interpretation of arousal, rather than the intensity or specific nature of the body's arousal, that determines the conscious experience of emotions. (pp. 404–405)

b. & c. The findings of these studies do not indicate that a minimum level of arousal is necessary for an emotional experience nor that applying a cognitive label must be simultaneous with the arousal.

16. **c.** is the answer. As heightened arousal may reflect feelings of anxiety or irritation rather than of guilt, the polygraph, which simply measures arousal, may easily err. (p. 387)

a. Misuse and invasion of privacy are valid issues, but Lykken primarily objects to use of lie detectors because of their inaccuracy.

b. Although there are discrepancies on the various measures of arousal, this was not what Lykken objected to.

d. The lie detector errs about one-third of the time.

17. **d.** is the answer. (pp. 393–394)

a. Because most fears are acquired through learning, people acquire highly individual fears.

b. & c. Only a few basic fears are biologically determined and present at birth.

18. **b.** is the answer. (p. 395)

19. **d.** is the answer. (p. 402)

20. **c.** is the answer. (p. 391)

a. & b. These are true of cultures that emphasize individuality rather than interdependence.

True-False Items

1. True (pp. 384–385)
2. False (p. 389)
3. True (p. 384)
4. True (p. 384)
5. True (pp. 391–392)
6. False (p. 403)
7. False (pp. 397, 401)
8. True (p. 404)
9. False (p. 406)
10. False (p. 404)

CHALLENGE TEST

1. **b.** is the answer. The James-Lange theory proposes that the experienced emotion is an awareness of a prior body response: Your pulse races, and so you feel nervous. (p. 402)

a. According to the Cannon-Bard theory, your body's reaction would occur simultaneously with, rather than before, your experience of the emotion.

c. The opponent-process theory states that each time an emotion occurs, an opposing emotion is triggered as well.

d. The adaptation-level principle concerns our tendency to judge stimuli on the basis of recent experience.

2. **b.** is the answer. Professor Simon's judgment of his office is affected by his recent experience: When that experience was of a smaller office, his new office seemed terrific; now, however, it is commonplace. (p. 398)

a. Relative deprivation is the sense that one is better or worse off than those with whom one compares oneself.

c. This is the theory that every emotion triggers an opposing emotion.

d. This is the principle that there is an inverse relationship between the difficulty of a task and the optimum level of arousal.

3. **b.** is the answer. The parasympathetic division is involved in calming arousal. (p. 384)

a. The sympathetic division is active during states of arousal and hence would *not* be active in the situation described.

c. The somatic division is involved in transmitting sensory information and controlling skeletal muscles; it is not involved in arousing and calming the body.

d. This answer is too general, since the peripheral nervous system includes not only the parasympathetic division but also the sympathetic division and the somatic division.

4. **a.** is the answer. According to the James-Lange theory, Maria's emotions should be greatly diminished since her brain is unable to sense physical arousal. (p. 403)

b. Cannon and Bard would have expected Maria to experience emotions normally because they believed that the experiencing of emotions occurs separately from the body's responses.

c. & d. The opponent-process theory and adaptation-level principle make no particular prediction regarding the importance of physical arousal in the conscious experience of emotion.

5. **b.** is the answer. Expressions may amplify the associated emotions. (p. 392)

a. Laboratory studies have shown that facial expressions intensify emotions.

c. Arousal of the sympathetic nervous system, such as occurs when one is afraid, slows digestive function.

d. Increased body temperature accompanies anger but not fear.

6. **d.** is the answer. In keeping with the catharsis hypothesis, Jane feels less angry after releasing her aggression. (p. 395)

a. Adaptation level is our tendency to judge things relative to our experiences.

b. The opponent-process theory states that every emotion triggers its opposing emotion and that, with repeated stimulation, the former becomes weaker and the latter stronger.

c. Relative deprivation is the sense that one is better or worse off relative to those with whom one compares oneself.

7. **d.** is the answer. According to the two-factor theory, it is cognitive interpretation of the same general physiological arousal that distinguishes the two emotions. (pp. 404–405)

a. According to the James-Lange theory, if the same physical arousal occurred in the two instances, the same emotions should result.

b. The Cannon-Bard theory argues that conscious awareness of an emotion and body reaction occur at the same time.

c. The opponent-process theory, which states that every emotion triggers an opposing emotion, has no particular relevance to the example.

8. **d.** is the answer. (p. 387)

9. **d.** is the answer. (pp. 385–386)

10. **c.** is the answer. Because physical arousal tends to intensify emotions, Dan (who is likely to be physically aroused after playing tennis) will probably be angrier than Bob or Veronica, who are in more relaxed states. (pp. 404–405)

11. **d.** is the answer. (pp. 390–391)

a. & c. The Cannon-Bard and two-factor theories of emotion do not address the universality of emotional expressions.

b. Even if it is true that emotional expressions are acquired at an early age, this would not necessarily account for the common facial expressions of children from around the world. If anything, the different cultural experiences of the children might lead them to express their feelings in very *different* ways.

12. **d.** is the answer. In Asian and Third World cultures that emphasize human connections and interdependence, negative emotional displays are rare and typically brief. (p. 391)

a., b., & c. In cultures that encourage individuality, as in Western Europe, Australia, and North America, emotional displays often are intense and prolonged.

13. **c.** is the answer. (p. 385)

a. Individuals with more active right frontal lobes tend to be less cheerful and are more likely to be depressed.

b. In fact, just the opposite is true: People with greater left frontal activity tend to be better able to turn off upsetting feelings.

d. The text does not suggest that greater left or right frontal activity influences a person's ability to express his or her feelings.

14. **a.** is the answer. As people experience negative emotions, such as anger, the right hemisphere becomes more electrically active. (p. 385)

c. & d. The EEG measures electrical activity on the surface of the cortex, not at the level of structures deep within the brain, such as the amygdala.

15. **c.** is the answer. (p. 385)

a., b., & d. Direct stimulation of these brain areas will not trigger fear or rage.

16. **c.** is the answer. People who are in a good mood are more likely to help others. Bonnie, who is probably pleased with herself following her graduation from college, is likely to be in a better mood than Drew, Leon, or Nancy. (p. 396)

17. **d.** is the answer. (pp. 395–396)

a. Venting anger immediately may lead you to say things you later regret and/or may lead to retaliation by the other person.

b. Going over the reasons for your anger merely prolongs the emotion.

c. Counting to ten may give you a chance to calm down, but "blowing off steam" may rekindle your anger.

18. **d.** is the answer. Cindy is unhappy with her promotion because she feels deprived relative to Janice. (p. 401)

a. The adaptation-level phenomenon would predict that Cindy's raise would cause an increase in her happiness, since her most recent experience was to earn a lower salary.

b. The opponent-process theory states that every emotion triggers an opposing emotion that lingers after the first emotion is extinguished. Cindy's mood change, however, is the result of comparing herself to Janice, not the extinction of her pleasure at being promoted.

c. The catharsis hypothesis maintains that venting one's anger may relieve aggressive urges.

19. **c.** is the answer. (p. 400)

a., b., & d. The James-Lange, Cannon-Bard, and two-factor theories of emotion do not address situations such as Rosalina's, in which conflicting emotions are experienced.

20. **c.** is the answer. (p. 392)

Essay Question

All emotions involve some degree of physiological arousal of the sympathetic nervous system. Although the arousal that occurs with different emotions is in most ways undifferentiated, there may be subtle differences in the brain pathways and hormones associated with different emotions.

Other examples of the influence of biological factors on emotion are the universality of facial expressions of emotion and the fact that humans seem biologically predisposed to learn some fears more quickly than others.

Unlike facial expressions of emotion, the meaning of many gestures is culturally determined. Culture also influences how people express their feelings. In cultures that encourage individuality, for example, emotional displays often are intense and prolonged. In cultures that emphasize human interdependence, negative emotions that might disrupt group harmony are rarely expressed, while "other-sensitive" emotions such as sympathy, respect, and shame are more common than in the West.

KEY TERMS

1. **Emotion** is a response of the whole organism involving three components: (1) physical arousal, (2) expressive reactions, and (3) conscious experience. (p. 383)

2. The **polygraph**, or lie detector, is a device that measures physical arousal of the sympathetic nervous system. (p. 386)

3. **Catharsis** is emotional release; according to the catharsis hypothesis, by expressing our anger, we can reduce it. (p. 395)

4. The **adaptation-level phenomenon** refers to our tendency to judge things relative to our prior experience. (p. 398)

5. The principle of **relative deprivation** states that we judge our situation in relation to what we perceive other people's situations to be. (p. 401)

Example: The concept of **relative deprivation** helps explain why the relatively well-off tend to be somewhat more satisfied with life than the relatively poor.

6. The **James-Lange theory** states that emotional experiences are based on an awareness of body responses to emotion-arousing stimuli: a stimulus triggers body responses that in turn trigger the experienced emotion. (p. 402)

7. The **Cannon-Bard theory** states that the conscious experience of an emotion occurs at the same time as the body's physical reaction. (pp. 402–403)

8. The **two-factor theory** of emotion proposes that emotions have two ingredients: physical arousal and a cognitive label. Thus, physical arousal is a necessary, but not a sufficient, component of emotional change. For an emotion to be experienced, arousal must be attributed to an emotional cause. (p. 404)

14 / Personality

Chapter Overview

Personality refers to each individual's relatively distinctive and consistent pattern of thinking, feeling, and acting. Chapter 14 examines four perspectives on personality. The psychoanalytic theory emphasizes the unconscious and irrational aspects of personality. The trait theory led to advances in techniques for evaluating and describing personality. The humanistic theory draws attention to the concept of self and to human potential for healthy growth. The social-cognitive perspective emphasizes the effects of our interactions with the environment. The text first describes and then evaluates the contributions and shortcomings of each perspective.

NOTE: Answer guidelines for all Chapter 14 questions begin on page 297.

Guided Study

The text chapter should be studied one section at a time. Before you read, preview each section by skimming it, noting headings and boldface items. Then read the appropriate section objectives from the following outline. Keep these objectives in mind and, as you read the chapter section, search for the information that will enable you to meet each objective. Once you have finished a section, write out answers for its objectives.

The Psychoanalytic Perspective (pp. 412–421)

1. Describe how Freud's search for the psychological roots of nervous disorders led to his study of the unconscious and explain psychoanalysis.

2. Describe Freud's views of personality structure.

   Freud - psychoanalytic theory emphasizes childhood sexuality & unconscious motivations as possible causes of personality.

3. Outline and describe Freud's psychosexual stages of personality development.

   Oral (0-18 mo.) - pleasure centers on mouth.
   Anal - (18-3 emos.) - focus on bowel/bladder elimination; coping w/ demands for control.
   Phallic - (3-6 years) pleasure zone is genitals; coping w/ incestuous sexual feelings
   Latency (6 to pub) - repressed sexual "

   Genital (pub →) maturation or sexual interests

4. Explain Freud's view of maladaptive behavior and describe how defense mechanisms operate.

5. Discuss the major ideas of the neo-Freudians.

6. Explain how projective tests are used to assess personality and describe research findings regarding their validity and reliability.

7. Evaluate the psychoanalytic perspective.

The Trait Perspective (pp. 421–427)

8. Discuss trait theories of personality and trace their history.

9. Identify the "big five" personality factors and describe the assessment techniques associated with the trait perspective.

10. Evaluate the trait perspective on personality and describe research findings regarding the consistency of behavior over time and across situations.

The Humanistic Perspective (pp. 428–434)

11. Describe the humanistic perspective on personality and discuss the basic ideas of Maslow and Rogers.

12. Describe recent research on the way people view themselves.

13. Evaluate the humanistic perspective.

The Social-Cognitive Perspective (pp. 434–439)

14. Describe the social-cognitive perspective and define reciprocal determinism, giving three examples.

15. Discuss research findings on personal control.

16. Describe how social-cognitive researchers study behavior and evaluate this perspective on personality.

Chapter Review

When you have finished reading the chapter, work through the material that follows to review it. Complete the sentences and answer the questions. As you proceed, evaluate your performance for each section by consulting the answers on page 299. Do not continue with the next section until you understand each answer. If you need to, review or reread the appropriate section in the textbook before continuing.

1. An individual's characteristic pattern of _thinking_, _feeling_, and _acting_ constitute that individual's _personality_.

2. The four major perspectives on personality discussed in this chapter are the _psychoanalytic_ _trait_, _humanistic_, and _social-cognitive_ theories.

The Psychoanalytic Perspective (pp. 412–421)

3. The psychoanalytic perspective on personality was proposed by _Sigmund Freud_.

4. The technique used by Freud, in which the patient relaxes and says whatever comes to mind, is called _free association_.

5. Freud called his treatment technique, which exposes painful unconscious memories, _psychoanalysis_.

6. According to this theory, the mind is like an iceberg in that many of a person's thoughts, wishes, and feelings are hidden in a large _unconscious_ region. Some of the thoughts in this region can be retrieved at will into consciousness; these thoughts are said to be

preconscious. Many of the memories of this region, however, are blocked, or _repressed_, from consciousness.

7. Freud believed that a person's _unconscious_ wishes are often reflected in his or her dreams and _slip_ of the tongue. Freud called the remembered content of dreams the _manifest_ _content_, which he believed to be a censored version of the dream's true _latent_ _content_.

8. Freud believed that all facets of personality arise from conflict between our _aggressive, pleasure-seeking_ impulses and the _social_ restraints _biological_ against them.

9. According to Freud, personality consists of three structures: the _id_, the _ego_, and the _superego_.

10. The id is a reservoir of energy that is primarily _unconscious_ (conscious/unconscious) and operates according to the _pleasure_ principle.

11. The ego develops _after_ (before/after) the id and consists of perceptions, thoughts, and memories that are mostly _conscious_ (conscious/unconscious). The ego operates according to the _reality_ principle.

Explain why the ego is considered the "executive" of personality.

12. The personality structure that reflects moral values is the _superego_.

13. A person with a _weak_ (strong/weak) superego may be self-indulgent; one with an unusually _strong_ (strong/weak) superego may be continually guilt-ridden.

14. According to Freud, personality is formed as the child passes through a series of _psychosexual_ stages.

15. The first stage is the _oral_ stage, which takes place during the first 18 months of life. During this stage, the id's energies are focused on behaviors such as _sucking_.

16. The second stage is the _anal_ stage, which lasts from about age _18_ months to _3_ years.

17. The third stage is the _phalic_ stage, which lasts roughly from ages _3_ to _6_. During this stage the id's energies are focused on the _genitals_. Freud also believed that during this stage children develop sexual desires for the _opposite_ (same/opposite)-sex parent. Freud referred to these feelings as the _Oedipus complex_ in boys. Some psychologists believe that girls experience a parallel _Electra complex_.

18. Freud believed that _identification_ with the same-sex parent is the basis for _gender identity_.

Explain how this complex of feelings is resolved through the process of identification.

19. During the next stage, sexual feelings are repressed; this phase is called the _latency_ period and lasts until adolescence.

20. The final stage of development is called the _genital_ stage.

21. According to Freud, it is possible for a person's development to become blocked in any of the stages; in such an instance, the person is said to be ~~repressed~~ _fixated_

22. The ego attempts to protect itself against anxiety through the use of _~~reaction~~ defense ~~formation~~ mec!_ The process underlying each of these mechanisms is _repression_.

23. Dealing with anxiety by returning to an earlier stage of development is called _regression_.

24. When a person reacts in a manner opposite that of his or her true feelings, _reaction formation_ is said to have occurred.

25. When a person attributes his or her own feelings to another person, _projection_ has occurred.

26. When a person offers a false, self-justifying explanation for his or her actions, _rationalization_ has occurred.

27. When impulses are directed toward an object other than the one that caused arousal, _displacement_ has occurred.

28. When unacceptable impulses are channeled into socially acceptable activities, _sublimation_ has occurred.

Matching Items

Match each defense mechanism in the following list with the proper example of its manifestation.

Defense Mechanisms

f c   **1.** displacement
e f   **2.** projection
c e   **3.** reaction formation
_____ d   **4.** rationalization
_____ a   **5.** regression
_____ b   **6.** sublimation

Manifestations

a. nail biting or thumb sucking in an anxiety-producing situation
b. artistic achievements through which unacceptable urges may somehow be expressed
c. over-zealous crusaders against "immoral behaviors," who don't want to acknowledge their own sexual desires
d. saying you drink "just to be sociable" when in reality you have a drinking problem
e. thinking someone hates you when in reality you hate that person
f. a child who is angry at his parents and vents this anger on the family pet, a less threatening target

29. Defense mechanisms are _unconscious_ (conscious/unconscious) processes.

30. The theorists who established their own, modified versions of psychoanalytic theory are called _neo_-_freudians_. These theorists typically place _more_ (more/less) emphasis on the conscious mind than Freud did and _less_ (more/less) emphasis on sex and aggression.

Briefly summarize how each of the following theorists departed from Freud.

a. Adler and Horney _more on social._

b. Fromm _____

c. Erikson _lifelong psychosocial._

d. Jung _collective unconscious_

31. Tests that provide subjects with ambiguous stimuli for interpretation are called _projective_ tests.

32. Henry Murray introduced the personality assessment technique called the _Thematic Apperception_ Test.

33. The most widely used projective test is the _Rorschach_, in which subjects are

shown a series of _ink blots_. Generally, these tests appear to have _little_ (little/significant) validity.

34. Contrary to Freud's theory, research indicates that human development is _lifelong_ (fixed in childhood/lifelong), children gain their gender-identity at a(n) _earlier_ (earlier/later) age, and the presence of a same-sex parent _is not_ (is/is not) necessary for the child to become strongly masculine or feminine.

35. Recent researchers primarily perceive the unconscious not as the site of instinctual urges, but as where _information_ is processed without awareness.

Give several examples of Freudian ideas that are *not* widely accepted by contemporary psychologists.

36. Criticism of psychoanalysis as a scientific theory centers on the fact that it provides after-the-fact explanations and does not offer _testable_ _hypothesis_.

The Trait Perspective (pp. 421–427)

37. Gordon Allport developed trait theory, which defines personality in terms of people's characteristic __behaviors__ and conscious __motives__.

38. Trait theorists are generally less interested in __explaining__ individual traits than they are in __describing__ them.

39. The ancient Greeks classified people according to four types: __melancholic__, or depressed; __sanguine__, or cheerful; __phlegmatic__, or unemotional; and __choleric__, or irritable.

40. Sheldon identified three body types: the jolly __endomorph__ type, the bold __mesomorph__ type, and the high-strung __ectomorph__ type.

41. The widely used __Myers__-__Briggs__ __Type__ __Indicator__ classifies people according to Carl Jung's personality types.

42. The Eysencks argue that two personality dimensions are sufficient: __extrovert__-__introvert__ and emotional __stable__-__unstable__.

43. More recently, researchers have arrived at a cluster of five factors that seem to describe the major features of personality. List and briefly describe the "Big Five."
    a. __Emotional Stability__
    b. __Extroversion__
    c. __Openness__
    d. __Agreeableness__
    e. __Conscientiousness__

44. Questionnaires that categorize personality traits are called __personality__ __inventories__. The most widely used of all such personality tests is the __Minnesota__ __Multiphasic__ __Personality__ __Inventory__. This test was developed by testing a large pool of items and selecting those that differentiated particular individuals; in other words, the test was __empirically__ derived.

45. Human behavior is influenced both by our inner __traits__ and by the external __situation__.

46. To be considered a personality trait a characteristic must persist over __time__ and across __situations__.

47. Research on children's propensity to cheat, for example, indicates that people's behavior on different occasions is generally quite __variable__. (variable/consistent).

48. An individual's score on a personality test __is not__ (is/is not) very predictive of his or her behavior in any given situation.

Write a sentence defending trait theory against the criticism that people seem not to have clear, consistent personalities.

The Humanistic Perspective (pp. 428–434)

49. Two influential theories of humanistic psychology were proposed by __Maslow__ and __Rogers__.

50. According to Maslow, humans are motivated by needs that are organized into a __hierarchy__. Maslow refers to the process of fulfilling one's potential as __self__-__actualization__.

List some of the characteristics Maslow associated with those who fulfilled their potential.

51. According to Rogers, a person nurtures growth in a relationship by being __accepting__, __genuine__, and __empathetic__. People who are accepting of others offer them

unconditional positive regard.

52. For both Maslow and Rogers, an important feature of personality is how an individual perceives himself or herself; this is the person's self-concept.

53. Since the 1940s, research on the self has greatly increased (increased/decreased).

54. Hazel Markus and colleagues introduced the concept of an individual's possible selves to emphasize how our aspirations motivate us through specific goals.

55. According to the humanists, personality development hinges on our feelings of self-worth, or self-esteem. People who feel good about themselves are relatively independent (dependent on/independent of) outside pressures, while people who fall short of their ideals are more prone to anxiety and depression.

56. In a series of experiments, researchers found that people who were made to feel insecure were more (more/less) critical of other persons.

57. Research has shown that most people tend to have high (low/high) self-esteem.

58. The tendency of people to judge themselves favorably is called the self-serving bias.

State three criticisms that have been made of humanistic psychology.

59. Responsibility for success is generally accepted more (more/less) readily than responsibility for failure.

60. Most people perceive their own behavior and

traits as being above (above/below) average.

The Social-Cognitive Perspective (pp. 434–439)

61. Social-cognitive theorists focus on how the individual and the environment interact. One such theorist is Bandura.

62. Social-cognitive theorists propose that personality is shaped by the mutual influence of our behaviors, personal/cognitive factors, and environmental factors. This is the principle of reciprocal determinism.

Describe three different ways in which the environment and personality interact.

63. Individuals who believe that they control their own destinies are said to perceive an internal locus of control. Individuals who believe that their fate is determined by outside forces are said to perceive an external locus of control.

64. Seligman found that exposure to inescapable punishment produced a passive resignation in behavior, which he called learned helplessness.

65. People become happier when they are given more (more/less) control over what happens to them.

66. One measure of a person's feelings of effectiveness is their degree of optimism.

Describe two criticisms that have been made of the social-cognitive perspective.

67. List the major contributions of each perspective to our understanding of personality.

a. Psychoanalytic _____

_____

b. Trait _____

_____

c. Humanistic _____

_____

d. Social-Cognitive _____

_____

FOCUS ON PSYCHOLOGY:
Personality Over the Life Span

Do personalities change significantly over the life span? Many people think so, but this may be a result of their tendency to overestimate changes in personality. In one study that supports such a finding, a group of college students rated themselves on several personality traits. Twenty-five years later, they rated themselves again, not only as they saw their current personalities, but also as they thought they had been during college. Only the *original* college rating and the current rating were similar; there was little similarity between how people remembered themselves as having been during college and either their current ratings or their original ratings as college students. These results support the idea that there is an underlying consistency to personality, a consistency that people often underestimate.

In another study, the personality traits of 2000 men, who ranged in age from their 20s to their 90s, were compared several times over a 10-year period. Three personality dimensions remained stable over the course of the longitudinal study: *neuroticism* (the tendency toward feelings of anxiety, worry, and depression); *extraversion* (the tendency to be outgoing, active, and assertive); and *openness* (the tendency to be receptive to new ideas and experiences).

Compared with those who scored low on neuroticism, men who scored high on this dimension consistently tended to complain more about their health, were more likely to be heavy drinkers and smokers, more often reported financial and sexual problems, and were generally dissatisfied with life.

Men who scored high on extraversion were happier, showed stronger signs of well-being, and were more likely to seek out jobs dealing with other people than men who scored low on this dimension. With the exception of a tendency to become less independent with age, the extraverted men also demonstrated stable personality traits throughout adulthood.

Compared with those who scored low on openness, those who scored high on this dimension also tended to score high on aesthetic and theoretical values, had above-average intelligence scores, and were more likely to change jobs, have "eventful" lives, and experience both positive and negative emotions with greater intensity.

Although the stability of personality remains a controversial issue, these results suggest that certain core personality traits remain stable throughout life — unless there are sudden, critical breaks in the continuity of a person's life situation. As developmental psychologist Kathleen Berger notes, "Anxious, neurotic people are likely to be so throughout life. Similarly, the very outgoing college student is likely to be, in middle age, the kind of person who speaks to everyone at work, who spends a lot of time interacting with friends, family members, and neighbors, and who is involved in community activities. . . ."

Berger suggests three reasons for the apparent consistency in personality. First, there is evidence that some aspects of temperament, such as reactivity, emotionality, and sociability, are probably inherited. Second, numerous studies have shown that the experiences of childhood have a long-lasting impact on personality. Growing up in an affectionate and supportive family, for example, seems to foster openness and a tendency toward extraversion. Third, choices made in early adulthood regarding career, marriage, and friends often reinforce already established personality traits.

Sources: Berger, K. S., & Straub, R. O. (1989). Instructor's Resource Manual for use with *The Developing Person Through the Life Span* (2nd ed.). New York: Worth Publishers, Inc., pp. 388–389.

Berger, K. S. (1988). *The Developing Person Through the Life Span* (2nd ed.). New York: Worth Publishers, Inc., pp. 515–517.

McCrae, R. R., & Costa, P. T. (1987). Validation of the five factor model of personality across instruments and observers. *Journal of Personality and Social Psychology, 52*, 81–90.

Progress Test 1

Multiple-Choice Questions

Circle your answers to the following questions and check them with the answers on page 301. If your answer is incorrect, read the explanation for why it is incorrect and then consult the appropriate pages of the text (in parentheses following the correct answer).

1. How is personality defined in your text?
   a. as the set of personal attitudes that characterizes a person
   b. as an individual's characteristic pattern of thinking, feeling, and acting
   c. as a predictable set of responses to environmental stimuli
   d. as an unpredictable set of responses to environmental stimuli

2. Which of the following places the greatest emphasis on the unconscious mind?

   a. the humanistic perspective
   b. the social-cognitive perspective
   c. the trait perspective
   d. the psychoanalytic perspective

3. Which of the following is the correct order of psychosexual stages proposed by Freud?

   a. oral stage; anal stage; phallic stage; latency period; genital stage
   b. anal stage; oral stage; phallic stage; latency period; genital stage
   c. oral stage; anal stage; genital stage; latency period; phallic stage
   d. anal stage; oral stage; genital stage; latency period; phallic stage

4. According to Freud, defense mechanisms are methods of reducing:

   a. anger.   c. anxiety.
   b. fear.   d. lust.

5. Tests that provide ambiguous stimuli the subject must interpret are called:

   a. personality tests.
   b. personality inventories.
   c. subjective scales.
   d. projective tests.

6. Neo-Freudians such as Adler, Fromm, and Erikson believed that:

   a. Freud placed too great an emphasis on the conscious mind.
   b. Freud placed too great an emphasis on sexual and aggressive instincts.
   c. the years of childhood were more important in the formation of personality than Freud had indicated.
   d. Freud's ideas about the id, ego, and superego as personality structures were incorrect.

7. Research on locus of control indicates that internals are _____ than externals.

   a. more dependent
   b. more intelligent
   c. better able to cope with stress
   d. more sociable

8. Which two dimensions of personality have the Eysencks emphasized?

   a. extraversion-introversion and emotional stability-instability
   b. internal-external locus of control and extraversion-introversion
   c. internal-external locus of control and emotional stability-instability
   d. melancholic-phlegmatic and choleric-sanguine

9. With regard to personality, it appears that:

   a. there is little consistency of behavior from one situation to the next and little consistency of traits over the life span.
   b. there is little consistency of behavior from one situation to the next but significant consistency of traits over the life span.
   c. there is significant consistency of behavior from one situation to the next but little consistency of traits over the life span.
   d. there is significant consistency of behavior from one situation to the next and significant consistency of traits over the life span.

10. The humanistic perspective on personality:

    a. emphasizes the driving force of unconscious motivations in personality.
    b. emphasizes the growth potential of "healthy" individuals.
    c. emphasizes the importance of interaction with the environment in shaping personality.
    d. describes personality in terms of scores on various personality scales.

11. According to Rogers, three conditions are necessary to promote growth in personality. These are:

    a. honesty, sincerity, and empathy.
    b. high self-esteem, honesty, and empathy.
    c. genuineness, acceptance, and empathy.
    d. high self-esteem, acceptance, and honesty.

12. Regarding the self-serving bias, humanistic psychologists have emphasized that self-affirming thinking:

    a. is generally maladaptive to the individual because it distorts reality by overinflating self-esteem.
    b. is generally adaptive to the individual because it maintains self-confidence and minimizes depression.
    c. tends to prevent the individual from viewing others with compassion and understanding.
    d. tends not to characterize people who have experienced unconditional positive regard.

13. Which of Freud's ideas would not be accepted by most contemporary psychologists?

    a. Development is essentially fixed in childhood.
    b. Sexuality is a potent drive in humans.
    c. The mind is an iceberg with consciousness being only the tip.
    d. Repression can be the cause of forgetting.

14. The concept of a collective unconscious was developed by:

    a. Freud.   c. Jung.
    b. Fromm.   d. Bandura.

15. Projective tests such as the Rorschach inkblot test have been criticized because:
    a. their scoring system is too rigid and leads to unfair labeling.
    b. they were standardized with unrepresentative samples.
    c. they have low reliability and low validity.
    d. it is easy for people to fake answers in order to appear healthy.

16. A major criticism of trait theory is that it:
    a. places too great an emphasis on early childhood experiences.
    b. overestimates the consistency of behavior in different situations.
    c. underestimates the importance of heredity in personality development.
    d. places too great an emphasis on positive traits.

17. For humanistic psychologists, many of our attitudes and behaviors are ultimately shaped by whether our _____ is _____ or _____.
    a. ego; strong; weak
    b. locus of control; internal; external
    c. personality structure; introverted; extraverted
    d. self-concept; positive; negative

18. In studying personality, a trait theorist would *most likely*:
    a. use a projective test.
    b. observe a person in a variety of situations.
    c. use a personality inventory.
    d. use the method of free association.

19. Id is to ego as _____ is to _____.
    a. reality principle; pleasure principle
    b. pleasure principle; reality principle
    c. conscious forces; unconscious forces
    d. conscience; "personality executive"

20. Which of the following is a major criticism of the social-cognitive perspective?
    a. It focuses too much on early childhood experiences.
    b. It focuses too little on the inner traits of a person.
    c. It provides descriptions but not explanations.
    d. It lacks appropriate assessment techniques.

Matching Items

Match each definition or description with the appropriate term.

Definitions or Descriptions

f _____ 1. redirecting impulses to a less threatening object

j _____ 2. test consisting of a series of inkblots

b _____ 3. the conscious executive of personality

h _____ 4. personality inventory

_____ 5. disguising an impulse by imputing it to another person

d _____ 6. switching an unacceptable impulse into its opposite

a _____ 7. the unconscious repository of instinctual drives

g _____ 8. redirecting impulses into a more socially acceptable channel

c _____ 9. personality structure that corresponds to a person's conscience

e _____ 10. providing self-justifying explanations for an action

i _____ 11. a projective test consisting of a set of ambiguous pictures

Terms

a. id
b. ego
c. superego
d. reaction formation
e. rationalization
f. displacement
g. sublimation
h. projection
i. TAT
j. Rorschach
k. MMPI

Progress Test 2

Progress Test 2 should be completed during a final chapter review. Answer the following questions after you thoroughly understand the correct answers for the Chapter Review and Progress Test 1.

Multiple-Choice Questions

1. Which perspective on personality emphasizes the interaction between the individual and the environment in shaping personality?
   a. psychoanalytic
   b. trait
   c. humanistic
   d. social-cognitive

2. According to Freud's theory, personality arises in response to conflicts between:
   a. our unacceptable urges and our tendency to become self-actualized.
   b. the process of identification and the ego's defense mechanisms.
   c. the collective unconscious and our individual desires.
   d. our biological impulses and the social restraints against them.

3. The _____ classifies people according to Carl Jung's personality types.
   a. Myers-Briggs Type Indicator
   b. MMPI
   c. Locus of Control Scale
   d. Kagan Temperament Scale

4. Seligman has found that humans and animals who are exposed to aversive events they cannot escape may develop:
   a. an internal locus of control.
   b. a reaction formation.
   c. learned helplessness.
   d. neurotic anxiety.

5. Research has shown that individuals who are made to feel insecure are subsequently:
   a. more critical of others.
   b. less critical of others.
   c. more likely to display a self-serving bias.
   d. less likely to display a self-serving bias.

6. An example of the self-serving bias described in the text is the tendency of people to:
   a. see themselves as better than average on nearly any desirable dimension.
   b. accept more responsibility for successes than failures.
   c. be overly critical of other people.
   d. do both a. and b.

7. The Minnesota Multiphasic Personality Inventory (MMPI) is:
   a. a projective personality test.
   b. a personality test that is empirically derived and objective.
   c. a personality test developed mainly to assess job applicants.
   d. a personality test used primarily to assess locus of control.

8. Trait theory attempts to:
   a. show how development of personality is a life-long process.
   b. describe and classify people in terms of their predispositions to behave in certain ways.
   c. determine which traits are most conducive to individual self-actualization.
   d. explain how behavior is shaped by the interaction between traits and the environment.

9. With which of the following statements would a social-cognitive psychologist agree?
   a. People with an internal locus of control achieve more in school.
   b. "Externals" are better able to cope with stress than "internals."
   c. "Internals" are less independent than "externals."
   d. All of the above are true.

10. Which of the following statements about self-esteem is *not* correct?
    a. People with low self-esteem tend to be negative about others.
    b. People with high self-esteem are less prone to drug addiction.
    c. People with low self-esteem tend to be nonconformists.
    d. People with high self-esteem suffer less from insomnia and ulcers.

11. The Oedipus and Electra complexes have their roots in the:
    a. anal stage.
    b. latency stage.
    c. phallic stage.
    d. genital stage.

12. Which of the following is a common criticism of the humanistic perspective?
    a. Its concepts are vague and subjective.
    b. The emphasis on the self encourages selfishness in individuals.
    c. Humanism fails to appreciate the reality of evil in human behavior.
    d. All of the above are common criticisms of humanism.

13. In studying personality, a social-cognitive theorist would *most likely* make use of:
    a. personality inventories.
    b. projective tests.
    c. observations of behavior in different situations.
    d. factor analyses.

14. A major difference between the psychoanalytic and trait perspectives is that:

   a. trait theory defines personality in terms of behavior; psychoanalytic theory, in terms of its underlying dynamics.

   b. trait theory describes behavior but does not attempt to explain it.

   c. psychoanalytic theory emphasizes the origins of personality in childhood sexuality.

   d. All of the above are differences.

15. A statistical technique that can be used to identify clusters of basic personality traits is:

   a. the MMPI.

   b. the personality inventory.

   c. factor analysis.

   d. free association.

16. The "Big Five" personality factors are:

   a. emotional stability, openness, introversion, sociability, locus of control.

   b. neuroticism, extraversion, openness, emotional stability, sensitivity.

   c. neuroticism, gregariousness, extraversion, impulsiveness, conscientiousness.

   d. emotional stability, extraversion, openness, agreeableness, conscientiousness.

17. Which of the following was *not* mentioned in the text as a criticism of Freud's theory?

   a. The theory is sexist.

   b. It offers few testable hypotheses.

   c. There is no evidence of anything like an "unconscious."

   d. The theory ignores the fact that human development is lifelong.

18. According to Freud, _____ is the process by which children incorporate their parents' values into their _____.

   a. reaction formation; superegos

   b. reaction formation; egos

   c. identification; superegos

   d. identification; egos

19. A major criticism common to all four personality perspectives covered in the text is that:

   a. as scientific theory, each falls short.

   b. each overemphasizes the power of social situations.

   c. none is supported by valid research.

   d. each uses objective research to explain subjective behavior.

20. In promoting personality growth, the person-centered perspective emphasizes all but which of the following?

   a. empathy   c. genuineness

   b. acceptance   d. altruism

Matching Items

Match each term with the appropriate definition or description.

Terms

___g___ 1. projective test
___i___ 2. identification
___h___ 3. collective unconscious
___j___ 4. reality principle
___d___ 5. psychosexual stages
___a___ 6. pleasure principle
___k___ 7. psychosocial stages
___f___ 8. reciprocal determinism
___e___ 9. personality inventory
___b___ 10. Oedipus complex
___c___ 11. preconscious

Definitions or Descriptions

a. the id's demand for immediate gratification

b. a boy's sexual desires toward the opposite-sex parent

c. information that is retrievable but currently not in conscious awareness

d. stages of development proposed by Freud

e. questionnaire used to assess personality traits

f. the two-way interactions of behavior with personal and environmental factors

g. personality test that provides ambiguous stimuli

h. the repository of universal memories, proposed by Jung

i. the process by which children incorporate their parents' values into their developing superegos

j. the process by which the ego seeks to gratify impulses of the id in nondestructive ways

k. stages of development proposed by Erikson

Challenge Test

Answer these questions the day before an exam as a final check on your understanding of the chapter's terms and concepts.

Multiple-Choice Questions

1. Bill is muscular and physically strong. Sheldon would classify him as a(n):

   a. endomorphic type.

b. mesomorphic type.

c. ectomorphic type.

d. dysmorphic type.

2. A psychoanalyst would characterize a person who is impulsive and self-indulgent as possessing a strong _____ and a weak _____.

    a. id and ego; superego

    b. id; ego and superego

    c. ego; superego

    d. id; superego

3. Because Ramona identifies with her politically conservative parents, she chose to enroll in a conservative college. After four years in this environment Ramona's politics have become even more conservative. Which perspective best accounts for the mutual influences of Ramona's upbringing, choice of school, and political viewpoint?

    a. psychoanalytic

    b. trait

    c. humanistic

    d. social-cognitive

4. Jill has a biting, sarcastic manner. According to Freud:

    a. she is projecting her anxiety onto others.

    b. she is probably fixated in the oral stage of development.

    c. she is probably fixated in the anal stage of development.

    d. she is displacing her anxiety onto others.

5. James attributes his failing grade in chemistry to an unfair final exam. His attitude exemplifies:

    a. internal locus of control.

    b. unconditional positive regard.

    c. the self-serving bias.

    d. reciprocal determinism.

6. According to Freud, a person who is overzealous in campaigning against pornography may be displaying:

    a. sublimation.

    b. displacement.

    c. rationalization.

    d. reaction formation.

7. Randy "lives for the moment," squandering his paycheck as soon as he receives it. According to Freud, Randy's behavior is dominated by the:

    a. id.

    b. ego.

    c. superego.

    d. self-serving bias.

8. A psychologist at the campus mental health center administered an empirically derived personality test to diagnose an emotionally troubled student.

Which test did the psychologist *most likely* administer?

    a. the MMPI

    b. the TAT

    c. the Rorschach

    d. the Locus of Control Scale

9. The personality test Teresa is taking involves her describing random patterns of dots. What type of test is she taking?

    a. an empirically derived test

    b. the MMPI

    c. a personality inventory

    d. a projective test

10. Dr. Gonzalez believes that most students can be classified as "Type A" or "Type B" according to the intensities of their personalities and competitiveness. Evidently, Dr. Gonzalez is working within the _____ perspective.

    a. psychoanalytic   **c.** humanistic

    b. trait   **d.** social-cognitive

11. According to the psychoanalytic perspective, a child who frequently "slips" and calls her teacher "mom" *probably*:

    a. has some unresolved conflicts concerning her mother.

    b. is fixated in the oral stage of development.

    c. did not receive unconditional positive regard from her mother.

    d. can be classified as having a weak sense of personal control.

12. Isaiah has a sober and reserved personality; Rashid is fun-loving and affectionate. The Eysencks would say that Isaiah _____ and Rashid _____.

    a. has an internal locus of control; has an external locus of control

    b. has an external locus of control; has an internal locus of control

    c. is an extravert; is an introvert

    d. is an introvert; is an extravert

13. In high school Britta and Debbie were best friends. They thought they were a lot alike, as did everyone else who knew them. After high school they went on to very different colleges, careers, and life courses. Now, at their twenty-fifth reunion, the two are shocked at how little they have in common. Bandura would suggest that their differences reflect the interactive effects of environment, personality, and behavior—effects he refers to as:

    a. reciprocal determinism.

    b. personal control.

    c. identification.

    d. the self-serving bias.

14. For his class presentation, Bruce plans to discuss the "Big Five" personality factors that people throughout the world use to describe others or themselves. Which of the following is *not* a factor that Bruce will discuss?

    a. extraversion
    b. openness
    c. independence
    d. conscientiousness

15. Dayna is not very consistent in showing up for class and turning in assignments when they are due. Research studies would suggest that Dayna's inconsistent behavior:

    a. indicates that she is emotionally troubled and may need professional counseling.
    b. is a sign of learned helplessness.
    c. is not necessarily unusual.
    d. probably reflects a temporary problem in another area of her life.

16. Andrew's grandfather, who has lived a rich and productive life, is a spontaneous, loving, and self-accepting person. Maslow might say that he:

    a. has an internal locus of control.
    b. is an extravert.
    c. has attained the psychosocial stage of integrity.
    d. is a self-actualizing person.

17. The school psychologist believes that having a positive self-concept is necessary before students can achieve their potential. Evidently, the school psychologist is working within the _____ perspective.

    a. psychoanalytic
    b. trait
    c. humanistic
    d. social-cognitive

18. Wanda wishes to instill in her children an accepting attitude toward other people. Maslow and Rogers would probably recommend that she:

    a. teach her children first to accept themselves.
    b. use discipline sparingly.
    c. be affectionate with her children only when they behave as she wishes.
    d. do all of the above.

19. Suzy bought a used, high-mileage automobile because it was all she could afford. Attempting to justify her purchase, she raves to her friends about the car's attractiveness, good acceleration, and stereo. According to Freud, Suzy is using the defense mechanism of:

    a. displacement.
    b. reaction formation.
    c. rationalization.
    d. sublimation.

20. Nadine has a relatively low level of brain arousal. The Eysencks would probably predict that she is:

    a. an extravert.
    b. an introvert.
    c. an unstable person.
    d. both a. and c.

Essay Question

You are an honest, open, and responsible person. Discuss how these characteristics would be explained according to the four major perspectives on personality. (Use the space below to list points you want to make and organize them. Then write the essay on a separate sheet of paper.)

Key Terms

Using your own words, write a brief definition or explanation of each of the following terms.

1. personality

2. free association

3. psychoanalysis

4. unconscious

5. preconscious

6. id

7. pleasure principle

8. ego

9. reality principle

10. superego

11. psychosexual stages

12. oral stage

13. anal stage

14. phallic stage

15. Oedipus complex

16. identification

17. gender identity

18. latency stage

19. genital stage

20. fixation

21. defense mechanisms

22. repression

23. regression

24. reaction formation

25. projection

26. rationalization

27. displacement

28. sublimation

29. collective unconscious

30. projective tests

31. Thematic Apperception Test (TAT)

32. Rorschach inkblot test

33. traits

34. personality inventory

35. Minnesota Multiphasic Personality Inventory-2 (MMPI-2)

36. empirically derived test

37. self-actualization

38. unconditional positive regard

39. self-concept

40. self-esteem

41. self-serving bias

42. reciprocal determinism

43. personal control

44. external locus of control

45. internal locus of control

46. learned helplessness

ANSWERS

GUIDED STUDY

The following guidelines provide the main points that your answers should have touched upon.

1. Freud discovered that, under hypnosis, his patients were sometimes able to talk freely about their neurological symptoms, which led to their improvement. He later began using free association instead of hypnosis, believing that this technique triggered a chain of thoughts leading into a patient's unconscious, thereby retrieving and releasing painful unconscious memories.

   Psychoanalysis is based on Freud's belief that below our surface consciousness is a much larger, unconscious region that contains thoughts, feelings, wishes, and memories of which we are unaware. Although some of these thoughts are held in a preconscious area and can be retrieved at will into consciousness, some unacceptable thoughts and wishes are forcibly blocked, or repressed, from consciousness. These unconscious thoughts and urges often are expressed in troubling symptoms.

2. To Freud, personality is composed of three interacting, and often conflicting, systems: the id, ego, and superego. Operating on the pleasure principle, the unconscious id strives to satisfy basic drives to survive, reproduce, and aggress. Operating on the reality principle, the ego seeks to gratify the id's impulses in realistic and nondestructive ways. The superego, which represents the individual's internalization of the morals and values of parents and culture, forces the ego to consider not only the real but the ideal. Because the ego must intervene among the impulsive demands of the id, the restraining demands of the superego, and those of the external world, it is the personality "executive."

3. Freud believed that children pass through a series of psychosexual stages, during which the id's pleasure-seeking energies focus on particular erogenous zones. Between birth and 18 months (oral stage), pleasure centers on the mouth. Between 18 and 36 months (anal stage), pleasure focuses on bowel and bladder retention and elimination. Between 3 and 6 years (phallic stage), the pleasure zone shifts to the genitals and boys develop unconscious sexual desires for their mothers and the fear that their fathers will punish them (Oedipus complex). Children eventually cope with these threatening feelings by identifying with their same-sex parent.

   Between 6 years of age and puberty (latency stage), sexual feelings are repressed and redirected. At puberty, sexual interests mature as youths begin to experience sexual feelings toward others (genital stage).

4. According to Freud, maladaptive adult behavior results from unresolved conflicts during earlier psychosexual stages. Such unresolved conflicts may cause the person's pleasure-seeking energies to become fixated in one psychosexual stage, leading to later problem behaviors or distinctive personality characteristics.

   Defense mechanisms are the ego's attempt to reduce or redirect anxiety by distorting reality. Examples of defense mechanisms include the banishing of thoughts from consciousness (repression), retreating to behavior characteristic of an earlier stage (regression), turning threatening impulses into their opposites (reaction formation) or attributing them to others (projection), self-justification of unacceptable actions (rationalization), diverting sexual or aggressive impulses to a more acceptable object (displacement), and transforming unacceptable impulses into socially valued motivations (sublimation).

5. The neo-Freudians placed more emphasis than Freud on the role of the conscious mind in determining personality, and less emphasis on sex and aggression as all-consuming motivations. Alfred Adler and Karen Horney emphasized the importance of social rather than sexual tensions in the formation of the child's personality. Erich Fromm and the other "ego psychologists" deemphasized sexual and aggressive impulses and viewed the ego as striving for unity, love, truth, and freedom, rather than merely mediating between the id and superego. Erik Erikson outlined a sequence of psychosocial stages of development that encompass the whole life span. Carl Jung expanded Freud's view of the unconscious into the idea of a collective unconscious, a common reservoir of thoughts derived from the experiences of our ancestors.

6. Projective tests, such as the Thematic Apperception Test and the Rorschach inkblot test, ask people to describe or tell a story about an ambiguous stimulus that has no inherent meaning. In doing so, people presumably project their own interests and conflicts and provide a sort of psychological "x-ray" of their personalities. Despite their widespread use, projective tests are considered by most researchers to be lacking in validity and reliability. For example, there is no single accepted scoring system for interpreting the Rorschach, so two raters may not interpret a subject's responses similarly. Furthermore, the test is not very successful at predicting future behavior.

7. Freud's idea that development is fixed in childhood has been contradicted by research showing that development is lifelong. It is also clear that children gain their gender identity earlier than Freud believed and become strongly feminine or masculine even without a same-sex parent present. Freud's theory of dreams, memory losses, and defense mechanisms as disguising unfulfilled or repressed urges also has been disputed, as has his idea that sexual repression causes psychological disorder. In addition, Freud's theory has been criticized for offering after-the-fact explanations of behavior, yet failing to generate testable predictions of those behaviors. Freud's ideas concerning our limited access to all that goes on in the mind, the importance of sexuality, and the tension between our biological impulses and our social well-being have endured, however.

8. Trait theories define personality in terms of identifiable behavior patterns and conscious motives. As compared with psychoanalytic theories, they are less concerned with explaining personality and more concerned with its description.

The ancient Greeks classified people according to four bodily "humors": melancholic (depressed), sanguine (cheerful), phlegmatic (unemotional), and choleric (irritable). William Sheldon classified people according to their body types, as endomorphs (relaxed and jolly), mesomorphs (bold and physically active), or ectomorphs (high strung and solitary).

A popular procedure today, especially in business and career counseling, is to classify people according to Carl Jung's personality types using the "Myers-Briggs Type Indicator."

The statistical technique called factor analysis is used to identify clusters of personality test items that make up basic traits. Hans and Michael Eysenck believe that many of the personality traits researchers have identified using factor analysis can be reduced to two genetically influenced dimensions: extraversion-introversion and emotional stability-instability. They further believe that extraverts seek stimulation because their level of brain arousal is relatively low.

9. Across the world people describe others in terms roughly consistent with five trait dimensions: emotional stability, extraversion, openness, agreeableness, and conscientiousness.

To assess traits, psychologists use trait scales that measure single traits or personality inventories that assess several traits at once. In contrast to the subjectivity of projective tests, personality inventories are scored objectively. The most widely used personality inventory is the Minnesota Multiphasic Personality Inventory (MMPI-2) for assessing psychological disorders. The MMPI-2 is an empirically derived test that contains ten clinical scales, several validity scales, and fifteen content scales.

10. To be a genuine personality trait, a characteristic must persist over time and across situations. Critics of this perspective question the consistency of traits. Although people's traits do seem to persist over time, research has revealed much less consistency of specific behaviors from one situation to another. However, although people do not act with perfect consistency, their *average* behavior over *many* situations is predictable.

11. The humanistic perspective emerged as a reaction against several other perspectives on personality. In contrast to Freud's study of the negative motives of "sick" people, the humanistic psychologists have focused on the strivings of "healthy" people. Unlike the trait theorists, they view people as whole persons, rather than collections of individual traits. And in contrast to the behaviorists,

they emphasize the importance of personal experiences in personality development.

Maslow proposed that people are motivated by a hierarchy of needs and that if basic needs are fulfilled, people will strive to reach their highest potential (self-actualization). Carl Rogers agreed with much of Maslow's thinking, adding that people nurture others' actualizing tendencies by being genuine, accepting, and empathic. For both theorists a central feature of personality is a person's self-concept.

12. Research on the self documents the importance of people's visions of the self or selves they would like to become in motivating their behavior. Another recent finding is that people with high self-esteem have fewer physical problems, strive more at difficult tasks, and are happier than people with low self-esteem. One of the most firmly established findings is people's readiness to perceive themselves favorably through the self-serving bias. This bias is revealed in the willingness of people to accept responsibility for good deeds and successes more readily than for bad deeds and failures, and in the tendency of people to see themselves as better than average on nearly any desirable dimension.

13. The ideas of humanistic psychologists have influenced counseling, education, child-rearing, and management. Critics contend, however, that the concepts of humanistic psychology are vague, subjective, and so focused on the individual that they promote self-indulgence, selfishness, and an erosion of moral restraints. Furthermore, the humanistic psychologists have been accused of being naively optimistic and unrealistic, and of failing to appreciate the human capacity for evil.

14. The social-cognitive perspective applies principles of learning, cognition, and social behavior to personality and emphasizes the ways in which our personalities shape and are shaped by external events. Reciprocal determinism refers to the ways in which our personalities are influenced by the interaction of our situations, our thoughts and feelings, and our behaviors. There are many examples of reciprocal determinism. For one, different people choose different environments. For another, our personalities shape how we interpret and react to events. Finally, our personalities help create situations to which we react.

15. Whether people see themselves as controlling, or being controlled by, their environments is an important aspect of their personalities. Research reveals that people who perceive an internal locus of control achieve more and are more independent, less depressed, and better able to cope with various

life stresses than people who perceive an external locus of control. Seligman found that animals and people who experience uncontrollable negative events may perceive a lack of control in their lives and develop the passive resignation of learned helplessness. One measure of how helpless or effective people feel is whether they generally are optimistic or pessimistic.

16. Social-cognitive researchers study personality by exploring the effect of differing situations on people's behavior patterns and attitudes. This perspective has increased our awareness of how social situations influence, and are influenced by, individuals. Critics contend, however, that the theory explains behavior after the fact and that it focuses so much on the situation that it ignores the importance of people's inner traits, unconscious motives, and heredity in the formation of personality.

CHAPTER REVIEW

1. thinking; feeling; acting; personality
2. psychoanalytic; trait; humanistic; social-cognitive
3. Sigmund Freud
4. free association
5. psychoanalysis
6. unconscious; preconscious; repressed
7. unconscious; slips; manifest content; latent content
8. biological; social
9. id; ego; superego
10. unconscious; pleasure
11. after; conscious; reality

The ego is considered the executive of personality because it directs our actions as it intervenes among the impulsive demands of the id, the reality of the external world, and the ideals of the superego.

12. superego
13. weak; strong
14. psychosexual
15. oral; sucking (also biting, chewing)
16. anal; 18; 3
17. phallic; 3; 6; genitals; opposite; Oedipus complex; Electra complex
18. identification; gender identity

Children eventually cope with their feelings for the opposite-sex parent by repressing them and by identifying with the rival (same-sex) parent. Through this process children incorporate many of their parents' values, thereby strengthening the superego.

19. latency
20. genital

21. fixated
22. defense mechanisms; repression
23. regression
24. reaction formation
25. projection
26. rationalization
27. displacement
28. sublimation

Matching Items

1. f
2. e
3. c
4. d
5. a
6. b

29. unconscious
30. neo-Freudians; more; less

   a. Adler and Horney emphasized the social, rather than the sexual, tensions of childhood.

   b. Fromm emphasized the ego and its *conscious* strivings for unity, love, truth, and freedom.

   c. Erikson emphasized *lifelong* psycho*social* stages of development.

   d. Jung emphasized an inherited collective unconscious.

31. projective
32. Thematic Apperception
33. Rorschach; inkblots; little
34. lifelong; earlier; is not
35. information

Psychologists today do not widely accept Freud's ideas that conscience and gender identity are formed by resolution of the Oedipus (or the Electra) complex, that dreams are disguised wish fulfillments, that women have weak superegos, that repression is the main cause of memory loss, and that the unconscious mainly contains unacceptable desires and repressed memories.

36. testable hypotheses (or predictions)
37. behaviors; motives
38. explaining; describing
39. melancholic; sanguine; phlegmatic; choleric
40. endomorph; mesomorph; ectomorph
41. Myers-Briggs Type Indicator
42. extraversion-introversion; stability-instability
43. **a.** Emotional stability: calm vs. anxious; secure vs. insecure

   b. Extraversion: sociable vs. retiring

   c. Openness: preference for variety vs. routine

   d. Agreeableness: soft-hearted vs. ruthless

   e. Conscientiousness: disciplined vs. impulsive

44. personality inventories; Minnesota Multiphasic Personality Inventory; empirically
45. traits (or dispositions); situation (or environment)
46. time; situations
47. variable
48. is not

At any given moment a person's behavior is powerfully influenced by the immediate situation, so that it may appear that the person does not have a consistent personality. But averaged over many situations a person's outgoingness, happiness, and carelessness, for instance, are more predictable.

49. Maslow; Rogers
50. hierarchy; self-actualization

For Maslow, such people were self-aware, self-accepting, open, spontaneous, loving, caring, secure, and problem-centered rather than self-centered.

51. genuine; accepting; empathic; unconditional positive regard
52. self-concept
53. increased
54. possible selves
55. self-esteem; independent of; anxiety; depression
56. more
57. high
58. self-serving

Humanistic psychology is criticized for being vague and subjective, for encouraging self-indulgence and selfishness, and for failing to appreciate the capacity of humans for evil.

59. more
60. above
61. environment; Bandura
62. behaviors; personal/cognitive; environmental; reciprocal determinism

Different people choose different environments based partly on their dispositions. Our personality shapes how we interpret and react to events. It also helps create the situations to which we react.

63. internal locus of control; external locus of control
64. learned helplessness
65. more
66. optimism

One criticism is that the theory offers only after-the-fact explanations and thus can "explain" anything. Another is that the theory has overemphasized situational influences to the neglect of inner traits.

67. **a.** The psychoanalytic perspective has drawn attention to the unconscious and irrational aspects of personality.

b. The trait perspective has systematically described and measured important components of personality.

c. The humanistic perspective emphasizes the healthy potential of personality and the importance of our sense of self.

d. The social-cognitive perspective emphasizes that we always act in a particular situational context.

PROGRESS TEST 1

Multiple-Choice Questions

1. **b.** is the answer. Personality is defined as patterns of response—of thinking, feeling, and acting—that are relatively consistent across a variety of situations. (p. 411)

2. **d.** is the answer. (p. 413)

a. & b. Conscious processes are the focus of these perspectives.

c. The trait perspective focuses on description of behaviors.

3. **a.** is the answer. (pp. 414–415)

4. **c.** is the answer. According to Freud, defense mechanisms reduce anxiety unconsciously, by disguising one's threatening impulses. (p. 415)

a., b., & d. Unlike these specific emotions, anxiety need not be focused. Defense mechanisms help us cope when we are unsettled but are not sure why.

5. **d.** is the answer. They are so called because the individual supposedly projects his or her feelings into the ambiguous test stimuli. (p. 418)

a. Not all personality tests provide ambiguous stimuli.

b. Personality inventories are objective tests such as the MMPI.

c. There are no such tests.

6. **b.** is the answer. (p. 416)

a. According to most neo-Freudians, Freud placed too great an emphasis on the *unconscious* mind.

c. Freud placed great emphasis on early childhood, and the neo-Freudians basically agreed with him. Erikson, however, placed *less* emphasis on childhood, with the idea that development is a lifelong process.

d. The neo-Freudians accepted Freud's ideas about the basic personality structures.

7. **c.** is the answer. (p. 436)

a. & d. In fact, just the opposite is true.

b. Locus of control is not related to intelligence.

8. **a.** is the answer. (p. 423)

b. & c. Locus of control is emphasized by the social-cognitive perspective.

d. This is how the ancient Greeks described personality.

9. **b.** is the answer. Studies have shown that people do not act with predictable consistency from one situation to the next. But, over a number of situations, consistent patterns emerge, and this basic consistency of traits persists over the life span. (pp. 426–427)

10. **b.** is the answer. (pp. 428–429)

a. This is true of the psychoanalytic perspective.

c. This is true of the social-cognitive perspective.

d. This is true of the trait perspective.

11. **c.** is the answer. (p. 429)

12. **b.** is the answer. Humanistic psychologists emphasize that for the individual, self-affirming thinking is generally adaptive (therefore, not a.); such thinking maintains self-confidence, minimizes depression, and enables us to view others with compassion and understanding (therefore, not c.); unconditional positive regard tends to promote self-esteem and thus self-affirming thinking (therefore, not d.). (p. 432)

13. **a.** is the answer. Developmental research indicates that development is lifelong. (p. 419)

b., c., & d. To varying degrees, research has partially supported these Freudian ideas.

14. **c.** is the answer. (p. 417)

a. Freud based his theory on an individual, rather than collective, unconscious.

b. & d. There is no mention of an "unconscious" in Fromm's or Bandura's theory.

15. **c.** is the answer. As scoring is largely subjective and the tests have not been very successful in predicting behavior, their reliability and validity have been called into question. (p. 419)

a. This is untrue.

b. Unlike empirically derived personality tests, projective tests are not standardized.

d. Although this may be true, it was not mentioned as a criticism of projective tests.

16. **b.** is the answer. In doing so it underestimates the influence of the environment. (pp. 426–427)

a. The trait perspective does not emphasize early childhood experiences.

c. This criticism is unlikely since trait theory does not seek to explain personality development.

d. Trait theory does not look on traits as being "positive" or "negative."

17. **d.** is the answer. (p. 429)

a. & c. Personality structure, of which the ego is a part, is a concern of the psychoanalytic perspective.

b. Locus of control is a major focus of the social-cognitive perspective.

18. **c.** is the answer. (p. 424)

 a. & d. A psychoanalytic theorist would be most likely to use a projective test or the technique of free association.

 b. This would most likely be the approach taken by a social-cognitive theorist.

19. **b.** is the answer. In Freud's theory, the id operates according to the pleasure principle; the ego operates according to the reality principle. (pp. 413–414)

 c. The id is presumed to be unconscious.

 d. The superego is, according to Freud, the equivalent of a conscience; the ego is the "personality executive."

20. **b.** is the answer. The social-cognitive theory has been accused of putting so much emphasis on the situation that inner traits are neglected. (p. 439)

 a. Such a criticism has been made of the psychoanalytic perspective but is not relevant to the social-cognitive perspective.

 c. Such a criticism might be more relevant to the trait perspective; the social-cognitive perspective offers an explanation in the form of reciprocal determinism.

 d. There are assessment techniques appropriate to the theory, namely, questionnaires and observations of behavior in situations.

Matching Items

1. f (p. 416)	**5.** h (p. 416)	**9.** c (p. 414)
2. j (p. 418)	**6.** d (p. 415)	**10.** e (p. 416)
3. b (p. 414)	**7.** a (p. 413)	**11.** i (p. 418)
4. k (p. 424)	**8.** g (p. 416)	

PROGRESS TEST 2

Multiple-Choice Questions

1. **d.** is the answer. (p. 435)

 a. This perspective emphasizes unconscious dynamics in personality.

 b. This perspective is more concerned with *describing* than *explaining* personality.

 c. This perspective emphasizes the healthy, self-actualizing tendencies of personality.

2. **d.** is the answer. (p. 413)

 a. Self-actualization is a concept of the humanistic perspective.

b. Through identification, children *reduce* conflicting feelings as they incorporate their parents' values.

c. Jung, rather than Freud, proposed the concept of the collective unconscious.

3. **a.** is the answer. (p. 422)

4. **c.** is the answer. In such situations, passive resignation, called learned helplessness, develops. (p. 436)

 a. This refers to the belief that one controls one's fate; the circumstances described lead to precisely the opposite belief.

 b. Reaction formation is a defense mechanism in which unacceptable impulses are channeled into their opposites.

 d. Seligman did not specify that neurotic anxiety occurs.

5. **a.** is the answer. Feelings of insecurity reduce self-esteem, and there is a tendency for those who feel negative about themselves to feel negative about others as well. (p. 430)

6. **d.** is the answer. (p. 431)

7. **b.** is the answer. The MMPI was developed by selecting from many items those that **differentiated** between the groups of interest; hence it was empirically derived. That it is an objective test is shown by the fact that it can be scored by computer. (p. 424)

 a. Projective tests present ambiguous stimuli such as inkblots or drawings for people to interpret; the MMPI is a questionnaire.

 c. Although sometimes used to assess job applicants, the MMPI was developed to assess emotionally troubled people.

 d. The MMPI does not focus on control, but rather, measures various aspects of personality.

8. **b.** is the answer. Trait theory attempts to describe behavior and not to develop explanations or applications. The emphasis is more on consistency than on change. (p. 422)

9. **a.** is the answer. "Internals," or those who have a sense of personal control, have been shown to achieve more in school. Relative to externals, they also cope better with stress and are more independent. (p. 436)

10. **c.** is the answer. In actuality, people with *high* self-esteem are generally more independent of pressures to conform. (p. 430)

11. **c.** is the answer. (p. 414)

12. **d.** is the answer. (p. 434)

13. **c.** is the answer. In keeping with their emphasis on

interactions between people and situations, social-cognitive theorists would most likely make use of observations of behavior in relevant situations. (p. 439)

a. & d. Personality inventories and factor analyses would more likely be used by a trait theorist.

b. Projective tests would more likely be used by a psychologist working within the psychoanalytic perspective.

14. **d.** is the answer. Trait theory defines personality in terms of behavior and is therefore interested in describing behavior; psychoanalytic theory defines personality as dynamics underlying behavior and therefore is interested in explaining behavior in terms of these dynamics. (pp. 413–414, 421–422)

15. **c.** is the answer. (p. 423)

a. & b. The MMPI is a personality inventory, and personality inventories are questionnaires, not statistical techniques.

d. Free association is the psychoanalytic method of exploring the unconscious in which the person says whatever comes to mind.

16. **d.** is the answer. (p. 424)

17. **c.** is the answer. Although many researchers think of the unconscious as information processing without awareness rather than as a reservoir of repressed information, they agree with Freud that we do indeed have limited access to all that goes on in our minds. (p. 420)

18. **c.** is the answer. (pp. 414–415)

a. & b. Reaction formation is the defense mechanism by which people transform unacceptable impulses into their opposites.

d. It is the superego, rather than the ego, that represents parental values.

19. **a.** is the answer. None of these perspectives claim to fulfill the requirements of testable prediction required to validate a scientific theory. They offer instead distinct points of view that provide valuable insights into various aspects of personality. (pp. 439–440)

20. **d.** is the answer. (p. 429)

Matching Items

1. g (p. 418)	5. d (p. 414)	9. e (p. 424)
2. i (pp. 414–415)	6. a (p. 413)	10. b (p. 414)
3. h (p. 417)	7. k (p. 417)	11. c (p. 413)
4. j (p. 414)	8. f (p. 435)	

CHALLENGE TEST

Multiple-Choice Questions

1. **b.** is the answer. (p. 422)

a. Endomorphs are overweight.

c. Ectomorphs are thin.

d. This is not one of Sheldon's types.

2. **d.** is the answer. Impulsiveness is the mark of a strong id; self-indulgence is the mark of a weak superego. Because the ego serves to mediate the demands of the id, the superego, and the outside world, its strength or weakness is judged by its decision-making ability, not by the character of the decision—so the ego is not relevant to the question asked. (pp. 413–414)

3. **d.** is the answer. The social-cognitive perspective emphasizes the reciprocal influences between people and their situations. In this example, Ramona's parents (situational factor) helped shape her political beliefs (internal factor), which influenced her choice of colleges (situational factor), and created an environment that fostered her predisposed political attitudes. (p. 435)

4. **b.** is the answer. Sarcasm is said to be an attempt to deny the passive dependence characteristic of the oral stage. (p. 415)

a. A person who is projecting attributes his or her own feelings to others.

c. Such a person might be either messy and disorganized or highly controlled and compulsively neat.

d. Displacement involves diverting aggressive or sexual impulses onto a more acceptable object than that which aroused them.

5. **c.** is the answer. (p. 431)

a. A person with an internal locus of control would be likely to *accept* responsibility for a failing grade.

b. Unconditional positive regard is an attitude of total acceptance directed toward others.

d. Reciprocal determinism refers to the mutual influences among personality, environment, and behavior.

6. **d.** is the answer. The ego unconsciously makes unacceptable impulses look like their opposites. The person vehemently crusading against pornography would be moved by sexual desires he or she found unacceptable. (pp. 415–416)

a. Sublimation refers to transforming unacceptable impulses into socially valued behaviors.

b. Displacement refers to diverting aggressive or sexual impulses toward an object other than the one responsible for the impulses.

c. To rationalize is to generate inaccurate, self-justifying explanations for our actions.

7. **a.** is the answer. Operating according to the pleasure principle, the id's impulses, unless checked by the ego, might lead to such behavior. (p. 413)

   b. The ego is the rational part of the personality that mediates between the demands of the id, the superego, and reality. If the ego dominates, such pleasure-seeking is unlikely.

   c. The superego is the conscience of personality; if it is dominant, such pleasure-seeking behavior is unlikely.

   d. The self-serving bias is the tendency of people to perceive themselves favorably; it is not part of Freud's theory.

8. **a.** is the answer. (p. 424)

   b. & c. The TAT and Rorschach are projective tests that were not empirically derived.

   d. A personality test that measures locus of control would not be helpful in identifying troubled behaviors.

9. **d.** is the answer. Projective tests provide ambiguous stimuli, such as random dot patterns, in an attempt to trigger in the test-taker projection of his or her personality. (p. 418)

10. **b.** is the answer. (p. 422)

    a. The psychoanalytic perspective emphasizes unconscious processes in personality dynamics.

    c. The humanistic perspective emphasizes each person's potential for healthy growth and self-actualization.

    d. The social-cognitive perspective emphasizes the reciprocal influences of personality and environment.

11. **a.** is the answer. Freud believed that dreams and such slips of the tongue reveal unconscious conflicts. (p. 413)

    b. A person fixated in the oral stage might have a sarcastic personality; this child's slip of the tongue reveals nothing about her psychosexual development.

    c. & d. Unconditional positive regard and personal control are not psychoanalytic concepts.

12. **d.** is the answer. (p. 423)

    a. & b. The traits of Isaiah and Rashid reveal nothing about their sense of personal control.

13. **a.** is the answer. Reciprocal determinism refers to the mutual influences among personal factors, environmental factors, and behavior. (p. 435)

    b. Personal control is one's sense of controlling, or being controlled by, the environment.

    c. In Freud's theory, identification is the process by which children incorporate parental values into their developing superegos.

    d. The self-serving bias describes our readiness to perceive ourselves favorably.

14. **c.** is the answer. (p. 424)

15. **c.** is the answer. (p. 427)

16. **d.** is the answer. (p. 428)

    a. & b. These are concepts used by trait theorists rather than humanistic theorists such as Maslow.

    c. This reflects Erikson's viewpoint.

17. **c.** is the answer. (p. 429)

    a., b., & d. The self-concept is not relevant to the psychoanalytic, trait, or social-cognitive perspectives.

18. **a.** is the answer. (pp. 428–429)

    b. The text does not discuss the impact of discipline on personality.

    c. This would constitute *conditional*, rather than unconditional, positive regard and would likely cause the children to be *less* accepting of themselves and others.

19. **c.** is the answer. Suzy is trying to justify her purchase by generating (inaccurate) explanations for her behavior. (p. 416)

    a. Displacement is the redirecting of impulses toward an object other than the one responsible for them.

    b. Reaction formation is the transformation of unacceptable impulses into their opposites.

    d. Sublimation refers to transforming unacceptable impulses into socially valued behaviors.

20. **a.** is the answer. The Eysencks believe that extraverts are predisposed to seek stimulation because their normal level of brain arousal is relatively low. (p. 423)

    c. Nadine's low level of brain arousal would, if anything, be related to a *stable* personality, according to the Eysencks.

Essay Question

Since you are apparently in good psychological health, according to the psychoanalytic perspective you must have experienced a healthy childhood and successfully passed through the various stages of psychosexual (Freud) or psychosocial (Erikson) development. Freud would also say that your ego is functioning well in balancing the demands of your id with the restraining demands of your superego and reality. Freud might also say that your honest nature reflects a well-developed superego, while Jung might say it derives from a universal value found in our collective unconscious.

Trait theorists would be less concerned with explaining these specific characteristics than with describing them, determining their consistency, and classifying your personality type. Some trait theorists, such as Allport, Eysenck, and Kagan, attribute certain trait differences to biological factors such as autonomic reactivity and heredity.

According to the humanistic perspective, your open and honest nature indicates that your basic needs have been met and you are in the process of self-actualization (Maslow). Furthermore, your openness indicates that you have a healthy self-concept and were likely nurtured by genuine, accepting, and empathic caregivers (Rogers).

According to the social-cognitive perspective, your personal/cognitive factors, behavior, and environmental influences interacted in shaping your personality and behaviors. The fact that you are a responsible person indicates that you perceive yourself as controlling, rather than being controlled by, your environment.

KEY TERMS

1. **Personality** is an individual's relatively consistent pattern of thinking, feeling, and acting. (p. 411)

2. **Free association** is the Freudian technique in which the person is encouraged to say whatever comes to mind as a means of exploring the unconscious. (pp. 412–413)

3. In Freud's theory, **psychoanalysis** refers to the analysis of the tensions within a patient's unconscious, using methods such as free association. (p. 413)

4. In Freud's theory, the **unconscious** is the repository of thoughts, wishes, feelings, and memories of which we are unaware. According to contemporary psychologists, it is a level of information processing of which we are unaware. (p. 413)

   Example: According to Freud, much of the content of the **unconscious** is so threatening and unacceptable that it is repressed from awareness.

5. In Freud's theory, the **preconscious** area is a region of the unconscious that contains material that is retrievable at will into conscious awareness. (p. 413)

   Example: The Freudian notion of a **preconscious** is similar to the concept of long-term memory: Material is accessible but not currently in our awareness.

6. In Freud's theory, the **id** is the system of personality consisting of instinctual drives for survival, reproduction, and aggression, that supplies psychic energy to personality. (p. 413)

7. In Freud's theory, the **pleasure principle** refers to the id's demands for immediate gratification. (p. 413)

Example: Governed only by the id, the newborn infant demands immediate gratification of its physical needs according to the **pleasure principle**.

8. In psychoanalytic theory, the **ego** is the conscious division of personality that attempts to mediate between the demands of the id, the superego, and reality. Neo-Freudians such as Erich Fromm differed from Freud in proposing that, instead of just sublimating the id's baser motives, the ego consciously strives for unity, love, truth, and freedom. (p. 414)

9. The **reality principle** refers to the ego's tendency to gratify the desires of the id in ways that are realistic. (p. 414)

   Example: Operating according to the **reality principle**, the ego referees the continual battle between the pleasure-seeking demands of the id and the voice of conscience of the superego.

10. In Freud's theory, the **superego** is the division of personality that contains the conscience and develops by incorporating the perceived moral standards of society. (p. 414)

    Example: If a person has an overdeveloped **superego**, he or she might have a very rigid lifestyle and yet be continually guilt ridden.

11. Freud's **psychosexual stages** are developmental periods children pass through during which the id's pleasure-seeking energies are focused on different erogenous zones. (p. 414)

    Example: Freud's analysis of his patients' problems led to his conclusion that personality is fixed early in life as children pass through a series of **psychosexual stages**.

12. During the **oral stage**, which lasts throughout the first 18 months of life, pleasure centers on activities of the mouth. (p. 414)

13. The **anal stage**, lasting from 18 months to 3 years, shifts the source of gratification to bowel and bladder retention and elimination. (p. 414)

14. During the **phallic stage**, from 3 to 6 years, the genitals become the pleasure zone. (p. 414)

15. According to Freud, boys in the phallic stage develop a collection of feelings, known as the **Oedipus complex**, that center on sexual attraction to the mother and resentment of the father. Some psychologists believe girls have a parallel Electra complex. (p. 414)

    Example: According to Freud, resolution of the **Oedipus complex** occurs as the boy represses his feelings of hatred and identifies with his father.

16. In Freud's theory, **identification** is the process by which the child's superego develops and incorpo-

rates the parents' values. Freud saw identification as crucial, not only to resolution of the Oedipus complex, but also to the development of gender identity. (p. 415)

17. **Gender identity** is a person's sense of being male or female. (p. 415)

18. During the **latency stage**, from about age 6 to puberty, sexual impulses are dormant. (p. 415)
Memory aid: Something that is **latent** exists but is not manifesting itself.

19. At puberty the repressed sexual feelings of the latency stage give way to the **genital stage** and the maturation of sexual interests. (p. 415)

20. In Freud's theory, **fixation** occurs when development becomes arrested in an immature psychosexual stage. (p. 415)
Example: The "odd couple," consisting of one compulsively neat and one messy roommate, represents two manifestations of **fixation** in the anal stage.

21. In Freud' theory, **defense mechanisms** are the ego's methods of unconsciously protecting itself against anxiety by distorting reality. (p. 415)

22. The basis of all defense mechanisms, **repression** is the unconscious exclusion of painful impulses from the conscious mind. Repression is an example of motivated forgetting: One "forgets" what one really does not wish to remember. (p. 415)

23. **Regression** is the defense mechanism in which the person reverts to a less mature pattern of behavior. (p. 415)
Example: One defense mechanism that people sometimes use during frustrating arguments is to storm away—a classic example of **regressing** to an immature behavior pattern.

24. **Reaction formation** is the defense mechanism in which the ego converts unacceptable feelings into their opposites. (p. 415)
Memory aid: Social reformers often protest too vehemently. Their critics then cite their overreaction as an example of **reaction formation**.

25. In psychoanalytic theory, **projection** is the unconscious attribution of one's own unacceptable feelings, attitudes, or desires to others. (p. 416)
Memory aid: To project is to thrust outward. **Projection** is an example of thrusting one's own feelings outward to another person.

26. **Rationalization** is the defense mechanism in which one devises self-satisfying but incorrect reasons for one's behavior. (p. 416)
Example: A student who flunks out of school because of not studying may engage in **rationaliza-**

tion by claiming that all along he or she had wanted to be out in the "real world" anyway.

27. **Displacement** is the defense mechanism in which an impulse is shifted to an object other than the one that originally aroused the impulse. (p. 416)
Example: An employee who is angry at his or her boss might **displace** this anger onto a subordinate or some other safe target.

28. **Sublimation** is the defense mechanism in which an instinctual impulse is modified in a socially acceptable manner. (p. 416)
Memory aid: Sublimate and *sublime* derive from the same Latin root, meaning "to raise, uplift, or ennoble; of high spiritual, moral, or intellectual value."

29. The **collective unconscious** is Jung's concept of an inherited unconscious shared by all people and deriving from our early ancestors' universal experiences. (p. 417)

30. **Projective tests**, such as the TAT and Rorschach, present ambiguous stimuli onto which people supposedly *project* their own inner feelings. (p. 418)
Example: A major criticism of **projective tests** is that the interpretations of a subject's responses are, like the test stimuli themselves, ambiguous.

31. The **Thematic Apperception Test (TAT)** is a projective test that consists of ambiguous pictures about which people are asked to make up stories. (p. 418)

32. The **Rorschach inkblot test**, the most widely used projective test, consists of ten inkblots that people are asked to interpret. (p. 418)

33. **Traits** are people's characteristic predispositions to act in certain ways. (p. 422)
Example: Five **traits** that describe the major features of personality are emotional stability, extraversion, openness, agreeableness, and conscientiousness.

34. **Personality inventories**, associated with the trait perspective, are questionnaires used to assess personality traits. (p. 424)

35. Consisting of ten clinical scales, the **Minnesota Multiphasic Personality Inventory (MMPI)** is the most widely used personality inventory. (p. 424)

36. An **empirically derived test** is one developed by testing many items to see which best distinguish between groups of interest. (p. 424)
Example: The MMPI is an **empirically derived test**, since the questions chosen for it were those that best differentiated groups of interest, namely, "normal" and disordered people.

37. In Maslow's theory, **self-actualization** describes the process of fulfilling one's potential and becoming spontaneous, loving, creative, and self-accepting. Self-actualization is at the very top of Maslow's need hierarchy and therefore becomes active only after the more basic physical and psychological needs have been met. (p. 428)

38. **Unconditional positive regard** is, according to Rogers, an attitude of total acceptance and one of the three conditions essential to a "growth-promoting" climate. (p. 429)

39. **Self-concept** refers to one's personal awareness of "who I am." In the humanistic perspective, self-concept is a central feature of personality; life happiness is significantly affected by whether self-concept is positive or negative. (p. 429)

40. In humanistic psychology, **self-esteem** refers to an individual's sense of self-worth. (p. 430)

41. The **self-serving bias** is the tendency to perceive oneself favorably. (pp. 430–431)

    Example: The pervasiveness of the **self-serving bias** is indicated by the fact that most people tend to see themselves as relatively superior on just about every ability and personality dimension.

42. According to the social-cognitive perspective, personality is shaped through **reciprocal determinism**, or the interaction among situations, thoughts and feelings, and behaviors. (p. 435)

43. **Personal control** refers to a person's sense of controlling the environment. (p. 435)

44. **External locus of control** is the belief that one's fate is determined by forces not under personal control. (p. 436)

45. **Internal locus of control** is the belief that to a great extent one controls one's own destiny. (p. 436)

46. **Learned helplessness** is the passive resignation and perceived lack of control that a person or animal develops from repeated exposure to inescapable aversive events. (p. 436)

    Example: Following repeated exposure to inescapable shock, Seligman's dogs developed **learned helplessness**; later, when they could escape simply by jumping a hurdle, they failed to do so.

15 / Psychological Disorders

Chapter Overview

Although there is no clear-cut line between normal and abnormal behavior, we can characterize as abnormal those behaviors that are atypical, disturbing, maladaptive, and unjustifiable. Chapter 15 discusses types of anxiety, somatoform, dissociative, mood, schizophrenic, and personality disorders, as classified by the *Diagnostic and Statistical Manual of Mental Disorders* (DSM-III-R). Although this classification system follows a medical model, in which disorders are viewed as illnesses, the chapter discusses psychological as well as physiological factors. Thus, psychoanalytic theory, learning theory, social-cognitive theory, and other psychological perspectives are drawn on when relevant. The chapter concludes with a discussion of the advantages and problems connected with the use of diagnostic labels.

Your major task in this chapter is to learn about psychological disorders, their various subtypes and characteristics, and their possible causes. Since the material to be learned is extensive, it may be helpful to rehearse it by mentally completing the Chapter Review several times.

NOTE: Answer guidelines for all Chapter 15 questions begin on page 321.

Guided Study

The text chapter should be studied one section at a time. Before you read, preview each section by skimming it, noting headings and boldface items. Then read the appropriate section objectives from the following outline. Keep these objectives in mind and, as you read the chapter section, search for the information that will enable you to meet each objective. Once you have finished a section, write out answers for its objectives.

Perspectives on Psychological Disorders (pp. 445–451)

1. List the criteria for judging whether behavior is disordered.

2. Explain and contrast two perspectives on psychological disorders.

3. Describe the system used to classify psychological disorders and explain the reasons for its development.

Anxiety Disorders (pp. 451–454)

4. Describe the various anxiety disorders and discuss their possible causes.

Somatoform Disorders (pp. 454–455)

Dissociative Disorders (pp. 455–458)

5. Describe the nature and possible causes of somatoform and dissociative disorders.

Mood Disorders (pp. 458–465)

6. Describe the mood disorders and discuss the alternative explanations for their occurrence.

Schizophrenic Disorders (pp. 466–471)

7. Describe the symptoms of schizophrenic disorders and discuss research on the causes of schizophrenia.

Personality Disorders (pp. 471–472)

8. Describe the nature and causes of personality disorders and the specific characteristics of the antisocial personality disorder.

The Commonality of Psychological Disorders (pp. 472–473)

9. Briefly discuss the prevalence of psychological disorders.

Labeling People: The Power of Preconceptions (pp. 473–474)

10. Discuss the controversy surrounding the use of diagnostic labels.

Chapter Review

When you have finished reading the chapter, work through the material that follows to review it. Complete the sentences and answer the questions. As you proceed, evaluate your performance for each section by consulting the answers on page 323. Do not continue with the next section until you understand each answer. If you need to, review or reread the appropriate section in the textbook before continuing.

Perspectives on Psychological Disorders (pp. 445–451)

1. In order to be classified as psychologically disordered, behavior must be atypical,

disturbing, maladaptive, and
unjust. This definition emphasizes
that standards of acceptability for behavior are
variable (constant/variable).

2. The view that psychological disorders are
sicknesses is the basis of the medical
model. One of the first reformers to advocate
this position and call for providing more humane
living conditions for the mentally ill was
Pinel.

3. Psychiatrist Thomas Szasz has argued against
this model, which emphasizes mental health and
mental illness, on the grounds that psychological
disorders are not defined medically, but rather
Socially.

4. Freud's theory is consistent
(consistent/inconsistent) with the idea that
behavior disorders are sicknesses.

Summarize the viewpoint of those who disagree with
the medical model.

5. Major psychological disorders such as
depression and schizophrenia are
universal; others, such as anorexia
nervosa, are culture-bound.

6. Mental health workers today believe that
disorders are influenced by
genetic predispositions,
physiological states, inner
psychological dynamics, and
social circumstances.

7. The most widely used system for classifying
psychological disorders is the American
Psychiatric Association manual, commonly
known by its abbreviation,
DSM-III-R.

8. The revised manual has deemphasized the
formerly important distinction between

psychotic disorders,
or psychological illnesses that are severely
impairing, and neurotic
disorders, or psychological
illnesses that allow the person to function
socially. In general, it now seeks to list and
describe the disorders, rather
than attempting to explain them.

9. Independent diagnoses made with the current
manual show (show/do not
show) high levels of agreement.

Anxiety Disorders (pp. 451–454)

10. Two-thirds of those who suffer persistent and
distressing anxiety are women
(women/men).

11. When a person tends to feel anxious for no
apparent reason, he or she is diagnosed as
suffering from a generalized
anxiety disorder.

12. When a person has an irrational fear of a
specific object or situation, the diagnosis is a
phobic disorder.

13. When a person cannot control repetitive thoughts
and actions, an obsessive-
compulsive disorder is diagnosed.

14. In generalized anxiety disorder, which Freud
called free-floating
anxiety, the body reacts physiologically with the
arousal of the autonomic nervous
system. In some instances the anxiety of this
disorder may intensify dramatically and be
accompanied by trembling or fainting; this is
called a panic
attack.

15. Compared with other disorders, phobias typically
appear at a(n) earlier (earlier/
later) age, often in the sufferer's
teens.

16. Psychoanalytic theory assumes that anxiety
disorders are symptoms of submerged mental
energy that derives from intolerable impulses
that were repressed during
childhood.

17. Learning theorists, drawing on research in which rats are given unpredictable shocks, view anxiety as a response to feelings of _helplessness_

18. The anxiety response probably _is_ (is/is not) genetically influenced.

19. PET scans of persons with obsessive-compulsive disorder reveal excessive activity in a region of the _frontal_ lobes. Antidepressant drugs may reduce this activity by influencing the neurotransmitter _seretonin_.

Contrast the explanations of anxiety disorders proposed by the psychoanalytic, learning, and biological perspectives.

Somatoform Disorders (pp. 454–455)

20. When a neurotic symptom is expressed bodily, as in vomiting, dizziness, or blurred vision, the diagnosis is a _Somatoform_ disorder.

21. Generalized bodily complaints are relatively common in _China_, where people less often express the emotional aspects of distress.

22. Freud believed that the _conversion_ disorder resulted when anxiety was transformed into a very specific physical symptom. Today, this disorder is relatively _rare_ (rare/common).

23. When normal aches and pains are interpreted as serious illnesses, the person is said to suffer from _hypochondrias_.

Dissociative Disorders (pp. 455–458),

24. In dissociative disorders, _conscious awareness_ becomes dissociated, or _seperated_, from previous memories, thoughts, and feelings. These disorders are relatively _rare_ (common/rare).

25. A person who experiences a sudden loss of memory is suffering from _Amnesia_. If the loss of memory has occurred in response to intolerable stress, the person is said to have _psychogenic amnesia_. Such memory loss is usually for _selective_ (all/ selective) memories.

26. When an individual not only loses memory but also runs away, a _fugue_ has occurred.

27. A person who develops two or more distinct personalities is suffering from a _multiple_ _personality_ disorder. Those who accept this as a genuine disorder point to evidence that differing personalities may be associated with distinct _brain_ and _body_ states. The psychoanalytic and learning perspectives view dissociative disorders as ways of dealing with _anxiety_.

28. Nicolas Spanos has argued that such people may merely be playing different _roles_.

Identify two pieces of evidence brought forth by those who do not accept multiple personality as a genuine disorder.

Mood Disorders (pp. 458–465)

29. When a person experiences prolonged depression with no discernible cause, the disorder is called _major_ _depression_.

30. When a person's mood alternates between depression and the hyperactive state of

manced, a
bipolar disorder is diagnosed.

31. Among Americans born since World War II, depression has _increased_ (increased/decreased) dramatically, especially among _~~_____~~ young adults_ and _women_.

32. The possible signs of depression include _poor appetite, insomnia, lethargy feelings of worthlessness, loss of interest_

33. Major depression occurs when its signs persist _2_ _weeks_ or more with no apparent cause.

34. Symptoms of mania include _euphoria, hyperactivity, wild optimistic state_ The bipolar disorder occurs in approximately _1_ percent of men and women.

35. Depressed persons usually _can_ (can/cannot) recover without therapy.

36. It usually _is_ (is/is not) the case that a depressive episode has been triggered by a stressful event.

State the psychoanalytic explanation of depression.

37. Mood disorders _tend_ (tend/ do not tend) to run in families.

38. Certain types of depression may be caused by _low_ (high/low) levels of _norepinephrine_ or _serotonin_, two neurotransmitters.

39. According to the social-cognitive perspective, depression may be linked with beliefs that are _self_ – _defeating_. Such beliefs, in turn, might be linked to _learned_ _helplessness_, the feeling that can arise when the individual repeatedly experiences uncontrollable aversive events.

Describe how depressed people differ from others in their explanations of failure and how such explanations tend to feed depression.

40. Research studies suggest that depressing thoughts usually _coincide w/_ (precede/ follow/coincide with) a depressed mood.

41. A depressed person tends to elicit social _rejection_ (empathy/rejection).

Outline the vicious cycle of depression.

Schizophrenic Disorders (pp. 466–471)

42. Schizophrenia, or "split mind," refers not to a split personality but rather to a split from _reality_.

43. Three manifestations of schizophrenia are disorganized _thinking_, disturbed _perceptions_, and inappropriate _emotions_ and _actions_.

44. The distorted, false beliefs of schizophrenia patients are called _delusions_.

45. Many psychologists attribute the disorganized thinking of schizophrenia to a breakdown in the capacity for _selective_ _attention_.

46. The disturbed perceptions of people suffering from schizophrenia may take the form of _hallucinations_, which usually are _auditory_ (visual/auditory).

47. The term _schizophrenia_ describes a _cluster of disorders_ (single disorder/cluster of disorders).

48. *Positive symptoms* of schizophrenia include disorganized & diluted thinking, inappropriate emotions. *Negative symptoms* include toneless voices, expressionless faces, mute or rigid bodies. When schizophrenia develops slowly, recovery is less (more/less) likely than when it develops rapidly in reaction to particular life stresses.

49. The brain tissue of schizophrenia patients has been found to have an excess of receptors for the neurotransmitter dopamine. Drugs that block these receptors have been found to decrease (increase/decrease) schizophrenia symptoms.

50. Brain scans have shown that many people suffering from schizophrenia have a shrinkage of brain tissue or abnormal patterns of brain activity in the frontal lobes.

51. Twin and adoptive studies support (support/do not support) the contention that heredity plays a role in schizophrenia.

52. It appears that for schizophrenia to develop there must be both a genetic predisposition and some psychological trigger.

List several of the warning signs of schizophrenia in high-risk children.

Personality Disorders (pp. 471–472)

53. Personality disorders exist when an individual has character traits that are enduring and impair social functioning.

54. An individual who seems to have no conscience, lies, steals, is generally irresponsible, and may be criminal is said to have an antisocial personality. Previously, this person was labeled a psychopath.

55. Studies of the children of convicted criminals suggest that there is (is/is not) a biological predisposition to such traits.

56. When awaiting electric shocks, antisocial persons show less (more/less) arousal of the autonomic nervous system than do control subjects.

The Commonality of Psychological Disorders (pp. 472–473)

57. Research reveals that approximately 32 percent of American adults have at some time experienced a psychological disorder and that approximately 20 percent have an active disorder.

58. In terms of age of onset, most psychological disorders appear by early (early/middle/late) adulthood. Some, such as the anti-social personalities and phobias, appear during childhood.

Labeling People: The Power of Preconceptions (pp. 473–474)

59. Studies have shown that labeling has a significant (little/a significant) effect on our interpretation of individuals and their behavior.

Outline the pros and cons of labeling psychological disorders.

FOCUS ON PSYCHOLOGY:
Seasonal Affective Disorder (SAD)

A new category may soon need to be added to the bipolar family of psychological disorders. Persons with seasonal affective disorder, dubbed "SAD" for short, experience months of depression that begin each year in October or November and gradually give way to a more normal, occasionally manic mood as spring and summer approach. During the winter, SAD victims complain of loss of energy, sadness or hopelessness,

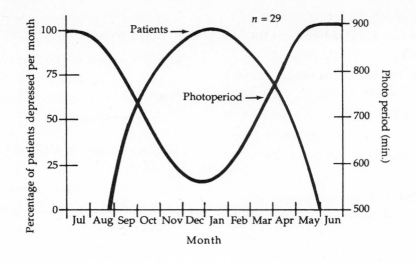

and a desire to withdraw socially. Other symptoms include oversleeping and eating and a drop in sexual arousal.

Depressive episodes among SAD patients are closely linked to the average temperature and number of hours of sunlight per day, as shown in the figure on this page. So strong are these relationships that when SAD patients travel south during the winter their depression often eases, returning to full intensity only when they come back to northern climates.

Although the prevalence of SAD is unknown, researchers at the National Institutes of Mental Health estimate that approximately 20 percent of the population experiences marked mood swings as the seasons change. Women suffering from SAD outnumber men 4 to 1, and the disorder has been identified in children as well as adults.

Several biological factors have been linked to SAD. In one study, nearly 75 percent of SAD patients were discovered to have relatives who also suffered from affective disorders, suggesting a possible genetic component to the disorder. Another study found that the hormone prolactin reached abnormally high levels during the winter depressions of those with SAD, suggesting a possible biochemical factor as well.

Some people apparently suffer a reverse form of SAD, experiencing depression during the spring and summer and an elevation in mood during winter. Although the basic symptoms are the same for both types of SAD, other evidence indicates that the reverse SAD pattern may involve a more serious form of depression. For example, suicide rates typically peak during the spring. Similarly, psychiatric hospital admissions for the most serious forms of depression peak in the spring.

Although much further research is needed, experts believe that it may be possible to prevent seasonal mood swings by manipulating environmental factors such as temperature and hours of daylight. In one

treatment program, patients are exposed to bright, white "growlights" placed in key locations in their homes and set to artificially lengthen the daylight hours. Relief following this type of treatment often occurs within days.

Although anyone with serious depression should consult a doctor, people who feel mild SAD symptoms are advised to increase their exposure to available sunlight during the gray days of winter. Because the timing, rather than total hours, of light exposure seems to be critical, they should focus on the morning hours. Taking early morning walks and avoiding the urge to hibernate during winter are two steps sufferers of seasonal mood swings are advised to try.

Sources: Rosenhan, D. L., & Seligman, M. E. P. (1989). *Abnormal psychology* (2nd ed.). New York: W. W. Norton, 354–355.

Adelmann, P. (1988, Feb. 26). Moods swing by season. *Detroit Free Press*, 3B.

Progress Test 1

Multiple-Choice Questions

Circle your answers to the following questions and check them with the answers on page 324. If your answer is incorrect, read the explanation for why it is incorrect and then consult the appropriate pages of the text (in parentheses following the correct answer).

1. Amnesia, fugue state, and multiple personality are all examples of:
   a. anxiety disorders.
   b. mood disorders.
   c. somatoform disorders.
   d. dissociative disorders.

2. The criteria for classifying behavior as psychologically disordered:
   a. vary from culture to culture.
   b. vary from time to time.

c. are characterized by both a. and b.

d. have remained largely unchanged over the course of history.

3. Most mental health workers today take the view that disordered behaviors:

   a. are usually genetically triggered.

   b. are organic diseases.

   c. arise from the interaction of nature and nurture.

   d. are the product of learning.

4. The French reformer who insisted that madness was not demon possession and who called for humane treatment of patients was:

   a. Nadel.   **c.** Szasz.

   b. Freud.   **d.** Pinel.

5. Which of the following is the most pervasive of the psychological disorders?

   a. depression

   b. schizophrenia

   c. hypochondriasis

   d. generalized anxiety disorder

6. Which of the following is *not* true concerning depression?

   a. Depression is more common in females than in males.

   b. Most depressive episodes appear not to be preceded by any particular factor or event.

   c. Most depressive episodes last less than 3 months.

   d. Most people recover from depression without professional therapy.

7. Which of the following is *not* true regarding schizophrenia?

   a. It affects men and women about equally.

   b. It occurs more frequently in the lower socioeconomic classes.

   c. It occurs more frequently in industrialized countries.

   d. It usually appears during adolescence or early adulthood.

8. Evidence of environmental effects on psychological disorders is seen in the fact that certain disorders, such as _____, are universal, while others, such as _____, are culture-bound.

   a. schizophrenia; depression

   b. depression; schizophrenia

   c. antisocial personality; neurosis

   d. depression; anorexia nervosa

9. The effect of drugs that block receptors for dopamine is to:

   a. alleviate schizophrenia symptoms.

   b. alleviate depression.

   c. increase schizophrenia symptoms.

   d. increase depression.

10. The diagnostic reliability of DSM-III-R:

    a. is unknown.

    b. depends on the age of the patient.

    c. is very low.

    d. is relatively high.

11. Behavior is classified as disordered when it is:

    a. atypical.

    b. maladaptive.

    c. unjustifiable.

    d. disturbing.

    e. all of the above.

12. (Close-Up) The terms *sanity* and *insanity* refer to:

    a. legal definitions.

    b. psychotic disorders only.

    c. personality disorders only.

    d. both psychotic disorders and personality disorders.

13. Phobias and obsessive-compulsive behaviors are classified as:

    a. anxiety disorders.

    b. somatoform disorders.

    c. dissociative disorders.

    d. personality disorders.

14. According to the social-cognitive perspective, a person who experiences unexpected aversive events may develop helplessness and manifest:

    a. an obsessive-compulsive disorder.

    b. a dissociative disorder.

    c. a personality disorder.

    d. a mood disorder.

15. Which of the following was presented in the text as evidence of biological influences on anxiety disorders?

    a. Identical twins often develop similar phobias.

    b. PET scans of persons with obsessive-compulsive disorder reveal unusually high activity in an area of the frontal lobes.

    c. Drugs that affect the neurotransmitter serotonin may control obsessive thoughts.

    d. All of the above were presented.

    e. None of the above was presented.

16. According to psychoanalytic theory, memory of losses, especially in combination with internalized anger, is likely to result in:

    a. learned helplessness.

    b. the self-serving bias.

    c. weak ego-defense mechanisms.

    d. depression.

17. When expecting to be electrically shocked, people with an antisocial disorder, as compared to normal people, show:
   a. less fear and greater arousal of the autonomic nervous system.
   (b.) less fear and less autonomic arousal.
   c. greater fear and greater autonomic arousal.
   d. greater fear and less autonomic arousal.

18. Hearing voices would be a(n) _____; believing that you are Napoleon would be a(n) _____.

   a. obsession; compulsion
   b. compulsion; obsession

c. delusion; hallucination
(d.) hallucination; delusion

19. In treating depression, a psychiatrist would probably prescribe a drug that would:
   a. increase levels of acetylcholine.
   b. decrease levels of dopamine.
   (c.) increase levels of norepinephrine.
   d. decrease levels of serotonin.

20. When schizophrenia is slow to develop, called _____ schizophrenia, recovery is _____.
   a. reactive; unlikely   (c.) process; unlikely
   b. process; likely   d. reactive; likely

Matching Items

Match each term with the appropriate definition or description.

Terms

__f__ 1. fugue
__d__ 2. psychotic disorder
__a__ 3. mood disorders
__i__ 4. dissociative disorders
__g__ 5. neurotic disorder
__b__ 6. mania
__k__ 7. obsessive-compulsive disorder
__j__ 8. schizophrenia
__c__ 9. somatoform disorder
__e__ 10. panic attack
__h__ 11. hypochondriasis

Definitions or Descriptions

a. psychological disorders marked by emotional extremes
b. an extremely elevated mood
c. a disorder in which symptoms take a bodily form
d. any psychological disorder that is severely debilitating and involves bizarre thinking and behavior
e. a sudden escalation of anxiety often accompanied by a sensation of choking or other physical symptoms
f. a dissociative disorder in which the person flees from home and identity
g. any psychological disorder in which the person continues to think rationally and function socially
h. a disorder in which normal physical aches and pains are misinterpreted as symptoms of a dread disease
i. disorders such as fugue, amnesia, or multiple personality
j. a group of disorders marked by disorganized thinking, disturbed perceptions, and inappropriate emotions and actions
k. a disorder characterized by repetitive thoughts and actions

Progress Test 2

Progress Test 2 should be completed during a final chapter review. Answer the following questions after you thoroughly understand the correct answers for the Chapter Review and Progress Test 1.

Multiple-Choice Questions

1. Which of the following is true concerning abnormal behavior?
   (a.) Definitions of abnormal behavior are culture-dependent.

b. A behavior cannot be defined as abnormal unless it is considered harmful to society.

c. Abnormal behavior can be defined as any behavior that is atypical.

d. Definitions of abnormal behavior are based on physiological factors.

2. According to the psychoanalytic perspective, phobias are:

   a. conditioned fears.

   b. displaced responses to incompletely repressed impulses.

   c. biological predispositions.

   d. manifestations of self-defeating thoughts.

3. The textbook suggests that the disorganized thoughts of people with schizophrenia may be attributed to a breakdown in:

   a. selective attention.

   b. memory storage.

   c. motivation.

   d. memory retrieval.

4. The most widely used system of classifying and describing disordered behavior in the United States is the:

   a. *Diagnostic and Statistical Manual of Mental Disorders (Third Edition – Revised).*

   b. *World Health Organization's International Classification of Diseases.*

   c. *Mental Measurements Yearbook.*

   d. *Psychiatric Reference Book.*

5. Somatoform disorders are more common in countries such as China, where:

   a. schizophrenia is rare.

   b. psychological explanations of anxiety are less acceptable.

   c. mood disorders are also common.

   d. there are more elderly people.

6. Our early ancestors commonly attributed disordered behavior to:

   a. "bad blood."   **c.** brain injury.

   b. evil spirits.   **d.** laziness.

7. The dissociative disorder that usually begins as a response to intolerable psychological stress is:

   a. conversion disorder.

   b. psychogenic amnesia.

   c. process schizophrenia.

   d. bipolar disorder.

8. Which of the following statements concerning the labeling of disordered behaviors is *not* true?

   a. Labels interfere with effective treatment of psychological disorders.

   b. Labels promote research studies of psychological disorders.

   c. Labels may create preconceptions that bias people's perceptions.

   d. Labels may influence behavior by creating self-fulfilling prophecies.

9. What does Nicolas Spanos believe about multiple personality disorder?

   a. It is a genuine disorder.

   b. It is merely role playing.

   c. It cannot be explained according to the learning perspective.

   d. He believes both a. and c.

10. Which neurotransmitter is present in overabundant amounts during the manic phase of bipolar depression?

   a. dopamine   **c.** epinephrine

   b. serotonin   **d.** norepinephrine

11. Psychiatrist Thomas Szasz has argued that:

   a. the medical model has played a valuable role in shaping the therapeutic process.

   b. psychological disorders will not be truly treatable until the underlying biochemical mechanisms are identified.

   c. the medical model errs in viewing psychological disorders as diseases.

   d. disordered behavior typically results from stress, and treatment must therefore aim at alleviating stress.

12. If a person experiences blindness, paralysis, or some other physical ailment for which no physiological cause can be found, the diagnosis would be:

   a. hypochondriasis.

   b. a conversion disorder.

   c. neurosis.

   d. schizophrenia.

13. Both the medical model and the psychoanalytic model:

   a. have in recent years been in large part discredited.

   b. view psychological disorders as sicknesses that are diagnosable and treatable.

   c. emphasize the role of physiological factors in disorders over that of psychological factors.

   d. advocate all of the above.

14. Psychoanalytic and learning theorists both agree that dissociative, somatoform, and anxiety disorders are symptoms that represent the person's attempt to deal with:

   a. unconscious conflicts.

   b. anxiety.

   c. unfulfilled wishes.

   d. unpleasant responsibilities.

15. The early warning signs of schizophrenia, based on studies of high-risk children, include all *but* which of the following?
    a. having a severely schizophrenic mother
    b. having been separated from parents
    c. having a short attention span
    d. having matured physically at a very early age

16. Many psychologists dislike using DSM-III-R because of its:
    a. failure to emphasize observable behaviors in the diagnostic process.
    b. learning theory bias.
    c. medical model bias.
    d. psychoanalytic bias.

17. Which of the following is *not* a symptom of schizophrenia?
    a. inappropriate emotions
    b. disturbed perceptions

    c. panic attacks
    d. disorganized thinking

18. Social-cognitive theorists believe that depression is linked with:
    a. negative moods.
    b. maladaptive explanations of failure.
    c. self-defeating beliefs.
    d. all of the above.

19. Most of the hallucinations of schizophrenia patients involve the sense of:
    a. smell.   c. hearing.
    b. vision.   d. touch.

20. Among the following, which is generally accepted as a possible cause of schizophrenia?
    a. an excess of endorphins in the brain
    b. being a twin
    c. extensive learned helplessness
    d. a genetic predisposition

Matching Items

Match each term with the appropriate definition or description.

Terms

___f___ 1. multiple personality
___e___ 2. phobic disorder
___a___ 3. dopamine
___i___ 4. conversion disorder
___c___ 5. antisocial personality
___b___ 6. norepinephrine
___g___ 7. serotonin
___h___ 8. bipolar disorder
___d___ 9. delusions

Definitions or Descriptions

a. a neurotransmitter for which there are excess receptors in some schizophrenia patients
b. a neurotransmitter that is overabundant during mania and scarce during depression
c. an individual who seems to have no conscience
d. false beliefs that may accompany psychological disorders
e. an anxiety disorder marked by a persistent, irrational fear of a specific object or situation
f. a type of dissociative disorder
g. a neurotransmitter possibly linked to obsessive-compulsive behavior
h. a type of mood disorder
i. a type of somatoform disorder

Challenge Test

Answer these questions the day before an exam as a final check on your understanding of the chapter's terms and concepts.

Multiple-Choice Questions

1. Joe has an intense, irrational fear of snakes. He is suffering from a(n):
    a. generalized anxiety disorder.
    b. obsessive-compulsive disorder.
    c. phobic disorder.
    d. somatoform disorder.

2. While mountain climbing Jack saw his best friend killed by an avalanche. Jack himself was found months later, hundreds of miles away. On questioning, he claimed to be another person and, indeed, appeared to have no knowledge about any aspect of his former life. Most likely, Jack was suffering from:
    a. a fugue state.
    b. the conversion disorder.
    c. multiple personality disorder.
    d. psychogenic amnesia.

3. Bob has never been able to keep a job. He's been in

and out of jail for charges such as theft, sexual assault, and spouse abuse. Bob would most likely be diagnosed as having:

a. a multiple personality.
b. major depression.
c. schizophrenia.
d. an antisocial personality.

4. Julia's psychologist believes that Julia's fear of heights can be traced to a conditioned fear she developed after falling from a ladder. This explanation reflects a _____ perspective.

a. medical
b. psychoanalytic
c. social-cognitive
d. learning

5. Before he can begin studying, Rashid must arrange his books, pencils, paper, and other items on his desk so that they are "just so." The campus counselor suggests that Rashid's compulsive behavior may help alleviate his anxiety about failing in school, which reinforces the compulsive actions. This explanation of obsessive-compulsive behavior is most consistent with which perspective?

a. learning
b. psychoanalytic
c. humanistic
d. social-cognitive

6. Sharon is continually tense, jittery, and apprehensive for no specific reason. She would probably be diagnosed as suffering a(n):

a. phobic disorder.
b. conversion disorder.
c. obsessive-compulsive disorder.
d. generalized anxiety disorder.

7. Jason is so preoccupied with staying clean that he showers as many as ten times each day. Jason would be diagnosed as suffering from a(n):

a. somatoform disorder.
b. conversion disorder.
c. personality disorder.
d. obsessive-compulsive disorder.

8. Lee is convinced that the eyestrain he feels after a day of working at his computer is caused by a detached retina. Although several doctors have assured him that he is fine, Lee continues to worry. His behavior is an example of:

a. a conversion disorder.
b. schizophrenia.
c. a panic attack.
d. hypochondriasis.

9. Claiming that she heard a voice commanding her to warn other people that eating is harmful, Sandy attempts to convince others in a restaurant not to eat. The psychiatrist to whom she is referred finds that Sandy's thinking and speech are often fragmented and incoherent. In addition, Sandy has an unreasonable fear that someone is "out to get her" and consequently trusts no one. Her condition is most indicative of:

a. schizophrenic disorders.
b. generalized anxiety disorder.
c. phobic disorders.
d. obsessive-compulsive disorder.

10. Irene occasionally experiences unpredictable episodes of intense dread accompanied by chest pains and a sensation of smothering. Since her symptoms have no apparent cause, they would probably be classified as indicative of:

a. schizophrenia.
b. hysteria.
c. hypochondriasis.
d. panic attack.

11. To which of the following is a person *most* likely to acquire a phobia?

a. heights
b. being in public
c. being dirty
d. All of the above are equally likely.

12. Dr. Jekyll, who suffered from multiple personality disorder, had a(n) _____ disorder.

a. anxiety
b. somatoform
c. dissociative
d. mood

13. For the past 6 months, a woman has complained of feeling isolated from others, dissatisfied with life, and discouraged about the future. This woman could be diagnosed as suffering from:

a. bipolar disorder.
b. major depression.
c. somatoform disorder.
d. dissociative disorder.

14. On Monday, Matt felt optimistic, energetic, and on top of the world. On Tuesday, he felt hopeless and lethargic, and thought that the future looked very grim. Matt would *most* likely be diagnosed as having:

a. bipolar disorder.
b. major depression.
c. somatoform disorder.
d. dissociative disorder.

15. Connie's therapist has suggested that her depression stems from unresolved anger toward her parents. Evidently, Connie's therapist is working within the _____ perspective.

a. learning
b. social-cognitive
c. biological
d. psychoanalytic

16. Ken's therapist suggested that his depression is a result of his self-defeating thoughts and negative assumptions about himself, his situation, and his future. Evidently, Ken's therapist is working within the _____ perspective.
    - **a.** learning
    - **b.** social-cognitive
    - **c.** biological
    - **d.** psychoanalytic

17. Alicia's doctor, who believes that Alicia's depression has a biochemical cause, prescribes a drug that:
    - **a.** reduces norepinephrine.
    - **b.** increases norepinephrine.
    - **c.** reduces serotonin.
    - **d.** increases acetylcholine.

18. Wayne's doctor attempts to help Wayne by prescribing a drug that blocks receptors for dopamine. Wayne has apparently been diagnosed with a(n) _____ disorder.
    - **a.** mood
    - **b.** anxiety
    - **c.** dissociative
    - **d.** schizophrenic

19. In many movies, soap operas, and novels, the hero or heroine, who is under great stress, experiences a sudden loss of memory without leaving home or establishing a new identity. This is an example of:
    - **a.** a dissociative disorder.
    - **b.** fugue.
    - **c.** psychogenic amnesia.
    - **d.** both a. and c.

20. Janet, whose class presentation is entitled "Current Views on the Causes of Schizophrenia," concludes her talk with the statement:
    - **a.** "Schizophrenia is caused by intolerable stress."
    - **b.** "Schizophrenia is inherited."
    - **c.** "Genes may predispose some people to react to particular experiences by developing a schizophrenic disorder."
    - **d.** "As of this date, schizophrenia is completely unpredictable and its causes are unknown."

Essay Question

Clinical psychologists label people disordered if their behavior is (1) atypical, (2) disturbing, (3) maladaptive, and (4) unjustifiable. Demonstrate your understanding of the classification process by giving examples of behaviors that might be considered atypical, disturbing, maladaptive, or unjustifiable but, because they do not fit all four criteria, would not necessarily be labeled disordered. (Use the space below to list the points you want to make and organize them. Then write the essay on a separate piece of paper.)

Key Terms

Using your own words, write a brief definition or explanation of each of the following terms.

1. psychological disorder

2. medical model

3. DSM-III-R

4. neurotic disorders

5. psychotic disorders

6. anxiety disorders

7. generalized anxiety disorder

8. phobic disorder

9. obsessive-compulsive disorder

10. panic attack

11. somatoform disorders

12. conversion disorder

13. hypochondriasis

14. dissociative disorders

15. amnesia

16. fugue

17. multiple personality disorder

18. mood disorders

19. major depression

20. bipolar disorder

21. mania

22. schizophrenia

23. delusions

24. personality disorder

25. antisocial personality

ANSWERS
GUIDED STUDY

The following guidelines provide the main points that your answers should have touched upon.

1. In order to be classified as psychologically disordered, behavior must be atypical, disturbing to others, maladaptive, and unjustifiable.

2. According to the medical perspective, psychological disorders are sicknesses that can be diagnosed on the basis of their symptoms and cured through therapy. Psychologists who reject the medical model contend that disorders arise from the inter-

action of genetic, physiological, psychological, and social factors.

3. DSM-III-R groups some 230 psychological disorders into 17 major categories. Diagnostic classification is intended to describe a disorder, predict its future course, imply its appropriate treatment, and stimulate research into its causes.

4. There are three types of anxiety disorder: generalized anxiety disorder, in which a person feels inexplicably tense and apprehensive; phobic disorder, in which a person has an irrational fear of a specific object or situation; and obsessive-compulsive disorder, in which a person is troubled by repetitive thoughts or actions.

   According to the psychoanalytic perspective, an anxiety disorder is a manifestation of repressed impulses, ideas, and feelings that influence the sufferer's actions and emotions. Learning theorists see generalized anxiety as a form of learned helplessness, phobias as conditioned fears, and obsessive-compulsive behaviors as responses reinforced because they reduce anxiety. Biologically oriented researchers believe that some people are genetically predisposed to particular fears and high anxiety. The anxiety of persons with obsessive-compulsive disorder, for example, is measurable as unusually high activity in a particular region of the frontal lobes.

5. In somatoform disorders, distressing symptoms take a bodily form such as vomiting, dizziness, blurred vision, or unexplained pain. In one type, conversion disorder, anxiety is converted into a physical symptom. In another, hypochondriasis, people interpret normal sensations as symptoms of a disease.

   In dissociative disorders, a person experiences a sudden loss of memory (amnesia) or change in identity (fugue) in response to extreme stress. Even more mysterious is the multiple personality disorder, in which people have two or more distinct personalities; however, some skeptics believe that such persons are merely enacting a role for strategic reasons.

   Psychoanalysts view the symptoms of these disorders as defenses against anxiety. Learning theorists see them as behaviors reinforced by anxiety reduction. Some theorists see dissociative behaviors as protective escape responses to traumatic experiences.

6. There are two principal mood disorders: major depression and the bipolar disorder. Major depression, the "common cold" of psychological disorders, occurs when signs of depression last 2 weeks or more without any discernible cause. Alternating between depressive episodes and the hyperactive, wildly optimistic state of mania is characteristic of the bipolar disorder.

   According to the psychoanalytic perspective, depression occurs when significant losses evoke feelings associated with losses experienced in childhood and when unresolved anger is directed inward against the self.

   According to the biological perspective, mood disorders involve genetic predispositions, and biochemical imbalances in which norepinephrine is elevated during mania and scarce during depression.

   According to the social-cognitive perspective, depression is a vicious cycle in which stressful experiences trigger self-focused negative thinking and a self-blaming style of explaining events that hamper the way the person thinks and acts, which leads to further negative experiences.

7. Schizophrenia is a cluster of disorders in which there is a split from reality that shows itself in disorganized thinking, disturbed perceptions, and inappropriate emotions and actions. *Positive symptoms* of schizophrenia include disorganized or deluded thinking and speech, and inappropriate emotions. *Negative symptoms* include toneless voices, expressionless faces, or mute and rigid bodies. Schizophrenia may develop gradually (chronic, or process, schizophrenia), in which case recovery is doubtful, or rapidly (acute, or reactive, schizophrenia) in response to stress, in which case recovery is much more likely.

   Some schizophrenia patients have an excess of brain receptors for dopamine. Others have abnormally low brain activity in the frontal lobes or enlarged fluid-filled areas and a corresponding shrinkage of cerebral tissue. Studies of identical twins and adopted children reveal a strong genetic link to schizophrenia. Genes may predispose some people to react to particular experiences by developing a form of schizophrenia. Psychological causes of schizophrenia are difficult to pinpoint due to the variety of forms of the disorder.

8. Personality disorders are inflexible and enduring behavior patterns, such as attention-getting emotionality or exaggerated self-importance, that impair one's social functioning. Those with the antisocial personality disorder display a lack of conscience at an early age, as they begin to lie, steal, fight, or evidence unrestrained sexual behavior. As adults their antisocial behavior may manifest itself in an inability to hold down a job, in marital and parental irresponsibility, or in criminal behavior. Twin and adoption studies suggest that some individuals may possess a genetic vulnerability to the antisocial personality disorder, which is manifested under stress.

9. Research reveals that approximately 32 percent of American adults have experienced a psychological disorder at some time in their lives and that 20 percent have an active disorder. Those who experience a psychological disorder usually do so by early adulthood. Some disorders, such as the antisocial personality and phobic disorders, often appear earlier, during childhood.

10. Most clinicians believe that diagnostic labels help in describing, treating, and researching the causes of psychological disorders. Critics contend that these labels are arbitrary value judgments that create preconceptions that can bias our perceptions and interpretations. Labels can also affect people's self-images and stigmatize them in others' eyes. Finally, labels can change reality.

CHAPTER REVIEW

1. atypical; disturbing; maladaptive; unjustifiable; variable
2. medical; Pinel
3. socially
4. consistent

Critics of the medical model maintain that disorders are caused by psychological as well as physical factors. They contend that *all* behavior arises from the interaction of nature and nurture. Therefore, abnormal behavior cannot be viewed simply as an internal "sickness."

5. depression; schizophrenia; anorexia nervosa
6. genetic; physiological; psychological; social
7. DSM-III-R
8. psychotic disorders; neurotic disorders; describe; explain
9. show
10. women
11. generalized anxiety
12. phobic
13. obsessive-compulsive
14. free-floating; autonomic; panic attack
15. earlier; teens
16. repressed
17. helplessness
18. is
19. frontal; serotonin

The psychoanalytic explanation is that phobias represent incompletely repressed impulses over which the person is anxious. When repression is incomplete, the anxiety is displaced onto the phobic stimulus. The learning explanation is that phobias are conditioned

fears. Since avoiding the feared situation reduces anxiety, the phobic behavior is reinforced. According to the biological perspective, anxiety disorders have evolutionary, genetic, and physiological causes. Some people, for example, may be genetically predisposed to develop particular fears and high anxiety. Others may have unusually high activity in certain regions of the brain.

20. somatoform
21. China
22. conversion; rare
23. hypochondriasis
24. conscious awareness; separated; rare
25. amnesia; psychogenic amnesia; selective
26. fugue
27. multiple personality; brain; body; anxiety
28. roles

Skeptics point out that the recent increase in the number of reported cases of multiple personality indicates that it has become a fad. The fact that the disorder is almost nonexistent outside North America also causes skeptics to doubt the disorder's genuineness.

29. major depression
30. mania; bipolar
31. increased; young adults; women
32. poor appetite, insomnia, lethargy, feelings of worthlessness, loss of interest in family, friends, and activities
33. 2 weeks
34. euphoria, hyperactivity, a wildly optimistic state; 1
35. can
36. is

The psychoanalytic perspective suggests that adulthood depression can be triggered by losses that evoke feelings associated with earlier, childhood losses—feelings that often include anger. Since this anger is unacceptable to the superego, the emotion is turned inward and takes the form of depression.

37. tend
38. low; norepinephrine; serotonin
39. self-defeating; learned helplessness

Depressed people are more likely than others to explain failures or bad events in terms that are *stable* (it's going to last forever), *global* (it will affect everything), and *internal* (it's my fault). Such explanations lead to feelings of hopelessness, which in turn feed depression.

40. coincide with
41. rejection

Depression is often brought on by stressful experiences. Depressed people brood over such experiences with maladaptive explanations that produce self-blame and amplify their depression, which in turn triggers other symptoms of depression. In addition, being withdrawn and complaining tends to elicit more social rejection and other negative experiences.

42. reality

43. thinking; perceptions; emotions; actions

44. delusions

45. selective attention

46. hallucinations; auditory

47. cluster of disorders

48. disorganized and deluded thinking, inappropriate emotions; toneless voices, expressionless faces, mute or rigid bodies; less

49. dopamine; decrease

50. shrinkage; activity

51. support

52. genetic; psychological

Such signs may include severe, long-lasting schizophrenia in the mother; complications at birth and low birth weight; separation from parents; short attention span and poor coordination; and behavioral problems at school.

53. social functioning

54. antisocial; psychopath or sociopath

55. is

56. less

57. 32; 20

58. early; antisocial personality; phobias

59. a significant

Psychological labels may be arbitrary. They can create preconceptions that bias our perceptions and interpretations and they can affect people's self-images. Moreover, labels can even change reality, by serving as self-fulfilling prophecies. Despite these drawbacks, labels are useful in describing, treating, and researching the causes of psychological disorders.

PROGRESS TEST 1

Multiple-Choice Questions

1. **d.** is the answer. In each of these disorders a person's conscious awareness becomes dissociated, or separated, from previous memories, thoughts, and feelings. (pp. 455–456)

2. **c.** is the answer. (pp. 446–447)

3. **c.** is the answer. Most clinicians agree that psychological disorders may be caused by both psychological (d.) and physical factors (a. and b.). (p. 448)

4. **d.** is the answer. (p. 447)

5. **a.** is the answer. (p. 458)

6. **b.** is the answer. Usually, depression is preceded by a stressful event related to work, marriage, or a close relationship. (p. 459)

7. **c.** is the answer. The incidence of schizophrenia does not vary significantly from country to country. (p. 466)

8. **d.** is the answer. Although depression is universal, anorexia nervosa is rare outside the United States. (p. 448)

   a. & b. Schizophrenia and depression are both universal.

   c. The text mentions only schizophrenia and depression as universal disorders. Furthermore, neurosis is no longer used as a category of diagnosis.

9. **a.** is the answer. (p. 468)

   b. & d. Thus far, it is norepinephrine and serotonin that have been implicated in depression and bipolar disorder.

   c. Schizophrenia has been associated with an excess of dopamine receptors. Blocking them alleviates, rather than increases, schizophrenia symptoms.

10. **d.** is the answer. (pp. 450–451)

    b. The textbook does not mention DSM-III-R's reliability in terms of a person's age.

11. **e.** is the answer. Behavior is considered disordered when it is atypical, maladaptive, unjustifiable, and disturbing. (p. 447)

12. **a.** is the answer. (p. 449)

13. **a.** is the answer. (p. 451)

    b. The somatoform disorders include hypochondriasis and the conversion disorder.

    c. The dissociative disorders include amnesia, fugue, and multiple personality.

    d. The personality disorders include the antisocial and histrionic personalities.

14. **d.** is the answer. Learned helplessness may lead to self-defeating beliefs, which in turn are linked with depression, a mood disorder. (p. 462)

15. **d.** is the answer. (p. 454)

16. **d.** is the answer. A loss may evoke feelings of anger associated with an earlier loss. Such anger is unacceptable to the superego and is turned against the self. This internalized anger results in depression. (pp. 460–461)

    a. Learned helplessness would be an explanation offered by the social-cognitive perspective.

    b. The self-serving bias is not discussed in terms of its relationship to depression.

c. This is the psychoanalytic explanation of anxiety.

17. **b.** is the answer. Those with antisocial personality disorders show less autonomic arousal in such situations, and emotions, such as fear, are tied to arousal. (p. 472)

18. **d.** is the answer. Hallucinations are false sensory experiences; delusions are false beliefs. (pp. 452, 466)

a. & b. Obsessions are repetitive and unwanted thoughts. Compulsions are repetitive behaviors.

19. **c.** is the answer. Drugs that relieve depression tend to increase levels of norepinephrine. (p. 462)

a. Acetylcholine is a neurotransmitter involved in muscle contractions.

b. It is in certain types of schizophrenia that decreasing dopamine levels is known to be helpful. Although researchers are investigating a possible role for dopamine in depression, answers have not yet been obtained.

d. On the contrary, it appears that a particular type of depression may be related to *low* levels of serotonin.

20. **c.** is the answer. (p. 468)

Matching Items

1. f (p. 456) 5. g (p. 450) 9. c (p. 454)
2. d (p. 450) 6. b (p. 459) 10. e (p. 451)
3. a (p. 458) 7. k (pp. 452–453) 11. h (p. 455)
4. i (pp. 455–456) 8. j (pp. 466–467)

PROGRESS TEST 2

Multiple-Choice Questions

1. **a.** is the answer. Different cultures have different standards for behaviors that are considered acceptable and normal. (pp. 466–467)

b. Some abnormal behaviors are simply maladaptive for the individual.

c. Many individuals who are atypical, such as Olympic gold medalists, are not considered abnormal. There are other criteria that must be met in order for behavior to be considered abnormal.

d. Although physiological factors play a role in the various disorders, they do not define abnormal behavior. Rather, behavior is said to be abnormal if it is atypical, disturbing, maladaptive, and unjustifiable.

2. **b.** is the answer. (p. 453)

a. This answer reflects the learning perspective.

c. Although certain phobias are biologically predisposed, this could not fully explain phobias, nor is it the explanation offered by psychoanalytic theory.

d. Social-cognitive theorists propose self-defeating thoughts as a cause of depression.

3. **a.** is the answer. Schizophrenia sufferers are easily distracted by irrelevant stimuli, evidently because of a breakdown in the capacity for selective attention. (p. 466)

4. **a.** is the answer. (p. 450)

5. **b.** is the answer. Apparently, because psychological explanations of anxiety are less acceptable in China, anxiety is expressed in bodily form. (pp. 454–455)

a., c., & d. None of these is true of China, or linked to the incidence of somatoform disorders.

6. **b.** is the answer. (p. 447)

7. **b.** is the answer. (pp. 455–456)

a., c., & d. These are somatoform, schizophrenic, and mood disorders, respectively.

8. **a.** is the answer. In fact, just the opposite is true. Labels are useful in promoting effective treatment of psychological disorders. (p. 473)

9. **b.** is the answer. (p. 457)

c. Playing a role is most definitely a learned skill.

10. **d.** is the answer. In bipolar disorder, norepinephrine appears to be overabundant during mania and in short supply during depression. (p. 462)

a. There is an overabundance of dopamine receptors in some schizophrenia patients.

b. Serotonin sometimes appears to be scarce during depression.

c. Epinephrine has not been implicated in psychological disorders.

11. **c.** is the answer. Szasz believes that psychological disorders are socially, not medically, defined and that treating them as medically defined diseases is wrong and has negative consequences. (p. 448)

12. **b.** is the answer. (p. 455)

a. In hypochondriasis, the person believes there is something physically wrong when nothing is.

c. *Neurosis* is Freud's term for the process by which unconscious conflicts create anxiety.

d. Schizophrenia is characterized by disorganized thinking, disturbed perceptions, and inappropriate emotions and actions.

13. **b.** is the answer. (pp. 447–448)

a. This isn't the case; in fact, the medical model has gained credibility from recent discoveries of genetic and biochemical links to some disorders.

c. The psychoanalytic perspective tends to place equal, if not more, emphasis on psychological factors.

14. **b.** is the answer. The psychoanalytic explanation

is that these disorders are a manifestation of incompletely repressed impulses over which the person is anxious. According to the learning perspective, the troubled behaviors that result from these disorders have been reinforced by anxiety reduction. (p. 457)

a. & c. These are true of the psychoanalytic, but not the learning, perspective.

15. **d.** is the answer. There is no evidence that early physical maturation is an early warning sign of schizophrenia. (p. 470)

16. **c.** is the answer. DSM-III-R was shaped by the medical model. (p. 450)

a. In fact, just the opposite is true. DSM-III-R was revised in order to improve reliability by basing diagnoses on observable behaviors.

b. & d. DSM-III-R does not reflect either a learning theory or a psychoanalytic bias.

17. **c.** is the answer. Panic attacks are characteristic of certain anxiety disorders, not of schizophrenia. (pp. 466–467)

18. **d.** is the answer. (pp. 462–464)

19. **c.** is the answer. (pp. 466–467)

20. **d.** is the answer. Risk for schizophrenia increases for individuals who are related to a schizophrenia victim, and the greater the genetic relatedness, the greater the risk. (p. 468)

a. Schizophrenia victims have an overabundance of the neurotransmitter dopamine, not endorphins.

b. Being a twin is, in itself, irrelevant to developing schizophrenia.

c. Although learned helplessness has been suggested by social-cognitive theorists as a cause of self-defeating depressive behaviors, it has not been suggested as a cause of schizophrenia.

Matching Items

1. f (p. 456)   4. i (p. 455)   7. g (p. 454)
2. e (p. 452)   5. c (p. 471)   8. h (p. 459)
3. a (p. 468)   6. b (p. 462)   9. d (p. 466)

CHALLENGE TEST

Multiple-Choice Questions

1. **c.** is the answer. An intense fear of a specific object is a phobia. (p. 452)

a. His fear is focused on a specific object, not generalized.

b. In this disorder a person is troubled by repetitive thoughts and actions.

d. This disorder is characterized by a bodily symptom that has no apparent physical cause.

2. **a.** is the answer. A fugue involves totally fleeing one's identity and home. (p. 456)

b. A conversion disorder is diagnosed when a psychological problem is expressed in a bodily symptom.

c. In multiple personality disorder, two or more personalities exist simultaneously, which is not the case in the example.

d. Psychogenic amnesia is generally a selective forgetting; it does not involve physical flight or total loss of identity.

3. **d.** is the answer. Repeated wrongdoing and aggressive behavior are part of the pattern associated with the antisocial personality disorder, which may also include marital problems and an inability to keep a job. (p. 471)

a. Although multiple personalities may involve an aggressive personality, there is nothing in the example to indicate a dissociation.

b. Nothing in the question indicates that Bob is passive and resigned and having the self-defeating thoughts characteristic of depression.

c. Bob's behavior does not include the disorganized thinking and disturbed perceptions typical of schizophrenia.

4. **d.** is the answer. In the learning perspective, a phobia, such as Julia's, is seen as a conditioned fear. (pp. 453–454)

a. Because the fear is focused on a specific stimulus, the medical model does not easily account for the phobic disorder. In any event, it would presumably offer an internal, biological explanation.

b. The psychoanalytic view of phobias is that they represent incompletely repressed anxieties that are displaced onto the feared object.

c. The social-cognitive perspective emphasizes a person's conscious, cognitive processes, not reflexive conditioned responses.

5. **a.** is the answer. According to the learning view, compulsive behaviors are reinforced because they reduce the anxiety created by obsessive thoughts. Rashid's obsession concerns failing, and his desk-arranging compulsive behaviors apparently help him control these thoughts. (p. 454)

b. According to the psychoanalytic view, obsessive thoughts are a symbolic representation of forbidden impulses. These thoughts may prompt the person to perform compulsive acts that counter these impulses.

c. & d. The textbook does not offer explanations of obsessive-compulsive behavior based on the humanistic or social-cognitive perspectives. Presumably, however, these explanations would emphasize growth-blocking difficulties in the person's environment (humanistic perspective) and the reciprocal influences of personality and environment (social-cognitive perspective), rather than symbolic expressions of forbidden impulses.

6. **d.** is the answer. (p. 451)

   a. In phobic disorders, anxiety is focused on a specific object.

   b. In conversion disorders, anxiety is manifested in physical symptoms.

   c. The obsessive-compulsive disorder is characterized by repetitive and unwanted thoughts and/or actions.

7. **d.** is the answer. Jason is obsessed with cleanliness; as a result, he has developed a compulsion to shower. (pp. 452–453)

   a. & b. In these disorders the symptoms take the form of physical symptoms.

   c. This disorder is characterized by maladaptive character traits.

8. **d.** is the answer. Lee is interpreting a normal sensation as a disease symptom. (p. 455)

   a. In a conversion disorder, a genuine physical ailment is exhibited.

   b. Schizophrenia is not characterized by such fears of illness.

   c. In a panic attack, the person has a sudden escalation of anxiety.

9. **a.** is the answer. Because Sandy experiences hallucinations (hearing voices), delusions (fearing someone is "out to get her"), and incoherence, she would most likely be diagnosed as suffering from schizophrenia. (pp. 466–467)

   b., c., & d. Anxiety disorders such as these are not characterized by disorganized thoughts and perceptions.

10. **d.** is the answer. These symptoms are characteristic of a panic attack, which is an episode of heightened anxiety. (p. 451)

    a. Baseless physical symptoms rarely play a role in schizophrenia.

    b. This is an older, Freudian term for somatoform disorders.

    c. In hypochondriasis, normal aches and pains are falsely interpreted as illness.

11. **a.** is the answer. Humans seem biologically prepared to develop a fear of heights and other dangers that our ancestors faced. (p. 452)

12. **c.** is the answer. (p. 456)

13. **b.** is the answer. The fact that this woman has had these symptoms for more than 2 weeks indicates that she is suffering from major depression. (p. 458)

14. **a.** is the answer. Matt's alternating states of the hopelessness and lethargy of depression and the energetic, optimistic state of mania are characteristic of bipolar disorder. (p. 459)

    b. Although depressed much of the time, Matt's manic states indicate that he is not suffering from major depression.

    c. That Matt has no apparent bodily symptoms indicates that he is not suffering from a somatoform disorder.

    d. That Matt has not lost his memory or changed his identity indicates that he is not suffering from a dissociative disorder.

15. **d.** is the answer. Freud believed that the anger once felt toward parents who were "abandoning" or "rejecting" is unacceptable to the superego, so the emotion is internalized and produces depression. (pp. 460–461)

    a. & b. The learning and social-cognitive perspectives focus on environmental experiences, conditioning, and self-defeating attitudes in explaining depression.

    c. The biological perspective focuses on genetic predispositions and biochemical imbalances in explaining depression.

16. **b.** is the answer. (pp. 462–464)

17. **b.** is the answer. Norepinephrine, which increases arousal and boosts mood, is scarce during depression. Drugs that relieve depression tend to increase norepinephrine. (p. 462)

    c. Increasing serotonin, which is sometimes scarce during depression, might relieve depression.

    d. This neurotransmitter is involved in motor responses but has not been linked to psychological disorders.

18. **d.** is the answer. Schizophrenia patients sometimes have an excess of receptors for dopamine. Drugs that block these receptors can therefore reduce symptoms of schizophrenia. (p. 468)

    a., b., & c. Dopamine receptors have not been implicated in these psychological disorders.

19. **d.** is the answer. Psychogenic amnesia, which is a dissociative disorder, involves a sudden memory loss brought on by extreme stress. (pp. 455–456)

    b. Fugue is a dissociative disorder in which flight from one's home and identity accompanies amnesia.

20. **c.** is the answer. (pp. 468–469)

Essay Question

There is more to a psychological disorder than being different from other people. Gifted artists, athletes, and scientists have atypical capabilities, yet are not considered psychologically disordered. To be considered disordered, other people must find the atypical behavior disturbing. But what is disturbing in one culture may not be in another, or at another time. Homosexuality, for example, was once classified as a psychological disorder, but it is no longer. Similarly, nudity is common in some cultures and disturbing in others. Atypical and disturbing behaviors are more likely to be considered disordered when judged as maladaptive to the individual. Prolonged feelings of depression or the use of drugs to avoid dealing with problems are examples of maladaptive behaviors that may signal a psychological disorder if they become disabling. Finally, abnormal behavior is most likely to be considered disordered when others find it unjustifiable. A student loudly reciting the Greek alphabet in public, for example, who can justify his or her unusual behavior as being part of a fraternity or sorority ritual, would not be considered psychologically disordered.

KEY TERMS

1. In order to be classified as a **psychological disorder**, behavior must be atypical, disturbing, maladaptive, and unjustifiable. (p. 447)

2. The **medical model** holds that psychological disorders are illnesses that can be diagnosed, treated, and cured, using traditional methods of medicine and psychiatry. (p. 447)

3. **DSM-III-R** is a short name for the American Psychiatric Association's *Diagnostic and Statistical Manual of Mental Disorders (Third Edition – Revised)*, which provides a widely used system of classifying psychological disorders. (p. 450)

4. **Neurotic disorders** is a former term for psychological disorders that, while distressing, still allow a person to think normally and function socially. The term is used mainly in contrast to *psychotic disorders*. (p. 450)

5. **Psychotic disorders** is a former term for psychological disorders that are severely debilitating and involve bizarre thoughts and behavior, and a break from reality. (p. 450)

6. **Anxiety disorders** involve distressing, persistent anxiety and/or maladaptive behaviors that reduce anxiety. (p. 451)

7. In the **generalized anxiety disorder**, the person is continually tense, apprehensive, and in a state of autonomic arousal for no apparent reason. (p. 451)

8. The **phobic disorder** is an anxiety disorder in which a person is irrationally afraid of a specific object or situation. (p. 451)
Example: Many **phobias** may actually be classically conditioned fears: The new irrational fear remains

even though the conditioning experience may have long since been forgotten.

9. The **obsessive-compulsive disorder** is an anxiety disorder in which the person experiences uncontrollable and repetitive thoughts (obsessions) and actions (compulsions). (p. 451)

10. A **panic attack** is an episode of intense dread accompanied by chest pain, dizziness, or choking. Panic attacks are essentially an escalation of the anxiety associated with generalized anxiety disorder. (p. 451)

11. **Somatoform disorders** involve physical symptoms with no apparent physical cause. (p. 454)
Memory aid: *Somatic* means "bodily." A **somatoform disorder** is one in which the disorder appears in bodily form.

12. The **conversion disorder** is a somatoform disorder in which there are very specific physical symptoms (e.g., paralysis, blindness, or inability to swallow) with no apparent physiological cause. (p. 455)
Memory aid: The **conversion disorder** is so named because Freud believed that in this disorder anxiety was *converted* into bodily symptoms.

13. **Hypochondriasis** is the somatoform disorder in which a person interprets normal aches and pains as symptoms of disease. (p. 455)

14. **Dissociative disorders** involve a separation of conscious awareness from one's previous memories, thoughts, and feelings. (p. 455)
Memory aid: To *dissociate* is to separate or pull apart. In the **dissociative disorder** a person becomes dissociated from his or her memories and identity.

15. **Amnesia** is a selective loss of memory. Amnesia may be caused by illness or head injuries, but the dissociative disorder, psychogenic amnesia, is usually precipitated by extreme stress. (p. 455)

16. **Fugue** is a dissociative disorder in which forgetting occurs and the person physically runs away from home and identity. (p. 456)
Memory aid: **Fugue** and *fugitive* both derive from the same Latin root, meaning "to flee."

17. The **multiple personality disorder** is a dissociative disorder in which a person exhibits two or more personalities. (p. 456)
Example: A common pattern in the **multiple personality disorder** is for one personality to be rather inhibited and shy while the second is more impulsive and uninhibited.

18. **Mood disorders** are characterized by emotional extremes. (p. 458)

19. **Major depression** is the mood disorder that occurs

when a person exhibits the passive, resigned, and self-defeating thoughts and behaviors of depression for more than a 2-week period and for no discernible reason. Because of its relative frequency, depression has been called the "common cold" of psychological disorders. (p. 458)

20. The **bipolar disorder** is the mood disorder in which a person alternates between depression and the euphoria of a manic state. (pp. 458–459)

    Memory aid: *Bipolar* means having two poles, that is, two opposite qualities. In the **bipolar disorder**, the opposing states are mania and depression.

21. **Mania** is the euphoric, hyperactive state that alternates with depression in the bipolar disorder (p. 459)

22. **Schizophrenia** refers to the group of disorders whose symptoms may include disorganized thinking, inappropriate emotions and actions, and disturbed perceptions. (p. 466)

23. **Delusions** are false beliefs that often are symptoms of schizophrenia. (p. 466)

24. **Personality disorders** are characterized by enduring maladaptive character traits. These disorders may, but need not, involve anxiety, depression, or dissociation from reality. (p. 471)

    Example: Examples of **personality disorders** include sexual deviations, the "asthenic personality," in which a person has a marked incapacity for enjoyment, and the "explosive personality," characterized by outbursts of verbal or physical aggressiveness.

25. The **antisocial personality** is a personality disorder in which the person is aggressive, ruthless, and shows no sign of a conscience that would inhibit wrongdoing. (p. 471)

    Example: Once called sociopaths or psychopaths, those with **antisocial personalities** are emotionally flat persons who express little remorse over violating others' rights.

16 / Therapy

Chapter Overview

Chapter 16 discusses the major psychotherapies and biomedical therapies for maladaptive behaviors. The various psychotherapies all derive from the psychological perspectives discussed earlier, namely, the psychoanalytic, humanistic, behavioral, and cognitive perspectives. The chapter groups the therapies by perspective but also emphasizes the common threads that run through them. In evaluating the therapies, the chapter points out that, although people who are untreated often improve, those receiving psychotherapy tend to improve somewhat more, regardless of the type of therapy they receive.

The biomedical therapies discussed are drug therapies; electroconvulsive therapy; and psychosurgery, which is seldom used. By far the most important of the biomedical therapies, drug therapies are being used in the treatment of psychotic, anxiety, and mood disorders.

Because the origins of problems often lie beyond the individual, the chapter concludes with approaches that aim at preventing psychological disorders by focusing on the family or on the larger social environment as possible contributors to psychological disorders.

NOTE: Answer guidelines for all Chapter 16 questions begin on page 342.

Guided Study

The text chapter should be studied one section at a time. Before you read, preview each section by skimming it, noting headings and boldface items. Then read the appropriate section objectives from the following outline. Keep these objectives in mind and, as you read the chapter section, search for the information that will enable you to meet each objective. Once you have finished a section, write out answers for its objectives.

The Psychological Therapies (pp. 480–502)

1. Briefly explain the current approach to therapy.

2. Discuss the aims and methods of psychoanalysis and explain the critics' concerns with this form of therapy.

3. Identify the basic themes of humanistic therapies and describe Rogers' person-centered approach.

4. Describe Perls' Gestalt therapy and discuss the application of humanistic principles in group therapies.

5. Identify the basic assumptions of behavior therapy and discuss the classical conditioning therapies.

6. Describe behavior modification and explain the critics' concerns with this therapeutic approach.

7. Identify the basic assumptions of the cognitive therapies and discuss their goals.

8. Discuss the findings regarding the effectiveness of the psychotherapies.

9. Discuss the commonalities among the psychotherapies.

The Biomedical Therapies (pp. 502–506)

10. Identify the common forms of drug therapy.

11. Describe the use of electroconvulsive therapy and psychosurgery in the treatment of psychological disorders.

Preventing Psychological Disorders (pp. 506–507)

12. Explain the rationale and goals of preventive mental health programs.

Chapter Review

When you have finished reading the chapter, work through the material that follows to review it. Complete the sentences and answer the questions. As you proceed, evaluate your performance for each section by consulting the answers on page 344. Do not continue with the next section until you understand each answer. If you need to, review or reread the appropriate section in the textbook before continuing.

1. Therapies are divided into two types:

_____ and _____ therapies.

The Psychological Therapies (pp. 480–502)

2. Psychological therapy is more commonly called

_____ .

3. Therapists who blend several psychotherapy techniques are said to take an

_____ approach.

4. The major psychotherapies are based on four perspectives: the _____ ,

_____ , _____ , and

_____ perspectives.

5. Freud's technique in which a client says whatever comes to mind is called

_____ _____ .

6. When, in the course of therapy, a person omits shameful or embarrassing material, _____ is occurring. Insight is facilitated by the analyst's _____ of the meaning of such omissions, of dreams, and of other information revealed during therapy sessions.

7. Freud referred to the hidden meaning of a dream as its _____ _____.

8. When strong feelings, similar to those experienced in other important relationships, are developed toward the therapist, _____ has occurred.

9. Humanistic therapies attempt to help people meet their potential for _____ – _____.

List several ways that humanistic therapy differs from psychoanalysis.

10. The humanistic therapy based on Rogers' theory is called _____ – _____, which is described as _____ therapy because the therapist _____ (interprets/does not interpret) the person's problems.

11. In order to promote growth in clients, Rogerian therapists exhibit _____, _____, and _____.

12. Rogers' technique of restating and clarifying what a person is saying is called _____ _____.

The computer program that is based on this listening technique is _____.

13. Another type of humanistic psychotherapy aims at helping people become more aware of and better able to express their feelings. It is known

as _____ therapy and was developed by _____.

14. This type of therapy focuses on bringing unconscious feelings to awareness, as _____ theory emphasized, and on clients taking responsibility for themselves in the present, as emphasized by the _____ perspective.

List several advantages of group therapy.

15. "T-groups" refer to groups of individuals participating in _____ training.

16. Rogers and other therapists developed a form of intensive group therapy known as the _____ group.

17. The type of group interaction that focuses on the social context in which the individual exists is _____ _____.

Contrast the assumptions of the behavior therapies with those of psychoanalysis and humanistic therapy.

18. One cluster of behavior therapies is based on the principles of _____ _____, as developed in Pavlov's experiments. This technique in which a new, incompatible response is substituted for a maladaptive one is called _____. Two examples of this technique are _____ _____ and _____ _____.

19. The technique of systematic desensitization has been most fully developed by the therapist _____. The assumption behind this technique is that one cannot simultaneously be _____ and relaxed.

20. The first step in systematic desensitization is the construction of a _____ of anxiety-arousing stimuli. The second step

involves training in _____. In the final step, the person is trained to associate the _____ state with the _____-arousing stimuli.

21. In aversive conditioning, the therapist attempts to substitute a _____ (positive/ negative) response for one that is currently _____ (positive/negative). In this technique, unwanted behaviors become associated with _____ consequences.

22. Therapies that influence behavior by controlling its consequences are called _____ _____. Such therapies are based on principles of _____ conditioning.

23. One application of this form of therapy to institutional settings is the

_____ _____, in which desired behaviors are rewarded.

24. Behavior therapies are generally most successful with problems that are _____ (specific/generalized).

25. Therapists who teach people new, more constructive ways of thinking are using _____ therapy.

26. The form of cognitive therapy that attempts to eliminate irrational thinking is

_____-_____ therapy. Its creator is _____. A technique that attempts to reverse the negative attitudes associated with depression by helping people see their irrationalities was developed by

_____.

27. A form of cognitive therapy developed by Adele Rabin builds on the finding that depressed people _____ (do/do not) exhibit the self-serving bias.

28. Treatment that combines an attack on negative thinking with the use of behavior modification techniques is known as _____ _____ therapy.

29. In contrast to earlier times, most therapy today

_____ (is/is not) provided by psychiatrists.

30. A majority of psychotherapy clients express _____ (satisfaction/ dissatisfaction) with their therapy.

31. A long-term study of 500 Massachusetts boys found that those who received intensive counseling _____ (had/did not have) significantly fewer problems than a control group.

32. The debate over the effectiveness of psychotherapy began with a study by _____; it showed that the rate of improvement for those who received therapy _____ (was/was not) higher than the rate for those who did not.

33. A statistical technique that makes it possible to combine the results of many different psychotherapy outcome studies is called

_____-_____. Overall, the results of such analyses indicate that psychotherapy is _____ (somewhat effective/ineffective).

34. As a rule, psychotherapy is most effective with problems that are _____ (specific/nonspecific).

35. Comparisons of the effectiveness of different forms of therapy reveal _____ (clear/no clear) differences.

36. With phobias, compulsions, and other specific behavior problems, _____ therapies have been the most effective. For depression, the _____ therapies have been the most successful.

37. The beneficial effect of a person's belief in treatment is called the _____

_____.

38. Several studies found that treatment for mild problems offered by paraprofessionals _____ (is/is not) as effective as that offered by professional therapists.

The Biomedical Therapies (pp. 502–506)

39. The most widely used biomedical treatments are the _____ therapies.

40. The field that studies the effects of drugs on the mind and behavior is _____.

41. When neither the subjects nor those assessing them are aware of which condition a given individual is in, a _____ _____ experiment is being conducted.

42. One effect of _____ drugs, such as _____, is to help those experiencing _____ (positive/ negative) symptoms of schizophrenia by decreasing their responsiveness to irrelevant stimuli; schizophrenia patients who are apathetic and withdrawn may be more effectively treated with the drug _____. These drugs work by blocking the receptor sites for the neurotransmitter _____.

43. Valium and Librium are classified as _____ drugs. These drugs depress activity in the _____ _____.

44. Drugs that are prescribed to alleviate depression are called _____ drugs. These drugs work by increasing levels of the neurotransmitters _____ and _____. One example of this type of drug is _____.

45. In order to stabilize the mood swings of a bipolar disorder, the drug _____ is often prescribed.

46. The therapeutic technique in which the patient receives an electric shock to the brain is referred to as _____ therapy, abbreviated as _____.

47. ECT is most often used with patients suffering from severe _____. One theory of how this treatment works suggests that it increases release of the neurotransmitter _____.

48. The biomedical therapy in which a portion of brain tissue is removed or destroyed is called _____.

49. In the 1930s, Moniz developed an operation called the _____. In this procedure, the _____ lobe of the brain is disconnected from the rest of the brain.

50. Today, most psychosurgery has been replaced by the use of _____ or some other form of treatment.

Preventing Psychological Disorders (pp. 506–507)

51. Unlike the psychotherapies and biomedical therapies, which focus on treatment of the _____, psychologists who practice preventive mental health believe that it is necessary to work on changing _____ conditions.

FOCUS ON PSYCHOLOGY:
Job-Related Psychotherapy

In his classic book, *A General Introduction to Psychoanalysis*, Sigmund Freud wrote that a healthy adult was one who could love and work. While Freud focused on issues more closely related to love than work, contemporary psychotherapists are finding that the nature of their clients' jobs is an increasingly important factor in their psychological well-being.

Many research studies have demonstrated the importance of work. Researchers have found, for example, that people who are out of work often feel depressed and empty. And, when people are asked what they would do if they suddenly became millionaires, more than 80 percent say they would continue to work at their regular jobs (Berger, 1988). As psychologist Douglas LaBier, author of *Modern Madness: The Emotional Fallout of Success*, puts it, increasingly for many of us "career and identity are inextricably bound up: Indeed they are almost equivalent."

Evidence for this career-identity merger comes from research showing that troubled behavior, including depression, anxiety, and drug abuse, is often a reaction to difficulties at work rather than a symptom of an underlying personality disorder. Other evidence comes from the trend toward occupational specialization among psychotherapists. According to science writer Ronni Sarnoff, "Work-proud dentists, police officers, middle managers, tennis champions, stockbrokers and other professionals have begun searching for therapists who talk their language and appreciate the tremendous importance of work in their lives."

Specialization exemplifies the spirit of eclectic therapy discussed in the text: Some forms of therapy are more effective than others for certain problems and, apparently, for certain professions. Stress-management techniques such as biofeedback and counterconditioning—both types of behavior therapy—have proven especially beneficial in treating stress-related problems. One New York therapist, for example, specializes in treating stress-related hypertension and headaches in corporate executives whose complaints have been diagnosed as psychophysiological.

Performance enhancement, also a form of behavior therapy, has been especially successful with clients in sales and business management. Originally developed by sports psychologists, performance enhancement helps people to attain "peak performance" in their events, or jobs, through visualization and rehearsal of critical situations and the application of other behavior modification techniques.

Traditional psychoanalysis seems to be most effective with artists, actors and actresses, writers, and people in the helping professions (including psychotherapy). Through free association, dream analysis, and therapist interpretation, such clients are able to deeply probe their problems and gain insight into their causes.

Group therapy is another technique that is becoming popular with therapists who are also occupational specialists. With this approach people employed in the same line of work are able to confront their problems together. Not only may they be able to help each other, but they are also better able than outsiders to empathize with the troubled individual.

As our identities and well-being become even more closely connected with our work, the trend toward occupational specialization in psychotherapy can certainly be expected to continue. The healthy adult may become the one who can love and work and find the right therapist for his or her profession should troubled times arise.

Sources: Berger, K. S. (1988). *The developing person through the life span* (2nd ed.). New York: Worth Publishers, p. 449.

Sarnoff, R. (1989, July/August). Is your job driving you crazy? *Psychology Today*, pp. 41–45.

Progress Test 1

Multiple-Choice Questions

Circle your answers to the following questions and check them with the answers on page 345. If your answer is incorrect, read the explanation for why it is incorrect and then consult the appropriate pages of the text (in parentheses following the correct answer).

1. Electroconvulsive therapy is most useful in the treatment of:
   a. schizophrenia.
   b. depression.
   c. personality disorders.
   d. anxiety disorders.

2. The technique in which a person is asked to report everything that comes to his or her mind is called _____ _____; this technique is favored by _____ therapists.
   a. active listening; cognitive
   b. spontaneous remission; humanistic
   c. free association; psychoanalytic
   d. systematic desensitization; behavior

3. Of the following categories of psychotherapy, which is known for its nondirective nature?
   a. psychoanalysis
   b. humanistic therapy
   c. behavior therapy
   d. cognitive therapy

4. Which of the following is *not* a common criticism of psychoanalysis?
   a. It emphasizes awareness of past feelings.
   b. It provides interpretations that are hard to disprove.
   c. It is generally a very expensive process.
   d. It gives therapists too much control over patients.

5. The computer program ELIZA was designed to simulate a:
   a. psychoanalyst.
   b. behavior therapist.
   c. cognitive therapist.
   d. humanistic therapist.

6. Which of the following is *not* necessarily an advantage of group therapies over individual therapies?
   a. They tend to take less time for the therapist.
   b. They tend to cost less money for the client.
   c. They are more effective.
   d. They allow the client to test new behaviors in a social context.

7. Which biomedical therapy is *most* likely to be practiced today?
   a. psychosurgery
   b. electroconvulsive therapy
   c. drug therapy
   d. counterconditioning

8. The effectiveness of psychotherapy has been assessed both through clients' perspectives and through controlled research studies. What have such assessments found?
   a. Clients' perceptions and controlled studies alike strongly affirm the effectiveness of psychotherapy.
   b. Whereas clients' perceptions strongly affirm the effectiveness of psychotherapy, studies point to more modest results.
   c. Whereas studies strongly affirm the effectiveness of psychotherapy, many clients feel dissatisfied with their progress.
   d. Clients' perceptions and controlled studies alike paint a very mixed picture of the effectiveness of psychotherapy.

9. Which of the following best describes the results of the 30-year follow-up study of 500 Massachusetts boys who had been considered predelinquents?
   a. Predelinquent boys who received counseling had fewer problems as adults than untreated predelinquent boys.
   b. Predelinquent boys who did not receive counseling had slightly fewer problems as adults than boys who received counseling.
   c. Predelinquent boys who underwent behavior therapy had fewer problems as adults than boys who underwent psychoanalysis.
   d. Predelinquent boys who underwent psychoanalysis had fewer problems as adults than boys who underwent behavior therapy.

10. The results of meta-analysis of the effectiveness of different psychotherapies reveals that:
    a. no single type of therapy is consistently superior.
    b. behavior therapies are most effective in treating specific problems, such as phobias.
    c. cognitive therapies are most effective in treating depressed emotions.
    d. all of the above are true.

11. The antipsychotic drugs appear to produce their effects by blocking the receptor sites for:
    a. dopamine.   c. norepinephrine.
    b. epinephrine.   d. serotonin.

12. Psychologists who advocate a _____ approach to mental health believe that many psychological disorders could be prevented by changing the disturbed individual's _____.
    a. biomedical; diet
    b. family; behavior
    c. humanistic; feelings
    d. preventive; environment

13. An eclectic psychotherapist is one who:
    a. takes a nondirective approach in helping clients solve their problems.
    b. views psychological disorders as usually stemming from one cause, such as a biological abnormality.
    c. uses one particular technique, such as psychoanalysis or behavior modification, in treating disorders.
    d. uses a variety of techniques, depending on the client and the problem.

14. The technique in which a therapist echoes and restates what a person says in a nondirective manner is called:
    a. active listening.
    b. free association.
    c. systematic desensitization.
    d. meta-analysis.

15. Which form of therapy emphasizes bringing unconscious feelings into awareness and taking full responsibility for oneself in the present?
    a. psychoanalysis
    b. behavior therapy
    c. Gestalt therapy
    d. person-centered therapy

16. The technique of systematic desensitization is based on the premise that maladaptive symptoms are:
    a. a reflection of irrational thinking.
    b. conditioned responses.
    c. expressions of unfulfilled wishes.
    d. all of the above.

17. The operant conditioning technique in which desired behaviors are rewarded with points or poker chips that can later be exchanged for various rewards is called:
    a. counterconditioning.
    b. systematic desensitization.
    c. a token economy.
    d. rational-emotive therapy.

18. One variety of _____ therapy is based on the finding that depressed people often attribute their failures to _____.
    a. humanistic; themselves
    b. behavior; external circumstances
    c. cognitive; external circumstances
    d. cognitive; themselves

19. A person can derive benefits from psychotherapy simply by believing in it. This illustrates the importance of:

a. spontaneous remission.
b. the placebo effect.
c. the transference effect.
d. interpretation.

20. Before 1950, the main mental health providers were:

a. psychologists.
b. paraprofessionals.
c. psychiatrists.
d. members of the clergy.

Matching Items

Match each term with the appropriate definition or description.

Terms

_____ **1.** cognitive therapy
_____ **2.** behavior therapy
_____ **3.** systematic desensitization
_____ **4.** rational-emotive therapy
_____ **5.** person-centered therapy
_____ **6.** Gestalt therapy
_____ **7.** aversive conditioning
_____ **8.** psychoanalysis
_____ **9.** preventive mental health
_____ **10.** biomedical therapy
_____ **11.** counterconditioning

Definitions or Descriptions

a. associates unwanted behavior with unpleasant experiences
b. associates a relaxed state with anxiety-arousing stimuli
c. emphasizes the social context of psychological disorders
d. attempts to eliminate irrational thinking through a confrontational approach
e. category of therapies that teach people more adaptive ways of thinking and acting
f. helps people become aware of unconscious feelings and assume responsibility for them in the present
g. therapy developed by Carl Rogers
h. therapy based on Freud's theory of personality
i. treatment with psychosurgery, electroconvulsive therapy, or drugs
j. classical conditioning procedure in which new responses are conditioned to stimuli that trigger unwanted behaviors
k. category of therapies based on learning principles derived from classical and operant conditioning

Progress Test 2

Progress Test 2 should be completed during a final chapter review. Answer the following questions after you thoroughly understand the correct answers for the Chapter Review and Progress Test 1.

Multiple-Choice Questions

1. Carl Rogers was a _____ therapist who was the creator of _____ therapy.

a. behavior; desensitization
b. psychoanalytic; insight
c. humanistic; person-centered
d. cognitive; rational-emotive

2. Using techniques of classical conditioning to develop an association between unwanted behavior and an unpleasant experience is known as:

a. aversive conditioning.
b. systematic desensitization.
c. transference.
d. electroconvulsive therapy.

3. Which type of psychotherapy emphasizes the individual's inherent potential for self-fulfillment?

a. behavior therapy
b. psychoanalysis
c. humanistic therapy
d. biomedical therapy

4. Which type of psychotherapy combines the psychoanalytic emphasis on making clients aware of unconscious feelings with the humanistic emphasis on taking responsibility for those feelings?

a. person-centered therapy
b. Gestalt therapy
c. rational-emotive therapy
d. cognitive therapy

5. Which type of psychotherapy focuses on changing unwanted behaviors rather than on discovering their underlying causes?

   a. behavior therapy   **c.** humanistic therapy
   b. cognitive therapy   **d.** psychoanalysis

6. The techniques of counterconditioning are based on principles of:

   a. observational learning.
   b. classical conditioning.
   c. operant conditioning.
   d. behavior modification.

7. In which of the following does the client learn to associate a relaxed state with a hierarchy of anxiety-arousing situations?

   a. rational-emotive therapy
   b. aversive conditioning
   c. counterconditioning
   d. systematic desensitization

8. Principles of operant conditioning underlie the techniques of:

   a. behavior modification.
   b. counterconditioning.
   c. systematic desensitization.
   d. rational-emotive therapy.

9. Which of the following is *not* a common criticism of behavior therapy?

   a. Clients may not develop intrinsic motivation for their new behaviors.
   b. Behavior control is unethical.
   c. Although one symptom may be eliminated, another may replace it unless the underlying problem is treated.
   d. All of the above are criticisms of behavior therapy.

10. Which type of therapy focuses on eliminating irrational thinking?

   a. Gestalt therapy
   b. person-centered therapy
   c. rational-emotive therapy
   d. behavior therapy

11. Antidepressant drugs are believed to work by affecting one or more of each of the following neurotransmitters *except*:

   a. dopamine.   **c.** norepinephrine.
   b. serotonin.   **d.** acetylcholine.

12. The following are some of the conclusions drawn in the textbook regarding the effectiveness of psychotherapy. For which of these conclusions did the Massachusetts study of predelinquent boys provide evidence?

   a. Clients' perceptions of the effectiveness of therapy usually are very accurate.
   b. Clients' perceptions of the effectiveness of ther-

apy differ somewhat from the objective findings.

   c. Individuals who receive treatment do somewhat better than individuals who do not.
   d. Overall, no one type of therapy is a "winner," but certain therapies are more suited to certain problems.

13. Which of the following is the drug most commonly used to treat the bipolar disorder?

   a. Valium   **c.** Librium
   b. chlorpromazine   **d.** lithium

14. The most widely prescribed drugs in biomedical therapy are the:

   a. antianxiety drugs.
   b. antipsychotic drugs.
   c. antidepressant drugs.
   d. amphetamines.

15. Which form of therapy is *most* likely to be successful in treating depression?

   a. behavior therapy
   b. psychoanalysis
   c. cognitive therapy
   d. humanistic therapy

16. Although Moniz won the Nobel prize for developing the lobotomy procedure, the technique is not widely used today because:

   a. it produces a lethargic, immature personality.
   b. it is irreversible.
   c. calming drugs became available in the 1950s.
   d. of all of the above reasons.

17. A meta-analysis of research studies comparing the effectiveness of professional therapists with paraprofessionals found that:

   a. the professionals were much more effective than the paraprofessionals.
   b. the paraprofessionals were much more effective than the professionals.
   c. except in treating depression, the paraprofessionals were about as effective as the professionals.
   d. the paraprofessionals were about as effective as the professionals.

18. Among the common ingredients of the psychotherapies is:

   a. the offer of a therapeutic relationship.
   b. the expectation among clients that the therapy will prove helpful.
   c. the chance to develop a fresh perspective on oneself and the world.
   d. all of the above.

19. Family therapy differs from other forms of psychotherapy because it focuses on:

   a. using a variety of treatment techniques.

b. conscious rather than unconscious processes.

c. the present instead of the past.

d. how family tensions may cause individual problems.

20. One reason that aversive conditioning may only be temporarily effective is that:

  a. for ethical reasons, therapists cannot use sufficiently intense unconditioned stimuli to sustain classical conditioning.

  b. patients are often unable to become sufficiently relaxed for conditioning to take place.

  c. patients know that outside the therapist's office they can engage in the undesirable behavior without fear of aversive consequences.

  d. most conditioned responses are elicited by many nonspecific stimuli and it is impossible to countercondition them all.

Matching Items

Match each term with the appropriate definition or description.

Terms

_____ 1. active listening
_____ 2. token economy
_____ 3. placebo effect
_____ 4. lobotomy
_____ 5. lithium
_____ 6. meta-analysis
_____ 7. psychopharmacology
_____ 8. double-blind technique
_____ 9. Valium
_____ 10. free association

Definitions or Descriptions

a. type of psychosurgery

b. procedure for statistically combining the results of many experiments

c. antidepressant drug

d. empathic technique used in person-centered therapy

e. the beneficial effect of a person's expecting that treatment will be effective

f. antianxiety drug

g. technique of psychoanalytic therapy

h. an operant conditioning procedure

i. the study of the effects of drugs on the mind and behavior

j. experimental procedure in which both the patient and staff are unaware of a patient's treatment condition

Challenge Test

Answer these questions the day before an exam as a final check on your understanding of the chapter's terms and concepts.

Multiple-Choice Questions

1. During a session with his psychoanalyst, Jamal hesitates while describing a highly embarrassing thought. In the psychoanalytic framework, this is an example of:

  a. transference. **c.** mental repression.
  b. insight. **d.** resistance.

2. During psychoanalysis, Jane has developed strong feelings of hatred for her therapist. The analyst interprets Jane's behavior in terms of a _____ of her feelings toward her father.

  a. projection **c.** sublimation
  b. resistance **d.** transference

3. Given that Jim's therapist attempts to help him by offering genuineness, acceptance, and empathy, she is probably practicing:

  a. psychoanalysis.
  b. behavior therapy.
  c. Gestalt therapy.
  d. person-centered therapy.

4. To help Sam quit smoking, his therapist blew a blast of smoke into Sam's face each time Sam inhaled. Which technique is the therapist using?

  a. rational-emotive therapy
  b. behavior modification
  c. systematic desensitization
  d. aversive conditioning

5. After Darnel dropped a pass in an important football game, he became depressed and vowed to quit the team because of his athletic incompetence. The campus psychologist challenged his illogical reasoning and pointed out that Darnel's "incompetence" had earned him an athletic scholarship. The

psychologist's response was most typical of a _____ therapist.

- **a.** Gestalt
- **b.** psychoanalytic
- **c.** person-centered
- **d.** rational-emotive

6. Seth enters therapy to talk about some issues that have been upsetting him. The therapist prescribes some medication to help him. The therapist is most likely a:

- **a.** psychologist.
- **b.** psychiatrist.
- **c.** psychiatric social worker.
- **d.** clinical social worker.

7. In an experiment testing the effects of a new antipsychotic drug, neither Dr. Cunningham nor her patients know whether the patients are in the experimental or the control group. This is an example of the _____ technique.

- **a.** meta-analysis
- **b.** within-subjects
- **c.** double-blind
- **d.** single-blind

8. Brad is seeking a psychotherapist who will help him get in touch with himself by bringing unconscious feelings into awareness and focusing on his present problems. Brad should probably choose a _____ therapist.

- **a.** psychoanalytic
- **b.** Gestalt
- **c.** humanistic
- **d.** behavioral

9. A relative wants to know which type of therapy works best. You should tell your relative that:

- **a.** psychotherapy does not work.
- **b.** behavior therapy is the most effective.
- **c.** cognitive therapy is the most effective.
- **d.** no one type of therapy is consistently the most successful.

10. Leota is startled when her therapist says that she needs to focus on eliminating her problem behavior rather than gaining insight into its underlying cause. Most likely, Leota has consulted a _____ therapist.

- **a.** behavior
- **b.** humanistic
- **c.** cognitive
- **d.** psychoanalytic

11. In order to help him overcome his fear of flying, Duane's therapist has him construct a hierarchy of anxiety-triggering stimuli and then learn to associate each with a state of deep relaxation. Duane's therapist is using the technique called:

- **a.** systematic desensitization.
- **b.** aversive conditioning.
- **c.** shaping.
- **d.** free association.

12. A patient in a hospital receives poker chips for making her bed, being punctual at meal times, and maintaining her physical appearance. The poker chips can be exchanged for privileges, such as television viewing, snacks, and magazines. This is an example of the _____ therapy technique called _____.

- **a.** Gestalt; systematic desensitization
- **b.** behavior; token economy
- **c.** cognitive; token economy
- **d.** humanistic; systematic desensitization

13. Ben is a cognitive behavior therapist. Compared to Rachel, who is a behavior therapist, Ben is more likely to:

- **a.** base his therapy on principles of operant conditioning.
- **b.** base his therapy on principles of classical conditioning.
- **c.** address clients' attitudes as well as behaviors.
- **d.** focus on clients' unconscious urges.

14. A psychotherapist who believes that the best way to treat psychological disorders is to prevent them from developing would be *most* likely to view disordered behavior as:

- **a.** maladaptive thoughts and actions.
- **b.** expressions of unconscious conflicts.
- **c.** conditioned responses.
- **d.** an understandable response to stressful social conditions.

15. Linda's doctor prescribes medication that blocks the activity of dopamine in her nervous system. Evidently, Linda is being treated with an _____ drug.

- **a.** antipsychotic
- **b.** antianxiety
- **c.** antidepressant
- **d.** anticonvulsive

16. Abraham's doctor prescribes medication that increases the availability of norepinephrine in his nervous system. Evidently, Abraham is being treated with an _____ drug.

- **a.** antipsychotic
- **b.** antianxiety
- **c.** antidepressant
- **d.** anticonvulsive

17. In concluding her talk entitled "Psychosurgery Today," Ashley states that:

- **a.** "Psychosurgery is still widely used throughout the world."
- **b.** "Electroconvulsive therapy is the only remaining psychosurgical technique that is widely practiced."
- **c.** "With advances in psychopharmacology, psychosurgery has largely been abandoned."
- **d.** "Although lobotomies remain popular, other psychosurgical techniques have been abandoned."

18. A psychiatrist has diagnosed a patient as having bipolar disorder. It is likely that she will prescribe:

- **a.** an antipsychotic drug.
- **b.** lithium.
- **c.** an antianxiety drug.
- **d.** a drug that blocks receptor sites for serotonin.

19. Which type(s) of psychotherapy would be most likely to use the interpretation of dreams as a technique for bringing unconscious feelings into awareness?
    a. psychoanalysis   d. all of the above
    b. Gestalt therapy   e. both a. and b.
    c. cognitive therapy

20. Of the following therapists, who would be most likely to interpret a person's psychological problems in terms of repressed impulses?
    a. a behavior therapist
    b. a cognitive therapist
    c. a humanistic therapist
    d. a psychoanalyst

Essay Question

Willie has been diagnosed as suffering from major depression. Describe the treatment he might receive from a psychoanalyst, a cognitive therapist, and a biomedical therapist. (Use the space below to list points you want to make and organize them. Then write the essay on a separate piece of paper.)

Key Terms

Using your own words, write a brief definition or explanation of each of the following terms.

1. psychotherapy

2. eclectic approach

3. psychoanalysis

4. free association

5. resistance

6. interpretation

7. transference

8. person-centered therapy

9. active listening

10. Gestalt therapy

11. family therapy

12. behavior therapy

13. counterconditioning

14. systematic desensitization

15. aversive conditioning

16. behavior modification

17. token economy

18. cognitive therapy

19. rational-emotive therapy

20. meta-analysis

21. psychopharmacology

22. lithium

23. electroconvulsive therapy (ECT)

24. psychosurgery

25. lobotomy

ANSWERS

GUIDED STUDY

The following guidelines provide the main points that your answers should have touched upon.

1. Psychotherapy is the planned treatment of mental and emotional problems based on the interaction between a socially sanctioned healer and a sufferer. The various types of psychotherapy derive from psychology's major personality theories: psychoanalytic, humanistic, behavioral, and cognitive. Half of all contemporary psychotherapists take an eclectic approach, using a blend of therapies tailored to meet their clients' particular problems.

2. Psychoanalysis assumes that psychological problems are caused by repressed unconscious conflicts that develop during childhood, and so its goal is to bring these feelings into conscious awareness and help the person work through them.

   Psychoanalysts may ask their patients to report everything that comes to mind (free association). Blocks in the flow of retrieval (resistance) are believed to indicate the repression of sensitive material. The analyst's interpretations of resistances aim to provide the patient with insight into their underlying meaning. Psychoanalysts interpret dreams for their latent content and the transference of feelings from early relationships in order to expose repressed feelings.

   Psychoanalysis has been criticized for offering after-the-fact interpretations that are impossible to prove or disprove and for being a lengthy and expensive process that only the relatively well-off can afford.

3. Humanistic therapists aim to boost self-fulfillment by helping people grow in self-awareness and

self-acceptance. Carl Rogers' nondirective person-centered therapy, which is based on the assumption that most people have within themselves the resources for growth, aims to provide an environment in which therapists exhibit genuineness, acceptance, and empathy. Humanistic therapists often use *active listening* to provide a psychological mirror that helps clients see themselves more clearly.

4. Perls' Gestalt therapy combines the psychoanalytic emphasis on bringing unconscious feelings into awareness with the humanistic emphasis on taking responsibility for oneself in the present. By using role-playing and other techniques, Gestalt therapists encourage clients to become more aware and expressive of their feelings.

   Group therapies based on humanistic approaches provide a social context which allows people to discover that others have similar problems and to try out new ways of behaving. Encounter, self-help, and support groups are examples of the group approach to psychotherapy. Another is family therapy, which treats individuals within their family system.

5. Behavior therapy applies learning principles to eliminate unwanted behavior. Counterconditioning describes classical-conditioning procedures that condition new responses to stimuli that trigger unwanted behaviors. One type of counterconditioning, systematic desensitization, is used to treat phobias, for example, by conditioning people to associate a pleasant, relaxed state with gradually increasing anxiety-provoking stimuli. Aversive conditioning is a type of counterconditioning that associates unwanted behavior (such as drinking alcohol) with unpleasant feelings (such as nausea).

6. Behavior modification is the use of operant conditioning procedures to treat behavior problems. In institutional settings, for example, behavior therapists may create a token economy to shape desired behaviors. With this procedure, patients earn tokens for exhibiting desired behavior, then exchange the accumulated tokens for various privileges.

   Critics note that because behavior modification depends on extrinsic rewards, the appropriate behaviors may disappear when the person leaves the conditioning environment. Second, critics question whether it is ethical for a therapist to exercise so much control over a person's behavior.

7. The cognitive therapies assume that our thinking influences our feelings and that maladaptive thinking patterns can be replaced with new, more constructive ones. Rational-emotive therapy is a confrontational cognitive therapy that challenges people's illogical, self-defeating attitudes and actions. Cognitive therapy for depression helps people to discover and reform their habitually negative patterns of thinking. Cognitive behavior therapy expands upon standard cognitive therapy to include helping people to practice their newly learned positive approach in everyday settings.

8. The effectiveness of psychotherapy depends on how it is measured. Although clients' testimonials and clinicians' perceptions strongly affirm the effectiveness of psychotherapy, controlled research studies, such as those originated by Hans Eysenck, report a similar improvement rate among treated and untreated people. More recent research using meta-analysis—combining the results of many different studies—reveals that psychotherapy is somewhat effective and that it is cost-effective compared with the greater costs of physician care for underlying psychological ailments. The same research revealed that although no particular type of therapy proved consistently superior, certain therapies work best with certain disorders. Behavioral conditioning therapies, for example, work best with specific behavior problems. With depression, the cognitive therapies prove most successful.

9. First, because they enable people to believe that things can and will get better, psychotherapies provide hope for demoralized people. This placebo effect explains why all sorts of treatments may produce cures. Second, therapy offers people a plausible explanation of problems and alternative ways of responding. Third, therapy establishes an empathic, trusting, caring relationship between client and therapist.

10. Discoveries in psychopharmacology revolutionized the treatment of disordered people and greatly reduced the need for psychosurgery or hospitalization. Antipsychotic drugs, such as Thorazine and Clozaril, are used to reduce positive and negative symptoms of schizophrenia, respectively. These drugs work by blocking receptor sites for the neurotransmitter dopamine. Antianxiety drugs, such as Valium and Librium, reduce tension and anxiety by depressing central nervous system activity. Antidepressant drugs elevate mood by increasing the availability of the neurotransmitters norepinephrine and serotonin; fluoxetine (Prozac) blocks the reabsorption of serotonin at the synapse. The drug lithium is used to stabilize the manic-depressive mood swings of the bipolar disorder.

11. Electroconvulsive therapy (ECT), which is used by psychiatrists to treat severe depression, produces marked improvement in 80 percent or more of patients without discernible brain damage. ECT

may work by increasing the release of norepineph-rine, or by inducing seizures that calm neural centers where overactivity produces depression.

Because its effects are irreversible, psychosurgery, which removes or destroys brain tissue to change behavior, is the most drastic biomedical intervention. The best known form of psychosurgery, the lobotomy, was developed by Moniz in the 1930s to calm emotional and violent patients. During the 1950s, with advances in psychopharmacology, psychosurgery was largely abandoned.

12. Psychotherapists who view psychological disorders as responses to a disturbed and stressful society believe that the best approach is to prevent problems from developing by treating not only the person, but also the person's social context. Accordingly, programs that help alleviate poverty, discrimination, constant criticism, unemployment, sexism, and other demoralizing situations that undermine people's sense of competence, personal control, and self-esteem are believed to be effective in reducing people's risk of psychological disorders.

CHAPTER REVIEW

1. psychological; biomedical
2. psychotherapy
3. eclectic
4. psychoanalytic; humanistic; behavioral; cognitive
5. free association
6. resistance; interpretation
7. latent content
8. transference
9. self-fulfillment

Unlike psychoanalysis, humanistic therapy is focused on the present instead of the past, on awareness of feelings as they occur rather than on achieving insights into the childhood origins of the feelings, on conscious rather than unconscious processes, on promoting growth and fulfillment instead of curing illness, and on helping clients take immediate responsibility for their feelings and actions rather than on uncovering the obstacles to doing so.

10. person-centered; nondirective; does not interpret
11. genuineness; acceptance; empathy
12. active listening; ELIZA
13. Gestalt; Perls
14. psychoanalytic; humanistic

Group therapy saves therapists time and clients money. The social context of group therapy allows people to discover that others have similar problems and to try out new ways of behaving.

15. sensitivity
16. encounter
17. family therapy

Whereas psychoanalysis and humanistic therapies assume that problems diminish as self-awareness grows, behavior therapists doubt that self-awareness is the key. Instead of looking for the inner cause of unwanted behavior, behavior therapy applies learning principles to directly attack the unwanted behavior itself.

18. classical conditioning; counterconditioning; systematic desensitization; aversive conditioning
19. Wolpe; anxious
20. hierarchy; relaxation; relaxed; anxiety
21. negative; positive; aversive
22. behavior modification; operant
23. token economy
24. specific
25. cognitive
26. rational-emotive; Ellis; Beck
27. do not
28. cognitive behavior
29. is not
30. satisfaction
31. did not have
32. Eysenck; was not
33. meta-analysis; somewhat effective
34. specific
35. no clear
36. behavior; cognitive
37. placebo effect
38. is
39. drug
40. psychopharmacology
41. double-blind
42. antipsychotic; chlorpromazine (Thorazine); positive; clozapine (Clozaril); dopamine
43. antianxiety; central nervous system
44. antidepressant; norepinephrine; serotonin; fluoxetine (Prozac)
45. lithium
46. electroconvulsive; ECT
47. depression; norepinephrine
48. psychosurgery
49. lobotomy; frontal
50. drugs
51. individual; environmental or social

PROGRESS TEST 1

Multiple-Choice Questions

1. b. is the answer. Although no one is sure how ECT works, one possible explanation is that it increases release of norepinephrine, the neurotransmitter that elevates mood. (p. 505)

2. c. is the answer. (p. 480)

a. Active listening is a humanistic technique in which the therapist echoes, restates, and seeks clarification of the client's statements.

b. Spontaneous remission, which is not mentioned in the text, refers to improvement without treatment.

d. Systematic desensitization is a process in which a person is conditioned to associate a relaxed state with anxiety-triggering stimuli.

3. b. is the answer. (p. 483)

4. d. is the answer. This is not among the criticisms commonly made of psychoanalysis. (It would more likely be made of behavior therapies.) (pp. 481–482)

5. d. is the answer. ELIZA simulates the active listening technique of Rogerian therapy. (pp. 483–484)

6. c. is the answer. Meta-analysis of the relative effectiveness of different therapies reveals no clear winner; the other factors mentioned are advantages of group therapies. (pp. 486, 500)

7. c. is the answer. (p. 502)

a. The fact that its effects are irreversible makes psychosurgery a drastic procedure, and with advances in psychopharmacology, psychosurgery has been largely abandoned.

b. ECT is still widely used as a treatment of major depression, but in general it is not used as frequently as drug therapy.

d. Counterconditioning is not a biomedical therapy.

8. b. is the answer. Clients' testimonials regarding psychotherapy are generally very positive. The research, in contrast, seems to show that therapy is only *somewhat* effective. (pp. 496, 499)

9. b. is the answer. Although many of those who received counseling felt it had saved their lives, on a number of measures these men exhibited slightly *more* problems than those who had not received counseling. (p. 497)

a. Boys who received counseling had slightly *more* problems as adults.

c. & d. This study did not compare the effectiveness of different forms of psychotherapy.

10. d. is the answer. (p. 500)

11. a. is the answer. By occupying receptor sites for dopamine, these drugs block its activity and reduce its production. (p. 503)

12. d. is the answer. (p. 506)

13. d. is the answer. Today, half of all psychotherapists describe themselves as eclectic—as using a blend of therapies. (p. 480)

a. An eclectic therapist may use a nondirective approach with certain behaviors; however, a more directive approach might be chosen for other clients and problems.

b. In fact, just the opposite is true. Eclectic therapists generally view disorders as stemming from many influences.

c. Eclectic therapists, in contrast to this example, use a combination of treatments.

14. a. is the answer. (p. 483)

15. c. is the answer. (p. 485)

a. Psychoanalysis is generally more concerned with past experiences and conflicts than with the present.

b. Behavior therapy is unconcerned with such explanations of behavior, focusing instead on the modification of symptoms.

d. Person-centered therapy is not concerned with the unconscious.

16. b. is the answer. (p. 488)

a. This reflects a cognitive perspective.

c. This reflects a psychoanalytic perspective.

17. c. is the answer. (p. 490)

a. & b. Counterconditioning is the replacement of an undesired response with a desired one by means of aversion therapy or systematic desensitization.

d. Rational-emotive therapy is a cognitive approach that challenges people's self-defeating attitudes.

18. d. is the answer. (pp. 494–495)

19. b. is the answer. (pp. 500–501)

a. Spontaneous remission refers to improvement without any treatment.

c. Transference is the psychoanalytic phenomenon in which a client transfers feelings from other relationships onto his or her analyst.

d. Interpretation is the psychoanalytic procedure through which the analyst helps the client become aware of resistances and understand their meaning.

20. c. is the answer. (p. 495)

Matching Items

1. e (p. 491)   5. g (p. 483)   9. c (p. 506)
2. k (p. 487)   6. f (p. 485)   10. i (p. 502)
3. b (p. 488)   7. a (pp. 488–489) 11. j (p. 487)
4. d (p. 492)   8. h (p. 480)

PROGRESS TEST 2

Multiple-Choice Questions

1. **c.** is the answer. (p. 483)

   a. This answer would be a correct description of Joseph Wolpe.

   b. There is no such thing as insight therapy.

   d. This answer would be a correct description of Albert Ellis.

2. **a.** is the answer. (pp. 488–489)

   b. In systematic desensitization, a hierarchy of anxiety-provoking stimuli is gradually associated with a relaxed state.

   c. Transference refers to a patient's transferring of feelings from other relationships onto his or her psychoanalyst.

   d. Electroconvulsive therapy is a biomedical shock treatment.

3. **c.** is the answer. (p. 482)

   a. Behavior therapy focuses on behavior, not self-awareness.

   b. Psychoanalysis focuses on bringing repressed feelings into awareness.

   d. Biomedical therapy focuses on physical treatment through drugs, ECT, or psychosurgery.

4. **b.** is the answer. As a humanistic therapy, Gestalt therapy emphasizes being in touch with one's feelings, but it also shares with psychoanalysis an interest in unconscious feelings. (p. 485)

   a. Person-centered therapy emphasizes personal growth in a supportive environment.

   c. & d. Cognitive therapies, such as rational-emotive therapy, emphasize getting people to change self-defeating attitudes and assumptions.

5. **a.** is the answer. For behavior therapy, the problem behaviors *are* the problems. (p. 487)

   b. Cognitive therapy teaches people to think and act in more adaptive ways.

   c. Humanistic therapy promotes growth and self-fulfillment by providing an empathic, genuine, and accepting environment.

   d. Psychoanalytic therapy focuses on uncovering and interpreting repressed feelings.

6. **b.** is the answer. Counterconditioning techniques involve taking an established CS, which triggers an undesirable CR, and pairing it with a new UCS in order to condition a new, and more adaptive, CR. (p. 487)

   a. As indicated by the name, counterconditioning techniques are a form of conditioning; they do not involve learning by observation.

   c. & d. The principles of operant conditioning are the basis of behavior modification, which in contrast to counterconditioning techniques, involves use of reinforcement.

7. **d.** is the answer. (pp. 487–488)

   a. This is a confrontational therapy aimed at teaching people to think and act in more adaptive ways.

   b. Aversive conditioning is a form of counterconditioning in which unwanted behavior is associated with unpleasant feelings.

   c. Counterconditioning is a general term, including not only systematic desensitization, in which a hierarchy of fears is desensitized, but also other techniques, such as aversive conditioning.

8. **a.** is the answer. (p. 490)

   b. & c. These techniques are based on classical conditioning.

   d. This is a type of cognitive therapy.

9. **d.** is the answer. (pp. 490–491)

10. **c.** is the answer. (p. 492)

   a. Gestalt therapy aims to help people become more aware of and able to express their present-day feelings.

   b. In this humanistic therapy, the therapist facilitates the client's growth by offering a genuine, accepting, and empathic environment.

   d. Behavior therapy concentrates on modifying the actual symptoms of psychological problems.

11. **d.** is the answer. (p. 504)

12. **b.** is the answer. Although many of the treated men offered glowing reports of the effectiveness of their therapy, these testimonials did not accurately reflect the results. (p. 497)

   a. In fact, as this study showed, clients' perceptions of the effectiveness of psychotherapy are often very positive but inaccurate.

   c. On some measures, the treated men exhibited slightly *more* problems than the untreated men.

   d. This study did not compare the effectiveness of different forms of psychotherapy.

13. **d.** is the answer. Lithium works as a mood stabilizer. (p. 504)

   a. & c. Valium and Librium are antianxiety drugs.

   b. Chlorpromazine is a major tranquilizer.

14. a. is the answer. Antianxiety drugs are among the most heavily prescribed of all drugs. (p. 504)

15. c. is the answer. (p. 500)

a. Behavior therapy is most likely to be successful in treating specific behavior problems, such as phobias.

b. & d. The textbook does not single out particular disorders for which these therapies tend to be most effective.

16. d. is the answer. (pp. 505–506)

17. d. is the answer. Even when dealing with seriously depressed adults, the paraprofessionals were as effective as the professionals. (p. 502)

18. d. is the answer. (p. 501)

19. d. is the answer. (p. 486)

a. This is true of most forms of psychotherapy.

b. & c. This is true of humanistic, cognitive, and behavior therapies.

20. c. is the answer. Although aversive conditioning may work in the short run, the person's ability to discriminate between the situation in which the aversive conditioning occurs and other situations can limit the treatment's effectiveness. (pp. 489–490)

a., b., & d. These were not offered in the textbook as limitations of the effectiveness of aversive conditioning.

Matching Items

1. d (p. 483)   5. c (p. 504)   9. f (p. 504)
2. h (p. 490)   6. b (p. 498)   10. g (p. 480)
3. e (pp. 500–501)   7. i (p. 502)
4. a (p. 505)   8. j (p. 503)

CHALLENGE TEST

Multiple-Choice Questions

1. d. is the answer. Resistances are blocks in the flow of free association that hint at underlying anxiety. (p. 481)

a. In transference, a patient attributes feelings from other relationships to his or her analyst.

b. The goal of psychoanalysis is for patients to gain insight into their feelings.

c. Although such hesitation may well involve material that has been repressed, the hesitation itself is a resistance.

2. d. is the answer. In transference, the patient develops toward the therapist feelings that were experienced in important early relationships but were repressed. (p. 481)

a. Projection is a defense mechanism in which a person imputes his or her own feelings to someone else.

b. Resistances are blocks in the flow of free association that indicate repressed material.

c. Sublimation is a defense mechanism in which a person channels unacceptable impulses into socially desirable activities.

3. d. is the answer. According to Rogers' person-centered therapy, the therapist must exhibit genuineness, acceptance, and empathy if the client is to move toward self-fulfillment. (p. 483)

a. Psychoanalysts are much more directive in providing interpretations of clients' problems than are humanistic therapists.

b. Behavior therapists focus on modifying the behavioral symptoms of psychological problems.

c. Like psychoanalysts, Gestalt psychologists emphasize bringing unconscious conflicts into conscious awareness.

4. d. is the answer. Aversive conditioning is the classical conditioning technique in which a positive response is replaced by a negative response. (In this example, the UCS is the hot blast of smoke, the CS is the taste of the cigarette as it is inhaled, and the intended CR is aversion to cigarettes.) (pp. 488–489)

a. Rational-emotive therapy is a confrontational cognitive therapy.

b. Behavior modification applies the principles of operant conditioning and thus, in contrast to the example, uses reinforcement.

c. Systematic desensitization is used to help people overcome specific anxieties.

5. d. is the answer. Because the psychologist is challenging Darnel's illogical, self-defeating attitude, this response is most typical of rational-emotive therapy. (p. 492)

a. Gestalt therapists combine the psychoanalytic emphasis on bringing unconscious feelings to awareness with the humanistic emphasis on getting in touch with oneself.

b. Psychoanalysts focus on helping patients gain insight into previously repressed feelings.

c. Person-centered therapists attempt to facilitate clients' growth by offering a genuine, accepting, empathic environment.

6. b. is the answer. Psychiatrists are physicians who specialize in treating psychological disorders. As doctors they can prescribe medications. (p. 496)

a., c., & d. These professionals cannot prescribe drugs.

7. c. is the answer. (p. 503)

a. This is a statistical technique used to combine the results of many different research studies.

b. In this design, which is not mentioned in the text, there is only a single research group.

d. This answer would be correct if the experimenter but not the subjects knew which condition was in effect.

8. **b.** is the answer. Gestalt therapists combine the psychoanalytic emphasis on bringing unconscious feelings into awareness with the humanistic emphasis on getting in touch with oneself. (p. 485)

a. Psychoanalysts place more emphasis on understanding of past feelings than on self-awareness of current problems.

c. & d. These therapies make no reference to unconscious processes.

9. **d.** is the answer. (pp. 499–500)

a. Psychotherapy has proven "somewhat effective" and more cost-effective than physician care for psychological disorders.

b. & c. Behavior and cognitive therapies are effective in treating specific behavior problems and depression, respectively, but not necessarily in treating other problems.

10. **a.** is the answer. (p. 487)

b. & c. These therapists are more concerned with promoting self-fulfillment (humanistic) and healthy patterns of thinking (cognitive) than with correcting specific problem behaviors.

d. Psychoanalysts see the behavior merely as a symptom and focus their treatment on its presumed underlying cause.

11. **a.** is the answer. (p. 488)

b. Aversive conditioning associates unpleasant states with unwanted behaviors.

c. Shaping is an operant conditioning technique in which successive approximations of a desired behavior are reinforced.

d. Free association is a psychoanalytic technique in which a patient says whatever comes to mind.

12. **b.** is the answer. (p. 490)

13. **c.** is the answer. (p. 495)

a. & b. Behavior therapists make extensive use of techniques based on both operant and classical conditioning.

d. Neither behavior therapists nor cognitive behavior therapists focus on clients' unconscious urges.

14. **d.** is the answer. (p. 506)

a. This would be the perspective of a cognitive behavior therapist.

b. This would be the perspective of a psychoanalyst or Gestalt therapist.

c. This would be the perspective of a behavior therapist.

15. **a.** is the answer. (p. 503)

16. **c.** is the answer. (p. 504)

17. **c.** is the answer. (p. 505)

18. **b.** is the answer. (p. 504)

19. **e.** is the answer. Both psychoanalysis and Gestalt therapy seek insight into a patient's unconscious feelings. The analysis of dreams, slips of the tongue, and resistances are believed to be a window into these feelings. (pp. 480, 485)

c. Cognitive therapists avoid reference to unconscious feelings and would therefore be uninterested in interpreting dreams.

20. **d.** is the answer. A key aim of psychoanalysis is to unearth and understand repressed impulses. (p. 480)

a., b., & c. Behavior and cognitive therapists avoid concepts such as "repression" and "unconscious"; behavior and humanistic therapists focus on the present rather than the past.

Essay Question

Psychoanalysts assume that psychological problems such as depression are caused by unresolved, repressed, and unconscious impulses and conflicts from childhood. A psychoanalyst would probably attempt to bring these repressed feelings into Willie's conscious awareness and help him gain insight into them. He or she would likely try to interpret Willie's resistance during free association, the latent content of his dreams, and any emotional feelings he might transfer to the analyst.

Cognitive therapists assume that a person's emotional reactions are influenced by the person's thoughts in response to the event in question. A cognitive therapist would probably try to teach Willie new and more constructive ways of thinking in order to reverse his catastrophizing beliefs about himself, his situation, and his future.

Biomedical therapists attempt to treat disorders by altering the functioning of the patient's brain. A biomedical therapist would probably prescribe an antidepressant drug such as fluoxetine to increase the availability of norepinephrine and serotonin in Willie's nervous system. If Willie's depression is especially severe, a *psychiatrist* might treat it with several sessions of electroconvulsive therapy.

KEY TERMS

1. **Psychotherapy** is the psychological treatment of mental and emotional problems, based on the interaction between therapist and client. (p. 480)

   Example: Four major **psychotherapies** are the psychoanalytic, humanistic, behavior, and cognitive therapies.

2. With an **eclectic approach**, therapists are not locked into one form of psychotherapy, but draw on whatever combination seems best suited to a client's needs. (p. 480)

   Example: The **eclectic approach** in psychotherapy is much more common today than in the past, when therapists were more likely to practice only one approach.

3. **Psychoanalysis**, the therapy developed by Freud, attempts to give clients self-insight by bringing into awareness and interpreting previously repressed feelings. (p. 480)

   Example: The tools of the **psychoanalyst** include free association, the analysis of dreams and transferences, and the interpretation of repressed impulses.

4. **Free association** is a psychoanalytic technique in which a person says everything that comes to mind. (p. 480)

5. **Resistance** is the psychoanalytic term for the blocking from consciousness of anxiety-provoking memories. Hesitation during free association may reflect resistance. (p. 481)

6. **Interpretation** is the psychoanalytic term for the analyst's helping the client to understand resistances and other aspects of behavior, so that the client may gain deeper insights. (p. 481)

7. **Transference** is the psychoanalytic term for a patient's attributing to the analyst emotions from other relationships. (p. 481)

   Example: Perhaps the best example of **transference** in psychoanalysis is when patients transfer long-repressed feelings about their parents to the analyst.

8. **Person-centered therapy** is a humanistic therapy developed by Rogers, in which growth and self-awareness are facilitated in an environment that offers genuineness, acceptance, and empathy. (p. 483)

9. **Active listening** is a nondirective technique of person-centered therapy, in which the listener echoes, restates, clarifies, but does not interpret, clients' remarks. (p. 483)

10. **Gestalt therapy** is a humanistic therapy developed by Perls that combines the humanistic emphases with those of psychoanalysis in an effort to help people become more aware of and responsible for their feelings in the present. (p. 485)

11. **Family therapy** views problem behavior as partially engendered by the client's family system and environment. Therapy therefore focuses on relationships and problems among the various members of the family. (p. 486)

    Example: A school psychologist who felt that a student's behavioral problems in the classroom reflected difficulties in the home environment might recommend counseling with a **family therapist**.

12. **Behavior therapy** is therapy that applies principles of operant or classical conditioning to the treatment of problem behaviors. (p. 487)

    Example: One criticism of **behavior therapy** is that it treats only the symptoms, rather than the causes, of problems. Critics fear that such treatment may merely result in the substitution of one symptom of the problem for another.

13. **Counterconditioning** is a category of behavior therapy in which new responses are classically conditioned to stimuli that elicit unwanted behaviors. (p. 487)

14. **Systematic desensitization** is a type of counterconditioning in which a state of relaxation is classically conditioned to a hierarchy of gradually increasing anxiety-provoking stimuli. (p. 488)

    Memory aid: This is a form of counterconditioning in which sensitive, anxiety-triggering stimuli are *de*sensitized in a progressive, or **systematic**, fashion.

15. **Aversive conditioning** is a form of counterconditioning in which an unpleasant state becomes associated with an unwanted behavior. (pp. 488–489)

    Example: **Aversive conditioning** has been tried with limited success as a behavior therapy for alcoholism, smoking, and certain sexual deviations.

16. **Behavior modification** refers to any technique of psychotherapy that is based on operant conditioning. Thus, behavior modification typically involves shaping behavior by giving and withholding rewards. (p. 490)

17. A **token economy** is an operant conditioning procedure in which desirable behaviors are promoted in people by rewarding them with tokens, or secondary reinforcers, which can be exchanged for privileges or treats. For the most part, token economies are used in hospitals, schools, and other institutional settings. (p. 490)

18. **Cognitive therapy** focuses on teaching people new and more adaptive ways of thinking and act-

ing. The therapy is based on the idea that our feelings and responses to events are strongly influenced by our thinking, or cognition. (p. 491)

19. **Rational-emotive therapy** is a confrontational therapy that maintains that irrational thinking is the cause of many psychological problems. (p. 492)

20. **Meta-analysis** is a procedure for statistically combining the results of many different research studies. (p. 498)

    Example: A **meta-analysis** of nearly 500 psychotherapy outcome studies indicated that the average therapy client ends up better off than about 80 percent of untreated individuals.

21. **Psychopharmacology** is the study of the effects of drugs on mind and behavior. (p. 502)

    Memory aid: Pharmacology is the science of the uses and effects of drugs. *Psycho*pharmacology is the science that studies the psychological effects of drugs.

22. **Lithium** is an antidepressant drug that is commonly used to stabilize the manic-depressive mood swings of the bipolar disorder. (p. 504)

23. In **electroconvulsive therapy (ECT)**, a biomedical therapy often used to treat major depression, electric shock is passed through the brain. ECT may work by increasing the availability of norepinephrine, the neurotransmitter that elevates mood. (pp. 504–505)

24. **Psychosurgery** is a biomedical therapy that attempts to change behavior by removing or destroying brain tissue. Since drug therapy became widely available in the 1950s, psychosurgery has been infrequently used. (p. 505)

25. Once used to control violent patients, the **lobotomy** is a form of psychosurgery in which the nerves linking the emotion centers of the brain to the frontal lobes are severed. (p. 505)

17 / Stress and Health

Chapter Overview

Behavioral factors play a major role in maintaining health and causing illness. The effort to understand this role more fully has led to the emergence of the interdisciplinary field of behavioral medicine. The field is notable for its "systems theory" perspective: Illness is assumed to result, not from a single cause, but from the interactions of various systems. The subfield of health psychology focuses on systems within the domain of psychology.

Chapter 17 addresses key topics in health psychology. First and foremost is stress—its nature, its effects on the body, and ways in which it can be managed. Second, the chapter looks at the psychology of illness, for example, at people's reactions to illness and the patient role. The chapter concludes by examining several factors that affect health, including smoking, nutrition, and obesity, and by looking at behaviors that promote good health.

NOTE: Answer guidelines for all Chapter 17 questions begin on page 363.

Guided Study

The text chapter should be studied one section at a time. Before you read, preview each section by skimming it, noting headings and boldface items. Then read the appropriate section objectives from the following outline. Keep these objectives in mind and, as you read the chapter section, search for the information that will enable you to meet each objective. Once you have finished a section, write out answers for its objectives.

1. Explain the "systems theory" perspective of behavioral medicine and identify the major concerns of health psychology.

Stress and Illness (pp. 512–524)

2. Define *stress* and describe the body's response to stress.

3. Discuss research findings on the health consequences of stressful life events, as well as the factors that influence our vulnerability to stress.

4. Discuss the role of stress in coronary heart disease and contrast Type A and Type B personalities.

5. Describe how the immune system defends the body and discuss the effect of stress on the immune system.

Reactions to Illness (pp. 524–528)

6. Discuss the relationship between symptoms and awareness of illness and identify the factors that influence the decision to seek medical treatment.

7. Discuss the patient's role in coping with the stress of medical treatment and identify factors that influence patients' compliance with medical instructions.

Promoting Health (pp. 528–546)

8. Identify and discuss different strategies for coping with stress.

9. Explain why people smoke and discuss ways of preventing and reducing this health hazard.

10. Discuss the relationship between nutrition and physical well-being.

11. Discuss the factors that contribute to obesity.

12. Explain whether heredity plays no role, some role, or an exclusive role in causing obesity.

13. (Close-Up) Identify several recommendations for dieters, as noted in the textbook.

Chapter Review

When you have finished reading the chapter, work through the material that follows to review it. Complete the sentences and answer the questions. As you proceed, evaluate your performance for each section by consulting the answers on page 365. Do not continue with the next section until you understand each answer. If you need to, review or reread the appropriate section in the textbook before continuing.

1. The four leading causes of serious illness and death in the United States are _____,

_____, _____,

and _____.

2. Today, half the mortality from the 10 leading

causes of death can be traced to people's

_____.

3. List several of the behaviors that have been linked to the leading causes of death: _____

_____.

4. The new field that integrates behavioral and medical knowledge relevant to health and disease is _____

_____.

Explain the "systems theory" of illness and how it differs from the traditional medical view.

5. The subfield of psychology related to behavioral medicine is called _____ psychology.

Stress and Illness (pp. 512–524)

6. The process by which we perceive environmental events as threatening or challenging and respond accordingly is called _____.

7. In the 1920s, physiologist Walter _____ began studying the effect of stress on the body. He discovered that the hormones _____ and _____ are released into the bloodstream in response to stress. This and other bodily changes due to stress are mediated by the _____ nervous system, thus preparing the body for "_____ _____ _____."

8. More recently, physiologists have discovered that stress also triggers release of the hormone

_____.

9. In studying animals' reactions to stressors, Selye repeatedly found three physiological effects: enlargement of the _____ cortex, shrinkage of the _____ gland, and formation of _____ in the stomach. He referred to this bodily

response to stress as the _____

_____ _____.

10. During the first phase of the GAS—the _____ reaction—the person is in a state of shock due to the sudden arousal of the _____ nervous system.

11. This is followed by the stage of _____, in which the body's resources are mobilized to cope with the stressor.

12. If stress continues, the person enters the stage of _____. During this stage a person is _____ (more/less) vulnerable to disease.

13. In one study of catastrophic events, it was found that following the eruption of Mount Saint Helens there was an increase in the number of

_____

_____.

14. Research studies have found that people who have recently been widowed, fired, or divorced are _____ (more/no more) vulnerable to illness than other people.

15. A person's total score on a life stress scale generally _____ (is/is not) an accurate predictor of his or her future health. Explain why this is so.

16. For most people, the most significant sources of stress are _____ _____. Persistent on-the-job stress can lead to the physical, mental, and emotional exhaustion called

_____.

17. One source of everyday stress is being pulled by two attractive but incompatible goals; this is the _____–_____ conflict. Being forced to choose between two undesirable alternatives is an example of an _____–_____ conflict. When one is both attracted and repelled by the

same goal the _____ –
_____ conflict is operating.

18. People are more likely to suffer ill health if they perceive a loss of _____ over their lives. People who have an _____ attitude are *less* likely than others to suffer ill health.

19. In animals and humans, sudden lack of control is followed by a drop in immune responses and a rise in the levels of

_____ .

20. The leading cause of death in North America is

_____ _____

_____ . List several risk factors

for developing this condition: _____

_____ .

21. Taken together, these factors _____ (account/do not account) for most instances of heart disease.

22. Friedman and Rosenman discovered that tax accountants experience an increase in blood _____ level and blood- _____ speed during tax season. This showed there was a link between coronary warning indicators and _____ .

Friedman and Rosenman's subsequent study grouped people into Type A and Type B personalities. Characterize these types and indicate the difference that emerged between them over the course of this 9-year study.

23. Type A persons tend to engage in certain behaviors that contribute to risk of coronary disease, including _____

_____ .

24. In relaxed situations, Type A persons _____ (differ/do not differ) from Type B persons in measures of physiological reactivity.

25. An experiment by Williams showed that when Type A students were challenged, their output of stress hormones was _____ (greater than/the same as) that of their Type B classmates. These hormones may increase the buildup of _____ in the artery walls. The hardening of the arteries that may result is called _____ .

26. When a person is angered, blood flow is diverted away from the internal organs, including the liver, which is responsible for removing _____ and fat from the blood. This finding may explain why _____ (Type A/Type B) persons have elevated levels of these substances in the blood.

27. Recent research _____ (has/ has not) consistently shown that Type A behaviors lead to heart attacks. The Type A characteristic that is most strongly linked with coronary heart disease is _____

_____ .

28. In _____ illnesses, physical symptoms are produced by psychological causes. Examples of such illnesses are certain forms of _____ , _____ , and _____ . Such illnesses are not associated with any known _____ disorder, but appear to be linked to _____ .

29. The body's system of fighting disease is the _____ system. This system includes two types of white blood cells, called _____ : the _____ _____ , which fight bacterial infections, and the _____ _____ , which, for example, attack foreign substances. Another immune agent, called the _____ , pursues and ingests foreign substances.

30. Stress can suppress the lymphocyte cells, resulting in a(n) _____ (increase/decrease) in disease resistance.

Characterize the link between stress and cancer.

Explain why patients may not follow doctors' orders.

Promoting Health (pp. 528–546)

38. Sustained exercise that increases heart and lung fitness is known as _____ exercise. Experiments _____ (have/have not) been able to demonstrate conclusively that such exercise reduces stress, anxiety, and depression.

31. Experiments by Ader and Cohen demonstrate that the functioning of the body's immune system _____ (can/cannot) be affected by conditioning.

39. A system for recording a physiological response and providing information concerning it is called _____. The instruments used in this system _____ (provide/ do not provide) the individual with a means of controlling physiological responses.

Reactions to Illness (pp. 524–528)

32. Most people _____ (are/are not) very accurate at diagnosing their physical state.

40. Lowered blood pressure and strengthened immune defenses have been found to be characteristic of people who regularly practice _____.

33. People tend to notice symptoms that fit with their preexisting disease _____. For this reason women may tend to overestimate the effects of _____ syndrome. Contrary to the presumptions of some employers, women's physical and mental skills _____ (do/do not) fluctuate noticeably with their menstrual cycles.

41. Meyer Friedman found that modifying Type A behavior in a group of heart attack survivors _____ (reduced/did not significantly reduce) the rate of recurrence of heart attacks.

42. Researchers have found that life events may be less stressful for people who have a good sense of _____.

34. In terms of medical treatment, _____ (men/women) report more symptoms, visit physicians more often, and use more drugs.

43. Another buffer against the effects of stress is _____ support.

35. Taylor refers to patients who are cooperative, unquestioning, and undemanding as playing the _____–_____ role. Patients who are demanding and uncooperative are playing the _____–_____ role.

Summarize the potential effects of stress and the factors that explain why some people are better able than others to cope with stress.

36. Researchers have found that giving patients a more active role in decision making _____ (increases/reduces) their stress.

37. Recent studies have reported that as many as _____ of all patients do not consistently follow their doctor's recommendations.

44. Advocates of behavioral medicine believe that creating programs to _____ disease by promoting healthy life-styles will result in lower health-care costs than will focusing only on _____ existing diseases.

45. The largest preventable cause of illness and premature death, smoking usually begins during _____ _____.

    According to _____–_____ theory, those who start smoking have friends who model smoking and pressure them to start.

46. By terminating an aversive state, smoking provides a person with a powerful _____ reinforcer. In addition, nicotine triggers the release of epinephrine and norepinephrine, which increase _____, and of neurotransmitters that calm _____ and reduce _____ _____. For these reasons, most programs to help people quit smoking _____ (are/are not) very effective in the long run. The decline in the smoking rate among Americans is most pronounced among _____ (males/females) and those at _____ (higher/lower) socioeconomic levels.

47. A study found that seventh graders who were taught to cope with peer pressure and advertisements for smoking were _____ (more/less) likely to begin smoking than were students in a control group.

48. Certain foods may affect mood and behavior by influencing the formation of specific _____.

49. A relaxed state may be facilitated by eating certain _____, which increase the amount of tryptophan that the brain receives and can thus be used for synthesizing the neurotransmitter _____.

Concentration and alertness, in contrast, may be improved by meals that are low in _____ but have a high _____ content.

50. People with high blood pressure tend to have a higher-than-normal intake of _____ but a lower-than-normal intake of _____. Certain forms of cancer have been linked with diets that are high in _____.

51. A person is said to be obese when he or she is _____ percent or more overweight.

Cite some of the ways in which obesity is a threat to physical and psychological health.

52. The energy equivalent of a pound of fat is approximately _____ calories. The immediate determinant of body fat is the size and number of _____ one has. This number is, in turn, determined by several factors, including _____ _____.

53. The size of fat cells _____ (can/cannot) be decreased by dieting; the number of fat cells _____ (can/cannot) be decreased by dieting.

54. Fat tissue has a _____ (higher/lower) metabolic rate than lean tissue. The result is that fat tissue requires _____ (more/less) food energy to be maintained.

55. Obese persons tend to be more responsive than others to external food cues and, as a result, may secrete more _____, which triggers hunger.

Explain why, metabolically, many obese people find it so difficult to become and stay thin.

56. Studies of adoptees and twins _____ (do/do not) provide evidence of a genetic influence on obesity.

57. The weight resemblance between identical twin women is _____ (less than/the same as/greater than) that between identical twin men.

58. Obesity is _____ (more/less) common among lower-class than upper-class women and _____ (does/does not) vary from culture to culture.

59. Most obese persons who lose weight _____ (gain/do not gain) it back.

FOCUS ON PSYCHOLOGY:
Job-Related Stress: Who's in Charge Here?

It's almost a cliché: If you are an ambitious manager, chief executive officer, or professional, you are a prime candidate for heart disease. The psychological stresses of decision making and being "in charge" presumably cause this dismal prognosis. A public health study has contradicted this widespread belief by demonstrating that employees nearer to the *bottom* of the corporate ladder may be under even greater psychological stress than those at the top.

Industrial sociologist Robert Karasek and his colleagues evaluated the nature of the jobs held by more than 4,800 male heart attack victims. The jobs were scored according to several criteria, including how physically and psychologically demanding they were and the degree of decision-making power exerted by the workers who held them. Surprisingly, the researchers found that most of the heart attack victims had not been employed in managerial positions or professional occupations; rather, they tended to be assembly-line workers, cooks, waiters, and laborers, for example. In fact, the rate of heart attacks among employees in such occupations was nearly three times that of those employed in managerial jobs.

According to the researchers, the stress of lower-echelon jobs is more than merely physical: "Job demands are potential sources of stress," they explain, "but how much freedom a worker has in deciding how to meet those demands will determine if they actually produce stress." Clearly, there are significant differences in the level of job control exerted by workers at the top and those at the bottom. Science writer Valerie Adler notes that in comparison to professionals such as doctors and lawyers, who have control over almost everything they do, low-status workers typically have little or no control over their work methods, schedules, or co-workers. This lack of control is a major factor in creating stress, and thus heart disease.

Although there have been fewer studies on the relationship between job stress and heart disease in women, Adler notes that the available evidence supports the low-control, high-stress hypothesis. The ongoing Framingham Heart Study, for example, has found that women having low-control clerical jobs have twice the incidence of heart disease as women whose jobs give them substantial personal control.

The results of these studies are consistent with the text discussion of the relationship between perceived control and stress. People who perceive that they have little control over their lives tend to suffer greater health problems. Even among laboratory rats, "helpless" rats that receive uncontrollable electric shocks are more likely to develop ulcers than those that control whether they are shocked.

These findings paint a rather bleak picture for workers who have little control in their jobs. There is hope, however. To reduce job-related stress, workers should try to become involved in whatever ways they can. For example, by discussing work conditions and procedures with management and other workers, they will increase their feelings of involvement and control—and this might even produce improved work conditions. The perception of control alone, even if not completely accurate, may help workers cope with the stresses of low-control jobs.

Sources: Adler, V. (1989, April). Little control = lots of stress. *Psychology Today*, 18–19.

Karasek, R., Theorell, T., Schwartz, J. E., Schnall, P. L., Pieper, C. F., & Michela, J. L. (1988, August). Job characteristics in relation to the prevalence of myocardial infarction in the US health examination survey and the health and nutrition examination survey. *American Journal of Public Health*, 78, 910–918.

Progress Test 1

Circle your answers to the following questions and check them with the answers on page 366. If your answer is incorrect, read the explanation for why it is incorrect and then consult the appropriate pages of the text (in parentheses following the correct answer).

1. Behavioral and medical knowledge about factors influencing health form the basis of the field of:
   a. health psychology.
   b. holistic medicine.
   c. behavioral medicine.
   d. osteopathic medicine.

2. The stress hormones epinephrine and norepinephrine are released by the _____ gland in response to stimulation by the _____ branch of the nervous system.
   a. pituitary; sympathetic
   b. pituitary; parasympathetic
   c. adrenal; sympathetic
   d. adrenal; parasympathetic

3. During which stage of the general adaptation syndrome is a person especially vulnerable to disease?
   a. alarm reaction   c. stage of exhaustion
   b. stage of resistance d. stage of adaptation

4. The leading cause of death in North America is:
   a. lung cancer.
   b. AIDS.
   c. coronary heart disease.
   d. alcohol-related accidents.

5. Researchers Friedman and Rosenman refer to individuals who are very time-conscious, supermotivated, verbally aggressive, and easily angered as:
   a. ulcer-prone personalities.
   b. cancer-prone personalities.
   c. Type A.
   d. Type B.

6. One effect of the hormones epinephrine, norepinephrine, and cortisol is to:
   a. lower the level of cholesterol in the blood.
   b. promote the buildup of plaques on the artery walls.
   c. divert blood away from the muscles of the body.
   d. reduce stress.

7. Genuine illnesses that are caused by stress are called _____ illnesses.
   a. psychophysiological   c. psychogenic
   b. hypochondriacal   d. psychotropic

8. Stress has been demonstrated to place a person at increased risk of:
   a. cancer.   c. viral infections.
   b. tuberculosis.   d. all of the above.

9. Stress is defined as:
   a. unpleasant or aversive events that cannot be controlled.
   b. situations that threaten health.
   c. the whole process by which we perceive and respond to challenging or threatening events.
   d. anything that decreases immune responses.

10. In one experiment, both "executive" rats and "subordinate" rats received identical electric shocks, the only difference being whether the shocks could be:
    a. predicted.   c. shortened.
    b. weakened.   d. controlled.

11. Research has demonstrated that, for a patient's well-being, it is better for a doctor to be:
    a. nonspecific in answering questions about the patient's condition.
    b. reassuring in answering questions, even if the person's condition is grave.
    c. realistic in answering questions about the patient's condition.
    d. harsh, in order to impress on the patient the importance of treatment.

12. Studies have demonstrated that meals that are high in _____ promote relaxation because they raise levels of _____.
    a. carbohydrates; serotonin
    b. carbohydrates; cortisol
    c. protein; serotonin
    d. protein; cortisol

13. A study in which people were asked to confide troubling feelings to an experimenter found that subjects typically:
    a. were not truthful in reporting feelings and events.
    b. experienced a sustained increase in blood pressure until the experiment was finished.
    c. became physiologically more relaxed after confiding their problem.
    d. denied having any problems.

14. Research suggests that _____ influences often lead a person to start smoking, while _____ influences become important in explaining why people continue to smoke.
    a. biological; social   c. biological; cognitive
    b. social; biological   d. cognitive; biological

15. Research on life-change scales has shown that total score generally:

a. is an accurate predictor of future health.

b. is not an accurate predictor of future health.

c. is greater for females than males.

d. bears a strong relationship to ethnic background.

16. Research on genetic influences on obesity reveals that:

a. the body weight of adoptees correlates with that of their biological parents.

b. the body weight of adoptees correlates with that of their adoptive parents.

c. identical twins usually have very different body weights.

d. none of the above is true.

17. Which of the following was *not* mentioned in the text as a potential health benefit of exercise?

a. Exercise can increase ability to cope with stress.

b. Exercise can lower blood pressure.

c. Exercise can reduce depression and anxiety.

d. Exercise improves functioning of the immune system.

18. Research studies demonstrate that rates of _____ often increase after a catastrophe.

a. psychological disorders

b. stress-related illnesses

c. death

d. All of the above increase.

e. None of the above increases.

19. Which of the following is *least* likely to promote patients' adherence to treatment instructions?

a. clearly framed treatment instructions

b. a warm patient-doctor relationship

c. patients' perception that every aspect of their treatment is being planned for them

d. the patient's receiving immediate rewards for compliant behavior

20. Social support _____ our ability to cope with stressful events.

a. has no effect on

b. usually increases

c. usually decreases

d. has an unpredictable effect on

Progress Test 2

Progress Test 2 should be completed during a final chapter review. Answer the following questions after you thoroughly understand the correct answers for the Chapter Review and Progress Test 1.

Multiple-Choice Questions

1. The field of health psychology is concerned with:

a. the prevention and treatment of illness.

b. the promotion of health.

c. the improvement of health care systems.

d. all of the above.

2. In order, the sequence of stages in the general adaptation syndrome is:

a. alarm reaction, stage of resistance, stage of exhaustion.

b. stage of resistance, alarm reaction, stage of exhaustion.

c. stage of exhaustion, stage of resistance, alarm reaction.

d. alarm reaction, stage of exhaustion, stage of resistance.

3. Researchers have found that individuals who suppress their anger are especially prone to:

a. ulcers.   c. stroke.

b. hypertension.   d. cancer.

4. "Burnout" refers to:

a. physical, emotional, and mental exhaustion brought on by persistent job-related stress.

b. the formation of plaques in the coronary arteries.

c. uncooperative, complaining, and demanding patient behavior.

d. the suppression of immune responses.

5. Which of the following statements concerning Type A and B persons is true?

a. Even when relaxed, Type A persons have higher blood pressure than Type B persons.

b. When stressed, Type A persons show greater output of epinephrine, norepinephrine, and cortisol than Type B persons.

c. Type B persons tend to suppress anger more than Type A persons.

d. Type A persons tend to sleep more than Type B persons.

6. According to the textbook, one-half of all deaths from the 10 leading causes of death in the United States can be attributed to:

a. stress.   c. nutrition.

b. obesity.   d. behavior.

7. The disease- and infection-fighting cells of the immune system are:

a. B lymphocytes.   c. both a. and b.

b. T lymphocytes.   d. antigens.

8. One effect of stress on the body is to:
   a. suppress the immune system.
   b. facilitate the immune system response.
   c. increase disease resistance.
   d. increase the proliferation of B and T lymphocytes.

9. A person who is forced to choose between two attractive but incompatible goals is experiencing:
   a. approach-approach conflict.
   b. approach-avoidance conflict.
   c. avoidance-avoidance conflict.
   d. none of the above.

10. In response to uncontrollable shock, levels of stress hormones _____ and immune responses are _____ .
    a. decrease; suppressed   c. decrease; increased
    b. increase; suppressed   d. increase; increased

11. Concerning patient adherence to treatment instructions, which of the following is *not* true?
    a. About half of all patients fail to adhere to treatment instructions.
    b. The tendency to comply is influenced by the patient-doctor relationship.
    c. Severe conditions are associated with high rates of compliance.
    d. When patients fail to follow instructions, it is often because they do not understand them.

12. Research on cancer patients reveals that:
    a. those who bottle up their emotions have less chance of survival than those who express them.
    b. patients' attitudes can influence their rate of recovery.
    c. participating in support groups may enhance immune responses.
    d. all of the above are true.

13. The component of Type A behavior that is the most predictive of coronary disease is:
    a. time urgency.   c. high motivation.
    b. competitiveness.   d. anger.

14. Which of the following is true concerning smoking treatment programs?
    a. Most are effective in the long run.
    b. Hypnosis is more effective than behavior modification.
    c. Treatment programs are more effective with women than with men.
    d. Most participants eventually resume smoking.

15. During biofeedback training:
    a. a subject is given sensory feedback for a subtle bodily response.
    b. biological functions controlled by the autonomic nervous system may come under conscious control.
    c. the accompanying relaxation is much the same as that produced by other, simpler methods of relaxation.
    d. all of the above occur.

16. Research on obesity indicates that:
    a. pound for pound, fat tissue requires more calories to maintain than lean tissue.
    b. once fat cells are acquired they are never lost, no matter how rigorously one diets.
    c. one pound of weight is lost for every 3500-calorie reduction in diet.
    d. compared to normal-weight persons, those who are obese secrete less insulin (which suppresses appetite) in response to external food cues.

17. The number of fat cells a person has is influenced by:
    a. genetic predisposition.
    b. childhood eating patterns.
    c. adulthood eating patterns.
    d. all of the above.

18. Relaxation is the most effective technique for preventing:
    a. alcoholism.
    b. a stressful environment.
    c. smoking.
    d. a repeat heart attack.

19. Which of the following was offered in the text as a reason people continue to smoke?
    a. Social pressure from peers is strong.
    b. Cigarettes serve as powerful negative reinforcers.
    c. Regular use of nicotine impairs the brain's ability to produce neurotransmitters such as serotonin.
    d. Most adults who smoke don't really want to quit.

20. The text suggests that a person's adopting the good-patient role may:
    a. enhance the effectiveness of their treatment.
    b. increase feelings of helplessness and anxiety.
    c. contribute to the placebo effect of the treatment.
    d. increase their sense over control over their treatment.

True-False Items

Indicate whether each statement is true or false by placing *T* or *F* in the blank next to the item.

_____ 1. Most obese people who lose weight eventually gain it back.

_____ 2. Stressors tend to increase activity in the immune system and in this way make people more vulnerable to illness.

_____ 3. Most patients are good at following their doctor's instructions.

_____ 4. Patients are better able to cope with medical trauma when they are given realistic information.

_____ 5. The single most important factor in causing obesity is heredity.

_____ 6. An approach-avoidance conflict occurs when a person is both attracted and repelled by the same goal.

_____ 7. Optimists cope more successfully with stressful events than pessimists.

_____ 8. Type A persons are more physiologically reactive to stress than Type B persons.

_____ 9. Chronic stress can lead to ulcers, headaches, and hypertension.

_____ 10. People with few social and community ties are more likely to die prematurely than are those with many social ties.

Challenge Test

Answer these questions the day before an exam as a final check on your understanding of the chapter's terms and concepts.

Multiple-Choice Questions

1. Which of the following is *not* necessarily a reason that obese people have trouble losing weight?
   a. Fat tissue has a lower metabolic rate than lean tissue.
   b. Obese people are more responsive to external cues.
   c. Obese people have a stronger insulin reaction to external cues.
   d. Obese people tend to lack willpower.

2. After an initial rapid weight loss, a person on a diet loses weight much more slowly. This slowdown occurs because:
   a. most of the initial weight loss is simply water.
   b. when a person diets, metabolism decreases.
   c. people begin to "cheat" on their diets.
   d. insulin levels tend to increase with reduced food intake.

3. Virginia can't decide whether to spend winter break on a Caribbean cruise or going skiing with her friends. Virginia's dilemma is an example of:
   a. an approach-approach conflict.
   b. an approach-avoidance conflict.
   c. an avoidance-avoidance conflict.
   d. none of the above.

4. According to the text, the single most beneficial change in a person's behavior, from the point of view of heath, would be to:
   a. stop abusing alcohol and drugs.
   b. begin a vigorous daily exercise regime.
   c. go on a diet that is low in fat intake and high in fiber intake.
   d. stop smoking.

5. Ricardo has an important psychology exam in the afternoon. In an effort to improve his concentration and alertness, he orders a lunch that is high in _____ and low in _____.
   a. carbohydrates; protein
   b. carbohydrates; fat
   c. protein; carbohydrates
   d. protein; fat

6. (Close-Up) Which of the following would be the *worst* piece of advice to offer to someone trying to lose weight?
   a. "In order to treat yourself to one 'normal' meal each day, eat very little until the evening meal."
   b. "Reduce your consumption of saturated fats."
   c. "Boost your metabolism by exercising regularly."
   d. "Without increasing total caloric intake, increase the relative proportion of carbohydrates in your diet."

7. Each semester, Bob does not start studying until just before midterms. Then he is forced to work around the clock until after final exams, which makes him sick, probably because he is in the _____ phase of the _____.
   a. alarm; post-traumatic stress syndrome
   b. resistance; general adaptation syndrome
   c. exhaustion; general adaptation syndrome
   d. depletion; post-traumatic stress syndrome

8. Connie complains to the campus psychologist that she has too much stress in her life. The psychologist tells her that the level of stress people experience depends primarily on:
   a. how many activities they are trying to "juggle."
   b. how they appraise the events of life.
   c. their physical hardiness.
   d. how predictable stressful events are.

9. Calvin was a social worker who counseled troubled families. After several years of breaking up fights and removing abused children from their homes for their own protection, Calvin became so depressed and cynical about his job that he began finding it difficult to go to work. Calvin was probably suffering from:

a. an avoidance-avoidance conflict.
b. an approach-avoidance conflict.
c. the alarm reaction.
d. burnout.

10. Karen and Kyumi are taking the same course with different instructors. Karen's instructor schedules quizzes every Friday, while Kyumi's instructor gives the same number of quizzes on an unpredictable schedule. Assuming that their instructors are equally difficult, which student is probably under more stress?
    a. Karen
    b. Kyumi
    c. There should be no difference in their levels of stress.
    d. It is impossible to predict stress levels in this situation.

11. Jill is an easygoing, noncompetitive person who is happy in her job and enjoys her leisure time. She would *probably* be classified as:
    a. Type A.   c. Type C.
    b. Type B.   d. atherosclerotic.

12. A white blood cell that is formed in the thymus and that attacks cancer cells is:
    a. a macrophage.   c. a T lymphocyte.
    b. a B lymphocyte.   d. any of the above.

13. When would you expect that your immune responses would be *weakest*?
    a. during summer vacation
    b. during exam weeks
    c. just after receiving good news
    d. Immune activity would probably remain constant during these times.

14. Which of the following would be the *best* piece of advice to offer to a person who is trying to minimize the adverse effects of stress on his or her health?
    a. "Avoid challenging situations that may prove stressful."
    b. "Learn to play as hard as you work."
    c. "Maintain a sense of control and a positive approach to life."
    d. "Keep your emotional responses in check by keeping your feelings to yourself."

15. Dr. Mendoza is seeking ways to increase her patients' adherence to her instructions. According to the text, Dr. Mendoza should:
    a. frighten her patients by telling them their condition will worsen if they do not follow her advice.
    b. emphasize the long-range benefits of healthy behaviors.

c. encourage patients to adopt the "good-patient role."
d. stress immediate rewards for following her advice.

16. Kenny and his identical twin have nearly identical eating and exercise habits, yet Kenny is obese and his twin is very thin. The most likely explanation for the difference in their body weights is that they differ in:
    a. their set points.   c. both a. and b.
    b. their metabolic rates. d. none of the above.

17. Dr. Williams, a health psychologist who conducts smoking cessation clinics, explains to his clients that smoking is best understood as an interaction of psychological, biological, and social influences. Evidently, Dr. Williams is working within the _____ perspective.
    a. systems theory
    b. behavioral
    c. general adaptation syndrome
    d. psychophysiological

18. Philip's physician prescribes a stress management program to help Philip control his ulcer. The physician has apparently diagnosed Philip's condition as a _____ illness, rather than a physical disorder.
    a. psychogenic   c. psychophysiological
    b. hypochondriac   d. biofeedback

19. Camelia is worried that her 12-year-old son might begin smoking because many of his classmates do. According to the text, Camelia can most effectively help her son not begin smoking by:
    a. telling him about the dangers of smoking.
    b. telling him that if he begins smoking she will withhold his allowance.
    c. using role-playing to teach him refusal techniques to counteract peer pressure to smoke.
    d. insisting that he not associate with anyone who smokes.

20. You have just transferred to a new campus and find yourself in a potentially stressful environment. According to the text, which of the following would help you cope with the stress?
    a. believing that you have some control over your environment
    b. being able to predict when stressful events will occur
    c. feeling optimistic that you will eventually adjust to your new surroundings
    d. All of the above would help.

Essay Question

Discuss several factors that enhance a person's ability to cope with stress. (Use the space below to list the points you want to make and organize them. Then write the essay on a separate sheet of paper.)

Key Terms

Using your own words, write a brief definition or explanation of each of the following terms.

1. behavioral medicine

2. health psychology

3. stress

4. general adaptation syndrome (GAS)

5. burnout

6. coronary heart disease

7. Type A

8. Type B

9. psychophysiological illness

10. lymphocytes

11. aerobic exercise

12. biofeedback

13. obesity

ANSWERS

GUIDED STUDY

The following guidelines provide the main points that your answers should have touched upon.

1. According to the systems theory, illness results from the interaction of a person's biological, social, and psychological systems. Health psychology's major concerns include the following: how our emotions and responses to stress influence our risk of disease, how people decide they are sick and whether they will seek and follow treatment, what attitudes and behaviors help prevent illness and

promote health and well-being, and how we can reduce or control stress.

2. Stress is the whole process by which we appraise and respond to events that threaten or challenge us. Stress triggers an outpouring of epinephrine, norepinephrine, and cortisol from nerve endings in the adrenal glands of the sympathetic nervous system. These stress hormones increase heart rate and respiration, divert blood to the muscles, and release fat from the body's stores to prepare the body for "fight or flight." Selye saw the body's reaction to stress as having three phases (general adaptation syndrome): the alarm reaction, in which the body's resources are mobilized; resistance, in which stress hormones flow freely to help cope with the stressor; and exhaustion, when reserves are depleted and illness is more likely.

3. Some studies have shown that stressful events, such as catastrophes, are closely followed by an increase in emergency room visits, psychological disorders, and even deaths. The level of stress we experience depends on how we appraise such events. Catastrophes, significant life changes, and daily hassles are especially stressful when they are appraised as uncontrollable and negative, and when we have a pessimistic outlook. A perceived loss of control, for example, triggers an outpouring of stress hormones. In such circumstances, the mental, physical, and emotional exhaustion of burnout can occur and vulnerability to disease may increase.

4. Friedman and Rosenman discovered that stress triggers a variety of physical changes, such as increased cholesterol and blood-clotting speed, that may promote coronary heart disease. According to their designation, Type A people are competitive, hard-driving, impatient, verbally aggressive, and easily angered. In contrast, Type B people are more relaxed and easygoing.

5. The immune system includes two types of white blood cells (lymphocytes) that defend the body by destroying foreign substances. The B lymphocytes form in the bone marrow and release antibodies that combat bacterial infections. The T lymphocytes form in the thymus and attack cancer cells and viruses. Another immune agent, the macrophage, identifies and ingests harmful invaders.

Stress lowers the body's resistance to disease by suppressing the disease-fighting lymphocytes of the immune system. This may explain the link between stress and cancer. Animal research has shown that when the immune system is weakened by stress, tumor cells develop sooner and grow larger. Research has also shown that immune suppression can be classically conditioned. Conversely, studies of cancer patients demonstrate that

reducing stress and creating a hopeful, relaxed state may improve chances of survival.

6. Most people are not very accurate at judging their physiological responses or the early signs of illness. When symptoms *are* noticed, people tend to interpret them according to familiar disease schemas and to attribute negative feelings to them. People are more likely to seek treatment if they believe their symptoms have a physical rather than a psychological cause. Embarrassment and the potential expense and inconvenience of treatment may cause them to delay seeking help. Although men may be more disease-prone, women report more symptoms and visit physicians more often.

7. In hospitals, people who adopt the good-patient role—being cooperative, undemanding, and unquestioning—may feel more helpless, anxious, and depressed about their condition. Those who adopt the more uncooperative, complaining, demanding bad-patient role may alienate hospital personnel and in this way undermine their own treatment. To reduce the patient's stress, doctors should provide realistic information about what to expect during a hospital stay.

Research reveals that as many as half of all patients fail to follow their doctor's recommendations. This may be because they do not understand the instructions or because the delayed consequences of health-enhancing behaviors are overshadowed by the immediate reinforcement of their usual behaviors. Thus, to be effective, strategies for increasing patients' compliance need to stress immediate rewards for compliant behavior.

8. Stress management includes aerobic exercise, biofeedback, relaxation, and social support. Aerobic exercise can reduce stress, depression, and anxiety. Research has also shown that those who exercise regularly tend to live longer and suffer from fewer illnesses than those who don't. Exercise may produce its benefits by increasing the production of mood-boosting neurotransmitters, by strengthening the heart, and by lowering both blood pressure and the blood pressure reaction to stress.

Biofeedback systems allow people to monitor their subtle physiological responses and enjoy a calm, tranquil experience. Simple relaxation produces the same effects, however, including lowered blood pressure and strengthened immune defenses.

People with strong social support systems eat better, exercise more, smoke and drink less, and have more opportunities to confide painful feelings. Research shows that such people report fewer illnesses and are less likely to die prematurely than people who lack close supportive relationships.

9. Those who smoke usually begin during adolescence if their friends, parents, and siblings are smokers. Because adolescent smokers tend to be perceived by other teenagers as tough and sociable, self-conscious adolescents may begin to emulate these models in order to receive the social rewards of peer acceptance. People continue smoking because it serves as a negative reinforcer that terminates the aversive states that accompany nicotine withdrawal. Nicotine is also a positive reinforcer that triggers the release of epinephrine, norepinephrine, and other neurotransmitters, which boosts alertness and calms anxiety.

   Smoking prevention programs that "inoculate" adolescents against peer pressure to smoke by teaching refusal skills have proven effective in reducing the rate of smoking. Programs for adults —counseling, drug treatments, hypnosis, aversive conditioning, for example—are less effective since all but one-fifth of the participants eventually return to smoking.

10. High-carbohydrate foods increase the amount of the amino acid tryptophan reaching the brain, which raises the level of the relaxation-promoting neurotransmitter serotonin. Low-carbohydrate, high-protein foods improve alertness and concentration. Low-cholesterol, low-salt, and low-fat diets help reduce the risk of heart disease, hypertension, and cancer.

11. Obesity is a threat to both physical and psychological well-being. The number of fat cells in our bodies is determined by genetic predisposition, early eating patterns, and adult overeating. Fat cells may shrink in size with dieting, but they will never decrease in number. Because fat tissue has a low metabolic rate, it takes less food energy to maintain, and it is therefore difficult for dieters to lose weight. Dieters also become more responsive to external food cues that trigger the release of insulin and stimulate hunger. Because obese persons probably have a higher-than-average set-point weight, when they diet their hunger increases and metabolism decreases, making it even more difficult for them to lose weight.

12. Adoption and twin studies both provide evidence for the role of heredity in determining obesity. The fact that the weight resemblance between identical twins is less in females than males suggests that social pressure may also play a role. Moreover, heredity cannot explain the fact that obesity is much more common in lower-class than in upper-class women, more common among Americans than Japanese or Europeans, and more common today than at the beginning of the century.

13. Research suggests that dieters should do the following: minimize their exposure to food cues, exercise and modify their diets to boost metabolism, avoid binge eating, eat regular meals to prevent the slowed metabolism that comes with starvation diets, and set realistic goals.

CHAPTER REVIEW

1. heart disease; cancer; stroke; accidents
2. behavior
3. cigarette smoking, excessive alcohol consumption, maladaptive responses to stress, nonadherence to doctors' orders, insufficient exercise, use of illicit drugs, poor nutrition
4. behavioral medicine

Behavioral medicine's "systems theory" maintains that illness results from the interaction of the biological, psychological, and sociological systems within which a person exists. This contrasts with traditional efforts to link specific diseases to single causes, such as genes, germs, or emotions.

5. health
6. stress
7. Cannon; epinephrine, or adrenaline; norepinephrine, or noradrenaline; sympathetic; fight or flight
8. cortisol
9. adrenal; thymus; ulcers; general adaptation syndrome
10. alarm; sympathetic
11. resistance
12. exhaustion; more
13. emergency room visits, deaths, stress-related health complaints
14. more
15. is not

The stresses that most people face are seldom the major crises indexed by such rating scales. Furthermore, it is not the events themselves but how we appraise them that determines their stressfulness.

16. daily hassles; burnout
17. approach-approach; avoidance-avoidance; approach-avoidance
18. control; optimistic
19. stress hormones (cortisol)
20. coronary heart disease; smoking, obesity, family history, high-fat diet, physical inactivity, elevated blood pressure and cholesterol levels
21. do not account
22. cholesterol; clotting; stress

Type A people were competitive, hard-driving, super-motivated, impatient, verbally aggressive, and easily angered. Type B people were more relaxed and easygoing. Heart attack victims over the course of the study came overwhelmingly from the Type A group.

23. smoking, sleeping less, drinking more caffeinated beverages and less milk

24. do not differ

25. greater than; plaques; atherosclerosis

26. cholesterol; Type A

27. has not; the tendency to become angry (or negative emotions, or an aggressively reactive temperament)

28. psychophysiological; hypertension; ulcers; headaches; physical; stress

29. immune; lymphocytes; B lymphocytes; T lymphocytes; macrophage

30. decrease

Stress can affect the spread of cancer by weakening the body's defenses against malignant cells. When rodents were inoculated with tumor cells, tumors developed sooner in those that were also exposed to uncontrollable stress. Stress does not cause cancer, however; nor can relaxation prevent it. Cancer patients who remain hopeful and who share their negative emotions with others survive longer than those who keep their feelings bottled up.

31. can

32. are not

33. schemas; premenstrual; do not

34. women

35. good-patient; bad-patient

36. reduces

37. half

Some patients fail to follow their doctor's instructions simply because they don't understand them. Others do not follow instructions because the delayed rewards of doing so are overshadowed by immediate consequences.

38. aerobic; have

39. biofeedback; do not provide

40. relaxation

41. reduced

42. humor

43. social

Stressful events are potentially debilitating. Stress may contribute to heart disease and to a variety of psychophysiological illnesses. It can also weaken the immune system, making the person more vulnerable to disease. The negative impacts of stress can be buffered by a healthy life-style that includes regular exercise and relaxation and by the social support of friends and family, or increased where these factors are lacking.

44. prevent; treating

45. early adolescence; social-cognitive

46. negative; alertness; anxiety; pain sensitivity; are not; males; higher

47. less

48. neurotransmitters

49. carbohydrates; serotonin; carbohydrates; protein

50. salt; calcium; fat

51. 20

Obesity increases one's risk of diabetes, high blood pressure and heart disease, gallstones, arthritis, and certain types of cancer. It negatively affects self-image and the perceptions of others, particularly if the excess weight is seen as the fault of the individual.

52. 3500; fat cells; genetic predisposition, early childhood eating patterns, adult overeating

53. can; cannot

54. lower; less

55. insulin

Obese persons have higher set-point weights than nonobese persons. During a diet, metabolic rate drops to defend the set-point weight. The dieter therefore finds it hard to progress beyond an initial weight loss. When the diet is concluded, the lowered metabolic rate continues, so that relatively small amounts of food may prove fattening. Also, some people have lower metabolic rates than others.

56. do

57. less than

58. more; does

59. gain

PROGRESS TEST 1

1. c. is the answer. (p. 511)

    a. Health psychology is a subfield within behavioral medicine.

    b. Holistic medicine is an older term that refers to medical practitioners who take more of an interdisciplinary approach to treating disorders.

    d. Osteopathy is a medical therapy that emphasizes manipulative techniques for correcting physical problems.

2. c. is the answer. (p. 513)

    a., b., & d. The pituitary does not produce stress hormones nor is the parasympathetic division involved in arousal.

3. c. is the answer. (p. 514)

a. & b. During these stages the body's defensive mechanisms are at peak function.

d. This is not a stage of GAS.

4. **c.** is the answer. Coronary heart disease is followed by (all) cancer, stroke, and accidents (of whatever source). AIDS has not yet become one of the four leading causes of death in North America among the general population. (p. 518)

5. **c.** is the answer. (p. 519)

a. & b. Researchers have not identified such personality types.

d. Individuals who are more easygoing are labeled Type B.

6. **b.** is the answer. These stress hormones accelerate the buildup of plaques, or masses formed by cholesterol deposits, on the artery walls. This likely occurs because during arousal blood is diverted from internal organs such as the liver, which removes cholesterol from the blood, to the muscles of the body. These hormones comprise a part of the body's response to stress; they do not reduce stress. (pp. 519–520)

7. **a.** is the answer. (p. 520)

b. Hypochondriacs think something is wrong with them, but nothing physical can be detected.

c. *Psychogenic* means "originating in the mind." One's reaction to stress is partially psychological, but this term is not used to refer to stress-related illness.

d. There is no such term.

8. **d.** is the answer. Because stress depresses the immune system, stressed individuals are prone to all of these conditions. (p. 521)

9. **c.** is the answer. (p. 512)

a., b., & d. Whether an event is stressful or not depends on how it is appraised.

10. **d.** is the answer. (p. 517)

11. **c.** is the answer. When patients know what to expect, they may be less anxious and better able to cope with discomfort. Therefore, it is generally best for doctors to be realistic, rather than nonspecific or reassuring. There is no evidence that harshness is helpful. (p. 527)

12. **a.** is the answer. Certain high-carbohydrate foods raise the levels of serotonin, which facilitates relaxation by increasing the amount of tryptophan reaching the brain. (p. 537)

b. Cortisol is a stress hormone and hence not related either to carbohydrates or to relaxation.

c. & d. Meals that are high in protein promote alertness.

13. **c.** is the answer. The finding that talking about grief leads to better health makes a lot of sense in light of this physiological finding. (p. 533)

a., b., & d. The study by Pennebaker did not find these to be true.

14. **b.** is the answer. People generally *start* smoking in adolescence in order to gain peer acceptance; they continue smoking primarily because they have become addicted to nicotine. Thus, the factors that motivate people to start smoking are best described as social, while the factors that explain continued smoking are mainly biological. (pp. 534–535)

15. **b.** is the answer. These scales do not accurately predict future health because they fail to consider individual differences in appraising and coping with stressful situations. (p. 515)

16. **a.** is the answer. (p. 541)

17. **d.** is the answer. Regular aerobic exercise has been shown to increase ability to cope with stress, lower blood pressure, and reduce depression and anxiety. The textbook does not cite evidence that exercise enhances immune function. (pp. 528–529)

18. **d.** is the answer. (p. 514)

19. **c.** is the answer. Patients' adherence to treatment instructions improves when they are personally involved in planning their treatment. (pp. 527–528)

a., b., & d. These factors have been shown to promote patients' adherence to treatment instructions.

20. **b.** is the answer. (pp. 532–533)

PROGRESS TEST 2

Multiple-Choice Questions

1. **d.** is the answer. This chapter deals with the topics of health psychology, namely: preventing illness, as by developing better ways to cope with stress; improving health care systems, as by improving communication between doctors and patients; and promoting health, for example, through nutrition and weight control. (p. 512)

2. **a.** is the answer. (pp. 513–514)

3. **b.** is the answer. People who suppress their anger are prone to hypertension. (pp. 516, 520)

a., c., & d. Suppression of anger has not specifically been linked to these conditions.

4. **a.** is the answer. (p. 517)

b. This defines atherosclerosis.

c. This defines the bad-patient role.

5. **b.** is the answer. The greater reactivity of Type A people includes much higher levels of stress hormones in stress situations. (pp. 519–520)

a. Under relaxed situations, there is no difference in blood pressure.

c. Anger, expressed and suppressed, is more characteristic of Type A people.

d. Type A persons tend to sleep less.

6. **d.** is the answer. Behaviors that contribute to the leading causes of mortality include smoking, excessive alcohol consumption, maladaptive responses to stress, nonadherence to doctors' instructions, insufficient exercise, use of illicit drugs, and poor nutrition. (p. 511)

7. **c.** is the answer. B lymphocytes fight bacterial infections; T lymphocytes attack cancer cells, viruses, and foreign substances. (p. 521)

d. Antigens are substances that cause the production of antibodies when they are introduced into the body.

8. **a.** is the answer. A variety of studies have shown that stress depresses the immune system, increasing the risk and potential severity of many diseases. (p. 521)

9. **a.** is the answer. (p. 517)

b. In this type of conflict a person is simultaneously attracted and repelled by a situation, person, or object.

c. This is a conflict between two undesirable alternatives.

10. **b.** is the answer. Both human and animal studies indicate that uncontrollable negative events trigger an outpouring of stress hormones and a drop in immune responses. (pp. 517–518)

11. **c.** is the answer. Only about half of all patients follow instructions, even when there is a life-threatening problem such as breast cancer or dangerously high blood pressure. The patient-doctor relationship and the patient's understanding of the instructions are two key factors in compliance. (p. 527)

12. **d.** is the answer. (pp. 521–523)

13. **d.** is the answer. The crucial characteristic of Type A behavior seems to be a tendency to react with negative emotions, especially anger; other aspects of Type A behavior appear not to predict heart disease, and some appear to be helpful to the individual. (p. 520)

14. **d.** is the answer. No particular treatment seemed to stand out in terms of effectiveness. All but one-fifth of the people who quit smoking in such programs eventually return to the habit. (pp. 535–536)

15. **d.** is the answer. In biofeedback training, subjects are given sensory feedback about autonomic responses. Although biofeedback may promote relaxation, its benefits may be no greater than those produced by simpler, and less expensive, methods. (pp. 529–530)

16. **b.** is the answer. Fat cells may change in size as a person gains or loses weight, but their number never decreases. (p. 539)

a. In fact, because of its lower metabolic rate, fat tissue can be maintained on *fewer* calories.

c. Because metabolism slows as food intake is restricted, a 3500-calorie reduction may not reduce weight by one pound.

d. In fact, just the opposite is true. In response to external cues, obese people secrete *more* insulin. Furthermore, insulin *triggers* hunger, rather than suppressing it.

17. **d.** is the answer. (p. 540)

18. **d.** is the answer. Friedman's subjects who received counseling on relaxation experienced half as many repeat heart attacks as did a control group. (p. 531)

19. **b.** is the answer. By alleviating the aversive physiological state of nicotine withdrawal, cigarettes act as negative reinforcers. (p. 535)

a. This is one explanation of why adolescents *start* smoking.

c. There is no evidence that this occurs.

d. Most smokers would like to quit smoking.

20. **b.** is the answer. These patients experience the greatest loss of control, and loss of control is associated with feelings of helplessness and anxiety. (pp. 526–527)

a. By reducing the patient's perceived control, the good-patient role may *reduce* the effectiveness of treatment.

c. The placebo effect is the beneficial effect of a patient's expecting to be helped by treatment. There is no evidence that the good-patient role increases patients' belief in their treatment.

d. The good-patient role is associated with feelings of loss of control.

True-False Items

1. True (p. 542)	6. True (p. 517)
2. False (p. 521)	7. True (p. 518)
3. False (p. 527)	8. True (p. 519)
4. True (p. 527)	9. True (p. 520)
5. False (p. 541)	10. True (p. 533)

CHALLENGE TEST

Multiple-Choice Questions

1. **d.** is the answer. Most researchers today discount the idea that people are obese because they lack willpower. (p. 539)

2. **b.** is the answer. Following the initial weight loss, metabolism drops as the body attempts to defend its set-point weight. This drop in metabolism means that eating an amount that once produced a loss in weight may now actually result in weight gain. (p. 540)

3. **a.** is the answer. This is an example of choosing between two desirable, but incompatible, goals. (p. 517)

   b. This conflict occurs when a person is both attracted and repelled by the same goal.

   c. This conflict occurs when a person must choose between two undesirable alternatives.

4. **d.** is the answer. Approximately 30 percent of all cancer deaths and 30 percent or more of the deaths caused by heart disease in the United States are linked with cigarette smoking. (p. 534)

   a., b., & c. Although each of these is an important factor in promoting health, cigarette smoking is the largest preventable cause of illness and death.

5. **c.** is the answer. High-protein foods seem to improve alertness, whereas high-carbohydrate foods seem to promote relaxation. (p. 537)

6. **a.** is the answer. Dieting, including fasting, lowers the body's metabolic rate and reduces the amount of food energy needed to maintain body weight. (p. 544)

   b., c., & d. Each of these strategies would be a good piece of advice to a dieter.

7. **c.** is the answer. According to Selye's general adaptation syndrome, diseases are most likely to occur in this final stage. (pp. 513–514)

   a. & b. Resistance to disease is greater during the alarm and resistance phases, since the body's mobilized resources are not yet depleted.

   d. There is no such thing as the "depletion phase." Moreover, the post-traumatic stress syndrome refers to the haunting nightmares and anxiety of those who have suffered extreme stress, such as that associated with combat.

8. **b.** is the answer. (p. 516)

   a., c., & d. Each of these is a factor in coping with stress, but it is how an event is *perceived* that determines whether it is stressful or not.

9. **d.** is the answer. Burnout refers to the physical, mental, and emotional exhaustion that may emerge from unrelenting job-related stress. (p. 517)

   a. & b. Conflict occurs when one is forced to choose between two events.

   c. The alarm reaction is the first phase of the general adaptation syndrome.

10. **b.** is the answer. Unpredictable events are more stressful than predictable events. (p. 514)

11. **b.** is the answer. (p. 519)

    a. Type A persons are hard-driving and competitive.

    c. There is no such thing as a "Type C" person.

    d. Atherosclerosis refers to the blockage of the arteries that leads to coronary heart disease. Type A persons are more susceptible to atherosclerosis than Type B persons.

12. **c.** is the answer. (p. 521)

    a. Macrophages are immune agents that patrol the body in search of debris and bacteria.

    b. B lymphocytes form in the bone marrow and release antibodies that fight bacterial infections.

13. **b.** is the answer. Stressful situations, such as exam weeks, decrease immune responses. (p. 521)

14. **c.** is the answer. (pp. 517–518)

    a. This is not realistic.

    b. & d. These might actually *increase* the health consequences of potential stressors.

15. **d.** is the answer. (p. 528)

    a. The text does not suggest that fear tactics improve patients' adherence to instructions.

    b. Patients often fail to follow their doctor's instructions because the long-term benefits of a healthier life-style compete with the immediate discomfort or inconvenience of following the doctor's orders.

    c. Because playing the good-patient role may actually undermine the effectiveness of a patient's treatment, the text does not recommend it.

16. **b.** is the answer. Individual differences in metabolism explain why it is possible for two people, even identical twins, to have very different weights despite similar patterns of eating and exercise. (pp. 540–541)

    a. Being genetically identical and having experienced similar early eating habits, it is likely that Kenny and his twin have similar set points.

17. **a.** is the answer. (p. 511)

    b. The behavioral perspective would emphasize only learned factors in smoking.

    c. The general adaptation syndrome is a sequence of bodily responses to stress.

    d. Psychophysiological illnesses are illnesses not caused by any known physical disorder.

18. **c.** is the answer. (p. 520)

  a. The text does not discuss any such thing as a "psychogenic" illness.

  b. Hypochondriasis is the misinterpreting of normal physical sensations as symptoms of a disease.

  d. Biofeedback is a system for recording information regarding a subtle physiological state, such as blood pressure.

19. **c.** is the answer. (pp. 536–537)

20. **d.** is the answer. (pp. 514, 517–518)

Essay Question

When potentially stressful events occur, a person's appraisal is a major determinant of their impact. Catastrophes, significant life events, and daily hassles and conflicts are especially stressful when appraised as negative, unpredictable, and uncontrollable, and when the person has a pessimistic outlook on life. Under these circumstances, stressful events may suppress immune responses and make the person more vulnerable to disease. If stressors cannot be eliminated, aerobic exercise, biofeedback, relaxation, and social support can help the person cope. Aerobic exercise can reduce stress, depression, and anxiety, perhaps by increasing production of mood-boosting neurotransmitters. During biofeedback training, people enjoy a calm, relaxing experience that can be helpful in reducing stress. Research demonstrates that people who regularly practice relaxation techniques enjoy a greater sense of tranquility, and have lower blood pressure and stronger immune responses. People with strong social ties eat better, exercise more, and smoke and drink less. Social support may also help people evaluate and overcome stressful events. And, confiding painful feelings to others has been demonstrated to reduce physiological responses linked to stress.

KEY TERMS

1. **Behavioral medicine** is the interdisciplinary health field that applies behavioral and medical knowledge to the treatment of disease and the promotion of health. (p. 511)

2. **Health psychology** is a subfield of psychology that studies how health and illness are influenced by emotions, stress, personality, life-style, and other psychological factors. (p. 512)

3. **Stress** refers to the psychological and physiological processes by which people perceive and react to stressors, or events they perceive as threatening. (p. 512)

4. The **general adaptation syndrome (GAS)** is the three-stage sequence of bodily reaction to stress outlined by Hans Selye. (pp. 513–514)

  Example: According to Selye, during the final stage of the **general adaptation syndrome**, the stage of exhaustion, people become more vulnerable to "diseases of adaptation" such as hypertension, ulcers, and coronary heart disease.

5. **Burnout** refers to a state of physical, mental, and emotional exhaustion brought on by unrelenting job-related stress. (p. 517)

6. The leading cause of death in the United States today, **coronary heart disease** results from the narrowing of the coronary arteries and the subsequent reduction in blood and oxygen supply to the heart muscle. (p. 518)

7. **Type A** personality is Friedman and Rosenman's term for the coronary-prone behavior pattern of hard-driving, impatient, verbally aggressive, and anger-prone people. (p. 519)

8. **Type B** personality is Friedman and Rosenman's term for the coronary-resistant behavior pattern of easygoing people. (p. 519)

9. A **psychophysiological illness** is any genuine illness, such as hypertension, ulcers, and headaches, that is apparently linked to stress, rather than caused by a physical disorder. (p. 520)

  Memory aid: *Psycho-* refers to mind; *physio-* refers to body; a **psychophysiological** illness is a mind-body disorder.

10. **Lymphocytes** are the two types of white blood cells of the immune system that fight bacterial infections (B lymphocytes) and viruses, cancer cells, and foreign substances in the body (T lymphocytes). (p. 521)

11. **Aerobic exercise** is any sustained activity, such as running, swimming, or cycling, that promotes heart and lung fitness and may help alleviate depression and anxiety. (p. 528)

12. **Biofeedback** refers to a system that provides external sensory feedback on an internal physiological state. (p. 529)

  Memory aid: A **biofeedback** device, such as a brain-wave trainer, provides auditory or visual feedback about biological responses.

13. **Obesity** is said to occur when a person's weight is 20 percent or more above the optimum for that person's sex, height, and build. (p. 538)

18 / Social Psychology

Chapter Overview

Chapter 18 demonstrates the powerful influences of social situations on the behavior of individuals. Central to this topic are research studies on attitudes and actions, conformity, compliance, and group influence, and aggression, altruism, and attraction. The social principles that emerge help us to understand how individuals are influenced by advertising, political candidates, and the various groups to which they belong. Although social influences are powerful, it is important to remember the significant role of individuals in choosing and creating the social situations they are influenced by.

Although there is some terminology for you to learn in this chapter, your primary task is to absorb the findings of the many research studies discussed. The chapter headings, which organize the findings, should prove especially useful to you here. In addition, you might, for each main topic (conformity, group influence, aggression, etc.), ask yourself the question, "What situational factors promote this phenomenon?" The research findings can then form the basis for your answers.

NOTE: Answer guidelines for all Chapter 18 questions begin on page 385.

Guided Study

The text chapter should be studied one section at a time. Before you read, preview each section by skimming it, noting headings and boldface items. Then read the appropriate section objectives from the following outline. Keep these objectives in mind and, as you read the chapter section, search for the information that will enable you to meet each objective. Once you have finished a section, write out answers for its objectives.

Social Thinking (pp. 551–557)

1. Discuss attribution theory, focusing on the fundamental attribution error, and describe some possible effects of attribution.

2. Define attitude and identify the conditions under which attitudes predict behavior.

3. Describe how actions influence attitudes and explain how cognitive dissonance theory accounts for this phenomenon.

371

Social Influence (pp. 557–567)

4. Define stress and describe the body's response to stress.

5. Describe the results of Asch's experiments on conformity and distinguish between normative and informational social influence.

6. Summarize the findings from Milgram's obedience studies.

7. Discuss how the presence of others may produce social facilitation, social loafing, or deindividuation.

8. Describe group polarization and show how it can be a source of groupthink.

9. Discuss how personal control and social influence interact in guiding behavior and explain how a minority can influence the majority.

Social Relations (pp. 567–583)

10. Describe the impact of biology, unpleasant events, and learning experiences on aggressive behavior.

11. Discuss the effects of television violence and pornographic films on viewers.

12. Describe and explain the "bystander effect."

13. Discuss how social exchange theory, social norms, and sociobiology variously explain altruism.

14. Identify the determinants of social attraction and distinguish between passionate and companionate love.

Chapter Review

When you have finished reading the chapter, work through the material that follows to review it. Complete the sentences and answer the questions. As you proceed, evaluate your performance for each section by consulting the answers on page 387. Do not continue with the next section until you understand each answer. If you need to, review or reread the appropriate section in the textbook before continuing.

1. The scientific study of how we think about, influence, and relate to one another is _Social_ _psychology_ .

Social Thinking (pp. 551–557)

2. Heider's theory of how we explain others' behavior is the _attribution_ theory. According to this theory, we attribute behavior either to internal causes, or _dispositions_ , or to external causes, or _situations_ .

3. Most people tend to _underestimate_ (overestimate/underestimate) the extent to which people's actions are influenced by social situations because their _attention_ is focused on the person. This tendency is called the _fundamental attribution error_ . When a person is explaining his or her *own* behavior this tendency is _weaker_ (stronger/weaker). When observers view the world from others' perspectives, attributions are _reversed_ (the same/reversed).

Give an example of how attributions influence judgments.

4. Beliefs and feelings that predispose our responses are called _attitudes_ .

5. The many research studies on attitudes and actions conducted during the 1960s _challenged_ (challenged/supported) the common assumption that our actions are guided by our attitudes.

List three conditions under which our attitudes do predict our actions. Give examples.

6. Many research studies demonstrate that our attitudes are strongly influenced by our _actions_ . One example of this is the tendency for people who agree to a small request to comply later with a larger one. This is the _foot_ - _in_ - _the_ - _door_ phenomenon.

7. A set of behaviors expected of someone in a given social position is called a _role_ .

8. Taking on a set of behaviors, or acting in a certain way, generally _changes_ (changes/does not change) people's attitudes.

9. According to _cognitive dissonance_ theory, thoughts and feelings change because people are motivated to justify actions that would otherwise seem hypocritical. This theory was proposed by _Festinger_ .

10. Dissonance theory predicts that people induced (without coercion) to behave contrary to their true attitudes will be motivated to reduce the resulting _dissonance_ by changing their _attitudes_ .

Social Influence (pp. 557–567)

11. The term that refers to the tendency to adjust one's behavior to coincide with an assumed group standard is _Conformity_.

12. The psychologist who studied social influences on suggestibility using a stationary point of light in a dark room is _Sherif_.

13. The psychologist who studied the effects of group pressure on conformity is _Asch_.

14. In this study, when the opinion of other group members was contradicted by objective evidence, subjects _were_ (were/were not) willing to conform to the group opinion.

15. One reason that people comply with social pressure is to gain approval or avoid rejection; this is called _normative social influence_. Understood rules for accepted and expected behavior are called _norms_.

16. Another reason people comply is that they have genuinely been influenced by what they have learned from others; this type of influence is called _informational social influence_.

17. The classic social psychology studies of obedience were conducted by _Milgram_. When ordered by the experimenter to electrically shock the "learner," most subjects (the "teachers") in these studies _complied_ (complied/refused).

18. When subjects were asked to administer the test while another person delivered the shocks, compliance was _increased_ (reduced/increased).

19. People who are working simultaneously on the same noncompetitive task are called _co-actors_.

20. The tendency to perform a task better when other people are present is called _social facilitation_. In general, people become aroused in the presence of others, and arousal enhances the correct response on a(n) _easy_ (easy/difficult) task.

21. Researchers have found that the reactions of people in crowded situations are often _amplified_ (lessened/amplified).

22. Ingham found that people worked _less hard_ (harder/less hard) in a team tug-of-war than they had in an individual contest. This phenomenon has been called _social loafing_.

23. The feeling of anonymity and loss of restraint that an individual may develop when in a group is called _deindividuation_.

24. Over time, the initial differences between groups usually _increase_ (increase/decrease). This phenomenon is called _group polarization_.

25. When the desire for group harmony overrides realistic thinking in individuals, the phenomenon known as _groupthink_ has occurred.

26. A minority opinion will have most success in swaying the majority if it takes a stance that is _unswerving_ (unswerving/flexible).

Social Relations (pp. 567–583)

27. Aggressive behavior is defined by the textbook as _any physical or verbal behavior intended to hurt or destroy_.

28. Two theorists who proposed that aggression is instinctive are _Freud_ and _Lorenz_. Today most psychologists _don't believe_ (believe/do not believe) that human aggression is instinctive.

29. In humans, aggressiveness _varies_ (varies/does not vary) greatly from culture to culture.

30. That there are genetic influences on aggression can be shown by the fact that many species of animals have been _bred_ for aggressiveness.

31. Twin studies suggest that genes _do_ (do/do not) influence human aggression.

32. In humans and animals, aggression is activated and inhibited by _neural_ systems, such as those in the _limbic system_, which are in turn influenced by _hormones_ and other substances in the blood.

33. The aggressive behavior of animals can be manipulated by altering the levels of the hormone _testosterone_. When this level is _decreased_ (increased/decreased) aggressive tendencies are reduced.

34. One drug that reduces a person's natural restraints against aggression is _alcohol_.

35. According to the _frustration_-_aggression_ principle, inability to achieve a goal leads to anger, which may generate aggression.

36. Aggressive behavior can be learned through _rewards_, as shown by the fact that people use aggression where they've found it pays, and through _observation_ of others.

37. Violence on television appears to promote aggressive behavior as a result of four factors: the excitement of television causes _arousal_; seeing violence triggers _ideas_ related to violence; TV violence erodes viewers' _inhibitions_; and viewers tend to _imitate_ behaviors they have seen.

38. Most rapes _are not_ (are/are not) reported. Most rapes _are not_ (are/are not) committed by strangers.

39. Correlational studies of pornography and aggression _generally_ (generally/do not generally) show a relationship between availability of pornography and incidence of rape.

40. When other studies looked at *nonviolent* pornography, it was found that attitudes toward rape _were_ (were/were not) affected.

Comment on the impression of women that pornography frequently conveys and the effects this impression has on attitudes and behavior.

Summarize the findings of the Zillmann and Bryant study on the effects of pornography on attitudes toward rape.

41. Eron and Huesmann found that children were _less_ (less/no less) influenced by watching television violence if they had been taught that television portrays the world unrealistically.

Summarize the American Psychological Association's advice to parents on children's television viewing.

42. An unselfish regard for the welfare of others is called _altruism_.

43. According to Darley and Latané, people will help only if a three-stage decision-making process is completed: Bystanders must first _notice_ the incident, then _recognize_ it as an emergency, and finally _assume_ _responsibility_ for helping.

44. When people who overheard a seizure victim calling for help thought others were hearing the same plea, they were _less_ (more/less) likely to go to his aid than when they thought no one else was aware of the emergency.

45. In a series of staged accidents, Latané and Darley found that a bystander was _less_ (more/less) likely to help if other bystanders were present. This phenomenon has been called the _bystander_ effect.

Identify the circumstances in which a person is most likely to offer help during an emergency.

46. The idea that social behavior aims to maximize rewards and minimize costs is proposed by _Social_ _Exchange_ theory.

47. Some people exhibit a natural _empathy_ for others; that is, they easily feel what another feels.

48. One rule of social behavior tells us to return help to those who have helped us; this is the _reciprocity_ norm. Another tells us to help those who need our help; this is the _social_ _responsibility_ norm.

49. The study of how natural selection influences social behavior is called _sociobiology_. According to this theory, altruism may have a _biological_ basis: People tend to be _more_ (more/less) altruistic to close relatives than to distant ones, because of the greater proportion of shared _genes_.

Identify several predictors of heroic or sacrificial behavior.

50. A prerequisite for, and perhaps the most powerful predictor of, attraction is _proximity_.

51. When people are repeatedly exposed to unfamiliar stimuli, their liking of the stimuli _increases_ (increases/decreases). This phenomenon is the _mere_ _exposure_ effect.

52. Our first impression of another person is most influenced by the person's _appearance_.

53. In a sentence, list several of the characteristics that physically attractive people are judged to possess: _happier, more sensitive &_ _successful, & socially skilled._

54. A person's attractiveness _is not_ (is/is not) strongly related to his or her self-esteem.

55. Cross-cultural research reveals that men judge women as more attractive if they have a _youthful_ appearance, while women judge men who appear _mature_ as more attractive.

State the sociobiological explanation of this gender difference.

56. Relationships in which the partners are very similar are _more_ (more/less) likely to last.

57. Compared with strangers, friends and couples are more likely to be similar in terms of _attitudes,_ _religions, interest, race, age, intelligence_

Explain what a reward theory of attraction is and how it can account for the three predictors of liking— proximity, attractiveness, and similarity.

58. Hatfield has distinguished two types of love: _passionate_ love and _compassionate_ love.

59. According to the two-factor theory, emotions have two components: physical _arousal_ and a _cognitive_ label.

60. When college men were placed in an aroused state, their feelings toward an attractive woman _were_ (were/were not) more positive than those of men who had not been aroused.

61. Companionate love is promoted by _____equity_____—mutual sharing and giving by both partners. Another key ingredient of loving relationships is the revealing of intimate aspects of ourselves through _____self-disclosure_____.

FOCUS ON PSYCHOLOGY:
Games that Promote Cooperation

Social psychologists believe that many conflicts arise from destructive social processes, such as social traps. Social traps are situations in which conflicting parties become caught in mutually destructive behavior by not trusting each other and pursuing their individual interests.

Computer systems engineer Gerald Rabow suggests that the roots of social traps may lie in the games children are taught to play—games adults continue to play throughout their careers and personal lives. Football, basketball, and most board games engender "zero-sum" (ZS) thinking: When one player wins, the other loses. In such games, according to Rabow, "Any positive score by one side is in effect a negative score by the other; hence the name, zero sum." As adults, zero-sum thinking is evident whenever our actions are guided by the attitude that we lose if someone else wins.

Rabow believes that if children and adults learn to play games that promote cooperation, they might later avoid conflicts and reach better solutions to problems. These would be "non-zero-sum" (NZS) games, since "opposing" sides could both benefit from cooperation because the net score need not equal zero.

Rabow suggests that many familiar ZS games can be made into NZS versions in which cooperation, as well as competition, would be rewarded. In the traditional word game Scrabble, for example, players score points by forming words from letter tiles placed on a special game board. The game winner is the player with the highest score. Good strategy therefore includes not only forming high-scoring words to increase one's own point total, but also making it difficult for the other player to score.

The NZS version of Scrabble retains the central features of ZS Scrabble—players still try to form high-scoring words—but eliminates the benefits of obstructing the other player's scoring opportunities. Instead, the objective becomes to score as many points as possible, regardless of the other player's score. All players can in effect "win" by scoring more points than their previous personal bests. All players therefore benefit from high scores by inducing cooperative play from one another. In addition to promoting cooperation, the NZS version of the game has the advantage of placing even greater emphasis than regular Scrabble on word skills.

Rabow also believes that many team games can be converted into challenging and enjoyable NZS versions that retain most of the regular rules but do more to promote cooperation among players. In NZS basketball, for example, each player receives the conventional one to three points for making a basket, minus one-fifth the number of points scored by the other team during the time that player is in the game. The net result is that while the combined score of the two teams equals zero, each player receives an individual point total that can be compared with that of other players. As in regular basketball, NZS players must cooperate with team members in overcoming the other team's defense so scoring is possible at all. In the NZS version of the game, however, the focus of competition is shifted from team scoring to individual scoring. Since there are no team victories, coaches and players can focus on teaching and player skill development rather than on making sure the team wins. Younger and less-skilled players can get equal playing time, since there is no pressure on coaches to keep their top scorers in the game to ensure a win.

Rabow believes that many other common games can be converted into NZS games and that entirely new ones can easily be devised. The dynamics of NZS play, involving both cooperation and competition among players, should make the games enjoyable both to play and to watch. "And the new skills that they simulate can be useful in the real NZS world," says Rabow. "The strategies that successful players evolve may even provide some useful insights into solving real-world problems."

Source: Rabow, Gerald. (1988, January). The cooperative edge. *Psychology Today*, 54–58.

Progress Test 1
Multiple-Choice Questions

Circle your answers to the following questions and check them with the answers on page 388. If your answer is incorrect, read the explanation for why it is incorrect and then consult the appropriate pages of the text (in parentheses following the correct answer).

1. In his study of obedience, Stanley Milgram found that:
   a. most subjects refused to shock the learner even once.
   b. most subjects complied with the experiment until the "learner" first indicated pain.
   c. most subjects complied with the experiment until the "learner" began screaming in agony.
   d. most subjects complied with all the demands of the experiment.

2. According to the cognitive dissonance theory, dissonance is most likely to occur when:
   a. a person's behavior is not based on strongly held attitudes.
   b. two people have conflicting attitudes and find themselves in disagreement.
   c. an individual does something that is personally disagreeable.
   d. an individual is coerced into doing something that he or she does not want to do.

3. Which of the following statements about groups is true?
   a. Groups are almost never swayed by minority opinions.
   b. Group polarization is most likely to occur when group members frequently disagree with one another.
   c. Groupthink provides the consensus needed for effective decision making.
   d. A group that is like-minded will probably not change its opinions through discussion.

4. Conformity increased under which of the following conditions in Asch's studies of conformity?
   a. The group had three or more people.
   b. The group had high status.
   c. Individuals were made to feel insecure.
   d. All of the above increased conformity.

5. One reason that people comply with social pressure is to avoid rejection or gain approval. This is called:
   a. informational social influence.
   b. the fundamental attribution error.
   c. normative social influence.
   d. deindividuation.

6. The phenomenon in which individuals lose their identity and relinquish normal restraints when they are part of a group is called:
   a. groupthink.
   b. cognitive dissonance.
   c. empathy.
   d. deindividuation.

7. Subjects in Asch's line-judgment experiment conformed to the group standard when their judgments were observed by others but not when they were made in private. This tendency to conform in public demonstrates:
   a. social facilitation.
   b. overjustification.
   c. informational social influence.
   d. normative social influence.

8. In Milgram's studies of obedience, subjects were *least* likely to follow the experimenter's orders when:

a. they heard the "learner" cry out in pain.
b. they merely administered the test while someone else delivered the shocks.
c. the "learner" was an older person or mentioned having some physical problem.
d. they observed another subject disobey instructions.

9. Aggression is defined as behavior that:
   a. hurts another person.
   b. is intended to hurt another person.
   c. is hostile, passionate, and produces physical injury.
   d. has all of the above characteristics.

10. Findings from cross-cultural studies of aggression suggest that:
    a. aggression is not a human instinct.
    b. aggression is just one instinct among many.
    c. aggression is instinctive but shaped by learning.
    d. aggression is the most important of the human instincts.

11. Research studies have found a positive correlation between aggressive tendencies in animals and levels of the hormone:
    a. estrogen.   c. noradrenaline.
    b. adrenaline.   d. testosterone.

12. Research studies have indicated that the tendency of viewers to misperceive normal sexuality, devalue their partners, and trivialize rape:
    a. is increased by exposure to pornography.
    b. is not changed after exposure to pornography.
    c. is decreased in men by exposure to pornography.
    d. is decreased in both men and women by exposure to pornography.

13. Increasing the number of people that are present during an emergency tends to:
    a. increase the likelihood that people will cooperate in rendering assistance.
    b. decrease the empathy that people feel for the victim.
    c. increase the role that social norms governing helping will play.
    d. decrease the likelihood that anyone will help.

14. Which of the following is in keeping with the sociobiological theory of altruistic behavior?
    a. Altruism is never favored by natural selection.
    b. Some forms of altruism help perpetuate our genes.
    c. For biological reasons, there are gender differences in altruism, with altruistic behavior confined largely to females.
    d. Altruism has come to play a key role in the survival of our species because it promotes global harmony.

15. The mere exposure effect demonstrates that:
    a. familiarity breeds contempt.
    b. opposites attract.
    c. birds of a feather flock together.
    d. familiarity breeds fondness.

16. In one experiment, college men were physically aroused and then introduced to an attractive woman. Compared to men who had not been aroused, these men:
    a. reported more positive feelings toward the woman.
    b. reported more negative feelings toward the woman.
    c. were more likely to feel that the woman was "out of their league" in terms of attractiveness.
    d. focused more on the woman's attractiveness and less on her intelligence and personality.

17. The deep affection that is felt in long-lasting relationships is called _____ love; this feeling is fostered in relationships in which _____.
    a. passionate; there is equity between the partners
    b. passionate; traditional roles are maintained
    c. companionate; there is equity between the partners
    d. companionate; traditional roles are maintained

18. Which of the following is associated with an increased tendency on the part of a bystander to offer help in an emergency situation?
    a. being in a good mood
    b. having recently needed help and not received it
    c. observing someone refusing to offer help
    d. being a female

19. Which of the following best expresses the relationship between aversive events and aggression?
    a. Only aversive stimuli that produce frustration increase anger.
    b. Aversive stimuli increase hostility in males but not in females.
    c. Foul odors, heat, smoke, and other aversive stimuli can provoke hostility.
    d. Only aversive stimuli that block our attempts to achieve some goal arouse hostility.

20. According to the social exchange theory, a person's tendency toward altruistic behavior is based on:
    a. a determination of the relatedness of those who will be affected.
    b. a cost-benefit analysis of any action.
    c. social norms.
    d. all of the above.

Matching Items

Match each term with the appropriate definition or description.

Terms
1. social facilitation
2. social loafing
3. empathy
4. norms
5. roles
6. normative social influence
7. informational social influence
8. group polarization
9. co-actors
10. attribution
11. altruism
12. mere exposure effect

Definitions or Descriptions
a. a causal explanation for someone's behavior
b. people working at the same task at the same time
c. people work less hard in a group
d. performance is improved by an audience
e. a set of social expectations for a position
f. the effect of social approval or disapproval
g. rules for acceptable behavior
h. group discussion enhances prevailing tendencies
i. the effect of accepting others' opinions about something
j. unselfish regard for others
k. feeling what another feels
l. the increased liking of a stimulus that results from repeated exposure to it

Progress Test 2

Progress Test 2 should be completed during a final chapter review. Answer the following questions after you thoroughly understand the correct answers for the Chapter Review and Progress Test 1.

Multiple-Choice Questions

1. Which theorist argued that aggression was a manifestation of a person's "death instinct" redirected toward another person?
   a. Wilson   c. Lorenz
   b. Freud   d. Janis

2. Research studies of selective breeding suggest that:
   a. aggressive behavior may have a genetic basis.
   b. aggressive behavior is primarily a learned rather than a genetically determined behavior.
   c. aggressive behavior cannot be increased through breeding.
   d. both b. and c. are true.

3. Regarding the influence of alcohol and testosterone on aggressive behavior, which of the following is true?
   a. Consumption of alcohol increases aggressive behavior; injections of testosterone reduce aggressive behavior.
   b. Consumption of alcohol reduces aggressive behavior; injections of testosterone increase aggressive behavior.
   c. Consumption of alcohol and injections of testosterone both promote aggressive behavior.
   d. Consumption of alcohol and injections of testosterone both reduce aggressive behavior.

4. Most people prefer mirror-image photographs of their faces. This is best explained by:
   a. the principle of equity.
   b. the principle of self-disclosure.
   c. the mere exposure effect.
   d. mirror-image perceptions.

5. Research studies have shown that frequent exposure to sexually explicit films:
   a. may promote increased acceptance of promiscuity.
   b. diminishes the attitude that rape is a serious crime.
   c. may lead individuals to devalue their partners.
   d. may produce all of the above effects.

6. Research studies indicate that in an emergency situation the presence of others often:
   a. prevents people from even noticing the situation.
   b. prevents people from interpreting an unusual event as an emergency.
   c. prevents people from assuming responsibility for assisting.
   d. leads to all of the above.

7. Which of the following best expresses the social exchange theory of altruistic behavior?
   a. People help others because they have learned that it is right to help those who have helped them.
   b. People help others out of a sense of guilt or pity.
   c. People help others because they expect to benefit from doing so.
   d. People are most likely to extend help to those who are related to them.

8. Which of the following factors is the most powerful predictor of friendship?
   a. similarity in age
   b. common racial and religious background
   c. similarity in physical attractiveness
   d. physical proximity

9. Most researchers agree that:
   a. television violence leads to aggression.
   b. although there is a correlation between television watching and aggressiveness, it's impossible to establish causation.
   c. paradoxically, watching excessive television violence ultimately diminishes an individual's aggressive tendencies.
   d. television violence is too unreal to promote aggression in viewers.

10. When subjects in an experiment were told that a woman to whom they would be speaking had been instructed to act in a friendly or unfriendly way, most of them subsequently attributed her behavior to:
    a. the situation.
    b. both the situation and her personal disposition.
    c. her personal disposition.
    d. their own skill or lack of skill in a social situation.

11. Which of the following is true?
    a. Attitudes and actions rarely correspond.
    b. Attitudes predict behavior about half of the time.
    c. Attitudes are excellent predictors of behavior.
    d. Attitudes predict behavior under certain conditions.

12. An individual may work harder when alone than as a member of a group. This phenomenon is called:
    a. social loafing.   c. empathy.
    b. social facilitation.   d. group polarization.

13. Which of the following most accurately states the effects of crowding on behavior?

a. Crowding makes people irritable.

b. Crowding sometimes intensifies people's reactions.

c. Crowding promotes altruistic behavior.

d. Crowding usually weakens the intensity of people's reactions.

14. Research has found that for a minority to succeed in swaying a majority, the minority must:

    a. make up a sizable portion of the group.

    b. express its position as consistently as possible.

    c. express its position in the most extreme terms possible.

    d. be able to convince a key leader of the majority.

15. Which of the following conclusions did Milgram derive from his studies of obedience?

    a. Even ordinary people, without any particular hostility, can become agents in a destructive process.

    b. Most people are able, under the proper circumstances, to suppress their natural aggressiveness.

    c. The need to be accepted by others is a powerful motivating force.

    d. All of the above conclusions were reached.

16. Which of the following best summarizes the relative importance of personal control and social control of our behavior?

    a. Situational influences on behavior generally are much greater than personal influences.

    b. Situational influences on behavior generally are slightly greater than personal influences.

    c. Personal influences on behavior generally are much greater than situational influences.

    d. Situational influences and personal influences interact in determining our behavior.

17. Which of the following pairs of individuals would be considered "co-actors"?

    a. debaters on opposing teams

    b. two members of an audience watching a play

    c. the pitcher and batter during a baseball game

    d. psychology lab partners collecting data during an experiment

18. Which of the following is important in promoting conformity in individuals?

    a. whether an individual's behavior will be observed by others in the group

    b. whether the individual is male or female

    c. the size of the room in which a group is meeting

    d. the age of the members in a group

19. Which theory describes how we explain other's behavior as being due to internal dispositions or external situations?

    a. social exchange theory

    b. reward theory

    c. two-factor theory

    d. attribution theory

20. Which of the following is most likely to promote groupthink?

    a. The group's leader fails to take a firm stance on an issue.

    b. A minority faction holds to its position.

    c. The group consults with various experts.

    d. Group polarization is evident.

True-False Items

Indicate whether each statement is true or false by placing *T* or *F* in the blank next to the item.

__T__ 1. When explaining another's behavior, we tend to underestimate situational influences.

__F__ 2. When explaining our own behavior, we tend to underestimate situational influences.

__T__ 3. An individual is more likely to conform when the rest of the group is unanimous.

__T__ 4. The tendency of people to conform is influenced by the culture in which they were socialized.

__F__ 5. A bystander is more likely to offer help in an emergency if other bystanders are present.

__T__ 6. Counter-attitudinal behavior (acting contrary to our beliefs) often leads to attitude change.

__F__ 7. Human aggression is instinctual.

__F__ 8. Group polarization tends to prevent groupthink from occurring.

__F__ 9. Crowded conditions usually subdue people's reactions.

__T__ 10. When individuals lose their sense of identity in a group, they often become more uninhibited.

Challenge Test

Answer these questions the day before an exam as a final check on your understanding of the chapter's terms and concepts.

Multiple-Choice Questions

1. After waiting in line for an hour to buy concert tickets, Teresa is told that the concert is sold out. In her anger she pounds her fist on the ticket counter, frightening the clerk. Teresa's behavior is best explained by the:

    a. theory of sociobiology.

    b. reciprocity norm.

    c. social exchange theory.

    d. frustration-aggression principle.

2. Before she gave a class presentation favoring gun control legislation, Wanda opposed it. Her present attitude favoring such legislation can best be explained by:
   a. attribution theory.
   b. cognitive dissonance theory.
   c. social exchange theory.
   d. sociobiological theory.

3. Which of the following would most likely be subject to social facilitation?
   a. running quickly around a track
   b. proofreading a page for spelling errors
   c. typing a letter with accuracy
   d. playing a difficult piece on a musical instrument

4. Jane and Sandy were best friends as freshmen. Jane joined a sorority; Sandy didn't. By the end of their senior year, they found that they had less in common with each other than with the other members of their respective circles of friends. Which of the following phenomena most likely explains their feelings?
   a. group polarization   c. deindividuation
   b. groupthink   d. social facilitation

5. The board members of Acme Truck Company are so afraid of going against the chairman's ideas and breaking the "team spirit" that they often conceal their true opinions. This group is a victim of:
   a. social facilitation.
   b. cognitive dissonance.
   c. informational social influence.
   d. groupthink.

6. José is the one student member on the college board of trustees. At the board's first meeting, José wants to disagree with the others on several issues but in each case decides to say nothing. Studies on conformity suggest all except one of the following are factors in José's not speaking up. Which one is *not* a factor?
   a. The board is a large group.
   b. The board is prestigious and most of its members are well known.
   c. The board members are already aware that José and the student body disagree with them on these issues.
   d. Because this is the first meeting José has attended, he feels insecure and not fully competent.

7. After Marilyn Monroe committed suicide, there was an increase in suicides in the United States. This has been attributed to the social influence of:
   a. conformity.   c. compliance.
   b. suggestibility.   d. all of the above.

8. An army captain who gives a controversial order to destroy a village is concerned about whether the soldiers will comply. Which of the following would promote the greatest compliance?
   a. Orders are given immediately prior to the time fixed for the attack.
   b. A decision is made to launch the attack by air.
   c. Reinforcements are sent in to assist in the attack.
   d. When several soldiers balk at the orders, they are severely reprimanded in front of the others.

9. Maria recently heard a speech calling for a ban on aerosol sprays that endanger the earth's ozone layer. Maria's subsequent decision to stop using aerosol sprays is an example of:
   a. informational social influence.
   b. normative social influence.
   c. deindividuation.
   d. social facilitation.

10. Lynn has just joined a sorority and feels awkward during rituals and sorority functions. After playing this role for some time, she will probably:
    a. experience an increase in awkwardness.
    b. continue to feel awkward but learn to hide these feelings.
    c. begin to resent the group.
    d. begin to feel more comfortable in her role.

11. Which of the following situations should produce the *greatest* cognitive dissonance?
    a. A soldier is forced to carry out orders he finds disagreeable.
    b. A student who loves animals has to dissect a cat in order to pass biology.
    c. As part of an experiment, a subject is directed to deliver electric shocks to another person.
    d. A student volunteers to debate an issue, taking the side he personally disagrees with.

12. Professor Washington's students did very poorly on the last exam. The tendency to make the fundamental attribution error might lead Professor Washington to conclude that the class did poorly because:
    a. the test was unfair.
    b. not enough time was given for students to complete the test.
    c. students were distracted by some social function on campus.
    d. students were unmotivated.

13. Which of the following would be the best advice to give parents who are concerned about the effects of television violence on their children?
    a. "Don't worry, there is in fact little solid evidence that viewing violence actually leads to violence."

b. "Limit television watching and discuss the programs with your children."

c. "Allow children to watch a few extremely violent programs so that they will see the absurdity of television's portrayal of the world."

d. "Ban all television viewing."

14. After Sandy helped Jack move into his new apartment, Jack felt obligated to help Sandy when she moved. Jack's sense of responsibility can best be explained by:

a. sociobiological theory.

b. two-factor theory.

c. the social responsibility norm.

d. the reciprocity norm.

15. Ahmed and Monique are on a blind date. Which of the following factors will probably be *most* influential in determining whether they like each other?

a. their personalities

b. their beliefs

c. their social skills

d. their physical attractiveness

16. Opening her mail, Joan discovers a romantic greeting card from her boyfriend. According to the two-factor theory, she is likely to feel the most intense romantic feelings if she has just:

a. completed her daily run.

b. finished reading a chapter in her psychology textbook.

c. awakened from a nap.

d. finished eating lunch.

17. Driving home from work, Althea saw a car run off the road and burst into flames. Althea stopped her car, ran to the burning vehicle, and managed to pull the driver to safety before the car exploded. With which of the following theories of altruistic behavior does Althea's behavior *conflict*?

a. social exchange theory

b. sociobiological theory

c. two-factor theory

d. reward theory

18. Having read the chapter, which of the following is best borne out by research on attraction?

a. Birds of a feather flock together.

b. Opposites attract.

c. Familiarity breeds contempt.

d. Absence makes the heart grow fonder.

19. Dr. Schachter, who studies how people think about, influence, and relate to one another is *probably* a:

a. sociobiologist.

b. social exchange theorist.

c. social psychologist.

d. cognitive psychologist.

20. Which of the following is an example of the foot-in-the-door phenomenon?

a. To persuade a customer to buy a product a store owner offers a small gift.

b. After agreeing to wear a small "Enforce Recycling" lapel pin, a woman agrees to collect signatures on a petition to make recycling required by law.

c. After offering to sell a car at a ridiculously low price, a car salesperson is forced to tell the potential purchaser the car will cost $1000 more.

d. All of the above are examples.

Essay Question

The PanHellenic Council on your campus has asked you to make a presentation on the topic "Social Psychology" to all freshmen who have signed up to "rush" a fraternity or sorority. In a fit of cynicism following your rejection last year by a prestigious fraternity or sorority, you decide to speak on the negative influences that groups may have on the behavior of individuals. What will you discuss? (Use the space below to list the points you want to make and organize them. Then write the essay on a separate sheet of paper.)

Key Terms

Using your own words, write a brief definition or explanation of each of the following terms.

1. social psychology

2. attribution theory

3. fundamental attribution error

4. attitudes

5. foot-in-the-door phenomenon

6. role

7. cognitive dissonance theory

8. conformity

9. normative social influence

10. norms

11. informational social influence

12. co-actors

13. social facilitation

14. social loafing

15. deindividuation

16. group polarization

17. groupthink

18. aggression

19. frustration-aggression principle

20. altruism

21. bystander effect

22. social exchange theory

23. empathy

24. sociobiology

25. mere exposure effect

26. passionate love

27. companionate love

28. equity

29. self-disclosure

ANSWERS
GUIDED STUDY
The following guidelines provide the main points that your answers should have touched upon.

1. According to attribution theory, people explain others' behavior as being due either to their dispositions or to their situations. Because people have enduring personality traits, we tend to overestimate the influence of personality and underestimate the impact of situational influences, particularly when explaining others' behavior. This is called the fundamental attribution error. When explaining our own behavior, or when we take another's perspective, we are less likely to make this type of error. Our attributions, of course, have important practical consequences. For example, there are political implications to the question of whether people's behavior is attributed to social conditions or to their own choices, abilities, and shortcomings.

2. Attitudes are beliefs and feelings that predispose our reactions to objects, people, and events. Our attitudes are most likely to guide our actions when outside influences on what we say and do are minimal, when the attitude is specifically relevant to the behavior, and when we are aware of our attitudes.

3. Studies of the foot-in-the-door phenomenon and role playing demonstrate that our actions can influence our attitudes. The foot-in-the door phenomenon is the tendency for people who agree to a small request to comply later with a larger one. Similarly, people who play a role tend to adjust their attitudes to coincide with behavior enacted while playing the role. The theory of cognitive dissonance maintains that when our thoughts and behaviors don't coincide, we experience tension. To relieve this tension we bring our attitudes into line with our actions.

4. Suggestibility studies conducted by Solomon Asch demonstrate that when we are unsure about our behavior or thinking, we are more likely to conform to a group standard, even if it is incorrect. Conformity is promoted when people feel incompetent or insecure, when they are in groups of three or more, when the group is unanimous and of high status, when no prior commitment has been made, when behavior will be observed, and when people have been socialized in a culture that encourages respect for social standards. We conform to gain social approval (normative social influence) or because the group provides valuable information (informational social influence).

5. Subjects in Milgram's experiments were ordered to teach a list of word pairs to another person by punishing the learner's wrong answers with electric shocks. Obedience was highest when the experimenter was nearby and was perceived as a legitimate authority supported by a prestigious institution, when the victim was depersonalized or at a distance, and when there was no role model for defiance.

6. Social facilitation occurs when tasks are simple or well-learned but not when they are difficult or unfamiliar. When observed by others, people become aroused. Arousal *facilitates* the most likely response—the correct one on an easy task, an incorrect one on a difficult task. Social loafing occurs when people who work anonymously as part of a group exert less effort than those individually accountable for performance. Deindividuation occurs when group participation makes individuals feel aroused, anonymous, and less self-conscious. The uninhibited and impulsive behavior of mobs may occur as a result of this phenomenon.

7. Group polarization refers to the enhancement of a group's prevailing tendencies that occurs when like-minded members discuss issues and attitudes. The unrealistic group decision making called groupthink occurs when the desire for group harmony outweighs the desire for realistic thinking. It is fed by overconfidence, conformity, self-justification and group polarization. Groupthink can be prevented when the leader welcomes dissenting opinions and invites criticism.

8. The power of the situation (social control) and of the individual (personal control) interact in two significant ways. First, people often choose or help create the situations that influence their behavior. Second, the expectations people have about situations and behaviors may cause them to act in ways that trigger the expected results. In this way, expectations may be self-fulfilling.

   The impact that a minority can have in swaying the majority opinion illustrates the power of personal control. Research reveals that a minority that unswervingly holds to its position is more likely to be successful in swaying the majority than a minority that waffles.

9. Biology influences aggression at three levels—the genetic, the neural, and the biochemical. Studies of human twins and selective breeding in animals reveal that genes influence aggression. Electrical stimulation and injuries to certain regions of the limbic system, such as the amygdala, suggest that animal and human brains have neural systems that control aggressive behavior. Studies of animal aggression and violent criminals demonstrate that aggressive tendencies increase with blood levels of the hormone testosterone.

   A variety of psychological factors influence aggression. The frustration-aggression principle indicates that pain, insults, excessive heat, and other aversive stimuli can evoke hostility. Learning also plays a role in aggression. Aggressive reactions are more likely in situations in which experience has taught the individual that aggression will be rewarded. Furthermore, children who observe aggressive models often imitate their behavior.

10. Correlational studies reveal a link between children's viewing of violent television programs and their later aggressiveness as teenagers and young adults. Experts maintain that the effects of viewing violent programs stem from a combination of factors, including arousal by the violent excitement, the triggering of violence-related ideas, the erosion of inhibitions, and imitation.

    Research indicates that pornography tends to portray women as enjoying being the victims of sexual aggression, and this perception increases the acceptance of coercion in sexual relationships. Repeated viewing of such films also makes one's own partner seem less attractive.

11. The bystander effect states that a bystander is less likely to give aid if other bystanders are present. Darley and Latané maintain that bystanders will help only if they notice the incident, interpret it as an emergency, and assume responsibility for helping. At each step in this decision-making process the presence of other bystanders makes it less likely a helping decision will be made. Further research reveals that bystanders are most likely to help when they have seen someone else being helpful, when they are not in a hurry, when the victim appears similar to them and deserving of assistance, when they are in a small town or rural area, when they feel guilty, and when they are in a good mood.

12. The social exchange theory maintains that self-interest underlies all human interactions, including altruism, so that our constant goal is to maximize rewards and minimize costs. This theory helps explain why people often help those whose approval they seek or who can reciprocate favors in the future.

    People are also sensitive to social norms that promote helping. The reciprocity norm, for example, dictates that we should help those who have helped us. The social responsibility norm is the expectation that we should help those who need our help.

    Sociobiology suggests that natural selection influences social behavior and that people have a genetic bias to help close relatives in order to promote their shared genes.

13. Studies of attraction indicate that proximity is the most powerful predictor of friendship, in part because being repeatedly exposed to any person or thing tends to increase our liking for it (mere exposure effect). Experiments also reveal that physical appearance is the most powerful factor in the first impression a person triggers. Although many aspects of attractiveness vary with place and time, some may be universal. Once relationships are formed, similarity of attitudes, beliefs, interests, and other characteristics increases attraction between people.

Passionate love is an intense state of physical arousal triggered by another person, usually at the beginning of a relationship, that is cognitively labeled as love. Companionate love is the steadier, deeply felt attachment that emerges as love matures. Companionate love is fostered by feelings of equity between the partners in a relationship, and the acceptability of self-disclosures.

CHAPTER REVIEW

1. social psychology
2. attribution; dispositions; situations
3. underestimate; attention; fundamental attribution error; weaker; reversed

Our attributions—to individual's dispositions or to situations—have important practical consequences. A hurtful remark from an acquaintance, for example, is more likely to be forgiven if it is attributed to a temporary situation than to a mean disposition.

4. attitudes
5. challenged

Attitudes predict actions when other influences on the attitudes and actions are minimized, when the attitude is specifically relevant to the behavior, and when we are especially aware of our attitudes. Thus, our attitudes are more likely to predict behavior when we are not attempting to adjust our behavior to please others, when we are in familiar situations in which we don't have to stop and think about our attitudes, and when the attitude pertains to a specific behavior, such as purchasing a product or casting a vote.

6. actions; foot-in-the-door
7. role
8. changes
9. cognitive dissonance; Festinger
10. dissonance; attitudes
11. conformity

12. Sherif
13. Asch
14. were
15. normative social influence; norms
16. informational social influence
17. Milgram; complied
18. increased
19. co-actors
20. social facilitation; easy
21. amplified
22. less hard; social loafing
23. deindividuation
24. increase; group polarization
25. groupthink
26. unswerving
27. any physical or verbal behavior intended to hurt or destroy
28. Freud; Lorenz; do not believe
29. varies
30. bred
31. do
32. neural; limbic system (the hypothalamus or the amygdala); hormones
33. testosterone; decreased
34. alcohol
35. frustration-aggression
36. rewards; observation (or imitation)
37. arousal; ideas; inhibitions; imitate
38. are not; are not
39. generally
40. were

Pornography tends to portray women as enjoying being the victims of sexual aggression, and this perception increases the acceptance of coercion in sexual relationships.

The Zillmann and Bryant study found that after viewing sexually explicit films for several weeks, undergraduates were more likely to recommend a lighter prison sentence for a convicted rapist than were subjects who viewed nonerotic films.

41. less

The APA advises parents to limit their children's television watching, and to watch and discuss television with their children.

42. altruism
43. notice; interpret; assume responsibility
44. less

45. less; bystander effect

People are most likely to help someone when they have just observed someone else being helpful; when they are not in a hurry; when the victim appears to need and deserve help; when they are in some way similar to the victim; when in a small town; when feeling guilty; when not preoccupied; and when in a good mood.

46. social exchange

47. empathy

48. reciprocity; social responsibility

49. sociobiology; biological (or genetic); more; genes

Predictors include having caring parental models, close-knit families, and allegiance to religious or humanitarian convictions.

50. proximity

51. increases; mere exposure

52. appearance

53. Attractive people are perceived as happier, more sensitive, more successful, and more socially skilled.

54. is not

55. youthful; mature

According to sociobiology, this gender difference evolved because men drawn to healthy, fertile-appearing women and women drawn to men who appear able to provide support and protection stood a better chance of sending their genes into the future.

56. more

57. attitudes, beliefs, interests, religion, race, education, intelligence, smoking behavior, economic status, age

Reward theories of attraction say that we are attracted to, and continue relationships with, those people whose behavior provides us with more benefits than costs. Proximity makes it easy to enjoy the benefits of friendship at little cost, attractiveness is pleasing, and similarity is reinforcing to us.

58. passionate; companionate

59. arousal; cognitive

60. were

61. equity; self-disclosure

PROGRESS TEST 1

Multiple-Choice Questions

1. d. is the answer. In Milgram's initial experiments, about 65 percent of the subjects fully complied with the experiment. (p. 561)

2. c. is the answer. Cognitive dissonance is the tension we feel when we are aware of a discrepancy between our thoughts and actions, as would occur when we do something we find distasteful. (p. 557)

a. Dissonance requires strongly held attitudes, which must be perceived as not fitting behavior.

b. Dissonance is a personal cognitive process.

d. In such a situation the person is less likely to experience dissonance, since the action can be attributed to "having no choice."

3. d. is the answer. In such groups, discussion usually strengthens prevailing opinion; this phenomenon is known as group polarization. (p. 559)

a. Minority opinions, especially if consistently and firmly stated, can sway the majority in a group.

b. Group polarization, or the strengthening of a group's prevailing tendencies, is most likely in groups where members agree.

c. When groupthink occurs, there is so much consensus that decision making becomes less effective.

4. d. is the answer. (p. 559)

5. c. is the answer. (pp. 559–560)

a. Informational social influence results from accepting the opinions of others about a situation one is unsure of.

b. The fundamental attribution error is the tendency to underestimate situational influences on the behavior of others.

d. Deindividuation is the loss of self-consciousness that sometimes occurs in individuals in groups.

6. d. is the answer. (p. 564)

a. Groupthink refers to the mode of thinking that occurs when the desire for group harmony overrides realistic and critical thinking.

b. Cognitive dissonance refers to the discomfort we feel when two thoughts (which include the knowledge of our *behavior*) are inconsistent.

c. Empathy is feeling what another person feels.

7. d. is the answer. Normative social influence refers to influence on behavior that comes from a desire to look good to others. Subjects who were observed conformed because they didn't want to look like oddballs. (pp. 559–560)

a. Social facilitation is the better or faster performance of tasks that occurs in the presence of others.

b. Overjustification occurs when one is rewarded for doing something that is already enjoyable.

c. Informational social influence is the tendency of individuals to accept the opinions of others, especially in situations where they themselves are unsure.

8. **d.** is the answer. Role models for defiance reduced levels of obedience. (p. 562)

a. & c. These did not result in diminished obedience.

b. This "depersonalization" of the victim resulted in increased obedience.

9. **b.** is the answer. Aggression is any behavior, physical or verbal, that is intended to hurt or destroy. (p. 567)

a. A person may accidentally be hurt in a nonaggressive incident; and aggression does not necessarily prove hurtful.

c. Verbal behavior, which does not result in physical injury, may also be aggressive. Moreover, acts of aggression may be cool and calculated, rather than hostile and passionate.

10. **a.** is the answer. The very wide variations in aggressiveness from culture to culture indicate that aggression cannot be considered an instinct, or unlearned, universal characteristic of the species. (p. 568)

11. **d.** is the answer. (p. 569)

12. **a.** is the answer. (pp. 572–573)

13. **d.** is the answer. This phenomenon is known as the bystander effect. (pp. 575–576)

a. This answer is incorrect because individuals are less likely to render assistance at all if others are present.

b. Although people are less likely to assume responsibility for helping, this does not mean that they are less empathic.

c. This answer is incorrect because norms such as the social responsibility norm encourage helping others, yet people are less likely to help with others around.

14. **b.** is the answer. If altruism is directed toward our children and other close kin, it can help perpetuate our genes. (p. 577)

a. According to sociobiology, altruism is selected when it promotes the welfare of relatives.

c. According to sociobiology, altruism that favors perpetuation of the individual's genes would be advantageous to, and hence practiced by, both sexes.

d. Sociobiology argues that altruism limits global harmony, because it encourages individuals to favor their own.

15. **d.** is the answer. Being repeatedly exposed to novel stimuli increases our liking for them. (p. 579)

a. For the most part, the opposite is true.

b. & c. The mere exposure effect concerns our

tendency to develop likings on the basis, not of similarities or differences, but simply of familiarity, or repeated exposure.

16. **a.** is the answer. This result supports the two-factor theory of emotion and passionate attraction, according to which arousal from any source can facilitate an emotion, depending on how we label the arousal. (p. 581)

17. **c.** is the answer. Deep affection is typical of companionate love, rather than passionate love, and is promoted by equity, whereas traditional roles may be characterized by the dominance of one sex. (p. 582)

18. **a.** is the answer. (p. 576)

b. & c. These factors would most likely decrease a person's altruistic tendencies.

d. There is no evidence that one sex is more altruistic than the other.

19. **c.** is the answer. (p. 570)

a. & d. It is now believed that the frustration-aggression effect actually represents the aggression-eliciting effect of any aversive stimulus.

b. There is no documented sex difference in the effect of aversive stimuli on aggression.

20. **b.** is the answer. (pp. 576–577)

a. This is a tenet of sociobiological theory.

c. Social exchange theory focuses on costs and benefits, rather than on norms.

Matching Items

1. d (p. 563) 5. e (p. 556) 9. b (p. 563)
2. c (p. 564) 6. f (pp. 559–560) 10. a (p. 551)
3. k (p. 577) 7. i (p. 560) 11. j (p. 574)
4. g (p. 560) 8. h (p. 565) 12. l (p. 579)

PROGRESS TEST 2

Multiple-Choice Questions

1. **b.** is the answer. (p. 568)

a. Wilson originated the theory of sociobiology.

c. Lorenz, too, was an instinct theorist, but only Freud argued the existence of a "death instinct."

d. Janis studied the process that led to groupthink.

2. **a.** is the answer. Aggressiveness *can* be increased through selective breeding, which suggests that it is genetically influenced. (p. 568)

3. **c.** is the answer. (p. 569)

4. **c.** is the answer. The mere exposure effect refers to our tendency to like what we're used to, and we're used to seeing mirror images of ourselves. (p. 579)

a. Equity refers to equality in giving and taking between the partners in a relationship.

b. Self-disclosure is the sharing of intimate feelings with a partner in a loving relationship.

d. Although people prefer mirror images of their faces, mirror-image perceptions are often held by parties in conflict. Each party views itself favorably and the other negatively.

5. **d.** is the answer. (pp. 572–573)

6. **d.** is the answer. (p. 575)

7. **c.** is the answer. Social exchange theory says that our behaviors, including helping, constitute an exchange process, in which we aim to maximize benefits and minimize costs. (pp. 576–577)

a. Helping for this reason would be based above all on the norm of social responsibility.

b. According to social exchange theory, helping occurs when benefits are seen to outweigh costs. Alleviated guilt is a potential benefit, but many other costs and benefits would also be weighed.

d. This reflects a sociobiological point of view.

8. **d.** is the answer. Because it provides people with an opportunity to meet, proximity is the most powerful predictor of friendship, even though, once a friendship is established, the other factors mentioned become more important. (p. 578)

9. **a.** is the answer. (p. 571)

b. Although some researchers take this view, the consensus, as expressed by the National Institute of Mental Health and by the American Psychological Association, the American Medical Association, and the American Pediatric Association, is that violence on television does lead to aggressive behavior.

c. & d. Most viewers would maintain the opposite.

10. **c.** is the answer. In this example of the fundamental attribution error, even when given the situational explanation for the woman's behavior, students ignored it and attributed her behavior to her personal disposition. (p. 552)

11. **d.** is the answer. Our attitudes are more likely to guide our actions when other influences are minimal, when there's a specific connection between the two, and when we're keenly aware of our beliefs. The presence of other people would more likely be an outside factor that would lessen the likelihood of actions being guided by attitude. (pp. 554–555)

12. **a.** is the answer. (p. 564)

b. Social facilitation refers to the improvement in performance that may result when one is observed by others.

c. Empathy is feeling what another person feels.

d. Group polarization refers to the strengthening of prevailing group attitudes that occurs with discussion.

13. **b.** is the answer. (p. 563)

a. & c. Crowding may amplify irritability or altruistic tendencies that are already present. Crowding does not, however, produce these reactions as a general effect.

d. In fact, just the opposite is true. Crowding often intensifies people's reactions.

14. **b.** is the answer. (p. 567)

a., c., & d. These aspects of minority influence were not discussed in the text.

15. **a.** is the answer. (p. 562)

16. **d.** is the answer. The text emphasizes the ways in which personal and social control interact in influencing behavior. It does not suggest that one factor is more influential than the other. (p. 566)

17. **d.** is the answer. Co-actors are people who are simultaneously at work on the same noncompetitive task. Debaters (a.) are obviously engaged in a competitive event, as are a pitcher and a batter (c.), although their tasks are not the same. As part of an audience (b.), one is not engaged in a specific task, competitive or otherwise. (p. 563)

18. **a.** is the answer. As Solomon Asch's experiments demonstrated, individuals are more likely to conform when they are being observed by others in the group. The other factors were not discussed in the text and probably would not promote conformity. (p. 559)

19. **d.** is the answer. (p. 551)

20. **d.** is the answer. Group polarization, or the enhancement of a group's prevailing attitudes, promotes groupthink, which leads to the disintegration of critical thinking. (p. 565)

a. Groupthink is more likely when a leader highly favors an idea, which may make members reluctant to disagree.

b. A strong minority faction would probably have the opposite effect, in that it would diminish group harmony while promoting critical thinking.

c. Consulting with experts would discourage groupthink by exposing the group to other opinions.

True-False Items

1. True (p. 552)
2. False (p. 552)
3. True (p. 559)
4. True (p. 560)
5. False (p. 576)
6. True (pp. 555–556)
7. False (p. 568)
8. False (p. 565)
9. False (p. 563)
10. True (p. 564)

CHALLENGE TEST

1. **d.** is the answer. The frustration-aggression principle states that the blocking of an attempt to achieve some goal—in Teresa's case, buying concert tickets—creates anger and can generate aggression. (p. 570)

   a. Sociobiological theory maintains that aggressive behavior is a genetically based drive. Teresa's behavior clearly was a reaction to a specific situation.

   b. The reciprocity norm—that we should return help to those who have helped us—would not engender Teresa's angry reaction.

   c. Social exchange theory views behavior as an exchange process in which people try to maximize the benefits of their behavior by minimizing the costs. Teresa's behavior likely brought her few benefits while exacting some costs, including potential injury, embarrassment, and retaliation by the clerk.

2. **b.** is the answer. Dissonance theory focuses on what happens when our actions contradict our attitudes. (p. 557)

   a. Attribution theory holds that we give causal explanations for the behavior of others, often by crediting either the situation or people's dispositions.

   c. Social exchange theory maintains that social behaviors maximize benefits and minimize costs. It is not clear in this example whether Wanda perceives such costs and benefits.

   d. This is not a theory of social influence.

3. **a.** is the answer. Social facilitation, or better performance in the presence of others, occurs for easy tasks but not for more difficult ones. For tasks such as proofreading, typing, or playing an instrument, the arousal resulting from the presence of others can lead to mistakes. (p. 563)

4. **a.** is the answer. Group polarization means that the tendencies within a group—and therefore the differences among groups—grow stronger over time. Thus, because the differences between the sorority and nonsorority students have increased, Jane and Sandy are likely to have little in common. (pp. 564–565)

   b. Groupthink is the tendency for realistic decision making to disintegrate when the desire for group harmony is strong.

   c. Deindividuation is the loss of self-consciousness and restraint that sometimes occurs when one is part of a group.

   d. Social facilitation refers to improved performance of a task in the presence of others.

5. **d.** is the answer. (p. 565)

   a. Social facilitation refers to improved performance in the presence of others.

   b. Dissonance is the personal discomfort one feels when attitudes and behaviors are discrepant.

   c. Informational social influence refers to the tendency to seek the opinions of others when one is unsure about one's own attitudes or behavior.

6. **c.** is the answer. Prior commitment to an opposing view generally tends to work against conformity. In contrast, large group size, prestigiousness of a group, and an individual's feelings of incompetence and insecurity all strengthen the tendency to conform. (p. 559)

7. **b.** is the answer. Although the three concepts are related, it is suggestibility that specifically refers to the tendency to be influenced by or to imitate the behavior of others. Conformity is the tendency to adjust one's behavior to go along with a group standard. Compliance is the tendency to obediently follow the demands of another person. (p. 558)

8. **b.** is the answer. An air attack would depersonalize the villagers, leading to compliance from those who might not comply if they had to destroy the village at close range. The other factors should not promote compliance, which would, if anything, be reduced by the role models for defiance in d. (p. 562)

9. **a.** is the answer. As illustrated by Maria's decision to stop buying aerosol products, informational social influence occurs when people have genuinely been influenced by what they have learned from others. (p. 560)

   b. Had Maria's behavior been motivated by the desire to avoid rejection or to gain social approval (which we have no reason to suspect is the case), it would have been an example of normative social influence.

   c. Deindividuation refers to the sense of anonymity a person may feel as part of a group.

   d. Social facilitation is the improvement in performance of well-learned tasks that may result when one is observed by others.

10. **d.** is the answer. Research demonstrates that playing a particular role often leads to adoption of that role. (p. 556)

11. **d.** is the answer. In this situation, the counter-attitudinal behavior is performed voluntarily and cannot be attributed to the demands of the situation. (p. 557)

    a., b., & c. In these situations, the counter-attitudinal behaviors should not arouse much dissonance, since they can be attributed to the demands of the situation.

12. **d.** is the answer. The fundamental attribution error refers to the tendency to underestimate situational influences in favor of this type of dispositional attribution when explaining the behavior of other people. (pp. 551–552)

    a., b., & c. Each of these is a situational attribution.

13. **b.** is the answer. By limiting the number and types of programs children watch, and by pointing out television's unrealistic portrayal of violence, parents can minimize the effects of viewing this violence. (p. 574)

    a. There is a well-established relationship between viewing television violence and aggressiveness.

    c. Doing so would only further desensitize children to violence and would promote aggressiveness.

    d. This is unrealistic.

14. **d.** is the answer. (p. 577)

    a. Sociobiological theory maintains that altruistic actions are predisposed by our genes.

    b. The two-factor theory holds that emotions consist of physical arousal and an appropriate cognitive label.

    c. The social responsibility norm refers to the social attitude that we should help those who need our help.

15. **d.** is the answer. Hundreds of experiments indicate that first impressions are most influenced by physical appearance. (p. 579)

16. **a.** is the answer. According to the two-factor theory, physical arousal can intensify whatever emotion is currently felt. Only in the situation described in a. is Joan likely to be physically aroused. (p. 581)

17. **b.** is the answer. The theory of sociobiology maintains that people are genetically biased to behave altruistically toward their relatives. Since Althea's altruism was apparently directed at a stranger, sociobiology would have difficulty accounting for her behavior. (p. 577)

    a. The social exchange theory states that social behavior is an exchange process, the aim of which is to maximize benefits and minimize costs. Although Althea's altruistic behavior placed her own life in jeopardy, and thus potentially was very "costly," the theory would simply suggest that she must have derived benefits from her actions that outweighed the costs.

    c. The two-factor theory of *emotion*, which assumes that emotions are based on physical arousal

and a cognitive label, makes no predictions regarding altruism.

    d. The reward theory, which states that social behavior is maintained by rewards, would explain Althea's altruism as being due to her having previously been rewarded for similar actions.

18. **a.** is the answer. Friends and couples are much more likely than randomly paired people to be similar in views, interests, and a range of other factors. (pp. 578–579)

    b. The opposite is true.

    c. The mere exposure effect demonstrates that familiarity tends to breed fondness.

    d. This is unlikely, given the positive effects of proximity and intimacy.

19. **c.** is the answer. (p. 551)

    a. Sociobiologists study the evolution of social behavior.

    b. Social exchange theorists are social psychologists who believe that our social behaviors maximize our benefits and minimize our costs. There is nothing in this question to indicate that Dr. Schachter is working from this perspective.

    d. Cognitive psychologists are interested in thinking *per se*, not in the influence of other people on the way a person thinks.

20. **b.** is the answer. In the foot-in-the-door phenomenon, compliance with a small initial request, such as wearing a lapel pin, later is followed by compliance with a much larger request, such as collecting petition signatures. (p. 555)

Essay Question

Your discussion might focus on some of the following topics: normative social influence, suggestibility, conformity, obedience, group polarization, and groupthink.

As a member of any group with established social norms, individuals will often act in ways that enable them to avoid rejection or gain social approval. Thus, a fraternity or sorority pledge would probably be very suggestible and likely to eventually conform to the attitudes and norms projected by the group—or be rejected socially. In extreme cases of pledge hazing, acute social pressures may lead to atypical and antisocial individual behaviors—for example, on the part of pledges complying with the demands of senior members of the fraternity or sorority. Over time, meetings and discussions will probably enhance the group's prevailing attitudes (group polarization). This may lead to the unrealistic and irrational decision making that is groupthink. The potentially negative consequences of groupthink depend on the issues being discussed, but may include a variety of socially destructive behaviors.

KEY TERMS

1. **Social psychology** is the study of how people think about, influence, and relate to one another. (p. 551)

2. **Attribution theory** is the study of our causal explanations of behavior. We attribute behavior to the individual's disposition or to the situation. (p. 551)

3. The **fundamental attribution error** is our tendency to underestimate the impact of situations and to overestimate the impact of personal dispositions upon the behavior of others. (p. 552)

   Example: If we meet someone who is withdrawn because of some preoccupation we know nothing about, we're liable to commit the **fundamental attribution error** and attribute that person's behavior to shyness or unfriendliness.

4. **Attitudes** are personal beliefs and feelings that may predispose a person to act in particular ways to objects, people, and events. (p. 553)

5. The **foot-in-the-door phenomenon** is the tendency for people who agree to a small request to comply later with a larger request. (p. 555)

6. A **role** is a set of behaviors expected of someone in a particular social position. (p. 556)

7. **Cognitive dissonance theory** refers to the theory that we act to reduce the psychological discomfort we experience when our behavior conflicts with what we think and feel, or more generally, when two of our thoughts conflict. This is frequently accomplished by changing our attitude rather than our behavior. (p. 557)

   Memory aid: *Dissonance* means disagreeing, or "at variance." **Cognitive dissonance** occurs when two thoughts, or cognitions, are at variance with one another.

8. **Conformity** is the tendency to change one's attitudes or behavior to be more in line with a group standard. (p. 557)

   Example: Experiments by Solomon Asch demonstrated that **conformity** is especially likely when a person is made to feel insecure in the presence of a high-status group of three or more people.

9. **Normative social influence** refers to the pressure on individuals to conform in order to avoid rejection or gain social approval. (pp. 559–560)

   Memory aid: *Normative* means "based on a norm, or pattern regarded as typical for a specific group." **Normative social influence** is the pressure groups exert on the individual to be normal.

10. **Norms** are understood social prescriptions, or rules, for accepted and expected behavior. (p. 560)

11. **Informational social influence** results when one goes along with a group when one is unsure or lacks information. (p. 560)

12. **Co-actors** are people who are working at the same task at the same time. (p. 563)

    Memory aid: *Co-* means "together"; **co-actors** are people engaged in some action together.

13. **Social facilitation** is the improvement in performance of well-learned tasks that occurs when other people are present. (p. 563)

14. **Social loafing** is the tendency for individual effort to be diminished when one is part of a group working toward a common goal. (p. 564)

15. **Deindividuation** refers to the loss of self-awareness and self-restraint that sometimes occurs in group situations. (p. 564)

    Memory aid: As a prefix, *de-* indicates reversal or undoing. To **deindividuate** is to undo one's individuality.

16. **Group polarization** refers to the enhancement of a group's prevailing tendencies over time, which often has the effect of accentuating the group's differences from other groups. (p. 565)

    Memory aid: To *polarize* is to "cause thinking to concentrate about two poles, or contrasting positions."

17. **Groupthink** refers to the unrealistic thought processes and decision making that occurs within groups when the desire for group harmony becomes paramount. (p. 565)

    Example: The psychological tendencies of self-justification, conformity, and group polarization foster the development of the "team spirit" mentality known as **groupthink**.

18. **Aggression** is any physical or verbal behavior intended to hurt or destroy. (p. 567)

19. The **frustration-aggression principle** states that aggression is triggered when people become angry because their efforts to achieve a goal have been blocked. (p. 570)

    Example: Researchers have realized that the **frustration-aggression** effect is a more general one in that not only frustration but many other aversive events, including humidity, hot weather, and foul odors, promote anger.

20. **Altruism** is unselfish behavior that helps others. (p. 574)

21. The **bystander effect** is the tendency of a person to be less likely to offer help to someone if there are other people present. (p. 576)

    Example: Latané and Darley have argued that the **bystander effect** occurs because with others present, the individual is less likely to notice an incident, identify it as a true emergency, and assume responsibility for helping.

22. **Social exchange theory** states that our social behavior revolves around exchanges, in which we try to minimize our costs and maximize our benefits. (pp. 576–577)

23. **Empathy** is understanding and feeling what another person feels. (p. 577)

24. **Sociobiology** is the scientific study of the evolution of social behavior using the principles of natural selection. (p. 577)

25. The **mere exposure effect** refers to the fact that repeated exposure to an unfamiliar stimulus increases our liking of it. (p. 579)

26. **Passionate love** refers to intense emotional absorption in another person, especially at the beginning of a relationship. (p. 581)

27. **Companionate love** refers to a deep, enduring, affectionate attachment. (p. 582)

28. **Equity** refers to the condition in which there is mutual giving and receiving between the partners in a relationship. (p. 582)

29. **Self-disclosure** refers to a person's sharing intimate feelings with another. (pp. 582–583)

19 / Social Diversity

Chapter Overview

Chapter 19 explores social diversity as it pertains to culture and gender. Although for most traits variation within any group is greater than that between groups, our identity as an individual, male or female, and as a member of various ethnic and racial groups exerts a strong influence on our self-concept and judgments about others.

The chapter also discusses how people respond to diversity: by rejecting it, developing prejudice, and provoking conflict; or by accepting it and promoting cooperation, communication, and conciliation among groups. The social, cognitive, and, in some cases, biological roots of these responses are explored, as are steps that might be taken to further constructive social relations.

The chapter concludes with a discussion of situations that engender conflict, along with techniques that have been shown to promote conflict resolution. There is not a great deal of terminology for you to learn in this chapter. Your primary task is to absorb the findings of the many research studies discussed. This should be an interesting chapter for you, since it explores topics of considerable relevance to your everyday life.

NOTE: Answer guidelines for all Chapter 19 questions begin on page 408.

Guided Study

The text chapter should be studied one section at a time. Before you read, preview each section by skimming it, noting headings and boldface items. Then read the appropriate section objectives from the following outline. Keep these objectives in mind and, as you read the chapter section, search for the information that will enable you to meet each objective. Once you have finished a section, write out answers for its objectives.

Cultural Diversity (pp. 588–597)

1. Discuss the origins of social diversity and describe the influence of culture on behavior, noting why it is important to study this influence.

2. Discuss differences between individualist and collectivist cultures, and how these differences influence self-concept.

3. Discuss how culture influences social judgment and parent-child relations.

4. Distinguish among culture, ethnicity, and race, and discuss how ethnicity influences self-awareness and identity.

9. State two criticisms of sociobiology and two points of agreement between sociobiologists and their critics regarding gender differences.

10. Distinguish among gender identity, gender-typing, and gender role, and discuss three theories of gender-typing.

Gender Diversity (pp. 597–609)

5. Discuss gender similarities and differences in physical and cognitive traits.

11. Explain the importance of gender roles and identify cultural variations and contemporary changes in gender roles.

6. Discuss gender differences in social "connectedness."

12. Discuss changes in gender roles across the life span.

7. Identify gender differences in aggression, social dominance, and sexual initiative.

8. Discuss biological and evolutionary influences on gender differences.

Responding to Diversity (pp. 610–618)

13. Describe the roles of social inequalities, ingroup bias, and scapegoating in prejudice.

14. Discuss the cognitive roots of prejudice.

their bodies is called _personal_
space. Culture _do_
(does/does not) influence personal space.

Identify several cultural differences in personal space and in expressiveness and pace of life.

15. Identify factors that fuel conflict and discuss effective ways of resolving such conflict.

7. The precision with which various social
roles are defined, and people's preoccupation with meeting these expectations, _varies_ (varies/ does not vary) significantly from one culture to another.

Chapter Review

When you have finished reading the chapter, work through the material that follows to review it. Complete the sentences and answer the questions. As you proceed, evaluate your performance for each section by consulting the answers on page 410. Do not continue with the next section until you understand each answer. If you need to, review or reread the appropriate section in the textbook before continuing.

8. Most industrialized cultures, especially those based on _N. Europe_
_____ roles and norms, promote _indiv._ in identity. Cultures that give priority to the goals of their groups nurture _collectivism_. Examples of such cultures are those of _____ _Asia, Africa_ (name three).

1. Historically, we are all descendants of common ancestors: the _African_ race. This means that we share not only a common biological heritage but also common _behavior_ tendencies. The most important of these tendencies is our capacity to _learn_ and to _adapt_.

9. The individualist societies thus focus on the _Self_, as in _humanistic_ psychology's emphasis on getting in touch with oneself; collectivist societies, on the other hand, emphasize the person's _social_ _network_.

2. Our adaptive diversity includes both _individual_ and _group_ differences in traits.

Contrast the influences of individualism and collectivism on personal identity.

Cultural Diversity (pp. 588–597)

3. The enduring behaviors, ideas, attitudes, and traditions of a group of people defines its _culture_.

4. Today, cultural diversity in many countries is _greater than_ (greater than/about the same as/less than) in the past.

5. All cultural groups _do_ (do/do not) evolve their own social norms.

6. The buffer zone that people maintain around

10. Group stereotyping is less likely to be condoned in _ind._ (individualist/ collectivist) cultures. Personal attributes such as attractiveness matter less to _coll._ (individualists/collectivists). Collectivists are _____less_____ (more/less) vulnerable to the fundamental attribution error.

11. Japanese and Chinese parents foster _____greater_____ (greater/lesser) interdependence in their children than do parents in individualist cultures.

12. An individual's social identity defines his or her _____ethinicity_____.

13. A large human population that, because of its geographical and genetic history, shares certain physical characteristics is a _____race_____.

14. Culture, ethnicity, and race _____can_____ (can/cannot) be distinguished.

15. Race is defined biologically and _____socially_____. In nearly every trait, individual differences within racial groups are _____greater than_____ (less than/equal to/greater than) differences between groups.

Summarize James Jones's views on differences between Black and White American culture.

16. Our self-concept is a mixture of our _____personal_____ and _____social_____ identities. Which aspect of identity we focus on at any moment depends on our culture and the immediate _____context_____.

Discuss how our self-awareness of our distinctiveness influences our experiences.

17. According to identity researcher Phinney, a person who identifies both with the ethnic culture and the larger culture has a _____bi-cultural_____ identity.

18. Group identification _____does_____ (does/does not) promote the tendency in each of

us to favor our own group, which makes us feel good about ourselves. A positive ethnic identity can therefore contribute to positive _____self_____-_____esteem_____.

19. Bicultural people typically have a more _____positive_____ (positive/negative) self-concept than people who have neither an ethnic nor a mainstream identity.

Gender Diversity (pp. 597–609)

20. Gender is defined as _____.

21. Three traits in which there are no significant gender differences are _____vocabulary_____, _____intelligence_____ and _____happiness_____.

22. Compared to the average man, the average woman has _____more_____ (more/less) body fat, _____less_____ (more/less) muscle, is about _____5_____ inches shorter, enters puberty about _____2_____ years earlier, and is _____less_____ (more/less) likely to have color-deficient vision.

23. Place a check mark next to the sex that, on average:

	Female	Male
a. is more vulnerable to anxiety disorders	✓	
b. is more likely to display antisocial behavior		✓
c. has a better sense of smell	✓	
d. is more vulnerable to depression	✓	
e. is more vulnerable to alcoholism		✓
f. is more likely to become sexually rearoused immediately after orgasm	✓	
g. is more likely to commit suicide		✓
h. is more likely to be diagnosed as hyperactive		✓
i. is more likely to stutter		✓
j. scores higher in math computation	✓	⊗
k. scores higher in math problem solving		✓
l. excels at spatial abilities		✓

24. Gender differences in spatial ability may be due

to the different _Social_ _expectations_ that parents have for boys and girls, rather than to natural sex differences.

25. Compared to the 1970s, when research on gender differences _wasn't_ (was/was not) emphasized, researchers in the 1980s were _more_ (more/less) accepting of gender diversity.

26. Jean Miller and Carol Gilligan believe that _women_ (women/men) give greater priority to relationships and develop an identity based on their _social connections_.

27. In most of the caregiving professions _women_ (women/men) predominate.

28. Compared to boys, girls tend to play in _sm_ (larger/smaller) groups, play _less_ (more/less) competitively, and be _more_ (more/less) responsive to feedback.

29. Although women are _more_ (more/less) likely than men to describe themselves as having empathy, physiological measures reveal _less_ (more/less) of a gender gap.

30. In terms of reading others' emotional cues, _females_ (females/males) are better than those of the opposite sex.

31. Studies have indicated that marital satisfaction is higher in couples when both partners possess some traditional _feminine_ traits.

32. The greater social connectedness of _females_ (females/males) can be compared to the _collectiveness_ (individualist/collectivist) values of many Third World cultures.

33. Several lines of research suggest that _males_ are the more aggressive sex. Cross-cultural studies reveal that people rate men as more _dominate_, _aggressive_, and women as more _____.

34. As leaders, men tend to be _directive_ and _autocratic_, while women tend to be more _democratic_.

35. Studies of sexuality indicate that _males_ tend to be the more assertive sex.

36. If the sex hormone _testosterone_ does not trigger the development of male external sex organs, the embryo continues to develop as a _female_. Genetic females who are prenatally exposed to overdoses of this hormone tend to exhibit more "_tomboy_" behavior.

37. In some animal species aggressiveness can be increased by administering the hormone _test_. Violent criminals tend to have levels of this hormone that are _higher_ (higher/lower) than normal.

38. According to the sociobiological perspective, _____ _____ favors behaviors that enable women and men to survive and reproduce. A result is the tendency of females, for whom each offspring requires _____ (greater/lesser) parental investment, to be _____ (more/less) cautious than males in choice of a mate.

39. Sociobiology's critics argue that cultural diversity in complex human social behaviors is _____ (greater/less) than would be expected if our genes rigidly determined sex differences. Furthermore, critics contend that many sociobiological explanations are of limited use because they are made _____ _____ _____.

State two points on which sociobiologists and their critics agree regarding human sex differences.

40. Our personal sense of being male or female is called our _____ _____. The extent to which an individual displays traditionally defined masculine or feminine traits is called _____-_____.

41. Freud believed that children become gender-typed by _identifying_ with the same-sex parent. This theory is disputed, in part because children become gender-typed well _____ (before/after) the age predicted by Freud. Another problem with the theory is that children typically _____ (do/do not) become gender-typed when the same-sex parent is not present.

42. According to the _Social learning_ theory, children acquire gender-typed behaviors by observing others, and through rewards and punishments.

43. Bem has combined aspects of the social learning and cognitive theories into the _gender Schema-_ theory.

44. A set of expectations regarding how a female or male should act is called a _gender role_.

45. Gender roles vary _more_ (more/less) in industrial societies than in agricultural societies.

46. Across the world, socialization practices for girls and boys _____ (do/do not) vary significantly.

Describe several ways in which gender roles have and have not changed in recent years.

47. Many gender differences peak in _____. With age, women often become more _____ and _____-_____, and men become more _____ and less _____.

48. The theory that people develop previously repressed characteristics of the other sex during the second half of life was proposed by _____.

49. For most traits, variation _____ (between/within) the sexes is greater than variation _____ (between/within) the sexes.

Responding to Diversity (pp. 610–618)

50. Prejudice is an _____ and usually _____ attitude toward a group that involves overgeneralized beliefs known as _____.

51. Americans today express _____ (less/the same/more) racial and gender prejudice than they did two and three decades ago.

52. For those with money, power, and prestige, prejudice often serves as a means of _____ social inequalities.

53. Prejudice is also fostered by the _____ _____, a tendency to favor groups to which one belongs. This bias is especially potent in _____ (individualist/collectivist) cultures.

54. In collectivist cultures, conflict is more likely to occur _____ (between/within) groups.

55. That prejudice derives from attempts to blame others for one's frustration is proposed by the _____ theory.

56. Research suggests that prejudice may also derive from _____, the process by which we attempt to simplify our world by classifying people into groups. One by-product of this process is that people tend to _____ the similarity of those within a group.

57. Another factor that fosters the formation of group stereotypes and prejudice is the tendency to _____ from vivid or memorable cases.

58. The belief that people get what they deserve—that the good are rewarded and the bad punished—is expressed in the

   _____-_____

   phenomenon.

59. A perceived incompatibility of actions, goals, or ideas is called _____. This perception can take place between individuals, _____, or _____.

60. Two destructive social processes that contribute to conflict are _____ _____ and _____ perceptions.

61. When the "non-zero-sum game" is played, most people fall into the social trap by mistrusting the other player and pursuing their own

   _____-_____.

62. The diabolical images people in conflict form of each other are called _____-_____ perceptions.

63. Several psychological tendencies foster biased perceptions. First, leaders, like other people, tend to accept credit for good deeds but not blame for bad deeds, a phenomenon called the

   _____-_____

   _____. Second, conflicting parties tend to attribute the other's actions to a negative disposition, an example of the

   _____ _____

   _____. Preconceived attitudes, or _____, also contribute to the problem, as does the _____ that often emerges within a group as the members' attitudes become _____.

64. Conflict resolution is most likely in situations characterized by _____, _____, and _____.

65. In most situations, establishing contact between two conflicting groups _____ (is/is not) sufficient to resolve conflict.

66. In Sherif's study, two conflicting groups of campers were able to resolve their conflicts by

working together on projects in which they shared _____ goals.

67. When conflicts arise a third-party _____ may facilitate communication and promote understanding.

68. Osgood has advanced a strategy of conciliation called GRIT, which stands for _____ and _____ in _____-_____. The key to this method is each side's offering of a small _____ gesture in order to increase mutual trust and cooperation.

FOCUS ON PSYCHOLOGY:
Superordinate Allied Goals Lead to Victory in the Persian Gulf War

Winning the Persian Gulf war required the 37 allied nations that eventually joined the cause to overcome national self-interests in the pursuit of the shared goal of defeating Iraqi forces and forcing their withdrawal from Kuwait. Although the allies presented a public facade of unity throughout the war, officials have disclosed that tensions among the forces were frequent and potentially polarizing. Despite their differences, the allies were able to avoid public feuding and to defuse tensions in a masterful exhibition of cooperation among culturally diverse groups.

Much of the credit for the success of "Operation Desert Storm" must go to the commanders of the various forces, who exercised diplomatic and social psychological skills worthy of professional conflict mediators. Examples abound:

1. With more than 540,000 troops in the gulf region, the United States was the dominant player in the war. In recognition of Arab sensitivities, however, two parallel commands—one Western, one Arab—were established.
2. When British forces insisted on joining main flanking forces on the Saudi border, field commanders drew up new battle plans to avoid a messy confrontation.
3. Differences among the various navies that participated in the embargo against Iraq were extreme from the start. To promote cooperation and to coordinate the embargo, delegates at a 2-day meeting in Manama, Bahrain, made a series of reciprocated conciliatory gestures ensuring that each country would play a role consistent with its reasons for joining the effort.

The efforts of the 37-nation coalition are reminiscent of Muzafer Sherif's study of cooperation among competing groups at a children's summer camp. In both instances, potential enemies were transformed into comrades through superordinate goals—shared goals that overrode their differences and required their cooperation. Commenting on the coalition's success, then Soviet defense minister Marshal Dimitri Yazoz summed it up as eloquently as could a social psychologist: "There is a lot we can learn from the organization of coordination of states with different national languages and weapons in executing one goal." (This comment is particularly interesting now, given the attempted coups by the group of 8, including Yazoz, in the U.S.S.R. in August 1991.)

Source: Schmitt, E., and Gordon, M. R. (March 24, 1991). Tensions bedeviled allies all the way to Kuwait. *The New York Times*, p. 18L.

Progress Test 1

Circle your answers to the following questions and check them with the answers on page 411. If your answer is incorrect, read the explanation for why it is incorrect and then consult the appropriate pages of the text (in parentheses following the correct answer).

1. Historically, humans are descendants of:
   a. many different races.
   b. a single Asian race.
   c. the African race.
   d. an unknown number of races.

2. The enduring behaviors, ideas, attitudes, and traditions shared by a large group of people and transmitted from one generation to the next defines:
   a. a race.   c. ethnicity.
   b. a culture.   d. none of the above.

3. Within most countries today, cultural diversity is:
   a. less than in the 1980s.
   b. about the same as in the 1980s.
   c. greater than at any other time in history.
   d. greater than in the 1980s, but decreasing.

4. Regarding cultural differences in personal space, which of the following is true?
   a. Arabs prefer less personal space than do Latin Americans.
   b. North Americans prefer more personal space than do Scandinavians.
   c. The British prefer less personal space than do the French.
   d. Latin Americans prefer less personal space than do North Americans.

5. Collectivist cultures:
   a. give priority to the goals of their groups.
   b. value the maintenance of social harmony.
   c. foster social interdependence.
   d. are characterized by none of the above.
   e. are characterized by a., b., and c.

6. Individualist cultures:
   a. value communal solidarity.
   b. emphasize personal achievement and identity.
   c. are relatively rare in immigrant countries.
   d. are characterized by none of the above.
   e. are characterized by a., b., and c.

7. People with a bicultural identity tend to:
   a. feel alienated.
   b. have a more negative self-concept than people who have neither an ethnic nor a mainstream identity.
   c. have a more positive self-concept than people who have neither an ethnic nor a mainstream identity.
   d. have low self-esteem.

8. An individual's personal sense of being male or female is called:
   a. gender.   c. gender identity.
   b. gender role.   d. gender type.

9. On the Scholastic Aptitude Test (SAT):
   a. males have higher average scores than females on both the verbal and math portions.
   b. males have higher average scores than females on the verbal portion.
   c. males have higher average scores than females on the math portion.
   d. females have higher average scores than males on the math portion.

10. Which of the following is correct?
    a. The belief that males tend to be more aggressive than females is not validated in laboratory experiments.
    b. Throughout the world, hunting and fighting are primarily men's activities.
    c. In most cultures there is no gender difference in aggressiveness.
    d. Gender differences in aggressiveness are entirely caused by biological factors.

11. Boys tend to outperform girls on tasks involving _____ skills.
    a. verbal   c. spatial
    b. social   d. musical

12. During adulthood, gender differences tend to:
    a. remain constant.
    b. increase.
    c. decrease.
    d. first increase, then decrease.

13. According to sociobiologists, gender differences:
    a. reflect the transmission of culture from generation to generation.

b. are biologically based and reflect the processes of natural selection and evolution.

c. are much greater in lower mammals than in humans.

d. have greatly diminished in today's industrialized societies.

14. Genetically female animals given testosterone before birth:

   a. continue to develop as normal females in all respects.

   b. develop a masculine appearance but retain female behavior patterns.

   c. retain a feminine appearance but develop masculine behavior patterns.

   d. develop both a masculine appearance and masculine behavior patterns.

15. Which of the following is *not* true?

   a. Violent criminals tend to have higher than normal levels of testosterone.

   b. Aggressiveness can be increased by administering testosterone.

   c. The relationship between testosterone and aggression occurs in a variety of species.

   d. The relationship between testosterone and aggression is absent in animals.

16. The theory that children become gender-typed through identification with the same-sex parent was proposed by:

   a. Bem.   c. Jung.
   b. Kohlberg.   d. Freud.

17. Which theory states that children's evolving concepts of gender play a crucial role in gender-typing?

   a. social learning theory
   b. Freud's theory
   c. gender schema theory
   d. All of the above theories do so.

18. Social traps are situations in which:

   a. conflicting parties realize that they have shared goals, the attainment of which requires their mutual cooperation.

   b. conflicting parties have similar, and generally negative, views of one another.

   c. conflicting parties each pursue their self-interest and become caught in mutually destructive behavior.

   d. two conflicting groups meet face-to-face in an effort to resolve their differences.

19. Which of the following was *not* mentioned in the text's discussion of the roots of prejudice?

   a. people's tendency to overestimate the similarity of people within groups

   b. people's tendency to assume that exceptional,

or especially memorable, individuals are unlike the majority of members of a group

   c. people's tendency to assume that the world is just and that people get what they deserve

   d. people's tendency to discriminate against those they view as "outsiders"

20. The belief that those who suffer deserve their fate is expressed in the:

   a. just-world phenomenon.
   b. phenomenon of ingroup bias.
   c. fundamental attribution error.
   d. mirror-image perception principle.

Progress Test 2

Progress Test 2 should be completed during a final chapter review. Answer the following questions after you thoroughly understand the correct answers for the Chapter Review and Progress Test 1.

1. Regarding cultural diversity, which of the following is *not* true?

   a. Culture influences emotional expressiveness.
   b. Culture influences personal space.
   c. Culture does not have a strong influence on how strictly social roles are defined.
   d. All cultures evolve their own norms.

2. Most industrialized cultures nurture:

   a. collectivism.
   b. individualism.
   c. the formation of bicultural identities.
   d. both a. and c.
   e. none of the above.

3. Compared to those in collectivist cultures, people in individualist cultures:

   a. are less geographically bound to elderly parents.

   b. tend to be more alienated.

   c. are more vulnerable to stress-related disease.

   d. have all of the above characteristics.

4. People in _____ cultures tend to be more vulnerable to the fundamental attribution error.

   a. collectivist
   b. ethnically diverse
   c. ethnically homogeneous
   d. individualist

5. James Jones believes that, partly as a result of its African heritage and partly as an adaptation to the prevailing attitudes of the larger culture, Black American culture is more _____ than White culture.

   a. future-oriented   c. present-oriented
   b. rationalistic   d. reserved

6. One reason any minority group tends to be conscious of itself in contrast with the majority group is that:
   a. ethnic self-awareness among minorities tends to be discouraged.
   b. people tend to be conscious of ways in which they differ from those around them.
   c. ethnic identity is amplified in an ethnically homogeneous society.
   d. group identifications promote an ingroup bias.

7. A flaw in Freud's theory of gender-typing is that children may become gender-typed:
   a. even in the absence of a same-sex parent.
   b. well before the age of 10.
   c. well after they have acquired concrete operational skills.
   d. even if not exposed to gender-stereotyped books or television programs.

8. Which of the following is true?
   a. In both self-report and physiological reactivity, women show more empathy than men.
   b. In both self-report and physiological reactivity, men show more empathy than women.
   c. In self-report, but less consistently in physiological reactivity, women are more empathic than men.
   d. In self-report, but less consistently in physiological reactivity, men are more empathic than women.

9. A set of expected behaviors for males or females is called:
   a. gender assignment.   c. gender identity.
   b. gender.   d. gender role.

10. Antill found that among married couples marital satisfaction was highest when:
    a. both spouses were strongly gender-typed.
    b. the female possessed some masculine traits.
    c. either or both spouses scored high in self-confidence.
    d. either spouse possessed some feminine traits.

11. Which of the following best expresses the social learning theory of gender-typing?
    a. Children acquire behaviors deemed appropriate for their sex by observation, by imitation, and by being rewarded and punished.
    b. Children form a concept of gender, which then influences whom they imitate.
    c. Children develop schemas for maleness and femaleness, the content of which is determined by learning.
    d. Children imitate their same-sex parent after renouncing their attraction to the other-sex parent.

12. In her gender schema theory, Bem proposes that:
    a. gender identity is biologically determined.
    b. children become gender-typed despite their environments.
    c. children form a concept of gender and evaluate themselves against it.
    d. children who are not strongly gender-typed were probably raised in a single-parent home.

13. Which of the following statements concerning gender differences is true?
    a. In many traits, the sexes are alike.
    b. Most gender differences do not become obvious until adulthood.
    c. Gender differences peak in late adulthood.
    d. No consistent evidence has been found for a gender-based difference in any ability.

14. People with power and status may become prejudiced because:
    a. they tend to justify the social inequalities between themselves and others.
    b. those with less status and power tend to resent them.
    c. those with less status and power appear less capable.
    d. they feel proud and are boastful of their achievements.

15. Which of the following best describes how GRIT works?
    a. The fact that two sides in a conflict have great respect for the other's strengths prevents further escalation of the problem.
    b. The two sides engage in a series of reciprocated conciliatory acts.
    c. The two sides agree to have their differences settled by a neutral, third-party mediator.
    d. The two sides engage in cooperation in those areas in which shared goals are possible.

16. The theory of sociobiology has been criticized for:
    a. providing after-the-fact explanations.
    b. failing to appreciate the enormous cultural diversity in complex human social behaviors.
    c. failing to make testable predictions.
    d. all of the above reasons.

17. In considering the research on gender differences, it is important to keep in mind that:
    a. as yet, none of the proposed gender differences have been supported by solid evidence.
    b. diversity is usually greater between the sexes than within the sexes.
    c. in many ways males and females are very similar.

d. researchers have typically studied age groups in which gender differences are smaller than average.

18. If an embryo inherits a(n) _____ chromosome, then its biological sex will be _____.

a. X; male

c. Y; female

b. Y; male

d. X; female

19. Concerning historical changes in gender roles, which of the following statements is the most accurate?

a. Gender roles have become more distinct in North America.

b. Gender roles have shown virtually no change in the past 50 years.

c. In North America gender roles have been converging.

d. Gender roles have disappeared in many cultures.

20. According to Carol Gilligan, girls are more likely than boys to develop an identity based on:

a. nontraditional gender roles.

b. traditional gender roles.

c. their social connections.

d. their independence.

Challenge Test

Answer these questions the day before an exam as a final check on your understanding of the chapter's terms and concepts.

Multiple-Choice Questions

1. Which of the following would you most likely find on visiting other countries?

a. In most primitive societies, men and women share equally in hunting for game and in food gathering.

b. Among industrialized societies, the roles assigned to men and women vary enormously from country to country.

c. Gender-typed behaviors are less distinct in other countries than in the United States.

d. All of the above would likely be found.

2. In some countries, it is acceptable to belch loudly after a fine meal. In most Western countries, this behavior would be offensive. This example indicates that:

a. Western countries generally are collectivist cultures.

b. Western countries have more rigid norms.

c. norms vary from culture to culture.

d. all of the above are true.

3. You believe that all overweight people are friendly, jolly, and cuddly. This is an example of:

a. a stereotype.

c. discrimination.

b. prejudice.

d. all of the above.

4. After having a British houseguest for several weeks, a friend from Mexico complains that her houseguest was cold and standoffish whenever she attempted to have a conversation with him. Based on your study of the material in this chapter you wisely point out that:

a. people act more reserved when staying in another's home.

b. men tend to have a higher threshold for perceiving someone's warmth as a sexual come-on.

c. women are more likely to misread emotions in others.

d. the British prefer more personal space around the body than do Latin Americans.

5. Being fed up with your cultural background, you decide to move to a culture that places greater value on maintaining social harmony and family identity. To which of the following countries should you move?

a. the United States

c. Australia

b. Canada

d. Japan

6. Your parents raised you to "have good judgment" and to be independent and nonconforming. You were probably brought up in a country with a(n) _____ culture.

a. homogeneous

c. individualist

b. heterogeneous

d. collectivist

7. When told of someone's actions, people in _____ cultures are less likely to offer _____ explanations.

a. individualist; dispositional

b. collectivist; situational

c. collectivist; dispositional

d. individualist; inaccurate

8. Patty and Karen are 5-year-olds who enjoy playing with dolls and cooking utensils. While Patty also enjoys playing with trucks and guns, Karen does not. Which of the following is true of Patty, as compared with Karen?

a. She is less strongly gender-typed.

b. She is experiencing greater gender confusion.

c. She probably grew up in a more strongly gender-typed family.

d. Both a. and c. are true.

9. Compared to those of the other sex, you are less likely to be color-blind, generally have a better sense of smell, but are more vulnerable to anxiety disorders and depression. You are probably a:
   a. male.   b. female.

10. According to Bem's theory, people with the strongest gender schemas would tend to:
    a. be weakly gender-typed.
    b. be strongly gender-typed.
    c. experience gender identity confusion.
    d. be oblivious to gender.

11. College women who filled out a questionnaire in which they described themselves to a tall, unattached, male senior who liked traditional women:
    a. described themselves as less traditionally feminine than did women describing themselves to a man who liked nontraditional women.
    b. described themselves as more traditionally feminine than did women describing themselves to a man who liked nontraditional women.
    c. described themselves no differently than did women describing themselves to a man who liked nontraditional women.
    d. tended to focus on attributes that were neither traditionally feminine nor masculine.

12. According to Bem, parents who want to raise children who are less gender-typed should:
    a. make gender irrelevant to job assignments at home.
    b. completely reverse the traditional gender roles at home.
    c. avoid transmitting their social convictions to their children.
    d. encourage and reward strongly gender-typed behaviors.

13. Which of the following strategies would be *most* likely to foster positive feelings between two conflicting groups?
    a. Take steps to reduce the likelihood of social traps.
    b. Separate the groups so that tensions diminish.
    c. Have one representative from each group visit the other and field questions.
    d. Have the groups work on a superordinate goal.

14. Given the tendency of people to categorize information, which of the following stereotypes would Juan, a 65-year-old political liberal and fitness enthusiast, be most likely to have?
    a. "People who exercise regularly are very extraverted."
    b. "All political liberals are advocates of a reduced defense budget."
    c. "Young people today have no sense of responsibility."
    d. "Older people are lazy."

15. Ever since their cabin lost the camp softball competition, the campers have become increasingly hostile toward one camper in their cabin, blaming her for every problem in the cabin. This behavior is best explained in terms of:
    a. the ingroup bias.
    b. prejudice.
    c. the scapegoat theory.
    d. the reciprocity norm.

16. Mr. and Mrs. Samuels are constantly fighting, and each perceives the other as hard-headed and insensitive. Their conflict is being fueled by:
    a. self-disclosure.
    b. stereotypes.
    c. a social trap.
    d. mirror-image perceptions.

17. Students at State University are convinced that their school is better than any other; this most directly illustrates:
    a. an ingroup bias.
    b. prejudice and discrimination.
    c. the scapegoat effect.
    d. the just-world phenomenon.

18. Jason, age 7, puts on his father's clothes and pretends he is a businessman because he wants to be "just like Daddy." According to Freud, Jason's behavior illustrates the process of:
    a. natural selection.
    b. identification.
    c. empathy.
    d. gender-schema formation.

19. In everyday situations, men are more likely than women to talk assertively and to interrupt others. These behaviors are characteristic of:
    a. verbal ability.   c. empathy.
    b. gender identity.   d. social dominance.

20. Concern has been expressed that the study of gender differences:
    a. has thus far not received the attention it should.
    b. is being conducted primarily within the sociobiological framework.
    c. might lead to the exaggeration of people's perceptions of the differences between women and men.
    d. has led to public policies that discriminate against women.

Essay Question

Your wealthy neighbor is extremely prejudiced against welfare recipients. Discuss several of the possible social and emotional roots of your neighbor's prejudice. (Use the space below to list the points you want to make and organize them. Then write the essay on a separate sheet of paper.)

7. gender identity

8. gender-typing

9. gender schema theory

Key Terms

Using your own words, write a brief definition or explanation of each of the following terms.

1. culture

10. gender role

11. prejudice

2. personal space

12. stereotype

3. individualism

13. ingroup bias

4. collectivism

14. scapegoat theory

5. ethnicity

15. just-world phenomenon

6. gender

16. conflict

17. social traps

18. mirror-image perceptions

19. superordinate goals

20. GRIT

ANSWERS

GUIDED STUDY

The following guidelines provide the main points that your answers should have touched upon.

1. Although humans share a common biological ancestry, our capacity to learn and adapt has given rise to our tremendous social diversity. More so today than ever before we live in a global multicultural village and need to understand how our cultures influence us.

   A culture is the enduring traditions, behaviors, ideas, and attitudes shared by a large group of people and passed from one generation to the next. All cultural groups evolve their own norms for acceptable and expected behavior. Because of differing norms, personal space, expressiveness, and pace of life, for example, misunderstandings are commonplace.

2. Individualist cultures, such as those of industrialized countries that are based on northern European norms and roles, nurture the development of personal goals and define their identity in terms of individual attributes, rather than social groups.

Collectivist cultures, such as those of Asia, Africa, and Central and South America, give priority to the goals of their groups—often their extended family, work group, or tribe. Consequently, identity in collectivist cultures is based more on social interdependence. While individualists easily move in and out of social groups, collectivists have fewer but deeper, more stable attachments to their groups and friends. Collectivist cultures also place a premium on maintaining harmony and allowing others to save face. People in individualist cultures tend to be more competitive and independent, and to take more pride in personal achievements. But compared to collectivists, individualists also tend to be lonelier, more alienated, more likely to divorce, more homicidal, and more vulnerable to stress-related diseases.

3. Individualist cultures place a greater premium than collectivist cultures on avoiding group stereotypes. Because of this, individualists are more vulnerable than collectivists to the fundamental attribution error when explaining others' behavior. In contrast to collectivist cultures, which tend to foster social interdependence in their children, individualist cultures encourage independence and less concern for conformity, communal sensitivity, and cooperation.

4. A culture is a people's shared behaviors, ideas, attitudes, and traditions. Ethnicity is one's social identity defined by the ancestors, heritage, and traits shared with others. A race is a large population that, because of its geographical and genetic history, shares certain physical characteristics. In practice, however, race is defined socially as well as biologically, in part because in nearly every trait racial groups are much more alike than they are different.

   A person's self-concept is a combination of his or her personal and social identities. People become more conscious of their distinctiveness when they are around people who are different. This explains why a minority group tends to be conscious of itself in contrast with the majority. Although group identification promotes a tendency to favor one's own group (ingroup bias), a positive ethnic identity contributes to a positive self-concept.

5. Although men and women have many physical differences (for example, in body fat, muscle mass, height, longevity, vulnerability to hyperactivity, alcoholism, and anxiety and eating disorders), in many traits, such as vocabulary, intelligence, and happiness, the sexes are alike. Where gender differences do exist, they are often sharpest at the extremes of ability. Some differences, such as

those in spatial reasoning, grow with age and indicate that different social expectations for boys and girls account in part for differences in their interests and abilities.

6. Some researchers believe that, in terms of personal identity, women place a higher priority than men on social connections. This difference appears first in play behavior. Girls play in smaller, less competitive groups, and in a manner more imitative of human relationships. The play of boys tends to be in larger groups, with a focus on activity and little intimate discussion. Another difference indicating a gender gap in social connectedness is that females are better at reading others' emotional cues and are more likely than men to describe themselves as having empathy.

7. Surveys, laboratory experiments, and cross-cultural studies reveal that men are more physically aggressive than women. Men are perceived as more socially dominant and achievement-driven, women as more deferential, nurturant, and affiliative. As leaders of groups, men tend to be autocratic, whereas women tend to be more democratic. Males are much more likely than females to initiate sexual activity and tend to have a lower threshold for misattributing someone's warmth as a sexual come-on.

8. Eight weeks after conception our genes activate our biological sex. The presence of a Y chromosome directs the development of a male; in its absence, a female develops. Testosterone production by the testes triggers the development of external male sex organs. Genetically female infants who were exposed to excess prenatal testosterone may be born with masculine-appearing genitals, later act in more aggressive ways than most girls, and have spatial abilities more like those of the average boy.

   According to the theory of sociobiology, males and females are selected for gender differences that best perpetuate their genes. Thus, males are presumably selected for sexual initiative toward females and aggressive dominance in competing with other males for mating privileges. Because females have fewer eggs than males have sperm and invest enormous time and energy in nurturing a single offspring, they are believed to be more selective in choosing mates.

9. Critics argue that the cultural diversity in complex social behaviors—fathers' investment in infant care and relations between the sexes, for example—is too enormous to indicate a rigid biological determinism. Critics further note that sociobiology's evolutionary explanations are impossible to test because they are offered after the fact. Both

sides agree that sex differences that may have been adaptive for our hunter-gatherer ancestors may no longer be so. They also agree that human behavior is the product of biological *and* cultural history.

10. Gender identity is one's sense of being male or female. Gender roles are expected behaviors for males and females. Gender-typing is the acquisition of a masculine or feminine gender identity and role.

    Freud explained gender-typing with his theory that 5- to 6-year-old children resolve tensions linked with their attraction to the other-sex parent by identifying with their same-sex parent. Social learning theory maintains that children become gender-typed by imitating the behavior of others and being rewarded or punished. Gender schema theory maintains that children form a concept, or schema, for gender from their own culture and use this schema to adjust their behavior.

11. Although different societies socialize children for varying gender roles, around the world, men predominate in roles that emphasize aggressiveness and dominance, women, in roles that are based on caregiving and nurturance. These differences have important consequences, as demonstrated by research findings that people act to fulfill gender-role expectations. Furthermore, different roles foster different behaviors, which may perpetuate certain gender differences.

    Gender roles vary over time as well as across cultures. The most obvious shift in gender-role expectations is the increase in the rate of women's employment. Changes are also evident in the nature of women's employment. Between 1960 and 1990 there was a 7-fold increase in the number of female doctors and a 24-fold increase in the numbers of female lawyers and engineers. The revolution in men's roles has been more subtle. Compared with the mid 1960s, men are now devoting more time to family work. However, even in countries that have sought to equalize the roles of men and women, gender distinctions persist.

12. Gender differences peak in late adolescence and early adulthood and diminish as people age. Women tend to become more assertive and self-confident and men more empathic and less domineering. According to Jung, both masculine and feminine tendencies exist in everyone and, during later life, people develop their previously repressed traits. Others believe that early social expectations lead each sex to downplay traits that interfere with their roles as mates and parents. According to this viewpoint, as men and women get older they become freer to explore other roles.

13. Prejudice is an unjustifiable and usually negative

attitude toward a group. People who have money, power, and prestige may become prejudiced toward those less fortunate in order to rationalize social inequalities. The reactions provoked in victims of discrimination may further increase prejudice. The tendency to favor one's own group (ingroup bias) may also lead to prejudice. Ingroup bias is especially potent in collectivist cultures where group identity runs strong. According to the scapegoat theory of prejudice, when people are frustrated or angry, blaming another individual or group may provide an outlet for their anger.

14. Stereotyped beliefs emerge as a result of our tendency to cognitively simplify the world. One way to do this is by categorizing people into groups and then overestimating the similarity of people within groups other than our own. Group stereotypes are also influenced by vivid but exceptional cases involving individuals from other groups, because they are more readily available to memory. Another cognitive root of prejudice is the just-world phenomenon, or the idea that good is rewarded and evil is punished, so those who are successful are good and those who suffer are bad. Hindsight bias also fosters prejudice, as people blame victims after the fact for "getting what they deserved."

15. Conflict is a seeming incompatibility of actions, goals, or ideas between individuals, groups, or nations. Conflict is fostered by social traps in which conflicting parties get caught up in mutually destructive behavior by pursuing their own self-interests. Another factor that fuels conflict is the tendency for those in conflict to form diabolical images of each other (mirror-image perceptions). The psychological roots of distorted perceptions include the self-serving bias, the fundamental attribution error, stereotyping, group polarization, and groupthink.

   Conflict resolution is most likely in situations characterized by cooperation, communication, and conciliation. Studies by Sherif and others demonstrate that cooperation between groups in the pursuit of superordinate goals is more effective than mere contact between conflicting groups in reducing differences. Communication between conflicting groups can be facilitated by a third-party mediator when conflicts are so intense that civil discussion between the groups is not possible. When cooperation and communication are impossible between conflicting groups, Osgood's "Graduated and Reciprocated Initiatives in Tension-Reduction" (GRIT) may help reduce hostilities. GRIT promotes trust and cooperation between groups by having each group initiate one or more small, conciliatory acts.

CHAPTER REVIEW

1. African; behavior; learn; adapt
2. individual; group
3. culture
4. greater than
5. do
6. personal space; does

North Americans, the British, and Scandinavians prefer more personal space than do Latin Americans, Arabs, and the French. Cultural differences in expressiveness and the pace of life often create misunderstandings. For example, people with northern European roots may perceive people from Mediterranean cultures as warm and charming but inefficient and time wasting, while Mediterraneans may see the Northern Europeans as efficient but emotionally cold.

7. roles; varies
8. northern European; individualism; collectivism; Asia, Africa, and Central and South America
9. self; humanistic; social network

Collectivists give priority to one's family identity and have fewer but deeper and more stable attachments to their groups and friends. Individualists focus more on personal identity and easily move in and out of social groups.

10. individualist; collectivists; less
11. greater
12. ethnicity
13. race
14. can
15. socially; greater than

Jones believes that, partly as a result of its African heritage and partly as an adaptation to the prevailing attitudes of the larger culture, Black American culture is present-oriented, expressive, spiritual, and emotion-driven. In contrast, White culture is more future-oriented, reserved, rationalistic, and achievement driven.

16. personal; social; context

Our self-consciousness is amplified when those around us are different. This explains why any minority group is conscious of itself in contrast with the majority. Our experiences are obviously colored by our self-perceptions.

17. bicultural
18. does; self-esteem
19. positive
20. the characteristics by which people identify us as male or female
21. vocabulary; intelligence; happiness

22. more; less; 5; 2; less
23. a. female   g. male
    b. male   h. male
    c. female   i. male
    d. female   j. female
    e. male   k. male
    f. female   l. male
24. social expectations
25. was not; more
26. women; social connections
27. women
28. smaller; less; more
29. more; less
30. females
31. feminine
32. females; collectivist
33. males; dominant, aggressive, and achievement-driven; deferential, nurturant, and affiliative
34. directive; autocratic; democratic
35. males
36. testosterone; female; "tomboyish"
37. testosterone; higher
38. natural selection; greater; more
39. greater; after the fact

Both sides agree that sex differences that may have enhanced the survival of our ancestors may no longer be adaptive and that humans are the products of their evolutionary and cultural history.

40. gender identity; gender-typing
41. identifying; before; do
42. social learning
43. gender schema
44. gender role
45. more
46. do

Recent changes in women's roles have been dramatic: The number of homemakers has plunged and the proportion of women in the work force has increased to nearly 3 in 5, for example. More subtle changes in men's roles relate to their increasing involvement in family work.

47. late adolescence and early adulthood; assertive; self-confident; empathic; domineering
48. Jung
49. within; between
50. unjustifiable; negative; stereotypes
51. less
52. justifying

53. ingroup bias; collectivist
54. between
55. scapegoat
56. categorization; overestimate
57. overgeneralize
58. just-world
59. conflict; groups; nations
60. social traps; distorted
61. self-interests
62. mirror-image
63. self-serving bias; fundamental attribution error; stereotypes; groupthink; polarized
64. cooperation; communication; conciliation
65. is not
66. superordinate
67. mediator
68. Graduated; Reciprocated Initiatives; Tension-Reduction; conciliatory

PROGRESS TEST 1

1. **c.** is the answer. (p. 587)
2. **b.** is the answer. (p. 588)
   a. A race is a socially distinct group of people, defined by their genetically transmitted physical characteristics.
   c. Ethnicity is that part of one's social identity defined by the ancestors, heritage, and traits one shares with others.
3. **c.** is the answer. (p. 589)
4. **d.** is the answer. (p. 590)
5. **e.** is the answer. (p. 591)
6. **b.** is the answer. (p. 591)
   a. & c. These are characteristics of collectivist cultures.
7. **c.** is the answer. (p. 597)
   a., b., & d. These are more likely to be true of a person who lacks either a mainstream or an ethnic identity.
8. **c.** is the answer. (p. 604)
   a. Gender simply refers to the social category of male or female, not to the individual's sense of being male or female.
   b. Gender role refers to a set of socially expected sex-related behaviors.
   d. Gender-typing is the process by which gender roles and identities are acquired.
9. **c.** is the answer. (p. 598)
   a., b., & d. Although males and females score sim-

ilarly on the verbal portion of the SAT, on the math portion males average about 50 points higher.

10. **b.** is the answer. (p. 601)

    a. Laboratory experiments *confirm* that males tend to be more aggressive than females.

    c. Greater aggressiveness in males is one of the most reliable cross-cultural gender differences.

    d. Gender influences in aggressiveness appear to have social as well as biological roots: Aggressiveness tends to be encouraged in boys and discouraged in girls.

11. **c.** is the answer. (pp. 598–599)

    a., b., & d. Boys and girls perform comparably on all these tasks, and girls may actually outperform boys in verbal skills.

12. **c.** is the answer. Having peaked in late adolescence and early adulthood, gender differences tend to diminish thereafter. (p. 609)

13. **b.** is the answer. (p. 603)

    a. Sociobiologists argue that gender differences reflect biological rather than environmental or cultural influences.

    c. Sociobiologists view gender differences in humans and other mammals as similar.

    d. According to sociobiologists, gender differences, being biologically based, are present regardless of the type of society.

14. **d.** is the answer. (p. 602)

    a., b., & c. Experiments with many species confirm that female embryos given male hormones exhibit more masculine appearance and behavior.

15. **d.** is the answer. Increases in testosterone increase aggressiveness in a wide range of species. (p. 602)

16. **d.** is the answer. (p. 604)

    a. Bem proposed the gender schema theory.

    b. Kohlberg proposed a theory of moral development not discussed in this chapter.

17. **c.** is the answer. Gender schema theory states that children's concept formation provides the basis for gender-typing. (p. 605)

    a. & b. Concept formation is not a factor in these theories.

18. **c.** is the answer. Social traps foster conflict in that two parties, by pursuing their self-interests, create a result that neither group wants. (pp. 614–615)

    a. As Sherif's studies demonstrated, the possession of shared or superordinate goals tends to reduce conflict between groups.

    b. This is an example of mirror-image perceptions, which, along with social traps, foster conflict.

    d. Face-to-face confrontations between conflicting parties generally do not reduce conflict, nor are they social traps.

19. **b.** is the answer. In fact, people tend to overgeneralize from vivid cases, rather than assume that they are unusual. (pp. 612–614)

    a., c., & d. Each of these is an example of a cognitive (a. & c.) or a social (d.) root of prejudice.

20. **a.** is the answer. (pp. 613–614)

    b. Ingroup bias is the tendency of people to favor their own group.

    c. The fundamental attribution error is the tendency of people to underestimate situational influences when observing the behavior of other people.

    d. The mirror-image perception principle is the tendency of conflicting parties to form similar, diabolical images of each other.

PROGRESS TEST 2

1. **c.** is the answer. Culture *does* have a strong influence on how rigidly social roles are defined. (p. 591)

2. **b.** is the answer. (p. 591)

3. **d.** is the answer. (pp. 592–593)

4. **d.** is the answer. This is because individualists tend to attribute behavior to personal traits. (p. 593)

5. **c.** is the answer. (p. 595)

    a., b., & d. In James's theory, these are characteristics of White American culture.

6. **b.** is the answer. (p. 595)

    a. The text does not indicate that this is so.

    c. In fact, just the opposite is true.

    d. This may be true, but it has nothing to do with why a minority tends to be conscious of itself in contrast with the majority.

7. **a.** is the answer. Freud proposed that gender-typing arises when the child identifies with the same-sex parent, in an unconscious reaction to anxiety felt as a result of sexual attraction to the parent of the opposite sex. (p. 604)

    b. Freud's identification theory proposed that children become gender-typed by age 6, so gender-typing before 10 would not be a problem for the theory. (In reality, gender-typing appears to occur well before age 6.)

    c. Piaget's stages do not play a role in Freud's theory.

    d. The identification process centers on the parent; the influence of the mass media is not involved in any crucial way.

8. **c.** is the answer. (p. 600)

a. Although women report much stronger reactions than men to emotional distress in others, laboratory measures of heart rate and perspiration fail to confirm that women have a more empathic physiological response.

b. & d. Women are more empathic than men in self-reports; in laboratory studies there is little difference between the sexes.

9. **d.** is the answer. (p. 605)

a. In the past, when an infant's biological sex was ambiguous, physicians and parents chose the baby's gender. This was known as gender assignment. (Now tests can determine genetic sex.)

b. Gender refers to the social category of male or female.

c. Gender identity is an individual's sense of male or female.

10. **d.** is the answer. Strength of gender-typing in itself was not shown to correlate with marital satisfaction. (p. 600)

b. & c. Masculine traits, including self-confidence, appeared to be unrelated to marital satisfaction.

11. **a.** is the answer. (p. 604)

b. & c. These answers express the gender schema theory.

d. This answer expresses Freud's identification theory.

12. **c.** is the answer. (p. 605)

a. In fact, Bem argues that gender identity is largely a cognitive, rather than a biological, process.

b. For Bem, the formation of gender schemas is based on the assimilation of, and accommodation to, experiences in the environment.

d. Bem's theory makes no such prediction.

13. **a.** is the answer. (p. 597)

b. Many gender differences appear much earlier than adulthood.

c. Gender differences peak in late adolescence and early adulthood.

d. Some abilities, such as spatial and mathematical ability, do show consistent gender differences.

14. **a.** is the answer. Such justifications arise as a way to preserve inequalities. The just-world phenomenon presumes that people get what they deserve. According to this view, someone who has less must deserve less. (p. 614)

15. **b.** is the answer. (p. 618)

a. GRIT is a technique for reducing conflict through a series of conciliatory gestures, not for maintaining the status quo.

c. & d. These measures may help reduce conflict but they are not aspects of GRIT.

16. **d.** is the answer. (p. 603)

17. **c.** is the answer. Although certain gender differences in behavior and abilities have been found, by and large the sexes are similar. (p. 609)

a. There has been ample evidence of differences in aggressiveness, for example.

b. Within-sex diversity is generally greater than between-sex diversity.

d. In fact, researchers have most often studied young adults, the age group in which gender differences are greatest.

18. **b.** is the answer. (p. 602)

a. & d. These are inconclusive; both males and females inherit at least one X chromosome, but it is the presence or absence of a Y chromosome that determines biological sex.

19. **c.** is the answer. (pp. 607–608)

a. Expectations for men's and women's behavior have become *less* distinct.

b. In the past 50 years there have been significant changes in gender roles.

d. In no culture have gender roles disappeared.

20. **c.** is the answer. (p. 599)

CHALLENGE TEST

Multiple-Choice Questions

1. **b.** is the answer. (p. 606)

a. In most primitive societies men predominate in hunting large game, while women gather food and care for infants.

c. Gender-typed behaviors are no less distinct in countries other than the United States.

2. **c.** is the answer. (pp. 588–590)

a. In fact, most countries in the West have individualist cultures.

b. Although the rigidity of norms does vary from culture to culture, the text does not suggest that norms are more rigid in the West.

3. **a.** is the answer. (pp. 610–611)

b. & d. Prejudice and discrimination involve unjustifiable and negative attitudes and behaviors directed at another group.

4. **d.** is answer. (p. 590)

a. This may or may not be true. However, in this example it is clear that the cultural differences between the hostess and her guest account for the social awkwardness.

b. & c. In fact, just the opposites are true.

5. **d.** is answer. Of the countries listed, only Japan has a collectivist culture that emphasizes family identity and social harmony. (p. 591)

6. **c.** is the answer. (p. 591)

a. & b. It is the primary cultural influence on a child's upbringing, not whether or not the country includes a mixture of cultures, that influences self-concept as stated in this question.

d. Collectivist cultures nurture interdependence, rather than independence.

7. **c.** is the answer. Collectivists are less likely to focus on personal attributes in explaining others' behavior. (p. 593)

a. Individualists are very likely to offer dispositional explanations of others' behavior.

d. If anything, because of their vulnerability to the fundamental attribution error, individualists are likely to offer inaccurate explanations. The text does not suggest, however, that collectivists and individualists differ in the accuracy of their explanations.

8. **a.** is the answer. Patty enjoys toys associated with traditional male roles, as well as those connected with traditional female roles. She is therefore less strongly gender-typed than Karen, who plays only with "girls' toys." (p. 604)

b. Gender identity refers to self-concept, not to external behavior.

c. If anything, Patty probably grew up in a *less* strongly gender-typed family and imitated those behaviors.

9. **b.** is the answer. (p. 598)

10. **b.** is the answer. Gender-typing occurs as children compare themselves to their male or female schema. A stronger gender schema translates into more strongly gender-typed behavior. (p. 605)

a., c., & d. Those who have very fixed concepts of the genders are less likely to fuse traditionally male and female qualities, to experience gender-identity confusion, or to be oblivious to gender.

11. **b.** is the answer. The results of this study showed that men and women adjust their behavior to fulfill others' gender-role expectations. (p. 605)

12. **a.** is the answer. (p. 608)

b. Reversing the traditional gender roles would probably produce gender confusion or reverse gender-typing.

c. A parent wishing to raise less gender-typed children would probably want to transmit the conviction that gender differences are not crucial.

d. This strategy would probably result in an even more strongly gender-typed child.

13. **d.** is the answer. Sherif found that hostility between two groups could be dispelled by giving the groups superordinate, or shared, goals. (p. 616)

a. Although reducing the likelihood of social traps might reduce mutually destructive behavior, it would not lead to positive feelings between the groups.

b. Such segregation would likely increase ingroup bias and group polarization, resulting in further group conflict.

c. This might help, or it might increase hostilities; it would not be as helpful a strategy as communication through an outside mediator or, as in d., cooperation toward a superordinate goal.

14. **c.** is the answer. People tend to overestimate the similarity of people within groups other than their own. Thus, Juan is not likely to form stereotypes of fitness enthusiasts (a.), political liberals (b.), or older adults (d.), because these are groups to which he belongs. (p. 613)

15. **c.** is the answer. According to the scapegoat theory, when things go wrong, people look for someone on whom to take out their anger and frustration. (p. 613)

a. In this example the campers are venting their frustration on a member of their *own* cabin group (although this is not always the case with scapegoats).

b. Prejudice refers to an unjustifiable and usually negative attitude toward another group.

d. The reciprocity norm, which refers to our tendency to help those who have helped us, was not discussed as a root of prejudice.

16. **d.** is the answer. The couple's similar, and presumably distorted, feelings toward each other fuels their conflict. (p. 615)

a. Self-disclosure, or the sharing of intimate feelings, fosters love.

b. Stereotypes are overgeneralized ideas about groups.

c. Social traps are situations in which conflicting parties engage in mutually destructive behavior while pursuing their own self-interests.

17. **a.** is the answer. (p. 612)

b. Prejudices are unjustifiable and usually negative attitudes toward other groups. They may result from an ingroup bias, but they are probably not the reason students favor their own university.

c. Scapegoats are individuals or groups toward which prejudice is directed as an outlet for the anger of frustrated individuals or groups.

d. The just-world phenomenon is the tendency for people to believe others "get what they deserve."

18. b. is the answer. (p. 604)

a. Natural selection is the process by which evolution favors those organisms that are best equipped to survive and reproduce.

c. Empathy is the ability to understand and feel what another person feels.

d. Social dominance involves the expression of attitudes and behaviors that attempt to influence others.

19. d. is the answer. These behaviors are indicative of social dominance. (p. 601)

20. c. is the answer. Although the study of gender differences has tended to undermine the myth of women's inferiority, some critics remain concerned that the research might exaggerate people's perceptions of the differences between the sexes. (p. 609)

a. If anything, critics are concerned that gender differences are the focus of too much attention.

b. Gender differences are studied by researchers working in a wide variety of frameworks.

d. Critics do not claim that public policy has been adversely affected by the research; they are more concerned about possible effects on public opinion.

Essay Question

People who have money, power, or prestige often develop attitudes to justify social inequalities. Fueling this is the just-world phenomenon, in which people come to believe that others "get what they deserve." For these reasons, your wealthy neighbor may justify his or her good fortune, and the misfortune of those on welfare, by perceiving those less fortunate as lazy and irresponsible. It is also likely that your neighbor associates with others in similar positions of wealth, prestige, and power. The mere act of being in such a group is likely to trigger an ingroup bias and a tendency to be critical of, and possibly scapegoat, those in the "outgroup." Group interaction among your neighbor's friends may polarize these tendencies and lead to groupthink. Finally, the fundamental attribution error may cause your neighbor to mistakenly attribute the plight of those who are less fortunate as arising from dispositional, rather than situational, causes.

KEY TERMS

1. A **culture** is the enduring behaviors, ideas, attitudes, and traditions shared by a large group of people and transmitted from one generation to the next. (p. 588)

2. **Personal space** refers to the buffer zone, or mobile territory, that people like to maintain around their bodies. (p. 590)
   Example: Cross-cultural research indicates that **personal space** is a culture-specific distance.

3. **Individualism** is a cultural emphasis on personal goals over group goals, and defining one's identity in terms of personal attributes rather than group identifications. (p. 591)

4. **Collectivism** is a cultural emphasis on the goals of one's groups, and defining one's identity accordingly. (p. 591)

5. **Ethnicity** is that part of one's social identity defined by the ancestors, heritage, and traits one shares with others. (p. 594)

6. **Gender** is the socially defined, but biologically dictated, classification of male or female. (p. 597)

7. **Gender identity** refers to a person's sense of being male or female. (p. 604)

8. **Gender-typing** refers to the acquisition of a masculine or feminine gender identity and role. (p. 604)

9. The **gender schema theory** proposes that gender-typing occurs as children learn from their cultures the concepts of male and female that guide their later behaviors. (p. 605)

10. A **gender role** is a culturally prescribed set of behaviors for males and females. (p. 605)

11. **Prejudice** is an unjustifiable and usually negative attitude toward a group and its members. (p. 610)
    Example: There are many social and psychological roots of **prejudice**, including the ingroup bias and the tendency of people to simplify the world through categorization.

12. A **stereotype** is a generalized (often overgeneralized) attitude about a group of people. (p. 610)

13. The **ingroup bias** is the tendency to favor one's own group. (p. 612)

14. The **scapegoat theory** proposes that prejudice arises when people who are frustrated or angry seek a target on which to vent their feelings. (p. 613)

15. The **just-world phenomenon** is a manifestation of the commonly held belief that good is rewarded and evil is punished. The logic is indisputable: "If I am rewarded, I must be good." (pp. 613–614)

16. **Conflict** is a perceived incompatibility of actions or goals between individuals or groups. (p. 614)

17. **Social traps** are situations in which conflicting parties become caught up in mutually harmful behavior as they pursue their perceived best interests. (p. 615)

18. **Mirror-image perceptions** are the distorted but similar views of one another often held by individuals or groups in conflict. (p. 615)

19. **Superordinate goals** are mutual goals that require the cooperation of individuals or groups otherwise in conflict. (p. 616)

20. **GRIT** (Graduated and Reciprocated Initiatives in Tension-Reduction) is a strategy of conflict resolution based on the defusing effect that conciliatory gestures can have on parties in conflict. (p. 618)

Appendix: Statistical Reasoning in Everyday Life

Chapter Overview

A basic understanding of statistical reasoning has become a necessity in everyday life. Statistics are tools that help the psychologist and layperson to interpret the vast quantities of information they are confronted with on a daily basis. The text appendix discusses how statistics are used to describe data and to generalize from instances.

In studying this chapter you must concentrate on learning a number of procedures and understanding some underlying principles in the science of statistics. The graphic and computational procedures in the section called "Describing Data" include how data are distributed in a sample; measures of central tendency such as the mean, median, and mode; variation measures such as the range and standard deviation; and correlation, or the degree to which two variables are related. Most of the conceptual material is then covered in the section entitled "Generalizing from Instances." You should be able to discuss four important principles concerning populations and samples, as well as the concept of significance in testing differences. The ultimate goal is to make yourself a better consumer of statistical research by improving your critical thinking skills.

NOTE: Answer guidelines for all questions in the Appendix begin on page 426.

Guided Study

The text chapter should be studied one section at a time. Before you read, preview each section by skimming it, noting headings and boldface items. Then read the appropriate section objectives from the following outline. Keep these objectives in mind and, as you read the chapter section, search for the information that will enable you to meet each objective. Once you have finished a section, write out answers for its objectives.

Describing Data (pp. 622–630)

1. Explain how frequency distributions, histograms, and percentile ranks are used to describe data.

2. Define the three measures of central tendency and explain how they describe data differently.

3. Describe measures of variation and the normal curve.

4. Describe the correlation coefficient and explain its importance in assessing relationships between variables.

5. Identify factors that may contribute to illusory correlation and an illusion of control.

Generalizing from Instances (pp. 630–634)

6. Distinguish between a population and a sample and explain the importance of using samples.

7. Discuss four important principles in making generalizations about populations on the basis of samples.

8. Describe how psychologists make inferences about differences between groups.

Chapter Review

When you have finished reading the chapter, work through the material that follows to review it. Complete the sentences and answer the questions. As you proceed, evaluate your performance for each section by consulting the answers on page 427. Do not continue with the next section until you understand each answer. If you need to, review or reread the appropriate section in the textbook before continuing.

Describing Data (pp. 622–630)

1. A table that depicts the number of individual scores occurring at each equal-sized interval of a range is called a _____

_____.

2. A bar graph that depicts a frequency distribution is called a _____.

3. The percentage of scores in a distribution that fall below an individual score is that score's

_____ _____.

4. The three measures of central tendency are the _____, the _____, and the _____.

5. The most frequently occurring score in a distribution is called the _____.

6. The mean is computed as the _____ of all the scores divided by the _____ of scores.

7. The median is the score at the _____ percentile.

8. In a symmetrical distribution, the three measures of central tendency are likely to be _____ (similar/different).

9. The measures of variation include the _____ and the _____

_____.

10. The range is computed as the _____

_____.

11. The range provides a(n) _____ (crude/accurate) estimate of variation because it _____ (is/is not) influenced by extreme scores.

12. The standard deviation is a _____ (more accurate/less accurate) measure of variation than the range. Unlike the range, the standard deviation _____ (takes/does not take) into consideration information from each score in the distribution.

13. List the four steps in computing the standard deviation.
    a. _____
    b. _____
    c. _____
    d. _____

14. The bell-shaped distribution that often describes large amounts of data is called the

_____ _____.

15. In this distribution, approximately

_____ percent of the individual scores fall within 1 standard deviation on either side of the mean. Within 2 standard deviations on either side of the mean fall

_____ percent of the individual scores.

Calculate what a score of 116 on the normally distributed Wechsler IQ test would mean with regard to percentile rank. (Recall that the mean is 100; the standard deviation is ±15 points. Hint: You might find it helpful to first draw the normal curve.)

16. A graph consisting of points that depict the relationship between two sets of scores is called a _____.

17. A measure of the direction and extent of relationship between two sets of scores is called the _____ _____.
Numerically, this measure can range from
_____ to _____.

18. When there is no relationship at all between two sets of scores, the correlation coefficient is
_____. The strongest possible correlation between two sets of scores is either
_____ or _____. When the correlation between two sets of scores is negative, as one increases, the other

_____.

Cite an example of a positive correlation and a negative correlation. Your examples can be drawn from previous chapters of the textbook or can be based on observations from daily life.
An example of positive correlation is

An example of negative correlation is

19. The correlation coefficient _____ (gives/does not give) information about cause-and-effect relationships.

20. A correlation that is perceived but doesn't really exist is called an _____
_____.

21. When we believe a relationship exists between two things, we are most likely to recall instances that _____ (confirm/disconfirm) our belief.

22. That average results are more typical than extreme results is expressed in the phenomenon of _____ _____
_____ _____.

Generalizing from Instances (pp. 630–634)

23. All of the cases in a total group make up a
_____.

List four important principles in generalizing from samples to populations.

a. _____
_____

b. _____
_____

c. _____
_____

d. _____
_____

24. People have a tendency to _____
from unrepresentative but vivid cases.

25. A random sample is one in which each person in the population has
_____.

26. Small samples provide a _____

(more/less) reliable basis for generalizing than large samples.

27. Averages based on a large number of cases are _____ (more/less) reliable than those based on a few cases.

28. Averages are more reliable when they are based on scores with _____ (high/low) variability.

29. When people perceive little variability in individual instances, they are _____ (more/less) likely to generalize from them.

30. Tests of statistical _____ are used to estimate whether observed differences are reliable, that is, to make sure they are not simply the result of _____ variation.

FOCUS ON PSYCHOLOGY:
Could a Monkey Have Written This?

It has been said that given enough time, a monkey randomly striking the keys of a typewriter could theoretically turn out the great American novel. What is the actual probability of this occurring?

In this study guide there are approximately 200,000 letters, numbers, and spaces. The keyboard of the microcomputer that I used to type it has 63 keys on it. Therefore, at any given point in time, the monkey would have a 1 in 63 chance of striking the correct key. Sounds plausible, you say? To complete the entire study guide, our diligent ape would have to strike the correct key 200,000 times in succession. The probability of this occurring is computed as $1/63 = 0.016$ raised to the power of 200,000. To develop a feeling for how remote this probability is, 0.016 raised to the power of 2 is equal to 0.000256; 0.016 raised to the 20th power is equal to .00000000000000000000000000000000000 00121. Raised to the power of 200,000, the probability is so small that the decimal point is followed by more zeros than there are characters in this entire book.

Source: Suggested by Grasha, A. F. (1963). *Practical Applications of Psychology* (2nd ed.). Boston: Little, Brown.

Progress Test 1

Multiple-Choice Questions

Circle your answers to the following questions and check them with the answers on page 428. If your answer is incorrect, read the explanation for why it is incorrect and then consult the appropriate pages of the text (in parentheses following the correct answer). Use the page margins if you need extra space for your computations.

1. Percentile rank is defined as:
   a. the difference between the highest and lowest scores in a distribution.
   b. a statistical statement of the likelihood that an obtained result occurred by chance.
   c. the square root of the average of the squared deviations in a distribution.
   d. the percentage of the scores in a distribution that a given score exceeds.

2. What is the mean of the following distribution of scores: 2, 3, 7, 6, 1, 4, 9, 5, 8, 2?
   a. 5   c. 4.7
   b. 4   d. 3.7

3. What is the median of the following distribution of scores: 1, 3, 7, 7, 2, 8, 4?
   a. 1   c. 3
   b. 2   d. 4

4. What is the mode of the following distribution: 8, 2, 1, 1, 3, 7, 6, 2, 0, 2?
   a. 1   c. 3
   b. 2   d. 7

5. Compute the range of the following distribution: 9, 14, 2, 8, 1, 6, 8, 9, 1, 3.
   a. 10   c. 8
   b. 9   d. 13

6. Squaring the difference between each score in a distribution and the mean is the first step in computing the:
   a. median.   c. range.
   b. mode.   d. standard deviation.

7. If two sets of scores are negatively correlated, it means that:
   a. as one set of scores increases, the other decreases.
   b. as one set of scores increases, the other increases.
   c. there is only a weak relationship between the sets of scores.
   d. there is no relationship at all between the sets of scores.

8. Regression toward the mean is the:
   a. tendency for unusual scores to fall back toward a distribution's average.
   b. basis for all tests of statistical significance.
   c. reason the range is a more accurate measure of variation than the standard deviation.
   d. reason the standard deviation is a more accurate measure of variation than the range.

9. In a normal distribution, what percentage of scores

fall between $+2$ and -2 standard deviations of the mean?

a. 50 percent   **c.** 95 percent
b. 68 percent   **d.** 99.7 percent

10. Which of the following statistics must fall between -1.00 and $+1.00$?

a. the mean
b. the standard deviation
c. the correlation coefficient
d. none of the above

11. In generalizing from a sample to the population, it is important that:

a. the sample is representative of the population.
b. the sample is large.
c. the scores in the sample have low variability.
d. all of the above are observed.

12. When a difference between two groups is "statistically significant," this means that:

a. the difference is statistically real but of little practical significance.
b. the difference is probably the result of sampling variation.
c. the difference is not likely to be due to chance variation.
d. all of the above are true.

13. A listing of the number of scores that occur within each interval of some scale of measurement is called a:

a. percentile rank.
b. standard deviation.
c. frequency distribution.
d. correlation coefficient.

14. Which of the following is *not* a measure of central tendency?

a. mean   **c.** median
b. range   **d.** mode

15. Which of the following is the measure of central tendency that would be most affected by a few extreme scores?

a. mean   **c.** median
b. range   **d.** mode

16. The symmetrical, bell-shaped distribution in which most scores are near the mean and fewer near the extremes forms a:

a. skewed curve.   **c.** normal curve.
b. bimodal curve.   **d.** histogram.

17. A homogeneous sample with little variation in scores will have a(n) ———————— standard deviation.

a. small
b. moderate
c. large
d. unknown (It is impossible to determine.)

18. If there is no relationship between two sets of scores, the coefficient of correlation equals:

a. 0.00   **c.** $+1.00$
b. -1.00 **d.** 0.50

19. Illusory correlation refers to:

a. the perception that two negatively correlated variables are positively correlated.
b. the perception of a relationship between two unrelated variables.
c. an insignificant correlation coefficient.
d. a correlation coefficient that equals -1.00.

20. The correlation between two vivid events will most likely be:

a. significant.   **c.** negative.
b. positive.   **d.** overestimated.

Matching Items

Match each term with the appropriate definition or description.

Terms

_____ **1.** histogram
_____ **2.** median
_____ **3.** population
_____ **4.** sample
_____ **5.** mode
_____ **6.** range
_____ **7.** standard deviation
_____ **8.** scatterplot
_____ **9.** mean
_____ **10.** measures of central tendency
_____ **11.** measures of variation

Definitions or Descriptions

a. the mean, median, and mode
b. the difference between the highest and lowest scores
c. the arithmetic average of a distribution
d. the range and standard deviation
e. all of the cases in a group
f. the most frequently occurring score
g. a subset of a group
h. a bar graph depicting a frequency distribution
i. the middle score in a distribution
j. a graphed cluster of dots depicting the values of two variables
k. the square root of the average squared deviation of scores from the mean

Progress Test 2

Progress Test 2 should be completed during a final chapter review. Answer the following questions after you thoroughly understand the correct answers for the Chapter Review and Progress Test 1.

Multiple-Choice Questions

1. A bar graph that depicts a frequency distribution is called a:
  a. scatterplot.
  b. normal curve.
  c. coefficient plot.
  d. histogram.

2. What is the mean of the following distribution of scores: 2, 5, 8, 10, 11, 4, 6, 9, 1, 4?
  a. 2
  b. 10
  c. 6
  d. 15

3. What is the median of the following distribution: 10, 7, 5, 11, 8, 6, 9?
  a. 6
  b. 7
  c. 8
  d. 9

4. The highest percentile rank in a distribution:
  a. depends on the size of the distribution.
  b. will equal 100.
  c. will equal 99.
  d. will equal 50, since this is the midpoint.

5. Which statistic is the average amount by which the scores in a distribution vary from the average?
  a. standard deviation
  b. range
  c. median
  d. mode

6. The most frequently occurring score in a distribution is the:
  a. mean.
  b. median.
  c. mode.
  d. range.

7. In the following distribution, the mean is _____ the mode and _____ the median: 4, 6, 1, 4, 5.
  a. less than; less than
  b. less than, greater than
  c. equal to; equal to
  d. greater than; equal to

8. Which of the following is the measure of variation that is most affected by extreme scores?
  a. mean
  b. standard deviation
  c. mode
  d. range

9. What is the standard deviation of the following distribution: 3, 1, 4, 10, 12?
  a. 10
  b. 15
  c. $\sqrt{18}$
  d. 4

10. Which of the following sets of scores would likely be most representative of the population from which it was drawn?
  a. a sample with a relatively large standard deviation
  b. a sample with a relatively small standard deviation
  c. a sample with a relatively large range
  d. a sample with a relatively small range

11. The *value* of the correlation coefficient indicates the _____ of relationship between two variables, and the *sign* (positive or negative) indicates the _____ of the relationship.
  a. direction; strength
  b. strength; direction
  c. direction; reliability
  d. reliability; strength

12. If a difference between two samples is *not* statistically significant, which of the following can be concluded?
    a. The difference is probably not a true one.
    b. The difference is probably not reliable.
    c. The difference could be due to sampling variation.
    d. All of the above are true.

13. The first step in constructing a histogram is to create a:
    a. standard deviation.
    b. frequency distribution.
    c. correlation coefficient.
    d. range.

14. Why is the median at times a better measure of central tendency than the mean?
    a. It is more sensitive to extreme scores.
    b. It is less sensitive to extreme scores.
    c. It is based on more of the scores in the distribution than the mean.
    d. Both a. and c. explain why.

15. Standard deviation is to mode as _____ is to _____.
    a. mean; median
    b. variation; central tendency
    c. median; mean
    d. central tendency; variation

16. In a normal distribution, what percentage of scores fall between −1 and +1 standard deviation units of the mean?
    a. 50 percent   c. 95 percent
    b. 68 percent   d. 99.7 percent

17. The precision with which sample statistics reflect population parameters is greater when the sample is:
    a. large.
    b. characterized by high variability.
    c. small in number but consists of vivid cases.
    d. statistically significant.

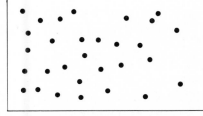

18. The above scatterplot depicts a correlation coefficient that would be close to:
    a. +1.0   c. 0
    b. −1.0   d. 0.50

19. Which of the following correlation coefficients indicates the strongest relationship between two variables?
    a. −.73   c. 0.00
    b. +.66   d. −.50

20. All the members of a group constitute a:
    a. sample.   c. mode.
    b. random sample.   d. population.

True-False Items

Indicate whether each statement is true or false by placing a T or F in the blank next to the item.

_____ 1. A percentile rank of 60 means that most of the scores in the distribution fall above it.

_____ 2. In almost all distributions, the mean, the median, and the mode will be the same.

_____ 3. When a distribution has a few extreme scores, the range is more misleading than the standard deviation.

_____ 4. If increases in the value of variable *x* are accompanied by decreases in the value of variable *y*, the two variables are negatively correlated.

_____ 5. Over time, extreme results tend to fall back toward the average.

_____ 6. If a sample was selected randomly, it cannot be representative of the population from which it was drawn.

_____ 7. The mean is always the most precise measure of central tendency.

_____ 8. Averages that have been derived from scores with low variability are more reliable than those derived from scores that are more variable.

_____ 9. If a difference between two groups is due to sampling variation, it cannot be statistically significant.

_____ 10. Small samples are less reliable than large samples for generalizing to the population.

Challenge Test

Answer these questions the day before an exam as a final check on your understanding of the chapter's terms and concepts.

Multiple-Choice Questions

1. Jack's score on the psychology exam was the highest in the class. What is his percentile rank for this score?
   a. 99

b. 100
c. 95
d. It cannot be determined from the information given.

2. Compute the standard deviation of the following distribution: 3, 5, 6, 2, 4.
   a. 1
   b. $\sqrt{2}$
   c. $\sqrt{10}$
   d. 4

3. Jane usually averages 175 in bowling. One night her three-game average is 215. What will probably happen to her bowling average over the next several weeks of bowling?
   a. It will return to about the level of her average.
   b. It will continue to increase.
   c. It will dip down to about 155.
   d. There is no way to predict what her scores will average.

4. If height and body weight are positively correlated, which of the following is true?
   a. There is a cause-and effect relationship between height and weight.
   b. As height increases, weight decreases.
   c. Knowing a person's height, one can predict his or her weight.
   d. All of the above are true.

5. The football team's punter wants to determine how consistent his punting distances have been during the past season. Which of the following should he compute?
   a. mean
   b. median
   c. mode
   d. standard deviation

6. If about two-thirds of the cases in a research study fall within 1 standard deviation from the mean, and 95 percent within 2 standard deviations, researchers know that their data form a:
   a. frequency distribution.
   b. scatterplot.
   c. normal curve.
   d. histogram.

7. Which of the following exemplifies regression toward the mean?
   a. In his second season of varsity basketball, Edward averaged 5 points more per game than in his first season.
   b. A gambler rolls 5 consecutive "sevens" using her favorite dice.
   c. After earning an unusually low score on the first exam in a class, a "B student" scores much higher on the second exam.

d. A student who usually earns Bs earns grades of A, D, D, and A on the four exams in a class, thus maintaining a B average overall for the class.

8. Which score falls at the 50th percentile of a distribution?
   a. mean
   b. median
   c. mode
   d. standard deviation

9. If scores on an exam have a mean of 50, a standard deviation of 10, and are normally distributed, approximately 95 percent of those taking the exam would be expected to score between:
   a. 45 and 55.
   b. 40 and 60.
   c. 35 and 65.
   d. 30 and 70.

10. Joe believes that his basketball game is always best when he wears his old gray athletic socks. Joe is a victim of the phenomenon called:
    a. regression toward the mean.
    b. the availability heuristic.
    c. illusory correlation.
    d. the gambler's fallacy.

11. Five members of Terry's sorority reported the following individual earnings from their sale of raffle tickets: $3, $6, $8, $6, and $12. In this distribution, the mean is _____ the mode and _____ the median.
    a. equal to; equal to
    b. greater than; equal to
    c. greater than; greater than
    d. equal to; less than

12. During elections, opinion researchers poll selected voters in order to try to gauge overall voter attitudes for or against specific issues and candidates. Pollsters consider all eligible voters the _____ and the selected voters the _____ .
    a. sample; representative sample
    b. population; sample
    c. frequency distribution; range
    d. normal distribution; population

13. In six tosses of a coin, which of the following outcomes of heads (H) and tails (T) could *not* be the result of chance?
    a. HHHTTT
    b. THTHTH
    c. HHHHHH
    d. All of the above could be the result of chance.

14. Which of the following sets of scores best fits the definition of a normal distribution?
    a. 1, 2, 4, 8, 16, 32
    b. 2, 2, 2, 2, 2, 2

c. 1, 2, 3, 4, 4, 4, 5, 6, 7
d. 2, 8, 10, 18, 35

15. Which of the following distributions has the largest standard deviation?

   a. 1, 2, 3   **c.** 6, 10, 14
   b. 4, 4, 4   **d.** 30, 31, 32

16. Bob scored 43 out of 70 on his psychology exam. He was worried until he discovered that most of the class earned the same score. Bob's score was equal to the:

   a. mean.   **c.** mode.
   b. median.   **d.** range.

17. The four families on your block all have annual household incomes of $25,000. If a new family with an annual income of $75,000 moved in, which measure of central tendency would be most affected?

   a. mean   **c.** mode
   b. median   **d.** standard deviation

18. How would you describe a scatterplot depicting a perfect correlation between two sets of scores?

   a. All the points fall on a straight line.
   b. The points are spread randomly about the graph.
   c. All the points fall on a curved line.
   d. It is impossible to determine from the information given.

19. Dr. Numbers passed back the exam and announced to the class that the mean, the median, and the mode of the scores were equal. This means that:

   a. the scores formed a normal distribution.
   b. the distribution had a large standard deviation.
   c. the students did very well on the exam.
   d. all of the above are true.

20. Dr. Salazar recently completed an experiment in which she compared reasoning ability in a sample of females and a sample of males. The means of the female and male samples equaled 21 and 19, respectively, on a 25-point scale. A statistical test revealed that her results were not statistically significant. What can Dr. Salazar conclude?

   a. Females have superior reasoning ability.
   b. The difference in the means of the two samples is probably due to chance variation.
   c. The difference in the means of the two samples is reliable.
   d. None of the above is true.

Essay Question

Discuss several ways in which statistical reasoning can improve your own everyday thinking. (Use the space below to list the points you want to make and organize them. Then write the essay on a separate sheet of paper.)

Key Terms

Using your own words, write a brief definition or explanation of each of the following terms.

  1. frequency distribution

  2. histogram

  3. percentile rank

  4. mode

  5. mean

  6. median

7. range

8. standard deviation

9. normal curve (normal distribution)

10. scatterplot

11. correlation coefficient

12. illusory correlation

13. regression toward the mean

14. population

15. statistical significance

ANSWERS

GUIDED STUDY

The following guidelines provide the main points that your answers should have touched upon.

1. Constructing a frequency distribution is the first step in organizing and describing a data set. A frequency distribution is a listing of the number of individual scores that occur within each equal-sized interval within a distribution. Frequency distributions provide a clear picture of how scores are distributed according to the variables being measured. Histograms, which are bar graphs depicting frequency distributions, make the distribution even easier to see and interpret. To help interpret any single score in a distribution a researcher can compute its percentile rank, which is simply the percentage of scores that fall below it in the distribution.

2. The mode is the most frequent score in a distribution. The mean, or arithmetic average, is the sum of the scores divided by the number of scores. Although the mean is the most commonly reported measure of central tendency, it is extremely sensitive to unusual scores and therefore is potentially misleading as a representation of the average of a distribution that is not symmetrical. In such cases, the median, or the score that falls at the 50th percentile, more accurately depicts the average, because it is not influenced by unusual scores.

3. The simplest measure of variation is the range, or the difference between the lowest and highest scores in a distribution. As a measure of variation, the range is rather crude because it is based on only the two extreme scores in a distribution. A better gauge of variation is the standard deviation, which is computed as the square root of the average squared deviation of the scores from the mean of the distribution. A symmetrical, bell-shaped distribution forms a normal curve in which the three measures of central tendency are equal, most cases fall near the mean, and fewer scores fall near either extreme. Furthermore, in a normal distribution roughly 68 percent of the cases fall within 1 standard deviation on either side of the mean, and 95 percent of the cases fall within 2 standard deviations.

4. The correlation coefficient, which can range from +1.00 through 0.00 to −1.00, is a statistical measure of how strongly related two sets of scores are. It is represented graphically on a scatterplot. A positive correlation means that one set of scores increases in direct proportion to the other. A negative correlation means that one set of scores goes

up as the other goes down. The strength of a relationship is indicated by the value of the correlation coefficient. A strong correlation is one that has a coefficient near +1.00 or −1.00. A correlation of 0.00 means that there is no predictive relationship between the sets of scores. While the correlation coefficient does not indicate a cause-and-effect relationship between two variables, it does reveal whether changes in one variable can be predicted from changes in another variable.

5. Illusory correlation is a perceived correlation that does not actually exist. Believing there is a relationship between two things may make one more likely to notice and recall instances that confirm this belief, and contribute to this misperception. Furthermore, because people are sensitive to unusual events they are likely to notice the occurrence of two such events in close proximity and incorrectly perceive the existence of a correlation between them. Illusory correlations contribute to the illusion that chance events are subject to personal control. This illusion is also fostered by the tendency for unusual events to be followed by more ordinary happenings. Failing to recognize this statistical principle (regression toward the mean) can mislead people into believing that they can control the events in question.

6. A population consists of all the cases in a group. A sample is a subset of a population. Because it often is impossible to study every member of a population, researchers observe a small sample and then generalize about the entire population.

7. Although it is tempting to overgeneralize from highly select samples, the most reliable inferences about a population are based on a representative sample. A good way to generate a representative sample is by selecting cases at random, so that each individual in the population has an equal chance of being selected. It is important to remember, however, that random samples, or sequences, often do not appear to be random. A third important principle is that averages based on more cases are more reliable than averages based on only a few cases. A fourth is that averages derived from samples with low variability are more reliable than those based on samples with high variability. Generalizing to the population from a small sample with high variability is therefore inadvisable and potentially misleading.

8. When psychologists compare two samples to determine if their difference is statistically significant, they want to know whether the difference is real and not due to chance variation between the samples. When sample averages are based on many observations that have low variability, and the difference between the averages for two samples is large, researchers can say that the difference has statistical significance.

CHAPTER REVIEW

1. frequency distribution
2. histogram
3. percentile rank
4. mean; median; mode
5. mode
6. sum; number
7. 50th
8. similar
9. range; standard deviation
10. difference in the lowest and highest scores in a distribution
11. crude; is
12. more accurate; takes
13. a. Calculate the deviation between each score and the mean.
    b. Square each deviation score.
    c. Determine the mean of the deviation scores.
    d. Take the square root of this mean.
14. normal curve
15. 68; 95

Since the mean equals 100 and the standard deviation is 15 points, a score of 116 is just over one standard deviation unit above the mean. Since 68 percent of the population scores fall within one standard deviation on either side of the mean, 34 percent fall between 0 and +1 standard deviation unit. By definition, 50 percent of the scores fall below the mean. Therefore, a score at or above 115 is higher than that obtained by 84 percent of the population (50 percent + 34 percent = 84 percent).

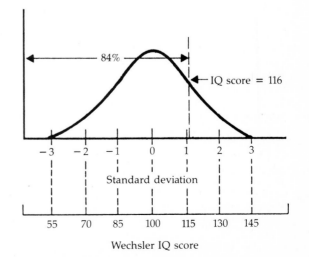

Wechsler IQ score

16. scatterplot
17. correlation coefficient; $+1.00$; -1.00
18. 0.00; $+1.00$; -1.00; decreases

An example of a positive correlation is the relationship between air temperature and ice cream sales: As one increases so does the other.

An example of a negative correlation is the relationship between good health and the amount of stress a person is under: As stress increases, the odds of good health decrease.

19. does not give
20. illusory correlation
21. confirm
22. regression toward the mean
23. population
    a. Representative samples are better than biased samples.
    b. Random sequences may not look random.
    c. Large samples yield more reliable statistics than small samples.
    d. Less variable observations are more reliable than more variable observations.
24. overgeneralize
25. an equal chance of being selected
26. less
27. more
28. low
29. more
30. significance; chance

PROGRESS TEST 1

Multiple-Choice Questions

1. **d.** is the answer. (p. 623)
    a. This is the range.
    b. This is a test of statistical significance.
    c. This is the standard deviation.

2. **c.** is the answer. The mean is the sum of scores divided by the number of scores. [$(2 + 3 + 7 + 6 + 1 + 4 + 9 + 5 + 8 + 2)/10 = 4.7$.] (p. 625)

3. **d.** is the answer. When the scores are put in order (1, 2, 3, 4, 7, 7, 8), 4 is at the 50th percentile, splitting the distribution in half. (p. 625)

4. **b.** is the answer. The mode is the most frequent score. Since there are more "twos" than any other number in the distribution, 2 is the mode. (p. 625)

5. **d.** is the answer. The range is the gap between the highest and lowest scores in a distribution. ($14 - 1 = 13$.) (p. 625)

6. **d.** is the answer. (p. 626)

7. **a.** is the answer. (p. 627)

b. This situation indicates that the two sets of scores are positively correlated.
c. Whether a correlation is positive or negative does not indicate the strength of the relationship, only its direction.
d. In negative correlations, there *is* a relationship; the correlation is negative because the relationship is an inverse one.

8. **a.** is the answer. (p. 629)
    b. Regression toward the mean has nothing to do with tests of statistical significance.
    c. In fact, just the opposite is true.
    d. This is true, but not because of regression toward the mean.

9. **c.** is the answer. (p. 626)
    a. 50 percent of the normal curve falls on either side of its mean.
    b. 68 percent of the scores fall between -1 and $+1$ standard deviation units.
    d. 99.7 percent fall between -3 and $+3$ standard deviations.

10. **c.** is the answer. (p. 627)

11. **d.** is the answer. (pp. 630–631, 633–634)

12. **c.** is the answer. (p. 621)
    a. A statistically significant difference may or may not be of practical importance.
    b. This is often the case when a difference is *not* statistically significant.

13. **c.** is the answer. (p. 634)
    a. Percentile rank refers to the percentage of scores in a distribution that a particular score exceeds.
    b. The standard deviation is the average amount by which scores in a distribution differ from the mean of the distribution.
    d. The correlation coefficient is an index of the degree to which two sets of scores are related.

14. **b.** is the answer. The range is a measure of variation. (p. 625)

15. **a.** is the answer. As an average, calculated by adding all scores and dividing by the number of scores, the mean could easily be affected by the inclusion of a few extreme scores. (p. 625)
    b. The range is not a measure of central tendency.
    c. & d. The median and mode give equal weight to all scores; each counts only once and its numerical value is unimportant.

16. **c.** is the answer. (p. 626)
    a. A skewed curve is formed from an asymmetrical distribution.

b. A bimodal curve has two modes; a normal curve has only one.

d. A histogram is a bar graph depicting a frequency distribution.

17. **a.** is the answer. The standard deviation is the average deviation in a distribution; therefore, if variation (deviation) is small, the standard deviation will also be small. (p. 626)

18. **a.** is the answer. (p. 627)

b. & c. These are "perfect" correlations of equal strength.

d. This indicates a much stronger relationship between two sets of scores than does a coefficient of 0.00.

19. **b.** is the answer. (p. 628)

20. **d.** is the answer. (pp. 628–629)

a., b., & c. Each of these may or may not be true, but they cannot be determined from the information given.

Matching Items

1. h (p. 623) 5. f (p. 625) 9. c (p. 625)
2. i (p. 625) 6. b (p. 625) 10. a (p. 625)
3. e (p. 630) 7. k (p. 626) 11. d (pp. 625–626)
4. g (p. 630) 8. j (pp. 626–627)

PROGRESS TEST 2

Multiple-Choice Questions

1. **d.** is the answer. (p. 623)

a. A scatterplot is a depiction of the nature and degree of relationship between two variables.

b. A normal curve is the symmetrical distribution that describes the frequency of many psychological and physical characteristics in a population.

c. There is no such thing as a coefficient plot.

2. **c.** is the answer. The mean is the sum of the scores divided by the number of scores. (60/10 = 6.) (p. 625)

3. **c.** is the answer. When the scores are put in order (5, 6, 7, 8, 9, 10, 11), 8 is at the 50th percentile, splitting the distribution in half. (p. 625)

4. **c.** is the answer. (p. 623)

a. The highest score always has a percentile rank of 99, regardless of the size of the distribution.

b. Since a score cannot exceed itself, the percentage of scores *below* the highest score cannot equal 100.

d. The highest percentile rank exceeds all the others, not 50 percent of them.

5. **a.** is the answer. (p. 626)

b. The range is the difference between the highest and lowest scores in a distribution.

c. The median is the score that falls at the 50th percentile.

d. The mode is the most frequent score.

6. **c.** is the answer. (p. 625)

a. The mean is the arithmetic average.

b. The median is the score that splits the distribution in half.

d. The range is the difference between the highest and lowest scores.

7. **c.** is the answer. The mean, median, and mode are equal to 4. (p. 625)

8. **d.** is the answer. Since the range is the difference between the highest and lowest scores, it is by definition affected by extreme scores. (p. 625)

a. & c. The mean and mode are measures of central tendency, not of variation.

b. The standard deviation is less affected than the range because, when it is calculated, the deviation of *every* score from the mean is computed.

9. **c.** is the answer. The answer is calculated as follows (p. 626):

i. The mean = $(3 + 1 + 4 + 10 + 12)/5 = 6$.

ii. The deviation scores are $3 - 6 = -3$; $1 - 6 = -5$; $4 - 6 = -2$; $10 - 6 = 4$; $12 - 6 = 6$.

iii. The squared deviation scores are $-3^2 = 9$; $-5^2 = 25$; $-2^2 = 4$; $4^2 = 16$; $6^2 = 36$.

iv. The mean of the squared deviation scores is $(9 + 25 + 4 + 16 + 36)/5 = 18$.

v. The square root of this mean, and the standard deviation of the distribution, is $\sqrt{18}$.

10. **b.** is the answer. Averages derived from scores with low variability tend to be more reliable estimates of the populations from which they are drawn. Thus, a. and c. are incorrect. Because the standard deviation is a more accurate estimate of variability than the range, d. is incorrect. (pp. 626, 633)

11. **b.** is the answer. (p. 627)

12. **d.** is the answer. A difference that is statistically significant is a true difference, rather than an apparent difference due to factors such as sampling variation, and it is reliable. (p. 634)

13. **b.** is the answer. A histogram is a bar graph based on a frequency distribution. (p. 623)

14. **b.** is the answer. (p. 625)

a. In fact, just the opposite is true.

c. Both the mean and the median are based on all the scores in a distribution. The median is based on the number of scores, while the mean is based on the average of their sum.

15. **b.** is the answer. Just as the standard deviation is a measure of variation, so the mode is a measure of central tendency. (pp. 625–626)

16. b. is the answer. (p. 626)

a. 50 percent of the scores in a normal distribution fall on one side of the mean.

c. 95 percent fall between -2 and $+2$ standard deviations.

d. 99.7 percent fall between -3 and $+3$ standard deviations.

17. a. is the answer. Figures based on larger samples are more reliable. (p. 633)

b. & c. These sample characteristics would tend to lower precision.

d. A test of significance is a determination of the likelihood that an obtained result is real.

18. c. is the answer. (p. 627)

19. a. is the answer. The closer the correlation coefficient is to either $+1$ or -1, the stronger the relationship between the variables. (p. 627)

20. d. is the answer. (p. 630)

a. A sample is a subset of a population.

b. A random sample is a subset of a population in which every member of the population has the same chance of being selected.

c. The mode is the most frequent score in a distribution.

True-False Items

1. False (p. 623)
2. False (p. 625)
3. True (pp. 625–626)
4. True (p. 627)
5. True (p. 629)
6. False (p. 630)
7. False (p. 625)
8. True (p. 633)
9. True (p. 634)
10. True (p. 633)

CHALLENGE TEST

Multiple-Choice Questions

1. a. is the answer. The percentile rank of a score is the percentage of scores in a distribution that a given score exceeds. The highest score in the class exceeds 99 percent of the scores in the distribution —that is, all the scores except itself. (p. 623)

2. b. is the answer. The answer is calculated as follows (p. 626):

i. The mean $= (3 + 5 + 6 + 2 + 4)/5 = 4$.

ii. The deviation scores are $3 - 4 = -1$; $5 - 4 = 1$; $6 - 4 = 2$; $2 - 4 = -2$; $4 - 4 = 0$.

iii. The squared deviation scores are $-1^2 = 1$; $1^2 = 1$; $2^2 = 4$; $-2^2 = 4$; $0^2 = 0$.

iv. The mean of the squared deviation scores is $(1 + 1 + 4 + 4 + 0)/5 = 2$.

v. The square root of this mean, and the standard deviation of the distribution, is $\sqrt{2}$.

3. a. is the answer. Although Jane's individual scores cannot be predicted, over time her scores will fall close to her average. This is the phenomenon of regression toward the mean. (p. 629)

4. c. is the answer. If height and weight are positively correlated, increased height is associated with increased weight. Thus, one can predict a person's weight from his or her height. (pp. 627–628)

a. Correlation does not imply causality.

b. This situation depicts a negative correlation between height and weight.

5. d. is the answer. A small or large standard deviation indicates whether a distribution is homogeneous or variable. (p. 626)

a., b., & c. These statistics would not give any information regarding the consistency of performance.

6. c. is the answer. (p. 626)

a. A frequency distribution is a listing of the number of scores that occur within each interval of some scale of measurement.

b. A scatterplot is a graph that depicts the nature and degree of relationship between two variables.

d. A histogram is a bar graph that depicts a frequency distribution.

7. c. is the answer. Regression toward the mean is the phenomenon that average results are more typical than extreme results. Thus, after an unusual event (the low exam score in this example) things tend to return toward their average level (in this case, the higher score on the second exam). (p. 629)

a. Edward's improved average indicates only that, perhaps as a result of an additional season's experience, he is a better player.

b. Because the probability of rolling 5 consecutive "sevens" is very low, the gambler's "luck" will probably prove on subsequent rolls to be atypical and things will return toward their average level. This answer is incorrect, however, because it states only that 5 consecutive "sevens" were rolled.

d. In this example, although the average of the student's exam grades is her usual grade of B, they are all extreme grades and do not regress toward the mean.

8. b. is the answer. (p. 625)

a. The mean is the arithmetic average of the scores in a distribution.

c. The mode is the most frequent score in a distribution.

d. The standard deviation is the average deviation of scores from the mean.

9. d. is the answer. 95 percent of the scores in a

normal distribution fall between 2 standard deviation units below the mean and 2 standard deviation units above the mean. In this example, the test score that corresponds to -2 standard deviation units is $50 - (2 \times 10) = 30$; the score that corresponds to $+2$ standard deviation units is $50 + (2 \times 10) = 70$. (p. 626)

10. **c.** is the answer. A correlation that is perceived but doesn't actually exist, as in the example, is known as an illusory correlation. (p. 628)

   a. Regression toward the mean is the tendency for extreme scores to fall back toward the average.

   b. The availability heuristic is the tendency of people to estimate the likelihood of something in terms of how readily it comes to mind.

   d. The gambler's fallacy is the false perception that the probability of a random event is determined by past events.

11. **c.** is the answer. In this case, the mean, or average (7), is greater than both the mode, or most frequent score (6), and the median, or middle score (6). (p. 625)

12. **b.** is the answer. The entire group that is of interest, in this case, all eligible voters, is the population; the subgroup actually polled is the sample. (p. 630)

   a. Pollsters will work to make their sample conform as closely as possible to the general voting population.

   c. & d. A frequency distribution is a listing of the number of scores within each range, while normal distribution refers to one possible shape for the curve; the difference between the highest and lowest scores in a distribution defines the range.

13. **d.** is the answer. In such a case, any sequence, no matter how "unrandom" it may look, can be the result of chance. (p. 631)

14. **c.** is the answer. This best approximates a normal distribution because most of the scores are near the mean, fewer scores are at the extremes, and the distribution is symmetrical. (p. 626)

15. **c.** is the answer. Even without actually computing its value, it is evident that the standard deviation of these three scores will be greater than that in a., b., or d. because the scores in this distribution are much more variable. (p. 626)

16. **c.** is the answer. (p. 625)

   a. The mean is computed as the sum of the scores divided by the number of scores.

   b. The median is the midmost score in a distribution.

   d. The range is the difference between the highest and lowest scores in a distribution.

17. **a.** is the answer. The mean is strongly influenced by extreme scores. In this example, the mean would change from \$25,000, to $(75,000 + 25,000 + 25,000 + 25,000 + 25,000)/5 = \$35,000$. (p. 625)

   b. & c. Both the median and the mode would remain \$25,000 even with the addition of the fifth family's income.

   d. The standard deviation is a measure of variation, not central tendency.

18. **a.** is the answer. (p. 627)

   b. This will occur when the correlation coefficient is near 0.00.

   c. Correlations are linear, rather than curvilinear, relationships.

19. **a.** is the answer. (pp. 625–626)

   b. & c. Neither of these can be determined from the information given.

20. **b.** is the answer. (p. 634)

   a. If the difference between the sample means is not significant, then the groups probably do not differ in the measured ability.

   c. When a result is not significant it means that the observed difference is unreliable.

Essay Question

The use of frequency distributions, histograms, and percentile ranks is helpful in accurately organizing, describing, and interpreting events, especially when there is too much information to remember and one wishes to avoid conclusions based on general impressions. Computing an appropriate measure of central tendency provides an index of the overall average of a set of scores. Knowing that the mean is the most common measure of central tendency, but that it is very sensitive to unusual scores, can help one avoid being misled by claims based on misleading averages. Being able to compute the range or standard deviation of a set of scores allows one to determine how homogeneous the scores in a distribution are and provides a basis for realistically generalizing from samples to populations. Understanding the correlation coefficient can help us to see the world more clearly by revealing the extent to which two things relate. Being aware that unusual results tend to return to more typical results (regression toward the mean) helps us to avoid the practical pitfalls associated with illusory correlation. Finally, understanding the basis for tests of statistical significance can make us more discerning consumers of research reported in the media.

KEY TERMS

1. A **frequency distribution** is a listing of the number of individual scores that occur within equal-sized intervals in a distribution. (p. 623)

2. A **histogram** is a bar graph that depicts a frequency distribution. (p. 623)

3. **Percentile rank** is the percentage of scores in a distribution that fall below a particular score. (p. 623)

   Example: A student whose **percentile rank** is 85 has outperformed 85 percent of all students.

4. The **mode** is the most frequent score in a distribution; it is the simplest measure of central tendency to determine. (p. 625)

5. The **mean** is the arithmetic average, the measure of central tendency computed by adding together the scores in a distribution and dividing by the number of scores. (p. 625)

6. The **median**, another measure of central tendency, is the score that falls at the 50th percentile, cutting a distribution in half. (p. 625)

   Example: When the *mean* of a distribution is affected by a few extreme scores, the **median** is the more appropriate measure of central tendency.

7. The **range** is a measure of variation computed as the difference between the highest and lowest scores in a distribution. (p. 625)

8. The **standard deviation** is the average amount by which the scores in a distribution deviate from the mean. Because it is based on every score in the distribution, it is a more precise measure of variation than the range. (p. 626)

9. The **normal curve**, or normal distribution, is the symmetrical curve that describes many types of data, with most scores centering around the mean and progressively fewer scores occurring toward the extremes. (p. 626)

10. A **scatterplot** is a depiction of the relationship between two sets of scores by means of a graphed cluster of dots. (pp. 626–627)

    Example: The extent to which the points in a scatterplot fall along a straight line indicates the strength of relationship between two sets of scores. The direction of slope indicates whether the relationship is positive or negative.

11. The **correlation coefficient** is an index of the strength and direction of relationship between two sets of scores. (p. 627)

    Example: When the **correlation coefficient** is positive, the two sets of scores increase together. When it is negative, increases in one set are accompanied by decreases in the other.

12. **Illusory correlation** is the false perception that a correlation exists. (p. 628)

    Example: Superstitious behaviors such as avoiding cracks in the sidewalk, wearing "lucky" clothing, and not walking under ladders exemplify **illusory correlation**—in this case, the illusion that uncontrollable events are correlated with our actions.

13. **Regression toward the mean** is the tendency for extreme scores to return back, or regress, toward the average. (p. 629)

    Example: A baseball player who usually bats around .250 may have several exceptional games in which he bats .750 but can then be expected to return to his usual .250 hitting, as a result of **regression toward the mean**.

14. A **population** refers to all the members of a group from which samples may be drawn for study. (p. 630)

    Example: Because it often is not practical to measure every member of the **population**, researchers carefully select and study a representative sample.

15. **Statistical significance** means that an obtained result, such as the difference between the averages for two samples, very likely reflects a real difference rather than sampling variation or chance factors. Tests of statistical significance help researchers decide when they can justifiably generalize from an observed instance. (p. 634)